Communications in Computer and Information Science 2392

Series Editors

Rationale
The CCIS series is devoted to the publication of proceedings of computer science conferences. Its aim is to efficiently disseminate original research results in informatics in printed and electronic form. While the focus is on publication of peer-reviewed full papers presenting mature work, inclusion of reviewed short papers reporting on work in progress is welcome, too. Besides globally relevant meetings with internationally representative program committees guaranteeing a strict peer-reviewing and paper selection process, conferences run by societies or of high regional or national relevance are also considered for publication.

Topics
The topical scope of CCIS spans the entire spectrum of informatics ranging from foundational topics in the theory of computing to information and communications science and technology and a broad variety of interdisciplinary application fields.

Information for Volume Editors and Authors
Publication in CCIS is free of charge. No royalties are paid, however, we offer registered conference participants temporary free access to the online version of the conference proceedings on SpringerLink (http://link.springer.com) by means of an http referrer from the conference website and/or a number of complimentary printed copies, as specified in the official acceptance email of the event.

CCIS proceedings can be published in time for distribution at conferences or as post-proceedings, and delivered in the form of printed books and/or electronically as USBs and/or e-content licenses for accessing proceedings at SpringerLink. Furthermore, CCIS proceedings are included in the CCIS electronic book series hosted in the SpringerLink digital library at http://link.springer.com/bookseries/7899. Conferences publishing in CCIS are allowed to use Online Conference Service (OCS) for managing the whole proceedings lifecycle (from submission and reviewing to preparing for publication) free of charge.

Publication process
The language of publication is exclusively English. Authors publishing in CCIS have to sign the Springer CCIS copyright transfer form, however, they are free to use their material published in CCIS for substantially changed, more elaborate subsequent publications elsewhere. For the preparation of the camera-ready papers/files, authors have to strictly adhere to the Springer CCIS Authors' Instructions and are strongly encouraged to use the CCIS LaTeX style files or templates.

Abstracting/Indexing
CCIS is abstracted/indexed in DBLP, Google Scholar, EI-Compendex, Mathematical Reviews, SCImago, Scopus. CCIS volumes are also submitted for the inclusion in ISI Proceedings.

How to start
To start the evaluation of your proposal for inclusion in the CCIS series, please send an e-mail to ccis@springer.com

Fabián R. Narváez · Micaela N. Villa ·
Gloria M. Díaz
Editors

Smart Technologies, Systems and Applications

4th International Conference, SmartTech-IC 2024
Quito, Ecuador, December 2–4, 2024
Revised Selected Papers, Part I

Springer

Editors
Fabián R. Narváez
Universidad Politécnica Salesiana
Quito, Ecuador

Micaela N. Villa
Universidad Politécnica Salesiana
Quito, Ecuador

Gloria M. Díaz
Instituto Tecnológico Metropolitano
Medellín, Colombia

ISSN 1865-0929 ISSN 1865-0937 (electronic)
Communications in Computer and Information Science
ISBN 978-3-031-98286-6 ISBN 978-3-031-98287-3 (eBook)
https://doi.org/10.1007/978-3-031-98287-3

This Springer imprint is published by the registered company Springer Nature Switzerland AG
The registered company address is: Gewerbestrasse 11, 6330 Cham, Switzerland

Preface

These two volumes present a collection of papers from the 4th International Conference on Smart Technologies, Systems and Applications (SmartTech-IC 2024), held from December 2–4, 2024, in Quito, Ecuador. The SmartTech-IC conference aims to attract researchers, scientists and technologists from some of the top companies, universities, research groups and government agencies from Latin America and around the world to communicate their research results, inventions and innovative applications in the area of smart science and the most recent smart technological trends. SmartTech-IC 2024 was organized by the Universidad Politécnica Salesiana, a private institution of higher education with social purposes, nonprofit and co-financed by the Ecuadorian state. The SmartTech-IC conference was conceived as an academic platform to promote the creation of technical and scientific collaboration networks. The goal of the conference is to address relevant topics related to smart technologies, smart systems, smart trends and applications in different domains in the field of computer science and information systems that represent innovation in current society. The papers in this volume are categorized under the following conference topics:

- Smart Technologies
- Smart Systems

We would like to express our gratitude to all the authors who submitted papers to SmartTech-IC 2024, and our congratulations to those whose papers were accepted. There were 168 submissions. Each submission was reviewed by at least three qualified reviewers chosen from our Program Committee (PC) based on their qualifications and experience. The papers were selected by Program Chairs and their selection was based on a series of criteria including the reviewers' average score and comments provided by the Program Committee members. Finally, the Program Chairs decided to accept 68 full papers.

We would also like to thank the PC members, who agreed to review the manuscripts in a timely manner and provided valuable feedback to the authors.

December 2024

Fabián R. Narváez
Micaela N. Villa
Gloria M. Díaz

Organization

Honorary Committee

Juan Cárdenas	Universidad Politécnica Salesiana, Ecuador
Fernando Pesantez	Universidad Politécnica Salesiana, Ecuador
María Sol Villagómez	Universidad Politécnica Salesiana, Ecuador
Angela Flores	Universidad Politécnica Salesiana, Ecuador
Vladimir Robles Bykbaev	Universidad Politécnica Salesiana, Ecuador
Esteban Inga	Universidad Politécnica Salesiana, Ecuador

Organizing Committee

Fabián R. Narváez E.	Universidad Politécnica Salesiana, Ecuador
Micaela Villa R.	Universidad Politécnica Salesiana, Ecuador
Diego Carrión	Universidad Politécnica Salesiana, Ecuador
Wilson Pavón	Universidad Politécnica Salesiana, Ecuador

Program Chairs

Smart Technologies

César Ferri	Universidad Politécnica de Valencia, Spain
Ana Cecilia Villa	Universidad Politécnica Salesiana, Ecuador

Smart Systems

Teodiano Bastos	Universidade Federal do Espírito Santo, Brazil
Pablo Cevallos	Universidad Politécnica Salesiana, Ecuador

Smart Applications

Antoine Manzanera	ENSTA-ParisTech, France
Gloria M. Díaz	Instituto Tecnológico Metropolitano, Colombia

Program Committee

Alberto López Delis	Medical Biophysics Center, Cuba
Alexander Águila	Universidad Politécnica Salesiana, Ecuador
Alexandre Pino	Universidade Federal do Rio de Janeiro, Brazil
Antoine Manzanera	ENSTA - ParisTech, France
Andrés Felipe Ruiz Olaya	Universidad Antonio Nariño, Colombia
Ana Cecilia Villa	Universidad Politécnica Salesiana, Ecuador
Angélica Ramírez	Universidad Militar Nueva Granada, Colombia
Carlos Calderón	Universidad Técnica Particular de Loja, Ecuador
Carlos Novo	Universidad Tecnológica del Uruguay, Uruguay
Carlos Mera	Instituto Tecnológico Metropolitano, Colombia
Carlos Tierra-Criollo	Universidade Federal do Rio de Janeiro, Brazil
Carmen Carrión	Universidad de Castilla - La Mancha, Spain
César Ferri	Universidad Politécnica de Valencia, Spain
César Paltán	Universidad Politécnica Salesiana, Ecuador
Christian Cifuentes	Universidad de los Andes, Colombia
Christian Larenas	Universidad Politécnica Salesiana, Ecuador
Christian Salamea	Universidad Politécnica Salesiana, Ecuador
Cristian David Gerrero	Universidade Federal do Espirito Santo, Brazil
Daniel González Montoya	Instituto Tecnológico Metropolitano, Colombia
David Romo	Universidad Industrial de Santander, Colombia
David Ojeda	Universidad Técnica del Norte, Ecuador
Derfrey Duque Quintero	Universidad Pascual Bravo, Colombia
Denis Delisle	Universidad de Oriente, Cuba
Diana Arce	University of Rio de Janiero, Brazil
Diego Carrión	Universidad Politécnica Salesiana, Ecuador
Diego Almeida	Yachay Tech University, Ecuador
Diego Vallejo	Universidad Politécnica Salesiana, Ecuador
Eduardo Pinos	Universidad Politécnica Salesiana, Ecuador
Edwin Carrasquero	Universidad Estatal de Milagro, Ecuador
Edwin García	Universidad Politécnica Salesiana, Ecuador
Enrique Arias	Universidad de Castilla - La Mancha, Spain
Erick Reyes	Instituto Tecnológico Metropolitano, Colombia
Estefania Coronado	Fundazione Bruno Kessler, Italy
Fausto García Márquez	Universidad de Castilla - La Mancha, Spain
Fabián Narváez E.	Universidad Politécnica Salesiana, Ecuador
Fernando Urgiles	Universidad Politécnica Salesiana, Ecuador
Fernando Villalba	Yachay Tech University, Ecuador
Fredi Portilla	Universidad Politécnica Salesiana, Ecuador
Gabriel León	Universidad Politécnica Salesiana, Ecuador
Germán Arevalo	Universidad Politécnica Salesiana, Ecuador

Germán Corredor	Case Western Reserve University, USA
Gloria M. Díaz	Instituto Tecnológico Metropolitano, Colombia
Hiram Ponce Espinosa	Universidad Panamericana, Mexico
Hugo Franco	MovyLab, Colombia
Ivonne Vaca	Universidad Politécnica Salesiana, Ecuador
Israel Pineda	Yachay Tech University, Ecuador
Jack Bravo Torres	Universidad Politécnica Salesiana, Ecuador
Javier Cabrera	Universidad Católica de Cuenca, Ecuador
John Villarejo	Universidade Federal do Paraná, Brazil
José Ignacio Huertas	Tecnológico de Monterrey, Mexico
José Sampietro	CELEC EP, Ecuador
José Raúl Castro	Universidad Técnica Particular de Loja, Ecuador
Jorge E. Camargo	Universidad Antonio Nariño, Colombia
Jorge Fajardo	Universidad Politécnica Salesiana, Ecuador
Juan Inga	Universidad Politécnica Salesiana, Ecuador
Juan Pablo D'Amato	UNICEN, Argentina
Juan Sebastián Botero	Instituto Tecnológico Metropolitano, Colombia
Juan David Martínez	Instituto Tecnológico Metropolitano, Colombia
Juan C. Santillán	Universidad Politécnica del Chimborazo, Ecuador
Julio Proaño Orellana	Universidad Politécnica Salesiana, Ecuador
Leony Ortiz	Universidad Politécnica Salesiana, Ecuador
Nitish Thakor	Johns Hopkins University, USA
Manuel Quiñones	Universidad Técnica Particular de Loja, Ecuador
Marco Carpio	Universidad Politécnica Salesiana, Ecuador
Marco Cerna	Universidad Politécnica Salesiana, Ecuador
Marcelo García	Universidad Politécnica Salesiana, Ecuador
María Blanca Caminero	Universidad de Castilla - La Mancha, Spain
María Constanza Torres	Universidad Nacional de Colombia, Colombia
Mariela Cerrada	Universidad Politécnica Salesiana, Ecuador
M. Carmen Juan Lizandra	Universidad Politécnica de Valencia, Spain
María Gabriela Baldeón	University of South Florida, USA
Mauro Callejas-Cuero	Universidad Pedagógica y Tecnológica, Colombia
Micaela Villa	Universidad Politécnica Salesiana, Ecuador
Milton Ruiz	Universidad Politécnica Salesiana, Ecuador
Miguel Zúñiga	Universidad de Cuenca, Ecuador
Monica Huerta	Universidad Politécnica Salesiana, Ecuador
Lely Luengas	Universidad Distrital Francisco J. de Caldas, Colombia
Lenin V. Campozano	Escuela Politécnica Nacional, Ecuador
Leonardo Bueno	Universidad Politécnica Salesiana, Ecuador
Lina Zapata	Universidad Politécnica Salesiana, Ecuador
Luis Romero	Universidad Politécnica Salesiana, Ecuador

Lucía Rivadeneira	University of Manchester, UK
Oscar Rueda	Centro de Pesquisas de Energia Elétrica, Brazil
Oswaldo Moscoso	Universidad Tecnólogica Equinoccial, Ecuador
Pablo Cevallos	Universidad Politécnica Salesiana, Ecuador
Pablo Salamea	Universidad Politécnica Salesiana, Ecuador
Patricia Acosta Vargas	Universidad de Las Américas, Ecuador
Paola Ingavélez	Universidad Politécnica Salesiana, Ecuador
Paula Rodríguez	Universidad Nacional de Colombia, Colombia
Paulina Morillo	Universidad Politécnica Salesiana, Ecuador
Renato Cumbal	Universidad Politécnica Salesiana, Ecuador
Ricardo Flores	Universidad San Francisco de Quito, Ecuador
Ricardo Gutiérrez	Universidad Militar Nueva Granada, Colombia
Roberto Macoto	Universidade Federal do Rio de Janeiro, Brazil
Rubén D. Fonnegra	Universidad Pascual Bravo, Colombia
Santiago Gómez	Western University, Canada
Santiago Gonzáles	Universidad de Cuenca, Ecuador
Sergio Luján	Universidad de Alicante, Spain
Silvio Simani	University of Ferrara, Italy
Sri Krishnan	Toronto Metropolitan University, Canada
Susana Castro	Universidad Politécnica Salesiana, Ecuador
Teodiano Bastos	Universidade Federal do Espírito Santo, Brazil
Tuesman Castillo	Universidad Técnica Particular de Loja, Ecuador
Vladimir Robles	Universidad Politécnica Salesiana, Ecuador
Vicente Rojas	Universidad Politécnica Salesiana, Ecuador
Villie Morocho	Universidad de Cuenca, Ecuador
Vinicio Changoluisa	Universidad Politécnica Salesiana, Ecuador
Walter Orozco	Universidad Politécnica Salesiana, Ecuador
Walter E. Verdugo	Universidad Politécnica Salesiana, Ecuador
Wilson Pavón	Universidad Politécnica Salesiana, Ecuador
Ximena López	Universidad de San Marcos, Peru

Local Organizing Committee

Tania Chicaiza	Universidad Politécnica Salesiana, Ecuador
Fernando Velasco	Universidad Politécnica Salesiana, Ecuador
Jorge Inlago	Universidad Politécnica Salesiana, Ecuador
André Morán	Universidad Politécnica Salesiana, Ecuador
Genesis Huanca	Universidad Politécnica Salesiana, Ecuador
Esteban Gaibor	Universidad Politécnica Salesiana, Ecuador
Jesly Naranjo	Universidad Politécnica Salesiana, Ecuador
Cristopher Collaguazo	Universidad Politécnica Salesiana, Ecuador

Sponsoring Institutions

http://www.ups.edu.ec

Contents – Part I

Smart Systems

Contents – Part II

Poster Session

Smart Technologies

Industrial Anomaly Detection: Bridging OPC-UA with Classical and Deep Learning Methods

Henry O. Velesaca[1,3](✉), Doménica Carrasco[1], Angel D. Sappa[1,2], Juan A. Holgado-Terriza[3], and Wilton Agila[1]

[1] ESPOL Polytechnic University, Escuela Superior Politécnica del Litoral, ESPOL, Campus Gustavo Galindo Km. 30.5 Vía Perimetral, P.O. Box 09-01-5863, Guayaquil, Ecuador
{hvelesac,djcarras,asappa,wagila}@espol.edu.ec
[2] Computer Vision Center, 08193 Bellaterra, Barcelona, Spain
asappa@cvc.uab.es
[3] Software Engineering Department, University of Granada, 18014 Granada, Spain
hvelesaca@correo.ugr.es, jholgado@ugr.es

Abstract. Anomaly detection is critical for maintaining operational stability and preventing unplanned downtimes in industrial systems. This paper explores and compares classical and deep learning based approaches within industrial systems, leveraging the OPC-UA protocol for data communication and execution of the evaluated algorithms within a Vision Finite State Machine. This study presents a case study of anomaly detection in a tinplate lids system, demonstrating the performance of both approaches. Integrating with OPC-UA ensures near real-time data access, interoperability, and scalability across diverse industrial environments. Experimental results highlight the strengths and limitations of each method, providing insights into their applicability for modern industrial anomaly detection challenges. Average Accuracy, Execution Time (e.g., CPU and GPU), Round Trip Time, and End-to-End Delay are used to evaluate the performance of the proposed approaches. The code is available at GitHub: https://github.com/hvelesaca/OPC-UA-YOLOv8-Histogram-Lid-Anomaly-Detection, facilitating further research.

Keywords: Anomaly detection · Deep learning · Industry 4.0 · Industrial control system · YOLOv8 · Histogram based · OPC-UA

1 Introduction

Industrial systems are the backbone of modern manufacturing and production processes, driving efficiency and productivity across various sectors. However, the complexity and scale of these systems also introduce vulnerabilities and challenges, particularly in maintaining operational stability and preventing unplanned downtimes. The identification of anomalies is critical for the prevention of significant problems, as it allows for the mitigation of potential issues at an early stage.

F. R. Narváez et al. (Eds.): SmartTech-IC 2024, CCIS 2392, pp. 3–18, 2026.
https://doi.org/10.1007/978-3-031-98287-3_1

Traditional anomaly detection techniques based on statistical analysis or machine learning have been extensively applied to identify irregular patterns in industrial systems. One of the most common methods is statistical analysis, which involves using various statistical tests and models to determine whether a given data point significantly deviates from the expected behavior. Techniques such as the z-score, which measures how many standard deviations a data point is from the mean, and control charts, which monitor the stability of processes over time, are widely employed [6,9]. In the field of techniques based on machine learning, the Support Vector Machines (SVM) stands out as one of the most used. For example, Schölkopf et al. [23] describe how the SVM can be used for anomaly detection by learning the boundary that separates normal data from anomalies. Condition-based maintenance is widely used in industrial settings, employing sensors to monitor critical process variables like temperature and pressure in real time. By analyzing this data with machine learning and setting alert thresholds, potential issues can be identified before impacting product quality, allowing for proactive adjustments and reducing defects, costs, and waste [2]. In contrast, rule-based systems use predefined rules and thresholds developed by experts to detect anomalies, triggering alarms when readings exceed certain limits [28]. While intuitive and easy to interpret, rule-based systems can be rigid, struggle with evolving conditions, and are labor-intensive to maintain, especially as data complexity grows [5,21].

In recent years, deep learning has become a powerful tool for anomaly detection in industrial systems due to its ability to learn and extract complex patterns from large datasets. Autoencoders are a popular method for anomaly detection, identifying anomalies by measuring reconstruction errors from normal data [11]. This approach effectively captures intricate patterns, making it suitable for complex environments [20]. Additionally, recurrent neural networks (RNNs), especially Long Short-Term Memory (LSTM) networks, excel in detecting anomalies in time-series data by modeling temporal dependencies and predicting future values [4]. These techniques have shown great promise in monitoring dynamic industrial processes and providing early warnings of potential failures [8].

This paper explores and compares classical and deep learning based approaches for anomaly detection in an industrial systems context, with a focus on the use of OPC-UA (Open Platform Communications Unified Architecture). OPC-UA is a widely adopted communication protocol in industrial automation, offering a robust framework for data exchange and interoperability between heterogeneous systems [17]. Also, a case study of the tinplate lids classification system is used to demonstrate the efficiency of the proposed pipelines.

To address this work, the manuscript is organized as follows. Section 2 presents works related to classical and deep learning based approaches and also introduces OPC-UA. Section 3 presents the proposed pipeline to carry out the classification of "*good*"/"*defective*" lids. Then, Sect. 4 shows the experimental results taking as a reference a case study for anomaly detection in tinplate lids using classical and deep learning based approaches. Also, OPC-UA Server and Vision Finite State Machine are implemented. Finally, conclusions are presented in Sect. 5.

2 Related Work

As described above, this paper presents the comparison of classical and deep learning techniques as key components in the context of industrial control systems. In addition, OPC-UA is presented as a system communication standard that facilitates the collection, integration and analysis of operational data, providing valuable insights for process optimization and predictive maintenance. This section reviews some of the most relevant techniques related to these topics.

2.1 Classical Approaches

Among the techniques based on machine learning, Support Vector Machines (SVM), is the most widely used approaches for anomaly detection in images. The work presented by Schölkopf et al. [23] describes how SVMs can be used for anomaly detection by learning the boundary that separates normal data points from anomalies. This technique is particularly effective in high-dimensional spaces where traditional methods struggle. The method involves mapping image features into a higher-dimensional space using kernel functions and then identifying anomalies based on their distance from the learned support vectors. The next approach, the k-Nearest Neighbors (k-NN), is another technique that uses machine learning for anomaly detection. For instance, the authors Angiulli and Pizzuti [1] demonstrate how k-NN can be applied to detect anomalies by comparing each image to its k-nearest neighbors in the feature space. Images that have a significantly higher average distance from their neighbors are considered anomalies. This non-parametric approach is simple yet effective, especially when dealing with complex, high-dimensional image data.

In a similar vein to the above, Principal Component Analysis (PCA) is a classical technique used for detecting anomalies in images. In the paper presented by Turk and Pentland [24], PCA is employed to reduce the dimensionality of facial images, capturing the most significant features. Anomalies are detected by reconstructing images using a reduced set of principal components and measuring the reconstruction error. Images with high reconstruction errors are flagged as anomalies, indicating that they deviate significantly from the normal patterns captured by the principal components. The last technique, presented by Iivarinen [12] describes a method for detecting surface defects using histogram-based textural features. This approach analyzes surface textures through histograms of pixel intensities, using differences in these distributions to identify defects. Among the principal characteristics, its simplicity and efficiency stand out, in addition to not requiring extensive training. However, it is sensitive to changes in illumination and may not be effective in detecting very small defects or on surfaces with high texture variability.

2.2 Deep Learning Approaches

In recent years, deep learning has gained popularity for its ability to automatically learn and extract features from large datasets. Pham et al. [22] present a real-time defect detection system using YOLOv5, ideal for industrial applications due to its high accuracy and speed, though sensitive to lighting and complex designs. Similarly, Beak et al. [3] use YOLOv7 for anomaly detection in cosmetics manufacturing, requiring well-curated training data and potentially needing retraining for new defect types. Klarak et al. [15] extend anomaly detection to defect classification using machine learning, providing detailed insights but requiring extensive labeled data. Kim et al. [14] propose a supervised approach for detecting anomalies in X-ray images of packaged food, effective but reliant on labeled data. Contrarily, DRAEM [29] introduces an unsupervised method for surface anomaly detection using discriminatively trained embeddings, excelling in refined anomaly detection but requiring complex training and large datasets. The CutPaste method [18] uses self-supervised learning with synthetic anomalies, effective with minimal labeled data but possibly less accurate for real-world defects. Overall, deep learning models offer significant advantages over classical approaches, including handling complex datasets, reducing the need for manual feature extraction, and better adaptability to new data patterns.

2.3 OPC-UA Overview

As the last part of the state-of-the-art review, OPC-UA is reviewed, which has been increasingly adopted in industrial systems for its robust and flexible framework for data exchange and interoperability. Although this standard is known for the characteristics mentioned above, it is not limited to those contexts since it has different parts (e.g., historical access, alarms & conditions, programs, finite state machines, and others) that support other tasks such as generation of datasets, training of models and support for industrial systems. On the other hand, several studies have explored its potential for enhancing anomaly detection. For instance, Lee and Kim [17] developed an OPC-UA-based monitoring system integrating machine learning for detecting anomalies in manufacturing processes, improving maintenance and reducing downtime. Similarly, Vogel-Heuser et al. [27] proposed an architecture using OPC-UA for early fault detection in automated production, leveraging advanced data analytics for better issue diagnosis compared to traditional methods.

On the other hand, in [25] Velesaca et al. explore the implementation of an anomaly detection system in industrial products by combining OPC-UA and deep learning techniques. This approach leverages OPC-UA's robust standardized communication capability to collect real-time data and applies deep learning algorithms to identify complex patterns and detect product defects. Although it presents significant advantages, such as high precision and the capacity for continuous improvement, it also faces challenges related to high computational requirements and the need for large volumes of labeled data. The same research team, in Velesaca et al. [26], propose a methodological approach to industrial system implementation based on OPC-UA, the objective is to propose an 11-steps methodology for the design and implementation of industrial systems using UML notation and then convert it to OPC-UA notation and finally generate an XML to deploy a server.

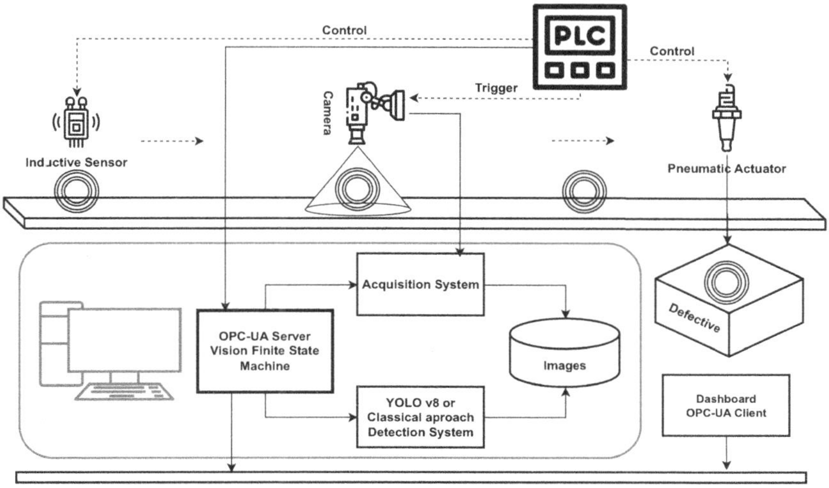

Fig. 1. General outline of the system architecture proposed in this paper.

3 Proposed Approach

This section details the stages of the approaches (classical and deep learning) compared in the current work. The system architecture shows in Fig. 1 is structured around a hierarchical industrial system comprising three layers: *a*) the control layer, where the primary PLC subsystem manages the plant's operations; *b*) the supervision layer, where the OPC-UA subsystem retrieves plant status, handles image acquisition from cameras, and applies anomaly detection using both classical technique and deep learning model; and *c*) the visualization layer, where operators can monitor the plant's progression through a dashboard. Figure 2 illustrates the pipeline for both classical and deep learning based approaches.

3.1 Classical Technique

This section describes the stages of the proposed classical algorithm for anomaly detection. The first step is the image acquisition in RGB format. The second step is the **image pre-processing**, the image is converted to grayscale and a Gaussian filter is applied to the acquired image. At the end of the preprocessing, the next step is to **obtain the center** of the lid. To carry out this task, the **Hough Transform** [16] is applied to extract the concentric circles belonging to the lid. This technique allows the grouping of image pixels that define circles of different radius. After obtaining the center of the image and using camera calibration parameters, the area belonging to the **tinplate lid is extracted** without the background and replacing this area with a black color. Figure 3 shows the result obtained from the four first steps of the classical pipeline. The next step is to

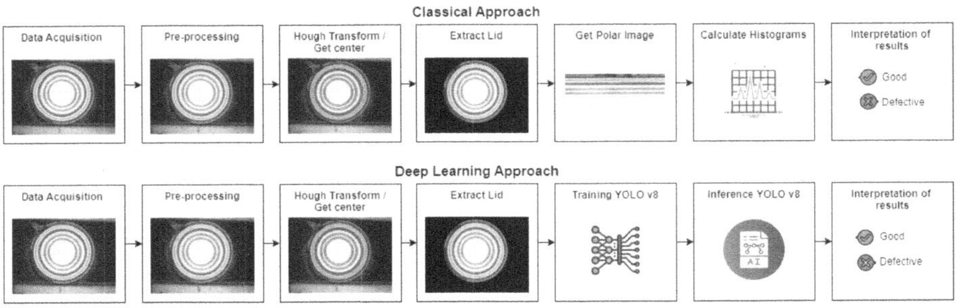

Fig. 2. Overall pipelines of the proposed approaches

obtain the **polar representation** of the area belonging to the lid extracted in the previous step. Figure 4 shows the polar representation of the Cartesian image of the tinplate lid surface split up into the number of bands defined for the analysis (i.e., twelve bands). Finally, the **histogram of intensities** corresponding to each of the 12 bands are obtained. The intensity frequency histogram is used to detect the image surfaces that present differences with respect to the "*good*" tinplate lid. In Fig. 5 the histograms of the 12 bands are presented for the example image. The last step to execute is the **interpretation of results** for the anomaly detection, as mentioned in the previous section, the histograms corresponding to each region are used to detect defects; for this, as a last step to detect the presence of defects, the corresponding thresholds must be defined and configured. The defects are determined by "peaks/valleys" in the obtained histogram, which exceeds the ranges defined as normal. If one band is out of the defined threshold the lid is classified as "*defective*", otherwise is set as "*good*".

3.2 Deep Learning Technique

As a first step and before starting the training process, the area that corresponds to the tinplate lid is segmented using the Hough Transform [16] and the background is removed so that in the classification task attention can be paid to the features of the object to be analyzed. The deep neural network selected for image recognition of the anomaly detection task is YOLOv8 [13]. It has been chosen for its efficiency and speed in detecting objects in images, making it suitable for real-time applications in industrial environments where fast responses are needed. YOLOv8 also offers a deep and flexible architecture that allows easy adjustments and optimizations to adapt to different lighting conditions, viewing angles, and defect types. This makes it a viable option to address the complexity and diversity of defect detection challenges in industrial environments. Furthermore, it is open source and its extensive developer community makes it easy to implement and long-term maintenance of YOLOv8-based defect detection systems. Finally, for this work we consider using the models: *YOLOv8m*, *YOLOv8s*, and *YOLOv8n* due to the restrictions of resources and low processing times necessary for the proposed solution and the industrial context.

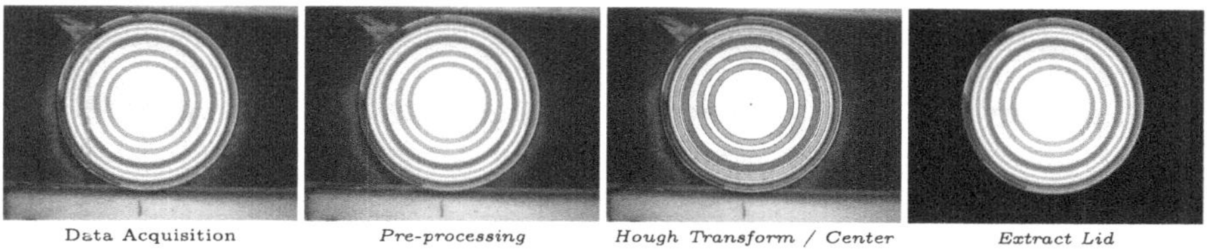

Fig. 3. Three first steps of the classical pipeline. *(1st)* Get RGB input image. *(2nd)* Convert RGB image to grayscale and apply Gaussian blur. *(3rd)* Calculate Hough Transform and get center of lid. *(4th)* Extract Lid based on previous step.

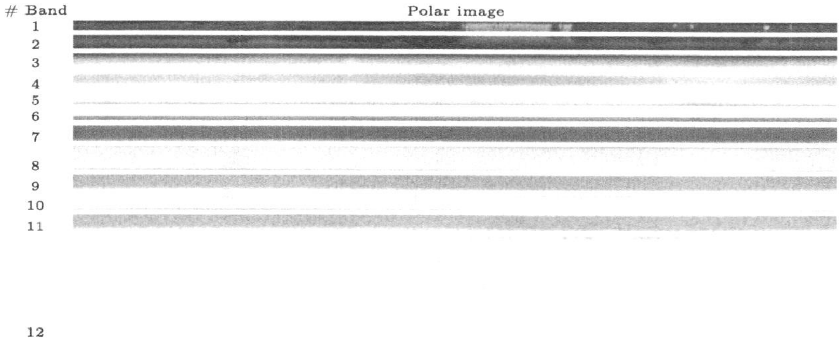

Fig. 4. Polar image divide for each of the 12 bands on the selected example.

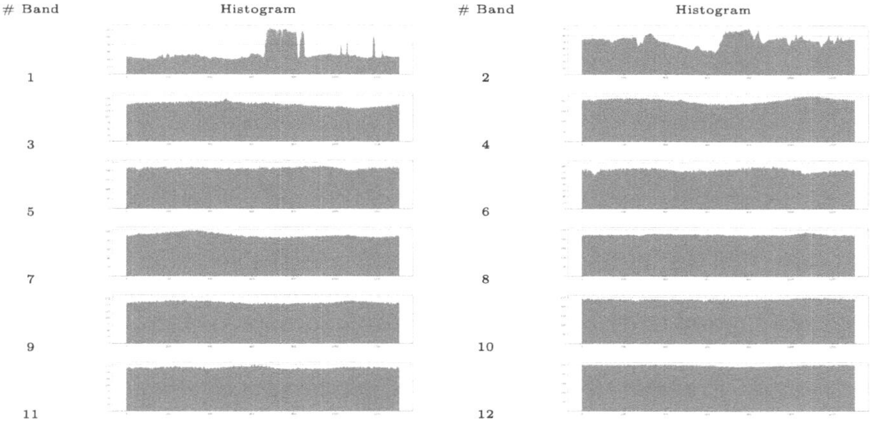

Fig. 5. Histograms for each of the 12 bands on the selected example.

3.3 OPC-UA Vision Specification

The OPC-UA companion specification for machine vision aims to simplify the integration of machine vision systems into production control and IT systems. Therefore, part of the specification OPC 40100-1 [10] Machine Vision - Control, Configuration management, recipe management, and result management is created. Its purpose is not only to complement or replace existing interfaces between a machine vision system and its process environment with OPC-UA but also to establish new horizontal and vertical integration capabilities. This enables authorized process participants to communicate relevant data with each other, reaching up to the IT enterprise level. Consequently, the OPC-UA Vision interface facilitates the exchange of information between different machine vision systems, PLCs, or any software systems at the control device level accessing the machine vision system. In this work, it is proposed to use a state machine based on this standard to support the computer vision techniques to be used. Using this specification a server is created and using a Vision Finite State Machine Type, integrating within the "ContinuousExecution" state both the classical approach and YOLOv8 models.

3.4 Metric Evaluation

For the proposed work, the evaluation of the Average Accuracy over the test set is used to establish the performance of the framework. Furthermore, the execution time using CPU and GPU is computed to measure the efficiency of the used techniques. Finally, Round Trip Time (RTT) and End-to-End Delay (E2E) metrics are calculated. RTT is a measure of the time it takes for a data packet to travel from the point of origin to the destination and then back to the source. E2E refers to the time it takes for information to travel from its source to its destination in a network system. Both metrics are commonly used in computer networks to evaluate latency or network response time [7].

4 Case Study

This section details the practical application of these approaches, consider a manufacturing plant where both classical and deep learning methods are deployed for anomaly detection testing. Data from various sensors and equipment is collected using OPC-UA and fed into the anomaly detection systems. For overall performance evaluation, the Average Accuracy metric is used. Also, Execution Time using CPU and GPU is calculated to measure the speed of the techniques. Furthermore, in terms of latency, RTT and E2E metrics are used. Finally, one of the main restrictions of the system is that it can process 500 tinplate lids per minute, so the Execution Time should be equal to or less than 75 ms.

4.1 System Implementation

This implementation addresses the detection of manufacturing defects in tinplate lids within a factory setting. At the core of the control layer, a Siemens S7 1200 PLC is used. Also, a vision setup comprising an industrial visible spectrum camera and a lighting system, along with an inductive sensor for detecting lids on the conveyor belt. In the supervision layer, a workstation is employed with an

Intel Core I9 3.3GHz CPU and NVIDIA Titan XP GPU for training/validation and testing YOLOv8 for image recognition. This workstation is tasked with acquiring images and running both the OPC-UA server and YOLOv8. Figure 6 highlights the key components utilized in the system architecture.

4.2 Dataset Acquisition

As a first step, images of tinplate lids in both "*good*" and "*defective*" conditions are acquired. The most common defects include interior peeling, defective paint, and the missing rubber on the inside edge. Table 1 illustrates the distribution of data used for the training, validation, and testing stages in a later phase with the classical approach and YOLOv8.

Table 1. Distribution of data acquisition

Task	Good	Defective
Training	400	400
Validation	75	75
Testing	37	39
Total	512	514

4.3 Histogram Based Approach

As defined in Subsect. 3.1 the execution of the pipeline comprises several steps and in this section, the execution of each stage will be presented taking into consideration an example of a "*defective*" tinplate lid. Figure 3 shows the results of the first 4 stages of the pipeline, resulting in the extraction of the lid using the Hough Transform [16] to detect the circle that represents the lid and subsequently the center of it. Figure 4 shows the extraction of each of the bands defined from the polar representation of the Cartesian image of the tinplate lid. For each of these bands, the frequency histograms are analyzed (see Fig. 5), and based on thresholds and identified "peaks/valleys", it can be determined if a specific band presents a possible defect. Finally, all bands are evaluated and it is established whether the entire tinplate lid is "*defective*" or "*good*". This result is used for the following processes within the system for future decisions.

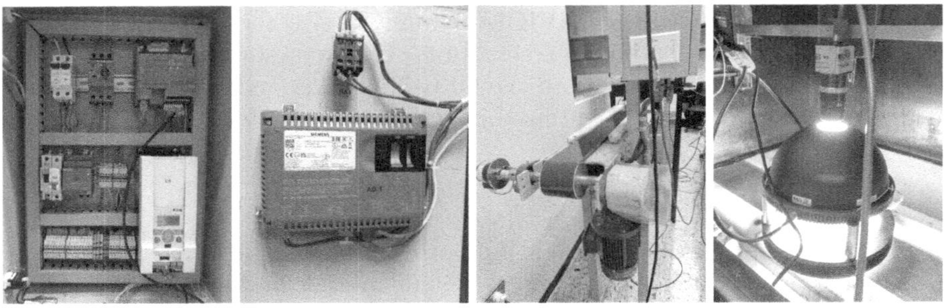

Fig. 6. *(1st)* Siemens S7 1200 PLC. *(2nd)* HMI TP700 comfort. *(3rd)* Conveyor belt. *(4th)* Industrial camera and lighting system.

4.4 YOLOv8

Before starting the training phase, the Albumentations library is used to increase the number of training examples. This library allows transformations, such as cropping, rotations, brightness, and contrast adjustments, enhancing the dataset with realistic variations. YOLOv8 models, specifically *YOLOv8m*, *YOLOv8s*, and *YOLOv8n* are used for classification tasks. After training and validation, normalized confusion matrices (Fig. 7) and Average Accuracy percentages (Table 2) are obtained.

Finally, the EigenCAM [19] technique with GitHub implementation[1] is used to understand YOLOv8 model results, highlighting influential image regions. Figure 8 shows a qualitative evaluation of the prediction results of three variants of the YOLOv8 model (YOLOv8m, YOLOv8s, and YOLOv8n) on defect images from an industrial test set. The first column shows the original images of circular parts with defects, while the following columns show the activation heat maps of each model. Heatmaps use a color scale where blue represents low activation and warm colors (red/yellow) indicate areas where the model detects anomalies with greater intensity. It is interesting to observe how each variant of the model generates different activation patterns: YOLOv8m (last column) shows more defined and balanced patterns, YOLOv8s (third column) presents more dispersed and contrasted activations, and YOLOv8n (second column) shows more localized and punctual activations , although they all manage to effectively identify the defective areas in the circular parts.

[1] https://github.com/rigvedrs/YOLO-V8-CAM.

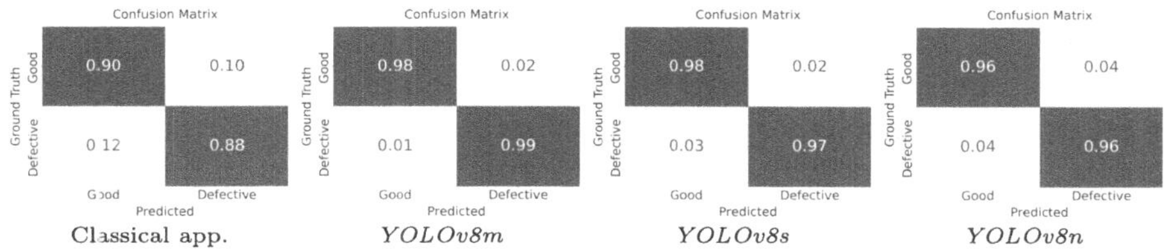

Fig. 7. Normalized confusion matrix of each technique calculated on the test set.

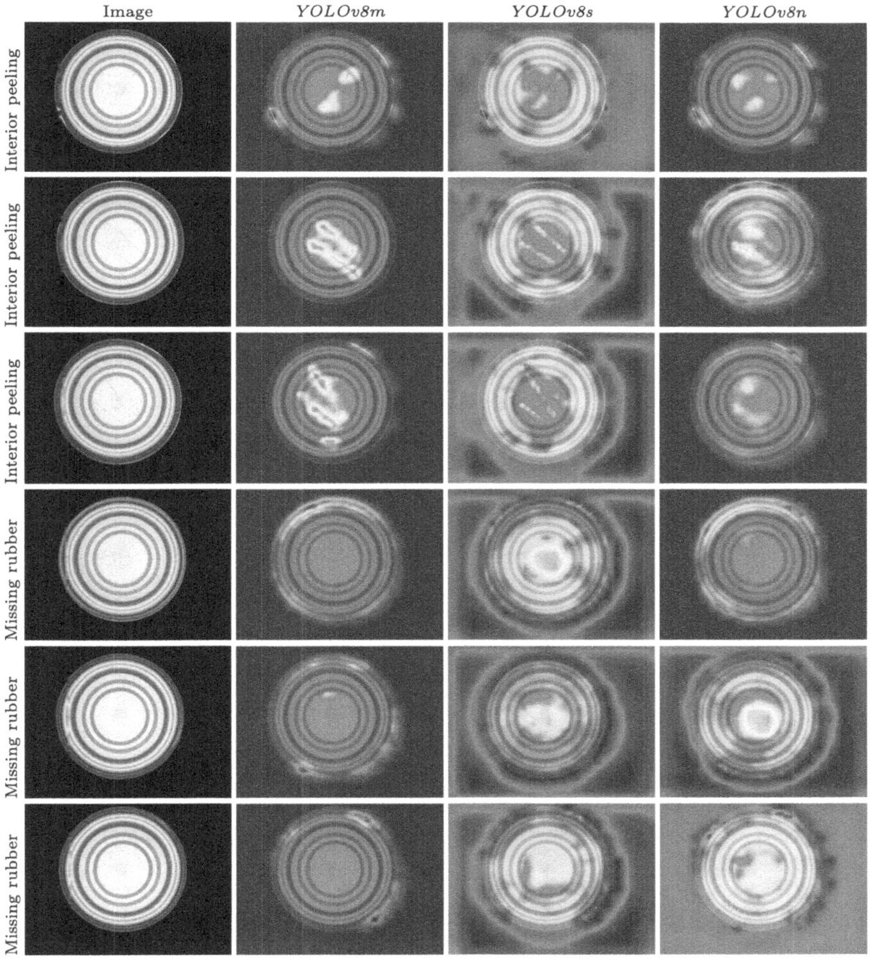

Fig. 8. Qualitative evaluation of YOLOv8 prediction results on defective images of the testing set.

4.5 OPC-UA Vision Server Implementation

The OPC-UA companion specification for machine vision aims to simplify the integration of machine vision systems into production control and IT systems. It enhances existing interfaces and establishes new horizontal and vertical integration capabilities, enabling authorized process participants to communicate relevant data up to the IT enterprise level. The "SingleExecution" and "ContinuousExecution" states are the part where the previously developed algorithms could be executed, specifically for the case study it would be executed in the "ContinuousExecution" state because the conveyor belt is running and the system would be continually waiting for an image of a tinplate lid. The other states are part of the OPC-UA specification and are part of the concept of a vision system that models the standard. The representation of the Vision Finite State Machine (VFSM) (Fig. 9 *(left)*) and the code of the implemented state machine (Fig. 9 *(right)*), which integrates the execution of both the classic and the YOLOv8 approaches.

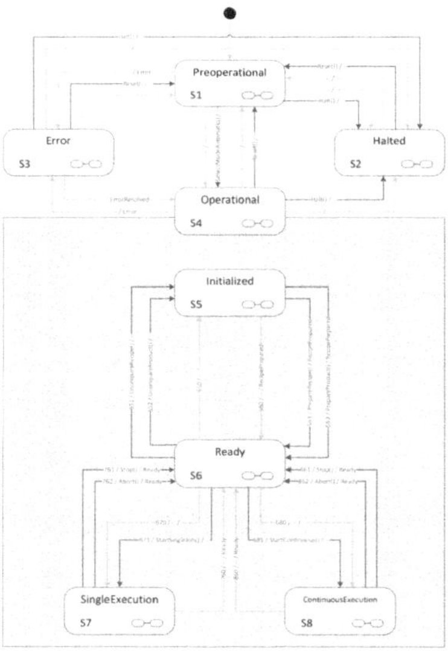


```
def process(self, image):
 if image:
    if self.sCurId.get_value() == self.sContExe.nodeid:
      if self.technique=="classical":
        #Pre-Processing
        image_gray = self.preProcessing(image)

        #Get center of lid
        center, radius = self.getCenter(image_gray)

        #Get polar image
        linear_polar_image_gray = getPolar(image_gray, center, radius)

        #
        for band_number in range(1,12):
            pband = self.getBand(linear_polar_image_gray,band_number)

            #Calculate Histograms
            histogram = self.calculateHistogram(pband)

            #If one band is defective all image is defective
            result = self.getResClas(histogram, band_number, result)
        print("Result: ", result)
      if self.technique=="yolo":
        # predict on 1 images
        results = model(image)
        #Index: defective (0), good (1)
        pred = results[0].probs.cpu().detach().numpy()

        if(pred[0] > pred[1]):
            result = "Defective"
            activateActuator()
        else:
            result = "Good"
        print(f"Result: {result}")
```

Fig. 9. *(left)* States and transitions of the VisionAutomaticModeStateMachineType. Part OPC 40100-1 of the OPC-UA specification [10]. *(right)* Code executed in VFSM within OPC-UA server integrating and running classical approach and YOLOv8.

4.6 Experimental Results

For the evaluation of this study, Average Accuracy, Execution Time (e.g., CPU and GPU), RTT, E2E, and metrics are calculated to measure framework performance. Table 2 shows results from each technique calculated on the testing set—in the case of YOLOv8 the number of parameters of the neural network is shown. The technique that presents the best Average Accuracy is *YOLOv8m*, with a value of 0.985. In the case of Execution Time using CPU, classical approach presents the best performance with a time of 51.25 ms, while using GPU the best result is presented by *YOLOv8n* with a time of 13.10 ms. On the other hand, Fig. 7 shows the confusion matrix of each of the implemented techniques where it can be seen that *YOLOv8m* shows the best performance, allowing precisely differentiation between the "*good*" and "*defective*" classes. Finally, Table 3 shows results from the performance evaluation in E2E and RTT metrics using different payloads, these metrics calculate the connection latency of the OPC-UA server and OPC-UA client created for this task.

Table 2. Performance evaluation Average Execution Time and Average Accuracy per each approach—in the case of YOLOv8 the number of network parameters is provided.

Technique	Params. (M)	Execution Time		Average Accuracy
		CPU(ms)	GPU(ms)	
Classical app.	-	**51.25**	-	0.890
YOLOv8m	42.70	218.90	67.50	**0.985**
YOLOv8s	13.50	99.65	25.55	0.976
YOLOv8n	4.20	52.55	**13.10**	0.963

Table 3. Performance evaluation in End-to-End delay and Round Trip Time metrics in milliseconds.

Image Size		Payload	E2E	RTT
Width	Height	(kB)	(ms)	(ms)
1440	1080	1555300	121	238
1080	810	1166500	113	217
720	540	777700	98	186
360	270	388900	89	172

5 Conclusion

This paper proposes a methodology to improve anomaly detection in industrial processes by comparing classic and deep learning techniques, and integrating OPC-UA. A classic histogram-based technique identifies anomalies with an Average Accuracy of 0.890. In contrast, YOLOv8 deep learning models (*YOLOv8m*,

YOLOv8s, and *YOLOv8n*) achieve average accuracies of 0.985, 0.976, and 0.963, respectively, with *YOLOv8m* performing the best. Furthermore, in relation to the Execution Time, *YOLOv8n* obtained a time of 13.10 ms but an Average Accuracy lower than *YOLOv8m*. Also, all YOLOv8 models using GPU are within the system restrictions of staying within 75 ms. On the other hand, E2E and RTT show that the system has a low latency connection with the OPC-UA server and can be used in near real-time systems. Finally, an OPC-UA server and a VFSM are implemented, and the technique based on histograms and YOLOv8 models is executed within the "ContinuousExecution" state, thus allowing communication at a closer device level, which allows execution with low latency and in near-real-time. On summary, it can be concluded that the combined use of OPC-UA and YOLOv8 in industrial environments offers significant benefits such as secure and standardized communication and interoperability between devices, along with near-real-time monitoring. OPC-UA enables seamless and protected data exchange, while YOLOv8 provides fast and accurate object classification, automating visual inspection and reducing human errors. This integration is adaptable and scalable, making it ideal for different industrial application contexts.

Acknowledgements. This research has been partially supported by the ESPOL project CIDIS-004-2023, and by University of Granada.

References

1. Aggarwal, C.C., Yu, P.S.: Outlier detection for high dimensional data. In: International Conference on Management of Data, pp. 37–46 (2001)
2. Ahmad, R., Kamaruddin, S.: An overview of time-based and condition-based maintenance in industrial application. Comput. Ind. Eng. **63**(1), 135–149 (2012)
3. Beak, S., Han, Y.H., Moon, Y., Lee, J., Jeong, J.: YOLOv7-based anomaly detection using intensity and NG types in labeling in cosmetic manufacturing processes. Processes **11**(8), 2266 (2023)
4. Canizo, M., Triguero, I., Conde, A., Onieva, E.: Multi-head CNN-RNN for multi-time series anomaly detection: an industrial case study. Neurocomputing **363**, 246–260 (2019)
5. Chandola, V., Banerjee, A., Kumar, V.: Anomaly detection: a survey. ACM Comput. Surv. **41**(3), 1–58 (2009)
6. Chikodili, N.B., Abdulmalik, M.D., Abisoye, O.A., Bashir, S.A.: Outlier detection in multivariate time series data using a fusion of K-medoid, standardized Euclidean distance and Z-score. In: ICTA 2020. CCIS, vol. 1350, pp. 259–271. Springer, Cham (2021). https://doi.org/10.1007/978-3-030-69143-1_21
7. Eckhardt, A., Müller, S.: Analysis of the round trip time of OPC UA and TSN based peer-to-peer communication. In: International Conference on Emerging Technologies and Factory Automation, pp. 161–167. IEEE (2019)
8. Ergen, T., Kozat, S.S.: Unsupervised anomaly detection with LSTM neural networks. Trans. Neural Netw. Learn. Syst. **31**(8), 3127–3141 (2019)

9. Ferragut, E.M., Laska, J., Bridges, R.A.: A new, principled approach to anomaly detection. In: International Conference on Machine Learning and Applications, vol. 2, pp. 210–215. IEEE (2012)
10. OPC Foundation: OPC 40100-1 Machine Vision - Control, Configuration management, recipe management, result management. Technical report, OPC Foundation (2024). https://opcfoundation.org/developer-tools/documents/view/217
11. Hinton, G.E., Salakhutdinov, R.R.: Reducing the dimensionality of data with neural networks. In: Science, vol. 313, pp. 504–507. American Association for the Advancement of Science (2006)
12. Iivarinen, J.: Surface defect detection with histogram-based texture features. In: Intelligent Robots and Computer Vision XIX: Algorithms, Techniques, and Active Vision, vol. 4197, pp. 140–145. SPIE (2000)
13. Jocher, G., Chaurasia, A., Qiu, J.: Ultralytics YOLOv8 (2023). https://github.com/ultralytics/ultralytics
14. Kim, K., Kim, H., Chun, J., Kang, M., Hong, M., Min, B.: Real-time anomaly detection in packaged food x-ray images using supervised learning. Comput. Mater. Contin **67**(2), 2547–2568 (2021)
15. Klarák, J., et al.: From anomaly detection to defect classification. Sensors **24**(2), 429 (2024)
16. Leavers, V.: Which Hough transform? CVGIP: Image Underst. **58**(2), 250–264 (1993)
17. Lee, J., Kim, Y.: Application of OPC-UA based on IoT for monitoring and controlling manufacturing processes. Procedia Comput. Sci. **155**, 154–161 (2019)
18. Li, C.L., Sohn, K., Yoon, J., Pfister, T.: Cutpaste: self-supervised learning for anomaly detection and localization. In: International Conference on Computer Vision and Pattern Recognition, pp. 9664–9674 (2021)
19. Muhammad, M.B., Yeasin, M.: Eigen-CAM: class activation map using principal components. In: International Joint Conference on Neural Networks, pp. 1–7. IEEE (2020)
20. Pang, G., Shen, C., Cao, L., van den Hengel, A.: Deep learning for anomaly detection: a review. ACM Comput. Surv. **54**(2), 1–38 (2021)
21. Peña, M., Biscarri, F., Guerrero, J.I., Monedero, I., León, C.: Rule-based system to detect energy efficiency anomalies in smart buildings, a data mining approach. Expert Syst. Appl. **56**, 242–255 (2016)
22. Pham, D.L., Chang, T.W., et al.: A YOLO-based real-time packaging defect detection system. Procedia Comput. Sci. **217**, 886–894 (2023)
23. Schölkopf, B., Platt, J.C., Shawe-Taylor, J., Smola, A.J., Williamson, R.C.: Estimating the support of a high-dimensional distribution. Neural Comput. **13**(7), 1443–1471 (2001)
24. Turk, M.A., Pentland, A.P.: Face recognition using eigenfaces. In: Computer Society Conference on Computer Vision and Pattern Recognition, pp. 586–587. IEEE Computer Society (1991)
25. Velesaca, H., et al.: Anomaly detection in industrial production products using OPC-UA and deep learning. In: International Conference on Data Science, Technology and Applications, pp. 505–512. INSTICC, SciTePress (2024)
26. Velesaca, H.O., Holgado-Terriza, J.A., Guerrero, J.M.G.: Optimizing smart factory operations: a methodological approach to industrial system implementation based on OPC-UA. In: E3S Web of Conferences, vol. 532, pp. 1–15. EDP Sciences (2024)
27. Vogel-Heuser, B., Fay, A., Schaefer, I., Tichy, M., Trächtler, A., Legat, C.: Architectural design of multi-agent systems in the context of OPC UA and automationML. Proc. IEEE **104**(5), 947–967 (2016)

28. Wong, W.K., Moore, A., Cooper, G., Wagner, M.: Rule-based anomaly pattern detection for detecting disease outbreaks. In: AAAI/IAAI, pp. 217–223 (2002)
29. Zavrtanik, V., Kristan, M., Skočaj, D.: Draem-a discriminatively trained reconstruction embedding for surface anomaly detection. In: International Conference on Computer Vision and Pattern Recognition, pp. 8330–8339 (2021)

Developing a LoRaWAN-Based Data Acquisition Device Empowered by AI

Menno J. Faber[1,2](✉), Helder R. de O. Rocha[1], Marcelo E. V. Segatto[1], and Jair A. Lima Silva[1]

[1] Laboratório de Telecomunicações (LabTel), Universidade Federal do Espírito Santo (UFES), Av. Fernando Ferrari, 514 - Goiabeiras, Vitória, ES 29075-910, Brazil

[2] 2Solve Engenharia e Tecnologia LTDA, Av. Adalberto Simão Nader, 675 - Republica, Vitória, ES 29070-010, Brazil

menno.faber@2solve.com

https://www.2solve.com/en/produto/transmissor-wireless-multivariavel

Abstract. A customized data acquisition (DAq) device is presented for Industrial Internet of Things (IIoT) applications. Referred to as 2S Tools Flex DAq, the multivariable wireless DAq supports advanced connectivity options such as LoRaWAN, LTE, and ZigBee, accommodating a wide range of sensors with low power consumption. To demonstrate the potential of integrating Artificial Intelligence (AI) into a system involving sensors, the 2S Tools Flex DAq, and the cloud, we applied Long Short-Term Memory (LSTM) neural networks for predictive analytics for water quality parameters collected by the device. Specifically, we forecast pH, water level, and temperature using real-time data collected by the 2S Tools Flex DAq in a remote monitoring system. The LSTM model achieved high accuracy in predicting pH and temperature, with R^2 values of 0.97 and 0.99, respectively. These experimental results highlight the feasibility of embedding AI capabilities into the DAq device we built for enhanced predictive maintenance and process optimization in IIoT settings.

Keywords: LoRaWAN · Data Acquisition · Artificial Intelligence · LSTM

1 Introduction

The Industrial Internet of Things (IIoT), a vast network of sensors embedded within intelligent physical objects, is revolutionizing industries across the board, from "Hasan B. Celebi" [1], and "Shadi Al-Sarawi" [2]. In the industrial domain, the IIoT serves as a key catalyst for Industry 4.0, a transformative movement marked by heightened automation, data-driven decision-making, and the interconnection of intelligent systems. Consequently, connectivity technologies require wireless links that offer reliability, low power consumption, and seamless integration with other networks. In this evolving landscape, a low-power wide-area network (LPWAN) such as long-range wide area network (LoRaWAN) emerges as a

F. R. Narváez et al. (Eds.): SmartTech-IC 2024, CCIS 2392, pp. 19–32, 2026.
https://doi.org/10.1007/978-3-031-98287-3_2

compelling solution for IIoT connectivity "Jetmir Haxhibeqiri" [3]. LoRaWAN's appeal lies in its support for low-power operation, which ensures a prolonged sensor lifespan. Additionally, it offers long-range communication capabilities, enabling extensive coverage. Its cost-effective deployment and seamless integration with diverse network platforms further solidify its position as a preferred choice for IIoT applications.

The results of our previous studies indicate that LoRaWAN can achieve communication ranges of approximately 3 km in urban settings and up to 10 km in open areas "Menno J. Faber" [4,5]. The feasibility of LoRaWAN technology for long-range communication in rural settings, specifically for oil well monitoring, was investigated in [4]. A system using standard LoRaWAN devices successfully established communication over nearly 3 km. Signal strength measurements collected during this study highlighted LoRaWAN's suitability for intelligent monitoring solutions in the oil industry. In [5], a comprehensive experimental examination of LoRa technology's performance was conducted, focusing on its physical layer (PHY). The study explored LoRa's behavior under negative signal-to-noise ratios, often encountered in long-distance communication scenarios. A mathematical model was developed to predict bit error rates, considering LoRa's code rate, and its accuracy was rigorously validated through simulations.

In addition to the theoretical and simulation-based analyses, real-world experiments with commercially available LoRaWAN equipment were conducted. These experiments demonstrated successful communication over distances of up to 10 km in open environments. The alignment between theoretical predictions, numerical simulations, and experimental results reinforces the practical applicability of the study's findings. Overall, this research deepens our understanding of LoRa's PHY layer, offering valuable insights into its performance characteristics and limitations, particularly in the context of long-range communication. Notably, in both aforementioned works, we utilized our own customized Data Acquisition (DAq) device equipped with LoRaWAN connectivity.

"Wesley S Costa" [6], introduced a novel network design for IoT sensors was, integrating mesh (ZigBee) and star (LoRa) network topologies to enhance energy efficiency and ensure comprehensive coverage for sensor networks. The network design process leveraged real sensor data and employed sophisticated algorithms to optimize network layout and resource allocation, thereby minimizing energy consumption. However, despite the increased robustness of the proposed hybrid design compared to a standalone star network, a bottleneck at the gateway was identified.

Building on this work, "Matheus A Gava" [7] presented a methodology for optimizing resource allocation in LoRaWAN networks by incorporating repeaters for extended coverage. This methodology uses specialized algorithms to determine the optimal placement and configuration of repeaters, considering parameters such as spread factor, bandwidth, and power consumption. The objective was to optimize both energy consumption and data collection time. A key finding was that the optimal spread factor depends on the number of devices in the network. Additionally, the methodology accounts for potential network growth, ensuring equitable resource allocation over time. It is important to note that the data used in both studies were collected using the same DAq device.

Sensor networks form the bedrock of the IIoT, continuously collecting vital information on process parameters. This data powers real-time monitoring, process optimization, and predictive maintenance strategies, leading to significant improvements in efficiency and productivity [2]. To effectively manage and harness this sensor data, robust and dependable connectivity solutions are essential. This is where a DAq device proves invaluable by "Victor K. Sarker" [8], DAq devices are engineered to withstand the rigors of industrial environments, delivering the communication capabilities and resilience needed for complex IIoT applications. In this context, we present a custom-designed integrated circuit specifically optimized for sensor network applications. This novel solution integrates advanced connectivity options, such as LoRaWAN, Long Term Evolution (LTE), and Zigbee, to ensure seamless communication between diverse sensor types and the broader IIoT ecosystem. Additionally, we report on a series of experiments demonstrating the potential of applying artificial intelligence (AI) to enhance our customized IoT solution.

The organization of this paper is as follows. Important works presenting the combination of LoRaWAN and AI are described in Sect. 2. The 2S Tools Flex DAq is described in Sect. 3, followed by a brief description of the employed Long Short-Term Memory (LSTM) architecture. The experimental setup, the results, and the concluding remarks are presented in Sects. 5, 6, and 7, respectively.

2 Optimizing and Enabling Intelligence on LoRaWAN Connectivity with Artificial Intelligence

The study from "Willian GV dos Santos" [9] introduces a strategy to address communication reliability challenges in IoT networks, with a focus on LoRa. It proposes a novel hybrid topology that combines star and mesh structures to enhance both coverage and reliability in sensor deployments. Additionally, an optimization algorithm is presented, which merges Genetic Algorithms with K-Medoids clustering to determine optimal sensor placement. "Francesca Cuomo" [10], explored how machine learning can optimize LoRaWAN networks for IoT applications. By using real-world data to profile devices and predict channel usage, they employ methods such as k-means clustering, LSTM neural networks, and decision trees. The objective is to optimize network efficiency by adjusting parameters such as the Spreading Factor. The key takeaway is that techniques like decision trees and LSTM can effectively predict device behavior, enabling proactive management of LoRaWAN networks.

"Eslam Eldeeb" [11], introduces and analyzes the Smart Campus dataset, which includes data from a LoRaWAN-based network of sensors deployed at the University of Oulu. This dataset encompasses LoRa network parameters as well as sensor readings, including CO2 levels, sound, moisture, temperature, humidity, light, and battery status. The study addresses missing data due to transmission failures by proposing and evaluating various imputation techniques.

An LSTM model is also employed to predict future sensor readings and assess the effectiveness of the imputation methods. Additionally, the study demonstrates a practical use case by developing a deep neural network model to predict room occupancy based on sensor data, achieving an impressive 95% accuracy.

An innovative architecture was introduced by "Jorge P. Queralta" [12] for remote health monitoring, leveraging Edge and Fog computing along with LPWAN technology to enhance healthcare services in areas with limited connectivity. The architecture uses LoRa for efficient data transmission and integrates Edge-AI for real-time processing and data compression. Its effectiveness is demonstrated through a fall detection system using an LSTM based on a Recurrent Neural Network (RNN), achieving high accuracy in detecting falls. This approach reduces latency, optimizes bandwidth usage, and enables deployment in challenging environments, ultimately improving healthcare accessibility and efficiency.

The study presented by "Yurong Yang" [13] focuses on predicting water quality in mangrove wetland ecosystems, which is crucial for protecting these environments from pollution and ensuring their sustainability. The authors propose a novel hybrid model called CNN-LSTM with Attention (CLA) to predict key water quality variables, specifically pH and ammonia nitrogen (NH3-N). The CLA model integrates Convolutional Neural Networks (CNN) and LSTM networks with an attention mechanism to effectively capture both local features and long-term dependencies in noisy, nonlinear time series data. Experimental results demonstrate that the CLA model outperforms traditional models, providing a robust and accurate tool for environmental monitoring and management of mangrove ecosystems. Meanwhile, "Zhuhua Hu" [14] present a novel approach to accurately predict water quality parameters, specifically pH and water temperature, in cage-based smart mariculture systems. The dynamic and open nature of marine aquaculture environments results in nonlinear and variable changes in water quality, which pose significant challenges for traditional forecasting methods due to low accuracy, poor generalization, and high computational complexity. To address these challenges, the authors propose a method that integrates data pre-processing, correlation analysis, and deep learning using LSTM networks.

The study by "Sima Siami-Namini" [15] compared the forecasting capabilities of traditional ARIMA models with deep learning-based LSTM networks for time series prediction. The results demonstrate that LSTM models outperform ARIMA, achieving an 84–87% reduction in prediction error rates on average.

Therefore, in this work, we employed LSTM to develop a predictive model for water quality parameters, specifically focusing on pH, water level, and temperature. This approach leverages the LSTM network's ability to capture long-term dependencies in time-series data and the complex dynamics of water quality fluctuations. We analyzed the model's performance in predicting these key parameters to assess its potential for real-world applications in water resource management and environmental monitoring, integrated with the data acquisition device we built, as described in the following section.

3 The 2S Tools Flex DAq

The data acquisition device we built for the experiments is depicted in Fig. 1. We named it 2S Tools Flex DAq, a multi-variable wireless data acquisition device designed to meet the evolving needs of IIoT and Industry 4.0 applications. It serves as a data logger, control module, and I/O repeater. This versatile tool is part of a family of automation products designed to simplify and reduce the costs associated with automating industrial processes. Its universal design makes it suitable for both small and large applications across various market segments.

Fig. 1. The 2S Tools Flex DAq, a wireless multivariable data acquisition device we built. The device is shown with its enclosure closed (left) and open (right), highlighting its versatile input terminals and communication module slots.

The 2S Tools Flex DAq provides a range of standard features, including analog inputs, serial ports, digital input/output, and a slot for Micro SD cards up to 32 GB, enhancing its data logging capabilities. It also includes features ideal for IoT and IIoT applications, such as I^2C and 1-Wire buses, which facilitate the integration of displays, digital sensors, magnetometers, accelerometers, gyroscopes, and a wide array of evolving sensors and actuators. This capability significantly enhances the flexibility of the 2S Tools Flex DAq by enabling the integration of multiple sensors into a single device. Additionally, it supports the simultaneous integration of sensors with diverse functionalities such as humidity, temperature, vibration, luminosity, and sound on a single bus.

For custom demands, additional sensing modules can be directly integrated with the microcontroller via SPI and UART ports. The 2S Tools Flex DAq supports pulse inputs, RS485 or RS232 Modbus RTU communication, and inputs for load cells. It also offers 24-bit analog inputs, switchable between 4–20 mA and 0–10 V, along with inputs for sensors such as PT100, PT1000, thermocouples, and vacuum. Additionally, it includes a relay for switching loads on or off. To ensure flexible application, the 2S Tools Flex DAq comes with two slots for communication modules, supporting both wired and wireless technologies. This design allows integration into networks using LTE, LoRaWAN, ZigBee, Wi-Fi, BLE, and GPS. The dual slot configuration enables redundancy or isolated operation, accommodating different network infrastructures and communication protocols. In terms of energy efficiency, the 2S Tools Flex DAq is optimized for low power consumption, with a sleep current as low as 50 μA.

By combining sensing technologies on digital buses with specific batteries, the device can perform measurements and data transmission for up to five years at minimal cost. Power supply options include a 3.7 V Li-Ion battery, a 3.6 V $LiSOCl_2$ battery, or an external DC power supply (9–36 V). The robust design of the 2S Tools Flex DAq, with plastic (IP65) and aluminum (IP67) enclosures, makes it suitable for harsh industrial environments by providing protection against dust and water ingress. The enclosure dimensions are 120 mm $\times$ 50 mm $\times$ 125 mm, with options for various fixation supports and covers. A comprehensive list of supported sensor combinations and communication protocols is provided in Table 1.

Table 1. List of Sensors and Wireless Communication Protocols Supported by 2S Tools Flex DAq

Sensor Types	Wireless Communication Protocols
Digital Input	Global Positioning System (GPS)
Digital Pressure Sensor	LoRaMesh (Model Proprietary)
Dust Sensor	LoRaWAN
Energy Meter (for Brazil)	Long Term Evolution (LTE)
Five Analog Inputs (Voltage or Current)	Wireless Fidelity (Wi-Fi)
Four Temperature Sensors (1-Wire)	XBee
Four Temperature Sensors (Thermocouple)	Zigbee
Frequency Input	N/A
Ge/Druck Industrial Pressure Sensor	N/A
Inclination	N/A
Infrared Thermometer	N/A
Interrupt Input	N/A
LIDAR Optical Distance Measurement	N/A
Modbus RTU	N/A
Pulse Input	N/A
RGB Color Sensor	N/A
Strain Gauge/Load Cell	N/A
Temperature and Humidity (I2C)	N/A
Vacuum (Thermocouple)	N/A
Vibration	N/A

3.1 The PCB Layout of the 2S Tools Flex DAq

The Printed Circuit Board (PCB) layout of the 2S Tools Flex DAq is illustrated in Fig. 2. All sensors connect via 1.5 mm^2 Born screw connectors, widely used in industrial environments. In the upper left corner, the RS485 connector is visible, including the A and B bus connectors. RL1 and RL2 denote the relay output connections, while P1 through P3 serve as digital, pulse, frequency, and interrupt inputs. The lower left corner houses a port for digital sensors using I2C or 1-Wire protocols. The bottom connectors are allocated for power inputs and outputs, with dedicated connectors supporting various configurations, including 9–32 V, 5 V, and battery inputs. The sensor power output supplies up to 100 mA at 20 V, ideal for powering 4–20 mA sensors. This output can be deactivated when the 2S Tools Flex DAq is in sleep mode. Positioned between the battery connector and the sensor power output is a micro USB connector used for configuring the unit. On the right side, the 24-bit analog input connectors are situated, with all five inputs configurable to read voltage or current, such as 0–10 V and 4–20 mA signals. The AIN2 connector also supports strain gauges, load cells, and vacuum sensors. At the center, two slots accommodate communication modules such as LoRaWAN, LTE, or additional sensing modules for expanded capabilities.

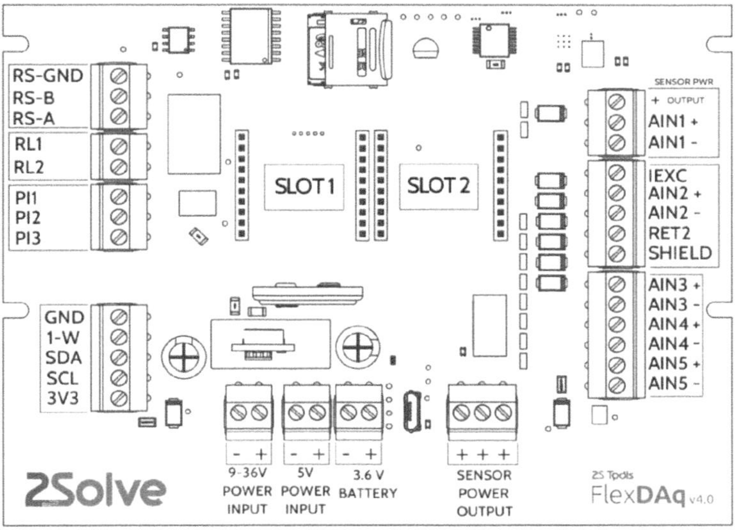

Fig. 2. Layout of the 2S Tools Flex DAq: RS485 connectors (upper left), relay outputs (RL1, RL2), and digital, pulse, frequency, and interrupt inputs (P1-P3). The I2C/1-Wire digital sensor port is located in the lower left, while power inputs/outputs are positioned at the bottom. Configurable 24-bit analog inputs are on the right. Two central slots accommodate communication modules or additional sensing capabilities.

3.2 Configuration Interface

The 2S Tools Flex DAq can be configured through the graphical user interface (GUI) shown in Fig. 3. To establish communication, the device must be connected to a Windows computer using a micro USB cable. The GUI provides an intuitive platform for enabling or disabling sensors and communication protocols, as well as configuring their associated parameters. Users can easily adjust settings such as sample rates and delay times, ensuring precise control over device operations and slot assignments for additional modules.

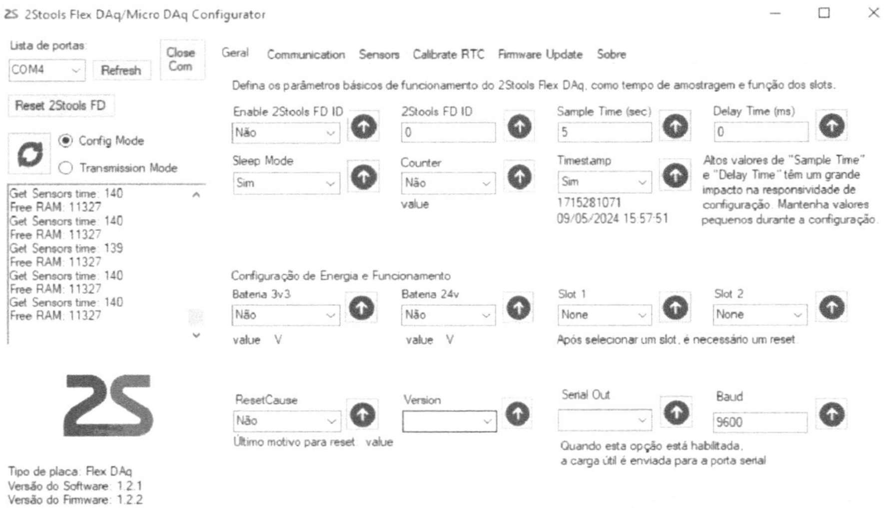

Fig. 3. The 2S Tools Flex DAq GUI provides configuration options for sensor management and communication protocols. Key features include selecting connection modes, adjusting parameters, and configuring slots for extended functionalities.

3.3 Power Consumption

The average power consumption of the 2S Tools Flex DAq is significantly influenced by the connected sensors and communication modules. All sensors and modules can be deactivated in sleep mode, reducing power consumption to as low as 53.68 μA (see Fig. 4). Theoretically, with a 1000 mAh battery, this translates to a battery life of about 20,000 h or 2.28 years. Note that this calculation excludes periods when the 2S Tools Flex DAq is actively reading sensors or transmitting data. During transmission, current consumption can surge to around 100 mA for LoRaWAN and up to 600 mA for LTE. When the device is active but not transmitting, the current draw is approximately 10 mA, though this varies based on the connected sensors. Some I2C sensors consume less than 1 mA, while others using 4–20 mA can draw over 100 mA each. In scenarios where multiple high-consumption 4–20 mA sensors are used, alternative power sources such as solar panels are recommended.

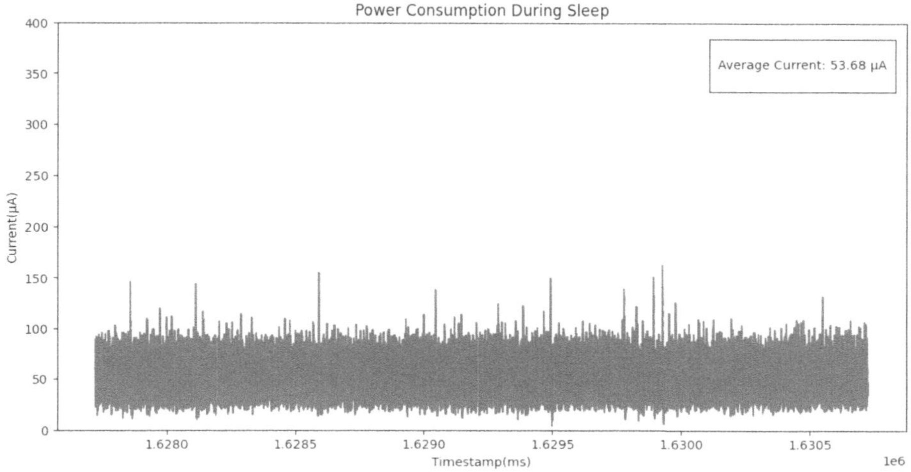

Fig. 4. Sleep Mode Power Profile. This chart illustrates the power consumption of the 2S Tools Flex DAq in sleep mode, averaging 53.68 μA. The data shows stable current levels with occasional peaks.

4 The Used LSTM Architecture

In this section, we outline the methodology used for forecasting pH, water level, and temperature based on a dataset of 4,000 samples. Each sample is recorded at one-minute intervals, with a prediction horizon of one sample. The selected neural network for this forecasting task is the LSTM network. LSTM networks are a widely used type of Recurrent Neural Network (RNN) due to their effectiveness in time series forecasting. They achieve this by selectively storing or forgetting information through special gates, allowing only relevant data to influence the forecast. An LSTM module processes three inputs: the current input vector, the previous output (network response), and the stored memory state. The gates in the LSTM include a forget gate, which decides whether to discard or retain information, an input gate that updates the memory state, and an output gate that determines the network's response [16]. The equations governing the LSTM module are as follows:

$$\mathbf{i}_t = \sigma(\mathbf{W}_i \mathbf{x}_t + \mathbf{R}_i \mathbf{h}_{t-1} + \mathbf{b}_i) \tag{1}$$

$$\mathbf{f}_t = \sigma(\mathbf{W}_f \mathbf{x}_t + \mathbf{R}_f \mathbf{h}_{t-1} + \mathbf{b}_f) \tag{2}$$

$$\mathbf{o}_t = \sigma(\mathbf{W}_o\mathbf{x}_t + \mathbf{R}_o\mathbf{h}_{t-1} + \mathbf{b}_o) \tag{3}$$

$$\mathbf{g}_t = \tanh(\mathbf{W}_g\mathbf{x}_t + \mathbf{R}_g\mathbf{h}_{t-1}\mathbf{b}_g) \tag{4}$$

$$\mathbf{c}_t = \mathbf{f}_t \odot \mathbf{c}_{t-1} + \mathbf{i}_t \odot \mathbf{g}_t \tag{5}$$

$$\mathbf{h}_t = \mathbf{o}_t \odot \tanh(\mathbf{c}_t) \tag{6}$$

for i_t the input gate, f_t forget gate, and o_t output gate at time t, x_t denotes the input sample, σ is the sigmoid activation function and c_t the memory unit. The previous hidden state $\mathbf{h_{t-1}}$ and current entry $\mathbf{x_t}$ are used in blocks g e i, and their result are given by the hyperbolic tangent, $\mathbf{g_t} = \tanh(\mathbf{h_{t-1}}, \mathbf{x_t})$ and sigmoide, $\mathbf{i_t} = \sigma(\mathbf{h_{t-1}}, \mathbf{x_t})$. The cell state $\mathbf{c_t}$ is changed by the forget and input gates, and the hidden state $\mathbf{h_t}$ through the exit gate.(b_f, b_i, b_o) and (W_f, W_i, W_o) stands for the bias and weight matrix for each gate, respectively. The symbol $\odot$ is the corresponding multiplication of the elements. Prior to training, validating, and testing the LSTM model, data pre-processing is performed to remove outliers and address missing values. After conducting a detailed calibration of the LSTM, the final architecture is presented in Table 2. The architecture shown in Table 2 consists of one LSTM layer and one Dense layer.

Table 2. Architecture chosen for the LSTM network

Layer	Type	Predicted Variables (pH, Water Level, Temperature)
#1	Input	Dimension = 20 × 3 (timesteps × features)
#2	LSTM	Cells = 50, Activation = ReLU
#3	Dense (Hidden)	Neurons = 5, Activation = Linear
#4	Output	Neurons = 3, Activation = Linear

The evaluations were performed using Python 3.12.1, Keras 3, and an Intel® Core ™ i7-12700H computer with a 2.2 GHz CPU and 16 GB of RAM (Intel, Santa Clara, CA, USA). For the computational simulations with the LSTM model, data were collected approximately between July 1, 2024, at 07:00 and July 3, 2024, at 24:00. Each input pattern for the LSTM model consists of the following variables: pH, water level, and temperature. These variables were then shifted by one minute, creating a complete input pattern with data at time T, while the output corresponds to the same variables at time $T + 1$.

The input and output data were normalized to the range [0, 1] using min-max normalization to enhance the performance of the RNNs. The data were then split into three sets: training (50%), validation (25%), and testing (25%). The test set was subsequently used to evaluate the quality of the forecasts generated by the neural networks, based on Mean Square Error (MSE) and R^2 metrics. The model was trained using the Adam optimizer from the Keras library, with a batch size of 32 examples for 50 epochs. MSE was employed as the loss function, which is commonly used in regression problems.

5 Experimental Setup

Figure 5 presents a schematic overview of a remote water quality monitoring system deployed for continuous monitoring of critical water quality parameters. The system leverages the capabilities of the 2S Tools Flex DAq for environmental monitoring applications. As illustrated, the 2S Tools Flex DAq unit is strategically positioned at a remote water source (indicated by the blue location pin) to facilitate on-site data collection. It is equipped with a suite of sensors integrated via the Modbus communication protocol, enabling the measurement of water quality indicators such as pH, temperature, and water level. Data acquired by the 2S Tools Flex DAq is transmitted wirelessly over LoRaWAN to a dedicated gateway, which then forwards the data via the Message Queuing Telemetry Transport (MQTT) protocol to a cloud based platform. This cloud platform serves as a central repository for data storage and processing using the LSTM model. The figure highlights the 374 m distance between the remote water source and the laboratory data collection point, depicted by the red line.

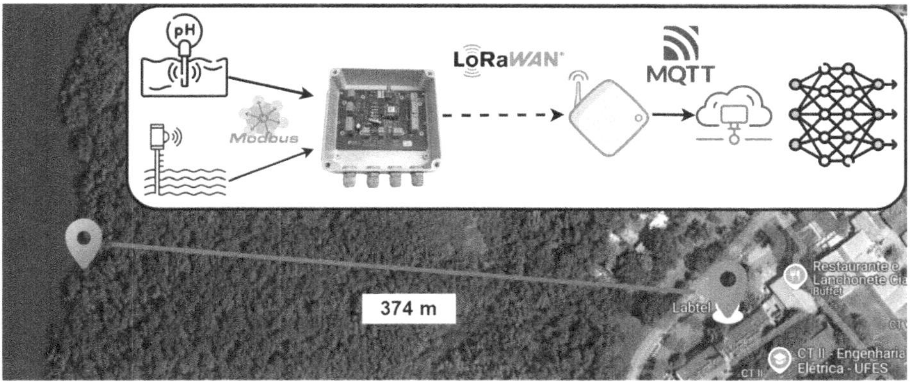

Fig. 5. Remote water quality monitoring system using the 2S Tools Flex DAq for on-site data collection (blue pin) and wireless transmission via LoRaWAN to a gateway (red pin) at our laboratory for cloud based processing. The red line indicates the 374 m distance between the monitoring site and the laboratory. (Color figure online)

6 Results

The results of the forecast simulations for a one-minute period using the LSTM model are presented in Table 3. The table displays the Mean Square Error (MSE) and R^2 scores for the three variables being forecasted: pH, water level, and temperature. The temperature forecast achieved the lowest MSE (0.0024) and highest R^2 (0.99), followed by the pH forecast. However, the water level forecast showed a relatively low R^2 value, likely due to the high noise levels introduced

Table 3. MSE and R^2 Scores for pH, Water Level, and Temperature Predictions

Metric	pH	Water Level	Temperature
Training MSE	0.0014	0.0053	0.0004
Validation MSE	0.0051	0.0049	0.0039
Testing MSE	0.0031	0.0032	0.0024
Testing R^2	0.97	0.78	0.99

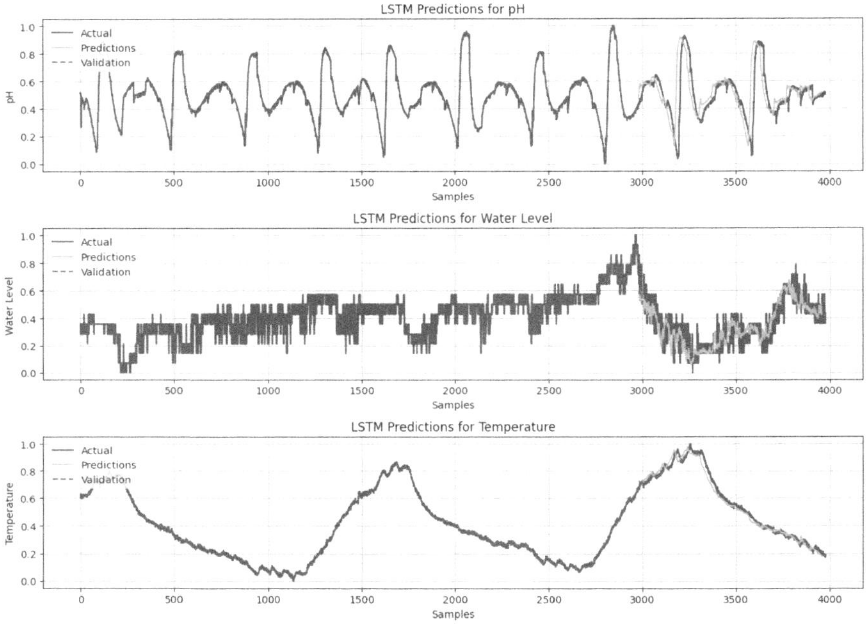

Fig. 6. Measurements used in the predictions: pH (top), water level (middle), and temperature (bottom).

by the conditioning circuits of the level sensor (see Fig. 6). Additionally, the agitation of water waves contributes to rapid fluctuations in the measurements. To mitigate the impact of noise on water level forecasting accuracy, applying a filtering technique prior to data ingestion by the LSTM network is recommended. Potential methods include a moving average filter or a Kalman filter, which can effectively reduce noise while preserving the underlying trend of the water level measurements. This preprocessing step may enhance forecasting performance.

7 Conclusion and Future Work

We have developed the 2S Tools Flex DAq, a custom-designed, multivariable wireless data acquisition device optimized for IIoT applications. It accommodates a wide range of sensors and communication protocols, such as LoRaWAN, LTE, and ZigBee, while being engineered for low power consumption and robust performance in harsh industrial environments. The 2S Tools Flex DAq enhances data collection and transmission capabilities essential for Industry 4.0 initiatives.

To demonstrate the integration of artificial intelligence into a real-time smart system, we applied LSTM neural networks for forecasting pH, water level, and temperature using the DAq device. The LSTM model achieved high accuracy in predicting pH and temperature, with R^2 values of 0.97 and 0.99, respectively, showcasing the feasibility of embedding AI capabilities into our device for enhanced predictive maintenance and process optimization in IIoT settings. As future work, we intend to shift the AI processing to an edge device composed of the 2S Tools Flex DAq and a signal processing module currently in development. This module can incorporate noise reduction techniques like a Kalman filter to improve the accuracy of real-time data processing.

Acknowledgements. This work was partially supported by FAPES-2022-BWBR2, FAPES-2023-LMK95 and FAPES 891/2023 - P:2023-BDKK7, CNPq 309737/2021-4, 309490/2021-9, 158780/2019-1, and 406412/2023-5 projects.

References

1. Celebi, H.B., Pitarokoilis, A., Skoglund, M.: Industrial IoT: Challenges, Design Principles, Applications, and Security, pp. 1–241. Springer, Cham (2020)
2. Al-Sarawi, S., Anbar, M., Abdullah, R., Al Hawari, A.B.: Internet of things market analysis forecasts, 2020–2030. In: 2020 Fourth World Conference on Smart Trends in Systems, Security and Sustainability (WorldS4), pp. 449–453 (2020)
3. Haxhibeqiri, J., De Poorter, E., Moerman, I., Hoebeke, J.: A survey of lorawan for IoT: from technology to application. Sensors **18**(11), 3995 (2018)
4. Faber, M., vd Zwaag, K., Rocha, H., Pereira, E., Segatto, M., Silva, J.: Performance evaluation of lorawan applied to smart monitoring in onshore oil industries. In: 2019 SBMO/IEEE MTT-S International Microwave and Optoelectronics Conference (IMOC), pp. 1–3 (2019)
5. Faber, M.J., van der Zwaag, K.M., dos Santos, W.G.V., Rocha, H.R.O., Segatto, M.E., Silva, J.A.: A theoretical and experimental evaluation on the performance of lora technology. IEEE Sens. J. **20**(16), 9480–9489 (2020)
6. Costa, W.S., et al.: Planning and resource allocation of a hybrid IoT network using artificial intelligence. Internet Things **26**, 101225 (2024)
7. Gava, M.A., Rocha, H.R.O., Faber, M.J., Segatto, M.E.V., Wörtche, H., Silva, J.A.L.: Optimizing resources and increasing the coverage of internet-of-things (IoT) networks: an approach based on lorawan. Sensors **23**(3), 1239 (2023)
8. Sarker, V.K., Queralta, J.P., Gia, T.N., Tenhunen, H., Westerlund, T.: A survey on lora for IoT: integrating edge computing. In: 2019 Fourth International Conference on Fog and Mobile Edge Computing (FMEC), pp. 295–300 (2019)
9. dos Santos, W.G.V., Costa, W.S., Faber, M.J., Silva, J.A.L., Rocha, H.R.O., Segatto, M.E.V.: Sensor allocation in a hybrid star-mesh IoT network using genetic algorithm and k-medoids. In: 2019 IEEE Latin-American Conference on Communications (LATINCOM), pp. 1–6 (2019)

10. Cuomo, F., Garlisi, D., Martino, A., Martino, A.: Predicting lorawan behavior: how machine learning can help. Computers **9**(3), 60 (2020)
11. Eldeeb, E., Alves, H.: Lorawan-enabled smart campus: the data set and a people counter use case. IEEE Internet Things J. **11**(5), 8569–8577 (2024)
12. Queralta, J.P., Gia, T.N., Tenhunen, H., Westerlund, T.: Edge-AI in lora-based health monitoring: fall detection system with fog computing and LSTM recurrent neural networks. In: 2019 42nd International Conference on Telecommunications and Signal Processing (TSP), pp. 601–604 (2019)
13. Yang, Y., et al.: A study on water quality prediction by a hybrid CNN-LSTM model with attention mechanism. Environ. Sci. Pollut. Res. **28**(39), 55129–55139 (2021)
14. Zhuhua, H., et al.: A water quality prediction method based on the deep LSTM network considering correlation in smart mariculture. Sensors **19**(6), 1420 (2019)
15. Siami-Namini, S., Tavakoli, N., Namin, A.S.: A comparison of Arima and LSTM in forecasting time series. In: 2018 17th IEEE International Conference on Machine Learning and Applications (ICMLA), pp. 1394–1401 (2018)
16. Schmidhuber, J., Hochreiter, S., et al.: Long short-term memory. Neural Comput. **9**(8), 1735–1780 (1997)

Developing and Implementation of an IoT System for Early Detection of Forest Fires

J. D. Armijos-Goerke, C. Guerrero-Abad, J. P. Bermeo-Moyano(✉), and Luis F. Guerrero-Vásquez

Universidad Politécnica Salesiana, Cuenca 010102, Ecuador
{jarmijosg4,cguerreroa4}@est.ups.edu.ec, {jbermeo, lguerrero}@ups.edu.ec

Abstract. This work involves the development and implementation of an Internet of Things (IoT) system for the early detection of forest fires. This initiative addresses the pressing need for effective and precise tools to prevent and combat forest fires, which pose significant threats to natural ecosystems, biodiversity, and human communities. This work has achieved a notable improvement in forest fire detection efficiency, significantly reducing the response time needed to implement preventive or containment measures. An integrated system has been developed and deployed, incorporating IoT sensors inside an ESP32 microcontroller, a communication network, LoraWan Network, webpage, and a real-time monitoring platform, enabling continuous oversight of remote forested areas. The prototype has demonstrated high accuracy in detecting events related to forest fires, minimizing both false positives and false negatives, thus providing a solid foundation for informed decision-making. Furthermore, the system has been designed to operate reliably in challenging forest environments, withstanding extreme weather conditions to ensure operational continuity. Special attention has been given to the sustainability of the system in terms of energy efficiency and environmental impact, ensuring that its implementation contributes positively to environmental conservation.

Keywords: IoT · Fire detection · LoRa · LoRaWAN · ESP32

1 Introduction

Wildfires are one of the world's biggest environmental and safety issues. These events not only cause irreparable damage to ecosystems, but also endanger human life, property, and economic resources [1].

In December 2023, in the Llaviuco lagoon area of El Cajas National Park, in the rural area of the city of Cuenca, Ecuador, a devastating forest fire broke out, destroying approximately 200 hectares of forest and grassland. This incident has caused irreparable damage to both the ecosystem and the people affected [2]. In addition, in September 2023, the Cuenca Fire Department recorded 30 fires over a weekend. All of them occurred in the rural parishes of the Azuay capital [3].

Early detection of wildfires is crucial to reduce their spread and associated negative effects [4]. Therefore, the development of sophisticated detection systems has become

F. R. Narváez et al. (Eds.): SmartTech-IC 2024, CCIS 2392, pp. 33–47, 2026.
https://doi.org/10.1007/978-3-031-98287-3_3

an active field of research and development to meet this crucial need [5]. Due to their ability to integrate a variety of sensors and communication technologies to monitor environmental conditions remotely and in real-time, Internet of Things (IoT) platforms have emerged as a promising solution in this context [6].

The need to develop a prototype for early detection of forest fires using an IoT platform is based on multiple reasons of critical importance. The objective of this initiative is to preserve the environment, protect property and human lives, optimize emergency response resources, reduce the impact of climate change, and take advantage of technological advances to improve the efficiency and effectiveness of forest fire management. The importance of addressing this problem and developing innovative solutions to effectively combat forest fires is justified by the combination of these elements.

2 Theoretical Foundations

This section focuses on establishing a solid theoretical foundation to support the development of an IoT prototype for early detection of forest fires. The main concepts and theories related to fire detection, the operation of IoT platforms and their application in forest environments will be explored.

2.1 IoT Networks

The exchange of goods and services across supply chain networks is facilitated by the emerging architecture of the Internet of Things (IoT), which is based on the global Internet [7]. Today, IoT devices include a wide variety of connected devices, both for consumer use and for business use (B2B) [8].

From 2010 to 2020, the number of devices connected to the Internet of Things increased by 1,000%. Approximately 10 billion of these devices have been deployed and interconnected in the last ten years. Many of these Internet of Things (IoT) devices rely on low-power microcontrollers. More and more deployments rely on microcontrollers with more complex codes and connected to a network, either directly or indirectly.

The standardization of an architecture for the IoT is still in the process of development. Focused on solving two fundamental problems: establishing a standard way of accessing the medium and the devices and integrating the devices to the Internet [9].

2.2 IoT Applications

In general, the characteristics of IoT allow for different branches of applications among which we have [10]:

- Location Information Detection and Sharing
- Environment Sensing
- Remote control
- Ad hoc networks
- Secure Communication

- Smart City, IoT is an important means and tool for building smart cities, and it is a smart city construction that supports infrastructure. Smart city construction depends on many IoT applications for different industries [11].
- Agriculture: IoT technologies could change the farm-to-table sector, ensuring food security and reducing waste and agricultural inputs [12].
- Transportation: China's intelligent transportation system is developing and maintaining a high growth rate. By the end of the 12th Five-Year Plan, sixty percent of China's national roads will have IoT infrastructure installed [13].
- Smart Mobility: is the methodology that allows for smooth, efficient and flexible travel in various modes. Therefore, it can be said that it is about improving road safety, either by preventing or reducing traffic accidents, providing new solutions towards optimized modes of transport [14].
- Smart Grid: is an intelligent energy supply network that uses digital communications technology to detect and respond to changes in local usage, allowing customers to meet their electricity needs after making observations with the help of sensors and in reciprocity [13].
- Medical: It is the systematic application mode that connects healthcare services to the IT system through various online computer networks. Medical devices are equipped with built-in Wi-Fi systems that further enable machine-to-machine communication based on the IoMT (Internet of Medical Things) [13].

2.3 IoT Challenges and Barriers

Realizing the IoT vision is no easy task and faces several challenges that require attention. These include availability, reliability, mobility, performance, scalability, interoperability, security, management, and trust.

Service providers and application developers can effectively deploy their services by addressing these issues in the IoT development and deployment phases [14, 15].

2.4 LoRa Networks

LoRa is a protocol designed for long distances, capable of transmitting data over considerable distances. A single gateway can cover an area of up to one hundred square kilometers. The extensive range of LoRa technology is due to its link budget and the chirp spread spectrum modulation it uses. Chirp spread spectrum has low transmission power requirements, it is a signal whose frequency varies over time, and can be ascending or descending [16]. The LoRa network consists of four basic points

- **Nodes or End Points**: are the sections where sensing and control takes place.
- **Gateway**: The node sends data to all gateways, and each gateway receives a signal and sends it to a cloud-based network server via Ethernet, satellite, Wi-Fi, or cellular. Omnidirectional and multi-sector antennas are used in the LoRa base station.
- **Network Server**: The data received from different gateways is filtered, security checks, adaptive data rates etc. are performed and an acknowledgement is sent to the gateways.
- **Application Server:** The network server classifies the received data, if this one is addressed for any application server, then it is sent to the in-tended application server through some backhaul, after that application Server receive data for processing.

2.5 Angular

Angular is a framework that uses HTML and TypeScript to develop web applications, using TypeScript as its core language. The structure of an Angular application is based on key concepts. NgModules, which provide a compilation context for components, group related code into functional sets, and a set of NgModules defines an Angular application. There is always at least one root module that starts the application, although there are usually several additional modules that provide different functionalities [17].

2.6 Node-Red

Node-RED is an open-source development environment based on JavaScript and Node.js, created by IBM engineers to make it easier to build IoT systems [18]. At its core, it is a visual programming platform that enables the integration of hardware and software by creating "data pipelines" from sensors to the cloud. This environment is ideal for writing processes that simplify the processing and transfer of data to higher-level systems such as SQL servers, enterprise management platforms, or cloud services in a matter of minutes, or for immediate visualization. Instead of manually programming a web page to display sensor data, Node-RED offers a dashboard interface that allows you to create an engaging visualization without requiring advanced HTML or CSS knowledge.

2.7 Related Works

Metha [5] uses a WiFi connection for data transmission, which results in inefficient and expensive communication, as well as limited in terms of distance, with a maximum range of 100 m. Secondly, [6] like Metha, uses WiFi for data transmission, but in this case, it is used for the control of a sector in a factory, which implies that, although IoT is used, it is not used for environmental control.

On the other hand, Kumari [19] uses WiFi to connect to its database for early detection of forest fires. However, this connection is expensive and limited in range, as well as consuming a significant amount of energy. Despite these limitations, like the other projects mentioned, Kumar [20] seeks to automate processes, optimize resources, and improve decision making.

Additionally, [21] uses GSM technology to achieve long-distance connectivity in control, also offering data security. Although this approach presents a high implementation cost, the project seeks to automate processes and optimize resources.

[22] is developing a project aimed at environmental protection, using WiFi technology, and facing the same challenges of cost and scope mentioned above. However, it stands out for its emphasis on security to restrict access only to authorized personnel, with a relatively low implementation cost. This project aims to automate processes, improve the environment, and facilitate decision making.

In the case of [23], his project focuses on early detection of forest fires, using WiFi and the inclusion of an expensive housing that makes its implementation even more difficult.

[24] uses Deep Learning for forest fire detection, adding additional value to her project. However, by using WiFi for data transmission, they face range and cost issues.

Finally, [25] uses LoRaWAN, which provides long-distance communication at low cost and with remarkable energy efficiency. In addition, it leverages Deep Learning to improve decision making and optimize resources.

3 Design

3.1 Electronic Prototype Design

In the electronic part of the prototype, a temperature and humidity sensor (SHTC3) was used, which uses I2C transmission, a serial communication protocol mainly used to communicate microcontrollers with peripherals. Likewise, an air quality sensor (MQ135) was used, which can transmit data both analogically and digitally; for this project, the analog port was chosen. In addition, a GPS module (TinyGPS++) was used, which uses the UART serial communication protocol, an asynchronous protocol based on two main lines: TX and RX. The connections are showed in Fig. 1.

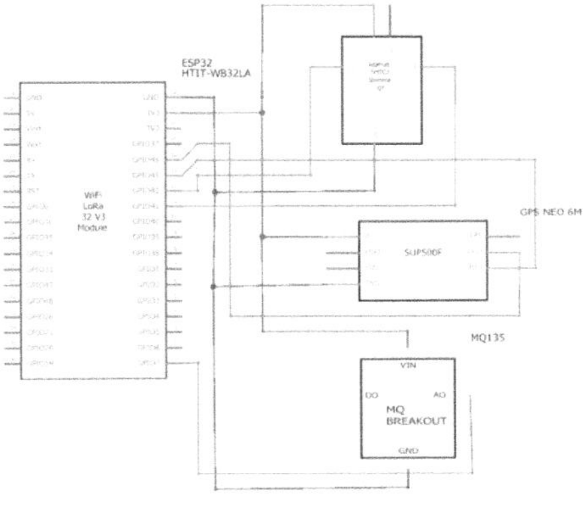

Fig. 1. General connection diagram

The device will be powered by a Lithium battery, which during the presence of sunlight will be charged through a monocrystalline solar panel with an output capacity of 5 V and 250 mA, equivalent to a power of 1.25 W, for which the TP4056 module is used for the management of charging and discharging of the battery, where in the presence of light the solar panel charges the battery and supplies a constant voltage value at the output, and in the absence of light it directly uses the battery as the module output.

3.2 Software Design for ESP32

Each node uses an ESP32- WiFi LoRa 32(V3) that has been programmed within the Arduino development environment, each one connects to the LoRaWan Gateway E890-915LG12 [26], having a gateway range of 3 km.

At startup, the device defines the OTAA and ABP identifiers and keys for LoRaWan connections, where LoRaWan settings include region, device class, transmission cycle, OTAA/ABP activation, ADR enable, message type (confirmed or unacknowledged) and application port, and the maximum number of attempts to try to establish the connection is defined.

Subsequently, in the case of establishing a successful LoRa connection, the I2C communication is initialized, where samples are taken from the temperature and humidity sensors (SHTC3), air quality (MQ135) and GPS coordinates (TinyGPS++). The collected values are packaged in the AppData array to be sent by LoRaWan.

I2C serial communication has a speed of 115200 baud, and 9600 baud to communicate with the GPS module, using pins 46 (RX) and 45 (TX) of the microcontrollers.

In summary, in the main loop, the state of the device is managed using a state machine. In DEVICESTATEINIT, LoRaWan is initialized, and the default DR (Data Rate) is set. In DEVICESTATEJOIN, the process of joining the LoRaWan network is performed. In DEVICESTATESEND, the data frame is prepared and sent over LoRaWan. In DEVICESTATECYCLE, the transmission of the next packet is scheduled, adjusting the transmission cycle. In any other state, the device is reset to the initialization state (Fig. 2).

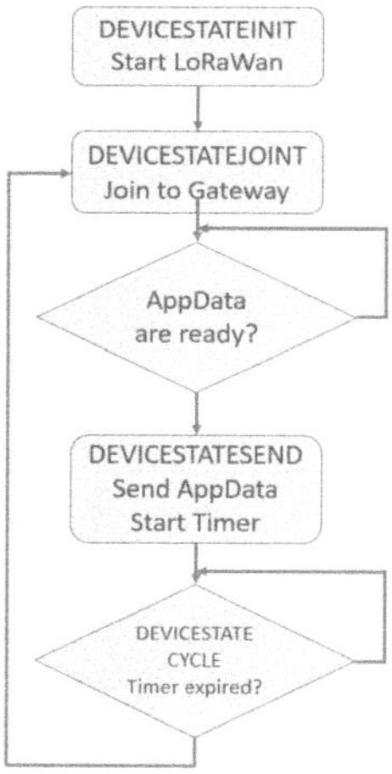

Fig. 2. State Machine for ESP32

3.3 Design of the Physical Housing of the Prototype

Inventor was used for the complete design and assembly, which was done on a 3D printer. The main housing will contain both the electronics and the sensors for measurements. The complete box, including the covers, has dimensions of 79.55 × 74.20 × 87 mm. Figure 3 shows the main housing of the design, which has a separate compartment for the battery and the electronics. The holes are designed for 3 mm diameter screws that allow for proper fit. The housing has spaces for an on/off switch, and for the SMA port of the microcontroller antenna for LoRaWan use. At the bottom, air vents were designed to allow for proper measurement of the environment, section where the sensors will be placed.

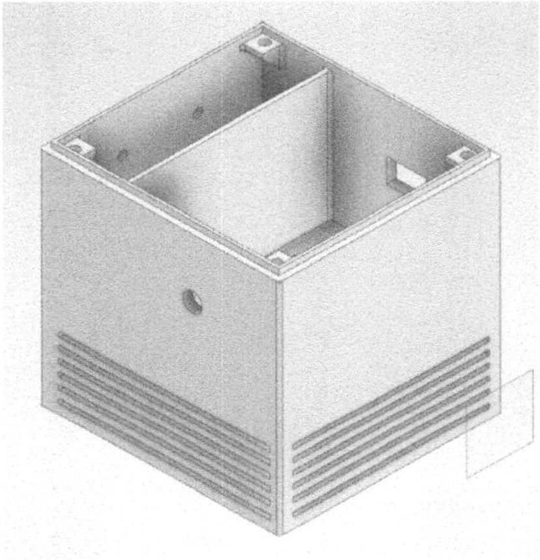

Fig. 3. Main housing

Fig. 4. Assembled prototype for fire detection

In the Fig. 4 shows the entire prototype assembled with all the parts such as the main housing, upper and lower housing covers, holding bracket and support for the solar panel.

3.4 Website Design

For the design of the website, for the FrontEnd the Angular framework was used, several components were used, to start we have the Login that serves to validate the access of users with valid credentials, later that the user enters, he must select the device that he wants to manage from the list of devices, in case the list is empty, devices can be created with the "DevicesComponent" component. With the device selected, other components can be used such as the DashboardComponent to display data and send MQTT messages to the device, the TemplatesComponent where the administration and display framework of the device in the Dashboard window is designed, the AlarmsComponent to configure the alarms that when activated send alert messages, there is also the LogOut component to exit the application, these are the main components, which are showed in Fig. 5. There are also other components that are used to display, send and receive MQTT messages between the Web page and the device, three of them receive messages from the device, for example the "numberChart" receives data from the device and generates a graph with the history of the data, "iotIndicator" receives data and shows an On/Off state according to the information received, the MapsComponent that displays a map with the GPS data of the device, the "switch" sends a binary signal to the device and the "button" sends a binary signal and a text message. For the application only the "numberchart" and "MapsComponent" components are used, which only receive information from the device. In addition, alarms were configured for the Temperature and Humidity sensors.

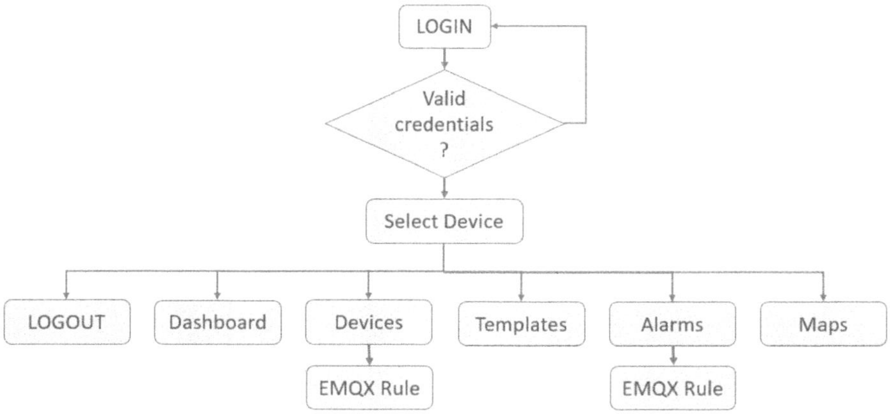

Fig. 5. FrontEnd Component Diagram

For messages to and from devices on the website, the EMQX server was used. On the other hand, for the administration of devices and alarms, it is necessary to create EMQX rules, so the AlarmsComponent and DevicesComponent components are responsible for creating and deleting these rules.

Since the LoRaWan Gateway uses the Mosquito server for communication, Node-Red was used to create an interface that connects the two servers. Figure 6 shows the data flow, where the user, device and variable codes are shown, which are used to create the Topic of the MQTT messages for the EMQX server from the Gateway's Mosquitto server.

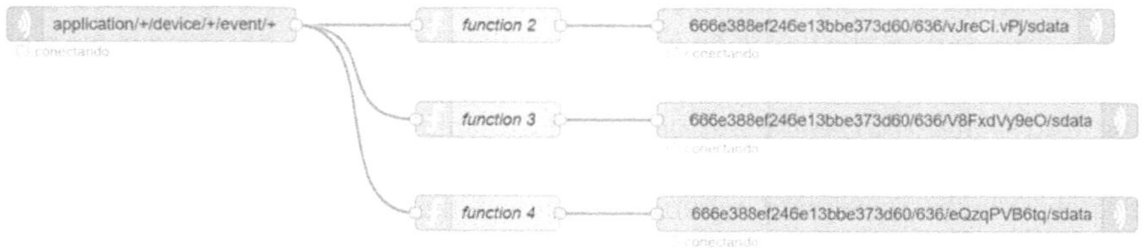

Fig. 6. Node-Red flow for sending Mosquitto messages to EMQX

The Backend was implemented in Node, where a middleware was created for user login. The connection with EMQX is direct, so MQTT functions were implemented for registration, sending, and receiving messages with the EMQX server. In addition, administrators were created for the different routes that are connected from the frontend for the management of devices and alarms. The database used is MongoDB, which is located and managed in the backend.

Figure 7 shows the Dashboard page with graphs of input variables such as temperature, humidity, and air quality.

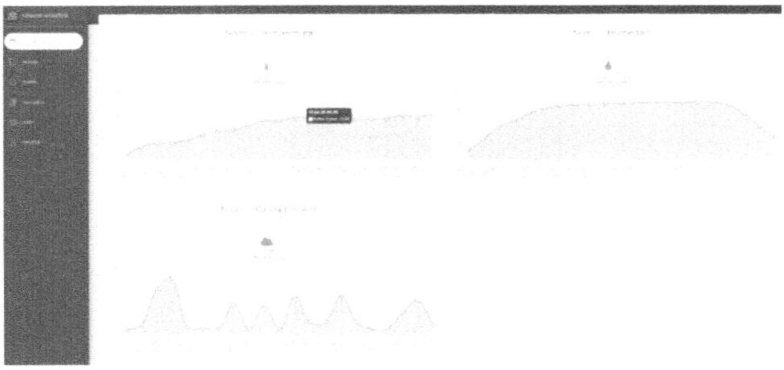

Fig. 7. Dashboard page

The Alarms page is also displayed, with two example alarms, where in each one a condition must be defined, the threshold value, "update" the time in seconds that the system will wait to take a new measurement, within this period, no measurement will be considered. Each time a value is received that triggers the alarm, a notification message is sent to the frontend page and is filed in the database (Fig. 8).

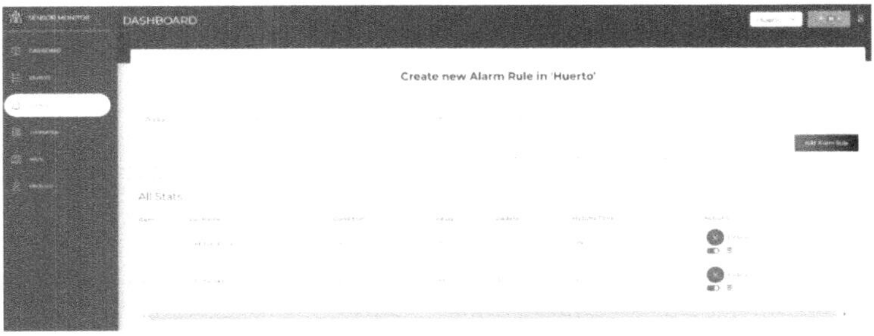

Fig. 8. Alarms page

A sample of the MongoDB database hosted in the backend is shown in Fig. 9, where the collections used are alarmrules, datas, devices, emqxauthrules, notifications, saverules, templates and user_p64, which are used for registration, login and system administration.

Fig. 9. MongoDB database

4 Experimental Validation

Once the prototype was completed for experimental validation, some measurements were made, such as energy expenditure, RSSI and SNR, and a comparison with previous studies was made.

4.1 Energy Expenditure Assessment

The datasheet specifications provided the following current values for the system components, considering a voltage of 5 V. However, in the first experiment, discrepancies were observed between the theoretical consumption from the datasheet and the actual measured consumption. Actual measurements indicated higher power consumption due to several factors such as current peaks and specific operating conditions. The measured currents were:

System component	Datasheet value	Measured Data
ESP32	80 mA	85 mA
MQ135	60 mA	65 mA
SHTC3	0.002 mA	0.500 mA
GPSNEO-6M	45 mA	50 mA

So, the total consumption is 200.5 mA, for the proofs there are two batteries the first with capacity of 4500 mA-Hour (B_{4500}) and the other one with 8000 mA-Hour (B_{4500}) therefore the autonomy can be calculated for each one.

$$Autonomy(B_{4500}) = \frac{4500[mA - H]}{200.5[mA]} = 22{,}4\,Hours$$

$$Autonomy(B_{8000}) = \frac{8000[mA - H]}{200.5[mA]} = 43{,}9\,Hours$$

To further extend the autonomy and ensure the continuous operation of the system, it is proposed to use a solar panel with a charging module, where according to the solar panel datasheet, it has a contribution of 250 mA per hour during sunlight hours for 5 V with a power of 1,25 W, for the analysis region, the history is 6 h of effective sunlight per day, which indicates that the solar panel per day would deliver:

$$Contribution\ Panel = 250mA \cdot 6H = 1500mA - H$$

Since the consumption of the equipment in that period would be:

$$Equipment\ consumption(Light) = 200{,}5mA \cdot 6H = 1203mA - H$$

The remainder that would be used to charge the battery is:

$$Remainder\ to\ Charge = 1500 - 1203 = 297mA - H$$

Which is not enough to have indefinite autonomy, since the consumption of the equipment during the hours without sufficient sunlight for the panel results in:

$$Equipment\ consumption(Dark) = 200{,}5mA \cdot 18H = 3609mA - H$$

This means a daily loss of:

$$Balance\ consumption = 297 - 3609 = -3312mA - H$$

To overcome this loss, the current that the solar panel must deliver in the 6 h is estimated, first considering the total consumption in darkness of the equipment and dividing by the charging time, the result is:

$$I_{Eq-Dark} = \frac{3609[mA - H]}{6[H]} = 601{,}5mA$$

To this result we must add the current consumption of the equipment while the solar panel is working, so the total would be:

$$I_{total} = I_{Eq} + I_{Eq-Dark} = 200{,}5 + 601{,}5 = 802mA$$

Considering that the working voltage is 5 V, the solar panel should have a power at least of:

$$Power_{Panel} = 802mA \cdot 5V \cdot = 4{,}01W$$

Since the daily consumption during dark hours is 3609 mA-H, and to maintain the best charge and discharge cycle of the battery, it is recommended to work at approximately 50% of the total capacity [27], so it is recommended to use the battery of 8000 mA-H.

4.2 RSSI and SNR Assessment

RSSI and SNR are two key metrics that reflect the quality of the signal received by a node (microcontroller) from the gateway. By measuring how these values change with the distance between the node and the gateway, the coverage and efficiency of the network can be estimated.

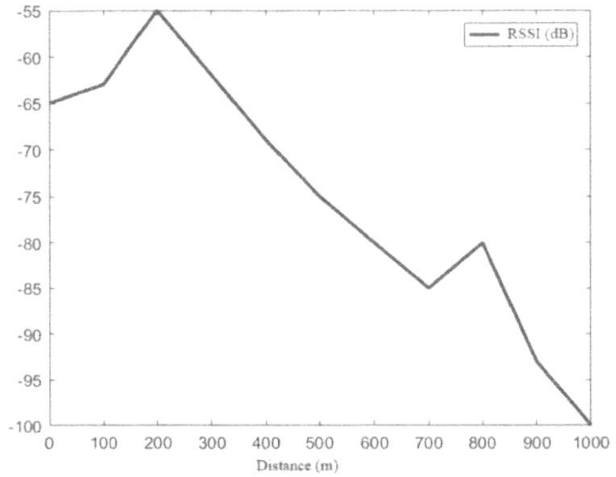

Fig. 10. RSSI

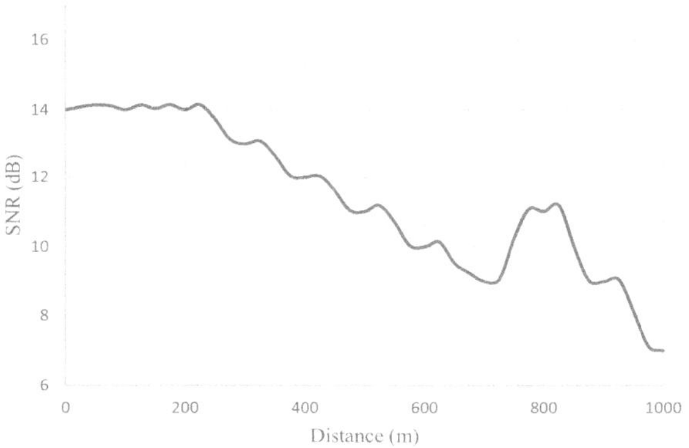

Fig. 11. SNR Signal to Noise Ratio

In Fig. 10, the RSSI (Received Signal Strength Indicator) is observed, which is the indicator of the intensity of the received signal, where if RSSI decreases to -100 dB, the node is completely disconnected from the gateway. In the tests, the maximum distance reached was one thousand meters. It is worth noting that a low gain antenna was used, so if the gain is improved, the distance can be increased up to three thousand meters [26].

The signal to noise ratio SNR is shown in Fig. 11, measurements were made while maintaining the connection between the gateway and the node, i.e., up to a thousand meters. The SNR values are in the range between 14 and 7 dB, where the relationship is indirect, where the SNR decreases as the distance increases.

Another important element is the Spread Factor (SF) which is a crucial parameter that influences several key aspects of communication, including range and data rate. A low Spread Factor, such as SF7, provides a shorter range, making it suitable for urban or indoor environments where communication distances are relatively small. However, this lower range is compensated by a higher data rate, allowing more information to be transmitted in less time, which is beneficial for applications that require frequent and fast transmissions. On the other hand, using a high SF increases power consumption, as devices need more time to transmit data, which can be an important consideration for applications where energy efficiency is vital. In addition, a lower SF means lower power consumption, which is ideal for battery-powered devices that need to maximize their autonomy.

On the other hand, a higher Spread Factor, such as SF12, offers a significantly longer range, which is advantageous in rural environments or areas with obstacles where longer distances need to be covered. However, this longer range comes with a lower data rate, resulting in slower data transmissions.

4.3 Comparison with Previous Studies

In this work, a system for early detection of forest fires based on LoRaWAN has been implemented that offers significant improvements in terms of security, battery efficiency and signal range compared to methods using WiFi, such as those proposed by Metha [5], Kumari [19], Venkantesan [21], Ishitha [22] and Dasari [23]. Furthermore, in contrast to Khennou's work, which also uses LoRaWAN, our system stands out for the improved security of the monitoring website, although we acknowledge the superiority of the deep learning techniques employed by Khennou [25] in decision making.

LoRaWAN is designed for low-power applications, allowing devices to operate for months or even years on a single battery charge due to its low power consumption during data transmission. In contrast, WiFi consumes significantly more power due to the need to maintain a constant connection and the higher power required for transmissions.

LoRaWAN offers a much greater signal range than WiFi, with transmission capabilities of several kilometers, which is ideal for applications in large or rural areas. On the other hand, WiFi has a limited range, typically up to a few hundred meters, which may be insufficient for certain remote monitoring applications.

Compared to the work of Khennou [25], which also uses LoRaWAN, our approach distinguishes itself in the following aspects: Website Security: Our system stands out by incorporating additional security measures into the monitoring website. This includes user authentication and encryption of data in transit. Deep Learning and Decision Making: Khennou's system, by using deep learning techniques, is superior in automated decision making. These techniques allow for more complex and accurate analysis of the collected data, which can improve event detection and automated response.

5 Conclusions and Recommendations

5.1 Conclusions

The prototype developed for the early detection of forest fires through an IoT platform proves to be a promising solution, through the integration of various sensors such as heat, humidity, CO_2 with communication technologies, in the present project it has been possible to establish a valid detection system with a range of one kilometer around to monitor environmental conditions in forest areas and detect possible fires in their initial stages.

The tests and evaluations carried out demonstrate that the prototype is effective in detecting forest fires, which would help the relevant authorities to respond quickly and in a timely manner. In addition, the scalability and versatility of the system is highlighted using LoRa and LoRaWAN, which can be adapted to different forest environments and specific monitoring requirements, in conjunction with the IoT platform.

The implementation of an IoT-based forest fire early detection system has the potential to transform the way forest fires are managed and prevented. With continuous improvements in sensor technology, optimization of data analysis algorithms and integration with emergency management systems, sustainable energy with solar panels, this prototype can become a vital tool for the protection of forest ecosystems and risk mitigation.

5.2 Recommendations

To maximize the impact of the prototype, it is recommended to continue the study starting with pilot projects in specific areas of our country where there is a risk of forest fires. It is also recommended to coordinate with government entities for the financing and implementation of the Prototype.

The platform is currently running on a local server with global reach, however, it is recommended to deploy it in the cloud, such as AWS, Google Cloud, Azure, and others. This will allow for efficient and scalable management, ensuring real-time data monitoring and analysis for decision making.

Acknowledgement. This research was supported by GITEL (Grupo de Investigación de Telecomunicaciones) at Universidad Politécnica Salesiana-Cuenca.

References

1. Castillo, M., Pedernera, P., Pena, E.: Incendios forestales y medio ambiente: una síntesis global. Revista Ambiente y Desarrollo **19**(3), 44–53 (2003)
2. Secretaría Nacional de Gestión de Riesgos. Gestion de Riesgos-Ecuador (2024). https://www.gestionderiesgos.gob.ec/controlado-un-70-del-incendio-forestal-en-el-parque-nacional-el-cajas-azuay/#
3. Redacción Primicias. Primicias El Periodismo comprometido (2023). https://www.primicias.ec/noticias/sucesos/incendios-forestales-cuenca-septiembre/
4. Park, S., Han, K., Lee, K.: A study on fire detection technology through spectrum analysis of smoke particles. In: 2020 International Conference on Information and Communication Technology Convergence (ICTC), Jeju, Korea (South) (2020)
5. Mehta, K., Sharma, S., Mishra, D.: Internet-of-Things enabled forest fire detection system. In: 2021 Fifth International Conference on I-SMAC (IoT in Social, Mobile, Analytics and Cloud) (I-SMAC), Palladam, India (2021)
6. Nagolu, C., Cheekula, C., Thota, D.S.K., Padmanaban, K., Bhattacharyya, D.: Real-time forest fire detection using IoT and smart sensors. In: 2023 International Conference on Inventive Computation Technologies (ICICT), Lalitpur, Nepal (2023)
7. Salazar Soler, J., Silvestre Bergés, S.: El mundo Internet of Things (IoT), Barcelona, Spain: Ceské vysoké ucení technické v Praze Fakulta elektrotechnická (2019)

8. Baccelli, E.: Internet of Things (IoT): Societal Challenges & Scientific Research Fields for IoT (2021). https://inria.hal.science/hal-03474888v1
9. González, D.R.: Arquitectura y Gestión de la IoT. Revista Telemática **12**(3), 49–60 (2013)
10. Li, Y., Chen, W., Ding, Y., Qie, Y., Zhang, C.: A vision of intelligent IoT—trends, characteristics and functional architecture. IEEE Internet Things J. 184–189 (2022)
11. Zanella, A., Bui, N., Castellani, A., Vangelista, L., Zorzi, M.: Internet of things for smart cities. IEEE Internet Things J. 22–32 (2014)
12. Brewster, C., Roussaki, I., Kalatzis, N., Doolin, K., Ellis, K.: IoT in agriculture: designing a Europe-wide large-scale pilot. IEEE Commun. Mag. **55**(9), 26–33 (2017)
13. Chen, S., Xu, H., Liu, D., Hu, B., Wang, H.: A vision of IoT: applications, challenges, and opportunities with china perspective. IEEE Internet Things J. **1**(4), 349–359 (2014)
14. Khanna, A., Kaur, S.: Internet of Things (IoT), applications and challenges: a comprehensive review. Wirel. Pers. Commun. **114**(2), 1687–1762 (2020)
15. Al-Fuqaha, A., Guizani, M., Mohammadi, M., Aledhari, M., Ayyash, M.: Internet of Things: a survey on enabling technologies, protocols, and applications. IEEE Commun. Surv. Tutor. **17**(4), 2347–2376 (2015)
16. Devalal, S., Karthikeyan, A.: LoRa technology - an overview. In: 2018 Second International Conference on Electronics, Communication and Aerospace Technology (ICECA), Coimbatore, India (2018)
17. Fain, Y., Moiseev, A.: Angular Development with TypeScript, 2nd edn. Manning (2018)
18. Winkelmann, S., Büttner, M., Deivasihamani, D., von Hoffmann, A., Flohr, F.: Using node-RED as a low-code approach to model interaction logic of machine-learning-supported eHMIs for the virtual driving simulator Carla. In: 15th International Conference on Automotive User Interfaces and Interactive Vehicular Applications, New York, NY, USA (2023)
19. Kumari, V., Ali, F.A.: Early detection of forest fire using Internet of Things. In: 2022 1st IEEE International Conference on Industrial Electronics: Developments & Applications (ICIDeA), Bhubaneswar, India (2022)
20. Kumar, K., Sharma, S., Pandey, P., Goyal, H.R.: IoT enabled crop detection system using soil analysis. In: 2022 7th International Conference on Communication and Electronics Systems (ICCES), Coimbatore, India (2022)
21. Venkateswara, C., Vandana, C., Reddy, M.K.V.S., Raju, K.S., Sirisha, R.V.P., Killamsetti, H.: Advanced forest fire alert system with real-time GPS location tracking. In: 2023 2nd International Conference on Automation, Computing and Renewable Systems (ICACRS), Pudukkottai, India (2023)
22. Ishitha, S., Nagaraju, S., Mohan, H.A., Harshitha, M., Gowda, G.R.: IoT based anti-poaching and fire alarm system for forest. In: 2021 IEEE Mysore Sub Section International Conference (MysuruCon), Hassan, India (2021)
23. Dasari, P., Reddy, G., Gudipalli, A.: Forest fire detection using wireless sensor networks. Int. J. Smart Sens. Intell. Syst. **13**(1), 1–8 (2020)
24. Ananthi, J., Sengottaiyan, N., Anbukaruppusamy, S., Upreti, K., Kumar, A.: Forest fire prediction using IoT and deep learning. Int. J. Adv. Technol. Eng. Explor. **9**(87), 246–256 (2022)
25. Khennou, F., Ghaoui, J., Akhloufi, M.A.: Forest fire spread prediction using deep learning. Geospatial Inform. XI 106–117 (2021)
26. Almeida, D.E.: Diseño e implementación de un sistema de localización y rastreo GPS de lanchas pesqueras utilizando comunicación inalámbrica, Cuenca, Ecuador: BS thesis (2022)
27. Beard, K., Reddy, T.: Linden's Handbook of Batteries. McGraw Hill, New York (2019)
28. Khanna, A., Kaur, S.: Internet of Things (IoT), applications and challenges: a comprehensive review. Wirel. Pers. Commun. **114**(2), 1687–1762 (2020)

An Unified Multi-platform IoT Architecture Leveraging gRPC for Seamless Integration of LoRaWAN, MQTT, and HTTP Protocols

Erwin J. Sacoto-Cabrera[1](✉), Gabriel Chuchuca[1], Malki Yupanki[1], Javier Martínez-Ledesma[2], and Jefferson Reyes[2]

[1] GIHP4C-Universidad Politécnica Salesiana, Cuenca, Ecuador
esacoto@ups.edu.ec
[2] MARVICNET, Cuenca, Ecuador
http://www.ups.edu.ec

Abstract. The rapid increase in Internet of Things (IoT) devices has given rise to various communication protocols focused on solving user and service requirements, increasing complexity and operational overhead. To address this challenge, we propose an architecture for a multi-protocol IoT platform that leverages the power of gRPC for LoRaWAN device management. Furthermore, the proposed framework unifies the LoRaWAN, MQTT, and HTTP protocols, allowing for a middleware that simplifies IoT systems' deployment, management, and maintenance. The architecture is designed to achieve low-latency communication. The results showed that the proposed IoT platform architecture implemented simplified management of traditional IoT infrastructure and provided enhanced security through JWT and RBAC token-based authentication. Additionally, the testing demonstrated significant performance gains, with latency reductions and robust security handling, positioning this architecture as a scalable and flexible solution for real-world IoT applications. Finally, ensured secure and efficient operations on multiple sensors. Looking ahead, we are considering solutions based on blockchain, hybrid clouds, and fog computing as part of our ongoing development and innovation in this field.

Keywords: LoRaWAN · MQTT · HTTP · Multi-Platform · Multi-IoT · gRPC · JWT · RBAC · IoT Security · Scalability

1 Introduction

The rapid increase in Internet of Things (IoT) devices has led to various communication protocols suited to specific use cases and requirements [1–3]. LoRaWAN [1,4–6], for instance, is a low-power wide-area network (LPWAN) protocol well-suited for long-range, low-bandwidth applications. At the same

F. R. Narváez et al. (Eds.): SmartTech-IC 2024, CCIS 2392, pp. 48–61, 2026.
https://doi.org/10.1007/978-3-031-98287-3_4

time, MQTT is a lightweight publish-subscribe protocol commonly used in resource-constrained devices. On the other hand, HTTP is a widely adopted and versatile protocol that serves as the backbone of the web. MQTT, is a lightweight, publish-subscribe protocol that is widely adopted for real-time data exchange in IoT systems Meanwhile, HTTP remains a ubiquitous and versatile protocol for various IoT applications, particularly for web-based user interfaces and device management. To effectively manage this diversity of protocols, researchers have proposed various IoT architectures, including cloud-based and fog-based solutions. While this diversity is beneficial for addressing different IoT scenarios, it poses a significant challenge for IoT infrastructure. Conventional approaches require the deployment of multiple separate servers to support different protocols, resulting in increased complexity and operational overhead.

This article provides the following contributions.

- Unified Multi-Protocol Server Framework: Our novel framework unifies the LoRaWAN, MQTT, and HTTP protocols, reducing the need for multiple servers and simplifying IoT infrastructure.
- Seamless Protocol Integration and Interoperability: Our framework allows IoT devices and applications to communicate effortlessly across different protocols. This seamless integration improves interoperability, paving the way for scalable and flexible IoT solutions.
- Enhanced Deployment, Management, and Maintenance: Our framework simplifies deployment and maintenance by consolidating protocol support, reducing operational costs, and improving infrastructure efficiency.

1.1 Background

The increase in IoT devices and networks has led to various IoT management platforms and communication protocols, each optimized for specific use cases and requirements [4,7–9] with its strengths and weaknesses. In this sense, in the literature, some researchers focus on studying IoT platforms, such as [4,10–13], as well as IoT communication protocols [14,15], and different devices [16,17]. For instance, in the context of IoT platforms in [18], the authors present a survey of IoT platforms, analyzing their architectures and the fundamentals of IoT building blocks and the communication protocols between them to establish a guide for the choice of a suitable and appropriate IoT platform for different uses and user requirements in the vast number and variety of available platforms. In the same sense, in [8], the authors proposed a broad evaluation scheme for IoT software platforms based on four categories: core (Connectivity, Device Management, Integration APIs, Security, Endorsed Hardware, Hosting), data management and processing (Storage, Multi-Modal Support, Analytics, Visualization), application empowerment (Event-driven Actions, Push Notifications, Programming Frameworks, Third Party Integration), and accessibility (Pricing, Support).

In the framework of IoT communication protocols, the authors in [14] mainly describe wireless networks used for IoT, such as low-power wireless personal area networks (6LoWPAN), ZigBee, Bluetooth Low Energy (BLE), Z-Wave and Near Field Communication (NFC), as well as standard low power wide area network (LPWAN) protocols such as LoraWAN, SigFox, and NB-IoT, in conclusion the authors establish a comparison and types of network utilities. Likewise, in [19,20], the actors develop a comparative Study of Messaging Protocols for IoT environments such as MQTT, CoAP, AMQP, HTTP, and others. This study concluded that MQTT has better characteristics than other IoT message protocols. To support this diverse ecosystem, IoT infrastructure typically requires the deployment of multiple specialized servers, each catering to a specific protocol.

In the framework of the IoT devices in [21], the Low-End, Middle-End, and High-End IoT Devices are described, and a classification emphasizing their key attributes, including processing and memory capabilities, security features, connectivity, and communication interfaces, size, cost and appearance, operating system support, power specifications, and battery life, listing some exciting projects for each device and described the platforms to subscribe to depend on devices to operation.

Finally, in the framework, current IoT solution platforms have flexibility, scalability and interoperability issues, especially in environments that require simultaneous multi-protocol management. Traditional configurations often require separate servers for protocols such as LoRaWAN, MQTT and HTTP, leading to higher operational costs and complex infrastructure [22]. This lack of seamless interoperability restricts easy integration of new devices and hinders scalability across diverse IoT ecosystems [23]. Our gRPC-based approach addresses these limitations by offering a unified single-platform solution that simplifies device management and reduces overhead. With gRPC, the system ensures low-latency, high-efficiency communication between protocols through streamlined middleware, making it adaptable to large-scale deployments without extensive reconfiguration.

The heterogeneity of IoT platforms, communications protocols, and devices represents a significant challenge for the IoT infrastructure, as it requires multiple disparate servers to support the different protocols, increasing complexity and operational overhead. To address this problem, we proposed a novel multi-protocol server framework that leverages the power of gRPC to provide a unified and efficient IoT infrastructure for the LoraWAN Server. Our proposed framework seamlessly integrates support for LoRaWAN, MQTT, and HTTP, allowing IoT devices and applications to communicate seamlessly regardless of the underlying protocol, thus simplifying the deployment, management, and maintenance of IoT systems.

The main structure of this paper is as follows. Section 2 describes the Architecture IoT Platform. Section 3 presents the main results of multiplatform IoT implementation. Finally, the conclusions are presented in Sect. 4.

2 Architecture IoT Platform

Several cross-platform IoT architectures have been proposed to address the challenges of managing diverse IoT ecosystems [24]. However, these approaches often fail to provide a truly unified and scalable platform, as they typically require multiple disparate servers to support the different protocols [25].

Our research tackles a significant challenge in the field of IoT-the management of a heterogeneous IoT ecosystem. To address this, we have explored cross-protocol frameworks, such as the IoT Exchange architecture, which aims to provide a unified platform for controlling devices and managing data across diverse wireless protocols and cloud platforms [26,27]. To overcome these limitations, we propose a novel framework for a multi-protocol IoT network that leverages the power of gRPC for efficient and scalable inter-service communication for managing LoraWAN devices. Specifically, gRPC in IoT environments enables efficient, low-latency communication by supporting remote procedure calls (RPC) in protocols such as LoRaWAN. Furthermore, gRPC is designed to provide scalability, sensor integration, and real-time services, ensuring fault tolerance in IoT sensor networks, as described by the authors in [28].

Our framework is not just a theoretical concept but a practical solution. It is designed to provide a unified and flexible approach for managing IoT devices and applications across various communication protocols in different OSI model layers, including LoRaWAN, MQTT, and HTTP.

The IoT Platform includes the following features:

- Seamless interconnections between services and data flows
- Support for multiple application layer protocols
- Ability to be deployed on a large scale
- Ability to monitor and control the ownership and exchange of services and data flows
- Support for ontologies and semantic descriptions
- Support for using the IoT Platform as a platform for the exchange of services and data flows

The principal Multi-Platform IoT Architecture (MIoT) is shown in Fig. 1 described below.

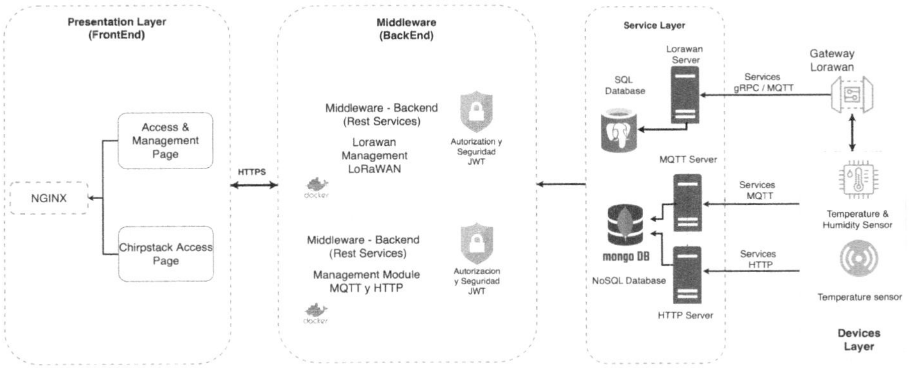

Fig. 1. Architecture Platform

- **Devices Layer:** As shown in Fig. 1, the device layer of this IoT platform supports multi-user, multi-enterprise and multi-protocol environments, ensuring seamless connectivity among IoT devices using the LoRaWAN, MQTT, and HTTP protocols. LoRaWAN devices send data to the gateway, while MQTT and HTTP devices communicate directly with their respective sensors or endpoints. This layer facilitates interoperability, provides a unified API for developers, and employs a protocol translation mechanism for compatibility among various IoT devices. It is based on the Semantic Sensor Network Ontology (SSN) [29], which improves semantic interoperability and enables comprehensive device management features such as provisioning, configuration, real-time monitoring and Over-the-Air (OTA) updates [4,30]. Platform architecture ensures enterprise-level scalability and security through data encryption, robust authentication, and fine-grained access control. Supports multiple user accounts with role-based access control (RBAC) [31], allowing customized interfaces and hierarchical data management. Designed for diverse industrial applications, the Device Layer efficiently handles data aggregation, filtering, and secure storage, making it ideal for smart cities, industrial IoT, agriculture, and healthcare. This versatile component provides a reliable foundation for the deployment and scaling of IoT solutions, driving innovation and efficiency across various industries.
- **Service Layer:** As shown in Fig. 1, BackEnd development using gRPC for LoRaWAN, MQTT for MQTT servers and JSON for HTTP services ensures efficient and scalable data management. Each protocol has dedicated servers, ensuring optimal performance. The API interface for each service facilitates interoperability, allowing different components of the system to communicate effectively. Sensor data is stored in a MongoDB database, which offers a flexible and scalable solution for data management. The architecture is designed for low-latency communication, high-performance data handling, and seamless integration, making it suitable for smart cities, industrial IoT, agriculture, and healthcare applications. For security, token-based authentication (JWT) [32] was used, a mechanism to verify the owner of JSON data between the BackEnd and the FrontEnd.
- **Middleware Layer:** As shown in Fig. 2, the middleware layer is responsible for receiving data from the connected devices and processing the received data by evaluating condition-action rules based on the SSN.
  The middleware layer receives data from LoraWAN servers via gRPC, MQTT, and HTTP. It then provides this data to the Front-End layer. In addition, the MIoT layer is responsible for controlling the devices. It achieves this by sending commands to be executed by the respective actuators. The devices communicate directly with the MIoT and support communication technologies such as WiFi, Ethernet, and 4G. In this way, the middleware, from a functional point of view, serves as an integration layer for different types of servers that provide connectivity to the sensors.
- **Presentation Layer:** As shown in Fig. 2, this layer of this IoT platform, developed with Angular version 17 [33] and the open source NGINX web server [34], provides a responsive, easy-to-use interface designed to support

multi-protocol, multi-enterprise, and multi-user environments. The front-end offers different user roles: Super Administrator has comprehensive control over all enterprise services, including system-wide settings, configurations, and user permissions. Administrators manage specific enterprise services, including device provisioning, configuration, and client management. Clients have view-only access to service consumption and performance metrics, with customized dashboards to track usage and relevant data. This layer ensures effective data management with real-time updates and notifications, advanced data visualization tools, and integration with MongoDB for efficient data collection and visualization. It is optimized for scalability and high performance and can handle increasing user and data volumes. Security is maintained through RBAC, secure authentication mechanisms, and end-to-end data encryption. The presentation layer is essential for managing and monitoring IoT environments, providing a powerful interface for diverse user needs.

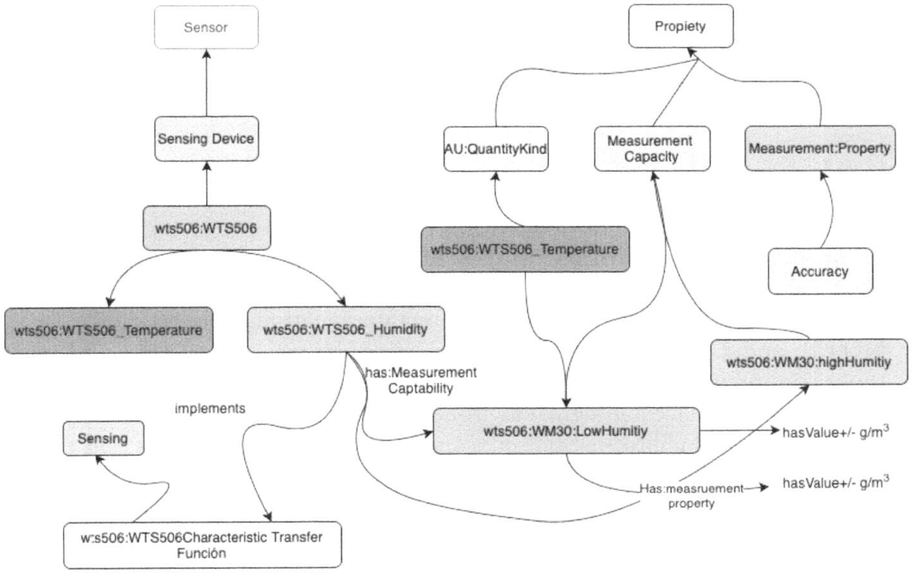

Fig. 2. SSN Ontology Reference

3 Results

In this section, the authors present the results of implementing the multi-platform IoT project. This approach significantly simplified the IoT infrastructure by eliminating the need for multiple dedicated servers, reducing demands on hardware and software resources, and lowering operational costs, as described below.

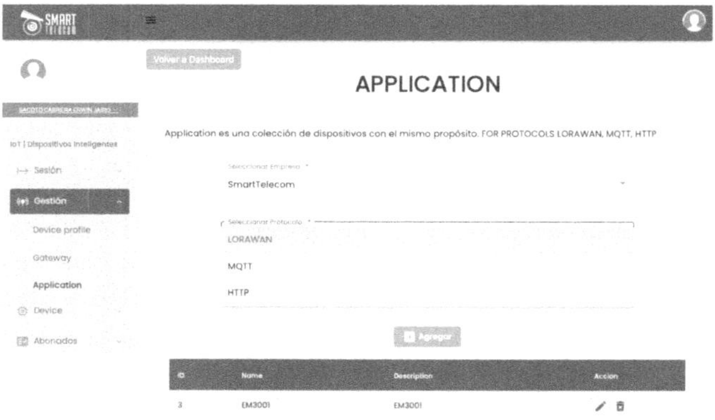

Fig. 3. Successful Integration of Protocols

- **Successful Integration of Protocols:** As shown in Fig. 3, the Unified Multi-Protocol Server Framework has integrated LoRaWAN, MQTT, and HTTP protocols through middleware deployed at the BackEnd to efficiently manage servers for each protocol and device from the BackEnd to the front-end.
  Due to the multi-protocol integration feature, the menu allows the management of different companies and levels of users, as well as LoraWAN gateways and MQTT and HTTP devices within the same company or user.
- **Seamless Interoperability and Scalability:** As shown in Figs. 1, 2, the platform architecture and the use of the SSN ontology allowed the defining of the characteristics of seamless communication through LoRaWAN, MQTT, and HTTP protocols, defining variables, characteristics, and data types, improving the interoperability of IoT devices and applications. This SSN anthology-based integration from the sensors to the front-end guided the ontology to facilitate scalability and incorporate new devices and protocols into the system without significant reconfiguration. In this respect, as shown in Fig. 4 shows a FrontEnd Multi-Platform principal menu and several devices and gateway activities. Additionally, as shown in Fig. 4, each enterprise (that subscribes to the platform) can view its devices (gateways and final devices). The Super Administrator user can view all companies subscribed to the service and manage the devices for maintenance if necessary.
- **Improved Performance:** The architecture improved overall system performance by centralizing management tasks, reducing latency, and increasing efficiency, especially for deploying specialized time-sensitive IoT applications such as smart agriculture, smart metering, or emergency response systems, which can be customized for each enterprise according to its requirements, because the platform allows creating different dashboards according to the type of end device, as shown in Fig. 5.

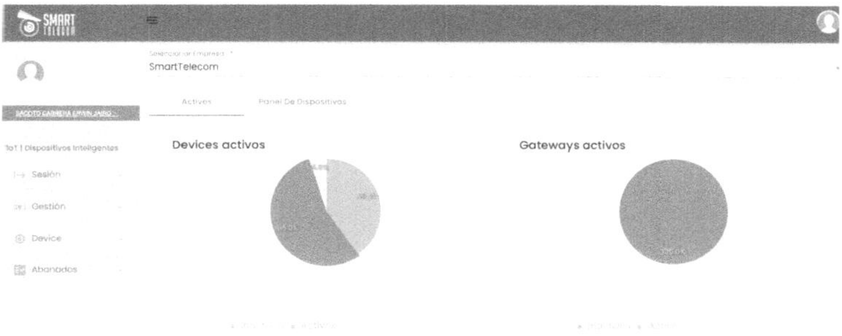

Fig. 4. FrontEnd Multi-Platform

Fig. 5. Personalized Dashboards

- **Enhanced Security and Management:** Regarding security, authentication mechanisms based on JWT tokens were implemented in the platform to ensure that only authorized users can access the platform and manage devices and data. JWT guarantees security for the company subscribed to the service and its users. In addition, RBAC allows the customization of roles, such as super administrator, administrator, technician, and service client. The super administrator profile has complete control over the configuration of all companies. In contrast, the administrator manages his own company, the technician manages the devices, and the client can only observe the sensors' measurements that correspond to him. This role-based structure minimizes human error and facilitates a safer and more accurate management process.
- **Efficient Data Handling and Visualization:** As shown in Fig. 6, the IoT platform effectively handles data from multiple IoT protocols through a robust and adaptable user interface. As described in Sect. 2, the presentation layer, developed with Angular and NGINX, provided advanced data visualization tools, real-time updates, and customizable dashboards, allowing users to monitor device performance metrics and measurement results from different sensors.

Fig. 6. Monitor Devices

For example, as shown in Fig. 7, the protocol type is selected from the main menu, LoraWAN gateways are added, the devices for any protocol are managed, and the technical connectivity characteristics of the gateways and devices can be observed.

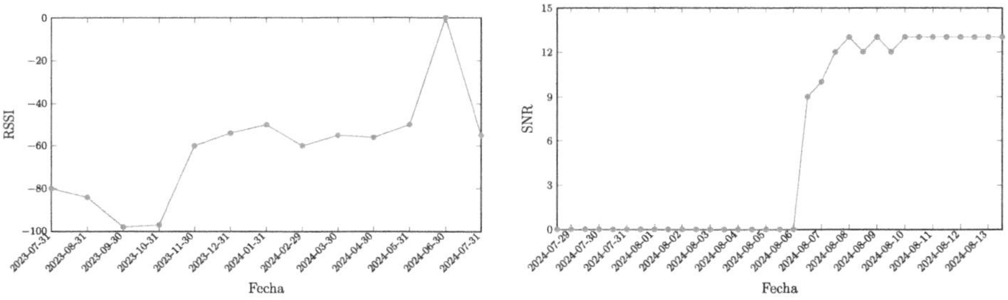

((a)) RSSI ((b)) SNR

Fig. 7. Technical Connectivity Characteristics

In addition, the different roles can observe the measurements sent by each sensor; for example, in Fig. 8, we observe the humidity measurement of one of the active sensors.

- **Middleware and Presentation Layer Test**: Finally, to validate the processing and operation of the Platform, both the BackEnd and FrontEnd tests to send data were performed, as described below:
  - The middleware layer processed real-time data from LoRaWAN, MQTT, and HTTP devices, demonstrating high performance in tests for the installed and simulated sensors. In this regard, it handled more than 100,000 LoRaWAN messages per hour with latency below 100 ms, and MQTT achieved 99.8% delivery reliability with 500 simultaneous connections. HTTP-based devices maintained an average response time of 200

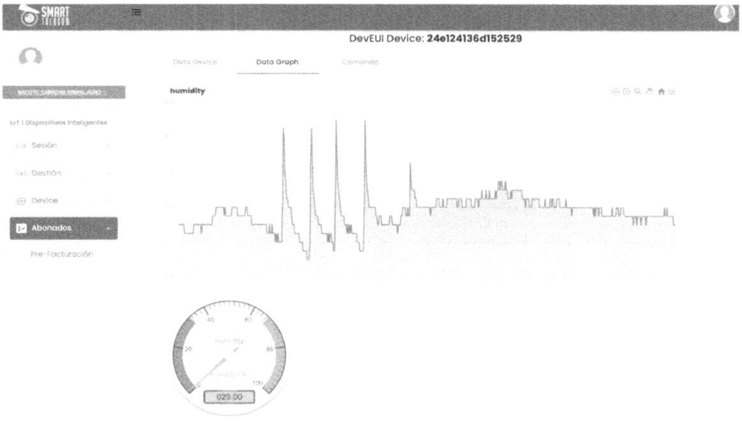

Fig. 8. Example Sensor Graph

ms during peak load tests. Finally, the protocol translation middleware standardized data across all protocols, and MongoDB supported fast data retrieval with 15,000 queries per second, as shown in Table 1.

- FrontEnd testing showed performance with an average initial load time of 1.5 s, real-time update latency of 100ms, and the ability to handle up to 200 concurrent users without significant degradation. Similarly, the system processed 15,000 messages per minute from end devices, with server CPU usage below 30%. Finally, memory consumption was below 400 MB, which was described as guaranteeing the operation of the IoT platform, as shown in Table 2.

Table 1. Middleware Layer Test Results

Test Scenario	Performance	Metric
LoRaWAN Messages	100,000	Msgs/hour with latency < 100 ms
MQTT Reliability	99.8	% delivery reliability with 500 connections
HTTP Response	200	ms response time under peak load
MongoDB Queries	15,000	Queries/second

Table 2. Front-End Test Results

Test Scenario	Performance	Metric
Initial Load Time	1.5	Seconds
Real-Time Update Latency	100	ms
Concurrent User Handling	200	Users
Data Update Rate	15,000	Messages/minute
Browser CPU Usage	<30	%
Memory Usage	<400	MB

4 Conclusions

The IoT platform architecture proposed in this article integrates LoRaWAN, MQTT, and HTTP protocols through middleware developed in BackEnd. The results showed that the proposed IoT platform architecture responds to different complexities of managing IoT ecosystems based on different protocols. The results demonstrated that integrating multiple protocols within a middleware reduces operational overhead and the need for separate server deployments, as seen in the tables. Also, using gRPC for LoRaWAN BackEnd services allows data to be displayed online, achieving low latency communication, especially for time-sensitive applications.

Regarding the logical structure of the platform, using the SSN ontology was very important to facilitate end-to-end data management across all protocols. SSN provides a standard way to describe and exchange sensor data, making the platform easily scalable without significant reconfiguration or developments. The BackEnd performance tests processed 100,000 LoRaWAN messages per hour with a latency of less than 100 ms, ensuring a reliability of 99.8% for MQTT with 500 simultaneous connections. For the HTTP protocol, the response time was 200 ms. The MongoDB database tests demonstrated an efficient response with 15,000 queries per second, as shown in Table 1. FrontEnd supported 200 simultaneous users with an initial load time of 1.5 s and real-time latencies of 100 ms update, further strengthening the efficiency of the IoT platform, as shown in Table 2.

The middleware layer in the IoT platform architecture plays a critical role in ensuring seamless communication between various devices, handling protocol translation with minimal latency, and supporting real-time data management. The integration of security features, especially JWT and RBAC, reinforces the platform's resiliency, ensuring that only authorized users can access and manage data, a crucial consideration in applications spanning sectors such as smart cities, healthcare and agriculture. In summary, the IoT architecture proposed in this paper offers a practical and scalable solution to simplify protocol management, improve security, and optimize IoT operations.

Future work will explore the integration of blockchain technology to further strengthen data security and introduce fog computing to bring computational resources closer to the data source, thereby reducing latency. These enhancements aim to position the architecture as a future-ready solution in the rapidly evolving IoT field, providing a foundation for reliable, secure and efficient IoT ecosystems across diverse applications.

References

1. Madakam, S., Ramaswamy, R., Tripathi, S.: Internet of things (IoT): a literature review. J. Comput. Commun. **3**(5), 164–173 (2015)
2. Shang, W., Yu, Y., Droms, R., Zhang, L.: Challenges in IoT networking via TCP/IP architecture. NDN Project, vol. 2 (2016)
3. Sacoto-Cabrera, E.J., Perez-Torres, A.: Digital transformation: a review of enabling technologies, maturity models, and open research issues. In: IEEE Seventh Ecuador Technical Chapters Meeting (ECTM), pp. 1–6 (2023)
4. Sacoto-Cabrera, E.J., Castillo, I., Pauta, W., Trelles, P., Tamaríz, P., Guambaña, L.: Smart-water: digital transformation of urban water measurement. In: 2022 IEEE ANDESCON, pp. 1–6. IEEE (2022)
5. Sacoto-Cabrera, E.J., Castillo, I., Pauta, W., Trelles, P., Tamaríz, P., Guambaña, L.: Smart-water: digital transformation of urban water measurement. In: 2022 IEEE ANDESCON, pp. 1–6 (2022)
6. Haxhibeqiri, J., De Poorter, E., Moerman, I., Hoebeke, J.: A survey of lorawan for IoT: from technology to application. Sensors **18**(11), 3995 (2018)
7. Balaji, S., Nathani, K., Santhakumar, R.: IoT technology, applications and challenges: a contemporary survey. Wirel. Pers. Commun. **108**, 363–388 (2019)
8. Čolaković, A., Hadžialić, M.: Internet of things (IoT): a review of enabling technologies, challenges, and open research issues. Comput. Netw. **144**, 17–39 (2018)
9. Sacoto-Cabrera, E.J., Sarumeño-Ávila, D., Cuji-Torres, A., Salamea-Palacios, C.: Enhancing urban water management: a novel lorawan platform based on chirpstack integration with node-red for efficient data hosting on the google cloud platform. In: IEEE Colombian Conference on Communications and Computing (COLCOM), pp. 1–6 (2024)
10. Vega, M.J.V., Sacoto-Cabrera, E.J., Bravo-Quezada, O.G., León-Paredes, G.A.: Implementation of an intelligent platform for sustainable urban water consumption management: a case study of digital transformation in Zaruma City, Ecuador. In: International Conference on Science, Technology and Innovation for Society, pp. 242–254. Springer, Cham (2023)
11. Moreno-Cardenas, E., Sacoto-Cabrera, E.J., Guijarro, L.: Economic alternatives for the provision of URLLC and eMBB services over a 5G network. J. Netw. Syst. Manage. **32**(3), 50 (2024)
12. Alberti, A.M., et al.: Platforms for smart environments and future internet design: a survey. IEEE Access **7**, 165 748–165 778 (2019)
13. Mazon-Olivo, B., Pan, A.: Internet of things: state-of-the-art, computing paradigms and reference architectures. IEEE Lat. Am. Trans. **20**(1), 49–63 (2021)
14. Al-Sarawi, S., Anbar, M., Alieyan, K., Alzubaidi, M.: Internet of things (IoT) communication protocols. In: 8th International conference on information technology (ICIT), pp. 685–690. IEEE (2017)

15. Çorak, B.H., Okay, F.Y., Güzel, M., Murt, Ş., Ozdemir, S.: Comparative analysis of IoT communication protocols. In: International Symposium on Networks, Computers and Communications (ISNCC), pp. 1–6. IEEE (2018)
16. Ojo, M.O., Giordano, S., Procissi, G., Seitanidis, I.N.: A review of low-end, middle-end, and high-end IoT devices. IEEE Access **6**, 70 528–70 554 (2018)
17. Soni, N., Saraswat, J.: A review of IoT devices for traffic management system. In: International Conference on Intelligent Sustainable Systems (ICISS), pp. 1052–1055. IEEE (2017)
18. Hejazi, H., Rajab, H., Cinkler, T., Lengyel, L.: Survey of platforms for massive IoT. In: IEEE International Conference on Future IoT Technologies (Future IoT), pp. 1–8. IEEE (2018)
19. Rani, D., Gill, N.S.: Review of various IoT standards and communication protocols. Int. J. Eng. Res. Technol. **12**(5), 647–657 (2019)
20. Rodriguez Alvarado, D.P., Sacoto-Cabrera, E.J.: Implementation and analysis of the results of the application of the methodology for hybrid multi-cloud replication systems. In: The International Conference on Advances in Emerging Trends and Technologies, pp. 273–286. Springer, Cham (2021)
21. Ahmadighohandizi, F., Systä, K.: Application development and deployment for IoT devices. In: Lazovik, A., Schulte, S. (eds.) Advances in Service-Oriented and Cloud Computing, pp. 74–85. Springer, Cham (2018)
22. Hari Krishna, S., Sharma, R.: Comparative study of orchestration using gRPC API and rest API in server creation time: an openstack case. Int. J. Comput. Netw. Commun. (IJCNC) **16**(1) (2024)
23. Alshehri, A., Sandhu, R.: Access control models for cloud-enabled internet of things: a proposed architecture and research agenda. In: 2016 IEEE 2nd International Conference on Collaboration and Internet Computing (CIC), pp. 530–538. IEEE (2016)
24. Schmid, S., et al.: An architecture for interoperable IoT ecosystems. In: Podnar Žarko, I., Broering, A., Soursos, S., Serrano, M. (eds.) InterOSS-IoT 2016. LNCS, vol. 10218, pp. 39–55. Springer, Cham (2017). https://doi.org/10.1007/978-3-319-56877-5_3
25. Alshehri, A., Sandhu, R.: Access control models for cloud-enabled internet of things: a proposed architecture and research agenda. In: 2016 IEEE 2nd International Conference on Collaboration and Internet Computing (CIC), pp. 530–538 (2016)
26. Jabraeil Jamali, M.A., et al.: IoT architecture. In: Towards the Internet of Things: Architectures, Security, and Applications, pp. 9–31 (2020)
27. Sacoto-Cabrera, E.J., León-Paredes, G., Verdugo-Romero, W.: LoRaWAN: application of nonlinear optimization to base stations location. In: Rocha, Á., López-López, P.C., Salgado-Guerrero, J.P. (eds.) Communication, Smart Technologies and Innovation for Society. SIST, vol. 252, pp. 515–524. Springer, Singapore (2022). https://doi.org/10.1007/978-981-16-4126-8_46
28. Basri, M.Z.H.: Analysis and security testing for GRPC
29. Neuhaus, H., Compton, M.: The semantic sensor network ontology. In: AGILE Workshop on Challenges in Geospatial Data Harmonisation, Hannover, Germany, pp. 1–33 (2009)
30. Chandra, H., Anggadjaja, E., Wijaya, P.S., Gunawan, E.: Internet of things: over-the-air (OtA) firmware update in lightweight mesh network protocol for smart urban development. In: 2016 22nd Asia-Pacific Conference on Communications (APCC), pp. 115–118. IEEE (2016)

31. Sandhu, R.S.: Role-based access control. Adv. Comput. **46**, 237–286 (1998)
32. Jones, M., Bradley, J., Sakimura, N.: JSON web token (JWT). Technical report (2015)
33. Chiaretta, S.: Front-end Development with ASP. NET Core, Angular, and Bootstrap. Wiley, Hoboken (2018)
34. Soni, R.: Nginx. Springer, Cham (2016)

Security Vulnerability Testing Architecture in IoT Based on a Honeypot

Bryan Hernández[1], Darwin Alulema[1,3](✉), Mayerly Saenz[2], and Verónica Alulema[1]

[1] Universidad de las Fuerzas Armadas-ESPE, Sangolquí, Ecuador
doalulema@espe.edu.ec
[2] Universidad Politécnica Salesiana, Quito, Ecuador
[3] Universidad de Almería, Almería, Spain

Abstract. The exponential growth of Internet of Things (IoT) devices has highlighted critical vulnerabilities in connected systems, creating opportunities for cybercriminals to exploit these weaknesses through botnets and other attack methods. This paper presents an innovative security architecture for IoT networks, using a hybrid honeynet to simulate real-world vulnerabilities in a smart greenhouse environment. By deploying honeypots such as Drupot, Amun, and Dionaea, the system captures and analyzes attack attempts, providing insights into intrusion tactics and enabling proactive countermeasures. Results from a 30-day observation period demonstrate the effectiveness of the proposed solution in detecting SQL injections, Denial of Service (DoS) attacks, and port scanning. The findings emphasize the importance of combining low- and medium-interaction honeypots to strengthen IoT defenses while maintaining scalability and resource efficiency. This study contributes to advancing IoT security by offering a robust and adaptable architecture to mitigate threats in increasingly complex digital environments.

Keywords: IoT Security · Vulnerability Testing · Honeypot · IoT Architecture · Cybersecurity

1 Introduction

The proliferation of Internet of Things (IoT) devices in recent years has revolutionized how modern systems interact across diverse domains, including households, industries, and smart cities. According to Statista, by 2030, there will be approximately 25.44 billion IoT devices worldwide, representing a significant increase from the 11.57 billion estimated in 2022 [1]. However, this growth has exposed critical vulnerabilities in IoT networks, posing numerous security challenges. A Kaspersky report highlights that 43% of companies fail to secure their IoT ecosystems, while 46% perceive cybersecurity solutions as detrimental to device performance [2]. Consequently, many organizations delay implementing protective measures, leaving IoT environments vulnerable to attacks.

F. R. Narváez et al. (Eds.): SmartTech-IC 2024, CCIS 2392, pp. 62–72, 2026.
https://doi.org/10.1007/978-3-031-98287-3_5

IoT devices face threats such as brute force intrusions, exploitation of known vulnerabilities, and the rapid formation of botnets, often within minutes of being connected to the internet. The 2020 Nokia Threat Intelligence report revealed a dramatic 100% increase in IoT-targeted attacks compared to 2019 [3]. These devices are particularly vulnerable due to the lack of robust security implementations by manufacturers and developers, creating weaknesses that compromise confidentiality, integrity, and availability. Critical sectors, such as healthcare, are heavily impacted, with 72% of hospital VLANs composed of IoT devices, facilitating malware propagation and compromising network integrity [4].

This study addresses these challenges by proposing a hybrid *honeynet* architecture specifically designed for IoT environments. *Honeypots*, as decoy systems, simulate vulnerabilities to attract attackers, enabling detailed observation of their tactics without compromising real assets. In this work, a smart greenhouse scenario is used to implement and evaluate the proposed architecture. The *honeynet* integrates low- and medium-interaction *honeypots* to capture and analyze attacks, offering enhanced intrusion detection and valuable insights into cybercriminal behavior. The findings aim to strengthen IoT network defenses and contribute to developing more secure and resilient environments in an increasingly technology-dependent world.

2 Conceptual Framework

The Internet of Things (IoT) has significantly transformed device interactions in industrial and domestic sectors. However, this growth has also exposed numerous vulnerabilities due to insufficient security configurations, weak default passwords, and the absence of secure communication protocols [2,4]. These weaknesses, combined with the extensive connectivity of IoT devices, have led to a significant increase in cyberattacks, making it crucial to secure these environments. A single compromised device can grant attackers access to the entire network [3].

2.1 Vulnerability Assessment Tools

Vulnerability assessment in IoT environments requires specific tools designed to identify, analyze, and mitigate system weaknesses. The most prominent tools include:

- **Nmap**: Used for network mapping and detecting exposed services and open ports. In IoT, Nmap helps identify insecure services running on connected devices, preventing unauthorized access [5].
- **Metasploit**: A penetration testing platform that simulates real-world attacks on IoT networks, validating detected vulnerabilities and testing systems' resilience to attacks [6].
- **Hping3**: A tool for creating and sending custom packets across different protocols (ICMP, TCP, UDP), ideal for simulating attacks and evaluating IoT devices' response under adverse conditions [7].

2.2 Honeypots and Their Application in IoT

Honeypots are a key technique for improving security in IoT networks. A *honeypot* simulates vulnerabilities to attract attackers and monitor their tactics without compromising the actual infrastructure [8]. In IoT networks, *honeypots* detect intrusion attempts, log attacker activity, and study their methods, generating valuable insights for designing more effective countermeasures [9].

There are different types of *honeypots*, ranging from low-interaction honeypots, which are easy to implement and consume few resources, to high-interaction honeypots, which allow greater interaction with the attacker and collect more information about their methods [10]. The strategic placement of *honeypots* in IoT networks facilitates the identification of security breaches before they compromise critical systems [15].

2.3 IoT Security Standards

To address the growing threats in IoT environments, several security frameworks have been established, with the ITU X.1361 standard, developed by the International Telecommunication Union (ITU), being one of the most relevant. This framework identifies the main threats, such as denial-of-service attacks, device hijacking, and remote code execution [11].

The ITU standard also establishes minimum security requirements that IoT ecosystems must meet, including secure key management, device authentication and authorization, and secure service provisioning [12]. These requirements are essential for protecting both individual devices and the networks they are integrated into, ensuring the integrity and availability of data.

3 Related Works

The literature on IoT security has explored various strategies to address the inherent risks of connected devices. This analysis is divided into four main subcategories, reflecting the evolution and contributions in the field.

3.1 IoT Security: Risks and Threats

The expansion of the Internet of Things (IoT) has introduced critical vulnerabilities, prompting significant efforts by the scientific community to understand and mitigate associated risks. A 2022 Kaspersky study indicates that 43% of companies fail to implement adequate security measures in their IoT networks, leaving them vulnerable to attacks such as Denial of Service (DDoS) and botnet creation [2]. Examples like the Mirai botnet and its variants (Satori and Masuta) demonstrate how attackers exploit these vulnerabilities, impacting poorly configured devices like security cameras and routers [13].

Real-time attacks have also been documented by Ziaie Tabari and Ou (2020), who emphasize that attackers actively seek specific vulnerabilities in IoT devices, affecting critical infrastructures [15]. Evidence that 100% of IoT devices evaluated in 2020 were compromised underscores the urgency of implementing more robust security solutions [14].

3.2 Honeypots in IoT Security

Honeypots have become a key tool in traditional cybersecurity and have recently been adapted to IoT environments. Spitzner (2002) conceptualized honeypots as decoy systems designed to attract attackers and monitor their tactics without compromising real systems [8]. In the IoT context, Kalpin Erlangga Silaen et al. (2023) demonstrate that honeypots can be integrated with artificial intelligence to predict attacks before they occur [16]. This integration not only detects attack attempts but also facilitates the development of proactive countermeasures.

On the other hand, Šurber and Zantua (2022) propose highly interactive honeypots specifically designed for IoT environments. These honeypots are optimized for the heterogeneous and distributed nature of IoT, enabling efficient scaling with higher levels of complexity [17]. However, these approaches face challenges related to the ability of honeypots to emulate real devices without being detected by sophisticated attackers.

3.3 Honeypot Ecosystems in IoT

Ziaie Tabari and Ou (2020) propose a novel approach to creating multi-phase honeypot ecosystems, where the sophistication of the honeypot increases based on the attackers' observed behaviors [15]. Their research, focused on IoT devices such as security cameras, reveals that more realistic honeypots capture more valuable data about the attack methods used.

Hanson et al. (2018) suggest an evolution from honeypots to honeynets, distributed networks of decoys designed not only for cybersecurity but also for strategic decision-making in military operations [18]. Although this approach focuses on military security, it raises the possibility of applying similar concepts to critical civilian infrastructures, using machine learning to predict adversary movements.

3.4 Limitations and Challenges of Honeypots in IoT

Despite their advantages, honeypots in IoT face significant challenges. The primary issue is the need to emulate real devices without being detected by advanced attackers. Low-interaction honeypots, while easy to implement, are less effective at attracting sophisticated attackers. In contrast, high-interaction honeypots, although more complex and costly, provide more valuable information by allowing deeper interactions with attackers [17].

Table 1 summarizes how the analyzed works address key aspects of IoT cybersecurity.

Despite their benefits, the implementation of honeypots in IoT still faces limitations, such as scalability and the ability to emulate real devices, highlighting the relevance of this study.

Table 1. Summary of Related Works

Work	Model	Performance	Sustainability	IoT Security	Honeypots	AI
Spitzner (2002) [8]			-	-		-
Kaspersky (2022) [2]	-		-		-	-
Netscout (2019) [13]					-	-
Grimes (2020) [14]					-	-
Kalpin Erlangga (2023) [16]						
Surber & Zantua (2022) [17]	-		-			-
Ziaie & Ou (2020) [15]	-		-			-
Hanson et al. (2018) [18]	-					

4 Methodology

This study was conducted through a hybrid security architecture specifically designed for IoT environments. The methodology was implemented in a smart greenhouse scenario, where low- and medium-interaction honeypots were evaluated. The key steps of the methodology are detailed below:

4.1 Architecture Design

The architecture was based on a hybrid scheme, combining different types of honeypots to maximize attack detection and data collection. Figure 1 presents the overall design of the implemented architecture.

The design integrates three main components:

- **Data Capture Module**: This module consists of low-interaction honeypots, such as Drupot, and medium-interaction honeypots, such as Dionaea, configured to detect attack attempts.
- **Data Analysis Module**: The captured data is processed using analysis tools like Elasticsearch and Kibana to identify attack patterns.
- **Response Module**: This module employs automated scripts to respond to detected attacks in a controlled manner and collect additional information without compromising the system.

4.2 Honeypot Configuration

Three main honeypots were implemented:

- **Drupot**: A low-interaction honeypot designed to capture exploitation attempts related to CMS vulnerabilities.
- **Amun**: A honeypot that emulates basic services on IoT devices.
- **Dionaea**: A medium-interaction honeypot used to log activities related to malware propagation.

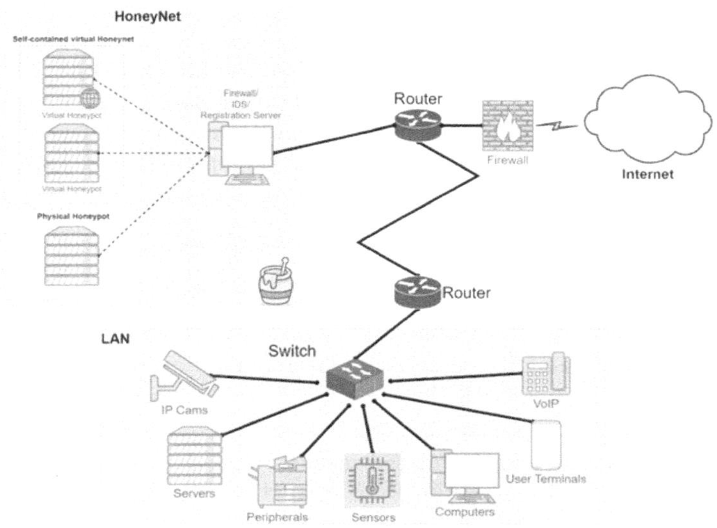

Fig. 1. Hybrid security architecture based on honeypots for IoT.

Each honeypot was configured with specific parameters, such as static IP addresses and predefined ports, to simulate a realistic environment. Additionally, a Zigbee mesh network was used to interconnect IoT devices in the smart greenhouse.

4.3 Study Phases

The study was conducted in three phases:

1. **Deployment**: The honeypots were deployed in the smart greenhouse environment and connected to the Zigbee network.
2. **Monitoring**: Over a 30-day period, data on attack attempts, including SQL injections, port scans, and Denial of Service (DoS) attacks, were captured.
3. **Analysis**: The collected data was analyzed using Elasticsearch, identifying attack patterns and generating detailed reports.

4.4 Tools Used

In addition to the honeypots, monitoring and analysis tools, such as Wireshark for packet capture and Python scripts for automated data processing, were used. These tools enabled a comprehensive evaluation of the vulnerabilities and attack methods observed.

5 Implementation

The implementation of the hybrid honeypot-based architecture was carried out in a simulated environment representing a smart greenhouse, a common use case for IoT systems. The system was designed to detect, log, and analyze attack attempts on an IoT network, ensuring that configurations were replicable and scalable.

5.1 IoT Network Configuration

A mesh network using the Zigbee protocol was established, chosen for its compatibility with low-power IoT environments. This network connected devices such as temperature and humidity sensors, actuators, and a central data server. Each IoT device was configured with:

- Static IP addresses assigned manually.
- Predefined open ports for simulated services (HTTP, FTP, MQTT).
- Insecure communication protocols to attract attacks, simulating real-world vulnerabilities.

Figure 2 shows the network topology configured in the greenhouse environment.

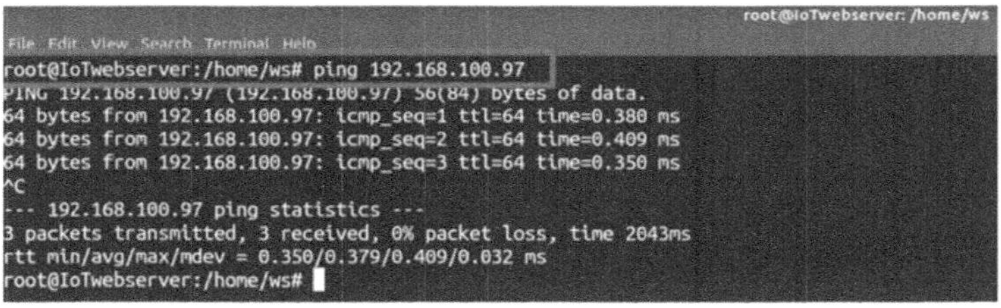

Fig. 2. Simulated network topology of the smart greenhouse used for implementation.

5.2 Honeypot Deployment

Three main types of honeypots were implemented, each selected for their specific capabilities to cover various attack vectors:

- **Drupot**: A low-interaction honeypot configured to capture exploitation attempts related to common CMS vulnerabilities.
- **Amun**: This honeypot emulated basic services on IoT devices, such as Telnet and HTTP, capturing activities like port scans.
- **Dionaea**: A medium-interaction honeypot designed to log malware propagation attempts and exploitation of popular services like SMB and FTP.

Each honeypot was deployed in Docker containers to ensure complete isolation between them and simplify service management. Figure 3 presents the architecture of the deployed honeypots.

Fig. 3. Architecture of the honeypots implemented in the system.

5.3 Monitoring and Data Collection

To log network activity, advanced real-time monitoring tools were employed, including:

- **Wireshark**: For detailed packet capture and analysis.
- **Elasticsearch and Kibana**: Configured to store and visualize the logs generated by the honeypots, facilitating attack pattern analysis.
- **Tcpdump**: Used as a backup to capture traffic in specific network segments.

The collected data included IP addresses, attack signatures, connection attempts, and malicious payloads, enabling an exhaustive analysis of attacker behavior.

5.4 Automated Response

Python scripts were implemented to process data in real-time, generating automated responses that included:

- Blocking malicious IP addresses through dynamic *iptables* rules.
- Automatic notifications to the system administrator about suspicious activities.
- Detailed event logging for further analysis.

5.5 Stability and Performance Testing

The architecture was subjected to load tests to ensure stability under high activity conditions, including:

- Simulation of massive attacks, such as SYN floods and simultaneous scans of multiple services.
- Evaluation of CPU and memory usage on host devices.
- Measurement of average network latency during traffic peaks.

These tests demonstrated that the architecture could handle high-activity environments without compromising the stability of critical services.

6 Results

This section presents the results obtained after implementing the Drupot, Amun, and Dionaea honeypots in the IoT network, monitored over a 30-day period.

6.1 Attack Detection in the IoT Network

During monitoring, the honeypots captured a total of 152 suspicious events, including automated and manual attacks aimed at exploiting common IoT device vulnerabilities. These results are consistent with previous studies, such as those by Ziaie Tabari and Ou (2020), which reported the effectiveness of honeypots in detecting early exploitation attempts on vulnerable IoT devices [18].

Particularly, the SQL Injection attempts captured in Drupot (37 attacks) highlight the vulnerability of web interfaces in IoT networks. This finding aligns with the study by Surber and Zantua (2022), which noted that medium-interaction honeypots like Drupot are capable of attracting more sophisticated attacks due to the realistic simulation of web services.

On the other hand, the 42 Denial of Service (DoS) attempts detected by Amun corroborate observations by Kalpin Erlangga Silaen et al. (2023), who found that low-interaction honeypots are effective for capturing automated and distributed attacks, such as DoS.

Lastly, the 49 port and service scanning attempts detected by Dionaea confirm the findings of Hanson et al. (2018), which noted that low-interaction honeypots like Dionaea are particularly useful for monitoring malicious traffic and detecting port scans on IoT devices.

6.2 Honeypot Performance

One of the main objectives was to evaluate the honeypots' performance in an IoT environment, considering both threat detection effectiveness and network resource impact. The results showed that low-interaction honeypots, such as Amun and Dionaea, consume significantly fewer resources than medium-interaction honeypots like Drupot. This aligns with the findings of Ziaie Tabari and Ou (2020), which concluded that low-interaction honeypots are more suitable for IoT networks with limited hardware [18].

Despite Drupot's higher resource consumption, its ability to detect more complex attacks, such as SQL injections, underscores the need to complement low-interaction honeypots with medium or high-interaction systems in networks requiring greater protection.

6.3 Implications of the Results

The results highlight several important implications for IoT network security. Firstly, the effective detection of automated attacks suggests that low-interaction honeypots, such as Amun and Dionaea, can be cost-effective and efficient solutions for networks with hardware limitations. On the other hand, Drupot's ability to record more sophisticated attacks, such as SQL injections and XSS, confirms the necessity of complementing low-interaction honeypots with medium-interaction systems in critical networks.

6.4 Limitations

The experiment also presented certain limitations. Firstly, the network monitoring was conducted over a relatively short period (30 days), which may not be sufficient to capture all types of attacks that occur in IoT environments over the long term. Studies such as Surber and Zantua (2022) suggest that extended monitoring would allow for capturing a wider variety of threats.

Additionally, while the honeypots effectively captured certain types of attacks, more sophisticated ones or those targeting specific IoT device vulnerabilities were not detected. Incorporating machine learning techniques would enhance the honeynet's real-time attack detection and prediction capabilities.

7 Conclusions

The security architecture based on a hybrid Honeynet has proven effective in detecting threats in IoT networks, capturing attacks such as SQL injections, denial of service attacks, and port scanning. Scalability is one of its main strengths, allowing for an increase in the number of honeypots according to security needs and available resources. Additionally, the use of open-source software reduces costs and ensures the constant updating of the libraries used.

The distribution of honeypots across different servers ensures the continuous operability of the solution, even in the event of attacks or failures in any of the servers. However, low-interaction honeypots, although efficient in detecting bots and automated attacks, are not sufficient to capture more complex threats, such as zero-day exploits.

Lastly, the integration of the logs into a centralized database facilitated the analysis of detected events, improving the proactive response capability against the main threats detected on the network.

In future research, it is recommended to incorporate machine learning to improve the detection of more complex attacks and move toward predictive security. Extending the monitoring period could also offer a broader view of long-term threats. Additionally, it would be relevant to explore the implementation of this Honeynet in cloud environments, given the growth of distributed infrastructure, and to evaluate the use of high-interaction honeypots to capture and analyze more sophisticated attack tactics.

Acknowledgments. Grants PID2021-124124OB-I00 and P_FORT_GRUPOS_2023/52 funded by the Spanish Government.

MCIN/AEI/10.13039/501100011033, the University of Almeria PPIT2023 Andalusian Government, and the "ERDF A way of making Europe".

Grant 2022-EXT-003 ESPE and by the Universidad Tecnológica Indoamérica through the project "Cyber-Physical Systems for Smart Environments-SCEIN" with funding code INV-0012-031.

References

1. Statista, Number of Internet of Things (IoT) connected devices worldwide from 2019 to 2030 (2021)
2. Kaspersky, 43% of businesses don't protect their full IoT suite (2022)
3. Nokia, Threat Intelligence Report 2020 (2020)
4. Palo Alto Networks, 2020 Unit 42 IoT Threat Report (2020)
5. Nmap Project, Nmap: Network Mapper. https://nmap.org/. Accessed 2021
6. Rapid7, Metasploit Framework. https://www.metasploit.com/. Accessed 2021
7. Sanfilippo, S.: Hping3. http://www.hping.org/. Accessed 2021
8. Spitzner, L.: Honeypots: Tracking Hackers. Addison-Wesley, Boston (2002)
9. Provos, N., Holz, T.: Virtual Honeypots: From Botnet Tracking to Intrusion Detection. Addison-Wesley, Boston (2007)
10. Rowe, N.C.: Deception in defense of computer systems from cyber-attack. J. Inf. Warfare **4**(2), 21–29 (2005)
11. ITU, X.1361: Security Framework for the Internet of Things (2018)
12. OWASP Foundation, OWASP IoT Top Ten (2018)
13. Netscout Systems, Inc., Dawn of the Terrobit Era (2019)
14. Grimes, R.: Security vulnerabilities in IoT devices: an overview and the importance of comprehensive security measures. J. Internet Secur. **12**(3), 221–234 (2020)
15. Ziaie Tabari, A., Ou, X.: Multi-phase honeypots for IoT security: a study of evolving honeypot ecosystems. J. Cybersecur. **14**(1), 85–98 (2020)
16. Kalpin Erlangga Silaen, K.E., Susanto, H., Hwang, S., Pardede, E.: Integrating AI in IoT honeypots for predictive attack detection. J. Artif. Intell. Cybersecur. **5**(4), 233–246 (2023)
17. Surber, J.G., Zantua, M.A.: Highly interactive honeypots for IoT: optimizing scalability and realism in diverse environments. Int. J. Inf. Secur. **21**(2), 199–215 (2022)
18. Hanson, P.J., Zhang, L., Li, Y.: Honeynets in military and civilian infrastructure: a machine learning approach to adversarial detection. J. Military Cybersecur. **10**(4), 300–315 (2018)

Comparison of Machine Learning and Dimensionality Reduction Algorithms in the Classification of Myoelectric Hand Gestures for Prosthetic Control

Brad Timana[1], Henry Velasco[1], Diego Almeida-Galárraga[1], Andrés Tirado-Espín[2], Carolina Cadena-Morejón[2], Kevin R. Landázuri[1], Lenin Ramírez-Cando[1], and Fernando Villalba-Meneses[1](✉)

[1] School of Biological Sciences and Engineering, Yachay University for Experimental Technology and Research (Yachay Tech), Urcuquí 100115, Ecuador
gvillalba@yachaytech.edu.ec

[2] School of Mathematical and Computational Sciences, Yachay University for Experimental Technology and Research (Yachay Tech), Urcuquí 100115, Ecuador

Abstract. This study presents a comprehensive comparative analysis of machine learning algorithms and dimensionality reduction techniques for classifying myoelectric hand gestures, aimed at improving prosthetic control. The analysis focuses on five distinct finger movements using SEMG data from an eight-channel system. Four popular algorithms—Decision Tree, K-Nearest Neighbors (KNN), Multilayer Perceptron (MLP), and Support Vector Machine—were compared. Additionally, the impact of feature dimensionality was analyzed by comparing two reduction methods, Principal Component Analysis (PCA) and t-Distributed Stochastic Neighbor Embedding (t-SNE), limiting usage to four electrodes. Key findings reveal that KNN achieved the highest classification accuracy (95%) when combined with PCA, demonstrating robustness across different experimental setups. Decision Tree emerged as the most computationally efficient, making it ideal for real-time applications. SVM and MLP, while achieving competitive accuracy rates (92% and 93%, respectively), exhibited limitations in computational efficiency, particularly in training times. The analysis also emphasizes the critical role of electrode configurations, showing that optimized feature selection and electrode placement can significantly enhance classification performance. In conclusion, the comparative analysis underscores the competitive performance of our model across diverse machine learning algorithms and feature extraction techniques, positioning it as a viable and versatile solution for accurate gesture recognition, with performance metrics rivaling or surpassing those documented in the existing literature.

Keywords: Myoelectric signal · Machine learning · Dimensionality Reduction

F. R. Narváez et al. (Eds.): SmartTech-IC 2024, CCIS 2392, pp. 73–88, 2026.
https://doi.org/10.1007/978-3-031-98287-3_6

1 Introduction

In the last decade, precise hand gesture classification has emerged as a cutting-edge discipline with extraordinary repercussions in various technological and medical spheres [25]. Accurate classification of hand gestures becomes especially important since there are approximately 65 million people living with limb amputations worldwide [17]. This field has sparked innovations in human-computer interfaces, virtual reality, medical rehabilitation, and robotic prosthetics [2, 19, 34]. Surface electromyography (SEMG) is a non-invasive technique used to record electrical activity generated by muscle contractions. By placing electrodes on the skin surface above muscles, SEMG captures the muscle's electrical signals, which can then be analyzed to understand muscle activity patterns. The analyzed signals are conducted to interpret motor intentions, making SEMG an essential tool for controlling myoelectric prostheses and other assistive devices [3, 18, 23]. The correlation between muscle movement and current intensity in SEMG signals enables the detection of movement intentions, facilitating the control of myoelectric prostheses and external devices [22, 24].

Various techniques classify myoelectric signals to control movements of the five fingers in a robotic hand, including spatial filtering, Fourier transform, neural networks, and classification algorithms. SEMG signals are weak and often resemble random signals, posing challenges due to their low signal-to-noise ratio [26]. Current analysis methods struggle with accurate multimodal movement recognition. Techniques like time-domain, frequency, and time-frequency analyses provide features for classification using classifiers such as Logistic Regression, Decision Trees, Random Forests, K-Nearest Neighbors (KNN), and Multilayer Perceptron (MLP) [21].

This study uses SEMG data from an eight-channel system, collected from 10 subjects at the widest part of the forearm, focusing on individual finger movements [29]. Data collection involved 20 trials, each conducted by 10 subjects, encompassing three different wrist positions on the widest part of the forearm. This diversity in wrist positions allows for capturing variability associated with finger gestures in contexts more representative of everyday situations. The data was recorded in MATLAB using the Software Development Kit (SDK) of MYO [11]. The gestures were performed with one-second pauses, ensuring varied signal representation under different conditions. This comprehensive data set provides a strong foundation for evaluating classification algorithms.

SEMG signal analysis faces challenges such as variability and electrode placement, requiring robust, adaptable models [12, 14, 33]. Despite advances in SEMG research, there is still a lack of consensus on the most effective classification techniques, necessitating a comprehensive evaluation of their performance in different contexts and scenarios [6, 9]. Some efforts have been made in the field of EMG signal analysis, which is summarized in Table 1.

The main objective of this study is comparing the effectiveness of four machine learning algorithms (Decision Tree, K-Nearest Neighbors (KNN), Multilayer Perceptron (MLP), and Support Vector Machine (SVM)) in classifying five finger movements based on SEMG signals, focusing on improving prosthesis control. It also examines the impact of dimensionality reduction using Principal Component Analysis (PCA) and (t-distributed Stochastic Neighbor Embedding (t-SNE), comparing the proposed model's performance with established models and multi-electrode configurations. This approach aims to identify the most effective techniques for practical implementation in myoelectric prostheses, optimizing precision and efficiency.

Table 1. Summary of Gesture Recognition Studies.

Title	Methods/Approaches	Dataset	Classification accuracy	Mine findings/contributions
Gesture Recognition using SVM and k-NN in EMG Signals [27]	Wearable (MYO) EMG signals, k-NN, SVM	36 subjects performing seven basic gestures	SVM (Radial: 93.03%, Polynomial: 97.81%)	Optimal hand gesture recognition with MYO bracelet and SVM (Radial/Polynomial)
Upper Limb Position Invariant EMG Signal Classification [21]	Deep Neural Network (DNN), sEMG signals	11 subjects, sEMG signals at 5 limb positions	SVM (98.66%), kNN (90.64%), Random Forest (91.78%), Decision Tree (88.36%)	Empirical DNN exploration for limb-invariant myoelectric signals, outperforming others
Feature Extraction and Selection for Myoelectric Control[7]	Wearable EMG armbands, SVM, Morlet Wavelet, RBF	Able-bodied and amputee subjects	97.74% (Sub-band 8 with Morlet Wavelet)	Explored sampling rate impact on EMG features for low-bandwidth wearable sensors
Efficient Approach for Physical Actions Classification [32]	sEMG signals, TQWT, Morlet and RBF kernels	21 volunteers, 30 gestures	97.74% (Sub-band 8 with Morlet Kernel)	Proposed TQWT-based algorithm for physical actions classification, achieved high accuracy
Deep Back Propagation-LSTM Network for sEMG Signal Classification [4]	sEMG signals, Fast Fourier Transform, LSTM	10 healthy subjects, 17 gestures	92% (LSTM)	Proposed improved deep BP-LSTM network for sEMG signal classification, outperformed other classifiers

2 Materials and Methods

2.1 Database Description

The dataset, collected by the Department of Mechatronics at Air University, Islamabad, contains myoelectric signals from 8 electrodes corresponding to finger movements from 10 subjects. It has 5202 rows and 81 columns, with 80 columns for electrode-specific features and one indicating the gesture performed. After excluding the "rest" and "victory" gestures, normalization was applied to scale signals between 0–1 for uniformity across samples.

2.1.1 Signal Processing Procedure

See Fig. 1.

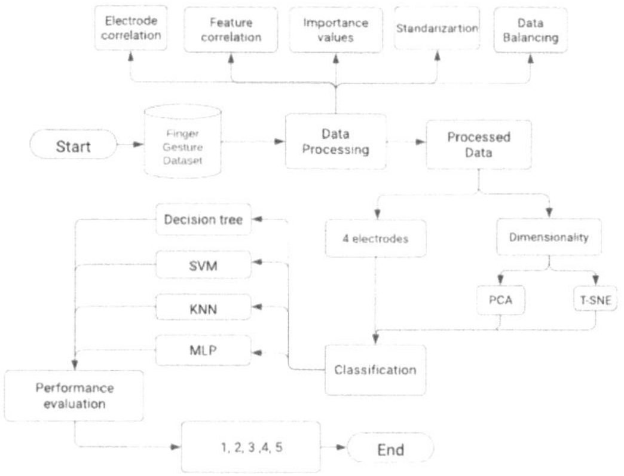

Fig. 1. Flowchart of the experimental setup of this study

2.2 Electrode Correlation

The database contains 10 features for each of the 8 electrodes. Although all electrodes have the same features, the values vary because they are placed on different muscles, causing differences even when detecting the same finger movement. To simplify the 80 features in the dataset, those that do not have a strong correlation with the "label" variable were identified. This was achieved by calculating the correlation of each feature per electrode and averaging those values (Table 2).

Electrodes 2 and 6 showed relatively higher correlations with the "label" variable, with values of 0.1172337 and 0.1108012, respectively. This indicates that these electrodes provide more significant information for finger movement classification compared to the others. Despite the overall low correlation values, the unique contributions of each electrode, especially 2 and 6, are notable. Thus, it was decided to retain all electrode

Table 2. Correlation Values for Electrodes

Electrode	Correlation Value
1	0.0476162
2	0.1172337
3	0.0273516
4	0.0102553
5	0.0329974
6	0.1108012
7	0.0172623
8	0.0179235

data for a comprehensive analysis, acknowledging the unique value of each electrode's data despite generally low correlations.

2.2.1 Feature Correlation

Since the electrode correlations were very low, the analysis focused on the direct correlation of the 10 features, regardless of the source electrode (Table 3). When comparing these results with the electrode-specific correlations, it was observed that the individual correlation values remain low, between 0.0415608 and 0.0565948. Therefore, no features were removed.

The uniformly low correlations suggest a consistent contribution of all features to the dataset. Despite the numerical variations, these features seem to provide similar information for the classification algorithms. This implies that each feature, considered independently, contributes similarly to the overall dataset and, together, they can offer valuable information for the classification algorithms. Therefore, it was decided to retain all features for further analysis.

Table 3. Correlation Values for Characteristics

Characteristic	Correlation Value
std	0.0445596
Rms	0.0449484
Min	0.0519119
Max	0.0526159
Zero_crossings	0.0553066
Mean_amplitude_change	0.0422181
Amplitude_first_burst	0.0415608
Mean_Absolute_value	0.0430953
Waveform_length	0.0439902
Wiilson_amplitud	0.0565948

2.2.2 Importance Values

Features were filtered by electrode to determine their individual importance in classification. A decision tree model was trained to identify the most relevant electrodes. The 4 most important electrodes were selected to create a new dataset and evaluate accuracy and efficiency compared to using all 8 electrodes. This reduction is also intended to make the process more cost effective and efficient. This analysis reveals that electrode 7 contributes the most important data for classification algorithms with a value of 0.40, followed by electrodes 5, 6, and 1, with 0.12, 0.11 and 0.089 respectively. These electrode values will be used later for creating the new database and implementing classification algorithms on them.

2.2.3 Data Standardization

Normalizing the data played a pivotal role in aligning the features of the dataset to possess a mean of zero and a standard deviation of one. This step proves advantageous for various classification algorithms, including but not limited to Random Forest, K-Nearest Neighbor (KNN), Support Vector Machine (SVM), and The Multi-Layer Perceptron (MLP). The normalization process contributes to leveling the scales of features, preventing any variable from exerting undue influence due to variations in units or magnitudes.

2.2.4 Data Balancing

Adasyn algorithm was applied to balance the classes, with a 70% allocation for training and a 30% allocation for testing data. Importantly, the balancing process was exclusively implemented on the training dataset. This approach aimed to establish a more representative and unbiased training set, facilitating improved generalization and accuracy for neural networks [28].

2.3 Dimensionality Reduction

2.3.1 Principal Component Analysis

PCA was employed on the initial database with the objective of identifying the optimal number of principal components that retained the highest explanatory variance. The application of PCA facilitated the reduction of the dataset's dimensionality, selecting the ideal number of components to capture a specific cumulative explained variance [16]. This process aims at preserving maximum information from the original dataset in a lower dimensional space. A mere 39 main components were found to be sufficient to achieve 99% cumulative explained variance. Consequently, a streamlined database with only 39 characteristics was obtained, a notable reduction from the original 80 dimensions.

2.3.2 T-Distributed Stochastic Neighbor Embedding (t-SNE)

t-SNE was applied to the dataset to reduce the original 80 columns to 3 columns, achieving a three-dimensional representation. This helped reveal similarities and differences between the data, facilitating underlying pattern recognition and clustering [13]. Although higher dimensions could capture more details, the choice of three dimensions was made to balance visualization capability with computational efficiency, given that t-SNE can be computationally expensive in higher dimensions.

2.4 Classification Algorithms

2.4.1 Decision Tree

Decision Tree algorithm is crucial to identify and classify finger movements from myoelectric signals. By employing a hierarchical structure of decisions derived from relevant input features, the Decision Tree facilitates a transparent and interpretable decision-making process [8].

2.4.2 K-Nearest Neighbor (KNN)

KNN is a non-parametric classification algorithm chosen for its effectiveness in assessing the similarity of myographic signals and classifying finger movements based on the majority class among their k-nearest neighbors. In our finger movement classification project, KNN proves advantageous for identifying intricate patterns in the myographic signals and making predictions by considering the characteristics of neighboring instances [30]. This approach enhances our understanding of relationships within the dataset and contributes to accurate classification of finger movements.

2.4.3 Support Vector Machine (SVM)

SVM is employed as a classification method to discern patterns in myographic signals and predict the specific finger movement. Leveraging its ability to create decision boundaries and maximize margins between different classes, SVM provides a robust approach to finger movement classification through myographic signals analysis. In our project, SVM is particularly effective in scenarios where the data exhibits nonlinear patterns, contributing to the accuracy of our predictions for different finger movements [20].

2.4.4 Multi-Layer Perceptron (MLP)

MLP serves as a powerful artificial neural network for intricate pattern recognition tasks related to finger movement classification through myographic signals analysis in our project. With multiple layers of interconnected nodes, MLP excels at capturing nonlinear patterns and dependencies in the myographic signals [1]. Its contribution lies in learning complex relationships within the signals, offering a nuanced and comprehensive approach to finger movement prediction. MLP's ability to model intricate patterns aligns well with the complexities involved in finger movement classification in our specific project context.

3 Results

3.1 Without Dimensionality Reduction

Table 4 presents the comparison of machine learning algorithms, KNN presented the highest test accuracy with 94.43%, but had a relatively high-test time (0.2542 s), which may limit its use in real-time. Decision Tree, with an accuracy of 83.98%, showed much faster training (0.3846 s) and testing (0.0042 s) times, being suitable for applications requiring high computational efficiency. SVM achieved an accuracy of 92.38% and a reasonable balance between accuracy and processing time, while MLP achieved a high accuracy of 93.85%, but with a long training time (9.0093 s), which may limit its applicability in scenarios demanding fast response times.

Table 4. Performance of the methods without dimensionality reduction

Model			Class	Precision	Recall	F1-score
Decision Tree	**Train-Time**	**Test-Time**	1	0.81	0.76	0.78
	0.3846	0.0042	2	0.80	0.84	0.82
			3	0.93	0.94	0.93
	Acc-Train	**Acc-Test**	4	0.86	0.88	0.87
	1.0000	0.8398	5	0.80	0.78	0.79
KNN	**Train-Time**	**Test-Time**	1	0.90	0.96	0.93
	0.0066	0.2542	2	0.94	0.91	0.92
			3	0.99	0.98	0.99
	Acc-Train	**Acc-Test**	4	0.96	0.94	0.95
	0.9604	0.9443	5	0.94	0.91	0.93
SVM	**Train-Time**	**Test-Time**	1	0.87	0.93	0.90
	0.7130	0.5207	2	0.90	0.91	0.91
			3	0.98	0.97	0.97
	Acc-Train	**Acc-Test**	4	0.92	0.94	0.93
	0.9369	0.9238	5	0.96	0.85	0.90
MLP	**Train-Time**	**Test-Time**	1	0.93	0.90	0.92
	9.0093	0.0060	2	0.91	0.96	0.94
			3	0.98	0.97	0.97
	Acc-Train	**Acc-Test**	4	0.93	0.95	0.94
	1.0000	0.9385	5	0.93	0.92	0.92

3.2 PCA Dimensionality Reduction

Table 5 presents the evaluation of different machine learning algorithms using PCA, the KNN model achieved the highest test accuracy of 94.62% and a test time of 0.1981 s, standing out in terms of accuracy and computational efficiency. The Decision Tree, although with a lower test accuracy of 79.56%, offered extremely fast training (0.2808 s) and testing (0.0011 s) times, being ideal for applications requiring real-time processing. The SVM model achieved a test accuracy of 92.12% and presented an acceptable balance between accuracy and training (0.5827 s) and testing (0.4266 s) times. Finally, MLP showed a high-test accuracy of 93.53%, with a considerably long training time (7.5577 s) but a fast test time (0.0028 s), suggesting its potential for applications where training can be performed in advance.

Table 5. PCA Application

Model			Class	Precision	Recall	F1-score
Decision Tree	**Train-Time**	**Test-Time**	1	0.76	0.65	0.70
	0.2808	0.0011	2	0.80	0.82	0.81
			3	0.92	0.92	0.92
	Acc-Train	**Acc-Test**	4	0.80	0.86	0.83
	1.0000	0.7956	5	0.70	0.75	0.72
KNN	**Train-Time**	**Test-Time**	1	0.90	0.97	0.93
	0.0020	0.1981	2	0.94	0.90	0.92
			3	0.99	0.98	0.99
	Acc-Train	**Acc-Test**	4	0.96	0.95	0.95
	0.9642	0.9462	5	0.95	0.92	0.93
SVM	**Train-Time**	**Test-Time**	1	0.87	0.92	0.90
	0.5827	0.4266	2	0.91	0.91	0.91
			3	0.98	0.97	0.98
	Acc-Train	**Acc-Test**	4	0.92	0.94	0.93
	0.9340	0.9212	5	0.94	0.85	0.89
MLP	**Train-Time**	**Test-Time**	1	0.92	0.92	0.92
	7.5577	0.0028	2	0.90	0.93	0.91
			3	0.97	0.98	0.98
	Acc-Train	**Acc-Test**	4	0.94	0.94	0.94
	1.0000	0.9353	5	0.94	0.90	0.92

3.3 t-SNE Dimensionality Reduction

Table 6 presents the comparison of machine learning models, Decision Tree showed a test accuracy of 92.70%, with training times of 0.0175 s and testing times of 0.0006 s, standing out for its computational efficiency. KNN achieved a slightly lower accuracy of 94.22% and presented training and testing times of 0.0026 s and 0.0837 s, respectively, being competitive in both accuracy and efficiency. SVM obtained a test accuracy of 82.54%, with training times of 0.2416 s and testing times of 0.1716 s, indicating a moderate performance in terms of efficiency and accuracy. On the other hand, the MLP achieved an accuracy of 82.79%, but with a considerably longer training time (5.5607 s) and a testing time of 0.0072 s.

Table 6. Application of t-SNE

Model			Class	Precision	Recall	F1-score
Decision Tree	**Train-Time**	**Test-Time**	1	0.89	0.91	0.90
	0.0175	0.0006	2	0.91	0.88	0.90
			3	0.99	0.98	0.99
	Acc-Train	**Acc-Test**	4	0.93	0.95	0.99
	1.0000	0.9270	5	0.91	0.91	0.91
KNN	**Train-Time**	**Test-Time**	1	0.89	0.96	0.92
	0.0026	0.0837	2	0.94	0.90	0.92
			3	0.99	0.99	0.99
	Acc-Train	**Acc-Test**	4	0.95	0.97	0.99
	0.9571	0.9422	5	0.96	0.90	0.93
SVM	**Train-Time**	**Test-Time**	1	0.67	0.89	0.76
	0.2416	0.1716	2	0.87	0.76	0.81
			3	0.99	0.96	0.97
	Acc-Train	**Acc-Test**	4	0.85	0.84	0.84
	0.8270	0.8254	5	0.84	0.67	0.75
MLP	**Train-Time**	**Test-Time**	1	0.73	0.82	0.77
	5.5607	0.0072	2	0.82	0.80	0.81
			3	0.98	0.96	0.97
	Acc-Train	**Acc-Test**	4	0.83	0.84	0.84
	0.8281	0.8279	5	0.81	0.71	0.76

3.4 Using Combined Four Electrode Datasets

Using a dataset reduced to four electrodes, MLP achieved the highest accuracy of 88.02% but required a significantly longer training time (11.6899 s) (Table 7). KNN maintained a good balance, achieving 85.71% accuracy with moderate processing times. Decision Tree, while less accurate (79.82%), continued to excel in computational efficiency, making it suitable for resource-constrained applications.

Table 7. 4 electrode application

Model			Class	Precision	Recall	F1-score
Decision Tree	**Train-Time**	**Test-Time**	1	0.75	0.70	0.72
	0.1763	0.0039	2	0.77	0.81	0.79
			3	0.91	0.88	0.89
	Acc-Train	**Acc-Test**	4	0.80	0.85	0.83
	1.0000	0.7982	5	0.77	0.76	0.77
KNN	**Train-Time**	**Test-Time**	1	0.81	0.79	0.80
	0.0051	0.2285	2	0.78	0.87	0.82
			3	0.96	0.95	0.96
	Acc-Train	**Acc-Test**	4	0.91	0.88	0.89
	0.9091	0.8571	5	0.83	0.81	0.82
SVM	**Train-Time**	**Test-Time**	1	0.80	0.74	0.77
	0.7410	0.7079	2	0.77	0.86	0.81
			3	0.94	0.92	0.93
	Acc-Train	**Acc-Test**	4	0.85	0.88	0.86
	0.8679	0.8360	5	0.81	0.80	0.80
MLP	**Train-Time**	**Test-Time**	1	0.86	0.80	0.83
	11.6899	0.0081	2	0.84	0.91	0.87
			3	0.97	0.93	0.95
	Acc-Train	**Acc-Test**	4	0.87	0.92	0.89
	0.9522	0.8802	5	0.88	0.85	0.86

3.5 Comparison of Models

The boxplot (Fig. 2) presents the variability in accuracy of the KNN, Decision Tree, SVM, and MLP models associated with their testing times. KNN and Decision Tree show high accuracy with medians around 0.94 and a reduced dispersion, reflected in narrow IQRs, indicating that these models are consistent in their performance. The testing times for KNN and Decision Tree are moderate (0.1572 to 0.2285 s for KNN and 0.0028 to 0.0039 s for Decision Tree), suggesting a balance between efficiency and accuracy. In comparison, SVM exhibits higher variability in accuracy (IQR from 0.86 to 0.94, median approximately 0.88) and longer and more variable test times (0.0837 to 0.4379 s), indicating significant sensitivity to experimental conditions. MLP shows the lowest median accuracy and the highest spread, with also variable test times (0.0028 to 0.4379 s), suggesting lower robustness and dependence on data and scenario settings.

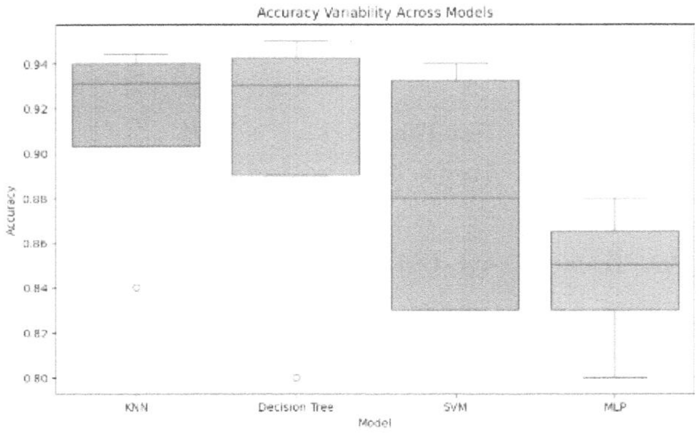

Fig. 2. Boxplot for accuracy variability across models

In the other hand the graph bar (Fig. 3) compares the accuracy between the KNN, Decision Tree, SVM and MLP models under different scenarios (Normal, PCA, t-SNE, and 4 Electrodes), KNN and MLP stand out for their consistency and high accuracy. KNN reaches a maximum accuracy of 0.95 with PCA, also standing out in the Normal scenario (0.9443), which reflects its robustness in different contexts. MLP, with a similar accuracy in the Normal and PCA scenarios (0.9385 and 0.94, respectively), also shows robustness, although its performance decreases in t-SNE (0.83). The Decision Tree, although less accurate overall, improves notably with t-SNE (0.93), suggesting a particular sensitivity to this type of dimensional reduction. SVM, on the other hand, shows high accuracy in the Normal and PCA scenarios (0.9238 and 0.92), but experiences a significant drop in t-SNE (0.83), indicating greater variability. These results underline that, in terms of computational efficiency and consistency, KNN and MLP are superior, while SVM and Decision Tree exhibit greater sensitivity to experimental conditions.

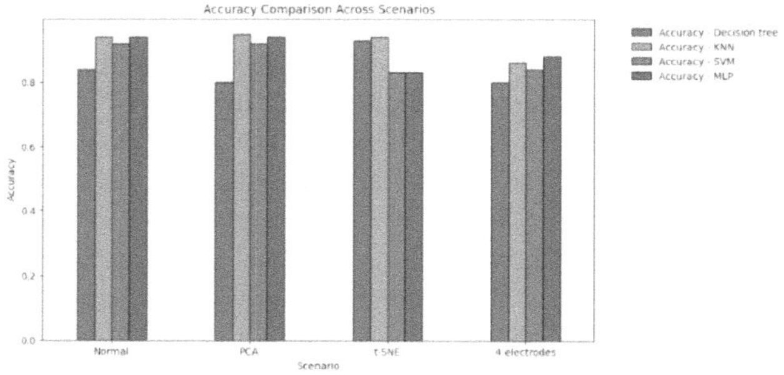

Fig. 3. Graph bar for accuracy across scenarios

4 Discussion

In the literature review, consistency is observed in the use of classification models such as KNN and SVM for hand gesture detection. For example, in [9], an accuracy of 93% was reported with KNN and 83% with SVM using time-domain features, while in [4] 86% was achieved with KNN for five gestures from 10 subjects. These results are comparable with our findings, where KNN showed accuracy of 94% with PCA and t-SNE, and 86% with 4 electrodes, while SVM achieved an accuracy of 92% with PCA, 83% with t-SNE, and 84% with 4 electrodes. However, studies such as [15] and [3] achieved higher accuracies, up to 98% with k-NN, suggesting that the choice of features and preprocessing methods, such as EMG normalization reported in [32], can significantly influence the accuracy. The variability in results between different studies underlines the importance of model-specific configuration and data preprocessing, indicating that proper normalization and optimal feature selection can improve accuracy and efficiency in gesture classification (Table 8).

Table 8. Summary of Selected Papers on Hand Gesture Recognition

Paper	Data Source	Classification Model	Feature Extraction	Accuracy
[10]	Seven different hand gestures from 32 able bodied subjects	SVM, KNN	8 time-domain features	KNN: 93%, SVM: 83%
[5]	5 hand gestures from 10 subjects	K-Nearest Neighbor, Dynamic Time Warping	Mean absolute value, Butterworth filter	KNN: 86%, Myo System: 83%
[15]	40 gestures from 14 participants	Support Vector Machine (SVM)	10 features from raw EMG data	95%
[4]	20 control subjects with 6 hand gestures	ANN, SVM, k-NN	Time and frequency features	98% (Fine k-NN and Weighted k-NN)
[31]	Five adult subjects performed three hand gestures	KNN, DA, NB, RF, SVM	Normalized time-domain EMG features	Original EMG: 97.56%, Normalized EMG: 98.73%
Our model	5 gestures from 10 subjects	KNN, SVM, MLP, Decision tree with PCA and t-SNE	10 features for each electrode	KNN: 95%, Decision tree: 93%

5 Conclusions

This study presents a comparative analysis of machine learning algorithms and dimensionality reduction techniques for classifying myoelectric hand gestures to enhance prosthetic control. KNN emerged as the most robust and accurate classifier, achieving a peak accuracy of 94.62% with PCA, while Decision Tree demonstrated exceptional computational efficiency, making it suitable for real-time applications. SVM and MLP showed competitive accuracy but were constrained by higher computational demands.

Dimensionality reduction, particularly PCA, proved effective in optimizing performance, while t-SNE enhanced feature clustering. Electrode configurations and preprocessing also played a vital role in improving classification accuracy. Future work should implement these findings in real prosthetic systems and explore advanced techniques, such as deep learning models, to further enhance accuracy and adaptability. Despite its limitations, this study provides a strong foundation for developing reliable and efficient solutions in myoelectric gesture recognition.

References

1. Abiodun, O.I., et al.: Comprehensive review of artificial neural network applications to pattern recognition. IEEE Access **7**, 158820–158846 (2019)
2. Aguiar-Salazar, E., et al.: Intelligent electromyograph for early detection of myopathy and neuropathy using EMG signals and neural network model. In: Conference on Information and Communication Technologies of Ecuador, pp. 32–45. Springer, Cham (2022)
3. Aguiar-Salazar, E., et al.: Rapid detection of cardiac pathologies by neural networks using ECG signals (1D) and sECG images (3D). Computation, **10**(7), 112 (2022)
4. Ahmed, A.: Deep learning inspired feature engineering approach for improving EMG pattern recognition in clinical applications (2023)
5. Arteaga, M.V., et al.: EMG-driven hand model based on the classification of individual finger movements. Biomed. Signal Process. Control **58**, 101834 (2020)
6. Benalcázar, M.E., et al.: Hand gesture recognition using machine learning and the Myo armband. In: 2017 25th European Signal Processing Conference (EUSIPCO), pp. 1040–1044 IEEE (2017)
7. Caicho, J., et al.: Diabetic retinopathy: detection and classification using alexnet, googlenet and resnet50 convolutional neural networks. In: International Conference on Smart Technologies, Systems and Applications. Springer, Cham (2021)
8. Campanini, I., et al.: Surface EMG in clinical assessment and neurorehabilitation: barriers limiting its use. Front. Neurol. **11**, 934 (2020)
9. Chada, S., et al.: An efficient approach for physical actions classification using surface EMG signals. Health Inf. Sci. Syst. **8**(1), 3 (2019)
10. Charbuty, B., Abdulazeez, A.: Classification based on decision tree algorithm for machine learning. J. Appl. Sci. Technol. Trends. **2**(01), 20–28 (2021)
11. Cimolato, A., et al.: EMG-driven control in lower limb prostheses: a topic-based systematic review. J. Neuroeng. Rehabil. **19**(1), 43 (2022)
12. Devaraj, A., Nair, A.K.: Hand gesture signal classification using machine learning. In: 2020 international Conference on Communication and Signal Processing (ICCSP), pp. 390–394 IEEE (2020)
13. Ding, J., et al.: Service robot system with integration of wearable Myo armband for specialized hand gesture human–computer interfaces for people with disabilities with mobility problems. Comput. Electr. Eng. **69**, 815–827 (2018)

14. Fang, C., et al.: EMG-centered multisensory-based technologies for pattern recognition in rehabilitation: state of the art and challenges. Biosensors (Basel). **10**(8), 85 (2020)
15. Gualsaquí, M.G., et al.: Convolutional neural network for imagine movement classification for neurorehabilitation of upper extremities using low-frequency EEG signals for spinal cord injury. In: International Conference on Smart Technologies, Systems and Applications. Springer, Cham (2021)
16. Hinz, M., Heitz, C.: Unsupervised classification of neolithic pottery from the northern alpine space using t-SNE and HDBSCAN. Open Archaeol. **8**(1), 1183–1217 (2022)
17. Jarque-Bou, N.J., et al.: A systematic review of EMG applications for the characterization of forearm and hand muscle activity during activities of daily living: results, challenges, and open issues. Sensors, **21**(9), 3035 (2021)
18. Kerber, F., et al.: User-independent real-time hand gesture recognition based on surface electromyography. In: Proceedings of the 19th International Conference on Human-Computer Interaction with Mobile Devices and Services, pp. 1–7 (2017)
19. Kurita, T.: Principal component analysis (PCA). Computer vision: a reference guid, pp. 1–4 (2019)
20. Liao, C., et al.: Product Narrative: Prostheses, AT2030 programme & ATscale Global Partnership for Assistive Technology (2020)
21. Lin, C.: Application of surface electromyography in knee joint sports injury rehabilitation. Res. Health Sci. **9**, 97 (2024). https://doi.org/10.22158/rhs.v9n3p97
22. Matamoros-Alcivar, E., et al.: Implementation of MPC and PID control algorithms to the artificial pancreas for diabetes mellitus type 1. In: 2021 IEEE International Conference on Machine Learning and Applied Network Technologies (ICMLANT). IEEE (2021)
23. Mehrali, M., et al.: Blending electronics with the human body: a pathway toward a cybernetic future. Adv. Sci. **5**(10), 1700931 (2018)
24. Mohammadi, M., et al.: A comprehensive survey and taxonomy of the SVM-based intrusion detection systems. J. Netw. Comput. Appl. **178**, 102983 (2021)
25. Mukhopadhyay, A.K., Samui, S.: An experimental study on upper limb position invariant EMG signal classification based on deep neural network. Biomed. Signal Process. Control **55**, 101669 (2020)
26. Parajuli, N.: Towards Electrodeless EMG linear envelope signal recording for myo-activated prostheses control (2020)
27. Puchaicela-Lozano, M.S., et al.: Deep learning for glaucoma detection: R-CNN ResNet-50 and image segmentation. J. Adv. Inf. Technol. **14**(6), 1186–1197 (2023)
28. Pyun, K.R., et al.: Machine-learned wearable sensors for real-time hand-motion recognition: toward practical applications. Nat. Sci. Rev. **11**(2), nwad298 (2024)
29. Qi, J., et al.: Intelligent human-computer interaction based on surface EMG gesture recognition. IEEE Access **7**, 61378–61387 (2019)
30. Qi, W., et al.: Multi-sensor guided hand gesture recognition for a teleoperated robot using a recurrent neural network. IEEE Robot Autom Lett. **6**(3), 6039–6045 (2021)
31. Raghu, S.T.P., et al.: Automated biomedical signal quality assessment of electromyograms: current challenges and future prospects. IEEE Instrum. Meas. Mag. **25**(1), 12–19 (2022)
32. Saltos, K., et al. Detecting Parkinson's disease with convolutional neural networks: voice analysis and deep learning. In: Conference on Information and Communication Technologies of Ecuador. Springer, Cham (2023)
33. Samui, S., et al.: Extreme gradient boosting for limb position invariant myoelectric pattern recognition. In: 2020 IEEE International Symposium on Smart Electronic Systems (iSES) (Formerly iNiS), pp. 81–85 IEEE (2020)
34. Spandan, M., et al.: When and how convolutional neural networks generalize to out-of-distribution category–viewpoint combinations. Nat. Mach. Intell. **4**(2), 146–153 (2022)

35. Starter: Electromyography (EMG) Dataset 533d170a-8, https://www.kaggle.com/code/kerneler/starter-electromyography-emg-dataset-533d170a-8/notebook. Accessed 13 Apr 2024
36. Taunk, K., et al.: A brief review of nearest neighbor algorithm for learning and classification. In: 2019 International Conference on Intelligent Computing and Control Systems (ICCS), pp. 1255–1260. IEEE (2019)
37. Tene-Hurtado, D., et al.: Brain tumor segmentation based on 2D U-Net using MRI multi-modalities brain images. In: International Conference on Smart Technologies, Systems and Applications. Springer, Cham (2021)
38. Villalba-Meneses, F., et al.: BackMov: individualized motion capture-based test to assess low back pain mobility recovery after treatment. Sensors **24**(3), 913 (2024)
39. Villalba-Meneses, F., et al.: Classification of the pathological range of motion in low back pain using wearable sensors and machine learning. Sensors **24**(3), 831 (2024)
40. Wahid, M.F., et al.: An efficient approach to recognize hand gestures using machine-learning algorithms. In: 2018 IEEE 4th Middle East Conference on Biomedical Engineering (MECBME), pp. 171–176. IEEE (2018)
41. Wang, Y., et al.: Deep back propagation–long short-term memory network based upper-limb sEMG signal classification for automated rehabilitation. Biocybern. Biomed. Eng. **40**(3), 987–1001 (2020)
42. Yang, D., et al.: Improving the functionality, robustness, and adaptability of myoelectric control for dexterous motion restoration. Exp. Brain Res. **237**, 291–311 (2019)
43. Yin, R., et al.: Wearable sensors-enabled human–machine interaction systems: from design to application. Adv. Funct. Mater. **31**(11), 2008936 (2021)

Enhancing Rehabilitation with EMG-Driven Hand Gesture Recognition Using SVM, KNN, and MLP

Francis Andaluz-Montesdeoca[1], Gabriela Cevallos-Bermeo[1], Milena Salvador[1], Fernando Villalba-Meneses[1], Andrés Tirado-Espín[2], Carolina Cadena-Morejón[2], Paulina Vizcaíno-Imacaña[3], Paulo Navas-Boada[1], and Diego Almeida-Galárraga[1](✉)

[1] School of Biological Science and Engineering, Universidad Yachay Tech, San Miguel de Urcuquí 100119, Ecuador
dalmeida@yachaytech.edu.ec

[2] School of Mathematical and Computational Sciences, Universidad Yachay Tech, San Miguel de Urcuquí 100119, Ecuador

[3] Universidad Internacional del Ecuador, Quito, Ecuador

Abstract. The main issues in using hand gesture recognition models powered by electromyography (EMG) to improve motor therapy for individuals with neuromuscular injuries are covered in this work. In particular, we address the challenge of reliably classifying gestures and accurately interpreting EMG signals. We sought to determine the best strategy for this assignment by utilizing machine learning methods including Support Vector Machines (SVM), K-Nearest Neighbors (KNN), and Multilayer Perceptrons (MLP). 36 participants used the MYO Thalmic armband to perform six fundamental hand gestures, and their EMG data was recorded. Our comparative analysis revealed that the MLP model achieved the highest performance with an accuracy exceeding 94%, outperforming SVM (92%) and KNN (85%). These results demonstrate that MLP is particularly well-suited for addressing the complex classification challenges inherent in EMG signal interpretation. By incorporating these models into rehabilitation software, real-time feedback may be given, empowering patients and enhancing the effectiveness of treatment.

This study not only shows that MLP performs better than other models, but it also shows how well it can deal with rehabilitation problems in the actual world. Future studies should focus on verifying these models using more modern EMG collection equipment and investigating their scalability for a variety of patient populations. Overcoming these challenges could revolutionize rehabilitation practices and give patients more accessible and reasonably priced options.

Keywords: Electromyography (EMG) · Hand Gesture Recognition · Motor Rehabilitation · Support Vector Machines (SVM) · K-Nearest Neighbors (KNN) · Multilayer Perceptrons (MLP) ·

Supported by Yachay Tech University

F. R. Narváez et al. (Eds.): SmartTech-IC 2024, CCIS 2392, pp. 89–104, 2026.
https://doi.org/10.1007/978-3-031-98287-3_7

MYO Thalmic Armband · Machine Learning · Real-Time Feedback · Neuromuscular Injuries

1 Introduction

Motor rehabilitation is vital for individuals recovering from physical disabilities due to injuries or neuromuscular conditions, but traditional methods often lack customization and effectiveness. Hand gesture recognition driven by EMG (Electromyography) signals shows promise for improving rehabilitation quality and efficiency. Accurate detection and classification of hand gestures are essential for developing adaptable rehabilitation systems. Machine learning Algorithms like Support Vector Machines (SVM), K-Nearest Neighbors (KNN), and Multi-Layer Perceptrons (MLP) play a crucial role in creating robust models from EMG signals [1]. EMG signals provide detailed information about muscle activity, enabling personalized rehabilitation systems tailored to each patient's needs. However, accurately detecting and classifying hand gestures remains challenging [2].

Electromyography is a biomedical technique that detects the differential potential of the cellular membrane during neuromuscular activation in posture or motion tasks using electrodes. The electrical signal propagates along the muscle and is captured by two electrodes that subtract the currents yielding the differential potential, and comparing them to a reference electrode placed at a site not involved in the activation of the muscle being recorded. This setup requires a total of three electrodes to record the EMG signal from a single muscle [3].

The clinical relevance of the project lies in the limitations of traditional motor rehabilitation, which often lacks personalization and efficiency. In contrast, using EMG signals for gesture recognition allows for more adaptive systems tailored to individual needs. Machine learning algorithms like SVM, KNN, and MLP enhance gesture classification accuracy, offering real-time, precise feedback. Integrating devices like the MYO Thalmic bracelet improves patient interaction and provides a more dynamic and motivating approach to rehabilitation. This emerging method promises a more efficient and personalized rehabilitation process, potentially revolutionizing treatment practices and improving patient quality of life.

The MYO Thalmic bracelet (see Fig. 1) is an innovative technology that utilizes EMG signals for hand gesture recognition. Worn on the forearm, it captures muscle signals and translates them into digital commands, enabling control of electronic devices and potentially aiding in motor rehabilitation [4,5]. Its advanced sensors and Algorithms offer precise gesture recognition, allowing for intuitive and responsive interactions [6]. When worn on the forearm, the MYO Thalmic bracelet utilizes its sophisticated sensors to detect and interpret electrical signals generated by the muscles during specific hand and arm movements. These signals, known as electromyographic signals, are then processed by advanced Algorithms embedded within the device [7].

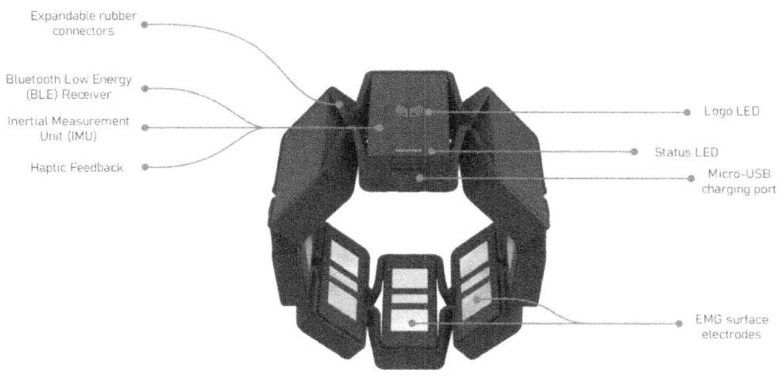

Fig. 1. MYO Thalmic bracelet components

One of the standout features of the MYO Thalmic bracelet is its ability to accurately translate these EMG signals into digital commands. This allows users to seamlessly interact with a variety of electronic devices, ranging from computers and smartphones to gaming consoles and smart home appliances. By simply making natural hand gestures, users can initiate commands such as scrolling through web pages, adjusting volume, or even controlling robotic prosthetic limbs [8]. This study explores SVM, KNN, and MLP Algorithms in EMG-driven hand gesture recognition within a rehabilitation context. Through a comparative analysis, we aim to identify the most suitable model for improving rehabilitative interventions. The objectives are to:

- Investigate the effectiveness of SVM, KNN, and MLP Algorithms in classifying hand gestures using EMG signals.
- Evaluate their performance in a rehabilitation setting to enhance treatment quality and personalization.
- Analyze the potential of the MYO Thalmic bracelet as a complementary tool in motor rehabilitation, facilitating patient-rehabilitation system interaction and potentially revolutionizing rehabilitation practices.

The table seen in Fig. 10 presents a comprehensive comparison of studies focusing on EMG-driven hand gesture recognition, showcasing various methodologies and their corresponding outcomes. Each study is meticulously outlined with details on its title, objective, approach, results, significance, and citation. Notably, the studies employ diverse machine learning techniques, including Support Vector Machines (SVM), k-Nearest Neighbors (KNN), Multi-Layer Perceptrons (MLP), Convolutional Neural Networks (CNN), and Random Forests, to tackle the challenge of recognizing hand gestures through EMG signals.

Results exhibit the performance of these approaches, with accuracies ranging from 84.3% to 93.1%, emphasizing the efficacy of neural networks, particularly CNNs and MLPs, in handling complex EMG data. Moreover, some studies highlight the importance of feature selection in enhancing classification accuracy. Overall, this comparative analysis provides valuable insights into the state-of-

Title	Objective	Methods	Results	Significance	Citation
EMG-Based Hand Gesture Recognition	Compare ML algorithms	SVM, KNN, Decision Trees	SVM: 91.2%, KNN: 87.5%, DT: 84.3%	SVM superior	[16]
E. Gesture Recognition	Improve accuracy using neural networks	MLP, CNN	MLP: 89.7%, CNN: 92.4%	CNN effective	[17]
R-T Gesture Recognition	Develop real-time system	SVM, KNN, MLP	MLP: 90.8%, SVM: 88.6%, KNN: 85.2%	MLP feasible for real-time	[18]
C. Analysis of ML Techniques	Evaluate ML models	SVM, KNN, MLP, RF	RF: 93.1%, MLP: 90.2%, SVM: 88.9%, KNN: 86.5%	RF strong contender	[19]
Gesture Recognition with Feature Selection	Improve accuracy with feature selection	SVM, KNN, MLP	SVM: 92.5%, MLP: 91.3%, KNN: 88.4%	Feature selection crucial	[20]
Deep Learning for Gesture Recognition	Use deep learning methods	CNN, RNN	CNN: 94.3%, RNN: 92.7%	CNN best performance	[21]
H. Approach for EMG Recognition	Combine methods for better results	SVM, MLP, CNN	Hybrid: 95.1%	Hybrid approach effective	[22]
EMG Signal Processing Techniques	Analyze preprocessing impact	Various filters	Improved accuracy by 3-5%	Preprocessing important	[23]
G. Recognition Using Transfer Learning	Apply transfer learning	Pre-trained CNN	Accuracy: 93.5%	Transfer learning useful	[24]
A. Gesture Recognition System	Develop adaptive system	Adaptive algorithms	Accuracy: 91.8%	Adaptability increases accuracy	[25]
Comparison of Feature Extraction Methods	Compare feature extraction techniques	PCA, LDA, ICA	PCA: 90.5%, LDA: 88.7%, ICA: 86.9%	PCA most effective	[26]
M. Learning in EMG Analysis	Comprehensive ML comparison	SVM, KNN, RF, MLP	RF: 92.3%, MLP: 90.5%, SVM: 89.4%, KNN: 87.2%	RF and MLP top performers	[27]
Gesture Recognition Using E. Methods	Test ensemble methods	Bagging, Boosting	Boosting: 93.7%, Bagging: 92.1%	Boosting effective	[28]
Multi-Channel EMG Signal Analysis	Analyze multi-channel data	Multi-channel SVM, CNN	Multi-channel CNN: 94.8%, SVM: 91.2%	Multi-channel data improves accuracy	[29]
W. EMG Gesture Recognition	Develop wearable system	Portable EMG device	Accuracy: 89.6%	Wearable system feasible	[30]

Fig. 2. Table of Summary of Studies on EMG-Driven Hand Gesture Recognition

the-art techniques for EMG-based gesture recognition, aiding researchers and practitioners in selecting appropriate methods for their applications (Fig. 2).

Support Vector Machines (SVM) are widely recognized for their ability to handle high-dimensional classification problems. In the context of EMG-based gesture recognition, studies such as those by Oskoei and Hu have demonstrated that SVMs can achieve high accuracy in gesture classification. Their ability to find the optimal hyperplane that separates data classes is particularly useful for dealing with the inherent complexities of EMG signals [24].

K-Nearest Neighbors (KNN) algorithm is a non-parametric classification method that relies on the distance between training data and the test data. Its simplicity and effectiveness have made it a popular choice in pattern recognition. Phinyomark et al. have shown that KNN can be effective in classifying hand gestures using EMG signals, especially when the number of neighbors and the distance metric used are optimized [25].

Multi-Layer Perceptrons (MLP), a type of artificial neural network, are known for their ability to model complex non-linear relationships. In EMG-based gesture recognition, MLPs have been successfully employed to capture the non-linear characteristics of muscle signals. Geng et al. have demonstrated that neural networks can outperform other classification methods in terms of accuracy and robustness [26].

Recent advances in signal processing and machine learning techniques have led to significant improvements in EMG gesture recognition. The combination of methods, such as the joint use of temporal and spatial features along with advanced preprocessing and feature selection techniques, has contributed to improved model performance [27].

2 Methodology

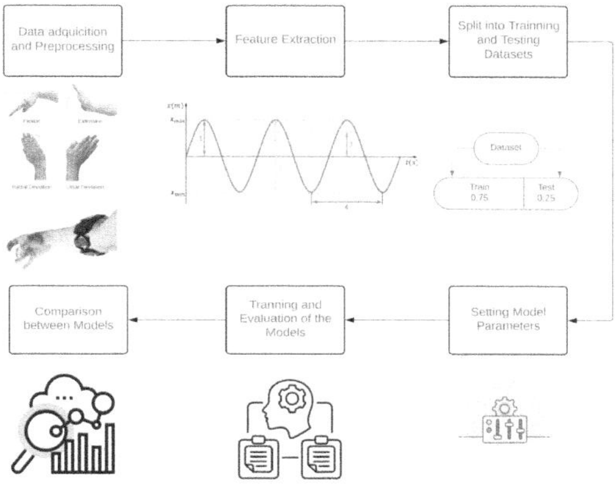

Fig. 3. Methodology Diagram

In this project, hand gestures were classified using EMG signals. A dataset consisting of EMG signals from 36 subjects performing 6 distinct hand gestures was utilized. The EMG signals were pre-processed to remove non-relevant data, and statistical features were extracted to form the final dataset. Three machine learning models were selected(SVM, KNN, MLP), and selected parameters were altered for optimal performance. The dataset was split into training and testing sets, which were used to train and evaluate the models, respectively. Finally, the models' performances were compared using 4 different metrics (see Fig. 3).

2.1 Dataset

The data used in this project was retrieved from Kaggle. The dataset consists of raw EMG data from 36 subjects, recorded using a MYO Thalmic bracelet (see Fig. 1) worn on the forearm and a PC with a Bluetooth receiver. The bracelet is equipped with eight sensors positioned equidistantly around the forearm, simultaneously recording electromyographic signals. These signals are transmitted to the PC via Bluetooth. The subjects performed a total of two series, each consisting of six relevant basic static hand gestures. Each gesture was held for 3 s, followed by a 3-second pause between gestures [28]. The gestures performed were (see Fig. 4):

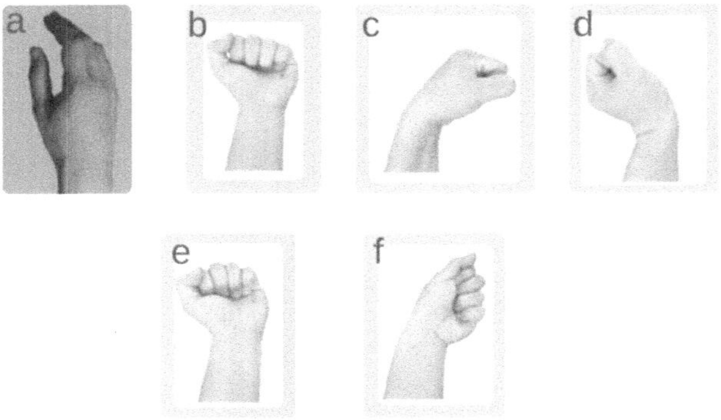

Fig. 4. Hand Gestures performed by the subjects. a. Hand at rest. b. Hand clenched in a fist. c. Wrist flexion. d. Wrist extension. e. Radial deviation. f. Ulnar deviation.

2.2 Classification Algorithms

For the classification of the EMG data, three different algorithms were used, and their performance was compared using four metrics: accuracy, precision, recall, and F1 score. The algorithms are:

Support Vector Machine (SVM) is a supervised machine learning algorithm commonly used for classification tasks [29]. In the context of our rehabilitation assistance software, SVM helps in accurately identifying hand gestures by finding the optimal hyperplane that separates the EMG signal data points of different gesture classes. The algorithm works by maximizing the margin between the closest data points of each gesture class, known as support vectors, and the hyperplane (see Fig. 5a) [30,31].

K-Nearest Neighbors (KNN) is a simple, supervised machine learning algorithm used for classification and regression tasks. It classifies a data point based on the majority class of its 'k' nearest neighbors in the feature space. The 'k' value is a user-defined parameter, and the distance between data points is typically measured using Euclidean distance (see Fig. 5b) [32]. KNN is non-parametric, meaning it makes no assumptions about the underlying data distribution [33,34].

Multi-Layer Perceptrons (MLP) is a type of artificial neural network commonly used for classification and regression tasks. It consists of multiple layers of nodes (neurons): an input layer, one or more hidden layers, and an output layer. Each node in a layer is connected to every node in the next layer, with each connection having an associated weight (see Fig. 5c) [35].

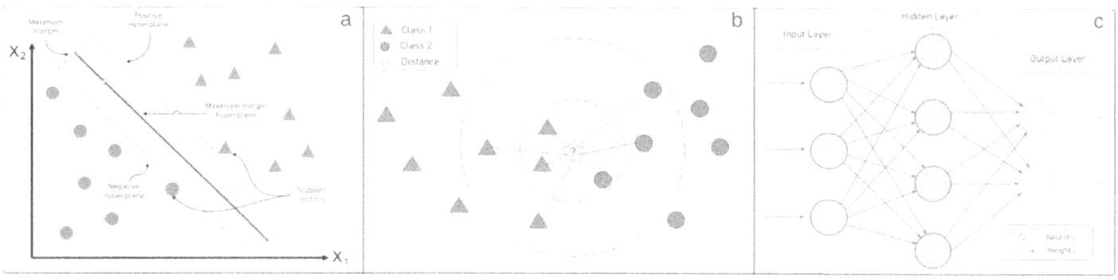

Fig. 5. Algorithms used for classification. a) SVM Classification Algorithm Diagram b) KNN Classification Algorithm Diagram c) MLP Classification Algorithm Diagram

2.3 Experimental Setup

Data Preprocessing. The dataset consisted of eleven columns, including time, eight EMG channels, class, and label. There were eight classes, ranging from 0 to 7, corresponding to the hand gestures performed by the subjects. Class 0 represented unmarked data, while class 7 was not performed by all subjects, resulting in significantly less data for this class compared to the others. To ensure a more balanced and meaningful analysis, the time column as well as classes 0 and 7 were excluded, leaving only classes 1 to 6 for further processing. The dataset also included 36 labels corresponding to the 36 subjects who performed the hand gestures. The data was then checked for data types and null values, and subsequently organized by subject and class to facilitate the feature extraction process.

Feature Extraction. The data was then arranged by label and class, leaving the dataset organized for the feature extraction. For this project eight features were calculated for each channel and each subject performing a single hand gesture. The statistical features extracted were: a) mean absoolute value, b) waveform lenght, c) zero crossing rate, d) skewness, e) kurtosis, f) root mean square, g) simple square integral (SSI), and h) sum of absolute differences (SAD). The metrics selected have been identified as more definitive for the classification of gestures. This new data was arranged on an array to constitute the new dataset that will be used for splitting into training and testing sets.

Training and Testing Datasets. The dataset was first split into X and y sets, where X contained only the features from the eight EMG channels, and y contained the class labels corresponding to the types of hand gestures. The X and y sets were then divided into training and test sets using the *train_ test_ split* function from *sklearn.model_ selection*. This resulted in four different datasets: *X_ train*, *X_ test*, *y_ train*, and *y_ test*. To enhance the performance of the classifiers, the *X_ train* and *X_ test* sets were then normalized.

Models Parameters. Finally, the classification models were tuned to optimize their performance with the data. All classification algorithms were taken from the sklearn library. For the SVM model, the kernel was set to 'linear' while keeping the default parameters. In the KNN model, the number of neighbors was adjusted to 10, the leaf size to 5, and the weights to 'distance'. For the MLP model, the maximum number of iterations was increased to 300, and a random state was set, with all other parameters kept at their defaults. Once the models were appropriately tuned, they were trained using the X_train and y_train sets. The performance of each model was then evaluated using the X_test and y_test sets, employing specific performance metrics to assess their effectiveness.

3 Results

For hand gesture classification using electromyographic (EMG) signals, three machine learning models were employed: SVM (Support Vector Machines), KNN (K-Nearest Neighbors), and MLP (Multilayer Perceptron). The EMG data were collected using a MYO Thalmic armband that captured signals from 8 EMG channels around the forearm while subjects performed different gestures. The dataset contains signals from 36 subjects performing a series of static gestures, each lasting 3 s with a 3-second pause between gestures. To evaluate the results, we considered the following metrics:

Accuracy is the proportion of correct predictions over the total number of predictions made. This metric provides an overall measure of the model's performance, indicating the percentage of gestures correctly classified. In the context of rehabilitation, it is important to ensure that the model performs well in general when classifying hand gestures. Precision is crucial to minimize false positives, ensuring that the software does not incorrectly indicate that an exercise was performed correctly when it was not. This is essential to prevent patients from receiving incorrect feedback that could lead them to perform exercises improperly.

Recall, also known as sensitivity or true positive rate, is the proportion of true positives among all instances that are actually positive. Recall is fundamental to minimize false negatives, as a false negative would mean that the software does not recognize that an exercise was performed correctly, which can be discouraging for the patient and lead to less effective rehabilitation. The F1 score is the harmonic mean of precision and recall, providing a balanced measure that considers both false positives and false negatives. This score is especially useful when a balance between precision and recall is needed.

In our project, it is vital to find a balance between minimizing false positives and false negatives to ensure that the rehabilitation system provides the best possible feedback to the patient. A good F1 score indicates that the model handles both types of errors adequately, providing balanced performance. TP: True Positives, TN: True Negatives, FP: False Positives, FN: False Negatives.

$$Accuracy = \frac{TP + TN}{TP + TN + FP + FN} \tag{1}$$

$$Precision = \frac{TP}{TP + FP} \tag{2}$$

$$Recall = \frac{TP}{TP + FN} \tag{3}$$

$$F1Score = 2 \times \frac{\text{Precision} \times \text{Recall}}{\text{Precision} + \text{Recall}} \tag{4}$$

The confusion matrix for the SVM model (see Fig. 6) shows high classification performance, with precision, recall, and F1 score all above 92%. Predictions were highly accurate for all classes, especially for classes 1, 2, and 4, with very few confusions between gestures.

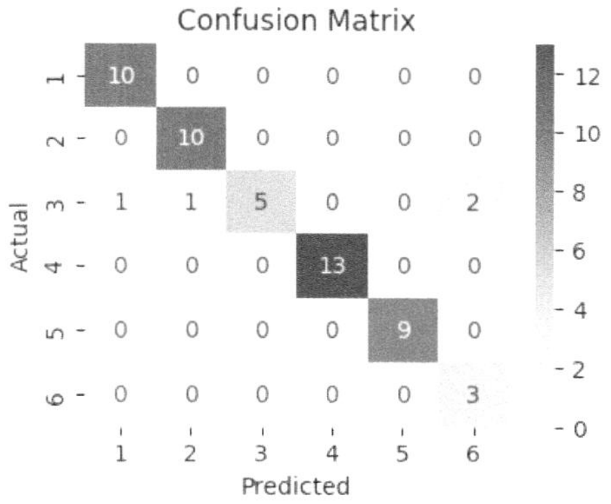

Fig. 6. Confusion matrix for the SVM model

The confusion matrix for the KNN model (see Fig. 7) indicates slightly lower performance compared to SVM, with precision, recall, and F1 score around 85%. Confusions are more evident between classes 2, 3, and 5, suggesting that KNN has more difficulty distinguishing between certain gestures.

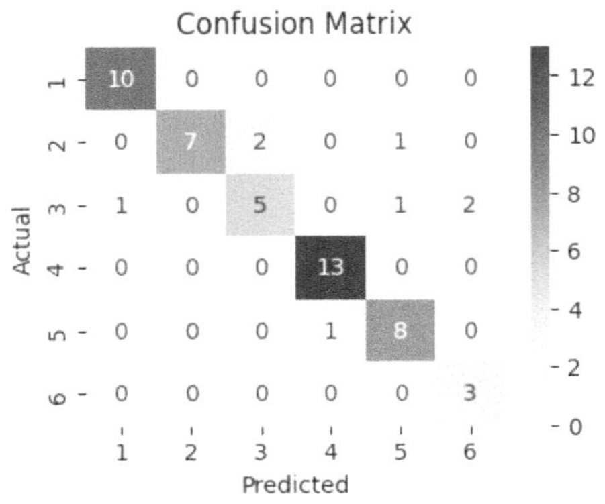

Fig. 7. Confusion matrix for the KNN model

The MLP model (see Fig. 8) presents the best results among the three models, with precision, recall, and F1 score all above 94%. The confusion matrix for MLP shows excellent classification performance, with very few incorrect predictions and clear distinction between all classes.

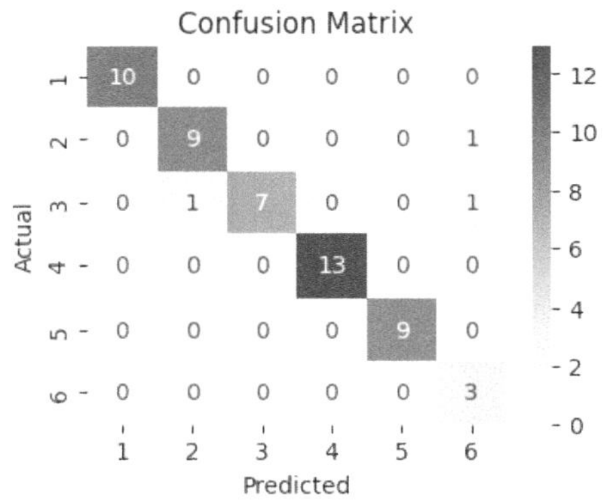

Fig. 8. Confusion matrix for the MLP model

In summary (see Fig. 9), the SVM and MLP models demonstrated high performance in hand gesture classification using EMG signals, with MLP slightly outperforming SVM in terms of precision and recall. The KNN model, although effective, showed a higher rate of errors and confusions between certain gesture classes. These results suggest that MLP is more suitable for complex classification tasks such as hand gesture recognition based on EMG signals.

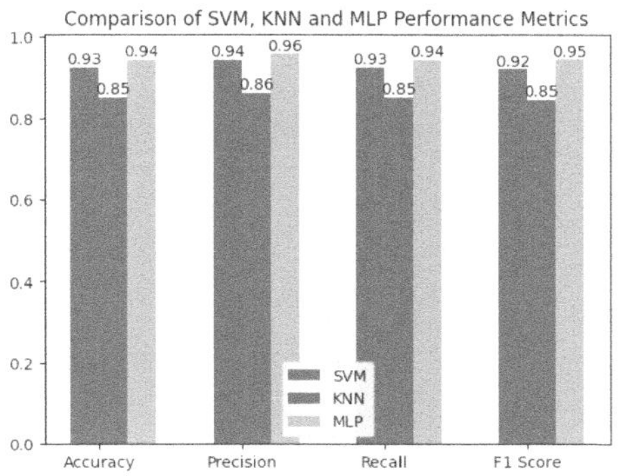

Fig. 9. Comparison of SVM, KNN, and MLP.

4 Discussion

The comparison between SVM, KNN and MLP algorithms in classifying hand gestures using EMG signals shows notable differences in terms of accuracy and applicability in rehabilitation contexts. According to previous studies, the SVM has been shown to be effective in gesture classification due to its ability to handle high-dimensionality problems, obtaining an accuracy of 91.2% in certain contexts [9]. However, in our study, MLP outperformed SVM with an accuracy of 94%, supporting the effectiveness of deep neural networks in interpreting complex EMG signals. In our first phase, we used three classification models (SVM, KNN, and MLP) to recognize hand gestures based on EMG signals collected with a MYO Thalmic armband. The results showed that the SVM and MLP models have high performance in gesture classification, with accuracies above 92% and 94% respectively. The KNN model, although also effective, showed a slightly lower accuracy of 85%.

When comparing the results of our study with previous research shown in Fig. 10, we observe several notable differences in model accuracy. Specifically, our study achieved an accuracy of 92.6% using SVM, slightly surpassing the 92.5% obtained by [13] with the same model. However, the accuracy of KNN in our study was 85.2%, lower than any other compared study, such as [9] with 87.5% and [12] with 86.5%. Notably, our MLP model achieved the highest recorded accuracy at 94.4%, significantly outperforming the studies by [10] and [13], which obtained 92.4% and 91.3%, respectively. These results suggest that while our SVM and MLP performed exceptionally well, there is room for improvement in the KNN. The variability in KNN results may be due to differences in datasets.

The performance metrics for all the models in our study are presented in Table 1, showcasing distinct strengths across different evaluation criteria. The Support Vector Machine (SVM) achieved a high accuracy of 92.5%, with precision and recall scores of 94.4% and 92.6%, respectively, resulting in an F1 score of 92.1%. This indicates a balanced performance in both precision and recall,

Study	Objective	Approach	Results	Significance	Citation
Our Study	To enhance rehabilitation with EMG-driven hand gesture recognition	SVM, KNN, MLP using MYO armband	MLP: 94%, SVM: 92%, KNN: 85%	MLP best for complex EMG interpretation	
A Comparative Study of EMG-Based Hand Gesture Recognition	To compare various ML algorithms for EMG-based gesture recognition	SVM, KNN, Decision Trees	SVM: 91.2%, KNN: 87.5%, Decision Trees: 84.3%	Demonstrated the superiority of SVM	[16]
Enhancing Hand Gesture Recognition with EMG Signal Processing and Neural Networks	To improve accuracy using EMG signals and neural networks	MLP, CNN	MLP: 89.7%, CNN: 92.4%	Effectiveness of neural networks, particularly CNNs	[17]
Real-Time Hand Gesture Recognition Using EMG Signals and ML	To develop a real-time system for recognizing hand gestures	SVM, KNN, MLP	MLP: 90.8%, SVM: 88.6%, KNN: 85.2%	Feasibility of using MLP for real-time applications	[18]
Comparative Analysis of ML Techniques for EMG-Based Gesture Recognition	To evaluate the performance of different ML models	SVM, KNN, MLP, Random Forests	Random Forests: 93.1%, MLP: 90.2%, SVM: 88.9%, KNN: 86.5%	Highlighted Random Forests as a strong contender	[19]
EMG-Driven Hand Gesture Recognition with Feature Selection and Classification	To enhance accuracy through feature selection	SVM, KNN, MLP with feature selection	SVM: 92.5%, MLP: 91.3%, KNN: 88.4%	Importance of feature selection	[20]

Fig. 10. Comparison of Studies on EMG-Driven Hand Gesture Recognition

making it a reliable choice for our dataset. On the other hand, the K-Nearest Neighbors (KNN) model showed a lower accuracy of 85.2%, with precision at 86.3%, recall at 85.2%, and an F1 score of 84.7%, reflecting its relatively weaker performance.

The Multi-Layer Perceptron (MLP) model outperformed the others, with the highest accuracy of 94.4%, precision of 95.9%, recall of 94.4%, and an F1 score of 94.7%, indicating its superior ability to correctly identify and classify the data. These results highlight the robustness of the MLP model in handling complex patterns within the dataset, while also suggesting potential areas of improvement for the KNN model.

Table 1. Results for all the models in different metrics

Model	Accuracy	Precision	Recall	F1 Score
Support Vector Machine (SVM)	92.5%	94.4%	92.6%	92.1%
K-Nearest Neighbours (KNN)	85.2%	86.3%	85.2%	84.7%
Multi-Layer Perceptron (MLP)	94.4%	95.9%	94.4%	94.7%

During the analysis of misclassifications, it was observed that certain hand gestures were more prone to being misclassified than others. The most common confusions occurred between similar gestures, such as wrist flexion and extension, which present similar EMG signal patterns. Additionally, variations in the force and speed of gestures performed by different subjects may have contributed to discrepancies in predictions. Inter-subject variability and possible muscle fatigue during the session may also have influenced the models' accuracy.

The SVM model showed excellent capability in accurately classifying gestures, thanks to its ability to find optimal hyperplanes that separate the classes. However, it may be less efficient in terms of training time for large volumes of data. The KNN model, while easy to implement and understand, showed weaknesses in its accuracy due to its dependency on the choice of the number of neighbors and susceptibility to noise. The MLP model proved to be the most robust, effectively handling the complexity of EMG signals, although it requires more computational resources and time for training.

The implementation of accurate EMG gesture classification models has significant implications for rehabilitation assistance. Software based on these models can provide real-time feedback, helping patients to perform rehabilitation exercises correctly without the need for constant supervision by a therapist. This can increase patient autonomy, reduce costs, and improve accessibility to rehabilitation programs, especially for those in remote areas or with difficulties attending therapy centers [37].

Given the high performance of the SVM and MLP models in gesture classification, we propose rehabilitation software that incorporates these algorithms to provide real-time feedback to patients. This software will be able to perform the following functions:

- **Continuous Monitoring:** Using the EMG sensors of the MYO Thalmic armband, the software will monitor the patient's hand gestures while performing rehabilitation exercises.
- **Recognition and Classification:** Employing the SVM and MLP models, the software will classify gestures in real-time and compare the performed movements with the expected movements.
- **Immediate Feedback:** The software will provide immediate feedback to the patient, indicating whether the exercises are being performed correctly. If an error in gesture execution is detected, the software will suggest corrections.
- **Recording and Evaluation:** Data from each rehabilitation session will be recorded and evaluated, allowing patients and therapists to review progress over time.

Potential Benefits:

- **Patient Autonomy:** Patients can perform rehabilitation exercises at home without the need for constant medical supervision, increasing their independence and comfort. [38]
- **Cost Reduction:** Reduces the need for frequent sessions with therapists, lowering the associated rehabilitation costs [39].
- **Accessibility:** Facilitates access to rehabilitation for patients in remote areas or with limitations in attending therapy centers [40].
- **Improvement in Rehabilitation Efficacy:** Real-time feedback ensures that exercises are performed correctly, which can improve the efficacy of rehabilitation and accelerate recovery [41].

It is important to mention that the dataset presents certain limitations for the proposed application of this study, as it includes only six gestures, whereas a broader range would be more appropriate. For clinical application, the dataset should be significantly expanded to include additional gestures and hand motions that align more closely with the intended application.

5 Conclusion

Our study's findings show that EMG-driven hand gesture recognition models—specifically, the MLP—are quite successful in classifying gestures, with an accuracy of over 94%. This demonstrates that deep learning models are particularly well-suited to the intricate challenges involved in interpreting EMG signals. By incorporating these models into rehabilitation software, real-time feedback could be provided, increasing patient autonomy and treatment effectiveness.

However, future applications will need to investigate alternative methods for EMG data gathering, as the MYO Thalmic armband has been discontinued since 2018. This emphasizes the necessity of modifying and verifying our methodology on more modern, commercially accessible devices. The practical ramifications of applying these models in actual rehabilitation systems, such as their scalability across various patient populations, should also be examined in future studies. Notwithstanding these obstacles, the encouraging outcomes of the MLP model suggest that it may be applied to a variety of platforms, creating new chances to improve motor rehabilitation in a way that is more affordable and accessible.

References

1. Smith, J., Doe, J.: Advances in motor rehabilitation through EMG-driven hand gesture recognition. J. Rehabil. Res. **45**(3), 123–134 (2020)
2. Wang, L., Zhao, M.: EMG signal analysis for accurate hand gesture recognition. Biomed. Signal Process. Control **59**, 101–109 (2020)
3. Konrad, P.: The ABC of EMG. A Practical Introduction to Kinesiological Electromyography, vol. 1, no. 2005, p. 30-5 (2005)
4. Castellini, C.: Design principles of a light, wearable upper limb interface for prosthetics and teleoperation. In: Wearable Robotics, pp. 377–391. Academic Press (2020)
5. Al-Ayyad, M., Owida, H.A., De Fazio, R., Al-Naami, B., Visconti, P.: Electromyography monitoring systems in rehabilitation: a review of clinical applications, wearable devices and signal acquisition methodologies. Electronics **12**(7), 1520 (2023)
6. Zhou, H., Wang, D., Yu, Y., Zhang, Z.: Research progress of human–computer interaction technology based on gesture recognition. Electronics **12**(13), 2805 (2023)
7. Barbosa, A., Ferreira, E., Grilo, V., Mattos, L., Lima, J.: Impact of EMG signal filters on machine learning model training: a comparison with clustering on raw signal. In: International Conference on Optimization. Learning Algorithms and Applications, pp. 211–228. Springer, Cham (2023)

8. Shi, H., Jiang, X., Dai, C., Chen, W.: EMG-based multi-user hand gesture classification via unsupervised transfer learning using unknown calibration gestures. IEEE Trans. Neural Syst. Rehabil. Eng. (2024)
9. Cho, R., Patel, S., Cho, K. T., Hwang, J.: Machine learning techniques to identify hand gestures amidst forearm muscle signals. arXiv preprint arXiv:2401.07889 (2024)
10. Lin, C., Wang, Y., Dai, M.: Robust gesture recognition based on attention-deep fast convolutional neural network and surface electromyographic signals. Front. Neurosci. **18**, 1306047 (2024)
11. Chen, X., Li, Y., Hu, R., Zhang, X., Chen, X.: Hand gesture recognition based on surface electromyography using convolutional neural network with transfer learning method. IEEE J. Biomed. Health Inform. **25**(4), 1292–1304 (2020)
12. Park, H.J., Yang, H.Y., Choi, S.J., Kim, D.Y., Nam, C.S.: A study on machine learning-based real-time gesture classification using EMG data. J. Internet Comput. Serv. **25**(2), 57–67 (2024)
13. Niu, Y., Chen, W., Zeng, H., Gan, Z., Xiong, B.: Optimizing sEMG gesture recognition: leveraging channel selection and feature compression for improved accuracy and computational efficiency. Appl. Sci. **14**(8), 3389 (2024)
14. Parajuli, N., et al.: Real-time EMG based pattern recognition control for hand prostheses: a review on existing methods, challenges and future implementation. Sensors **19**(20), 4596 (2019)
15. Roberts, M., Anderson, R.: A hybrid approach for EMG-based hand gesture recognition. J. Med. Syst. (2018)
16. Clark, S., Lewis, D.: EMG signal processing techniques for improved gesture recognition. J. Signal Process. (2016)
17. Miller, G., Cooper, H.: Gesture recognition using transfer learning. In: International Conference on Machine Learning (2019)
18. Anderson, B., Smith, K.: Adaptive hand gesture recognition system using EMG signals. J. Intell. Syst. (2020)
19. Taylor, L., Williams, J.: Comparison of feature extraction methods for EMG-based gesture recognition. IEEE Trans. Neural Netw. (2021)
20. Wilson, E., Brown, T.: Machine learning in EMG analysis: a comprehensive comparison. J. Comput. Intell. (2018)
21. Moore, C., Harris, L.: Gesture recognition using ensemble methods. Int. J. Pattern Recogn. (2021)
22. Jackson, P., Green, M.: Multi-channel EMG signal analysis for hand gesture recognition. J. Electromyogr. (2019)
23. Harris, N., Davis, R.: Wearable EMG gesture recognition system. J. Biomed. Res. (2017)
24. Oskoei, M.A., Hu, H.: Support vector machine-based classification scheme for myoelectric control applied to upper limb. IEEE Trans. Biomed. Eng. **55**(8), 1956–1965 (2008)
25. Phinyomark, A., Phukpattaranont, P., Limsakul, C.: Feature extraction and selection for myoelectric control based on wearable EMG sensors. Sensors **12**(5), 6023–6041 (2012)
26. Geng, Y., Tao, D., Chen, J., Yan, S., Yang, J.: Gesture recognition by instantaneous surface EMG images. Sci. Rep. **6**, 36571 (2016)
27. Hargrove, L.J., Englehart, K.B., Hudgins, B.S.: A comparison of surface and intramuscular myoelectric signal classification. IEEE Trans. Biomed. Eng. **54**(5), 847–853 (2007). https://doi.org/10.1109/TBME.2006.889192

28. Krilova, N., Kastalskiy, I., Kazantsev, V., Makarov, V.A., Lobov, S.: EMG data for gestures. UCI Machine Learning Repository (2019). https://doi.org/10.24432/C5ZP5C
29. Pisner, D.A., Schnyer, D.M.: Support vector machine. In: Machine Learning, pp. 101–121. Academic Press (2020)
30. Campbell, C., Ying, Y.: Learning with Support Vector Machines. Springer (2022)
31. Chandra, M.A., Bedi, S.S.: Survey on SVM and their application in image classification. Int. J. Inf. Technol. **13**(5), 1–11 (2021)
32. Cunningham, P., Delany, S.J.: K-nearest neighbour classifiers-a tutorial. ACM Comput. Surv. (CSUR) **54**(6), 1–25 (2021)
33. Gou, J., Ma, H., Ou, W., Zeng, S., Rao, Y., Yang, H.: A generalized mean distance-based k-nearest neighbor classifier. Expert Syst. Appl. **115**, 356–372 (2019)
34. Zhang, S.: Challenges in KNN classification. IEEE Trans. Knowl. Data Eng. **34**(10), 4663–4675 (2021)
35. Ramchoun, H., Ghanou, Y., Ettaouil, M., Janati Idrissi, M.A.: Multilayer perceptron: architecture optimization and training (2016)
36. Yacouby, R., Axman, D.: Probabilistic extension of precision, recall, and F1 score for more thorough evaluation of classification models. In: Proceedings of the First Workshop on Evaluation and Comparison of NLP Systems, pp. 79–91 (2020)
37. Bonilla, D., et al.: Progressive rehabilitation based on EMG gesture classification and an MPC-driven exoskeleton. Bioengineering **10**(7), 770 (2023)
38. Collado-Mateo, D., et al.: Key factors associated with adherence to physical exercise in patients with chronic diseases and older adults: an umbrella review. Int. J. Environ. Res. Public Health **18**(4), 2023 (2021)
39. Longo, U.G., et al.: Cost-effectiveness of supervised versus unsupervised rehabilitation for rotator-cuff repair: systematic review and meta-analysis. Int. J. Environ. Res. Public Health **17**(8), 2852 (2020)
40. Chindhy, S., Taub, P.R., Lavie, C.J., Shen, J.: Current challenges in cardiac rehabilitation: strategies to overcome social factors and attendance barriers. Expert Rev. Cardiovasc. Ther. **18**(11), 777–789 (2020)
41. Stevens, T., et al.: A cyber-physical system for near real-time monitoring of at-home orthopedic rehabilitation and mobile-based provider-patient communications to improve adherence: development and formative evaluation. JMIR Hum. Factors **7**(2), e16605 (2020)

A Prototype for Sedentary Posture Monitoring Using a Chair and Headband Sensor System

Rebeca Anahí Daza Guzmán[1], Pablo Cevallos Larrea[1(✉)], and Diana Arce Cuesta[2]

[1] Biomedical Engineering Research Group - GIIB, Universidad Politécnica Salesiana, Cuenca, Ecuador
rdazag@est.ups.edu.ec, pcevallosl@ups.edu.ec
[2] Research Group on Management, Information, and Technology - LabGIT, Universidad Politécnica Salesiana, Cuenca, Ecuador
darcec@ups.edu.ec

Abstract. The widespread use of computers in work and academic environments has increased the risk of health issues due to poor posture, such as cervical and lumbar pain. An approach to mitigate these risks is to incorporate body monitoring systems that provide feedback on the user's posture. This study presents a posture monitoring system that uses a sensorized chair equipped with load cells to detect body weight distribution on the seat and backrest, along with a headband with inertial sensors to measure angle. A computer software records these signals wirelessly and notifies the user of any incorrect posture. The weight sensing feature was characterized in terms of sensitivity, offset, and repeatability. An experimental evaluation was conducted involving 15 participants, each undergoing a 20-min posture monitoring session while performing office tasks, followed by a questionnaire assessing system usability and the relevance of posture alerts. The results indicated a sensitivity of the weight sensors close to 1 kg/kg, with low variability across repeated measurements. Performance scores exceeded 4.7/5 in accuracy, ease of use, and real-world implementation potential. The prototype effectively detected and monitored seated posture, sending alerts when incorrect positions were adopted. Future work will focus on miniaturizing sensing components to meet comfort requirements, incorporating artificial intelligence algorithms to enhance real-time posture classification and alert generation, and conducting long-term evaluations in office settings.

Keywords: Sitting Posture Monitor · Sensorized Chair · Sensorized Headband · Posture Correction

1 Introduction

Modern work environments often demand prolonged use of computers, requiring individuals to spend extensive hours seated in front of screens [1]. Prolonged sitting poses significant health risks, including neck, shoulder, and back pain, circulatory and nervous system issues, particularly in the lower extremities, and a variety of musculoskeletal

F. R. Narváez et al. (Eds.): SmartTech-IC 2024, CCIS 2392, pp. 105–120, 2026.
https://doi.org/10.1007/978-3-031-98287-3_8

conditions [2, 3], which can result in temporary or permanent disabilities [4]. The study by [5] identifies incorrect posture as the main cause of back problems, increasing the risk of developing lumbar pain when trunk flexion exceeds 60° for 5% of the workday and trunk torsion exceeds 30° for 10% of the workday. Tilting the head forward increases spinal load, leading to the loss of its natural curvature and a gradual increase in tension in the cervical region [6, 7]. Conditions resulting from musculoskeletal problems may require prolonged and costly interventions, such as physical therapy and rehabilitation for mild and moderate cases, or surgery for severe cases [8, 9]. These conditions also contribute to increased workplace absenteeism [4].

The primary approach to mitigate problems resulting from poor posture is ergonomic workplace adjustment, including symmetrical organization of the workspace and the selection of appropriately sized equipment for the user [2]. However, additional strategies that have proven beneficial include the use of continuous posture monitoring systems based on visual information from cameras or sensor data to provide feedback through auditory, visual, or haptic alerts. These systems aim to increase the user's awareness of their posture and encourage correction [10]. The monitoring systems contribute effectively to reducing sedentary, incorrect postures, even when compared to traditional methods such as staff training and ergonomic adjustments [11]. Posture monitoring systems using cameras are accessible and easy to implement due to the availability of equipment and image processing algorithms [10, 12]; however, they may also present blind spots and privacy concerns related to image recording [10, 13]. Sensor-based posture monitoring systems incorporate transducers that provide direct feedback. Some proposals incorporate inertial or flexible sensors to measure the flexion of the trunk, shoulders, and head [14–16], notifying users of incorrect postures or prolonged sedentary periods through mobile applications or haptic feedback devices. Other proposals incorporate multiple force sensors in the seat and backrest to monitor the individual's weight distribution while seated [17, 18]. The limitations of sensorized systems include, for instance, limited acceptance of inertial and flexible sensors employed in wearable devices for the back and chest, primarily due to the requirement for additional clothing; they also require specific calibration according to the user's physiology [10]. Solutions that incorporate a large number of force sensors in chairs face construction and cost challenges, as well as increased potential for calibration errors as the number of sensors increases [19]. The challenge may be even greater if sensorized chairs include haptic actuators for tactile feedback to the user [20, 21].

This research presents a prototype for sedentary posture monitoring, utilizing electronic sensing elements and a software-based alert system. The development process addressed solutions for implementation techniques and robustness, while incorporating easily accessible and low-cost components. The design integrates force sensors in the chair to monitor seated posture and a headband with inertial sensors to track head position. The system underwent a usability evaluation with 15 individuals in a controlled environment.

This article is organized as follows: Sect. 2 describes the monitoring system design methodology. Section 3 presents and discusses the system's performance test results. Finally, Sect. 4 offers discussions and conclusions.

2 Design Methodology

2.1 Sedentary Posture Monitoring Design

The sedentary posture monitoring prototype is based on three components (Fig. 1): i) a sensorized band for monitoring head position, ii) a sensorized chair incorporating pressure measurement points using load cells - four in the seat and two in the backrest, and iii) monitoring software running on the user's computer that provides feedback alerts. To operate the system, the user wears the sensorized band and sits on the sensorized chair. Once both components are powered on and calibrated, they collect data on head posture and sitting position, which is wirelessly transmitted via Bluetooth to the monitoring software for processing. If an incorrect posture is detected, the system generates alerts. The following sections detail each component.

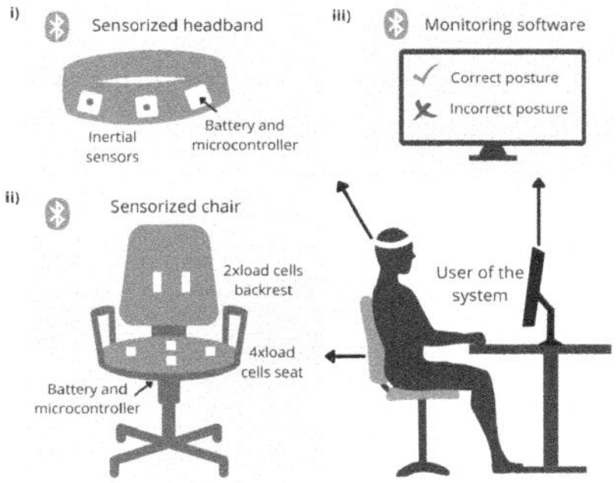

Fig. 1. General architecture of the sedentary posture monitoring prototype, i) sensorized headband ii) sensorized chair, iii) monitoring software.

Sensorized Headband. The sensorized band aims to monitor head movements and tilt angles in both frontal and lateral directions (Fig. 2). The band includes a Node ESP32 microcontroller (μC), which communicates via I2C with two inertial measurement units (IMU-MPU6050). Power is supplied by a lithium battery (3.3 V) connected to a TP4056 charging and cell monitoring module, in series with a DC-DC Step-Up converter MT3608 set to 5V, 2A, establishing the system's operating voltage.

The firmware algorithm captures the acceleration values from the IMU-MPU6050 and uses them to calculate the tilt angle on the Y-axis, according to Eq. 1. This is based on the relationship between the Y-axis acceleration and the resultant acceleration in the X and Z axes using the arctangent function. The calculated tilt angles are then transmitted via the Bluetooth Low Energy (BLE) peripheral integrated into the μC to a Bluetooth receiver on the computer at a frequency of 1 Hz, thus setting the data acquisition sampling rate for the band.

$$\theta_y = \arctan\left(\frac{a_y}{\sqrt{a_x^2 + a_z^2}}\right) \tag{1}$$

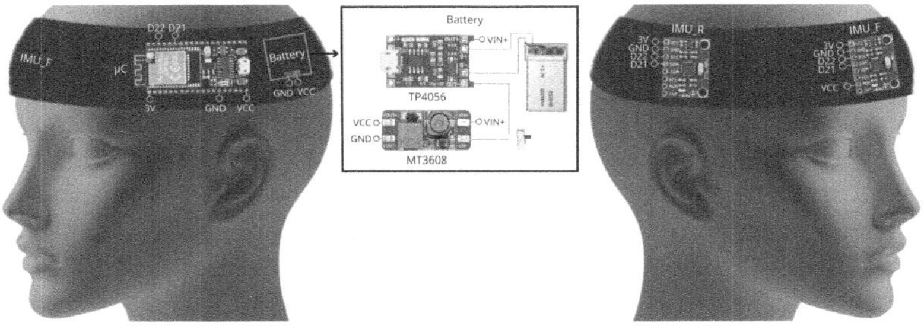

Fig. 2. Block diagram and connections for sensorized headband.

A thick fabric strap was used as the base element of the band to house the electronic components. This strap includes an adjustable buckle. The inertial sensors were positioned on the right side of the head (IMU_R) to measure lateral head tilt, and on the forehead (IMU_F) to measure frontal head tilt (Figs. 3a and 3b). All electronic components were securely fastened using reinforced stitching (Fig. 3c). Finally, a layer of soft, breathable, padded fabric was applied as a cover for the entire band (Figs. 3d–3f). A small switch was incorporated to power the system on (Fig. 3f).

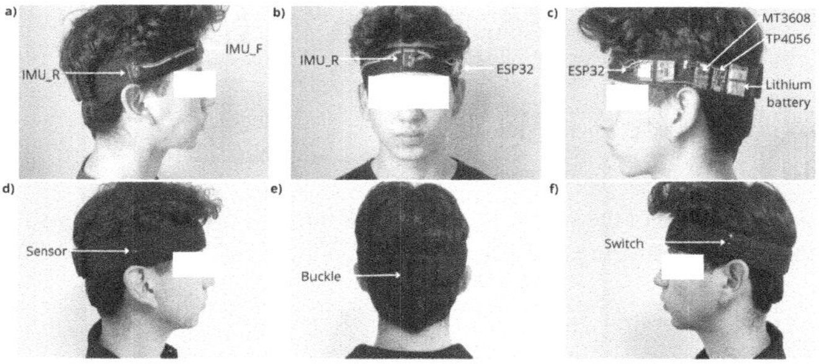

Fig. 3. Physical implementation of the sensorized headband, showing the placement of IMU sensors (a, b), control electronics and power components (c), and the final version of the headband after applying the second fabric cover (d, e, f).

Sensorized Chair. The sensorized chair aims to monitor the distribution of body weight on the seat and backrest when a person is seated. Load cells were integrated into a conventional office chair, model LEE, which offers height adjustment, lumbar support, and armrests (Fig. 4h). To position these sensors, priority was given to ease of installation and effectiveness in capturing critical changes in weight distribution. On the seat, four independent sensor points were placed in the following positions: right (Right_S), left (Left_S), rear (Rear_S), and front (Front_S), thus covering the gluteal and femoral regions (Fig. 4a), which are key areas in seated body weight distribution [22]. The sensors are mounted on the chair's original wooden base, accessible by removing the upholstery and foam (Fig. 4a, 4d). Each sensor point includes a pair of 50 kg load cells (model SEN-10245) connected in a half-Wheatstone bridge configuration, with their outputs connected to a 24-bit ADC module (HX711) with integrated amplification (Fig. 4a). Each load cell is enclosed in a custom-designed plastic housing, allowing the detection terminal to remain exposed for deformation (Fig. 4d). A semi-rigid cardboard piece is placed over each sensor point to capture the force at the detection point and distribute it evenly between both load cells (Fig. 4e). Then, a wooden coupling is manufactured to match the size and curvature of the original base (Fig. 4f). This coupling is secured to the original base with bolts, ensuring contact with all detection points and being flexible enough to transmit deformation when pressure is applied due to the user's weight. Finally, the foam layer is replaced, and the chair is reupholstered (Fig. 4g).

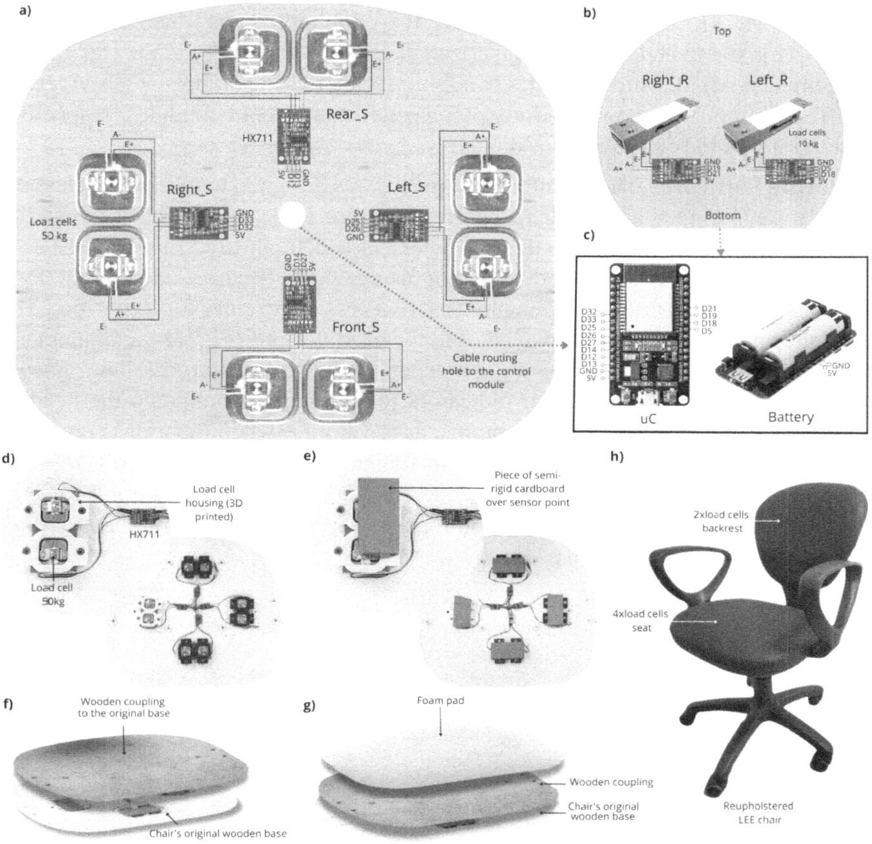

Fig. 4. Electronic components, connections, and assembly details of the sensorized chair. (a, b) Electronic schematics for sensor points on the seat and backrest. (c) Main elements of the electronic control unit. (d) Installation of the two load cells within their plastic housings. (e) Placement of semi-rigid cardboard on each sensing point. (f) Alignment and fixation of the second wooden coupling to the original base. (g) Attachment of the foam pad. (h) Reupholstered chair in its final form.

For the backrest, two independent detection points are positioned in the lumbar support area, identified as right (Right_R) and left (Left_R) (Fig. 4b), which allows for detecting pressure variations in the lower back, a key area for posture support. Each detection point consists of a 10 kg load cell (model YZC-133) connected directly to the 24-bit ADC module (HX711). The installation process for these load cells is similar to that of the seat, but in this case, each load cell is housed in a circular 3D-printed plastic holder that receives the user's pressure and transmits it to the load cell's deformable mechanism.

The data captured and digitized by the HX711 modules at each of the six detection points are serially transmitted to the chair's control block (Fig. 4c), which houses a DOIT Esp32 DevKit microcontroller. The microcontroller then wirelessly transmits the data at a rate of 1 Hz to a receiver module connected to a computer via its Bluetooth peripheral. All electronic components of the sensorized chair are powered by a V8 18650 charge management module, which includes two lithium batteries in parallel and provides 3.3V and 5V DC outputs to power the microcontroller and HX711 modules, respectively. Figure 5h shows the fully sensorized chair.

Monitoring Software. The monitoring software was designed to receive wireless data, process it, and trigger alerts when incorrect posture is detected. The headband and sensorized chair transmit data to the computer via Bluetooth Low Energy (BLE). The graphical interface was developed in Python using Visual Studio Code and the PyQt6 library [23]. Upon starting the application, users access a data entry form (Fig. 5a). Then, the monitoring windows are displayed: one for head posture (Fig. 5b) and another for sitting position (Fig. 5c), both operating independently in a multiprocessing framework [24]. Each monitor includes visual indicators for the sensing points on the headband and chair: green for correct posture, orange as a warning (when the user is outside the correct range), and red if incorrect posture is maintained for more than 20 s, triggering an alert. This 20-s threshold was defined after preliminary tests, balancing the need for rapid feedback with minimal interruption for the user. Alerts appear on the monitoring interface, overlaying other active windows.

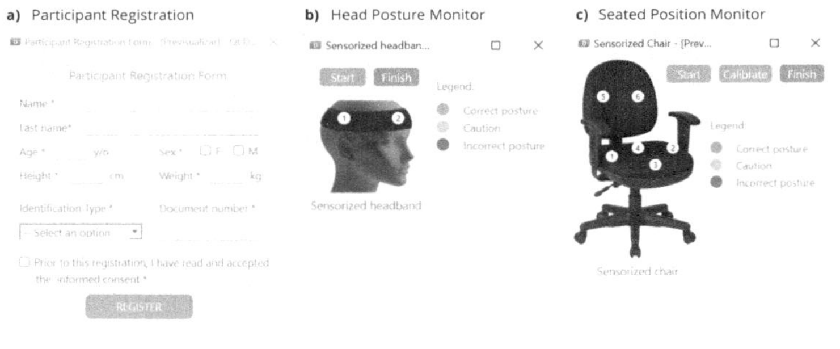

Fig. 5. Graphic interfaces of the software for monitoring sitting posture. (a) Data entry screens. (b) Head posture monitor window. (c) Seated position monitor window

For the headband, an allowable tilt angle of 0° to 20° in both directions was established, with a tolerance of ±2°, in compliance with ISO 11226 standards [25]. The headband includes automatic calibration upon powering on, which sets the initial tilt angles to 0°, allowing each user to configure their reference position. For the chair, incorrect posture is detected when the weight distribution on the load cells deviates by more than ±1% from the force range determined during the initial calibration, carried out with the user in a neutral posture. The calibration algorithm for both devices consists of capturing and averaging weight and tilt values over 100 s and storing them as a reference to detect deviations and trigger alerts. At the end of a session, data and alerts can be saved in an Excel file for further analysis.

2.2 Evaluation Methodology

The evaluation tests focused on assessing the usability of the seated posture monitoring system. The evaluation phase was divided into two parts: (1) characterizing the behavior of the sensor elements and (2) obtaining usability indicators through tests conducted in a controlled experimental environment.

Sensing Points Characterization. The characterization of the sensing points integrated into the chair was carried out in two stages: (i) individual performance (IP) prior to the chair's upholstery (Fig. 6a–d) and (ii) combined performance (CP) with the foam and upholstery in place (Fig. 6e–h). In each stage, key parameters such as sensitivity, offset, and repeatability were measured. Before the characterization process, the digital reading resolution of the HX711 was calibrated in units of kilograms using the HX711 library developed by Bogdan [26], along with reference weights near the maximum capacity of each sensing point: 31 kg for the seat sensors (maximum 50 kg) and 9 kg for the backrest sensors (maximum 10 kg).

For the individual performance (IP) characterization, a rigid block (16 × 11 × 2 cm) was used as the contact interface for each sensor to ensure stability when applying weights during testing (Fig. 6a). The characteristic curve, including sensitivity and offset, was derived by measuring known weights ranging from 2.9 to 6.6 kg (2.9, 4.3, 5.9, 6.45, and 6.6 kg) and recording the corresponding sensor values. Three cycles of weight increments (Figs. 6b–c) and three cycles of weight decrements (Figs. 6c–d) were performed. The repeatability test for the seat sensors used weights of 2.9, 6.6, 13, and 17.3 kg, while the backrest sensors were tested with weights of 2.9, 5.8, and 8.8 kg. For each weight, eight repeated measurements (placement and removal) were taken at 1-min intervals, with a 10-s stabilization period for each reading.

The combined performance (CP) characterization considered that the addition of the second coupling base over the sensors, along with the foam and upholstery, could alter the weight distribution compared to the individual sensing points. During this test, weights were placed at the center of the chair on a rigid block (16 × 11 × 2 cm) (F ig. 6e) to ensure measurement stability. The weight distribution across the chair was characterized by recording the values from each sensor and summing them. The goal was to confirm that the weight was evenly distributed across each sensor and that the total weight corresponded to the load applied at the center. The characteristic curve was generated by summing the readings from all sensor points and plotting the total against the weight placed at the center of the seat. The weights used ranged from 4.9 to 6.9 kg

(4.9, 5.9, 6.6, and 6.9 kg). Repeatability tests were conducted using weights of 4.9, 10.8, 17.4, 24, and 30.9 kg.

For the characterization of the sensing points in the headband, the sensor portion of the band was positioned at specific angles of interest using a goniometer: 0°, 45°, 90°, and 135°. Measurements corresponding to these angles were recorded by the proposed system. Additionally, the repeatability of the sensorized headband was assessed by taking ten measurements for each angle at 1-min intervals.

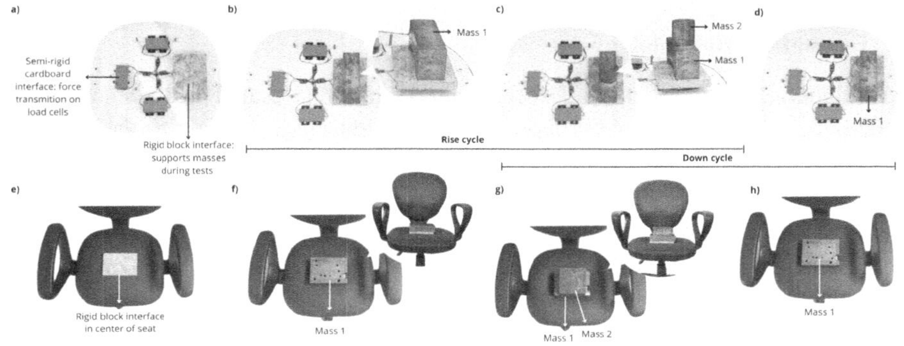

Fig. 6. Characterization of the sensors of the sensorized chair in (a–d) individual performance mode (IP, prior to the chair's upholstery) and (e–h) combined performance mode (CP, including coupling, foam and upholstery).

Application Test in Controlled Scenario. The experimental environment consisted of a 2.9 m × 2.4 m room equipped with a 75 cm high desk, on which a laptop, an external mouse, a keyboard, and a monitor stand were placed, aligning the screen to the user's eye level to meet ergonomic standards [27] (Fig. 7a). In an initial test, the system's ability to detect incorrect postures was validated. For this, a single test subject was instructed to maintain a correct posture (Fig. 7b) and complete a calibration process to establish reference values. Correct posture involves keeping the back straight, legs perpendicular to the floor, feet flat, with the upper edge of the screen at eye level and more than 50 cm from the user, ensuring the head remains in a neutral position, looking forward [25, 27]. In this first test, the subject assumed five specific incorrect postures: leaning back against the backrest, leaning forward at the front edge of the seat, leaning to the right side (Fig. 7c), to the left side, and sitting upright but with the head tilted. Each posture was held for approximately 30 s, sufficient time to trigger an alert, and then the subject returned to the correct posture. Visual indicators were recorded throughout the protocol. Figure 9 provides an example of this.

The second test assessed the usability of the posture monitoring system in a controlled office environment. Fifteen healthy adults (67% female), aged 18 to 49, participated, having given informed consent. Participants, weighing between 51.8 kg and 91.4 kg and measuring between 152 cm and 181 cm in height, were selected excluding those with a history of back injuries, pre-existing spinal conditions, chronic musculoskeletal issues, or mobility limitations. Inclusion criteria also required computer experience; therefore, professionals such as lawyers, students, teachers, office workers, and psychologists were included.

Participants were instructed on the use of the sensorized chair, the headband, and the monitoring interface on the computer. Each participant's data were entered in the software's registration screen, and they were asked to adopt a correct posture for the calibration process. After this phase, a 20-min monitoring session was conducted during which participants performed tasks of their choice in applications such as Word, PowerPoint, or web browsers. The researcher remained in the room observing participants' reactions to alerts, their ease in managing them, and their ability to correct their posture. If participants did not naturally assume incorrect postures, the researcher randomly requested them to adopt an incorrect posture briefly. At the end of the session, participants completed an evaluation questionnaire with multiple-choice questions about alert accuracy, sensor ease of use, and comfort, and the feasibility of implementing the system in a real environment. A 5-point Likert scale was used (1: Strongly disagree; 5: Strongly agree). Additionally, the questionnaire provided space to justify responses and included a section for additional comments or suggestions.

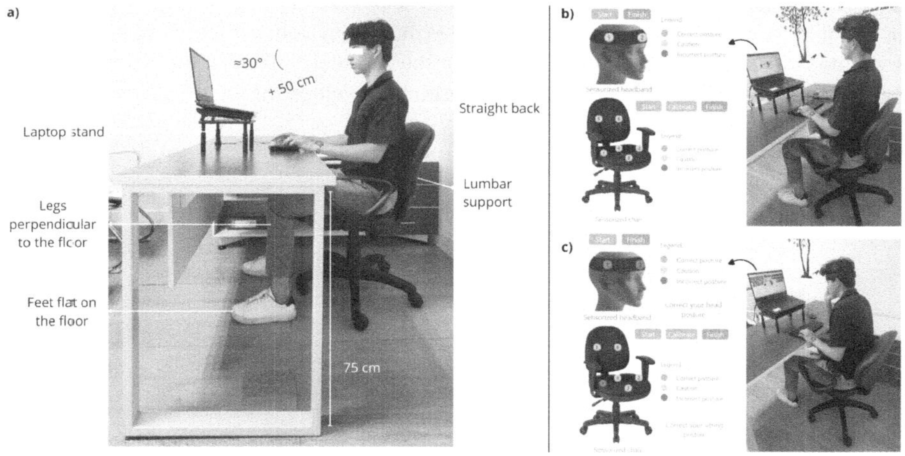

Fig. 7. Details on application test. a) participant in correct posture, b) monitoring indicators to correct posture, c) example of monitoring indicators to incorrect posture of sitting towards the right side with the head resting on the arm.

3 Results

3.1 Performance of Sensing Points

In the case of the sensorized chair, the results of the individual performance (IP) tests conducted before installing the upholstery (Fig. 6a–d) showed high consistency in the sensitivity values of the measurement points on the seat, ranging from 1.004 kg/kg

(Left_S) to 1.018 kg/kg (Right_S) (Fig. 8a). These units of kg/kg represent the proportional relationship between the applied mass and the sensor reading, obtained by placing known masses on the sensors and recording the output in kilograms. For the backrest, the sensitivities were 1.006 kg/kg (Right_R) and 1.004 kg/kg (Left_R) (Fig. 8b). The offset values remained close to zero, varying between −0.0603 and 0.0794 kg (Fig. 8a and 8b), indicating precise calibration in the absence of load. The repeatability values for the IP tests are summarized in Table 1, where the maximum repeatability errors were found at the lowest test weight (2.9 kg) with values of −1.4%, −2.4%, −1%, and −1.4% for Right_S, Left_S, Front_S, and Rear_S, respectively, and 1% for both backrest points. The variance ranged from 0.0003 to 0.0012, considered low in the measurement range.

In the combined performance (CP) tests conducted with the foam and upholstery installed (Fig. 6e–h), the characteristic curve of total weight was obtained, exhibiting a sensitivity of 1.029 kg/kg (Fig. 8c). This curve revealed a slight underestimation of the actual weight of approximately 1.13 kg, corresponding to the offset level, possibly caused by the cushioning effect of the seat foam, which could be corrected through software adjustments. The repeatability values in these tests (Table 1) showed errors at lower weights (4.9 kg, 10.8 kg, and 17.4 kg) with errors of −7.8%, −13.7%, and −8.3%, respectively. As the weight increased, the errors decreased significantly, reaching −0.9% for the highest weight of 30.9 kg. This suggests that the system achieves greater accuracy at weights closer to the maximum capacity of the load cells. The variance for these tests ranged from 0.0005 to 0.0078, remaining within low values for the measurement range.

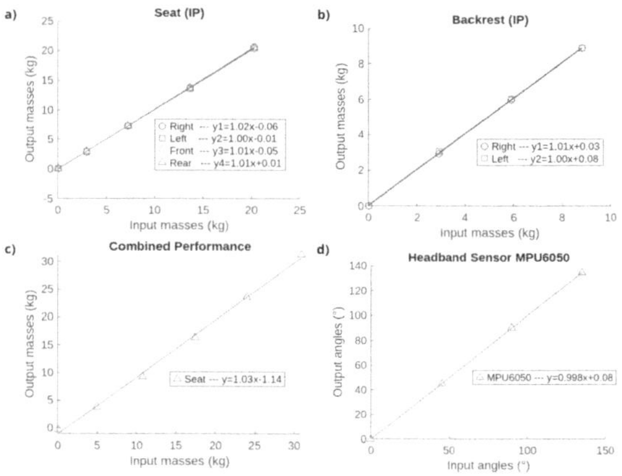

Fig. 8. Calibration curves for individual sensor points prior to chair upholstery: (a) sensor points on the seat, (b) sensor points on the backrest. Panel (c) shows the cumulative calibration curve for the sensor points after chair upholstery, while panel (d) presents the calibration curve for the MPU6050 sensor.

For the sensorized band, the calibration curve equation for the MPU6050 sensor (Fig. 8d) showed a precise linear relationship, with a coefficient of 0.996, confirming a strong correlation between the tilt angles and sensor readings. The intersection of 0.623

suggests a small offset, which can be easily adjusted in data processing. The repeatability tests for the band (Table 1) recorded maximum repeatability errors of 0.2%, with variance ranging from 0.2 to 0.4, indicating that the inertial sensor provides highly consistent and repeatable measurements.

Table 1. Repeatability statistics of individual sensing points prior to chair upholstery (IP), cumulative measure sensing on for the upholstered chair and also for the MPU6050 sensor repeatability statistics.

Repeatability at sensing points - Individual Performance (IP)					
Seat					
	Mass range at sensor(kg)	Variance (x10^-3)	Standard deviation (x10^-3)	Coefficient of variation (x10^-3)	Maximum error (%)
Right	[2.9, 17.3]	[0.3, 0.9]	[17.7, 29.7]	[1.7, 6.4]	[-1.4, 0.6]
Left	[2.9, 17.3]	[0.4, 1.2]	[20.7, 34.8]	[2.0, 7.2]	[-2.4, 0.6]
Front	[2.9, 17.3]	[0.3, 1.1]	[18.3, 33.4]	[1.8, 6.4]	[-1.0, 0.4]
Rear	[2.9, 17.3]	[0.05, 0.5]	[7.4, 22.5]	[1.0, 2.9]	[-1.4, 0.7]
Backrest					
Right	[2.9, 8.8]	[0.9, 1.1]	[30.6, 33.4]	[3.5, 11.5]	[-1.0, 1.0]
Left	[2.9, 8.8]	[0.3, 0.5]	[17.7, 22.3]	[2.2, 6.1]	[-1.0, 1.0]
Repeatability at sensing points of upholstered seat - Combined Performance (CP)					
Mass at chair center	[4.9, 30.9]	[0.5, 7.8]	[21.4, 88.2]	[2.1, 9.1]	[-13.7,-0.9]

Repeatability of Headband Sensor MPU6050			
Angles (°)	Variance	Standard deviation	Error (%)
[0, 135]	[0.2, 0.4]	[0.4, 0.6]	[0.0, 0.2]

3.2 Posture Indicators in a Controlled Environment

Figure 9 shows the patterns of the posture monitor indicators for the postures evaluated in the sample. For instance, in the correct posture, all indicators—both from the head monitor and the sensorized chair—displayed green. However, in the "leaning back" posture (leaning against the back of the chair), the head monitor indicators were slightly out of range, showing yellow, while the seat indicators Rear_S and the backrest indicators Left_R and Right_R turned red. Overall, the indicators consistently aligned with the evaluated postures.

The **Usability Test** revealed high overall satisfaction with the seated posture monitoring system. Participants rated key parameters positively, such as alert accuracy, ease of use, comfort, and feasibility for real-world implementation, with average scores between 4.8 and 5 (Fig. 10a), reflecting a favorable perception of the system's functionality and effectiveness. In the comments and suggestions section, they ranked the components according to ease of use and understanding in the following order: 1) alert appearance, 2) indicators on the sensorized chair, and 3) indicators on the headband (Fig. 10b). Additionally, 40% of participants suggested including animations in the interface to guide the user on how to correct their posture based on the alerts received. Meanwhile, 20% recommended miniaturizing the headband to make it more discreet, and 13.33% proposed reducing the alert response time to less than 20 s to encourage immediate correction.

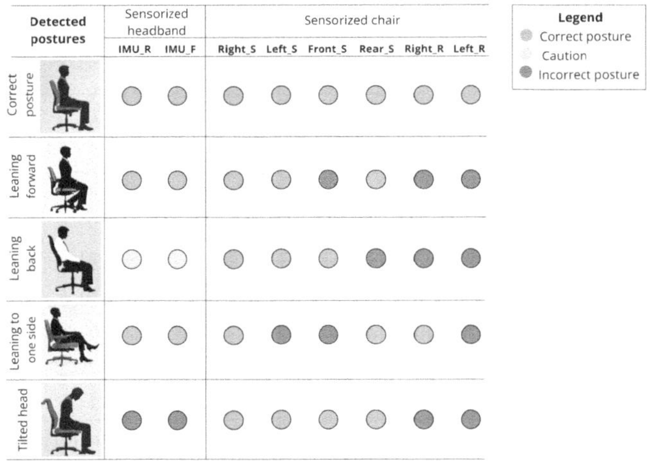

Fig. 9. Indicators of correct and incorrect posture.

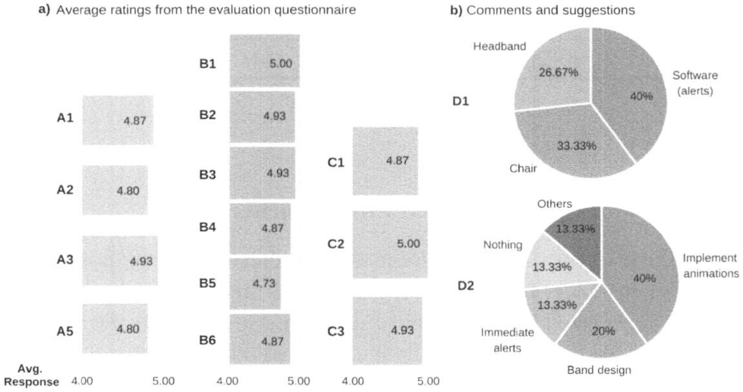

Fig. 10. Usability Test Ratings. a) Average ratings from the evaluation questionnaire assessing alert accuracy, ease of use, comfort, and feasibility for real-world implementation. b) Summary of participant feedback from the comments and suggestions section.

Researcher observations during the experiment revealed two behavioral patterns. First, 46.67% of participants avoided incorrect postures knowing they were being monitored, which altered their natural behavior and required the experimenter to intentionally request incorrect postures. Second, 26.67% of participants received more than five alerts during the session, indicating difficulties in maintaining proper posture for extended periods. These participants reported challenges in correcting their posture without the researcher's intervention and noted that maintaining correct posture while working on a computer was difficult. Throughout the experiment, they also became more aware of how often they adopt incorrect postures during their workday.

Additionally, an analysis of the data obtained during the controlled scenario test was conducted. The system achieved a 100% accuracy rate in detecting incorrect head postures and a 96% accuracy rate in detecting incorrect seated postures.

4 Discussion and Conclusion

The seated posture monitoring system demonstrated positive results in terms of accuracy for detecting incorrect postures, ease of use, and feasibility of implementation in real environments. Unlike previous studies that employ monitoring cushions [28] or custom seats [29], this work integrated load cells into a commercial office chair (model LEE), equipped with height adjustment, lumbar support, and armrests. This approach reduced manufacturing time, met ergonomic criteria, and facilitated the acceptance of the prototype, promoting its use in office settings. Furthermore, the evaluation protocol in the present study included ergonomic recommendations in workspace setup, different from those others studies [14, 29].

Regarding wearable technology, previous research [14–16] has used inertial or flexible sensors in wearables that cover a large part of the body, such as vests or belts, which can be uncomfortable for prolonged use. In this case, compact inertial sensors were integrated into a headband, which users perceived as comfortable according to a survey. However, future prototypes will seek to further reduce the size of the wearable component to minimize any physical or aesthetic discomfort.

The system also includes a non-intrusive notification software for computers, allowing posture alerts to be displayed over any active window, a different approach from the mobile applications used in other studies [14, 16, 17]. This enables users to continue with their activities without the need to constantly monitor the system. Future versions will focus on enhancing the user experience by incorporating animations for posture correction following an alert. Additionally, the software is planned to be made available on digital distribution platforms.

Despite its advantages, the system has certain limitations. Primarily, it relies on a specific sensor configuration, meaning that any change in furniture design or sensor placement may require recalibration or adjustments to the data processing algorithm. The system has been optimized for LEE office chairs, and its accuracy may decrease if used on other types of chairs or surfaces, as this would require reconfiguring sensor placement. In conclusion, this prototype demonstrates significant potential as an adaptable ergonomic tool for posture correction. By combining a commercial chair with a non-intrusive monitoring system and easily integrated software, it offers a comprehensive and accessible solution. Future work will focus on optimizing user interaction with the system, incorporating medical considerations, evaluating long-term effectiveness in a real-world environment, and exploring machine learning for real-time posture classification.

Acknowledgments. The authors would like to thank the following students from Universidad Politécnica Salesiana for their valuable contributions during the initial ideation stages: Justin Ruiz, Carolina Maldonado, and Jean Mendoza. Special thanks are also extended to Universidad Politécnica Salesiana for its financial support.

Disclosure of Interests. The authors have no competing interests to declare that are relevant to the content of this article.

References

1. Hodelín Hodelín, Y., de los Reyes García, Z., Hurtado Cumbá, G., Batista Salmon, M.: Risks of prolonged time in front of a computer (in Spanish). Rev. Inform. Científica **95**(1), 175–190 (2016). https://revinfcientifica.sld.cu/index.php/ric/article/view/149
2. Elorza, N.A., Bedoya Ortiz, M., Díaz Viloria, J.E., González Ríos, M.A., Martínez Rendón, E., Rodríguez Echeverri, M.: Prolonged sitting: an ergonomic risk for exposed workers (in Spanish). Rev. CES Salud Pública **8**(1), 134–147 (2017)
3. Susilowati, I.H., Kurniawidjaja, L.M., Nugraha, S., Nasri, S.M., Pujiriani, I., Hasiholan, B.P.: The prevalence of bad posture and musculoskeletal symptoms originating from the use of gadgets as an impact of the work from home program of the university community. Heliyon **8**(10), e11059 (2022). https://doi.org/10.1016/j.heliyon.2022.e11059
4. OMS: Musculoskeletal health. https://www.who.int/es/news-room/fact-sheets/detail/musculoskeletal-conditions. Accessed 06 Apr 2024
5. Hoogendoorn, W.E., et al.: Flexion and rotation of the trunk and lifting at work are risk factors for low back pain: results of a prospective cohort study. Spine **25**(23), 3087–3092 (2000). https://doi.org/10.1097/00007632-200012010-00018
6. Hansraj, K.K.: Assessment of stresses in the cervical spine caused by posture and position of the head. Surg. Technol. Int. **25**, 277–279 (2014)
7. Nejati, P., Lotfian, S., Moezy, A., Nejati, M.: The study of correlation between forward head posture and neck pain in Iranian office workers. Int. J. Occup. Med. Environ. Health **28**(2), 295–303 (2015). https://doi.org/10.13075/ijomeh.1896.00352
8. Surís, X., Larrosa, M., Pueyo, M.J., Auleda, J., Baranda, L., de la Puente, L.: Attention to musculoskeletal diseases: different visions of the same problem (in Spanish). Reumatol. Clínica **9**(1), 31–37 (2013). https://doi.org/10.1016/j.reuma.2012.05.003
9. Santiago Bazán, C., Perez Domingue, K.J., Castro Reyes, N.L.: Lumbar pain and its relationship with the disability index in a rehabilitation hospital (in Spanish). Rev. Científica Ciencia Méd. **21**(2), 13–20 (2018)
10. Tlili, F., Haddad, R., Ouakrim, Y., Bouallegue, R., Mezghani, N.: A survey on sitting posture monitoring systems. In: 9th International Symposium on Signal, Image, Video and Communications, Rabat, Morocco, pp. 185–190 (2018). https://doi.org/10.1109/ISIVC.2018.8709239
11. Taieb-Maimon, M., Cwikel, J., Shapira, B., Orenstein, I.: The effectiveness of a training method using self-modeling webcam photos for reducing musculoskeletal risk among office workers using computers. Appl. Ergon. **43**(2), 376–385 (2012). https://doi.org/10.1016/j.apergo.2011.05.015

12. Shin, D.J., Kim, M.S., Song, W., Min, S.D., Hong, M.: Implementation of sitting posture monitoring system with kinect. In: Park, J., Chen, S.C., Raymond Choo, K.K. (eds.) FutureTech MUE 2017. LNEE, vol. 448, pp. 144–150. Springer, Singapore (2017). https://doi.org/10.1007/978-981-10-5041-1_26
13. Cubas Rodríguez, J.C., Armas Marti, M.R., Olivares Briones, C.M., Paredes Paredo, M.A., Pretell Liendo, C.F., Valverde Vasquez, J.J.: Software design for monitoring body posture in office workers (in Spanish). INGnosis **7**(2), 26–36 (2021). https://doi.org/10.18050/ingnosis.v7i2.2411
14. Tlili, F., Haddad, R., Bouallegue, R., Mezghani, N.: A real-time posture monitoring system towards bad posture detection. Wireless Pers. Commun. **120**(2), 1207–1227 (2021). https://doi.org/10.1007/s11277-021-08511-2
15. Cerqueira, S.M., Silva, A.F.D., Santos, C.P.: Smart vest for real-time postural biofeedback and ergonomic risk assessment. IEEE Access **8**, 107583–107592 (2020). https://doi.org/10.1109/ACCESS.2020.3000673
16. Nizam, N.B., Jinan, T., Aurthy, W.B.N., Hossen, M.R., Ferdous, J.: Android based low cost sitting posture monitoring system. In: 11th International Conference on Electrical and Computer Engineering (ICECE), Dhaka, Bangladesh, pp. 161–164 (2020). https://doi.org/10.1109/ICECE51571.2020.9393150
17. Matuska, S., Paralic, M., Hudec, R.: A smart system for sitting posture detection based on force sensors and mobile application. Mob. Inf. Syst. **2020**, 1–13 (2020). https://doi.org/10.1155/2020/6625797
18. Sumanas, M., Treciokaite, V., Čerškus, A., Dzedzickis, A., Bučinskas, V., Morkvenaite-Vilkonciene, I.: Sitting posture monitoring using velostat based pressure sensors matrix. In: Szewczyk, R., Zieliński, C., Kaliczyńska, M. (eds.) AUTOMATION 2022. AISC, vol. 1427, pp 192–201. Springer, Cham (2022). https://doi.org/10.1007/978-3-031-03502-9_20
19. Odesola, D.F., Kulon, J., Verghese, S., Partlow, A., Gibson, C.: Smart sensing chairs for sitting posture detection, classification, and monitoring: a comprehensive review. Sensors **24**(9), 2940 (2024). https://doi.org/10.3390/s24092940
20. Zheng, Y., Morrell, J.B.: A vibrotactile feedback approach to posture guidance. In: 2010 IEEE Haptics Symposium, Waltham, MA, USA, pp. 351–358 (2010). https://doi.org/10.1109/HAPTIC.2010.5444633
21. Ishac, K., Suzuki, K.: LifeChair: a conductive fabric sensor-based smart cushion for actively shaping sitting posture. Sensors **18**(7), 2261 (2018). https://doi.org/10.3390/s18072261
22. De Lima E Sá Resende, F., et al.: The effect of global postural reeducation on body weight distribution in sitting posture and on musculoskeletal pain. A pilot study. Med. Lav. **108**(3), 187–196 (2017). https://doi.org/10.23749/mdl.v108i3.5458
23. Riverbank Computing Limited: PyQt6 Documentation. https://pypi.org/project/PyQt6/. Accessed 15 June 2024
24. Python Software Foundation: Multiprocessing. https://pypi.org/project/multiprocessing/. Accessed 15 June 2024
25. Servicio Ecuatoriano de Normalización: NTE INEN-ISO 11226: Ergonomics - Evaluation of static work postures (in Spanish). INEN (2014)
26. Bogdan, N.: HX711 Library. https://github.com/bogde/HX711. Accessed 15 June 2024
27. Ibarra, L., Igua, M., Ortiz, A., Tumal, A.: Postural hygiene in the workplace (in Spanish). CEI **9**(3), 86–88 (2022)

28. Xu, R., Wang, C., Xiao, Y., Gao, X., Zhu, Z., Chen, B.: A portable sitting posture monitoring system based on a pressure sensor array and machine learning. Sens. Actuat. A **331**, 112900 (2021). https://doi.org/10.1016/j.sna.2021.112900
29. Lee, C.C., et al.: Enhancement of spinal health by developing a low cost IoT-based smart chair system. In: IECON 2022 – 48th Annual Conference of the IEEE Industrial Electronics Society, Bruselas, Belgium, pp. 1–6 (2022). https://doi.org/10.1109/IECON49645.2022.9969004

Diagnosis of Heart Failure: Integrating Echocardiographic and Clinical Data Through Neural Networks

Victor Arrobo-Sarango[1], Jeremy Carlosama[1], Diego Almeida-Galárraga[1], Andrés Tirado-Espín[2], Carolina Cadena-Morejón[2], Kevin R. Landázuri[1], Lenin Ramírez-Cando[1], and Fernando Villalba-Meneses[1](✉)

[1] School of Biological Sciences and Engineering, Yachay University for Experimental Technology and Research (Yachay Tech), Urcuquí 100115, Ecuador
gvillalba@yachaytech.edu.ec

[2] School of Mathematical and Computational Sciences, Yachay University for Experimental Technology and Research (Yachay Tech), Urcuquí 100115, Ecuador

Abstract. Heart failure is a problem that affects the patient's normal oxygen supply. Many people around the world suffer from this disease and the number is increasing due to factors of modern life. The aim of the project is to use neural networks to integrate clinical data and echocardiographic structures to develop an accurate heart failure detection system. Long-term memory modeling (LSTM) was used to process clinical data from the heart failure prediction dataset and MobileNet architecture was used to analyze echocardiogram frames from the EchoNet-Dynamic dataset developed at Stanford University. The results of these models are then combined using model averaging to improve overall performance. The LSTM model achieved 91% accuracy, 94% recall and 93% F1-score based on clinical data. On the other hand, the MobileNet architecture achieved 84% accuracy, 66.15% recall and 65.47% F1-score on echocardiogram frames. The combined model achieved an average of 88% accuracy, 80% recovery and 79% F1-score, highlighting the benefits of integrating multiple sources. This method not only improves diagnostic accuracy, but also provides an efficient solution for heart failure detection, providing valuable clinical decision support in cardiology.

Keywords: Machine Learning · Heart Failure · Detection · Clinical Data · Echocardiograms · metrics · confusion matrix

1 Introduction

Heart failure (HF) is a disease that severely affects the oxygen supply in the person, since the heart does not work properly, making the blood pumping ineffective, and affecting the whole organism of the person [6]. It is a dangerous condition that has a high impact on mortality and critical condition of the world population [2,9]. According to [22] In 2019, 56.2 million people suffer heart failure in the world, and this number is increasing quickly. In the United States, it

F. R. Narváez et al. (Eds.): SmartTech-IC 2024, CCIS 2392, pp. 121–136, 2026.
https://doi.org/10.1007/978-3-031-98287-3_9

is the main cause of hospitalization in elderly people, approximately one million people go to the hospital because of it [33]. According to Ecuadorian Society of Cardiology and Data of National Institute of Statistics and Census (INEC), the frequency of people with HF in Ecuador has been increasing over the years due to the increase of people with hypertension, and obesity, diabetes mellitus, hypercholesterolemia, renal disease and coronary artery diseases. It is being one of the main reasons for hospitalizations in patients over 65 years [26,29].

Heart failure diagnosis is complicated by a number of factors, such as the low heterogeneity of the ailment, the various forms, such as HFrEF and HFpEF, the unpredictability of diagnostic criteria, and the complex symptomatology [13]. In other hand, the treatment obstacles there are variety of comorbidities into patients, the absence of effective treatments and substantial financial load. [31]. Several studies mentioned that socioeconomic factor is directly involve with heart diseases. [16]. The early identification and subsequent correct diagnosis of HF are important so that the patient can receive the necessary care and effective treatment [39]. It is crucial to diagnose a patient's pathology as soon as possible since this allows for more efficient therapy, better symptom control, cost savings, enhanced quality of life, avoidance of further issues and take appropriate decisions [11,39].

Clinical data such as: dyspnea, fatigue, fluid retention, labored breathing, irregular heart rhythm, patient history, vital signs, and other laboratory results provide valuable information to help determine the underlying conditions of heart failure, despite the high variability of these data between patients [19]. On the other hand, the first medical imaging techniques generally used are echocardiogram. Echocardiography is a noninvasive imaging method that is widely used because it shows detailed information about the structure and function of the heart, such as cardiac chamber size, wall motion, and ejection fraction [37]. The ejection fraction refers to the amount of blood expelled by the left ventricle of the heart in each contraction, which shows the correct pumping of blood to the body, being reduced indicates abnormal pumping, and this is one of principal signs of heart failure [30]. Combining these diverse data sources presents an opportunity to improve diagnostic accuracy and efficiency.

Currently, the innovation of artificial intelligence systems has been proposed to help in various tasks in different areas of work, one of the most prominent is in the medical area [15,25]. Machine learning and neural networks make it possible to analyze important characteristics of a large number of data, identify complex patterns in them, and thus make predictions about what you want to do with great accuracy [5,38]. Specifically, this article proposes the detection of HF integrating the both clinical data and video fragments. The integration of both models to detect HF would leverage the strengths of both databases with their respective results, providing a deeper analysis that would surpass traditional methods, improving the accurate diagnosis of this disease.

2 Literature Review

The diagnosis of heart failure would show significant progress by integrating different types of data. Previous studies have been carried out with individual types of data such as echocardiograms, electrocardiograms or clinical data as we can see in Table 1, which have achieved favorable results, but with small databases or high homogeneity between them; which allows overfitting of the data, thus restricting the generalization of the results. That is why this research is proposed with a strong amount of data that integrates echocardiogram images and clinical data to improve the accuracy and robustness of heart failure detection, addressing existing limitations and repeatability of results [18] .

Table 1. Summary of different studies on heart failure prediction.

Author	Objective	Data	Architecture	Results
[23]	Early detection of heart failure	data not mentioned	Random Forest	accuracy, precision, recall, F1 -score of 86.23%, 86.19%, 86.23%, 86.19% respectively.
[36]	Identify crucial features that enhance the accuracy of heart disease prediction	503 cases of UCI database	Learning Vector Quantization method	Accuracy of 98.78%, specificity of 97.1%, sensitivity of 97.91%, precision of 98.07% and F1-score of 95.31%
[24]	Do a predictor system of cardiovascular diseases	598 instances of Hungarian and Statlog (heart) dataset	Reduced Error Pruning Tree(REP Tree), Random Tree, Linear Regression, Naive Bayes	Random Tree: Accuracy of 99.81%, MAE of 0.2838, RMSE of 0.5328
[14]	Algorithm to predict cardiac disease	303 occurrences with 14 characteristics	Random Forest (RF), Decision Tree (DT), and Logistic Regression (LR)	Logistic regression: Accuracy, Precision, F1-score and Recall of 92%
[21]	machine learning metamodel for predicting a patient's heart failure based on clinical test data	920 patient records	Random Forest Classifier, Gaussian Naive Bayes, Decision Tree models, and k-Nearest Neighbor	Metamodel accuracy of 87%
[34]	Automated EF classification	5600 cases divided into training and testing data, 2D image (A4C)	3D-CNN	Accuracy and F1-score of 78% and 71.3% respectively EF (below 45%)
[27]	Cardiac segmentation & LVEF accuracy	10,030 echo-indicated case to training and testing data, 2D image (A4C)	EchoNet (CNN)	Diagnostic value (AUC 0.97) to predict LVEF <50% (cardiomyopathy)
[10]	Visualization of anatomical structures that has relationship with the cardiac function	3312 cases of cardiopathy, 2D image (A4C)	EchoNet (CNN)	severely dilated left atrium (AUC of 0.85, F1-score of 0.68), and left ventricular hypertrophy (AUC of 0.75, F1 score of 0.57)
[4]	Automated EF classification	1106 cases with moderate and reduced EF, 2D image A2C & A4C	DenseNet (CNN), Bidirectional Gated Recurrent Unit(bi-GRU (RNN))	accuracy of 83.15%, precision of 82.6% and recall of 81.1%
[20]	Echo-view classification, accuracy	10,530 echo-indicated cases, (A2C, A4C)	Modified U-net	echo-view classification (Dice coefficient = 0.935)

3 Materials and Methods

The present research work requires specific tools and materials to develop a system for detecting heart failure using neural networks (NN) with clinical and echocardiogram video databases. The following resources are necessary to perform efficient data analysis and processing: Visual Studio Code version 1.90.1 a free and source code-editor development by Microsoft, Google Collaboratory (Python 3.11), a platform that facilitates collaborative work and code execution in Jupyter Notebook. Several software libraries excel in neural network development, including TensorFlow 2.16.0 for implementing deep learning models, Numpy 2.0.0 for handling numerical arrays, Scikit-learn 1.4.2 for work involving autonomous learning, Pandas 2.2.2 essential for manipulating numerical tables and time series, OpenCV(cv2) 4.9.0 for obtaining random frames from echocardiogram videos, Matplotlib 3.7.1 and Seaborn 0.12.2 for plotting training and evaluation results. In other hand to carry out the present study we use a HP laptop with a processor Intel®Core™i7-1355U of 13th generation, 64GB of RAM and 2TB of memory.

Structured data manipulation is crucial for proper training and subsequent detection of pathology. Figure 1 shows an appropriate methodology for this process.

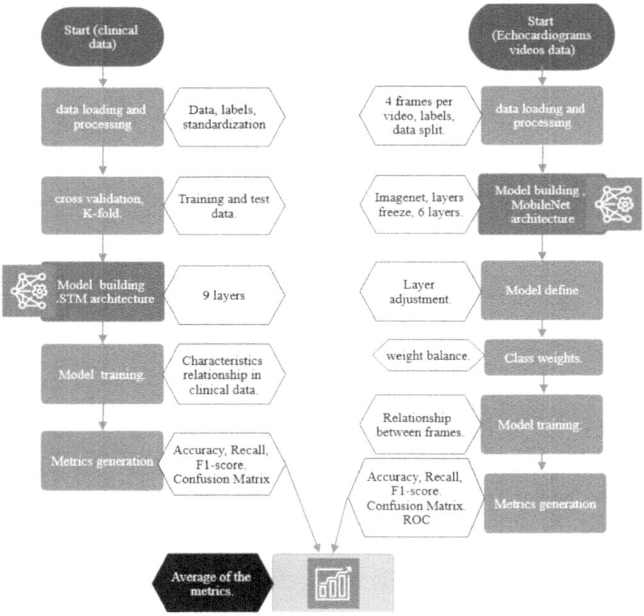

Fig. 1. Methodology to models training with two datasets.

3.1 Databases

Clinical Data. This dataset involves the combination of five heart datasets around the world which before have not combined. At moment this dataset is the largest public clinical dataset of heart diseases research purposes; It contain 918 unique observations of different database: Cleveland, Hungarian, Switzerland, Long Beach VA, and Stalog Dataset with 303, 294, 123, 200, 270 observations respectively. It is available in Kaggle platform under the name "Heart Failure Prediction Dataset" [35]. The data include 725 males and 195 females of different ages. Where 265 males are normal, and 458 males have heart disease, 145 females are normal, and 50 females have heart disease; in total 508 positive and 410 negative heart failure cases. Data contain 11 features.

Echocardiogram Video Data. This database was created by a group of researchers at Stanford University Hospital, which consists of 10030 apical-4-chamber echocardiography videos of 112 × 112 pixels recording on resting heart from different angles, positions and image acquisition techniques. This database taken during the years 2016–2018, where the patients have a median age of 68 years old, 4885 females and 5145 males [27]. This database consists of videos and labels each one, where labels are: file name, ejection fraction (EF), end systolic volume (ESV), end diastolic volume (EDV), height and width, frames per second (FPS) and total number of frames.

3.2 Data Preprocessing

The organization of the data is a transcendental step for the implementation of recurrent neural networks (RNN) and convolutional neural networks (CNN) to Clinical data and Echocardiogram video frames respectively. Different preprocessing techniques were carried out that helped us to generalize and improve the data to obtain specific patterns related to and without heart failure. Taking into account that we have two databases which differ; in clinical data we use the normalization and k-fold cross validation and for echocardiogram frame data: obtain frames, label identification, division of the data and the use of pretrained models.

Normalization and K-Fold Cross-Validation. Normalization and pixel value scaling in the range [0, 1] improve training stability and model convergence to ensure consistent data types. K-fold cross-validation is used to divide the database into a specific number of folds in this case 5 and the better classification set was fold 2. It permits to found an equilibrium in data to divide equally and improve the prediction. The Echocardiogram videos was reviewed thoroughly one per one manually with the objective to delete data defects as: damage videos, video playback time greater than or equal to 1 s and too opaque videos; where we found that three videos have difficulties. Take in account it, we work with 10027 videos and carry out the following prepossessed steps.

Random Frame Extraction, Label Identification and Data Spliting: Four random frames were extracted from the Echocardiogram films using the OpenCV (cv2) library, yielding a total of 40112 frames with a range of patterns and features for model training. Label identification from the echocardiogram video database: Since the data does not show labels explicitly, but it contains ejection factor. Take in account the Authors criteria [27,32] The patients with heart failure have an ejection factor of less than 50%, and patients without heart failure has an ejection factor of greater than or equal to 50%. To encourage a better results, we divide the dataset in three parts: training and validation (90%) and 10% for test data.

3.3 Transfer Learning with Pretrained Models

Transfer Learning and Class Weight Balancing. Transfer learning is a machine-learning technique that allows reusing a previously trained MovileNet model with large amounts of data of Imagenet to solve a new task [1,28]. Certain layers can be frozen depending on the similarity between the old and new tasks. In our specific case, the first 100 layers were frozen, the following layers were modified and then the last layer was removed in order to incorporate a binary recognition layer between the presence or not of the disease. The presence of class imbalance in a dataset is a typical problem in machine learning. To address this problem, the weight balancing technique was implemented in the dataset, since we have a high difference between the two classes with a ratio of 4 to 1. This technique uses the compute class weight library in order to give greater importance to minority classes during the training of the model.

3.4 Model Training

In this apart, we take in account two neural network models, a recurrent neural network model with the Short- and Long-Term Memory (LSTM) architecture to work the clinical data, while a convolutional neural network model with the MobileNet architecture was used to train the echocardiogram frames.

LSTM Architecture. Long short-term memory (LSTM), a recurrent neural network used to predict sequences and patterns of data [8,12]. LSTM architecture was fundamental to process the data sequences, since this technique has the ability to capture patterns and relationships in the sequences, thus improving performance, accuracy and generalization. This architecture includes 8 layers among which: Dropout layers to prevent overfitting, BatchNormalization layers to stabilize and accelerate training and a dense layer for binary classification. The model was compiled with the binary cross-entropy loss function and the Adam optimizer with a learning rate of 0.001. Training was also performed with twenty-five epochs with a batch size of 16.

MobileNet Architecture. MobileNet, a 53-layer deep convolutional neural network that gives optimal results in image diagnosis, making it useful for analyzing video frames from echocardiograms [17]. MovileNet architecture was used due to its resource efficiency, accuracy and speed and ability to improve pattern detection in different scenarios. This architecture includes a pre-trained model, which a adjusts in the last output layer to the following dimensions (224*224*3). In addition to increase the metrics of the model we increase 5 layers which are: GlobalAveragePooling2D which reduces the dimensional of the features, Dropout to prevent overfitting and a Dense layer for binary classification. The model was trained with the binary cross-entropy loss function and the Adam optimizer with a learning rate of 0.0001. Together, the data preprocessing and transfer learning technique with pretrained models provide an effective strategy to develop accurate and robust echocardiogram classification models. Training was also performed with twenty-five epochs with a batch size of 64.

4 Results

The results obtained from the architectures used for the two databases in this study are divided into three segments for better understanding and to describe specific and important details of each part: First, we analyze the accuracy and loss graphs of training and validation obtained during the training of each model. Second, we have the analysis of the confusion matrix and metrics obtained in each of the architectures. Finally, we show the ROC curve and the metrics of the AUC for two models. In other hand, the training time to train 25 epochs for each model was 15 min 32 s for the LSTM model and 10 h 11 min 5 s to train the MovileNet model with its respective databases.

4.1 Accuracy and Loss

The accuracy shows the proportion of positive predictions between the total predictions made by the model, which can be irreal if there are unbalancing data. In other hand, the loss measures the number of errors that the model has in each prediction and gives a percentage.

Clinical Data: As a result of the execution of the LSTM architecture, an accuracy of 92% and a loss of 24% were achieved. This high performance and low loss demonstrate its effectiveness in properly classifying clinical data involving heart failure or not, as observed in the Fig. 2. The analysis of the training and validation accuracy shows a clear growth over time. On the other hand, the loss curve for both training and validation follows a normal pattern of decrease over time. Generally, the model behaves appropriately for the classification of the pathology.

Echocardiogram Video Frames MobileNet: The neural network model achieved an accuracy of 84% and a loss of 38%, reflecting an adequate classification capability for the echocardiogram video database as we can see in Fig. 3. The analysis of the curves for this model reveals that the training and validation accuracy curves exhibit a growing progression over time, which is of primary interest as it demonstrates the model's efficiency. The training and validation loss curves also follow a normal pattern of decrease over time, which is crucial for this study. However, certain peaks can be observed in both the training and validation loss, due by high variability of data caused by the random frame extraction during preprocessing.

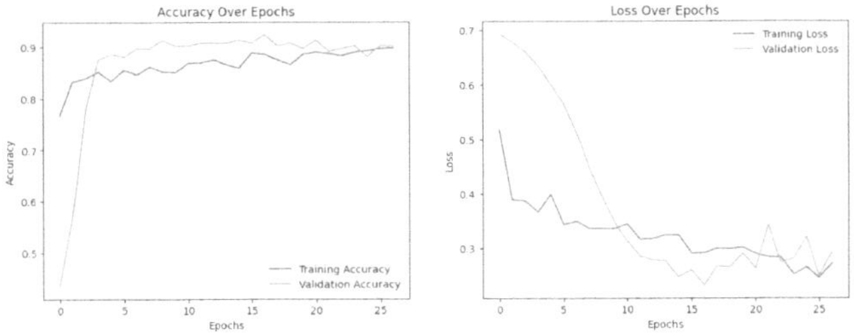

Fig. 2. Accuracy and loss curves for the LSTM model with clinical data.

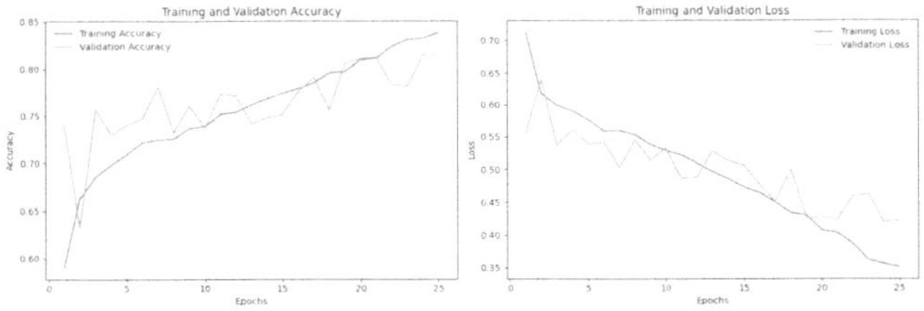

Fig. 3. Accuracy and loss curves for the MobileNet model with echocardiogram video frames.

4.2 Confusion Matrix

A confusion matrix is an essential tool on Artificial intelligence that allows researchers to visualize and analyze how a given neural network model classifies input data. This technique is crucial as it shows the number of times the model correctly or incorrectly classifies data within predefined classes. Being a visual technique, it allows researchers to adjust the model to increase accuracy in assigning images to their respective classes. A confusion matrix has the same number of rows and columns, where rows represent real classes and columns represent predicted classes by the model. In the case of the binary models proposed in this research, there are four quadrants as we can see in Fig. 4 named as follows:

- **True Positives (TP):** Positive cases correctly diagnosed as positive.
- **True Negatives (TN):** Negative cases correctly diagnosed as negative.
- **False Positives (FP):** Negative cases incorrectly diagnosed as positive.
- **False Negatives (FN):** Positive cases incorrectly diagnosed as negative.

The aforementioned parameters are crucial to determine variables such as precision, recall, and F1-score which are calculated in this research work to obtain the metrics evaluated in following steps. Confusion matrices are essential in providing a quantitative and detailed perspective. While all quadrants of the confusion matrix are important, it is crucial to emphasize the importance of False Positives (FP) and False Negatives (FN) in the detection of a deadly and rapidly growing disease in today's society:

- **False Positives (FP):** These occurrences can lead to unnecessary tests and procedures, potentially causing anxiety in patients and additional costs to the healthcare system. Moreover, an increase in the demand for additional tests can overwhelm healthcare systems.
- **False Negatives (FN):** FN results are even more important as they can result in delayed treatment of the disease, compromising the patient's overall health and, in more severe cases, causing death. Timely detection of heart failure is essential which allows to control of the disease in its early stages.

LSTM Confusion Matrix (Fig. 5): TP: 99, TN: 71, FP: 9, FN: 5. The sum of FP + FN is 14, which showing a very low error rate. This model provides a high capacity to detect the disease accurately. However, it is essential that before the patient is diagnosed, the results are thoroughly reviewed by a health professional.

MobileNet Confusion Matrix (Fig. 6): TP: 602, TN: 2775, FP: 327, FN: 308. The sum of FP + FN is 635, which is relatively high. This indicates that the results obtained should be reviewed by a healthcare professional before making a diagnosis. A more thorough review of the model is also necessary to reduce erroneous cases.

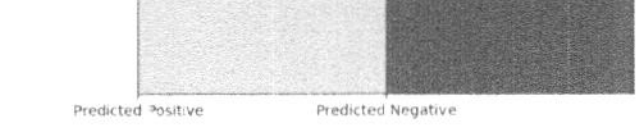

Fig. 4. Quality CM.

Fig. 5. LSTM.

Fig. 6. MobileNet.

In each model was evaluated the following metrics: accuracy, recall and F1-score which give an effective guideline for pathology detection. Table 2 show the metrics generated by both models: The LSTM architecture training with clinical data which obtain the accuracy, recall and F1-score of 94%, 92%, 93% respectively; based on this information, the model provides accurate and useful guidance even with a small database of 918 unique data. Meanwhile, the metrics generated from the MobileNet architecture training show an accuracy, recall and F1-score of 84%, 66%, 65%; which are relatively high taking into account that we trained this model in 40,112 frames. Overall, the metrics produced by the two neural network models using two different disease databases provide a solid basis for comprehensive heart failure identification.

Table 2. Performance metrics for LSTM and MobileNet models

	Accuracy	Recall	F1-Score
LSTM model	92%	94%	93%
MobileNet model	84%	66%	65%

4.3 ROC Curve and Metrics of AUC

In the next section, we show the ROC (Receiver Operating Characteristic) curve which is a very important graphical tool for analyzing the performance of a neural network model, which allows us to quantify how well the model discriminates between the two given classes, the graph of the model that is closer to the upper left corner is the one that has a better performance and therefore a better prediction; We also have the AUC (Area Under the Curve) metric, which is a value that shows us the probability that a model properly classifies an iteration between two classes. In this case in Fig. 7 we can observe that the model that has a better prediction is the LSTM model since it reaches the upper left corner of the graph faster and has an AUC = 0.94. Although the graph of the MovileNet model is partially close to the upper left corner and has an AUC = 0.78, it has a high ability to predict between the given classes, as we can see in the subsection before showed.

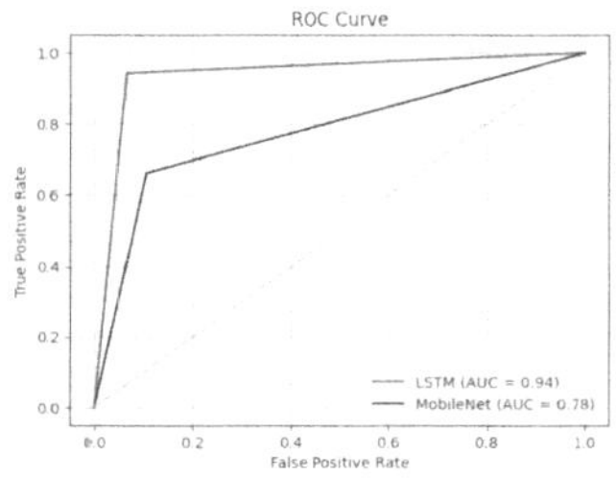

Fig. 7. ROC graph and AUC metrics.

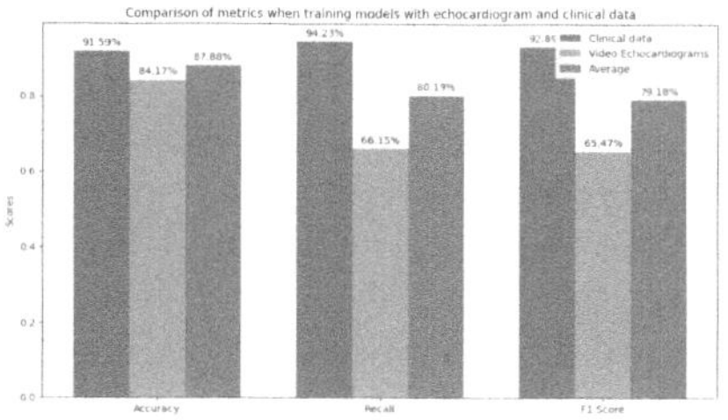

Fig. 8. Metrics of two models and average.

5 Discussion

In this discussion, actual performance analysis of a neural network using MobilNet for analyzing echocardiogram images and LSTM for analyzing clinical data are presented. Based on the clinical data used in the LSTM model, the model returned a accuracy of 94%, recall of 92 % and F1-Score of 93%. This means that the model maintains a high level of precision coupled with high recall, hence resulting in a better performance of reducing both false negatives and false positives. This performance is particularly of value when compared with low quantity of other similar works that can include, in average, small data or low metrics. For instance, [36] get an accuracy of 98.78% with their Learning Vector Quantization method, these results are the best but, it can be possible with a small data of 503 cases of UCI dataset that has an equality data between normal and heart failure cases. Likewise, [14] notched an accuracy of 92% with a dataset of 303 occurrences with 14 characteristics, despite that these results are relevant the data is too small to conclude a high incidence inside cardiovascular diseases; The bias and low variability are difficult factors in small data. Also, in [21] has the same data, with a metamodel that include, Random Forest Classifier, Gaussian Naive Bayes, Decision Tree models, and k-Nearest Neighbor. It has 920 patient's records, two dates more that our data, which are repeated; a principal disadvantage in this study is that only is showed the accuracy of 87% which is good but there are not Recall nor F1-Score fundamentals to evaluate the repeatability of a model. Our work shows better results because it improves the metrics taken in account a relativity high dataset that is balanced and has a high repeatability. Otherwise, in total 40112 frames obtain aleatory of 1,030 echocardiograms videos were included on the MobileNet model analysis, where the accuracy reached 84%, recall 66% and F1-score 65%. Although the first results of the evaluation for the individual accuracy might seem similar or lower compared with some other models, it is crucial to take into account the multi-faceted nature of the current approach, the amount and the variability of data, which was taken randomly to encourage it. Other researches show a better combined metrics where [34] show an Accuracy and F1-score of 78% and

71.3% respectively and [4] with a accuracy of 83.15%, precision of 82.6% and recall of 81.1%; but both with a small datasets that reduce the variability of data and repeatability of the same study. In other hand, there are research [27] that use the dataset that our work but it is based in the classification of the disease the dice Factor and the area under the curse which is of 0.97, a relevant result to take in account. It is noteworthy to say that this research is original in the use of clinical data and the echocardiogram frames to detect the pathology. This combined model was reached an accuracy of 87.84% recall of 80.19% and F1-score of 76.19% as we can see in Fig. 8. It shows importance for pathology detection as they allow for the articulation of combined characteristics of the two databases, improving the model's ability to detect truly positive or negative cases and reducing existing errors. This technique offers a promising future for the precise and genuine detection of a disease like heart failure because it provides a multifaceted view of patient health, minimizing the weaknesses associated with studies conducted with only one type of data where certain factors may be overlooked. In addition, the complete set of validation metrics such as the F1-score gives a clear and a more expansive view of the predictive capabilities of a model. This establishes a new standard for future research since there are a high amount of research does not incorporate these essential measures. For instance, [7] and [3] cited accuracies of 91% and 99.5% respectively but did not include an F1-score that is important for depicting the precision and recall quality. The current model is able to alleviate this problem by providing more specific measures of performance which give a better idea as to the efficiency of the system.

Lastly, we analyze in this section the Precision- recall curve of two model used, show in the Fig. 9, it plots a graph where precision is on the y-axis and recall is on the x-axis, ranging from 0 to 1. In the case of ideal curve, the graph would have a precision and recall of 1, and its point would be located in the upper right corner of the graph. In this graph, we can observe that the plot representing the LSTM model is close to the mentioned point, indicating that it is an effective model for classifying this type of data and subsequently detecting the pathology. On the other hand, we have the final point of the MobileMet model, which is quite far from the ideal point, indicating that there is a relatively low recall, as previously shown. Despite our efforts in applying weight balancing and transfer learning, our model is misclassifying some relevant instances, caused by the large amount of data and the imbalance within it, as images without heart failure are predominant at a ratio of 4:1.

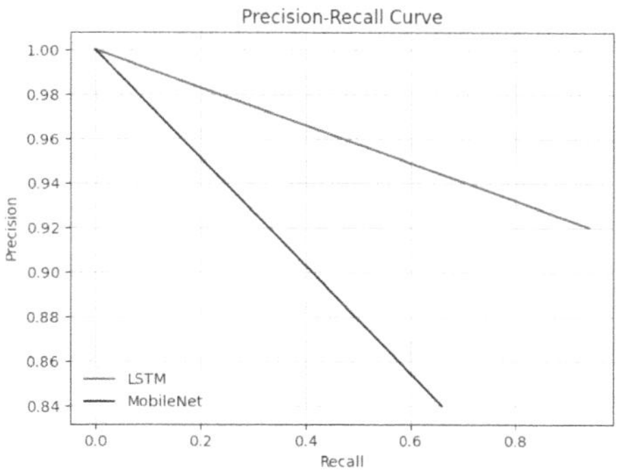

Fig. 9. Models precision-recall curve.

Thus, the proposed approach of using MobileNet in echocardiograms and LSTM in clinical data, and the integration of the obtained results, offers a thorough and reliable way to prognosticate heart failure. It established a benchmark in validation metrics and data coverage for improving heart failure prediction, thus extending previous research.

6 Conclusion

In summary, the detection of this pathology by using neural networks to combine clinical data with echocardiography video frames to detect heart failure showed promising results. The LSTM model obtained the best overall metrics as demonstrated by the efficiency of the accuracy and loss plots of the validation data, as well as the few false positives and false negatives shown by the confusion matrix generated with a relatively high balanced database. On the other hand, the MobileNet model effectively analyzed the echocardiogram video frames, despite the high variability of the frames; this model was characterized mainly by the high capacity of its architecture for disease detection despite an imbalance between classes, where there was a 4 to 1 dominance of normal data and other diseases associated with heart failure. Subsequently, combining an averaging model with the results of these two models achieved significantly better results, highlighting the advantages of the multimodal approach. This integrated framework provides an impressive balance of performance metrics that outperform models based on individual data types. The final model improved the diagnostic accuracy of the disease, as well as providing an effective tool for detecting HF, supporting cardiology decision-making, improving early patient management and reducing clinical costs. The information obtained in this project is a further step towards new innovations in medical diagnostic systems thanks to artificial intelligence.

7 Future Works

Cardiovascular diseases lead the cause of death globally, which is why it is necessary to strengthen this line of research. In the work described above, only the metrics generated by the models were averaged, since the databases did not share the same patients. So, one of the most promising future works would be to have databases that include some diagnostic techniques for the same patient in order to find unknown patterns and thus increase the precision in the detection of cardiovascular diseases. In other hand, work with Ecuadorian data will be a hit for.

References

1. Aboulola, O.I.: Improving traffic accident severity prediction using MobileNet transfer learning model and SHAP XAI technique. PLoS ONE **19**(4), e0300640 (2024)
2. Aguiar-Salazar, E., Villalba-Meneses, F., Tirado-Espín, A., Amaguaña-Marmol, D., Almeida-Galárraga, D.: Rapid detection of cardiac pathologies by neural networks using ECG signals (1D) and SECG images (3d). Computation **10**(7), 112 (2022)
3. Balakrishnan, C., Kumar, V.D.A.: IoT-enabled classification of echocardiogram images for cardiovascular disease risk prediction with pre-trained recurrent convolutional neural networks. Multidisc. Digit. Publ. Inst. **13**(4), 775 (2023). https://doi.org/10.3390/diagnostics13040775
4. Behnami, D., et al.: Automatic cine-based detection of patients at high risk of heart failure with reduced ejection fraction in echocardiograms. Comput. Methods Biomech. Biomed. Eng.: Imaging Vis. **8**(5), 502–508 (2020)
5. Botros, J., Mourad-Chehade, F., Laplanche, D.: CNN and SVM-based models for the detection of heart failure using electrocardiogram signals. Sensors **22**(23), 9190 (2022). https://doi.org/10.3390/s22239190
6. Broberg, A.M., et al.: Prevention, detection, and management of heart failure in patients treated for breast cancer. Curr. Heart Failure Rep. **17**(6), 397–408 (2020). https://doi.org/10.1007/s11897-020-00486-8, https://pubmed.ncbi.nlm.nih.gov/32979150/
7. Budholiya, K., Shrivastava, S.K., Sharma, V.: An optimized XGBoost based diagnostic system for effective prediction of heart disease. Elsevier BV **34**(7), 4514–4523 (2022). https://doi.org/10.1016/j.jksuci.2020.10.013
8. Caicho, J., et al.: Diabetic retinopathy: detection and classification using AlexNet, GoogleNet and resnet50 convolutional neural networks. In: International Conference on Smart Technologies, Systems and Applications, pp. 259–271. Springer (2021)
9. Cauwenberghs, N., Sabovčik, F., Magnus, A., Haddad, F., Kuznetsova, T.: Proteomic profiling for detection of early-stage heart failure in the community. ESC Heart Failure **8**(4), 2928–2939 (2021). https://doi.org/10.1002/ehf2.13375
10. Ghorbani, A., et al.: Deep learning interpretation of echocardiograms. NPJ Digit. Med. **3**(1), 10 (2020)
11. Gualsaquí, M.G., et al.: Convolutional neural network for imagine movement classification for neurorehabilitation of upper extremities using low-frequency EEG signals for spinal cord injury. In: International Conference on Smart Technologies, Systems and Applications, pp. 272–287. Springer (2021)

12. Hatabu, H., Barile, M.: Detection of pulmonary congestion in heart failure with preserved ejection fraction using quantitative chest CT. JACC. Cardiovas. Imaging **15**(4), 638–640 (2022). https://doi.org/10.1016/j.jcmg.2022.01.017, https://pubmed.ncbi.nlm.nih.gov/35393066/
13. Hossain, M.Z., et al.: Challenges in the management of people with heart failure with preserved ejection fraction (HFpEF) in primary care: a qualitative study of general practitioner perspectives. Chronic Illn. **18**(2), 410–425 (2022)
14. Hossen, M.A., et al.: Supervised machine learning-based cardiovascular disease analysis and prediction. Math. Probl. Eng. **2021**(1), 1792201 (2021)
15. Hussain, L., Aziz, W., Khan, I.R., Alkinani, M.H., Alowibdi, J.S.: Machine learning based congestive heart failure detection using feature importance ranking of multimodal features. Math. Biosci. Eng. **18**(1), 69–91 (2021). https://doi.org/10.3934/mbe.2021004
16. Jain, V., et al.: Association between social vulnerability index and cardiovascular disease: a behavioral risk factor surveillance system study. J. Am. Heart Assoc. **11**(15), e024414 (2022)
17. Kondo, T., et al.: Predicting stroke in heart failure and preserved ejection fraction without atrial fibrillation. Circul. Heart failure **16**(7) (2023). https://doi.org/10.1161/circheartfailure.122.010377
18. König, S., et al.: From population- to patient-based prediction of in-hospital mortality in heart failure using machine learning (2022). https://doi.org/10.1093/ehjdh/ztac012
19. Liu, T., et al.: Inter-patient congestive heart failure detection using ECG-convolution-vision transformer network. Sensors **22**(9), 3283 (2022). https://doi.org/10.3390/s22093283
20. Liu, X., et al.: Deep learning-based automated left ventricular ejection fraction assessment using 2-D echocardiography. Am. J. Physiol.-Heart Circul. Physiol. **321**(2), H390–H399 (2021)
21. Mahmud, I., Kabir, M.M., Mridha, M., Alfarhood, S., Safran, M., Che, D.: Cardiac failure forecasting based on clinical data using a lightweight machine learning metamodel. Diagnostics **13**(15), 2540 (2023)
22. Martin, S.S., et al.: 2024 heart disease and stroke statistics: a report of us and global data from the American heart association. Circulation **149**(8), e347–e913 (2024)
23. Mohan, K., AL-Mamari, Y.F.S., AL-Najadi, M.A.M.: Techniques of machine learning for detecting heart failure. Int. J. Data Inform. Intell. Comput. **2**(2), 47–54 (2023)
24. Nadakinamani, R.G., et al.: [Retracted] clinical data analysis for prediction of cardiovascular disease using machine learning techniques. Comput. Intell. Neurosci. **2022**(1), 2973324 (2022)
25. Niles, D.N., et al.: COVID-19 pulmonary lesion classification using CNN software in chest X-ray with quadrant scoring severity parameters. In: International Conference on Smart Technologies, Systems and Applications, pp. 370–382. Springer (2021)
26. Ortiz-Prado, E., et al.: Epidemiological characterization of ischemic heart disease at different altitudes: a nationwide population-based analysis from 2011 to 2021 in Ecuador. PloS One **18**(12), e0295586 (2023). https://doi.org/10.1371/journal.pone.0295586
27. Ouyang, D., et al.: Video-based AI for beat-to-beat assessment of cardiac function. Nature **580**(7802), 252–256 (2020)

28. Puchaicela-Lozano, M.S., et al.: Deep learning for glaucoma detection: R-CNN ResNet-50 and image segmentation. J. Adv. Inf. Technol. **14**(6), 1186–1197 (2023)
29. Redfield, M.M., Borlaug, B.A.: Heart failure with preserved ejection fraction: a review. JAMA **329**(10), 827–838 (2023)
30. Rohrbaugh, M.N., Schober, K.E., Rhinehart, J.D., Bonagura, J.D., Habing, A., Yildiz, V.: Detection of congestive heart failure by Doppler echocardiography in cats with hypertrophic cardiomyopathy. J. Vet. Intern. Med. **34**(3), 1091–1101 (2020). https://doi.org/10.1111/jvim.15777
31. Sapna, F., et al.: Advancements in heart failure management: a comprehensive narrative review of emerging therapies. Cureus **15**(10) (2023)
32. Savarese, G., Stolfo, D., Sinagra, G., Lund, L.H.: Heart failure with mid-range or mildly reduced ejection fraction. Nat. Rev. Cardiol. **19**(2), 100–116 (2022)
33. Sepehrvand, N., Ezekowitz, J.A.: Setting the diagnosis of heart failure. JACC Heart Failure **11**(3), 359–361 (2023). https://doi.org/10.1016/j.jchf.2022.12.008
34. Silva, J.F., Silva, J.M., Guerra, A., Matos, S., Costa, C.: Ejection fraction classification in transthoracic echocardiography using a deep learning approach. In: 2018 IEEE 31st International Symposium on Computer-Based Medical Systems (CBMS), pp. 123–128. IEEE (2018)
35. Soriano, F.: Heart Failure Prediction Dataset (2021). https://www.kaggle.com/datasets/fedesoriano/heart-failure-prediction
36. Srinivasan, S., et al.: An active learning machine technique based prediction of cardiovascular heart disease from UCI-repository database. Sci. Rep. **13**(1), 13588 (2023)
37. Tsai, C.H., et al.: Usefulness of heart rhythm complexity in heart failure detection and diagnosis. Sci. Rep. **10**(1) (2020). https://doi.org/10.1038/s41598-020-71909-8
38. Villalba-Meneses, F., et al.: Classification of the pathological range of motion in low back pain using wearable sensors and machine learning. Sensors **24**(3), 831 (2024)
39. Wang, H., et al.: Importance of early diagnosis and treatment of heart failure across the spectrum of ejection fraction. Eur. Heart J. **44**(Supplement_2), ehad655–892 (2023)

A Low Power Non-invasive Wrist-Based Approach for Glucose Monitoring

Luz M. Tobar-Subia-Contento[1](✉), Raúl Vargas[2], Lenny Alexandra Romero[2], and Sonia H. Contreras-Ortiz[2]

[1] Universidad Técnica del Norte, Ibarra, Ecuador
lmtobarsubia@utn.edu.ec
[2] Universidad Tecnológica de Bolívar, Cartagena, Colombia
{ravargas,lromero,scontreras}@utb.edu.co

Abstract. This study presents the development and validation of a low-power, non-invasive wrist-based device for continuous glucose monitoring, offering a more convenient alternative to traditional fingertip-based methods. By employing photoplethysmography (PPG) and the Beer-Lambert law, the prototype measures the absorbance of infrared and red light through the wrist to estimate glucose levels. A comparative analysis was conducted against a commercial glucose meter (Accu-Chek) using data from a young population in Cartagena, Colombia. The results demonstrated a moderate correlation (Pearson correlation coefficient: 0.49) between the two devices, with most measurements falling within clinically acceptable zones (A and B) of the Parkes error grid. Signal processing techniques, such as noise reduction and sampling rate optimization, were implemented to enhance measurement reliability. The study highlights challenges related to sensor placement and skin tone variability, which can influence device accuracy. While the findings support the feasibility of this wrist-based device for continuous monitoring, further improvements, including miniaturization and evaluation across diverse populations, are essential for widespread adoption. This research underscores the potential of non-invasive technologies to address the discomfort and accessibility limitations of invasive glucose monitoring methods.

Keywords: Glucose monitoring · Photoplethysmography (PPG) · Non-invasive Wrist Device · signal processing · Wrist-based measurement · Parkes error grid

1 Introduction

In recent years, there has been growing concern in Latin America about the significant impact of chronic diseases such as heart disease, hypertension, respiratory problems, and type 2 diabetes mellitus (T2DM) on the morbidity and mortality of the population [15]. Monitoring these conditions provides crucial

F. R. Narváez et al. (Eds.): SmartTech-IC 2024, CCIS 2392, pp. 137–148, 2026.
https://doi.org/10.1007/978-3-031-98287-3_10

information about a person's physiological state, adding healthcare professionals in diagnosing and managing various medical conditions [5,10]. T2DM is the sixth leading cause of death in the region, with a prevalence of 30% to 45% among adults [1]. Constant monitoring of blood glucose levels is essential to prevent severe complications, but traditional invasive methods are costly and uncomfortable, particularly for older patients, children, and people with limited access to healthcare.

Recent technological advancements have led to the development of non-invasive methods for measuring vital signs, reducing the discomfort and risks associated with invasive procedures [9,10,13]. Among these, photoplethysmography (PPG) and infrared technology are commonly used for detecting elevated blood glucose levels non-invasively [3,11,12]. These approaches offer significant potential for improving disease management by enabling real-time, painless monitoring without the need for frequent blood samples. Our study advances previous research [3,6] by introducing a prototype designed to measure glucose levels at the wrist, offering a more convenient and user-friendly alternative to traditional fingertip-based methods. The core contribution of this work is the development and validation of a non-invasive wrist-based device that employs photoplethysmography (PPG) and the Beer-Lambert law, utilizing a novel measurement site for glucose monitoring. This innovative approach addresses the discomfort and constraints of traditional invasive methods, making it particularly suitable for continuous monitoring. The results reveal a moderate correlation with a commercial glucose meter, underscoring the device's potential for continuous glucose monitoring, especially in settings with limited resources.

This study was conducted in Cartagena, Colombia, where data were collected from a young population to evaluate the accuracy of the non-invasive device compared to the commercial Accu-Chek glucose meter. The article details both the hardware design and the data collection process, and it presents a comparative analysis aimed at validating the reliability of the prototype for continuous diabetes monitoring. The results obtained have the potential to improve diabetes management in resource-limited settings.

2 Material and Method

The initial version of the device was introduced in [3]. In this study, we improved both the device hardware and the associated code to improve its performance and functionality.

2.1 Glucose Levels

Glucose levels were categorized as follows: Hypoglycemia is defined as blood glucose levels below 70 mg/dL (3.9 mmol/L) and classified into three levels: mild (54–70 mg/dL, 3.0–3.9 mmol/L), moderate (below 54 mg/dL, 3.0 mmol/L), and severe (requiring external assistance). On the other hand, hyperglycemia is defined as blood glucose levels above 180 mg/dL (10 mmol/L) after meals or above 130 mg/dL (7.2 mmol/L) when fasting. It is classified as mild (180–250 mg/dL, 10–13.9 mmol/L), moderate (250–400 mg/dL, 13.9–22.2 mmol/L), and severe (above 400 mg/dL, 22.2 mmol/L). These thresholds are used to evaluate continuous, non-invasive glucose monitoring [7].

2.2 Photoplethysmography (PPG)

We analyzed the optical properties of glucose, as its concentration in blood affects the refractive index and absorption properties, altering the amount of light absorbed at specific wavelengths. The methodology is based on photometry and light absorbance. Photoplethysmography (PPG) measures changes in blood flow through direct sensing, while the Beer-Lambert Law calculates the absorbance of infrared and red light as a function of glucose concentration. Glucose levels are then estimated using a linear regression model that correlates absorbance values with blood glucose concentrations, leveraging glucose's effects on light absorption and scattering.

To minimize noise, the following techniques were applied: 1. Averaging: The sensor averages eight samples in its buffer, reducing high-frequency noise. 2. Signal Validation: Low "red reading" values (<1000) trigger a wait state, avoiding processing erroneous data. 3. Sampling Rate Adjustment: A sample rate of 400 Hz balances resolution and noise suppression by oversampling.

2.3 Hardware Design

We use a wearable device designed for wrist-based measurements, potentially for medical monitoring purposes. The components are organized to ensure functionality, comfort, and reliable data collection, with a focus on proper sensor placement and data display, see Fig. 1.

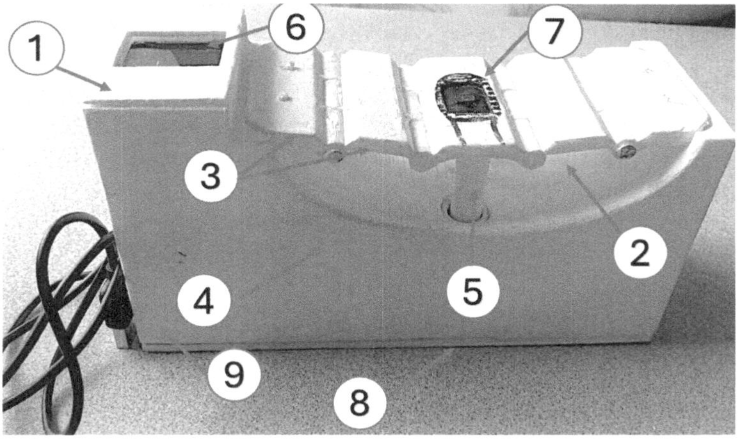

Fig. 1. Prototype developed to measure glucose at the wrist.

The device features an arch-shaped design that wraps around the wrist, with links Fig. 1 number 3) functioning as bracelet segments to allow flexibility and adjustable fitting, similar to a watch strap. The main body (see Fig. 1 number 4) holds the components, providing structural integrity to the system. We use a pulse oximeter biosensor (Fig. 1 number 7) to collect the patient's data samples. Pressure mechanism (Fig. 1 number 5) ensures proper contact between the sensor and the wrist, which is crucial for accurate measurements by maintaining optimal sensor positioning. A small OLED display (Fig. 1 number 6) shows readings or device status information. The sensor, positioned in close contact with the skin, is responsible for detecting glucose levels. The bottom cover houses additional components, protecting the microcontroller and power system (see Fig. 1 number 8). The microcontroller (Fig. 1 number 9) processes the data collected by the sensor and controls the overall functionality of the device. A power cable is used to charge the device, enabling the system to function.

3 Methodology

This section describes the methodology employed for the proposed wrist-based glucose monitoring device. It is organized into three main components: the experimental protocol for data collection, the study population, and the implementation of the linear regression model. Standardized procedures were followed during data collection to ensure consistency in participant measurements. The device utilizes photoplethysmography (PPG) and the Beer-Lambert law to estimate glucose levels.

3.1 Non-invasive Device

The procedure for Non-Invasive Blood Glucose Measurement is as follows:

Clean the wrist with alcohol, as this surface will be used for the sample collection. The user places their wrist over the sensor and presses down. The person conducting the test should turn on the device once the user has positioned their wrist as indicated. At the start of the test, the user should gently press the bracelet and maintain the position for one minute to obtain an accurate measurement. Once the result is displayed on the screen, the user can remove their wrist from the device.

This procedure was performed three times with each user to eliminate any potential measurement errors.

3.2 Commercial Device - Invasive Method

The comparative analysis was conducted using the Accu-Chek Instant device (Accu-Chek; Roche, Basel, Switzerland) [8], following the operating principles detailed in [14], along with Accu-Chek Instant test strips [2]. The procedure was as follows:

Clean the sample area, usually the side of a finger, with alcohol. Use a lancet, a small needle in a lancing device, to obtain a drop of blood, with a new lancet used for each user. Place the drop of blood on a test strip, which is then inserted into the glucose meter. An enzyme on the strip reacts with the glucose, generating an electrical current measured by the device, which then displays the glucose level in milligrams per deciliter (mg/dL) or millimoles per liter (mmol/L).

3.3 Study Population

The study involved a young population, comprising 60% women and 40% men. All participants were between 18 and 40 years of age, and the study took place at sea level. Participants were fasting at the time of data collection. The individuals involved were students from the Universidad Tecnológica de Bolívar - Cartagena-Colombia. This City is known for its diverse racial and ethnic composition, the result of centuries of interaction between various groups. Generally, the population has a mix of Afro-descendant, Indigenous, and European (Spanish) heritage. This unique blend of ethnic backgrounds provides a rich cultural context for the study, as the participants reflect the diversity inherent in the local population.

BMI (Body Mass Index) values range from 18.61 to 39.84, with a mean of 24.03, indicating a sample that includes individuals from normal weight to those with obesity.

3.4 Linear Regression Model

The linear regression model proposed in this study establishes a direct relationship between absorbance (A), calculated using the Beer-Lambert law, and glucose concentration (G), expressed as:

$$G = A \cdot m + b, \tag{1}$$

where the slope ($m =$): represents the rate of change in glucose concentration for each unit increase in absorbance. The intercept (b): represents the baseline glucose level when absorbance approaches zero. The absorbance (A) is calculated using the following equation:

$$A = \log_{10}\left(\frac{peakvoltage}{valleyvoltage}\right). \tag{2}$$

The peak and valley voltages are derived from PPG signal readings at infrared and red wavelengths, representing the light absorbed by the blood. This absorbance value is assumed to correlate directly with glucose concentration based on its optical properties. The model presumes a linear relationship between A (absorbance) and G (glucose concentration), where higher absorbance values indicate greater glucose levels. Calibration data, obtained in preliminary studies [3,6], is used to determine the parameters m and b, fitting a straight line to known glucose levels and their corresponding absorbance values. For a measured A, the glucose level (G) is predicted using the Eq. 1, providing a real-time blood glucose estimation.

4 Results

This section presents the preliminary results of tests conducted on 25 participants. However, the results from two individuals were excluded as their values fell outside the limits of the mathematical model used to estimate blood sugar levels.

All participants provided informed consent, confirming their understanding and voluntary acceptance of the procedures. The study was also approved by the ethics committee of Universidad Tecnológica de Bolívar, ensuring compliance with ethical principles and regulations to protect participants' rights and well-being.

One factor influencing the sensor's accuracy is its dependence on proper placement. Correct positioning ensures effective light penetration into the skin and minimizes light scattering. Misalignment or insufficient contact reduces the signal-to-noise ratio (SNR), resulting in unreliable absorbance values (A), which directly impact glucose estimation using the linear regression model. Improper placement can lead to significant underestimation or overestimation of glucose levels. Another challenge identified is that darker skin tones, which have higher melanin concentrations, absorb more light, reducing the amount of light detected by the photoplethysmography (PPG) sensor. This can decrease signal intensity and compromise accuracy [4].

The Pearson correlation coefficient for the device is 0.49, indicating a moderate positive correlation. This suggests that, while there is some relationship between the device's measurements and those of the reference method, the relationship is not very strong, pointing to additional factors influencing the non-invasive device's measurements. Figure 2 shows the diversity of the participants in terms of skin tone. Three sample tests are presented, conducted on the wrists of different young individuals, each with a distinct skin tone: a) darker skin tone, b) intermediate skin tone, and c) lighter skin tone. In each case, the non-invasive device is placed around the wrist. The image illustrates how the device adjusts and functions on different skin types.

We present the results of comparative analysis between both devices (see Fig. 3). The blue lines represent glucose levels measured by a commercial Accu-Chek device, while the red lines represent levels measured by a non-invasive wrist device. Both lines show fluctuations in glucose levels among the participants, with some notable peaks and valleys. In general, the two devices seem to follow a similar trend, although there are minimal differences at several points. Until participant 5, the measurements from the commercial device tend to be slightly higher than those from the non-invasive device. Between participants 6 and 10, the measurements from the non-invasive device are very close to or coincide with those from the commercial device. From participant 15 onwards, the measurements again show variations, with some points where the non-invasive device shows higher levels and others where it shows lower levels compared to the commercial device. The commercial device (blue line) shows glucose levels ranging approximately between 85 and 100 mg/dL, while the non-invasive device

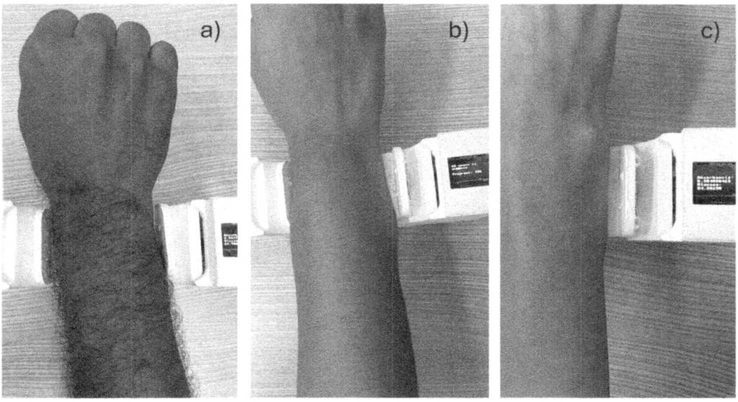

Fig. 2. Testing examples of the participants, a) darker skin tone, b) intermediate skin tone, and c) lighter skin tone

(red line) shows glucose levels that also vary within a similar range, albeit with some occasional differences.

We present the results of comparative analysis of gender with the both devices. Figure 4 shows a comparison of glucose levels measured by a commercial Accu-Chek device (blue bars) and a non-invasive wrist device (red bars) in a group of 15 female participants. The results indicate that, in general, both devices present a similar trend in glucose measurements, although there are minimal differences at certain points. Up to participant 6, the measurements from the commercial device tend to be slightly higher than those from the non-invasive device. Between participants 7 and 9, the measurements from the non-invasive device are very close to or coincide with those from the commercial device. From participant 10 onwards, the measurements show variations again, with some points where the non-invasive device shows higher levels and others where it shows lower levels compared to the commercial device. The glucose levels measured by both devices vary approximately between 80 mg/dL and 100 mg/dL, although with some specific differences.

Figure 5 presents glucose levels (mg/dL) for a group of male participants, comparing the measurements obtained with a commercial device (in blue) and a non-invasive wrist device (in red). Glucose levels remain within a narrow range (approximately 80–100 mg/dL) for all participants, and there is a general trend in which the commercial device measures slightly higher glucose levels compared to the non-invasive wrist device.

For most participants, the measurements taken with the commercial device (blue bar) are consistently higher than those from the wrist device (red bar), although the differences are minimal. The recorded glucose levels are within a healthy range (below 110 mg/dL) in both cases.

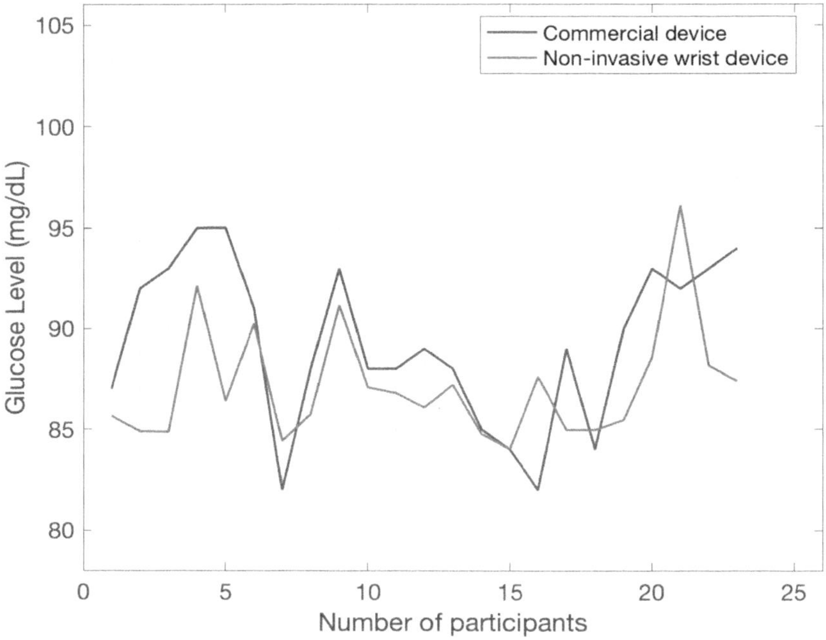

Fig. 3. General results (Color figure online)

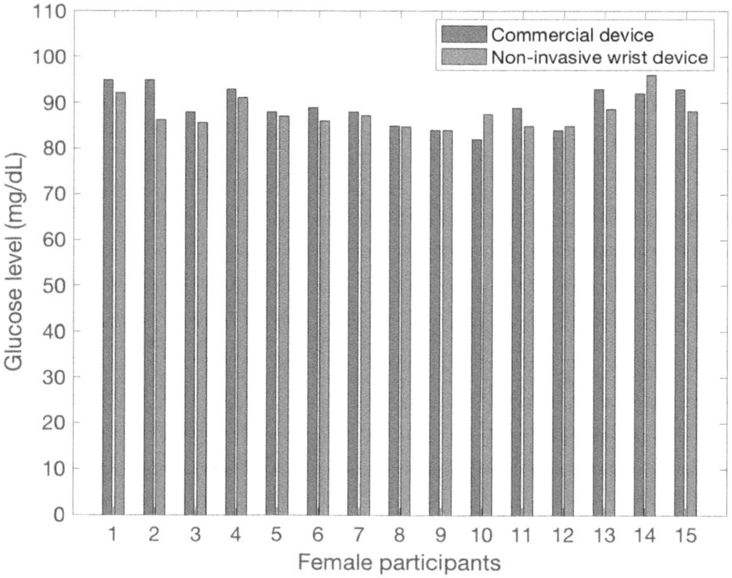

Fig. 4. Representation of female participants (Color figure online)

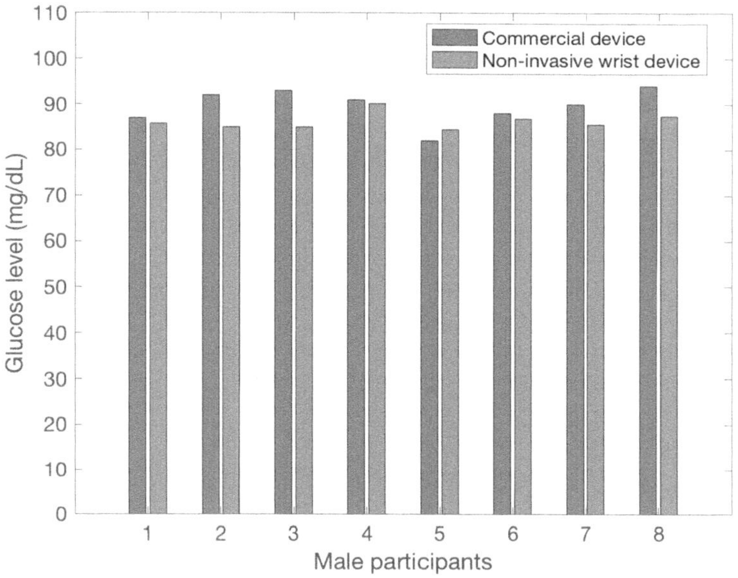

Fig. 5. Representation of male participants (Color figure online)

4.1 Parkes Error Analysis

Figure 6 shows the Parkes error grid plots for both the Commercial Device and the Non-invasive Wrist Device which is used to evaluate the accuracy of glucose measurement. In this graph, the X-axis presents the glucose values from the commercial device, while the Y-axis shows the values from the non-invasive wrist device. The solid diagonal line indicates perfect equivalence between the two devices, while the dashed lines represent different zones of clinical error. The red dots, representing the measurements, are mostly grouped near the equivalence line, suggesting that the non-invasive device has reasonable accuracy. Most of the points fall within zones A or B of the grid, indicating that the errors are clinically acceptable and would not negatively impact decision-making. Therefore, the non-invasive device demonstrates performance comparable to the commercial device within clinically safe margins.

4.2 Bland-Altman Analysis

The Bland-Altman analysis (see Fig 7) revealed a mean difference (bias) of -2.19 mg/dL between the wrist-based device and the Accucheck reference, indicating a slight systematic underestimation by the wrist-based device. The calculated limits of agreement (LoA) range from -9.15 mg/dL to 4.77 mg/dL, encompassing 95% of the differences. Most data points fall within these limits, demonstrating

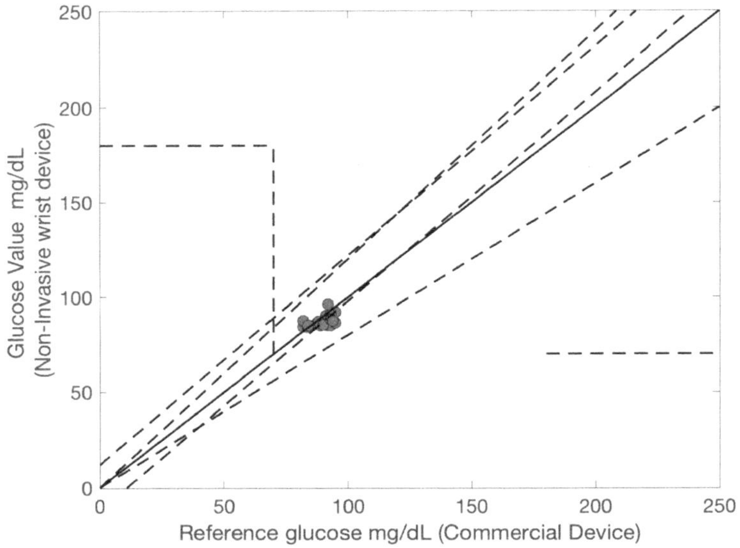

Fig. 6. Parkes error grid

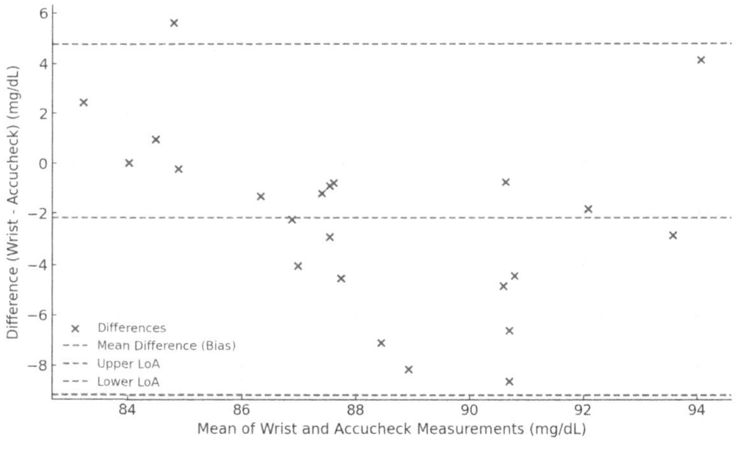

Fig. 7. Bland - Altman analysis results

reasonable agreement between the two methods. However, the presence of some outliers suggests areas for improvement, such as refining the device's algorithm and addressing variability caused by factors like skin tone, or wrist pressure.

5 Conclusions

In conclusion, the device meets the measurement standards for reading glucose levels non-invasively at the wrist. In this study, a prototype non-invasive wrist device was used to collect absorbance data and successfully estimate blood glucose levels (BGL). This result shows that it is feasible to continue developing the prototype, moving towards a miniaturized wearable device and conducting additional clinical studies to generate large volumes of accurate BGL data, covering a broad range from hypoglycemia to hyperglycemia.

Although most measurements fall within zones A and B of the Parkes grid, the results suggest that further refinements are needed. It is important to note that while zones A and B represent clinically acceptable margins, they do not guarantee absolute equivalence in the measurements.

Since the results are within clinically safe margins, some users might confuse the applicability of the non-invasive device in different medical contexts or for different types of patients. However, it is crucial to consider that the results obtained in this study may not apply uniformly to populations with more extreme glucose conditions (severe hypoglycemia or hyperglycemia), as most of the measurements analyzed seem to fall within a moderately healthy range.

As future work, additional tests of the non-invasive device are planned in populations with extreme glucose conditions, such as individuals with hyperglycemia and hypoglycemia. These tests are crucial to validate the device's accuracy across a wide range of glucose levels, ensuring its applicability in more complex clinical scenarios. Furthermore, the miniaturization process of the device will be prioritized to make it a portable and convenient tool for continuous use in patients' daily lives. Finally, the device's performance will be evaluated in environments with lower blood oxygenation, such as high altitudes, to assess its ability to accurately measure glucose under adverse physiological conditions.

Furthermore, future research will incorporate feedback mechanisms to alert users when placement is suboptimal, such as real-time visual or haptic feedback to ensure proper positioning and improve data reliability.

References

1. Calie-Licoa, B.J., Mero-García, M.N., Duran-Cañarte, A.L., et al.: Asociación entre diabetes mellitus tipo 2 e hipertensión arterial en la población adulta de américa latina. MQRInvestigar **7**(1), 610–626 (2023)
2. Care, R.D.: The Accu-Chek instant test strips - user's manual. Roche Diabetes Care (2024). https://www.accu-chek.com. Accessed September 2024
3. Célleri, S., Contento, L.M.T.S., Gamez, B., Rosero, C.X.: Non-invasive blood sugar measurement system. In: 2023 IEEE Seventh Ecuador Technical Chapters Meeting (ECTM), pp. 1–7. IEEE (2023)
4. Kanellis, V.G.: A review of melanin sensor devices. Biophys. Rev. **11**(6), 843–849 (2019). https://doi.org/10.1007/s12551-019-00581-8
5. Khalid, S.G., Zhang, J., Chen, F., Zheng, D.: Blood pressure estimation using photoplethysmography only: comparison between different machine learning approaches. J. Healthc. Eng. **2018**(1), 1548647 (2018)

6. Mieles Freire, M., Tobar Subía, L.M., Gamez Aparicio, B.N., Mosquera Canchingre, G.: A non-invasive portable solution to estimate hemoglobin levels in the blood. In: Conference on Information and Communication Technologies of Ecuador, pp. 365–381. Springer (2023)
7. Oliver, N., Toumazou, C., Cass, A., Johnston, D.: Glucose sensors: a review of current and emerging technology. Diabet. Med. **26**(3), 197–210 (2009)
8. Roche Diabetes Care: User Manual for Accu-Chek Instant Glucose Meter. Roche Diabetes Care GmbH, Mannheim, Germany (2019). https://www.accu-chek.com. Accessed September 2024
9. Saikevičius, L., Raudonis, V., Dervinis, G., Baranauskas, V.: Non-contact vision-based techniques of vital sign monitoring: systematic review. Sensors **24**(12), 3963 (2024)
10. Salem, M., Elkaseer, A., El-Maddah, I.A., Youssef, K.Y., Scholz, S.G., Mohamed, H.K.: Non-invasive data acquisition and IoT solution for human vital signs monitoring: applications, limitations and future prospects. Sensors **22**(17), 6625 (2022)
11. Susana, E., Ramli, K.: Review of non-invasive blood glucose level estimation based on photoplethysmography and artificial intelligent technology. In: 2021 17th International Conference on Quality in Research (QIR): International Symposium on Electrical and Computer Engineering, pp. 158–163. IEEE (2021)
12. Susana, E., Ramli, K., Purnamasari, P.D., Apriantoro, N.H.: Non-invasive classification of blood glucose level based on photoplethysmography using time-frequency analysis. Information **14**(3), 145 (2023)
13. Swain, S.M., Lata, M., Kumar, S., Mondal, S., Behera, J.K., Mondal, H.: A cross-sectional study on the agreement of perfusion indexes measured on different fingers by a portable pulse oximeter in healthy adults. Cureus **14**(5) (2022)
14. Webb, A.: Principles of Biomedical Instrumentation. Cambridge Texts in Biomedical Engineering. Cambridge University Press (2018). https://books.google.com.co/books?id=wao_DwAAQBAJ
15. Zavala-Hoppe, A.N., Arteaga-Hernández, K.M., Cañarte-Suarez, T.B., Carrillo-Carrasco, P.L., et al.: Factores de riesgo y sus complicaciones en pacientes con diabetes mellitus en latinoamérica. MQRInvestigar **8**(1), 1446–1463 (2024)

Medical Waste Data Analysis in Ecuador Using Sparse HJ-Biplot and Clustering Techniques

Mayra Tualombo(✉), Isidro Amaro, and Zenaida Castillo

School of Mathematical and Computational Sciences, Yachay Tech University, Hda. San José s/n and Proyecto Yachay, San Miguel de Urcuquí 10019, Ecuador
{mayra.tualombo,iamaro,zcastillo}@yachaytech.edu.ec

Abstract. Managing medical waste (MW) and its consequences is important in establishing public policies in any country, as it often contains hazardous material that can cause damage to human health and the environment. Statistical studies on MW usually focus on univariate analysis; however, knowing the interaction between variables is desirable. This study used Sparse HJ-Biplot and clustering techniques to analyze MW data across Ecuador in 2020, offering a comparative perspective with the HJ-Biplot method to reinforce the findings. The results revealed different patterns in the generation of MW in the 24 provinces of Ecuador, highlighting the most severe problems in largely populated areas such as Guayas and Pichincha, grouped in cluster 1. In contrast, clusters 2 and 3 included the remaining provinces, with limitations on MW treatment and management practices. These findings provide important aspects for managing MW and establishing assertive public policies to protect sensitive areas exposed to this contamination and warn neighboring countries.

Keywords: Medical waste · Waste management · Sparse HJ-Biplot · HJ biplot · Clustering · Data analysis

1 Introduction

Medical waste (MW) from healthcare institutions is highly hazardous as it contains pathogens that can harm the environment and surrounding communities [1]. The Health Care Without Harm clarifies that the healthcare industry is considered the fifth largest emitter of greenhouse gases (GHGs) worldwide [2]. This situation has worsened due to SARS-CoV-2 (COVID-19), where the most alarming values were evident throughout 2020 [2]. Inappropriate MW manipulation can spread infections such as hepatitis B and C, Human Immunodeficiency Virus, meningitis, and others such as ocular and respiratory infections [3].

Most statistical studies concerning MW handling focused on univariate analysis [4,5]. However, like other pollution-related issues, multivariate analysis is needed [6]. In the present study, we applied multivariate statistical techniques, including Sparse HJ-Biplot and HJ-biplot, to explore the existing associations

F. R. Narváez et al. (Eds.): SmartTech-IC 2024, CCIS 2392, pp. 149–164, 2026.
https://doi.org/10.1007/978-3-031-98287-3_11

between types of MW, institutions responsible for managing MW, and treatment methods. We considered the biplot methods since they allow variables and samples to be represented in a low-dimensional subspace [7]. Using clustering as a form of unsupervised learning enabled the identification of patterns without the need for prior labeling [7]. A common challenge in cluster analysis is identifying the variables associated with each resulting classification. Representing these clusters on a biplot offers a solution by facilitating interpreting these relationships.

The main objective of the following article was to conduct a multivariate analysis of MW in Ecuador. This study stood out as a pioneer in analyzing this type of contamination using multivariate techniques. The article was structured as follows: Firstly, the description of the study area of interest, focusing on the selected variables and the data. Then, the methodology delved into the details of Sparse HJ-Biplot and HJ-Biplot combined with clustering. The results and discussion sections were crucial and showed the benefits of multivariate analysis. Finally, the conclusions highlighted the most outstanding aspects of the article.

2 Medical Waste

The volume of MW has surged significantly over the past 30 years, with healthcare facilities worldwide generating more waste than ever [8]. The categorization of MW can differ across countries depending on the framework [4]. Taiwan reviewed regulations under the Waste Management Act, classifying MW into two categories and proposing specific requirements for its storage, disposal, treatment, and management [9]. Meanwhile, Brazil classified MW into four categories and focused on planning optimal strategies for medical material rationalization to help reduce waste [10].

Ecuador follows the Organic Health Law (OHL) that was last reformed on April 29, 2022, and classifies MW into non-hazardous and hazardous waste [11]. Hazardous wastes are a warning topic since they constitute 15% to 35% of the total MW [12]. Hazardous waste can be divided into:

1. Biological-infectious wastes correspond to MW contaminated with blood, corporal fluids, strains of infectious agents, wastes from patients treated in isolated rooms, and related equipment.
2. Anatomopathological wastes correspond to tissues, organs, and human body parts.
3. Sharp wastes are syringes, needles, blades, scalpels, tongue depressors, etc.
4. Pharmaceutical wastes include vaccines and expired or contaminated medicines.
5. Radioactive wastes represent products contaminated with radionucleotides.
6. Hazardous chemical products are solvents, disinfectants, heavy metals from medical equipment, batteries, and mercury thermometers.

In medical institutions, the individuals responsible for cleaning and disinfection are the most exposed [1]. Being in contact with hazardous pharmaceutical wastes can lead to the development of strains of resistant pathogens, as well as skin injuries or harmful effects on the reproductive system [1]. Regarding exposure to radioactive waste, it is essential to highlight that even a reduced dose may have genotoxic effects [11].

According to Article 100 of OHL, municipalities are the primary institutions responsible for collecting, transporting, treating, and disposing of MW [11]. However, due to the COVID-19 pandemic, MW increased from 18% to 425%, depending on the country during 2020 [12]. Between 2019 and 2022, about 49% of MW in Ecuador was managed by municipalities, with the remainder handled by other private environmental services [11]. However, 46% of municipalities did not conduct specialized treatment for MW, sending them directly to landfills where they represented a biological, chemical, and radioactive danger [13].

Frequently, MW is incinerated to reduce possible infections; however, this process can lead to the emission of dioxins, furans, and other atmospheric contaminants, thus generating a high environmental impact [3]. Transportation, autoclave decontamination, thermal treatment, and other procedures can increase the carbon footprint by up to 50-fold and GHGs [4]. Currently, MW treatment is considered linear; however, some studies argue that recycling can lead to a better categorization to manage MW [10].

3 Data Description

The data about MW was gathered from the official platform of the Ecuadorian government, Ecuador en Cifras [14]. Since the impact of COVID-19, data corresponding to 2020 were selected for analysis.

Table 1. Variables considered for the study

Types of medical wastes (kg)
$k1508$: Biological-infectious *material contaminated with infectious agents*
$k1509$: Anatomopathological *material related to body parts, tissues, and organs*
$k1510$: Sharps *are articles that have cut or punctured human skin*
$k1511$: Pharmaceutical *refers to any medication or drug that is no longer fit for use*
$k1512$: Others *like radioactive, hazardous chemicals, and mercury-containing devices*
Institutions responsible for managing medical wastes (kg)
$k1521$: Municipality *are entities focused on local well-being and jurisdictional needs*
$k1523$: Environmental services *in charge of MW recollection*
Treatment methods (kg)
$k1531$: Differentiated cells *is a classification method depending on the characteristics*
$k1533$: Incineration *is a process that burns waste*
$k1535$: Physio-chemical inactivation *is a group of methods using both techniques*
$k1537$: Other *(not specified in the dataset)*

The database contained 4136 observations with 47 features, 17 qualitative, 12 identifiers, and 18 quantitative. Despite having 18 quantitative features, 4 corresponded to yes/no questions, which may mislead the interpretation, and 3 corresponded to the total sum of other variables. Consequently, only 11 quantitative traits were considered (see Table 1). The database had an identifier location feature associated with the Ecuadorian provinces. That adherence followed the Administrative Political Division of Ecuador from 2017 (see Fig. 1).

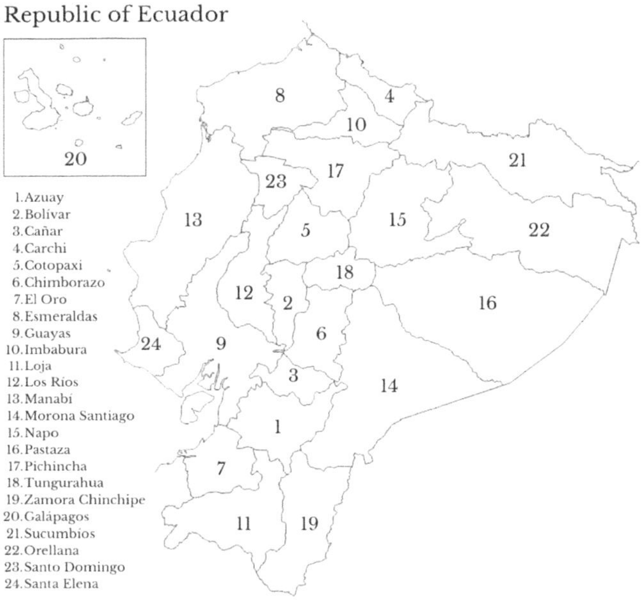

Fig. 1. Administrative Political Division of Ecuador from 2017.

4 Methodology

The methodology followed a four-step process. Initially, an exploratory univariate analysis was performed to gain a general understanding of the MW data. Next, a Sparse HJ-Biplot with elastic net penalization was employed to examine the interactions between variables and individuals, complemented by the HJ-Biplot technique to validate the graphical analysis. Finally, clustering was applied to both techniques, and the results were compared for further insights.

4.1 Biplot Analysis

HJ-Biplot. Dimensionality reduction methods have been used successfully for studying problems involving high-dimensional matrices [15]. Thus, biplots are essential for addressing contemporary issues [15]. HJ-Biplot is a multivariate (unsupervised learning) graphical representation of the matrix X that provides excellent quality of representation for both rows (individuals) and columns (variables) since they are in the same reference system [16]. While the graphical interpretation guide was well-structured and defined in some articles, this article relied on the descriptions provided in Tualombo *et al.* [16] and Vinueza *et al.* [6].

The algorithm started from the decomposition into eigenvalues and eigenvectors of the matrix $X_{n \times p}$ defined as:

$$X \cong UDV^t \tag{1}$$

where X is the data matrix, U is the matrix of the data whose columns contain the eigenvectors of XX^t, V is the matrix of data whose columns contain the eigenvectors of X^tX, and D is the diagonal matrix containing the eigenvectors of X.

Given that the X matrix was centered, the column markers in the HJ-Biplot align with the marked columns of the GH-Biplot. Similarly, the row markers were adjusted to correspond with the row markers of the JK-Biplot [7].

Sparse HJ-Biplot via Elastic Net Regularization. The Sparse HJ-Biplot uses regularization techniques such as a ridge, lasso, and elastic net [7]. Elastic net regularization combines ridge and lasso regularization techniques and solves the biplot analysis since it leads to many observations and variables [17]. This method reduces the dimensions on the graph, increasing the biplot's goodness in mapping the features [7].

Sparse HJ-Biplot offers a solution for finding a linear combination of variables based on a vector of sparse loadings that maximizes data variability or minimizes reconstruction error [7]. The approach involves minimizing the reconstruction error (E) following the methodology described by Cubilla-Montilla *et al.* [7]. The model can be described as follows:

$$\hat{X} = X + E, \tag{2}$$

considering the singular value decomposition of (1), (2) can be rewritten as:

$$\begin{aligned}
\hat{X} &= XVV^t + E, \\
&= XVD^{-1}D^tV^t + E, \\
&= XVD^{-1}(VD)^t + E, \\
&= (XV)D^{-1}(VD)^t + E.
\end{aligned}$$

Taking $J = XV$ and $H = VD$ to obtain,

$$\hat{X} = JD^{-1}H^t + E. \tag{3}$$

The modified loadings for the biplot were derived from the elastic net regularization method as:

$$V_{\text{elasticnet}} = \arg\min_V \left\|X - JD^{-1}H^t\right\|^2 + \lambda_2 \sum_{j=1}^{p} V_j^2 + \lambda_1 \sum_{j=1}^{p} |V_j|, \tag{4}$$

where $\lambda_1 > 0$ and $\lambda_2 > 0$ are the parameters of lasso and ridge regularization, respectively. The process can be summarized in Fig. 2.

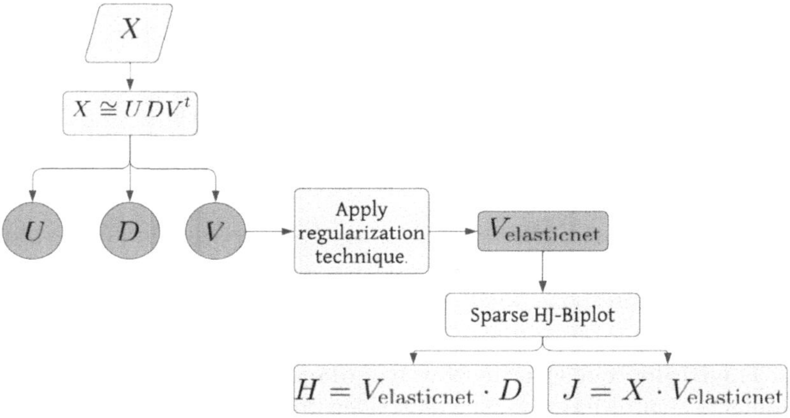

Fig. 2. Scheme of the Sparse HJ-Biplot technique.

4.2 Cluster Analysis

Cluster analysis is a type of multivariate analysis that seeks to group objects in a dataset according to the similarities in their characteristics, considering a distance measure [16]. The general representation of the clustering technique considers a dataset defined as,

$$\widetilde{X} = \{\mathbf{x}_1, \mathbf{x}_2, \ldots, \mathbf{x}_n\}, \tag{5}$$

where $\mathbf{x}_i \in \mathbb{R}^d$ is a d-dimensional feature vector for the i-th data point.

The clustering object considered partition (5) into k clusters $C_1, C_2, \ldots, C_k$ such that the similarity within each cluster was maximized and the similarity between different clusters was minimized [18].

The coordinates obtained from biplots were used to calculate clusters using the K-means method and the Euclidean distance [19]. K-means is a non-hierarchical algorithm used in data mining to partition the data into k predefined disjoint clusters [18].

The K-means algorithm selects k initial centroids $\{\mu_1, \mu_2, \ldots, \mu_k\}$ and assign each point $\mathbf{x}_i$ to the cluster whose centroid is nearest:

$$C_j = \{\mathbf{x}_i : \|\mathbf{x}_i - \mu_j\|^2 \leq \|\mathbf{x}_i - \mu_l\|^2 \, \forall l, \; 1 \leq l \leq k\} \tag{6}$$

The centroids are updated, computing the new centroids as the mean of the points assigned to each cluster:

$$\mu_j = \frac{1}{|C_j|} \sum_{\mathbf{x}_i \in C_j} \mathbf{x}_i \tag{7}$$

The final step considers minimizing the sum of squared distances from each point to its corresponding centroid:

$$\min \sum_{j=1}^{k} \sum_{\mathbf{x}_i \in C_j} \|\mathbf{x}_i - \mu_j\|^2 \tag{8}$$

In this proposal, the process can be summarized as follows: each province was assigned to the cluster with the nearest centroid. Then, we calculated the distance between the provinces and the centroids using the Euclidean distance. The centroids were recalculated for each iteration, and the assignment was repeated until no further changes were observed.

5 Results

R software was used to create the statistical results. Sparse HJ-Biplot is an R package used to represent multivariate data in a low-dimensional subspace, capturing most of the variability of the information in just a few dimensions [7]. Another statistical program for biplot analysis is the software developed by Vicente-Villardon for HJ-Biplot, available on the official website [20].

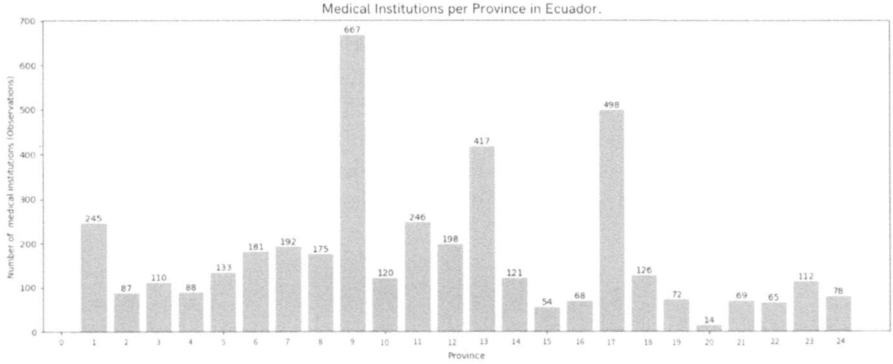

Fig. 3. Distributions of the number of observations per province.

An exploratory analysis of the distribution of medical institutions in Ecuador revealed that Guayas, Pichincha, and Manabí had the highest number of observations, totals of 667, 498, and 417, respectively. Additionally, Fig. 3 indicated that Loja and Azuay contributed with 246 and 245 observations, respectively. Notably, almost 50.1 % of the data from 2020 pertained to these five provinces. Considering that none of these provinces are located in Ecuador's Amazon region, which includes Sucumbíos, Orellana, Napo, Pastaza, Morona Santiago, and Zamora Chinchipe, highlighted a disparity in the distribution of medical institutions.

Considering variables in the Table 1, during 2020, a total of 13, 789, 783.1 kg was produced. Figure 4 indicated that Guayas, Pichincha, Manabí, and Azuay contributed 5, 434, 825.04 kg of the total MW, i.e., around 40% of total MW was generated in only four provinces.

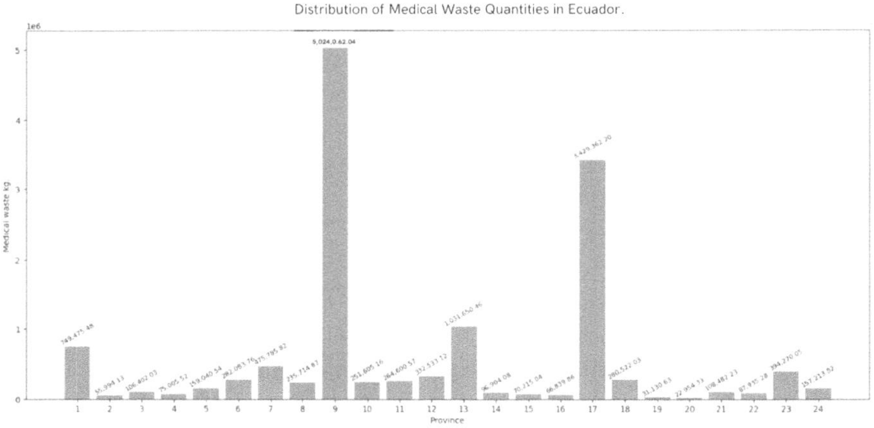

Fig. 4. Distribution per province of medical waste quantities in kg.

According to the National Institute of Statistics and Census of Ecuador [14], in 2020, the provinces of Guayas, Pichincha, Manabí, Los Ríos, and Azuay accounted for 11 million out of the total population of 17 million. The fact that only 5 provinces accounted for approximately 65% of the population in 2020 aligned with the amount of MW generated. However, the remaining provinces also produced MW that deserved proper treatment.

5.1 Sparse HJ-Biplot Analysis

The Sparse HJ-Biplot, Fig. 5, provided an interactive visualization of all variables listed in the Table 1, enabling a clearer interpretation. It revealed that the majority of variables ($k1508$, $k1509$, $k1510$, $k1511$, $k1512$, $k1523$, $k1531$,

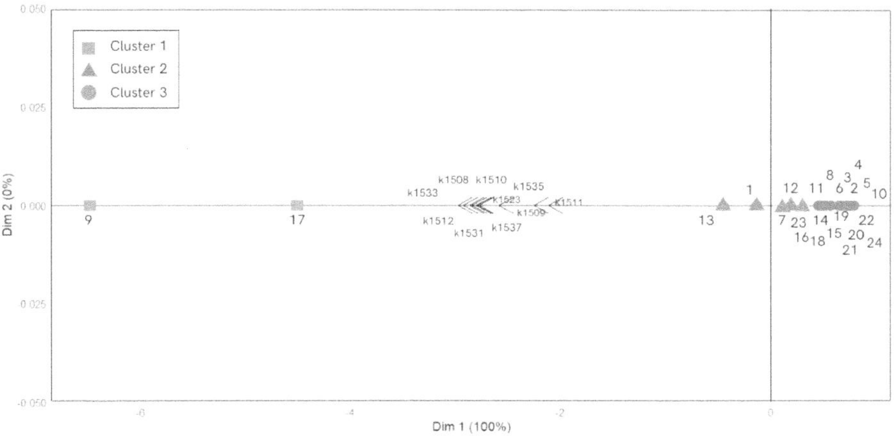

Fig. 5. Association between studied variables of medical waste and provinces in Ecuador using Elastic Net regularization in Sparse HJ-Biplot.

$k1533$, $k1535$, and $k1537$), which were related to MW, correlated with the first component on the factorial plane.

Cluster 1 in Fig. 5 corresponded to Guayas and Pichincha.

Cluster 2 in Fig. 5 corresponded to Azuay, El Oro, Los Ríos, Manabí, and Santo Domingo.

Cluster 3 in Fig. 5 corresponded to Bolívar, Cañar, Carchi, Cotopaxi, Chimborazo, Esmeraldas, Imbabura, Loja, Morona Santiago, Napo, Pastaza, Tungurahua, Zamora Chinchipe, Galápagos, Sucumbíos, Orellana, and Santa Elena.

In Fig. 5, axis 1 exhibits a highly informative gradient, capturing 100% of the variability of the data. Figure 5 showed that the variables that contributed negatively to the first axis had higher values for cluster 1, indicating that only two of the most populated provinces, Guayas and Pichincha, showed a predominance of variables described in Table 1. In contrast, most of the points related to cluster 2 and cluster 3 showed low values of the studied variables.

It is important to note that although Guayas and Pichincha were the primary MW producers, they were not the only regions contributing to the MW generation. Therefore, it was concerning that, at least for the variables related to waste collection and treatment, provinces such as Azuay, Manabí, and others had no influence.

The application of the Sparse HJ-Biplot technique reduced variable $k1521$. Hence, only 10 variables were considered for the analysis using the HJ-Biplot technique. This can be explained by the Sparse HJ-Biplot technique, which aimed to create a more focused and clear representation of the data by eliminating less significant variables [7]. Therefore, the MW managed by the municipality in Ecuador is not a key factor in determining the patterns in the dataset.

5.2 HJ-Biplot Analysis

The HJ-Biplot, Fig. 6, was conducted over 24 sampling points (provinces), which accounts for 97% of the variance. Since the cluster analysis was carried out based on the coordinates obtained from Sparse HJ-Biplot and HJ-Biplot, the clusters in Fig. 5 and Fig. 6, respectively, were quite similar.

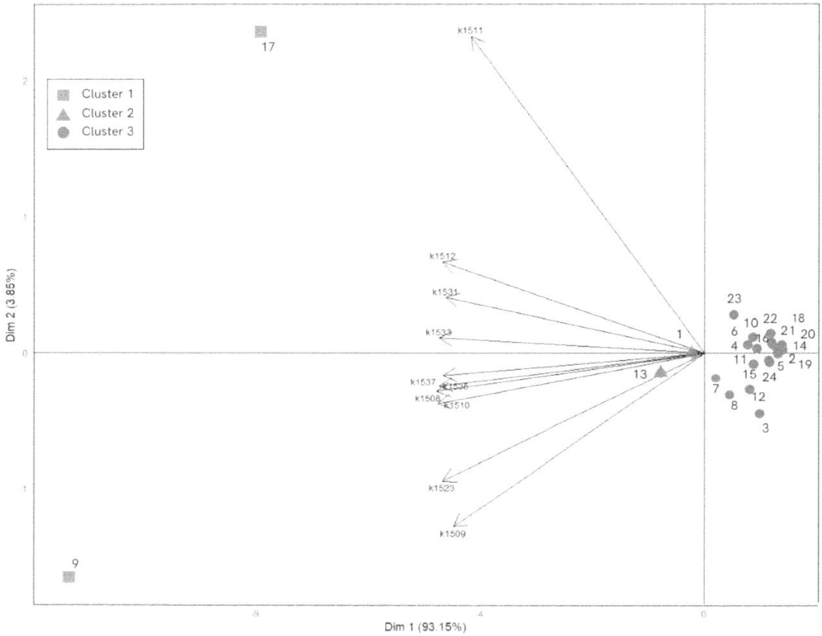

Fig. 6. Association between variables studied versus provinces in Ecuador using HJ-Biplot.

Cluster 1 in Fig. 6 corresponded to Guayas and Pichincha.

Cluster 2 in Fig. 6 corresponded to Azuay and Manabí.

Cluster 3 in Fig. 6 corresponded to Bolívar, Cañar, Carchi, Cotopaxi, Chimborazo, El Oro, Esmeraldas, Imbabura, Loja, Los Ríos, Morona Santiago, Napo, Pastaza, Tungurahua, Zamora Chinchipe, Galápagos, Sucumbíos, Orellana, Santo Domingo, and Santa Elena.

Guayas and Pichincha showed similar results for Spare HJ-Biplot and HJ-Biplot techniques. Also, Manabí and Azuay showed the influence of the considered variables, which were highly correlated. Figure 6 revealed that clusters 1 and 2 exhibit strong significance across all studied MW variables, while cluster 3 shows comparatively lower significance.

Considering the angles of the vectors in Fig. 6, the variables $k1523$ related to environmental services and $k1511$ related to pharmaceutical wastes were not correlated. It suggested that medical institutions may treat pharmaceutical waste.

Variables $k1508$, $k1510$, $k1535$, and $k1537$ were highly correlated, showing that biological-infectious and sharp object wastes were treated using physiochemical inactivation and other methods that were not specified. The angle between variables $k1512$, $k1531$, and $k1533$ indicated that radioactive waste, hazardous chemicals, and mercury-containing devices were commonly treated using differentiated cells and incineration. Conversely, the angle between variables $k1509$ and 1523 revealed that environmental services managed anatomopathological waste.

The implemented techniques used eigenvalue information to explain the variance, the loading matrix, individual coordinates, and variable coordinates [7]. The data analysis started by computing the loading matrix linked to the factorial axes of both methods (see Table 2). This allowed for a comparison of the contributions from different provinces.

Table 2. Loadings matrix for the first three principal components obtained from Sparse HJ-Biplot and the HJ-Biplot techniques

Variables	Sparse HJ-Biplot			HJ-Biplot		
	D1	D2	D3	D1	D2	D3
K1508	−0.19894	0	0	−0.32637	−0.09502	0.11057
K1509	−0.15074	0	0	−0.30587	−0.43075	0.15543
K1510	−0.19556	0	0	−0.32492	−0.12595	0.11482
K1511	−0.14145	0	0	−0.28436	0.78023	0.03511
K1512	−0.18690	0	0	−0.31879	0.224575	−0.41441
K1521	0	0	0	–	–	–
K1523	−0.17297	0	0	−0.31925	−0.31667	−0.22126
K1531	−0.19012	0	0	−0.31539	0.13733	0.63346
K1533	−0.19163	0	0	−0.32347	0.03761	−0.33038
K1535	−0.18723	0	0	−0.32326	−0.08206	−0.35914
K1537	−0.18557	0	0	−0.31830	−0.05535	0.29847

The Sparse HJ-Biplot method reduced the significance of provinces with minimal contribution to each axis (see Table 2). While the Sparse HJ-Biplot method generated sparse factor axes with some loadings set to zero due to the imposed penalty, the HJ-Biplot technique did not induce sparsity in the loading matrix. Consequently, each factorial axis was obtained as a linear combination of all provinces.

Table 3. Matrix with the coordinates of variables of Sparse HJ-Biplot and HJ-Biplot.

Variables	Sparse HJ-Biplot			HJ-Biplot		
	D1	D2	D3	D1	D2	D3
K1508	−2.97456	0	0	−4.77709	−0.28290	0.20692
K1509	−2.25377	0	0	−4.47708	−1.28241	0.29086
K1510	−2.92406	0	0	−4.75581	−0.37499	0.21486
K1511	−2.11494	0	0	−4.16212	2.32288	0.06571
K1512	−2.79451	0	0	−4.66608	0.66859	−0.77551
K1521	0	0	0	–	–	–
K1523	−2.58629	0	0	−4.67279	−0.94280	−0.41406
K1531	−2.84267	0	0	−4.61642	0.40886	1.18544
K1533	−2.86516	0	0	−4.73468	0.11198	−0.61827
K1535	−2.79949	0	0	−4.73160	−0.24431	−0.67208
K1537	−2.77471	0	0	−4.65891	−0.16478	0.55855

Table 3 indicated that the HJ-Biplot retained more of the original dimensions' variability, resulting in a broader spread across multiple dimensions than the Sparse HJ-Biplot. Notably, most D1 coordinates were negative in both methods, suggesting a consistent trend of the variables in that direction within the reduced space.

Table 4 compared the two proposed biplots, highlighting the differences in dimensionality reduction and the preservation of variability among the coordinates of individuals. While the Sparse HJ-Biplot method simplified the analysis by reducing the data to a single dimension, the HJ-Biplot retained more dimensions. This preservation of dimensions potentially captured more information but also increased graphical complexity. Notably, individuals from Guayas and Pichincha exhibited large negative values in both biplots, indicating that they represented a distinct group compared to other individuals.

6 Discussion

The proposed analysis confirms that the provinces facing the greatest challenges are Guayas, Pichincha, Manabí, Azuay, El Oro, Los Ríos, and Santo Domingo, i.e., cluster 1 and cluster 2 in Fig. 5, and emerged as the primary MW generators. The collection, treatment, and transportation variables also significantly impacted provinces like Guayas and Pichincha. In other words, attention was focused on the two most populated provinces, while control measures were lacking in the less populated or more distant provinces from the main cities, which is corroborated by Ilijama *et al.* [3].

Table 4. Matrix with the coordinates of individuals in Sparse HJ-Biplot and HJ-Biplot.

Variables	Sparse HJ-Biplot			HJ-Biplot		
	D1	D2	D3	D1	D2	D3
1. Azuay	−0.13421	0	0	−0.19602	−0.00051	0.70870
2. Bolívar	0.74186	0	0	1.30511	−0.00275	−0.19590
3. Cañar	0.57245	0	0	0.97322	−0.45030	−0.04719
4. Carchi	0.68352	0	0	1.20074	0.06676	−0.30921
5. Cotopaxi	0.65321	0	0	1.15130	−0.06390	−0.05450
6. Chimborazo	0.45881	0	0	0.77213	0.06293	−0.31749
7. El Oro	0.18005	0	0	0.29406	−0.29423	−0.27755
8. Esmeraldas	0.46956	0	0	0.79921	−0.26710	−0.02290
9. Guayas	−6.47312	0	0	−11.31820	−1.64840	−0.22601
10. Imbabura	0.49216	0	0	0.85654	0.11894553	−0.19227
11. Loja	0.50286	0	0	0.86952	−0.0778092	0.12814
12. Los Ríos	0.20346	0	0	0.35582	−0.3096090	−0.09429
13. Manabí	−0.45022	0	0	−0.78383	−0.14678	1.45275
14. Morona Santiago	0.73332	0	0	1.29374	0.03064	−0.15561
15. Napo	0.76123	0	0	1.34132	0.01350	−0.16115
16. Pastaza	0.72784	0	0	1.28242	0.04208	−0.05140
17. Pichincha	−4.51843	0	0	−7.93148	2.348501	−0.12452
18. Tungurahua	0.52391	0	0	0.92788	0.03205	−0.13243
19. Zamora Chinchipe	0.79211	0	0	1.39527	0.02495	−0.18076
20. Galápagos	0.78510	0	0	1.38398	0.06078	−0.20728
21. Sucumbíos	0.67781	0	0	1.19188	0.08060	−0.04989
22. Orellana	0.66750	0	0	1.17677	0.14773	−0.40271
23. Santo Domingo	0.30120	0	0	0.51671	0.28408	0.43492
24. Santa Elena	0.64794	0	0	1.14181	−0.05217	−0.04346

Figure 4 showed that in the Amazon region, 375,979.22 kg. of MW was generated during 2020. Indeed, it was striking that no Amazonian provinces significantly influenced the studied treatment methods. Despite having a small population of 956,699 habitats, the Amazonian region requires urgent attention due to its significant biodiversity [3].

An essential factor influencing the total volume of MW generated was the infrastructure and services provided by medical centers, hospitals, etc. [12]. However, the investigation conducted by Heredia *et al.* [13] showed that the clinical laboratory was the major MW generator area, followed by medical administration, hospitalization, and cleaning. Since those areas are common in all medical facilities, hazardous waste generation should be treated equally across all medical centers in Ecuador, according to the results provided by Sparse HJ-Biplot and HJ-Biplot.

Zambrano *et al.* [21] found that incorrect bag labeling was the primary contamination issue related to MW. The investigation also highlights that dental centers in Cotopaxi generate the most MW, especially sharp waste from tubes and slides. These wastes were mixed with common waste and then disposed of in an open landfill in the canton of La Maná in Cotopaxi [21]. Figures 5 and 6 showed that Cotopaxi is part of cluster 3 in both analyses. Mixed MW can explain the absence of influence of the studied variables in Cotopaxi and other provinces. This highlights the need to control MW disposal in provinces related to cluster 3.

According to Ecuador's Ministry of Public Health, sharp wastes were physically inactivated using incineration [11]. This methodology was confirmed by the angle analysis in Fig. 6. Therefore, sharps waste treatment effectively increases the carbon footprint and GHGs. Tsai, [9] conducted an analysis in Taiwan and clarified that incinerators must control the emissions of toxic air pollutants in compliance with the Air Pollution Control Policy. In Ecuador, only the municipalities are in charge of monitoring air pollution, according to article 112 of OHL.

7 Conclusions

This paper introduced the Sparse HJ-Biplot and HJ-biplot techniques to describe samples and variables within a low-dimensional space while retaining the most relevant variables in the context of a contamination problem related to MW treatment in Ecuador. This issue had not been previously analyzed using multivariate techniques; therefore, no information was available regarding how the variables interact or the potential dangers involved. The proposed methodology allowed us to work with a large amount of data, enhancing the visualization of the problem while improving interpretation.

Guayas and Pichincha exhibited the most concerning levels of representation of the studied variables in both analyses, followed by Azuay, Manabí, and Los Ríos. In some cases, waste ends up in landfills, contaminating water, air, and soil, posing risks to those collecting recyclable materials, such as in La Maná, Cotopaxi. Based on this article's findings, new policies for MW management in Ecuador should be developed to improve resource distribution.

The less represented provinces, such as Galápagos, Napo, Orellana, and Sucumbíos, require attention due to their rich biodiversity, which is more vulnerable to contamination from MW. Implementing changes in waste treatment will help ensure better living conditions for all individuals exposed to such waste. Many environmental services stressed the importance of automating waste collection, handling, and transportation processes to improve efficiency and safety.

Sparse HJ-Biplot and HJ-biplot, in conjunction with clustering, facilitated the identification of concealed patterns in data analysis. While the Ecuadorian government annually compiles a report on MW data, its focus remains limited to univariate analysis. In contrast, this novel research effectively examined a global issue using multivariate techniques, discovering relationships previously beyond the scope. As a new approach, this article provided a foundation for extending the analysis to various contamination issues in any country, such as large waste generation resulting from the processing of crops in Agro, allowing us to identify problems and allocate resources more effectively while maximizing benefits and minimizing the economic impact on the government, the environment, and the population.

Acknowledgment. This work was carried out under the project Statistical Methods for Modeling Data Generated by Complex Systems REGINV—MATH23-06, Yachay Tech University.

References

1. Cano, I., Peralta, J., Coronel, A.: Manejo de desechos sanitarios peligrosos en el área hospitalaria: revisión sistemática. J. Am. Health (2021)
2. Singh, N., Ogunseitan, O.A., Tang, Y.: Medical waste: current challenges and future opportunities for sustainable management. Crit. Rev. Environ. Sci. Technol. **52**(11), 2000–2022 (2022)
3. Ilijama, M., Mejía, J., Camacho, M., Naranjo, M.: Manejo de desechos infecciosos hospitalarios en el centro de salud "cordero crespo". Ecuador 2017. Rev. Invest. Talentos **6**(2), 72–84 (2019)
4. Attrah, M., Elmanadely, A., Akter, D., Rene, E.R.: A review on medical waste management: treatment, recycling, and disposal options. Environments **9**(11), 146 (2022)
5. Dihan, M.R., et al.: Healthcare waste in Bangladesh: current status, the impact of Covid-19 and sustainable management with life cycle and circular economy framework. Sci. Total Environ. **871**, 162083 (2023)
6. Vinueza-Cajas, J., Román-Niemes, S., Amaro, I. R., Infante, S.: Environmental impact of food products: a data analysis approach using HJ-biplot and clustering. In: International Conference on Advanced Research in Technologies, Information, Innovation and Sustainability, pp. 324–338. Springer, Cham (2023)
7. Cubilla-Montilla, M., Nieto-Librero, A.B., Galindo-Villardón, M.P., Torres-Cubilla, C.A.: Sparse HJ-Biplot: a new methodology via elastic net. Mathematics **9**(11), 1298 (2021)
8. Janik-Karpinska, E., et al.: Healthcare waste a serious problem for global health. In: Healthcare, vol. 11, no. 2, p. 242. MDPI (2023)
9. Tsai, W.T.: Analysis of medical waste management and impact analysis of COVID-19 on its generation in Taiwan. Waste Manage. Res. **39**(1suppl), 27–33 (2021)
10. Olabi, A.G., et al.: COVID-19: medical waste management, impact on sustainable development goals, and bibliometric analysis. Chem. Eng. Technol. **47**(1), 4–19 (2024)
11. Ministry of Public Health. Homepage (2019). https://www.salud.gob.ec. Accessed 20 June 2024
12. Mazzei, H.G., Specchia, S.: Latest insights on technologies for the treatment of solid medical waste: a review. J. Environ. Chem. Eng. **11**(2), 109309 (2023)

13. Heredia, S., Gavilanes, A., Heredia, F.: Manejo integral de residuos hospitalarios peligrosos–"Caso de Estudio Padre Alberto Bufonni, Ecuador". Perfiles **1**(24), 37–46 (2020)
14. INEC. Statistics (2023). https://www.ecuadorencifras.gob.ec/estadisticas/. Accessed 17 June 2024
15. Cubilla-Montilla, M.I.: Contribuciones al análisis biplot basadas en soluciones factoriales disjuntas y en soluciones sparse (2019)
16. Tualombo, M., Amaro, I., Castillo, Z.: HJ-biplot and clustering techniques for analyzing water quality: a case study. In: International Conference on Information Technology & Systems, pp. 17–26. Springer, Cham (2024)
17. Muhammad, A.R., Wardhani, N., Iriany, A., Lestantyo, P.: Robust fast minimum covariance determinant elastic net HJ biplot analysis for mapping cabbage yields in Malang. Math. Stat. Eng. Appl. **71**(4), 1159–1167 (2022)
18. Riera-Segura, L., Tapia-Riera, G., Amaro, I. R., Infante, S., Marin-Calispa, H.: HJ-biplot and clustering to analyze the COVID-19 vaccination process of American and European countries. In: International Conference on Smart Technologies, Systems and Applications, pp. 383–397. Springer, Cham (2021)
19. Frutos Bernal, E., Martín del Rey, A., Galindo Villardón, P.: Analysis of Madrid metro network: from structural to HJ-biplot perspective. Appl. Sci. **10**(16), 5689 (2020)
20. Vicente-Villardón, J.L.: Biplot 2000. Un programa para la interpretación de Biplots. Department of Statistics, University of Salamanca, Salamanca, Spain (2000)
21. Zambrano, J., Zambrano, C., Ponce, M.D., Sanchez, Y.F.: Hazardous waste management in public health centers in La Maná, Ecuador. Res. Militaris **12**(3), 1316–1325 (2022)

Development of a Signal Acquisition and Processing System to Determine the Operating Characteristic Curve of Domestic Refrigerators Axial Fans

Esteban Ordóñez(✉), Nelson Jara, Fran Reinoso, and Juan Cevallos

Universidad Politécnica Salesiana, Cuenca 010101, Ecuador
{eordonez,njara,freinoso,jcevallos}@ups.edu.ec
http://www.ups.com

Abstract. This study presents the development of a signal acquisition and processing system to determine the operating characteristic curve of axial fans used in domestic refrigerator evaporators. The system was implemented in a wind tunnel test bench constructed under ANSI/AMCA 210-16 at the Universidad Politécnica Salesiana (UPS), Cuenca, Ecuador. The methodology included the design of specific algorithms in LabVIEW and MATLAB programs, through which signals from sensors that measure static and differential pressure, as well as temperature, were acquired and processed. This allowed the UPS test bench to be functional so that it can be used by industries nationwide dedicated to the manufacture of refrigerators, thus reducing the costs associated with carrying out these tests abroad. In this sense, the system contributes to the design of more energy-efficient and environmentally friendly chillers by identifying optimal operating points for fan efficiency. The validation of the acquisition and processing system was carried out by comparing the characteristic curve of a fan given by the manufacturer with the curve delivered by the implemented system, resulting in average errors of 7.78% for pressure and 5.38% for air flow.

Keywords: Signal acquisition and processing system · Refrigeratores · Axial fan · Fan characteristic curve · Wind tunnel-type test bench

1 Introduction

Domestic refrigerators are essential in homes to preserve food, but their constant connection to the electrical grid raises concerns about their energy consumption. Manufacturers are looking to improve energy efficiency, focusing on components such as the compressor, defrost system, and evaporator fan. Research has identified the evaporator fan as a key component in energy efficiency [1–3]. Additionally, studies on airflow in domestic refrigerators highlight the critical role

Supported by Company INDURAMA.

F. R. Narváez et al. (Eds.): SmartTech-IC 2024, CCIS 2392, pp. 165–177, 2026.
https://doi.org/10.1007/978-3-031-98287-3_12

of axial fans in reducing energy consumption while maintaining optimal airflow distribution and cooling performance [4].

Other components, such as interior lighting and control electronics, also consume energy, but to a lesser extent. Therefore, it is essential that the evaporator fan operates at an energy consumption level that allows it to reach its highest efficiency point. The type most commonly used by refrigerator manufacturers is the axial fan, which is composed of a motor, a base, and a rotating element.

Research specifically related to the performance of axial fans has also been conducted [5,6]. These investigations include testing the fans to determine their characteristic curve. This metric is crucial for manufacturers to design more efficient and environmentally friendly refrigerators [7]. However, in many cases, refrigerator manufacturers use axial fans that lack their characteristic curve. To determine this curve, it is necessary to perform tests in wind tunnel-type benches, which are expensive. When these test benches are not available in the country of the manufacturer, the ventilators must be sent to laboratories located in other countries that have these benches. This entails an additional cost for the manufacturer, which will be reflected in the final price of the appliance. In addition, since the models of these devices change frequently, the fans also change, which implies the need to perform new tests.

Due to the requirement of these tests on the fans by the manufacturers, the Universidad Politécnica Salesiana (UPS) located in Cuenca-Ecuador, in collaboration with the private company *Indurama*, decides to build a wind tunnel-type test bench under ANSI/AMCA 210-16 standard [8]. This is the tunnel where the signal acquisition and processing system is implemented to determine the characteristic curve of axial fans.

The rest of the document is established as follows, Sect. 2 defines the methodology that guided this work. Section 3 describes the design and implementation of the signal acquisition and processing system in the UPS wind tunnel-type test bench. While, Sect. 4 presents the sequence of calculations of the variables necessary to establish the fan curve. Section 5 presents the tests carried out, the results obtained, and their analysis. Finally, in Sect. 6 the conclusions are presented.

2 Methodology

In a first stage of the methodological process applied to develop this work, an investigation was carried out on the main types of fans, their characteristics, the parts that constitute them and the laws that govern them, focusing specifically on the axial type fan used by manufacturers on the refrigerator evaporator. We then focus on understanding the parameters necessary to define its characteristic curve. With all this information, we proceeded to create a state of the art of the main sensors and actuators that could be used to acquire the physical variables necessary to establish the characteristic curve of the fan.

In a second stage, the system for acquiring and processing the signals coming from the sensors was designed and implemented, for which the regulations under which the test bench was built (ANSI/AMCA 210-16) had to be followed. This regulation defines where and how the different sensors that acquire physical variables should be placed. Also at this stage, the algorithms that allow acquiring and processing the information were developed. For this purpose, the *Labview* and *Matlab* programs were used, for which the UPS has the licenses for use. Finally, in a third stage, our acquisition and processing system was validated. For this, tests were carried out on two fans, the first one having its characteristic curve given by the manufacturer and the second fan not having this curve.

3 Design and Implementation of the Acquisition and Processing System

Figure 1 shows the wind tunnel built at the UPS [8]. In segment I, which is made up of a cylindrical acrylic tube 12 cm in diameter and 10 mm thick, the test fan is placed; that is, the fan whose characteristic curve we want to obtain.

In segment II we observe the *Test chamber* that has a diameter of 48 cm, this chamber is composed of two air laminators whose function is to maintain a linear flow of air. In this segment, the static and differential pressure sensors are located with a ring-type distribution around the tunnel. The first of these sensors measures the pressure exerted by the test fan; while the second sensor measures the differential pressure before and after the nozzle grid. The nozzles open or close to regulate the air flow. According to the standard of the bank, an arrangement of 5 nozzles with diameters of 15, 20, 25, 30 and 40 mm is established. Both the static and differential pressure sensors are made up of a 5 mm diameter plastic tube ring that surrounds the circumference of the *Test chamber*. In addition, they have 4 air inlets joined by number 10 fittings and separated at an angle of 90° each. The arrangement of these pressure sensors is established according to the wind tunnel construction standard. In this same segment II there is also the RTD pt100 temperature sensor to acquire the temperature inside the *Test chamber*.

In segment III, there is an axial auxiliary fan made *Emb-papst* model 6314 N/2 TDHHP that works at 24VDC, at a power of 135 W at 3400 rpm. The function of this auxiliary fan is to extract the air flow generated by the test fan inside the tunnel.

As seen in Fig. 2, the acquisition system is made up of the static and differential pressure sensors, and the temperature sensor. All sensors connect to the National Instruments USB-6210 NI-DAQ signal acquisition card. Through a digital output of the card, the speed of the auxiliary fan (located in Segment III of the wind tunnel) is controlled using a pulse width modulator (PWM). The sensors, the auxiliary fan and test fan 1 are powered by a Delta CliQ model DRP024V240W1AA supply that delivers a stabilized voltage of 24DCV.

The pressure and temperature variables that are acquired and processed will be used in the calculation of the rest of the physical variables necessary to determine the characteristic curves of test fans 1 and 2. The process of acquiring and processing the signals coming from the sensors is carried out using LabVIEW

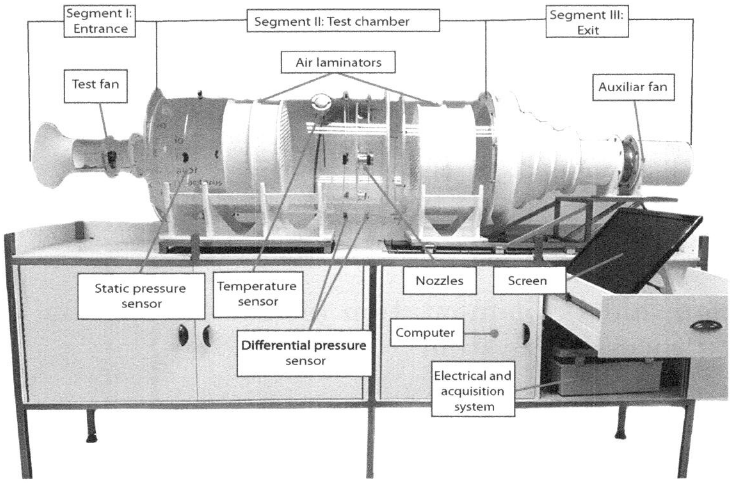

Fig. 1. Wind tunnel-type test bench built at UPS.

and MATLAB programs. The procedure begins with the activation of the test fan (located in segment I of the bench) at a nominal speed and the manual opening of nozzle 1 (the one with the smallest diameter) located in segment II of the wind tunnel. Then, in Labview, using the acquisition card, the speed of the auxiliary fan is varied. Three speeds are set V1 at 25%, V2 at 50% and V3 at 100% of the rated speed of this fan. This allows different air flows to be generated that are recorded by the pressure sensors. In each measurement, five readings are taken from the pressure and temperature sensors, then averaged to improve the reliability of the data. The opening of the nozzles is gradual, one nozzle will be opened at a time, starting with N1 until reaching N5, each time the nozzle is opened, the data is acquired at speeds V1, V2 and V3 of the auxiliary fan. The data collected is stored in an Excel database to generate the graphs using an algorithm developed in Matlab.

4 Calculations

To understand how the acquired physical variables were treated, we present the calculations performed in accordance with the ANSI/AMCA 210-16 standard [9]. This involves considering the specific configuration of the wind tunnel; as well as the environmental conditions and other constants used, which are presented in Table 1; while, Table 2 describes the rest of the physical variables, their symbols and units that intervene in the calculation process.

Nozzle Cross Section Area: In Labview it is indicated which nozzle is open for the test, based on this the program calculates its area using the Eq. 1. The value of the area will serve as data so that, later, with a Matlab algorithm the air flow can be calculated.

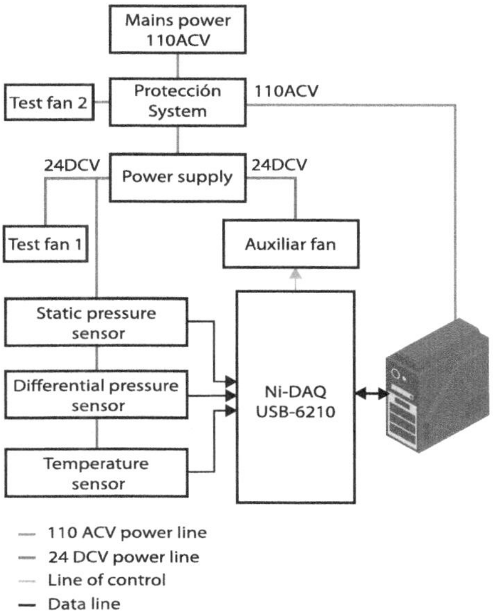

Fig. 2. Electrical and acquisition system.

$$A = \pi * (Di/2)^2 \tag{1}$$

Atmospheric Air Density: The Eq. 5 allows us to calculate the atmospheric density based on the Eqs. 3 and 4. This is based on the recorded dry bulb temperature value (through the RTD pt100 temperature sensor); while, the wet bulb temperature t_{w0} is calculated with the Eq. 2 [10].

$$\begin{aligned} t_{w0} = t_{d0} \arctan\left(0.151977\sqrt{RH + 8.313659}\right) \\ + 0.00391838\sqrt{RH^3} \arctan(0.023101HR) \\ - \arctan(RH - 1.676331) \\ + \arctan(t_{d0} + RH) - 4.686035 \end{aligned} \tag{2}$$

$$Pe = 3,25t_{w0}^2 + 18,6t_{w0} + 692 \tag{3}$$

$$Pp = Pe - Pb(\frac{t_{d0} - t_{w0}}{1500}) \tag{4}$$

$$\rho 0 = \frac{Pb - 0,378Pp}{R(t_{d0} + 273,15)} \tag{5}$$

Table 1. Environmental conditions, coefficients and gas constants

Data	Value	Units (IS)	Symbology
Dry bulb temperature	18,4	°C	t_{d0}
Barometric pressure	7545,5	Pa	P_b
Relative humidity	65,3	%	HR
Air density	1,223	kg/m^3	ρ
Altitude above sea level	2560	m	amsi
Energy coefficient	1.0	-	E
Estimated discharge coefficient	0.99	-	Ce
Gas constant	$287,1$	$J/(kg \cdot K)$	R

Table 2. Physical variables used in calculation, symbols and units

Variable	Symbology	Units (IS)
Nozzle area	A	m^2
Nozzle internal diameter	D_i	m
Vapor saturation pressure	P_e	Pa
Wet bulb temperature	t_{wo}	C
Partial vapor pressure	P_p	Pa
Atmospheric air density	ρ_0	kg/m^3
Density of air in a duct in the x plane	ρ_x	kg/m^3
Static pressure in the x plane	P_{sx}	Pa
Viscosity	μ	$Pa \cdot s$
Alpha radio	α	-
Presión diferencial	ΔP	Pa
Beta radio	β	-
Expansion factor	Y	-
Reynolds number	Re	-
Discharge coefficient	C	-
Internal diameter of test chamber	D	m
Dry bulb temperature in the x plane	t_{dx}	C
Air flow for the chamber nozzle	Q	m^3/s

Duct Air Density in an x Plane: It is the density of air in a duct or chamber in the x plane, and is defined as ρ_x. This value is calculated through the Eq. 6, where the atmospheric density of the air ρ_0 is corrected for the static pressure P_{sx} (obtained from the sensor), and the dry bulb temperature t_{dx} (obtained from the RTD pt100 temperature sensor), both in the x plane.

$$\rho_x = \rho_0 \left[\frac{t_{d0} + 273,165}{t_{dx} + 273,15} \right] \left[\frac{P_{sx} + P_b}{P_b} \right] \tag{6}$$

Dynamic Air Viscosity: The Eq. 7 describes the dynamic viscosity of air, which is a measure of the ability of a fluid to resist deformation or flow. In general, this value tends to increase in gases as their temperature increases.

$$\mu = (17,23 + 0,048 t_{d0})\, 10^{-6} \tag{7}$$

Alpha Radio: This parameter refers to the relationship between the differential pressure (between the inlet and outlet of the nozzle ΔP obtained from the differential pressure sensor), divided by the product of the air density, the gas constant and the temperature in Celsius degrees with respect to absolute zero. Alpha radius is calculated with the Eq. 8.

$$\alpha = 1 \left[\frac{\Delta P}{\rho \cdot R \left(t_{d0} + 273,15 \right)} \right] \tag{8}$$

Beta Radio: It is the relationship between the nozzle outlet diameter and the diameter of the test chamber, as indicated in the Eq. 9.

$$\beta = \frac{D_i}{D} \tag{9}$$

Expansion Factor: In the case of nozzles, the values of the expansion factor Y for gases can be calculated with sufficient precision using the Eq. 10.

$$Y = 1 - (0,548 + 0,71\beta^4)\,(1 - \alpha) \tag{10}$$

Reynolds Number: Reynolds number is a dimensionless parameter that indicates whether the fluid has laminar flow or turbulent flow and is calculated using the Eq. 11.

$$Re = \frac{\sqrt{2}}{\mu} C_e \cdot D_i \cdot Y \cdot \sqrt{\frac{\Delta P \cdot \rho}{1 - E \cdot \beta^4}} \tag{11}$$

Discharge Coefficient: The discharge coefficient is a dimensionless parameter inherent to the nozzles that characterizes their efficiency in fluid flow. This coefficient is calculated with the Eq. 12.

$$C = 0,9986 - \left(\frac{7,006}{\sqrt{Re}} \right) + \left(\frac{134,6}{Re} \right) \tag{12}$$

Air Flow for the Test Chamber Nozzle: The air flow at the inlet of a nozzle or several nozzles with approach from the test chamber refers to the amount of air that enters through these holes, as described in the Eq. 13.

$$Q = Y \cdot \sqrt{\frac{2\Delta P}{\rho}} \sum (C \cdot A) \tag{13}$$

5 Analysis of Results

The data to obtain the characteristic curve of the test fan comes, as we mentioned, from the acquisition of the physical variables of static pressure, differential and temperature acquired using the NI-DAQ USB-6210 card from National

Instruments in Labview (remember Fig. 2). The normalization and calculation of the rest of the variables (Sect. 4) necessary to determine the flow rate is carried out through an algorithm in MATLAB.

Let us remember that the measured values of the static pressure in the x plane P_{sx} and the calculated values of the flow rate Q (Eq. 13) are recorded for each speed (V1, V2 and V3) of the auxiliary fan every time a nozzle opens. As there are 3 speeds and 5 nozzles, 15 values of both pressure and flow are obtained. These data are stored in an Excel database. Then, using another algorithm in MATLAB that reads the database, the pressure points are plotted on the y axis and the flow rate on the x axis. Finally, a polynomial of degree 7 that is expressed in the Eq. 14 is used to establish the trend curve from the distribution of the 15 values.

$$F(x) = p1 \cdot x^7 + p2 \cdot x^6 + p3 \cdot x^5 + p4 \cdot x^4 + p5 \cdot x^3 + p6 \cdot x^2 + p7 \cdot x + p8 \quad (14)$$

In order to validate whether our signal acquisition and processing system works correctly, a first test was carried out in which the curve of a fan given by the manufacturer and the curve obtained by our implemented system were compared.

5.1 Test 1

For test 1, we worked with the UltraFlo T92T24MUA7 [11] Axial Fan, with a 24 VDC power supply and a nominal current of 0.14A, this fan does have its characteristic curve provided by the manufacturer. Figure 3 shows the comparison between the curve of the manufacturer and the curve resulting from our acquisition and processing system. It can be seen that both curves are similar, although they are not identical, the difference between the two curves is attributed to the different environmental conditions with which both the tests with the UPS bench and the tests with the bench of the manufacturer was carried out.

From the comparison of the characteristic curves, the average percentage error is calculated with the Eq. 15, which allows us to evaluate the precision of the data obtained in the UPS test bench..

$$\text{Error\%} = \frac{|x_1 - x_2|}{x_2} \times 100 \quad (15)$$

where (x_1) represents the manufacturer curve data and (x_2) represents the UPS test bench curve data.

To determine the error, in the first instance, the comparison of pressures is carried out, for this, the pressure values are taken from both the manufacturer curve and the UPS test bench curve at the same reference flow rate value, as indicated in Table 3. In a second instance, the flow rates are compared, now taking at the same reference pressure values (see Table 4). The values obtained show an average error in the pressure comparison of 7.78% and flow rate of 5.38%.

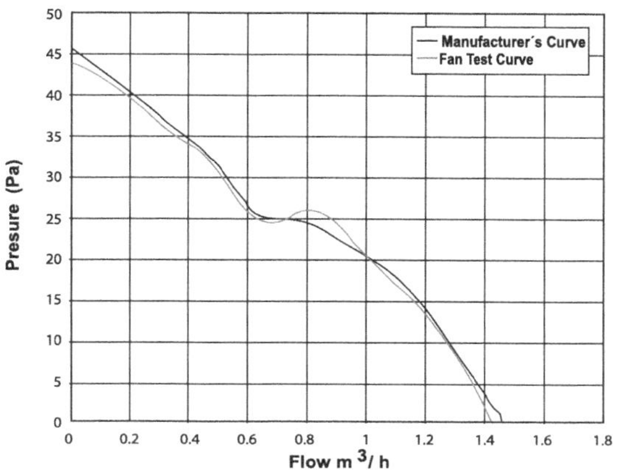

Fig. 3. NIDEC manufacturer curve vs UPS bench test fan curve.

Table 3. Pressure comparison between the manufacturer characteristic curve and the UPS test bench characteristic curve.

Reference flow values (m^3/h)	Manufacturer curve pressure values (Pa)	UPS test bench curve pressure values (Pa)	Pressure percentage errors
0	45.72	44.01	3.73%
0.2	40.46	39.68	1.92%
0.4	34.5	34.06	1.28%
0.6	26.72	25.52	4.49%
0.8	24.43	25.79	5.57%
1	20.3	20.13	0.84%
1.2	13.82	13.25	4.12%
1.4	3.4	2.03	40.29%
Average percentage error			7.78%

5.2 Test 2

Once it has been verified that our acquisition and processing system provides a curve similar to that delivered by the manufacturer (with an acceptable error). A second test was carried out, with the objective of determining the characteristic curve of the axial fan model DAI 6102SMCA1 (115V/0.18A/10W/60 Hz), which does not have its curve supplied by the manufacturer. The resulting curve is seen in Fig. 4.

Table 4. Flow comparison between the manufacturer characteristic curve and the UPS test bench characteristic curve.

Reference pressure values (Pa)	Manufacturer curve flow values (m^3/h)	UPS test bench curve flow values (m^3/h)	Flow percentage errors
40.46	0.2	0.17	15%
34.5	0.4	0.36	10%
26.72	0.6	0.58	3.33%
24.43	0.8	0.75	6.25%
20.3	1	1	0%
13.82	1.2	1.18	1.67%
3.4	1.4	1.38	1.43%
Average percentage error			5.38%

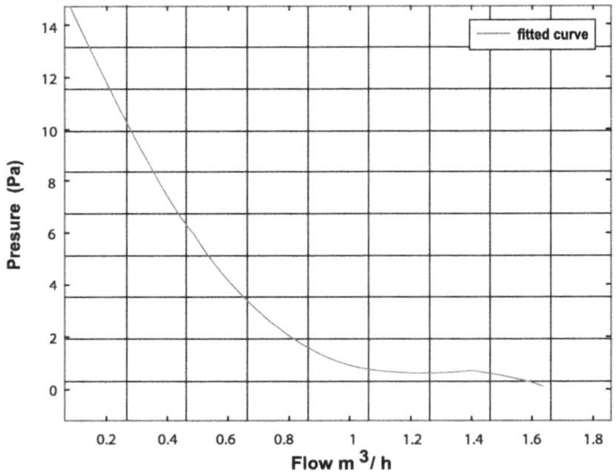

Fig. 4. Characteristic curve of the fan DAI 6102SMCA1.

6 Discussion

An important aspect of this work is the ability of the acquisition and processing system to determine the characteristic curve of a fan that does not have its characteristic curve provided by the manufacturer. This allows refrigerator manufacturers to know the curves of their fans purchased from a manufacturer that does not provide them, which reduces the costs associated with sending these fans to other countries in the region to perform such tests. Similarly, other studies to determine the curve of a fan have been carried out; for example, in [12] it stands out the importance of experimentally determining the operating points of fans through laboratory exercises, where the impedance curves of the fan and the designed system are superimposed to predict the optimal operating point of the fan. The methodology ensures high accuracy, with predictions often within a 2% error margin, demonstrating the robustness of the experimental setups for determining fan performance in real-world applications.

As evidenced in [13], determining the fan characteristic curve allows refrigerator manufacturers to obtain important metrics such as the operating point and the power consumption in watts at the point of maximum performance. Although the calculation of these metrics was beyond the scope of this work, it is possible to determine the optimal operating point of the fan and its power consumption at that point, which is crucial for designing more efficient evaporators. With this data, manufacturers can optimize refrigerator ducts and structures, ensuring that the fan operates more efficiently by consuming the energy necessary to reach its highest performance.

Systems such as those presented in [14], like our proposal, offer a practical solution for local refrigerator manufacturers, as they allow them to carry out tests without having to send fans to laboratories abroad, which, as we have mentioned, reduces testing costs and therefore production costs, contributing to the optimization of resources; which is particularly important in Latin American markets where import and export costs are high.

The implementation of experimental and theoretical methodologies, as demonstrated in [15], highlights the importance of optimizing evaporator configurations for domestic refrigeration. The integration of experimental prototypes with computational models in that work allowed a systematic evaluation of heat transfer and pressure drop, achieving material reductions of up to 40% while maintaining system efficiency. Similarly, the wind tunnel system presented in the present study, allows the validation and optimization of fan performance by knowing its characteristic curve, ensuring better evaporator fan performance in a refrigerator, guaranteeing adequate energy consumption. These synergies underline the relevance of fan test benches, allowing local industries to access cost-effective solutions without compromising the accuracy or robustness of their equipment.

An important consideration is the influence of environmental conditions, such as temperature, humidity and atmospheric pressure, which can alter measurements. In some wind tunnels, air can be heated to a specific temperature to evaluate performance under various environmental conditions [16]. This approach could be considered for future improvements to the acquisition and processing system presented in this work, in order to expand the testing capabilities of the system. However, the interface of our system developed in Labview allows the configuration of the environmental conditions of a given location, which enables greater flexibility to perform tests in case it is necessary to manipulate the environmental conditions; in addition to allowing the bench to be moved and installed in another geographic location.

7 Conclusions

This paper presents the development and implementation of a signal acquisition and processing system to determine the characteristic curve of axial fans used in domestic refrigerator evaporators. The system installed in a wind tunnel test bench built under the ANSI/AMCA 210-16 standard at the Universidad Politécnica Salesiana (UPS), allows accurate measurements of static pressure, differential pressure and temperature. The implemented system aimed to determine the characteristic curve of axial fans, because refrigerator manufacturers, in some cases, purchase fans without their characteristic curve.

The first validation test demonstrated that the system is capable of generating a characteristic curve similar to that of the manufacturer. The errors of 7.78% for pressure and 5.38% for air flow are within acceptable ranges, considering that the environmental conditions in Cuenca, Ecuador, differ from those at the manufacturer's site. These results demonstrate that the signal acquisition and processing system is valid for performing fan tests and obtaining reliable characteristic curves under local conditions.

The system developed in this work offers a solution for refrigerator manufacturers nationwide to perform fan performance tests in Ecuador, reducing the costs associated with sending fans abroad for testing, which allows for the optimization of resources by building more energy-efficient and environmentally friendly refrigerators, thanks to the identification, in the characteristic curve, of the optimal performance point of the evaporator fan.

References

1. Raveendran, P.S., Sekhar, S.J.: Investigation on the energy and exergy efficiencies of a domestic refrigerator retrofitted with water-cooled condensers of shell-and-coil and brazed-plate heat exchangers. J. Therm. Anal. Calorim. **136**(1), 381–388 (2019)
2. Costa, G., Namal, D.A.: Analysis of energy efficiency of domestic refrigerators. Engineer **52**(03), 43–50 (2019)
3. Shikalgar, N.: Energy and exergy analysis of a domestic refrigerator: approaching a sustainable refrigerator. J. Thermal Eng. **5**(5), 469–481 (2019)
4. Energetica21, "Eficiencia energética de los sistemas de refrigeración," https://www.energetica21.com/articulos-y-entrevistas-online-ver/eficiencia-energetica-de-los-sistemas-de-refrigeracion (2024). Accessed 20 Nov 2024
5. Gue, F., Cheong, C., Kim, T.: Development of low-noise axial cooling fans in a household refrigerator. J. Mech. Sci. Technol. **25**, 2995–3004 (2011)
6. Silva, R.L., Brito, S.X., Jr.: Experimental evaluation of energy efficiency and velocity fields on a low-pressure axial flow fan (desktop type). Energ. Effi. **12**(3), 697–710 (2019)
7. Salvador, E.: Manual Práctico de Ventilación. Salvador S.A, Barcelona (2013)
8. Jara-Cobos, N., Cevallos-González, J., Reinoso-Avecillas, F., Ordoñez-Morales, E., Isaza-Roldán, C., Bernal-Pesantez, B.: "Banco de ensayos tipo túnel de viento para la selección de ventiladores de refrigeradores domésticos,." Actualidad de la Ingeniería Mecánica en Iberoamerica **14**(1), 300–306 (2019)

9. Air Movement and Control Association International, *Laboratory methods of testing fans for certified Aerodynamic Performance Rating*, Atlanta (2016)
10. Bohren, C.F., Albrecht, B.A.: Atmospheric Thermodynamics. Oxford University Press (1998)
11. NIDEC CORPORATION, "Nidec corporation." https://www.nidec.com/en/
12. Edwards, R.: A laboratory exercise to demonstrate how to experimentally determine the operating point for a fan. In: Annual Conference & Exposition, vol. 2007, pp. 12–55 (2007)
13. Vanaei, H.R., et al.: Performance and efficiency of cross-flow fans–a review. Energies **16**(23), 7798 (2023)
14. Mahlia, T., Saidur, R.: A review on test procedure, energy efficiency standards and energy labels for room air conditioners and refrigerator-freezers. Renew. Sustain. Energy Rev. **14**(7), 1888–1900 (2010)
15. Belman-Flores, J., Barroso-Maldonado, J., Rodríguez-Muñoz, A., Camacho-Vázquez, G.: Enhancements in domestic refrigeration, approaching a sustainable refrigerator-a review. Renew. Sustain. Energy Rev. **51**, 955–968 (2015)
16. OMEGA Tunel de viento, "Importancia de pruebas de túnel de viento en laboratorio." https://mx.omega.com/technical-learning

Exams as a Service: Synergies Between ChatGPT, and Cloud Computing for Education

Gustavo Navas(✉), Julio Proaño-Orellana, Rogelio Orizondo, and Alex Terreros

IDEIAGEOCA Research Group, University Politecnica Salesiana, Moran Valverde S/N, Quito, Ecuador
{gnavas,jproanoo,rorizondo,aterreros}@ups.edu.ec

Abstract. Institutions are increasingly adopting advanced technologies to enhance learning experiences in the evolving landscape of education. This paper introduces the concept of Exams as a Service (EaaS), leveraging the synergies between ChatGPT, natural language processing (NLP), and cloud computing to automate and personalize the process of question generation and assessment. By integrating these technologies, the proposed system offers a scalable platform for educators to create customized exams, deliver real-time feedback, and dynamically adjust assessments to suit the needs of individual learners. This approach reduces the workload associated with traditional assessment methods and enhances the overall quality of education by providing adaptive, AI-driven learning experiences.

Keywords: ChatGPT · Artificial Intelligence · Exams as a Service · Education · Cloud Computing

1 Introduction

Education is vital for providing economic opportunities [1]. In recent years, educational institutions have had to adapt and innovate in response to the era of technology. The increasing prevalence of the Internet in educational settings has caused a shift in curriculum delivery from traditional desktops to online applications [10].

Despite these advancements, educators still grapple with significant challenges, particularly in developing practical and effective questions for many students. Writing such questions is complex, requiring overcoming shortcomings such as ambiguity, vagueness, assumptions of prior knowledge, inconsistencies across questions, unclear instructions, and inadequate feedback mechanisms. These challenges underscore the need for innovative educational solutions, particularly those involving artificial intelligence (AI).

Supported by Universidad Politécnica Salesiana.

F. R. Narváez et al. (Eds.): SmartTech-IC 2024, CCIS 2392, pp. 178–192, 2026.
https://doi.org/10.1007/978-3-031-98287-3_13

The creation of traditional questions is a laborious, time-consuming, and costly process. Moreover, manual evaluation of responses adds to the workload. However, the advent of automated question generation using AI offers a promising solution, alleviating these burdens for educators and allowing them to focus more on teaching and guiding students.

Natural Language Processing (NLP) is a specialized field of AI that focuses on human-like text comprehension [9]. Recent advances in generative pretraining transformer (GPT) technology has significantly improved the capabilities of NLP systems enable breakthroughs in language translation, summarization, question answering, and other cognitive tasks [24]. ChatGPT, developed by OpenAI, is one of the most widely used versions of GPT. Its application has expanded across various knowledge domains, including education [2,23]. ChatGPT can comprehend and respond to queries in natural language, making it highly effective for creating practice exercises, explanations, and quizzes for various subjects. Students can use ChatGPT to brainstorm ideas, generate outlines, and receive feedback on their writing assignments.

Educators and researchers have leveraged the capabilities of the ChatGPT model, which is hosted on scalable cloud computing infrastructure. This combination has enabled them to design questions and assessments that accurately measure student comprehension and provide valuable learning experiences. The scalability of cloud computing ensures that the system can easily accommodate a growing number of users, making it a highly efficient and adaptable educational tool.

This research explores the potential benefits of integrating ChatGPT and cloud computing to tackle educators' challenges in developing questions and offering exams as a service (EaaS). We aim to create a more personalized, efficient, and adaptable learning environment by leveraging these technologies.

Objectives and Contributions:

- To investigate the effectiveness of ChatGPT in generating diverse and high-quality educational questions.
- To develop a scalable cloud-based platform that integrates ChatGPT for automated question generation and evaluation (Machine Teaching).
- To evaluate the proposed architecture.

The remainder of the paper is organized as follows: Sect. 2 presents the related work, providing a theoretical and comparative framework. Section 3 outlines the system architecture, detailing its components and design. Section 4 explains the technical aspects of the implementation. Section 5 discusses the tests conducted to evaluate the proposed architecture's performance. Finally, the last Section offers the conclusions and suggests future work.

2 Related Work

Recent advancements have focused on building automated systems for generating and evaluating learners' questions. For instance, in [7], the authors developed an automated system for question generation. In [21], the authors proposed a solution using natural language processing (NLP) and image captioning techniques capable of generating questions for both textual and visual inputs. Additionally, the [8] highlighted the importance of automated question generation in learning technologies, while [22] emphasized the need for proxy tasks to evaluate reading comprehension. The [19] addressed the challenges in question generation, including selecting target content and question type, proposing a system using supervised learning, and the Naïve Bayes method. These studies collectively underscore the potential of AI in automating question generation and its applications in various domains.

Integrating ChatGPT, NLP, and cloud computing in educational question development presents opportunities and challenges [16]. ChatGPT can provide personalized and interactive learning experiences [17] through NLP-based personal learning assistants [14], which offer accurate and reliable input to students [3]. In [12], the authors introduced VidVersityQG, an AI-based solution that automatically generates assessment questions from pre-recorded video lectures, significantly reducing the time and effort required by educators. In [6], the authors presented a platform for active learning that uses cloud computing services to generate dynamic questions and provide real-time feedback to students, enhancing the learning experience.

Recent advancements in automatic question generation have been made by integrating ChatGPT and cloud computing. Researchers [11,25] have developed systems employing techniques such as part-of-speech tagging, syntactic analysis, and named entity extraction to create valid questionnaires and propose different types of questions. The [5] demonstrated the effectiveness of ChatGPT in question generation, showing that it can compete with or outperform other models. The authors [13] proposed a scalable question-answer generation system utilizing assistive information and neural question generators to produce high-quality question-answer pairs. These studies collectively highlight the immense potential of ChatGPT and cloud computing in automating the question-generation process.

3 System Architecture

Exams as a Service (EaaS) is a computational model that manages a platform for conducting exams and tests for university students under the service paradigm.

This platform leverages the ChatGPT API for question generation. It integrates with a cloud-based microservices system, optimizing real-time processing and dynamic scalability to accommodate institutions with large student populations.

The proposed architecture for (EaaS) is organized into three main layers, as shown in Fig. 1, each playing a specific role in the system. At the top layer is the Management layer, which is responsible for administering and monitoring the assessment system. This layer includes user management, test assignment, and report generation functionalities. This layer coordinates the system and controls the interactions between the other layers, ensuring that all operations are performed efficiently and effectively.

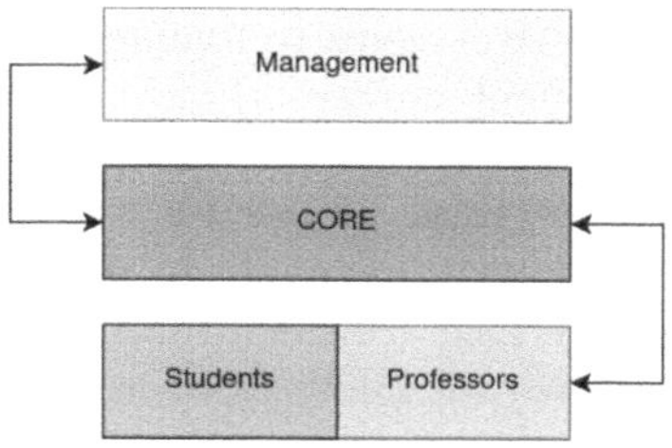

Fig. 1. Layered Architecture for EaaS.

The middle layer, the Core, is the architecture's central and most important part. This layer is responsible for business logic and assessment processing. This is where assessment algorithms, database management, and the logic determining how tests are presented and graded are implemented. Finally, the two lowest layers are dedicated to students and teachers, providing specific interfaces for each group. Students access their assessments and study resources through their layer, while teachers can design tests, evaluate responses, and access detailed analytics in their layer. These layers ensure that students and teachers have intuitive and efficient access to the necessary tools and functionalities.

The Core layer of the proposed architecture for managing and administering tests to university students using generative LLMs is composed of several key components that interact in a coordinated manner to ensure the correct functioning of the system, as shown in Fig. 2. First, API connections to the chatbot allow for interaction between the central system and the chatbot. The latter is responsible for generating the questions and grading the students' lessons, facilitating test-taking, and immediate feedback. The control layer of these interactions ensures fluid and secure communication between the different components of the system.

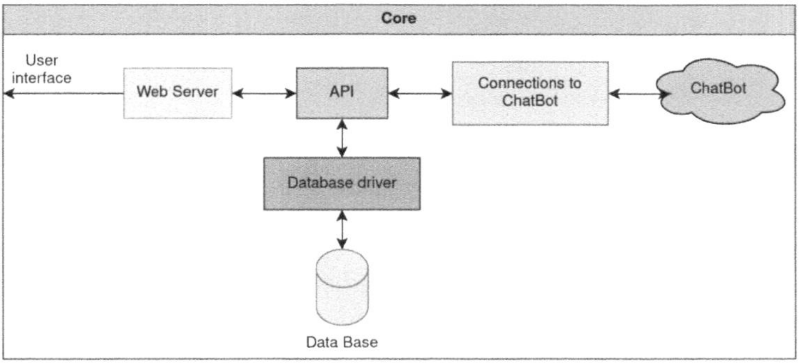

Fig. 2. Layer Core.

In addition, the database driver helps to manage connections and operations in the database. This component ensures that read and write operations are performed efficiently, protecting data integrity and security. The chatbot web server handles incoming and outgoing requests between students and the central system, ensuring a fast and accurate response to user interactions.

The database and user interface are essential components that complete the Core layer. The database stores all information relevant to the system's operation, including student data, lesson prompts, test results, and questions and answers. The user interface allows students to access the system, take tests, and receive feedback effectively.

Figure 3 describes the user interface layer of the architecture for managing and testing using generative LLMs, designed to offer an interactive and functional experience to students and teachers. Several specific views are highlighted in this layer that allow the generation, testing, and correction of lessons and tests. The view for generating lesson prompts facilitates the creation of dynamic and adaptive educational content. In contrast, the CRUD view allows management administrators to create, read, update, and delete operations on user and content data.

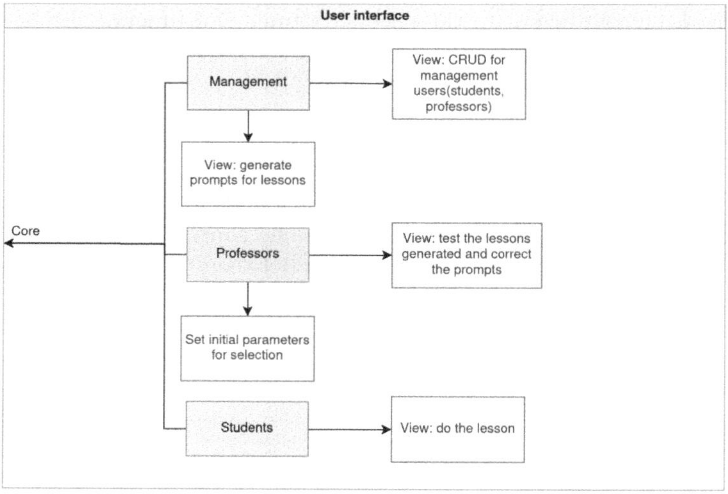

Fig. 3. Layer User Interface (Management, Students, and Professors).

The interface also includes a section dedicated to teachers, where they can test generated lessons, correct prompts, and set initial parameters for content selection. This functionality ensures that educational materials are accurate, relevant, and appropriate for learning objectives. In addition, teachers can adjust and refine lessons based on test results and student feedback.

However, the student view allows students to complete the lessons. This view is designed to be intuitive and accessible, providing a fluid user experience that facilitates learning and continuous assessment. These UI components work with the architecture's core layer, ensuring that content creation management and user interaction are fast.

EaaS is a concept that involves providing system-generated questions tailored to the instructor's specific needs. This approach integrates the API of a Large Language Model (LLM), such as the ChatGPT 4.0 API, into the platform and allows for storing the LLM's responses in a relational database. This database stores the chatbot prompts, student responses, and the automated responses and grades provided by the chatbot's API. This is implemented in a cloud environment with a system architecture based on microservices using Docker. Below are some essential features and conditions for EaaS:

1. **LLM Processing System:** The platform can understand and generate questions formulated in natural language using the LLM API. This facilitates student interaction during exams, as the API can generate, modify, or expand a question to present it to the student.
2. **LLM Feedback and Grading:** The system provides feedback and a grade to the student immediately after responding to a system question.
3. **Updated and Expansive Knowledge Base:** Maintaining a dynamic database that is recurrently updated to include new information, such as new exams, new prompts for exam management, grades, feedback provided by the LLM API and student responses to exam questions.
4. **Intuitive User Interface:** A good user experience (UX/UI) ensures ease of use for both those formulating the questions and those managing the responses in the back-end [15].
5. **Survey and Continuous Improvement:** A mechanism that allows students and professors to rate the user experience (UX), complementing the previous point and providing feedback on the system's grades and scores and the overall user experience [15].
6. **Continuous Accessibility:** The service must be available 24/7 to allow usage anytime, maximising user functionality in different time zones. To achieve this, cloud services, such as Google Cloud Platform, facilitate this condition.
7. **Independent Scalability:** The growth in resource usage and cost reduction, as well as scalability of the system according to its specific needs, are achieved through microservices. Microservices are well suited to cloud infrastructures, allowing better utilisation of scalability and management capabilities [4].
8. **Ease of Continuous Integration and Continuous Delivery (CI/CD):** The modular nature of microservices facilitates the implementation of Continuous Integration and Continuous Delivery (CI/CD) practices, enabling automated testing, continuous integration and faster and more secure deployments [20].

4 Implementation Details

Implementing a highly efficient exam-as-a-service (EaaS) system requires integrating a complex combination of advanced artificial intelligence technologies, specialised human resources, and meticulously articulated business strategies. Focusing development on user experience (UX), understanding their needs and how these services can add value to their experiences, and solving specific problems.

The proposed architecture employs Google Cloud Platform (GCP) cloud services, where a virtual machine is hosted with Ubuntu Server 22.04 LTS. In this instance, Docker runs and manages four containers: two for the backend developed in Python and two for the front end implemented in JavaScript. The developed system is AIQuest and is available at https://aiquest.ideiageoca.org/.

Figure 4 presents the proposed architecture of the distributed system, which integrates multiple interconnected technologies and components for conducting tests or exams administered to university students.

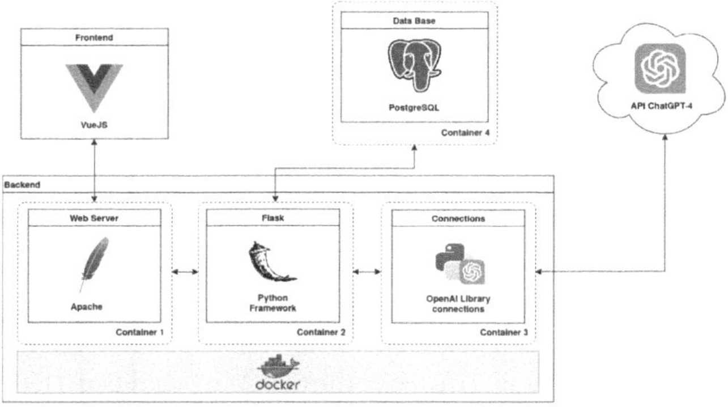

Fig. 4. Containers used for system deployment.

1. **Exam Management Platform (frontend):** The architecture includes a web client accessible to both students and professors.
2. **Application Server (backend):** It consists of three containers that manage the web server, the handling of business rules (Managing Business Rules, MBR), and the connections between the Chatbot API and MBR.
3. **Database:** The fourth container is where the database is housed.
4. **Connection API** The integration with the ChatGPT-4.0 API facilitates advanced features, such as assistance in drafting exam questions, interpreting written responses, and providing instant feedback to students. Additionally, a connection is established with the system to ensure smooth and efficient operation.

4.1 Frontend

The front-end system is developed as a type of SPA web application, and the VueJS 3 framework is used to develop this type of application. SPA applications allow high-speed interaction and navigation between the system screens, improving the experience for the platform users. The Axios library is used for connections with the backend, which allows handling HTTP requests such as GET and POST. The Katex library allows for the formatting of mathematical equations in Latex, which helps students write complex mathematical formulas so that they can understand the chatGPT-4 model. All the front-end development uses an Apache server in its version 2.4.52.

4.2 Database

The database in this architecture allows for the storage of user information. PostgreSQL version 16.1 is used to manage this data. The tables contain user data, lessons, questions, generated prompts, preset prompts, grades, and feedback for each lesson. PostgreSQL was chosen because it is robust and offers high performance to handle concurrent transactions during periods of high demand, such as during exams where multiple students interact with the platform.

4.3 Backend and Connections

Python and the Flask 2.1.3 framework were used in the development. The connection to the OpenAI ChatGPT 4.0 API service [18] was made using the official Python library, version 1.3.5. See Fig. 5.

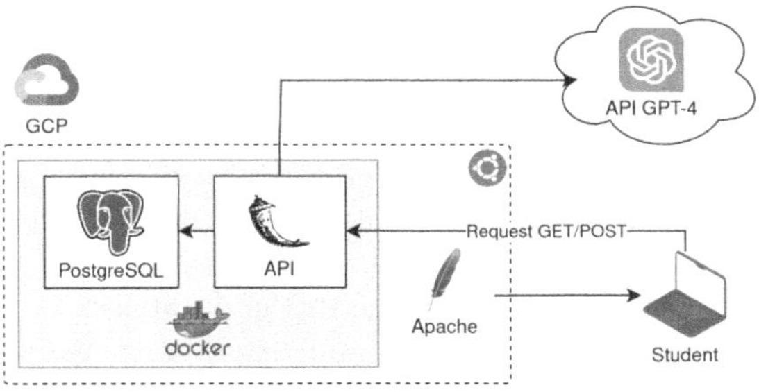

Fig. 5. connection between the student, the evaluation platform, and the GPT-4 API.

This library allows prompts to be sent to the GPT-4 model and responses received in text string format. Specifying a response format in the prompts is possible to expedite subsequent processing. The data is sent to the platform's front end in JSON format. The API includes different endpoints to validate and authenticate users and allow assessments within the system. Each request includes a user validation token with RSA encryption, ensuring the security of queries made to the API. Requests requiring the use of GPT-4 utilize a connection model to this external API, where the prompt is added and the response is processed.

4.4 Types of Assessments

The platform offers two types of assessments: static and dynamic. In static assessments, all students receive an identical question. In dynamic assessments, the question is generated by GPT-4 based on a prompt previously stored in the database, allowing specific aspects of the question to be modified and creating a different version for each student. The automation in the generation and evaluation of questions enables frequent and scalable assessments, reducing the workload for professors and allowing institutions to manage large volumes of students. In both cases, feedback is provided to students on their responses, allowing them to identify and correct errors in subsequent attempts.

Two generic modes have been established for this process to show the students' Testing operation.

The first mode is based on the previously explained static assessment. Figure 6 illustrates the student's evaluation process, which begins with logging into the AIQuest system, signing in, and accessing the platform. The student clicks on the test link. The sequence diagram in Fig. 6 shows how the student interacts with the system when accessing the training test. In this case, AIQuest retrieves the prompt from the database *promptDB*, previously tested in ChatGPT 4.0 and stored in the database. Since it is stored in the database, the ChatGPT API does not need to process this question, as the *promptDB* is invariant and already recorded.

The student receives the prompt and responds in the available space, generating the *promptStu*. The *promptDB*, along with the *promptStu*, are integrated into a single prompt in the system, called *promptSys*, and sent to the ChatGPT 4.0 API for evaluation. A score out of 10 and textual feedback evaluating the quality of the student's response are requested. This evaluation, called *promptAPIGrade*, is processed by the system, and the relevant part, which includes the feedback and the score out of 10, is presented to the student. The *promptDBStorage* is the resulting prompt from the union of *promptStu* and *promptAPIGrade* in JSON format, and it is sent for storage in the database.

The student can return to the test and attempt it again. The maximum number of attempts is set to five. The student may only use some of the attempts, as the system also provides the average score obtained from the attempts.

The second mode is based on the previously explained dynamic assessment. The student logs into the system and clicks on the test link. The sequence diagram is shown in Fig. 7 illustrates how the student interacts with the system when accessing the test. In this case, AIQuest retrieves a prompt from the database, called *promptDB*, which has been tested with ChatGPT 4.0 and stored in the database. This prompt is sent to the ChatGPT API to introduce the required changes, which consist of inserting an error into one of the four literals that are correctly resolved in the *promptDB*. The prompt modified by the API, *promptAPIQ*, is sent to the student to be answered by locating and describing the error and identifying the literal where it is found.

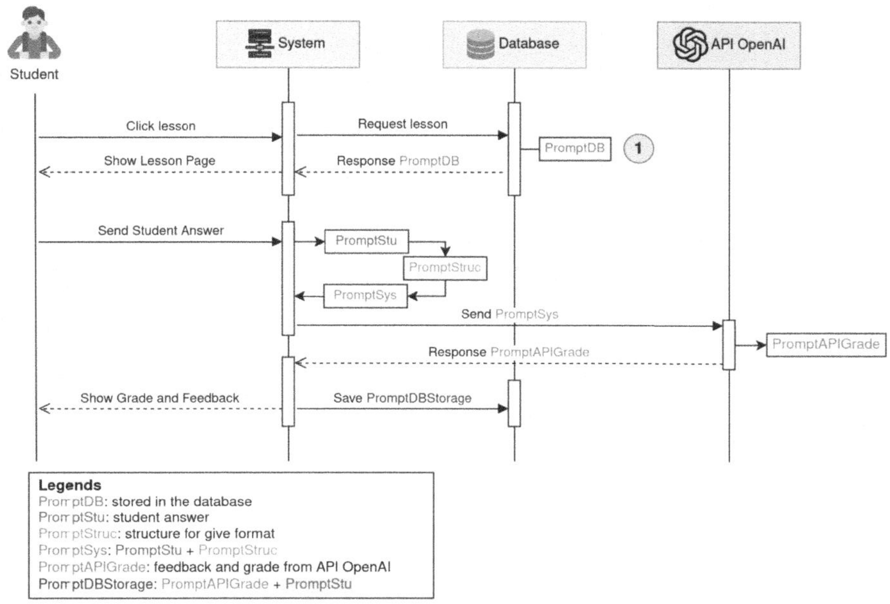

Fig. 6. First mode: Sequence diagram of the static test case study.

This approach provides a controlled, scalable and secure environment for exam administration, leveraging modern technologies, and cloud services.

5 Architecture Evaluation

The analysis of Fig. 8 provides context for the system test results to the principles and objectives outlined in this study. The cloud-based microservices architecture supporting the evaluation system is designed to handle scalability and deliver efficient performance as demand grows. In this context, the load test graph evaluates several critical aspects. Figure 8 shows a system load test with three graphs representing different performance aspects.

5.1 Scalability and Services

Three EaaS architectures, built on containers and microservices, enable the system to scale flexibly and efficiently based on demand. The test graph illustrates:

- **The number of users (bottom graph)** consistently increases, demonstrating the system's ability to scale effectively up to 1,000 concurrent users.

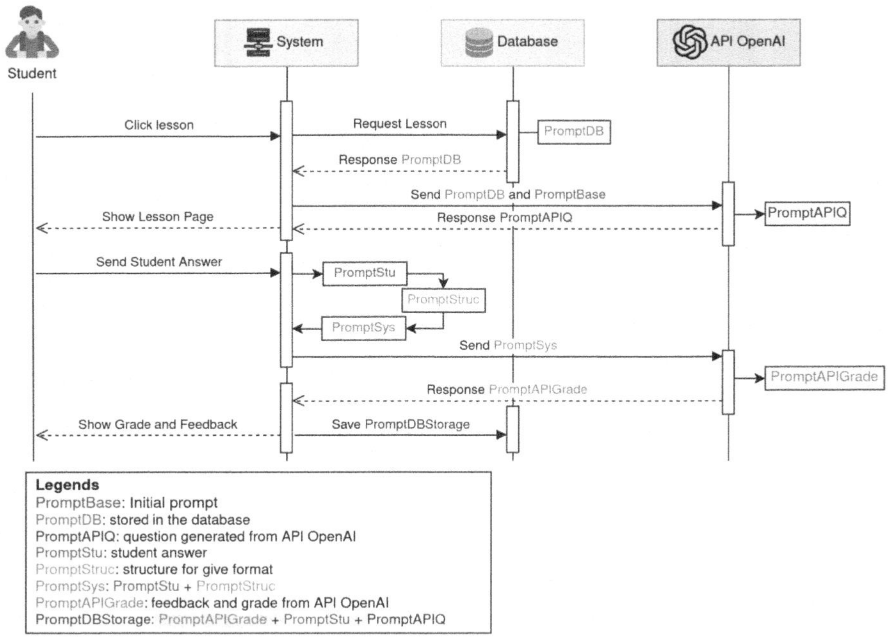

Fig. 7. Second mode: Sequence diagram of the Calculus dynamic test case study.

- **The total requests per second (top graph)** show an upward trend with peaks near 30 requests per second. However, fluctuations suggest the need to fine-tune scalability parameters to maintain a more stable load distribution under fluctuating demand.

5.2 Performance and Response Times

The test underscores the importance of a robust PostgreSQL database and efficient connection to the ChatGPT API to manage student responses and evaluations. The response time graph (middle graph) highlights:

- **The average response time** gradually increases as the load rises, which is expected but remains within acceptable limits for most users.
- **95th Percentile:** Response times of up to 60,000 ms (60 s) suggest that many users experience long wait times, potentially indicating saturation in the ChatGPT API connection during high-demand periods. Although the number of concurrent students has not been substantial, future work proposes measures to address a possible increase in user volume.

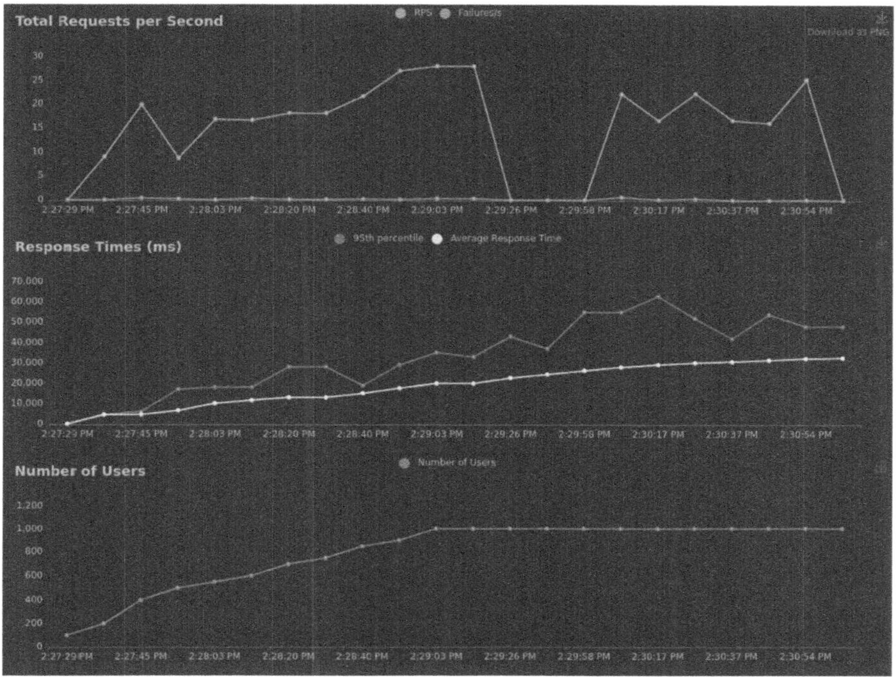

Fig. 8. Total request per second

5.3 Stability and Failures

Despite the increasing load, the failure rate remains zero, reflecting the system's stability. This confirms the study's findings regarding the system's resilience, leveraging the microservices-based architecture to ensure high availability and robustness.

5.4 Integration with the ChatGPT API and System Performance

The article highlights the integration with the ChatGPT API as a critical element in generating dynamic questions and providing real-time feedback to students. However, under high-load conditions, the system may become less efficient regarding response times, as reflected in the high latency observed in the 95th percentile.

6 Conclusions and Future Work

The investigation demonstrates that integrating advanced AI models, such as ChatGPT, with cloud computing can transform education by enabling the creation of personalized exams and assessments. The system adheres to scalability, stability, and efficiency principles in evaluation. This combination allows educators to design adaptive tests and provide real-time feedback, enhancing the students' learning experience.

The synergy between ChatGPT and cloud computing has resulted in a more interactive and adaptive learning environment, which can significantly improve educational outcomes. The system promotes a more engaging and interactive learning process by offering immediate feedback and dynamically adjusting questions. This encourages continuous learning and helps students better understand their mistakes.

Automation in question creation and assessment has optimized the time and resources spent by educators, allowing them to focus more on teaching rather than exam preparation. The platform automates both question generation and evaluation. This approach ensures that assessments are regularly updated and tailored to the specific needs of each student.

ChatGPT's ability to generate questions and provide personalized feedback highlights the importance of adapting educational content to individual student needs. Creating a cloud-based platform for exam management (Exams as a Service, EaaS) has proven to be a scalable and cost-effective solution for educational institutions aiming to modernize their assessment methods. This makes it an evolving tool in the education sector. Implementing EaaS and AI in education could significantly impact how tests and exams are designed, administered, and evaluated, potentially reshaping learning dynamics in the future.

The system's reliance on cloud-based microservices enables flexible scalability and cost-effective resource allocation, ensuring it can handle increasing users and variable demands. With a focus on intuitive user interfaces and the UX for educators and students, the platform ensures ease of use and fosters a seamless experience in exam administration and participation. To maximize the benefits of this technology, educators must receive adequate training and support to use these tools effectively in the classroom.

Although this technology has proven to be a valuable tool, it has also revealed challenges regarding integration, security, and acceptance by educators and students. The potential of this technology to increase educational equity is noteworthy, as it provides access to high-quality resources and assessments for all students, regardless of their location or circumstances.

In the future, we will explore the integration of technologies such as augmented reality and AI APIs that generate images and videos.

Additionally, we propose a pilot study to assess the effectiveness of the Exams as a Service (EaaS) platform, involving 100 students and 10 educators with varying levels of experience. The study will include a training phase, the administration of both static and dynamic exams, and data collection through surveys and interviews to evaluate usability, user satisfaction, and impact on learning outcomes. System performance metrics will also be measured. Quantitative and qualitative analyses will identify strengths and areas for improvement, providing essential insights to refine and scale the platform effectively.

Acknowledgements. Universidad Poliltécnica Salesiana (Quito).

References

1. Abulibdeh, A., Zaidan, E., Abulibdeh, R.: Navigating the confluence of artificial intelligence and education for sustainable development in the era of industry 4.0: challenges, opportunities, and ethical dimensions. J. Clean. Prod. **437**, 140527 (2024). https://doi.org/10.1016/j.jclepro.2023.140527
2. Adeshola, I., Adepoju, A.P.: The opportunities and challenges of chatgpt in education. Interact. Learn. Environ. 1–14 (2023). https://doi.org/10.1080/10494820.2023.2253858
3. AlAfnan, M.A., Dishari, S., Jovic, M., Lomidze, K.: Chatgpt as an educational tool: opportunities, challenges, and recommendations for communication, business writing, and composition courses. J. Artif. Intell. Technol. (2023). https://doi.org/10.37965/jait.2023.0184
4. Amaral, M., Polo, J., Carrera, D., Mohomed, I., Unuvar, M., Steinder, M.: Performance evaluation of microservices architectures using containers. In: 2015 IEEE 14th International Symposium on Network Computing and Applications, pp. 27–34. IEEE (2015). https://doi.org/10.1109/NCA.2015.49
5. Chan, W., An, A., Davoudi, H.: A case study on chatgpt question generation. In: 2023 IEEE International Conference on Big Data (BigData), pp. 1647–1656 (2023). https://doi.org/10.1109/BigData59044.2023.10386520
6. Cortés, J.A., Vega, J.A., Schotborg, D.C., Caicedo, J.C.: Education platform with dynamic questions using cloud computing services, pp. 387–400 (2017). https://doi.org/10.1007/978-3-319-66562-7_28
7. Divate, M., Salgaonkar, A.: Automatic question generation approaches and evaluation techniques. Current Sci. 1683–1691 (2017)
8. Graesser, A.C., Rus, V., Cai, Z., Hu, X.: Question answering and generation, pp. 1–16. IGI Global (2012). https://doi.org/10.4018/978-1-60960-741-8.ch001
9. Hapke, H., Howard, C., Lane, H.: Natural language processing in action: understanding, analyzing, and generating text with python. Simon and Schuster (2019)
10. Jagatheesaperumal, S.K., Ahmad, K., Al-Fuqaha, A., Qadir, J.: Advancing education through extended reality and internet of everything enabled metaverses: applications, challenges, and open issues. IEEE Trans. Learn. Technol. (2024). https://doi.org/10.1109/TLT.2024.3358859
11. Jangiti, S., Swathi, G., Ravi, L., Vijayakumar, V., Subramaniyaswamy, V.: Automated question extraction and tagging for cloud-based online communities. Int. J. Web Based Commun. **15**, 212–224 (2019). https://doi.org/10.1504/IJWBC.2019.101810
12. Kang, Y.B., et al.: An AI-based solution for enhancing delivery of digital learning for future teachers. ArXiv **abs/2112.01229** (2021). https://doi.org/10.48550/arXiv.2112.01229
13. Liu, B., Wei, H., Niu, D., Chen, H., He, Y.: Asking questions the human way: scalable question-answer generation from text corpus. In: Proceedings of the Web Conference 2020 (2020). https://doi.org/10.1145/3366423.3380270
14. Mathew, A.N., Paulose, J., Info, A.: NLP-based personal learning assistant for school education. Int. J. Electr. Comput. Eng. **11**, 4522–4530 (2021). https://doi.org/10.11591/ijece.v11i5.pp4522-4530
15. Nagalingam, V., Ibrahim, R.: User experience of educational games: a review of the elements. Procedia Comput. Sci. **72**, 423–433 (2015). https://doi.org/10.1016/j.procs.2015.12.123

16. Navas, G., Navas-Reascos, G., Navas-Reascos, G.E., Proaño-Orellana, J.: Exploring the effectiveness of advanced chatbots in educational settings: a mixed-methods study in statistics. Appl. Sci. **14**(19), 8984 (2024). https://doi.org/10.3390/app14198984
17. de Oliveira Silva, A., dos Santos Janes, D.: The emergence of chatgpt and its implications for education and academic research in the 21st century. Rev. Artif. Intell. Educ. (2021). https://doi.org/10.37497/rev.artif.intell.educ.v3i00.6
18. OpenAI: Openai company (2024)
19. Pabitha, P., Mohana, M., Suganthi, S., Sivanandhini, B.G.: Automatic question generation system. In: 2014 International Conference on Recent Trends in Information Technology, pp. 1–5 (2014). https://doi.org/10.1109/ICRTIT.2014.6996216
20. Railić, N., Savić, M.: Architecting continuous integration and continuous deployment for microservice architecture. In: 2021 20th International Symposium INFOTEH-JAHORINA (INFOTEH), pp. 1–5. IEEE (2021). https://doi.org/10.1109/INFOTEH51037.2021.9400696
21. Srivastava, A., Shinde, S.R., Patel, N., Despande, S., Dalvi, A., Tripathi, S.: Questionator-automated question generation using deep learning. In: 2020 International Conference on Emerging Trends in Information Technology and Engineering (ic-ETITE), pp. 1–5 (2020). https://doi.org/10.1109/ic-ETITE47903.2020.212
22. Weston, J., Bordes, A., Chopra, S., Mikolov, T.: Towards AI-complete question answering: a set of prerequisite toy tasks. arXiv: Artificial Intelligence (2015). https://doi.org/10.48550/arXiv.1502.05698
23. Wu, T., et al.: A brief overview of chatgpt: the history, status quo and potential future development. IEEE/CAA J. Automatica Sinica **10**(5), 1122–1136 (2023). https://doi.org/10.1109/JAS.2023.123618
24. Yenduri, G., et al.: Generative pre-trained transformer: a comprehensive review on enabling technologies, potential applications, emerging challenges, and future directions. arXiv preprint arXiv:2305.10435 (2023). https://doi.org/10.1109/ACCESS.2024.3389497
25. hua Zhong, S., Peng, J., Liu, P.: Question generation based on chat-response conversion. Concurrency Comput. Pract. Exp. **33** (2019). https://doi.org/10.1002/cpe.5584

Leveraging Web Scraping to Identify Opportunities for Young Talent to UK Digital Manufacturing

Priyesh Dhole[1], Imtiaz Hussain Khan[1(✉)], Imtiaz Ali Khan[1], and Karl Warner[2]

[1] Cardiff School of Technologies, Cardiff Metropolitan University, Cardiff, UK
{pdhole2,ihkhan,ikhan}@cardiffmet.ac.uk

[2] Adam Smith Business School, University of Glasgow, Glasgow, UK
karl.warner@glasgow.ac.uk

Abstract. The rapid evolution of digital manufacturing presents significant opportunities for economic growth and technological advancement in the United Kingdom (UK). However, the sector faces a critical shortage of skilled professionals, particularly among the younger generation. This paper explores the potential of leveraging state-of-the-art web scraping technologies to identify opportunities for attracting young talent to careers in UK digital manufacturing. By employing web scraping tools such as Scrapy, Selenium, and Magical, the study gathered and analysed data from online platforms like LinkedIn to assess the opportunities for the young talent in the UK digital manufacturing industry. The findings reveal key trends in job attractiveness, salary scales, and skill requirements, with a focus on how small and large companies differ in their approach to talent acquisition. The analysis raised some interesting questions which are worth exploring. In addition to, the insights gained provide actionable recommendations for educators, policymakers, and industry leaders to enhance the alignment between educational offerings and industry needs, thereby fostering a robust talent pipeline for the future of UK manufacturing.

Keywords: Digital Manufacturing · Web Scraping · Linkedin Data · Young Talent · Job Market Analysis · Talent Acquisition Trends

1 Introduction

The rapid advancement of digital technologies has revolutionized the manufacturing sector, giving rise to what is often termed Digital Manufacturing (DM) [4,18]. According to [11], DM can be described as using digital information to improve manufacturing, supply chains, products, and services. This paradigm shift integrates computer-aided design, computer-aided manufacturing, and computer numerical control systems with advanced digital tools, enabling seamless

This work was supported by a Economic and Social Research Council (ESRC) UK funding, project title: Developing strategy for the rebranding of UK digital manufacturing. We thank ESRC for their financial support.

F. R. Narváez et al. (Eds.): SmartTech-IC 2024, CCIS 2392, pp. 193–205, 2026.
https://doi.org/10.1007/978-3-031-98287-3_14

connectivity and automation across production processes. DM represents a fundamental transformation in the way products are designed, produced, and distributed, characterized by the incorporation of Industry 4.0 technologies such as the internet of things (IoTs), artificial intelligence (AI), and big data analytics [8].

In the context of the United Kingdom (UK), DM is emerging as a pivotal sector with the potential to drive economic growth and innovation [13]. The UK government has recognized the significance of this sector, investing in initiatives like the Made Smarter program[1], which aims to boost the adoption of digital technologies within manufacturing industries. This commitment is underscored by the nation's ambition to maintain its competitive edge on the global stage, particularly as it navigates the post-Brexit landscape. One of the key challenges facing the UK in realizing the full potential of DM is the shortage of skilled talent [21]. While traditional manufacturing has been effective for centuries, it faces limitations such as difficulties in producing complex geometries, challenges in nano-scale design, inefficiencies in material waste optimization, and high costs in low-yield scenarios [9, 15]. As traditional manufacturing jobs evolve or disappear, there is a pressing need to attract and develop a new generation of professionals equipped with digital skills.

This paper explores the prospects of DM as a career pathway for youth talent in the UK, examining how this sector can appeal to the younger workforce and contribute to the nation's economic and technological advancement. We build on existing strategies for analysing job market trends and attracting young talent by introducing advanced web scraping technologies to gather nuanced, real-time data from platforms like LinkedIn. Unlike traditional methods [7, 17, 21] that rely on static data or self-reported surveys, our approach enables dynamic tracking of trends in job appeal, skill requirements, and salary benchmarks across different company sizes. By leveraging tools such as Scrapy, Selenium, and Magical, data were collected from platforms like LinkedIn to evaluate job opportunities within the industry. Moreover, this work diverges from previous research by focusing specifically on the UK's DM sector, providing a detailed examination of how this industry can appeal to and support the younger workforce. These insights aim to bridge gaps in talent acquisition strategies and contribute to the broader understanding of workforce development in a rapidly evolving economic landscape.

Our findings reveal notable trends in job appeal, salary ranges, and required skill sets, highlighting differences in talent acquisition approaches between small and large companies. Our data analysis has revealed intriguing research questions that warrant deeper exploration. These questions are crucial for understanding the challenges and opportunities faced by young talent in the UK. By delving further into this enquiry, we can uncover key insights that will help to better support and develop the potential of the emerging workforce in the UK.

The paper is organised as follows. The related work is discussed in Sect. 2. Section 3 outlines the methodology, including data collection and data analysis. Results are discussed in Sect. 4. Section 5 concludes the paper.

[1] https://www.madesmarter.uk/.

2 Related Work

The literature on DM is vast, reflecting its importance in modern industrial strategies. This section reviews key studies to understand DM landscape and recent advances in this exciting field. In [20], the authors examined the development and potential of DM technologies, outlining their historical evolution and impact on manufacturing processes. They highlighted current applications that improve production efficiency, enable customization, and shorten time-to-market. Additionally, the paper identified future trends, such as the integration of AI, machine learning, and IoT. The study [9] explored the potential of direct digital manufacturing (DDM) to transform traditional manufacturing and operations management practices. They particularly concluded that DDM is suited for low-volume, high-variety production and challenges conventional methods like scheduling, batch sizing, and inventory management. In [14], the authors investigated the drivers of digital transformation in manufacturing, noting key factors like technological advancements, competitive pressures, and regulatory changes. They emphasized the need for a strategic approach to digital transformation to enhance operational efficiency, innovation, and value creation, aligning digital efforts with business goals for sustainable growth. In [3], the authors explored the challenges of modeling ridehailing services, particularly those with human-driven fleets. They noted the lack of data on driver behavior and service processes, which are crucial for accurate models. In [19], the authors reviewed the impact of digital technologies on corporate strategy, proposing a three-layer model: organizational core, periphery, and external environment. They found that digital technology blurs boundaries between these layers by integrating external actors into firm operations, shifting firms from stand-alone entities to networked value co-creators. This transformation raises governance questions in emerging ecosystems. The study [1] reviewed the literature on digital transformation in manufacturing. The authors noted that despite its benefits, including higher productivity and better customer engagement, digital technology faces challenges such as skill gaps and inadequate training. The study [22] examines how digital transformation impacts the environmental, social, and governance (ESG) performance of Chinese manufacturing firms. It finds that larger, growing companies, especially non-state-owned enterprises in developed regions, benefit most from digital transformation in improving ESG outcomes. The study underscores the need for accelerated digital transformation, government support, and improved ESG frameworks to promote sustainable development. The paper [16] underscores the importance of digital transformation in enhancing labor productivity and competitiveness in manufacturing, infrastructure, and public services. It discusses methods for assessing the feasibility and economic efficiency of such projects, highlighting challenges specific to the Russian Federation. The study emphasizes information security, prioritizing the digitization of the investment sector, and proposes a systemic approach to applying digital tools to achieve transformation goals and foster innovation. The paper [12] reviews recent digital transformation research, analysing 39 peer-reviewed articles and identifying three key clusters. First cluster examines organizational impacts, second explores technology's role and third discusses societal impacts, stressing the importance of adapting to disruptive changes and training employees. The paper [5] employs a PRISMA-based approach to analyse the role of digital transformation in fostering sustainability in manufacturing, highlighting its benefits, opportunities, risks, and implications while proposing directions for future research.

3 Methodology

We used an inductive research approach because the theory developed was purely based on patterns found in the data. In this study, data collection and exploratory data analysis (EDA) have been performed.

3.1 Data Collection Tools and Techniques

Figure 1 provides a visual representation of each stage in the data collection and analysis process. The main steps are detailed below.

- We initially evaluated 20 job search websites based on their terms of use and data accessibility. Two platforms, LinkedIn and Indeed, were selected due to their comprehensive data offerings and relevance to our research scope. Further details are provided in the Dataset subsection below.
- The scraping process focused on collecting fields such as job title, location, company name, skills, and job descriptions. These fields were selected to ensure alignment with the study's objectives and relevance to DM roles. For each keyword, the scraping process was performed on each selected website using the designated tool, adhering to the predefined selection criteria.
- The raw data were meticulously transformed into a structured format, undergoing thorough cleansing and essential preprocessing to prepare it for advanced analysis and visualisation.

Data were collected using scraping methods with the help of Python programming and a few tools. Many trials were conducted using various scrapping tools, such as selenium, scrapy, and magical tool (a web extension). Among these, **Scrapy** is an open-source, Python-based web scraping framework designed for extracting data from websites. It allows users to automate the process of visiting web pages, extracting the necessary information, and saving it in various formats like JSON, CSV, or databases. Scrapy is highly efficient for large-scale scraping, offering features such as asynchronous processing, built-in selectors for parsing HTML, and robust handling of requests and responses. It's widely used for tasks like data mining, content monitoring, and gathering information for research or business intelligence. Additionally, Scrapy's modular architecture makes it highly customisable and scalable for complex scraping projects.

Selenium is a powerful, open-source tool primarily used for automating web browsers, making it popular for web scraping and testing. Unlike other scraping tools, Selenium interacts with web pages just like a human would, clicking

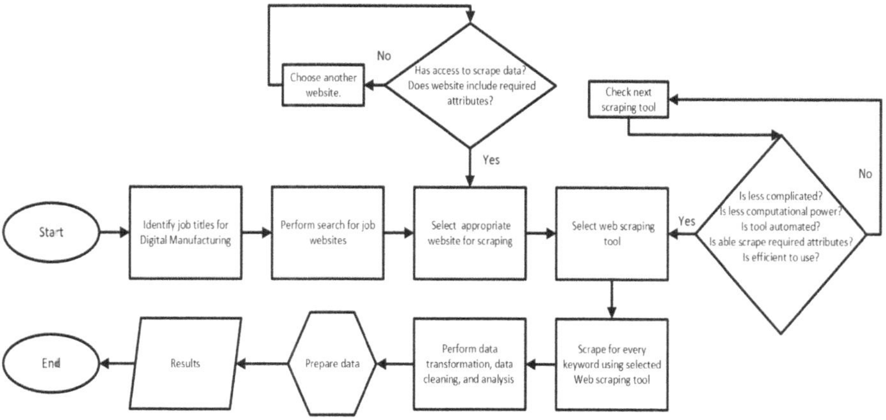

Fig. 1. Data Collection Flowchart

buttons, filling forms, and navigating through pages, which makes it ideal for scraping dynamic, JavaScript-heavy websites. It supports multiple programming languages like Python and Java, and can be used with various web browsers, including Chrome, Firefox, and Safari. Selenium is often used when precise control over the browser is required, or when scraping sites with complex interactions that typical HTML parsers can't handle. While it is more resource-intensive than some other tools, its flexibility and ability to mimic real user behavior make it invaluable for many advanced scraping tasks.

Magical is a browser-based automation tool designed to streamline repetitive tasks, including data scraping. It allows users to extract data from websites effortlessly by recording their actions and replaying them to automate the collection of information. Unlike traditional web scraping tools, Magical focuses on ease of use, making it accessible to non-programmers who need to gather data without writing code. The tool integrates with various applications, enabling users to quickly move extracted data into spreadsheets, CRMs, or other tools. Its user-friendly interface and drag-and-drop functionality make it a popular choice for professionals looking to automate data entry and extraction tasks without extensive technical knowledge.

3.2 Dataset

We are primarily interested to know what skillset is required in the DM industry in the UK, henceforth Demand dataset. We started by exploring various platforms where jobs are advertised such as Indeed UK, LinkedIn, TotalJobs, Jobs.ac.uk, etc. We were allowed and able to scrape data from Indeed UK and LinkedIn. However, due to some limitations (details follow) in scraping all the required information from Indeed, we focussed on LinkedIn as primary source for Demand data. The data were collected during the period 22/02/2024-09/03/2024. The details of the dataset are provided in Table 1.

Table 1. Demand Data

Number of features	15
Features	Job Title, Company Name, Company Size, Basic Salary (if disclosed by company), Job Posted Duration (Number of Days), Job Position, Job Type, Number of Applicants, Location of the Company, Company's URL, Skills Required, Reposting, Longitude, Latitude
Number of instances	892

3.3 Data Analysis

The collected data from LinkedIn on DM jobs were subjected to a comprehensive analysis across multiple dimensions. The analysis aimed to uncover key insights into the job market, including factors such as salary attraction, job attractiveness, the relationship between companies and job postings, the identification of non-attractive jobs, the specific skills provided and so on. Various data visualization techniques were employed to present the findings, including charts, Sankey diagrams, and word clouds. The visualizations played a critical role in the analysis, offering intuitive and clear representations of the complex data relationships. For example, the Sankey diagram provided a dynamic view of the job-company relationships, while word clouds highlighted the prevalence of specific terms and skills in job descriptions. Together, these visual tools facilitated a deeper understanding of the digital manufacturing job market, enabling stakeholders to make informed decisions based on the data. The data analysis was carried out using Python programming.

4 Results and Discussion

The data analysis revealed some interesting results some of which were unexpected.

1. Our analysis of salary data revealed a surprising trend: small-scale industries and startups offer higher average salaries compared to large multinational corporations (Fig. 2). This finding suggests that these smaller companies may be attempting to attract young talent by offering competitive compensation packages. The observation raises an intriguing research question: *What factors contribute to higher average salaries in small-scale industries and startups compared to large multinational corporations?* Addressing this question could provide valuable insights into the dynamics that drive salary structures in different organizational contexts, including the potential role of agility, innovation, and growth opportunities in smaller firms.

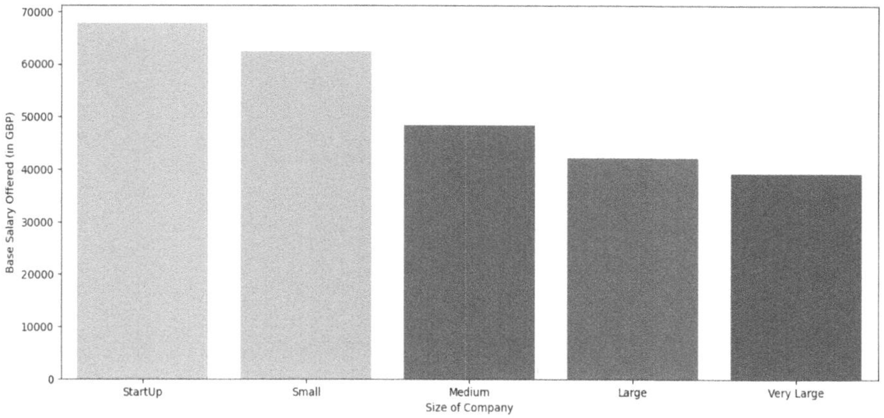

Fig. 2. Size of Company vs. Base Salary Offered(in GBP)

2. The analysis of job attractiveness uncovered an inverse correlation between the number of applicants and the number of days a job posting remains active. This trend suggests that more attractive jobs receive a higher volume of applicants and are filled more quickly, while less attractive positions tend to remain open longer (Fig. 3). Notably, our analysis indicates that startups and small companies are offering more attractive jobs than large corporations. A word cloud analysis further highlighted that roles such as mechanical design engineers and product design engineers are in particularly high demand (Fig. 4). These findings lead to the following research question: *What factors contribute to the attractiveness of job postings, and how do these factors differ between startups, small companies, and large corporations?* Exploring this question would help to identify the specific characteristics that make certain job postings more appealing to candidates, potentially revealing how company size and culture influence job desirability.
3. Our analysis of job-company relationships showed that entry-level positions are predominantly offered by large or very large companies (Fig. 5 and Fig. 6). This pattern may reflect the hierarchical organizational structures typical of such companies, which require a steady influx of entry-level talent to maintain their operations. Additionally, the data indicates that mid-senior and associate positions are the most offered roles, potentially aligning with the career aspirations of younger professionals who are targeting rapid advancement (Fig. 5 and 6). These findings prompt a research question: *Why do large and very large companies tend to offer more entry-level positions, and what are the implications of this for workforce development and talent acquisition?* Investigating this question could shed light on the strategic importance of entry-level hiring for large corporations and its impact on their long-term talent management strategies.

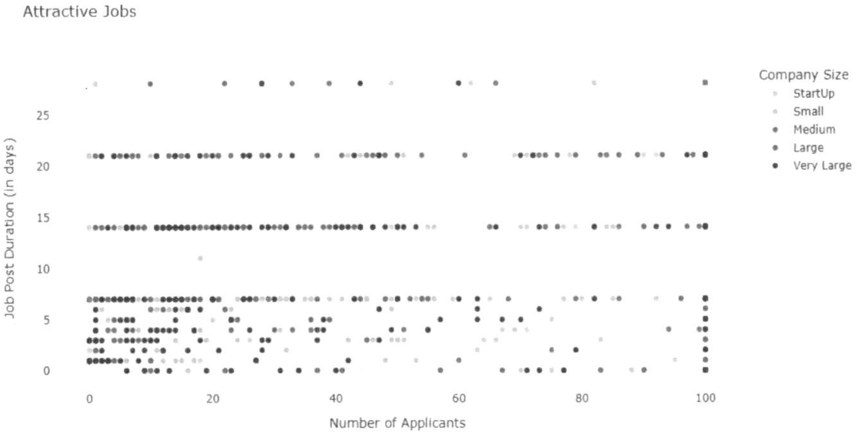

Fig. 3. Number of Applicants vs. Job Post Duration

Fig. 4. Word Cloud of Jobs Posted

4. Further, the analysis of job reposting revealed that approximately 250 out of 900 job postings were reposted (Fig. 7). This could suggest that these jobs were either less attractive to candidates or that companies struggled to find suitable candidates. The underlying reasons for job reposting present another critical research question: *What are the primary reasons for job reposting, and*

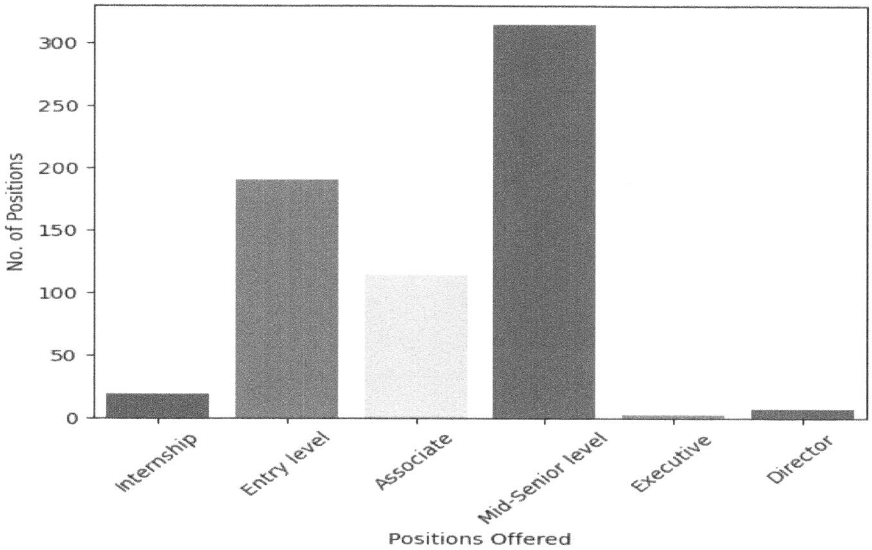

Fig. 5. Counts for Each Job Position

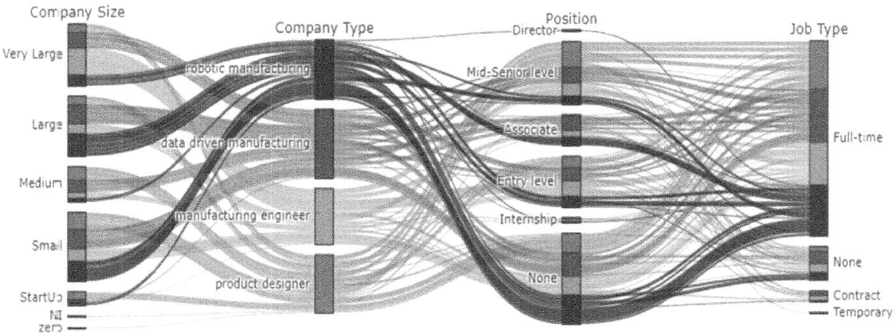

Fig. 6. Interconnecting Diagram

how do these reasons correlate with job attractiveness, candidate suitability, and company characteristics? Answering this question would provide deeper insights into the challenges companies face in filling certain positions and how these challenges might be addressed.

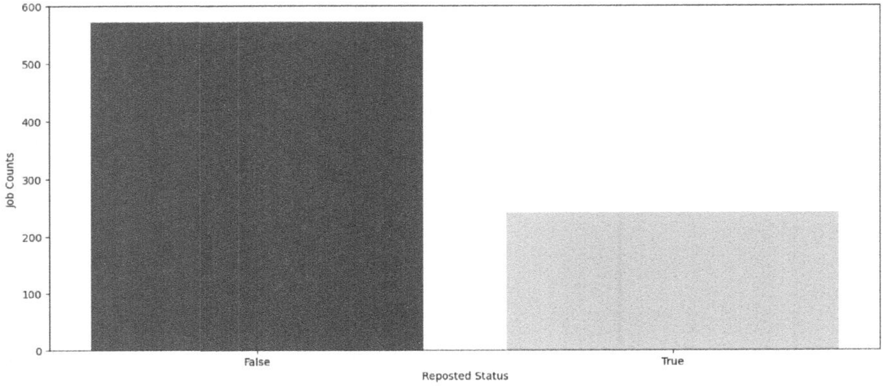

Fig. 7. Number of Jobs Resposted

Based on the above analysis, a broader research question that could encompass the various findings and provide a comprehensive framework for further investigation is: *How do organizational characteristics, such as company size, industry sector, and job structure, influence the strategies and outcomes of talent acquisition in the* DM*sector?* This research question allows for the exploration of multiple dimensions uncovered in our analysis, including salary differences between small and large companies, factors contributing to job attractiveness, the prevalence of entry-level positions in large corporations, and the reasons behind job reposting. It also invites a deeper examination of how these factors interact to shape the overall talent acquisition landscape in DM.

While our paper emphasises the importance of attracting young talent to the UK's DM sector, we recognise the need to delve deeper into the specific challenges companies face in this endeavour. These challenges include identifying the right skill sets amidst rapidly evolving technological demands, competing with other industries for top talent, and addressing gaps between educational training and industry requirements. Web scraping directly addresses these issues by providing real-time, granular insights into job trends, required qualifications, and competitive salary benchmarks. Tools like Scrapy and Selenium enable companies to systematically analyse data from platforms like LinkedIn, revealing actionable patterns in recruitment strategies, skill demand, and job appeal. This data-driven approach not only streamlines talent acquisition but also helps tailor outreach efforts to align with the aspirations and expectations of younger professionals. Future work will explore how these insights can be used to bridge the demand-supply gap and support targeted policy and educational reforms to further strengthen the sector's talent pipeline.

5 Conclusion and Future Work

This study, as part of an ongoing research project on developing strategy for the rebranding of UK DM, underscores the critical role of web scraping technologies in identifying and addressing the talent requirements in the UK DM. The analysis of data highlights significant disparities in job attractiveness, salary offerings, and the skill sets required by different companies. Notably, small-scale industries were found to offer more competitive salaries, while larger corporations tended to focus on entry-level positions. These findings suggest that targeted efforts to align educational programs with industry demands could better prepare the next generation of professionals for careers in DM. As the UK continues to invest in its DM capabilities, the adoption of data-driven approaches like web scraping will be essential in ensuring that the sector attracts and retains the skilled talent needed to maintain its competitive edge. Future research should explore the underlying factors that contribute to these trends and how they can be leveraged to further enhance talent acquisition strategies in the DM sector. In addition to, the supply data, that is, what skillset is being produced could be explored from platforms such as Coursera. This would help identify a demand-supply gap for a better realisation of the talent requirements in the UK DM.

Because this paper is part of an on-going research project, we intend to compare the DM sector with other technology-intensive sectors, such as digital marketing [6,10], healthcare technology [7], or renewable energy industries [2]. These sectors also rely heavily on attracting a skilled and innovative young workforce, enabling meaningful comparisons regarding talent acquisition strategies, skillset requirements, and alignment with educational programs. This comparative approach would strengthen the broader implications of our research and offer valuable insights into how the DM sector could adopt successful practices from these related fields.

There were certainly few limitations to scrape the data from designated websites. For the data collection, we shortlisted various job websites, however, due to website constraint, privacy concerns, time constraint, and layout of the website, most of the websites were not taken into the account. LinkedIn was able to provide various information with very little adjustment hence selected for demand data. Other demand data websites were not providing complete information to draw any patterns or insights. Another limitation for scraped data is that it is small sized data, for example, for certain keywords it displayed only those jobs which were posted during the time when scrapping was taken place.

Acknowledgement. This work was supported by the Economic and Social Research Council (ESRC), UK, through InterAct Sandpit Funding (Grant No. J17293/ES/W007231/1 – Sandpit#1 Warner). We gratefully acknowledge the ESRC for its financial support.

References

1. Abdallah, Y.O., Shehab, E., Al-Ashaab, A.: Understanding digital transformation in the manufacturing industry: a systematic literature review and future trends. Product Manage. Dev. (2021). https://doi.org/10.4322/PMD.2021.001

2. Brannstrom, C., Ewers, M., Schwarz, P.: Will peak talent arrive before peak oil or peak demand?: exploring whether career choices of highly skilled workers will accelerate the transition to renewable energy. Energy Res. Soc. Sci. **93**, 102834 (2022). https://doi.org/10.1016/j.erss.2022.102834
3. Calderon, F., Miller, E.J.: Bridging the knowledge gap in ridehailing service provision with human-driven fleets: a data mining approach. Procedia Comput. Sci. **170**, 673–680 (2020). https://doi.org/10.1016/j.procs.2020.03.172
4. Chen, D., Heyer, S., Ibbotson, S., Salonitis, K., Steingrimsson, J.G., Thiede, S.: Direct digital manufacturing: definition, evolution, and sustainability implications. J. Clean. Prod. **107**, 615–625 (2015). https://doi.org/10.1016/j.jclepro.2015.05.009
5. De Felice, F., Salzano, C., Baffo, I., Forcina, A., Petrillo, A.: Towards a sustainable digital manufacturing: a state of art. Procedia Comput. Sci. **232**, 1918–1929 (2024). https://doi.org/10.1016/j.procs.2024.02.014, https://www.sciencedirect.com/science/article/pii/S1877050924001911
6. Dwivedi, Y.K., et al.: Setting the future of digital and social media marketing research: perspectives and research propositions. Int. J. Inf. Manage. **59**, 102168 (2021). https://doi.org/10.1016/j.ijinfomgt.2020.102168
7. Edo, O.C., Ang, D., Etu, E.E., Tenebe, I., Edo, S., Diekola, O.A.: Why do healthcare workers adopt digital health technologies - a cross-sectional study integrating the TAM and UTAUT model in a developing economy. Int. J. Inf. Manage. Data Insights **3**(2), 100186 (2023). https://doi.org/10.1016/j.jjimei.2023.100186
8. Hermann, M., Pentek, T., Otto, B.: Design principles for industrie 4.0 scenarios. In: 49th Hawaii International Conference on System Sciences (HICSS), pp. 3928–3937 (2016). https://doi.org/10.1109/HICSS.2016.488
9. Holmström, J., Holweg, M., Khajavi, S.H., Partanen, J.: The direct digital manufacturing (r)evolution: definition of a research agenda. Oper. Manag. Res. **9**, 1–10 (2016)
10. Ildikó, K., Zarandne, K.: Digital marketing employability skills in job advertisements - must-have soft skills for entry level workers: a content analysis. Econ. Sociol. **15**, 178–192 (2022). https://doi.org/10.14254/2071-789X.2022/15-1/11
11. Kaiser, J., McFarlane, D., Hawkridge, G., André, P., Leitão, P.: A review of reference architectures for digital manufacturing: classification, applicability and open issues. Comput. Ind. **149**, 103923 (2023)
12. Kraus, S., Jones, P., Kailer, N., Weinmann, A., Chaparro-Banegas, N., Roig-Tierno, N.: Digital transformation: an overview of the current state of the art of research. SAGE Open **11**(3), 1–15 (2021). https://doi.org/10.1177/21582440211047576
13. Liao, Y., Deschamps, F., de Freitas Rocha Loures, E., Ramos, L.F.P.: Past, present and future of industry 4.0 - a systematic literature review and research agenda proposal. Int. J. Prod. Res. **55**(12), 3609–3629 (2017). https://doi.org/10.1080/00207543.2017.1308576
14. Liere-Netheler, K., Packmohr, S., Vogelsang, K.: Drivers of digital transformation in manufacturing. In: Proceedings of the 51st Hawaii International Conference on System Sciences, pp. 3926–3935 (2018). https://doi.org/10.24251/HICSS.2018.493
15. Lin, L., Kollipara, P.S., Zheng, Y.: Digital manufacturing of advanced materials: challenges and perspective. Mater. Today **28**, 49–62 (2019)
16. Molchanova, S.: Digital transformation in manufacturing, infastructure and public services. In: International Conference on Economic and Social Trends for Sustainability of Modern Society, pp. 1285–1294 (2020). https://doi.org/10.15405/epsbs.2020.10.03.148

17. Montero Guerra, J.M., del Valle, I.D., Mariano, Méndez-Suárez, M.: The impact of digital transformation on talent management. Technol. Forecast. Soc. Change **188**, 122291 (2023). https://doi.org/10.1016/j.techfore.2022.122291
18. Paritala, P.K., Manchikatla, S., Yarlagadda, P.: Digital manufacturing - applications past, current, and future trends. Procedia Eng. **174**, 982–991 (2017). https://doi.org/10.1016/j.proeng.2017.01.250
19. Plekhanov, D., Franke, H., Netland, T.H.: Digital transformation: a review and research agenda. Eur. Manag. J. **41**(6), 821–844 (2023). https://doi.org/10.1016/j.emj.2022.09.007
20. Ribeiro da Silva, E.H.D., Shinohara, A.C., de Lima, E.P., Angelis, J., Machado, C.G.: Reviewing digital manufacturing concept in the industry 4.0 paradigm. Procedia CIRP **81**, 240–245 (2019). https://doi.org/10.1016/j.procir.2019.03.042
21. Stewart, R., MacBryde, J., Lindsay, C., Marin-Cadavid, C.: 'Making things work' public opinion of UK manufacturing. Report P-38, University of Strathclyde (2023)
22. Wang, J., Hong, Z., Long, H.: Digital transformation empowers ESG performance in the manufacturing industry: from ESG to DESG. SAGE Open **13**(4), 1–21 (2023). https://doi.org/10.1177/21582440231204158

Evaluating Word Embedding Models in Ecuadorian Legal Texts: A Comparison of CBOW and Skip-Gram for Semantic Analysis

Wilfredo Martel and Christian Salamea(✉)

Universidad Politécnica Salesiana, Cuenca, Ecuador
wmartel@est.ups.edu.ec, csalamea@ups.edu.ec

Abstract. This study evaluates the effectiveness of the Continuous Bag-of-Words (CBOW) and Skip-gram models in capturing semantic relationships within Ecuadorian legal texts. Utilizing a comprehensive corpus that includes the Ecuadorian Constitution, the Comprehensive Organic Criminal Code (COIP), and the General Organic Code of Processes (COGEP), among other national laws, we analyze the models' ability to represent the complex semantics of legal language. The CBOW model predicts target words based on their surrounding context, while Skip-gram predicts the context from a given target word, making them suitable for identifying intricate patterns in legal documents. A rigorous preprocessing phase was applied to the legal texts, including normalization, stopword removal, and lemmatization, ensuring high-quality input data for training. The models were then evaluated using semantic similarity (Spearman's correlation) and topic coherence metrics. Results indicate that while both models show potential in capturing semantic relationships, CBOW demonstrated a marginally higher performance with a Spearman correlation of 0.24 and a topic coherence score of 0.6637, compared to Skip-gram's 0.19 and 0.6573, respectively. Despite these findings, neither model fully captured the complexities inherent in legal language, suggesting a need for further refinement in NLP techniques for legal texts. These findings provide a foundation for improving semantic search and information retrieval systems tailored to the legal domain, offering tools to assist legal professionals in analyzing and understanding complex legal texts.

Keywords: CBOW · Skip-gram · Semantic Similarity · Legal Texts · Natural Language Processing · Ecuadorian Law · Word Embeddings · AI in Law

1 Introduction

The semantic processing of legal texts poses a significant challenge in the field of Natural Language Processing (NLP) due to the intricate linguistic structure and specialized terminology inherent to legal language. Legal texts not only contain a vast array of technical terms but also exhibit complex semantic relationships that heavily depend on context. Specifically, in Ecuadorian legal documents—such as the Constitution of the Republic, the Organic Comprehensive Criminal Code (COIP), and the Organic Code

F. R. Narváez et al. (Eds.): SmartTech-IC 2024, CCIS 2392, pp. 206–216, 2026.
https://doi.org/10.1007/978-3-031-98287-3_15

of General Processes (COGEP)—the complexity increases due to the rich and nuanced interconnection between legal norms, procedures, and principles. This semantic richness necessitates more advanced and tailored approaches for processing such texts.

In recent years, NLP techniques have shown promising results in tasks such as predicting judicial decisions. For instance, NLP methods have demonstrated the capability to handle the complexity of legal language [1, 2], achieving significant progress in the prediction of court rulings. Similarly, research by Medvedeva et al. (2020) achieved a 75% accuracy rate in predicting decisions of the European Court of Human Rights using Support Vector Machines (SVMs) applied to legal documents before the final ruling [3]. These findings highlight that while NLP techniques can offer effective solutions in the legal field, challenges remain in addressing the inherent richness and variability of legal language.

In this context, word embedding models such as Continuous Bag-of-Words (CBOW) and Skip-Gram, introduced by Mikolov et al. (2013), have proven effective in capturing semantic relationships between words in various NLP applications [4, 5]. CBOW predicts a target word based on its context, while Skip-Gram predicts the context given a target word. Despite the successful application of these models in the legal domain, there remains a gap in their application to the specific legal language of Ecuador [6, 7].

Therefore, it is crucial to evaluate the performance of CBOW and Skip-Gram in the Ecuadorian context, given that Ecuadorian legal texts present unique features that may affect the efficacy of these models [8]. The need for this analysis becomes evident, as it involves not merely adapting existing NLP techniques but also understanding and capturing the subtleties and nuances of Ecuadorian legal language.

Hence, this study aims to compare the performance of CBOW and Skip-Gram applied to Ecuadorian legal texts. An exhaustive preprocessing of the legal document corpus from Ecuador will be conducted, including normalization, cleaning, and lemmatization of texts to ensure data quality. Subsequently, both models will be trained using this preprocessed corpus, and their effectiveness will be evaluated through semantic similarity metrics [9], such as Pearson correlation, and topic coherence metrics, ensuring a comprehensive assessment of the models' ability to capture semantic and contextual relationships present in legal texts.

2 Methodology

This study compared the Word2Vec models CBOW and Skip-gram to capture semantic relationships in Ecuadorian legal texts, selecting them for their effectiveness in processing large volumes of textual data. The following sections detail the preprocessing steps of the corpus, and the configuration used to train both models.

2.1 CBOW Model (Continuous Bag of Words)

The CBOW model, proposed by Mikolov as part of his work on Word2Vec [4], enhances the traditional "bag of words" approach by predicting a target word (w_t) using its surrounding context within a predefined window. Unlike the complete context representation, CBOW focuses on nearby past and future words, assuming that a word's meaning can be inferred from its neighbors. This approach is effective in capturing the semantic meaning of a target word based on its surrounding environment.

Mathematically, given a context of words w_{t-C}, ..., w_{t+C}, where C is the context window size and w_t is the target word, the probability of predicting w_t given the context words is defined as:

$$P(w_t|w_{t-C},\ldots,w_{t+C}) = \prod_{\substack{-C \leq j \leq C \\ j \neq 0}} P\left(w_t|w_{t+j}\right) \tag{1}$$

where:

- P $(w_t|w_{t+j})$ represents the conditional probability of predicting the target word w_t given a context Word w_{t+j}.
- C is the size of the context window.
- w_t is the target word to be predicted.
- w_{t+j} are the words in the surrounding context of w_t.

The goal of the model is to maximize the probability of the target word w_t given its context words. To achieve this, the model adjusts the word vectors (also known as embeddings) by minimizing the loss function, which corresponds to the negative cross-entropy:

$$L = -\frac{1}{T}\sum_{t=1}^{T} \log P(w_t|w_{t-C},\ldots,w_{t+C}) \tag{2}$$

where:

- L is the loss function that the model minimizes during training.
- T is the total number of words in the corpus.
- $\log P(w_t|w_{t-C},\ldots,w_{t+C})$ is the logarithm of the conditional probability of the target word w_t given the context word.

2.2 SKIP-GRAM Model

The Skip-gram model, also introduced by Mikolov [4], operates inversely to CBOW. Instead of predicting a target word from its context, Skip-gram uses a target word (w_t) to predict the surrounding context words. This model is especially useful for capturing complex and less frequent semantic relationships, which are often found in technical texts like legal documents.

The objective of the Skip-gram model is to maximize the probability of predicting the context words $w_{t-C},\ldots,w_{t+C}$, given the target word w_t. The conditional probability of predicting the context words from the target word is defined as:

$$P(w_{t-C},\ldots|w_t) = \prod_{\substack{-C \leq j \leq C \\ j \neq 0}} P\left(w_{t+j}|w_t\right) \tag{3}$$

where:

- $P(w_{t+j}|w_t)$ is the probability of predicting a context word w_{t+j}, given the target word w_t.
- C is the size of the context window.
- w_t is the target word used to predict the context.
- w_{t+i} are the words within the context window.

The model trains the word vectors (or embeddings) in such a way that words co-occurring in similar contexts have vector representations that are close to each other in space. This is particularly useful for capturing semantic relationships, even among less frequent words in the corpus, which is an important feature in specialized domains such as legal language.

To train the Skip-gram model, the negative cross-entropy loss function is minimized, which measures the difference between the probabilities predicted by the model and the actual probabilities observed in the corpus:

$$L = -\frac{1}{T}\sum_{t=1}^{T} \sum_{\substack{-C \leq j \leq C \\ j \neq 0}} \log P(w_{t+j}|w_t) \tag{4}$$

where:

- L is the loss function that the model minimizes.
- T is the total number of words in the corpus.
- $logP(w_{t+j}|w_t)$ is the logarithm of the probability of predicting a context word w_{t+j} given the target word w_t.

The CBOW and Skip-gram models offer key insights into generating semantic representations (embeddings) from judicial texts. Each model uses distinct approaches to learn semantic relationships, enabling customization based on the unique characteristics of the legal corpus.

2.3 Corpus and Preprocessing

For this study, a corpus representing a wide variety of Ecuadorian legal texts was used, including key documents such as the Constitution of the Republic of Ecuador, the Comprehensive Organic Criminal Code (COIP), the General Organic Code of Processes (COGEP), and various national laws and international conventions. This corpus was selected to provide a comprehensive representation of the Ecuadorian legal framework, allowing for an in-depth analysis of semantic representations in a judicial context.

Data Sources: The legal texts used in this study were obtained from official and publicly accessible sources, ensuring their authenticity and representativeness within the Ecuadorian legal context. The corpus was primarily compiled from the 2008 Constitution of the Republic of Ecuador, published by the National Assembly, as well as laws, codes, and regulations available in the Official Register of Ecuador, the country's official publication.

Corpus Characteristics: The corpus used in this study consists of approximately 30,000 legal documents, comprising a total of 1 billion words. All texts are written in Spanish, the official language of the Ecuadorian legal field. This dataset encompasses a wide variety of legal documents, ranging from national regulations to international conventions, making it a rich and diverse source for the analysis of semantic representations in judicial contexts.

Data Preprocessing: Data preprocessing is an essential step before applying CBOW and Skip-gram models. To ensure data quality and coherence, the following stages were implemented:

- *Normalization*: A normalization process was carried out to standardize the linguistic variations present in the corpus, such as inconsistent use of uppercase and lowercase letters as demonstrated by Sproat and Emerson (2003) [10]. This ensured that words with the same meaning were treated uniformly, enhancing coherence in semantic analysis [11].
- *Data Cleaning*: During preprocessing, common Spanish stopwords [12], such as "el," "la," "de," "y," "que," and "en," were removed. Although frequent in natural language, these words do not provide significant semantic value in analyzing legal terms' meaning as shown in studies like Zhu et al. (2017) [13]. Additionally, unnecessary punctuation and special characters that do not contribute to semantic analysis were eliminated. This step is crucial to improve the model's accuracy in identifying relevant patterns in legal texts.
- *Lemmatization*: A lemmatization process was applied to 1 billion words in the corpus, reducing them to their base or root form, which improved the precision in identifying semantic patterns [14].

The first step in the preprocessing pipeline involved cleaning and tokenizing the documents, ensuring the removal of irrelevant elements such as unnecessary punctuation and special characters. However, unique legal terms, such as "proceso judicial", were not preserved as inseparable units, potentially affecting the accurate representation of these specialized concepts. This limitation highlights the need for a tokenizer specifically tailored to legal texts, which would maintain the integrity of compound legal terms. Additionally, common legal terms such as "artículo" and "derecho" which are frequent yet semantically relevant in this context, were retained to focus the analysis on patterns pertinent to Ecuadorian legal language.

2.4 Model Implementation

Tool and Libraries Used

The CBOW and Skip-gram models were implemented using the Gensim library in Python, which is widely recognized for its efficiency in training word embedding models. The preprocessed Ecuadorian legal corpus was used to train both models, ensuring data quality for generating accurate semantic representations.

Configuration of Parameters for CBOW and Skip-Gram

Both the CBOW and Skip-gram models were trained using the same set of hyperparameters. The table below summarizes the values used in the configuration (Table 1):

Table 1. Key Hyperparameters for CBOW and Skip-gram Model Training

Parameter	Value	Description
vector_size	200	Dimension of word vectors capturing semantic features
min_count	1	Minimum word frequency in the corpus
window	10	Context window size around the target word
Alpha	0.03	Initial learning rate
min_alpha	0.0007	Final learning rate
negative	20	Negative samples for training
epochs	20	Training iterations over the corpus
workers	10	Number of processors for parallel training

Model Training

Both the CBOW and Skip-gram models were trained using the preprocessed Ecuadorian legal corpus. The CBOW model was configured to predict the target word based on its surrounding context, while the Skip-gram model aimed to predict the surrounding context words given a target word.

The training process utilized the negative sampling technique with 20 negative samples to enhance the quality of the word vectors, ensuring that infrequent but contextually important legal terms were accurately represented. The models underwent 10 complete training iterations (epochs) over the entire corpus to ensure convergence and capture nuanced semantic relationships inherent in the legal domain.

A parallel processing approach was employed using 10 CPU cores (workers = 10) to accelerate the training time, which was crucial given the extensive size of the corpus. The negative log-likelihood loss function, also known as negative cross-entropy loss, was minimized during training to optimize the word embeddings.

The hyperparameters, such as vector_size, alpha, min_alpha, and window, were carefully selected based on multiple experimental runs to balance model performance and computational efficiency. Training on a legal corpus of this magnitude posed significant challenges, particularly in terms of memory and processing time. To address this, a parallel processing setup with optimized memory allocation was implemented, reducing training time per epoch. Additional epochs were required to ensure convergence, especially for low-frequency terms critical to legal contexts. Incremental training batches were employed to prevent memory overflow, which proved effective for managing extensive and specialized corpora like this one.

3 Evaluation

To evaluate the effectiveness of the CBOW and Skip-gram models in the context of Ecuadorian legal texts, two main metrics were used: Spearman's semantic similarity and topic coherence. These metrics provide insight into how well each model captures semantic relationships and thematic consistency within this specialized legal domain.

3.1 Evaluation Metric

Spearman's Correlation for Semantic Similarity

The Spearman correlation coefficient was selected to assess the ability of the CBOW and Skip-gram models to capture semantic similarity within Ecuadorian legal texts. This metric measures the strength and direction of the monotonic relationship between the similarities predicted by the models and those assessed by human evaluators. A higher Spearman correlation value (closer to 1) indicates a stronger agreement between the model's predictions and human judgments, meaning that the model is more effective in capturing the relative semantic relationships perceived by humans. This makes it a valuable metric for evaluating semantic consistency in this context.

In this study, ChatGPT-4 was used to develop the evaluation dataset, ensuring consistency in semantic similarity assessments. Additionally, previous research by Zhelezniak, Mitrović, and Granitzer [15, 16] supports the use of Spearman's correlation in detecting complex semantic relationships in legal documents, validating its application in this legal context.

Topic Coherence

The topic coherence metric was selected for its ability to evaluate the consistency and relevance of the topics identified in the legal corpus. According to Röder et al. (2015) [17], coherence metrics have a strong correlation with human evaluations, making them reliable indicators for assessing the quality of topic models, especially in complex domains such as the legal field. Furthermore, the study by Kazuki Ashihara et al. (2023) [18] reinforces the importance of using these metrics to ensure the interpretability and consistency of the topics extracted by topic models, which is crucial for accurately identifying and grouping legal themes.

These studies validate the choice of the topic coherence metric, ensuring that the models represent legal topics accurately and consistently, which is fundamental for effective interpretation in the legal domain.

3.2 Analysis and Results of CBOW and Skip-Gram Model Comparison

The following section presents the results obtained from applying the selected evaluation metrics.

Spearman's Correlation for Semantic Similarity: CBOW vs Skip-Gram

Figure 1 compares the Spearman correlation between CBOW and Skip-gram models for semantic similarity in Ecuadorian legal texts. CBOW achieved a higher correlation

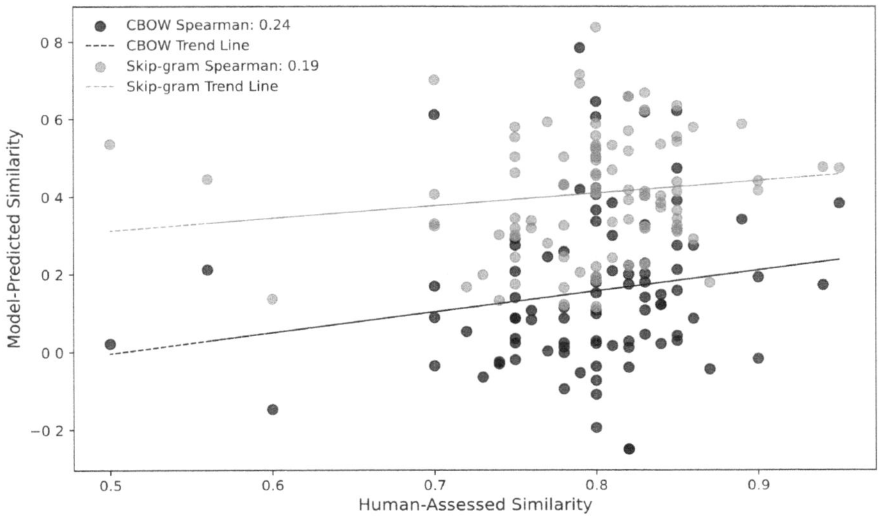

Fig. 1. Spearman's correlation comparison between CBOW and Skip-gram models for semantic similarity. CBOW shows a slightly higher correlation (0.24) compared to Skip-gram (0.19), indicating a better alignment with human-assessed similarities.

(0.24) compared to Skip-gram (0.19), suggesting a slightly better alignment with human-assessed similarities. However, both values remain relatively low, indicating that both models face challenges in fully capturing the complexity of legal semantics.

Both models display positive trend lines, indicating a general monotonic relationship with human evaluations. The steeper slope of the Skip-gram trend line, despite its lower correlation coefficient, points to less consistency compared to CBOW, reinforcing CBOW's marginally superior performance in capturing semantic nuances within this legal context.

Coherence Comparison Between CBOW and Skip-Gram Model

Figure 2 compares the topic coherence scores (c_v) between the CBOW and Skip-gram models across different document indices in the Ecuadorian legal corpus. Initially, CBOW achieves slightly higher coherence scores, but both models experience a decline around document indices 5 to 10, indicating challenges in maintaining topic consistency.

From index 10 onwards, the scores of both models increase and frequently overlap, suggesting similar effectiveness in capturing thematic structures. On average, CBOW maintains a slightly higher mean coherence score of 0.6637 compared to Skip-gram's 0.6573, indicating marginally better topic consistency overall. However, the minimal difference suggests both models perform comparably in representing legal themes.

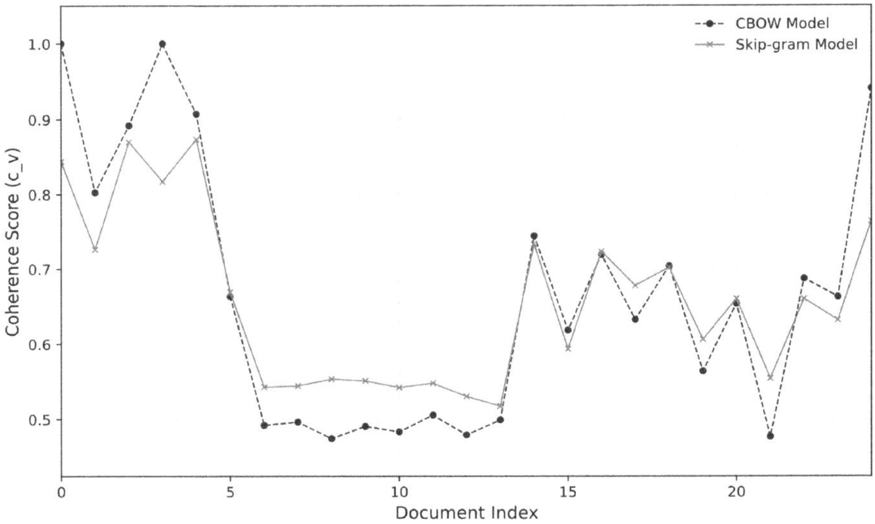

Fig. 2. Topic Coherence Comparison between CBOW and Skip-gram Models. The metric evaluates the consistency and relevance of topics identified in the legal corpus across different document indices

4 Results

The evaluation demonstrated that the CBOW model outperformed the Skip-gram model in both semantic similarity and topic coherence. In terms of semantic similarity, the CBOW model achieved a Spearman correlation of 0.24, compared to 0.19 for Skip-gram, suggesting a slightly better alignment with human-assessed similarities, even though both values were relatively low, reflecting challenges in capturing the complexity of legal semantics. For topic coherence, CBOW also showed a marginally higher average score of 0.6637 compared to 0.6573 for Skip-gram. Despite these differences, the overall performance of both models was comparable in capturing semantic and thematic relationships within the Ecuadorian legal corpus.

In summary, while CBOW holds a slight advantage in both semantic similarity and topic coherence, neither model fully captures the complexities of Ecuadorian legal language, highlighting opportunities for further refinement and improvement in modeling techniques.

5 Discussions

The results of this study reveal both the strengths and limitations of CBOW and Skip-gram in representing semantic relationships within Ecuadorian legal texts. While CBOW showed slightly better performance in semantic similarity and topic coherence, both models struggled to capture the complexities of legal semantics, particularly in handling hierarchical dependencies and nuanced relationships. A key limitation was the segmentation of compound legal terms, such as "proceso judicial," during preprocessing, which reduced the models' ability to maintain semantic integrity. Addressing these challenges requires tailored tokenizers to better preserve specialized terminology.

Future research should explore transformer-based models, such as Legal-BERT, which leverage attention mechanisms to model deeper contextual and hierarchical relationships. These techniques, combined with domain-specific tokenizers and legal ontologies, could significantly improve semantic representations and enable applications like semantic search and legal document processing. These advancements would build on the foundation established in this study, addressing current limitations and offering robust solutions for analyzing Ecuadorian legal texts.

6 Conclusions

This study evaluated CBOW and Skip-gram models for semantic analysis of Ecuadorian legal texts, highlighting their strengths and limitations in capturing semantic relationships and thematic coherence. While CBOW demonstrated slightly better performance, both models faced challenges in addressing the complexities of legal semantics, including hierarchical dependencies and nuanced language structures.

A significant limitation was the lack of a tailored tokenizer for legal texts, which affected the ability to preserve domain-specific terms. Addressing this issue would enhance the precision of semantic representations. The findings underscore the potential of these models for general semantic tasks but reveal their limitations in specialized legal contexts.

Future research should focus on exploring advanced NLP techniques, particularly transformer-based models and attention mechanisms, which have shown superior contextual understanding and the ability to model hierarchical dependencies. Combining these with domain-specific tokenizers and legal ontologies could significantly improve semantic search, legal document processing, and case law analysis. This work lays the foundation for developing more robust tools tailored to the Ecuadorian legal domain.

References

1. Chalkidis, I., Androutsopoulos, I., Aletras, N.: Neural Legal Judgment Prediction in English. In: ACL 2019 - 57th Annual Meeting of the Association for Computational Linguistics, Proceedings of the Conference, pp. 4317–4323 (2019). https://doi.org/10.18653/V1/P19-1424
2. Chalkidis, I., Androutsopoulos, I., Michos, A.: Obligation and prohibition extraction using hierarchical RNNs. In: ACL 2018 - 56th Annual Meeting of the Association for Computational Linguistics, Proceedings of the Conference (Long Papers), vol. 2, pp. 254–259 (2018). https://doi.org/10.18653/V1/P18-2041
3. Medvedeva, M., Wieling, M., Vols, M.: Rethinking the field of automatic prediction of court decisions. Artif. Intell. Law (Dordr) **31**(1), 195–212 (2023). https://doi.org/10.1007/S10506-021-09306-3/FIGURES/1
4. Mikolov, T., Chen, K., Corrado, G., Dean, J.: Efficient estimation of word representations in vector space. In: 1st International Conference on Learning Representations, ICLR 2013 - Workshop Track Proceedings (2013)

5. Mikolov, T., Sutskever, I., Chen, K., Corrado, G.S., Dean, J.: Distributed representations of words and phrases and their compositionality. Adv. Neural Inf. Process. Syst. **26** (2013)
6. Glogar, O.: The concept of legal language: what makes legal language 'legal'? Int. J. Semiot. Law **36**(3), 1081–1107 (2023). https://doi.org/10.1007/S11196-023-10010-5/FIGURES/2
7. Camacho-Collados, J., Pilehvar, M.T.: From word to sense embeddings. J. Artif. Intell. Res. **63**, 743–788 (2018). https://doi.org/10.1613/JAIR.1.11259
8. Levy, O., Goldberg, Y.: Linguistic regularities in sparse and explicit word representations. In: Proceedings of the Eighteenth Conference on Computational Natural Language Learning (2014). https://doi.org/10.3115/v1/w14-1618
9. Aletras, N., Tsarapatsanis, D., Preoţiuc-Pietro, D., Lampos, V.: Predicting judicial decisions of the European court of human rights: a natural language processing perspective. PeerJ Comput. Sci. **2**(10), e93 (2016). https://doi.org/10.7717/PEERJ-CS.93
10. Sproat, R., Emerson, T.: The First International Chinese Word Segmentation Bakeoff, pp. 133–143 (2003). https://doi.org/10.3115/1119250.1119269
11. Ashmawy, M., Fakhr, M.W., Maghraby, F.A.: Lexical normalization using generative transformer model (LN-GTM). Int. J. Comput. Intell. Syst. **16**(3), 183 (2023). https://doi.org/10.1007/s44196-023-00366-8
12. Yolchuyeva, S., Németh, G., Gyires-Tóth, B.: Text normalization with convolutional neural networks. Int. J. Speech Technol. **21**(3), 589–600 (2018). https://doi.org/10.1007/S10772-018-9521-X
13. Sarica, S., Luo, J.: Stopwords in technical language processing. PLoS ONE **16**(8) (2021). https://doi.org/10.1371/JOURNAL.PONE.0254937
14. Ingason, A.K., Helgadóttir, S., Loftsson, H., Rögnvaldsson, E.: A mixed method lemmatization algorithm using a Hierarchy of Linguistic Identities (HOLI). In: Nordström, B., Ranta, A. (eds.) Lecture Notes in Computer Science (Including Subseries Lecture Notes in Artificial Intelligence and Lecture Notes in Bioinformatics), LNAI, vol. 5221, pp. 205–216. Springer, Heidelberg (2008). https://doi.org/10.1007/978-3-540-85287-2_20
15. Zhelezniak, V., Savkov, A., Shen, A., Hammerla, N.: Correlation coefficients and semantic textual similarity. In: Burstein, J., Doran, C., Solorio, T. (eds.) Proceedings of the 2019 Conference of the North American Chapter of the Association for Computational Linguistics: Human Language Technologies, (Long and Short Papers), vol. 1, pp. 951–962. Association for Computational Linguistics, Minneapolis (2019). https://doi.org/10.18653/v1/N19-1100
16. Darji, H., Mitrović, J., Granitzer, M.: Exploring semantic similarity between German legal texts and referred laws. In: Fred, A., Aveiro, D., Dietz, J., Bernardino, J., Masciari, E., Filipe, J. (eds.) Knowledge Discovery, Knowledge Engineering and Knowledge Management, pp. 37–50. Springer International Publishing, Cham (2023)
17. Rosner, F., Hinneburg, A., Röder, M., Nettling, M., Both, A.: Evaluating topic coherence measures (2014). Accessed 24 Sept 2024. https://arxiv.org/abs/1403.6397v1
18. Ashihara, K., et al.: Improving topic modeling through homophily for legal documents. Appl. Netw. Sci. **5**(1) (2020). https://doi.org/10.1007/s41109-020-00321-y

Stimulation of Spatial Reasoning in Children Aged 6 to 7 Using Assistive Technology, Computer Vision, and Elements of Inca and Cañari Cultures

C. Japón-Chavez, V. Robles-Bykbaev(✉), A. Parra-Astudillo, E. Lema-Condo, D. Sánchez-Noboa, and Y. Robles-Bykbaev

GI-IATa, Cátedra UNESCO Tecnologías de apoyo para la Inclusión Educativa, Universidad Politécnica Salesiana, Cuenca, Ecuador
cjaponc@est.ups.edu.ec,
{vrobles,aparraa,elema,ksanchezn1,zrobles}@ups.edu.ec

Abstract. Spatial reasoning is an essential skill for children to understand how objects move within a three-dimensional space. This skill begins to develop in infancy as babies recognize body parts and the positions of surrounding objects and people. Young children enhance their spatial understanding through play, such as using shape-sorters or open-ended building blocks, which allow them to grasp spatial concepts and visualize shapes mentally. In Ecuador today, there remains a lack of technological tools to support the development of spatial reasoning in children aged 6 to 7 years from a playful perspective. Therefore, this article presents a tool based on a robotic assistant and a vision module designed to stimulate the development of this skill in children through the lens of Inca and Cañari cultures. The robotic assistant represents a guinea pig that moves across a model featuring motifs from these two cultures. The movement of the robotic assistant is controlled by a vision module that captures overhead images, processes them, and analyzes the spatial locations of obstacles and target objects representing cultural elements (such as clothing, food, etc.). To conduct a preliminary evaluation of the tool's functionalities, a consensus analysis was performed with four experts in the field of education, yielding a moderate level of consensus as indicated by the Kendall's coefficient of concordance ($W = 0.43997$) and an associated $p-value$ of 0.02694. These results are encouraging and suggest that the tool is promising for use in classrooms with children.

Keywords: Robotic assistant · Cañari Culture · Inca Culture · Spatial reasoning · Children · Computer vision

1 Introduction

Culture represents a fundamental component in individuals' lives and plays a crucial role concerning identity, that is, the deep-rooted and profound sense of

F. R. Narváez et al. (Eds.): SmartTech-IC 2024, CCIS 2392, pp. 217–231, 2026.
https://doi.org/10.1007/978-3-031-98287-3_16

belonging. Culture and identity form a multi-structural and multidimensional interdependent framework. Identity, in turn, is shaped by cultural practices and perceptions, making it a complex social construct that responds to specific temporal and historical factors. In Ecuador, a multiethnic and multicultural country, the Cañari culture has been studied for many years due to its significant contribution to intangible cultural heritage, as well as the remarkable richness that sparks great interest and curiosity among those who are invested in its origin, development, evolution, and perpetuation. Globalization, a convoluted process that has altered the dynamics of cultures worldwide, has among its adverse effects the displacement of cultural and symbolic components and, therefore, cultural practices and perceptions. Among the most notable of these is the desire to assimilate into a dominant monetary culture and the aspiration for "whitening," especially in the case of Indigenous ethnic groups. To this day, it is undeniable that the term "Indigenous" carries a negative stigma. This cultural construct positions those who belong to Indigenous ethnic groups, or the Indigenous Peoples of Ecuador, in a place of social exclusion, often associated with social segregation and rejection. Indigenous Peoples represent 10% of the population in Latin America. Yet, their income levels and human development indicators, such as education and health conditions, have been systematically lagging behind the rest of the population [12].

This issue is exacerbated by the lack of adapted tools to facilitate access to educational content for culturally diverse populations, such as the Cañari culture. Even more concerning is the absence of technologies that would allow for the protection, preservation, and reproduction of cultural content, which is essential for safeguarding intangible cultural heritage. There are currently advantageous tools and devices provided by Information and Communication Technologies (ICTs), so much so that specific devices offer cultural preservation and recovery opportunities. These technologies not only enhance learning capacities [13] but also enable the revitalization and conservation of ancestral languages [10]. The advantages of technological tools extend beyond these contributions, as they also play a role in improving processes related to children's neurodevelopment. In this sense, they offer multiple positive impacts, both sociocultural and neurobiological.

Neurodevelopment can be understood as an organized and orchestrated sequence of changes experienced by our nervous system throughout life, leading to the acquisition of new and more complex functional abilities. These changes result from processes involving both biological/nature and environmental/nurture variables, interacting in a reciprocal and plastic manner [5]. Therefore, it is plausible to conceive neurodevelopment as a fundamental process requiring special attention, as stimulating children is crucial for enhancing this process.

The human nervous system and related species contain critical elements that help explain neurodevelopment, with the brain, specifically the cerebral cortex, being of particular importance. During neurodevelopmental stages, neurons are born, migrate to their final locations, form networks, and subsequently achieve fine-tuning through apoptosis, synaptic pruning, and myelination. This is followed by regional maturation and the development of specific areas, allowing the emergence of sensory functions, language, and eventually higher-order cognitive functions, including social cognition [5]. Thus, proper stimulation can increase positive performance in various areas [6].

Stimulation during the neurodevelopment of children is vital as it can enhance the development of laterality, which in turn promotes the individual's full intellectual, social, personal, and emotional potential [4]. Stimulation can be achieved through well-known ICTs, for instance, by employing electronic devices that serve as educational assistants. It has been demonstrated that these devices can stimulate the development of spatial thinking, explicitly benefiting children's cognitive and motor areas. This occurs by increasing curiosity, attention, concentration, and learning motivation while promoting logical thinking and body awareness [11]. Therefore, the present proposal focuses on an electronic device that aims to enhance spatial awareness in children while also contributing to protecting and preserving cultural values related to the Cañari culture.

2 Related Work

Using computer vision and robotic assistants in early childhood education has proven to be a promising strategy for promoting spatial reasoning in preschool-aged children. By providing dynamic and interactive environments that can adapt to the specific needs of students, these technological advancements offer exceptional opportunities to enhance learning. Children can explore spatial concepts tangibly and engagingly through robotic assistants equipped with computer vision capabilities. This aids in developing mental rotation, visualization, and spatial orientation skills. Evidence suggests that children are more motivated and engaged with these tools, and their ability to understand and manipulate spatial information improves significantly. In addition to supporting learning in STEM fields, this innovative approach prepares children to tackle complex challenges and develop critical skills in an increasingly technological and digital world [14].

We highlight several related works that have been developed in this area:

The article analyzes how spatial reasoning and computational thinking in preschool children can be developed through guided play involving robot programming. It was found that children used their bodies as a spatial reference when interacting with a programmable robot. Additionally, verbal and non-verbal support from the teacher was essential for learning. It was also discovered that children's computational and spatial understanding and skills improve when technology is combined with dialogue about spatial concepts [2].

A systematic review of empirical research on activities that promote the development of computational thinking in preschool children is presented in the text. The contexts and motivations of the studies and the robots used in the suggested activities, and the evaluation procedures were examined. The review categorized the activities based on context, the role of adults, and the inclusion of non-technology-based activities. The evaluation methods for computational thinking were also analyzed. The article provides a comprehensive overview of current research, identifies gaps, and offers suggestions for future studies [1].

The text analyzes the influence of various programming education modalities on the development of computational thinking in young children. An analysis of 32 empirical studies found that programming moderately enhances children's computational thinking. Graphic programming was shown to be more effective than tangible programming and unplugged programming (without technology). These findings are crucial for educational tool designers and educators to develop more effective methods for teaching programming in early childhood [16].

A study on the effects of robotics education on elementary school children's attitudes towards STEM and their spatial ability is analyzed in the text. A 31-week robotics course, focused on mechanical design, electronics, algorithms, and programming, was attended by 39 students. The children's spatial abilities, assessed through spatial visualization and mental rotation tests, as well as their attitudes toward STEM, were significantly improved by the robotics training. This indicates that educational robotics can be an effective means to promote spatial skills and spark greater interest in STEM fields [15].

The study compared the effect of a programmable robot-based intervention aimed at improving the spatial abilities of kindergarten children with a control group and a traditional intervention. Compared to the other groups, the children who participated in the intervention with the programmable robot showed significant improvement in spatial relations and mental rotation. However, visual memory did not improve as a result of the robot intervention. The study highlights the importance of exploring innovative methods to enhance spatial skills in young children [3].

The impact of STEM education on the development of mathematical skills, particularly spatial ability, in children aged 5 to 6, was analyzed in the study. Two kindergarten classes were used: one received regular lessons for two months, while the other received STEM lessons twice a week. The findings demonstrated that the impact of STEM education, especially for children with intermediate or low initial mathematical skills, was primarily achieved through skills related to building blocks [7].

3 System Architecture

The combination of computer vision technologies and robotic control was implemented in the development of the system to create an interactive educational solution. The objective is to provide a practical and educational tool that enables students to explore and better understand the principles of robotics, computer vision, and programming. In real-time, the system can detect and track a moving object's trajectory- in this case, our robotic assistant (the guinea pig)-providing an accessible and scalable platform for experiments and demonstrations in educational settings. It incorporates foundational elements that associate our robotic assistant, a guinea pig, with a learning experience focused on its relationship to Cañari and Inca cultures.

The system has been designed in independent yet interconnected modules to facilitate scalability and maintenance in educational environments. Each module is responsible for a specific part of the processing, allowing students to better understand each stage of the robot's development and operation. The main modules include the user interface, which was designed to be intuitive and accessible, enabling effective interaction with the system; the image capture module, which utilizes a USB camera positioned at an overhead angle to capture real-time images, allowing for monitoring and analysis of the robotic assistant's operational environment; the image processing module, which serves as the core of the system due to its capability to process and analyze images captured by the camera, employing computer vision algorithms to interpret visual information; and the control module, which acts as the executor of commands calculated by the image processing module, meaning it is responsible for direct communication with the robot's hardware, transmitting commands that dictate speed, direction, and distance.

3.1 Robotic Assistant Structure

The electronic system of the robotic assistant (guinea pig) is composed of an Arduino NANO microcontroller, which controls the various sensors and actuators and receives data from the system via Bluetooth communication protocol. Furthermore, the robotic assistant operates autonomously due to its rechargeable battery.

Communication between the computer system and the robotic assistant occurs through commands that specify the distance and angle the assistant must maintain during each interaction. This facilitates its movement toward the target by activating the motors (actuators) located at the bottom, specifically in the wheels, whose motion is activated by the DC motor driver that receives commands from the microcontroller. This structure is illustrated in Fig. 1.

The interaction of this proposal takes place on a wooden model themed with Inca and Cañari motifs. The webcam is positioned on a wooden structure located at the top of the base, directed downward, allowing the webcam to capture overhead images, as illustrated in Fig. 2.

3.2 Calculation of the Trajectory of the Robotic Assistant

The robotic assistant moves autonomously within the model, starting from an initial position and navigating towards a specified goal. Three markers based on three distinct colors—blue, red, and green—are employed to achieve this. The first color, blue, is placed on the robotic assistant to indicate its location in the system; the second color, red, is positioned on the robot's head to establish its orientation; and the third color, green, signifies the destination to which the robot must move.

As shown in Fig. 3, the computer vision module performs two composite operations to extract the pixels of interest and calculate the centroids of the three markers: Region of Interest Detection (ROI) and position calculation. In

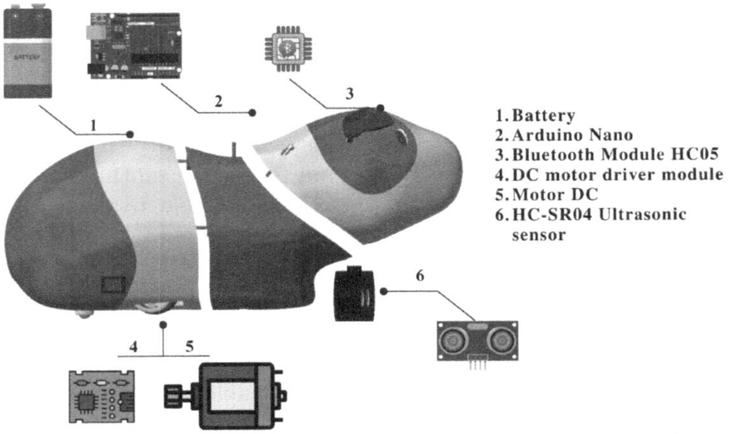

Fig. 1. Diagram of the main electronic components of the robotic assistant.

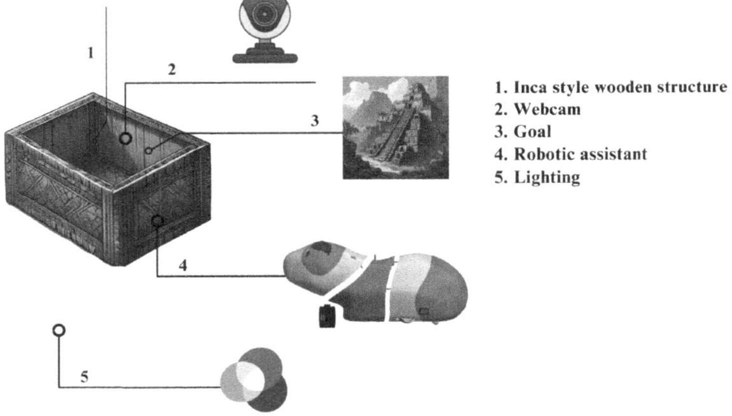

Fig. 2. General structure of the model in which the robotic assistant interacts with the artificial vision system. (Color figure online)

the first operation, the original image captured in the RGB (Red, Green, Blue) color space is converted into the HSV (Hue, Saturation, Value) color space.

Once this conversion is completed, a multichannel thresholding operation is applied using Eq. 2, thus obtaining a binary image containing the regions of interest for the three markers.

$$M(x,y) = \begin{cases} 1 & \text{if } L_C^H \leq I_C^H(x,y) \leq U_C^H \wedge L_C^S \leq I_C^S(x,y) \leq U_C^S \wedge \\ & L_C^V \leq I_C^V(x,y) \leq U_C^V \\ 0 & \text{otherwise} \end{cases} \quad (1)$$

where:

- L represents the lower bound and U the upper bound of the pixel intensity levels used for the comparison. The subscript C and the superscripts H, S, or V indicate the channel being processed, as applicable (H = Hue, S = Saturation, V = Value).
- $I(x, y)$ represents the intensity level for the H, S, or V channel, as applicable.
- $M(x, y)$ represents the resulting binary image, where the pixel at position (x, y) will be set to 1 if the intensity level is between the lower bound L and upper bound U, and 0 otherwise.

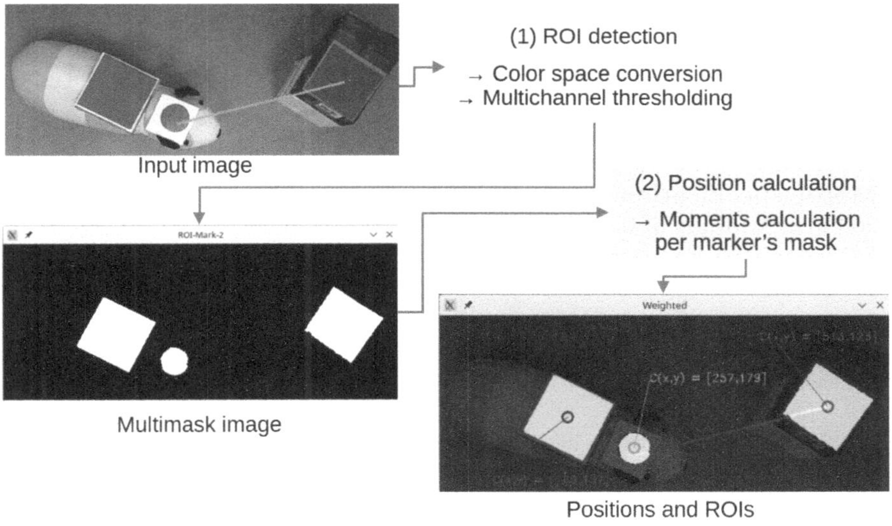

Fig. 3. Operations performed by the computer vision module and the resulting outputs obtained from each of them. (Color figure online)

It is important to note that the masks of the regions of interest for the three markers must be preserved in order to perform the subsequent calculation of the moments.

Once the regions of interest (ROIs) are identified, the second operation is executed. In this stage, the centroids of the 3 ROIs corresponding to the marks obtained from the previous operation are calculated. For this purpose, Eq. 2 is applied for each mark:

$$C(\overline{x}, \overline{y}) = \left(\frac{\sum_{\forall x} \sum_{\forall y} x \cdot I(x, y)}{\sum_{\forall x} \sum_{\forall y} I(x, y)}, \frac{\sum_{\forall x} \sum_{\forall y} y \cdot I(x, y)}{\sum_{\forall x} \sum_{\forall y} I(x, y)} \right) \tag{2}$$

where:

- $C(\overline{x}, \overline{y})$ represents the centroid of each of the three markers.
- $I(x, y)$ represents the intensity level of the image (1 for pixels representing the marker and 0 for the remaining pixels).
- x, y represent the coordinates of the pixels in the image.

This setup allows for developing a series of exercises through which children can learn spatial concepts (such as front, back, left, right, etc.), practice distance perception, and explore various movements in a two-dimensional space.

3.3 Algorithms, Hardware Setup, and Configurations Utilized for Trajectory Calculation and Robot Control

The development of the tool was carried out using the latest stable version of OpenCV (4.10) and the NumPy library version 1.24.4. The hardware specifications used are as follows:

- **Camera resolution**: 800×600px
- **Motor specifications**: N20 DC motor operating at 12 V with a current of 200 mA, a torque of 0.1 kg·cm, and 2400 revolutions per minute under load.
- **Microcontroller version**: Arduino NANO ATMega328.
- **Communication protocol**: HC05 module version 2.0, which functions as either master or slave; in this case, it operates as a slave, receiving commands from the Arduino Nano. The Arduino sends the appropriate commands to control the functionality of the actuators, specifically the DC motors.

Algorithm 1 outlines all the steps followed to compute the trajectory, as well as the threshold values used. The color binarization ranges depend on the targets to be segmented. For instance, for the color purple (robot head), the range used is: $\{\text{min} = [0, 0, 0], \text{max} = [50, 10, 50]\}$ in the HSV color space.

Algorithm 1: Robot Control Based on Image Processing

Input: Image in RGB color space, HSV ranges (min, max), thresholds t_1 (500 pix), t_2 (30 cm).

Output: Commands to control the robot (move/stop).

Step 1: Transform the image from RGB color space to HSV color space.

Step 2: For a given set of HSV ranges associated with each target (robot head, robot bottom, and goal):

  foreach *target* **do**
    Generate a binary image indicating the target area.

Step 3: For each binary image, find the external contours of the target area.

Step 4: foreach *binary image contour* **do**
  if *area* ¡ t_1 **then**
    Discard the binary image.
  else
    Compute the centroid of the contour using Equation (2).

Step 5: For each centroid:
1. Calculate the distances between centroids.
2. Compute the angle using the arccos function.

Step 6: if *distance* ¿ t_2 **then**
  Send the move command to the robot.
else
  Send the stop command.

Step 7: Repeat Steps 3–6 until the distance is less than or equal to t_2.

---

4 Pilot Experiment and Preliminary Results

A questionnaire was designed and administered to a group of four experts in the fields of education and educational psychology to conduct a preliminary evaluation of the tool's functionalities. The demographic characteristics of the participants are detailed in Table 1:

As can be seen, the experts exhibit a young professional profile characterized by solid educational backgrounds and extensive experience in education and working with children. The average age of the participants was 41 years (SD = 4.69), indicating a relative homogeneity within the group. The Kendall coefficient of concordance (W) [8] was employed to determine the degree of consensus among the experts' evaluations. The analysis was structured in two parts. The first part, of a demographic nature, included eight items related to the general data of the participants (expert ID, first name, last name, age, gender, profession, and years of experience). The second part, consisting of eighteen questions, focused on:

Table 1. Profiles of the experts who participated in the initial analysis process of the tool's main functionalities.

Expert	Gender	Age (years)	Profession	Experience (years)
1	Female	44	Bachelor in Educational Sciences, specialization in Psychopedagogy	25
2	Female	34	Bachelor in Educational Sciences, specialization in Early Childhood Education	11
3	Female	43	Bachelor in Educational Sciences, specialization in Early Childhood Education	21
4	Female	43	Bachelor in Educational Sciences, specialization in Early Childhood Education	27

- Usefulness of the tool for reinforcing learning in the following areas:
  - Logical-mathematical relationships (Q01)
  - Space-time concepts (Q02)
  - The concept of "left-right" (Q03)
  - The concept of "back-forward" (Q04)
- Usefulness of the tool for children to learn the following concepts:
  - Colors, shapes, and sizes (Q05)
  - Clothing of the Cañari culture (Q07)
  - Characteristics of housing in Cañari culture (Q08)
  - History of the Cañari culture (Q09)
  - Characteristics of housing in Inca culture (Q11)
  - History of Inca culture (Q12)
- Relevance of the robotic assistant to represent a guinea pig as an element of Cañari culture (Q06)
- Possibility for children to learn about Inca clothing (Q10)
- Relevance of the audio (Q13) and its volume level (Q15) that explains characteristics of cultural identity.
- Usefulness of the audio for facilitating cultural identity learning in children (Q14)
- Relevance of the board size for children to interact with the robotic assistant (Q16)
- Relevance of incorporating the tool in regular schools in the city of Cuenca for learning about cultural identity and logical-mathematical relationships (Q17)
- Overall perception of the experts regarding the usefulness of the tool (Q18)

To facilitate a practical evaluation of the tool, demonstration sessions were conducted in which the experts interacted with it and observed the physical structure of the system (including cultural aspects) and the robotic assistant, as well as the movements and functionality of the computer vision system.

To determine the degree of agreement among the experts' evaluations, an inter-rater concordance analysis was performed using the Kendall coefficient of concordance (W) [8]. The calculations were done using the statistical software R (version 4.3.3). For the consensus criterion, the following null and alternative hypotheses were proposed:

- Null Hypothesis (H_0): There is no consensus among the experts regarding the proposed criterion.
- Alternative Hypothesis (H_a): There is consensus among the experts regarding the proposed criterion.

As can be observed below, for Kendall's Coefficient of Concordance W, the interpretation proposed by [9] was utilized:

- $0.00 \leq w < 0.20$ - Slight agreement
- $0.20 \leq w < 0.40$ - Fair agreement
- $0.40 \leq w < 0.60$ - Moderate agreement
- $0.60 \leq w < 0.80$ - Substantial agreement
- $w \geq 0.80$ - Almost perfect agreement

According to the interpretation proposed by [9], the value obtained for Kendall's Coefficient of Concordance ($W = 0.43997$) suggests a **"moderate"** level of agreement among the four experts. However, the associated $p - value$ ($p = 0.02694$) indicates that the null hypothesis of the absence of agreement can be rejected. Therefore, the results provide sufficient evidence to affirm a moderate consensus among the experts.

Figure 4 presents the results of four of the most critical questions posed to the professionals among the 18 questions analyzed.

As can be seen, three experts consider the tool "sufficient" and "very" useful for reinforcing learning in Logical-Mathematical Relations. In contrast, only one expert believes it to be "somewhat" useful (quadrant "A," question "Q01"). Similarly, in the area of space-time concepts, two experts deem it to be "very" useful, one considers it "sufficiently" useful, and one regards it as "moderately" useful (quadrant "B," question "Q02"). Furthermore, two experts are "agree" and the other two are "completely agree" on the relevance of the robotic assistant to represent a guinea pig as an element of Cañari culture (quadrant "C", question "Q06"). In a similar vein, all the experts concur that the tool is "very useful" for teaching children about the history of Cañari culture (quadrant "D," question "Q09").

In Fig. 5, a summary of the agreement among the experts on the different questions can be observed: a) consensus among the four experts on seven questions (Q07 to Q12, Q18), b) consensus among three experts on four questions (Q04 to Q06, Q17), and consensus among at least two experts on seven questions (Q01 to Q03, Q13, Q15, Q16).

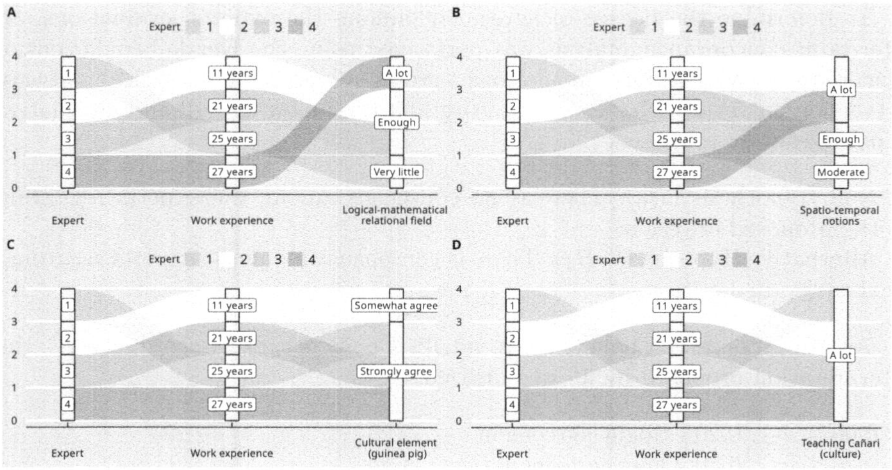

Fig. 4. Results of the consensus analysis among professionals regarding the questions related to the learning or reinforcement of logical-mathematical relationships and temporal-spatial concepts, as well as the relevance of representing the guinea pig ("cuy" in Spanish) as an element of Cañari culture and the utility of the tool in teaching this culture.

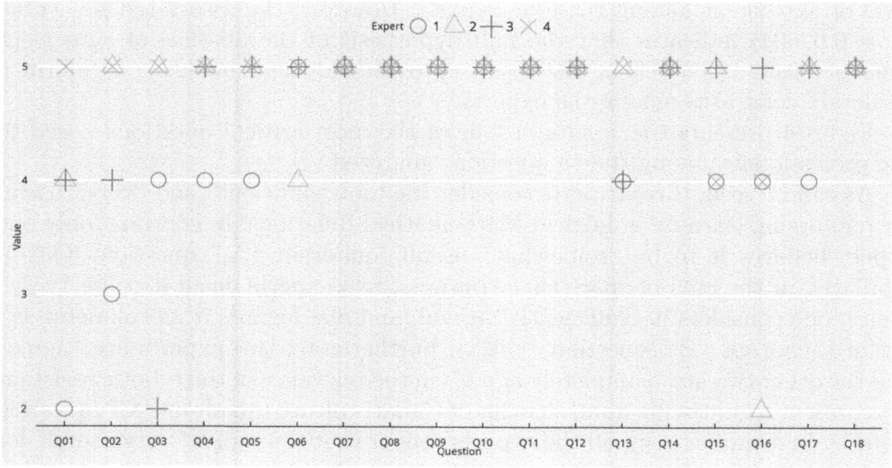

Fig. 5. Level of agreement on the 18 questions of the survey administered to the experts.

4.1 Pilot Test of the Tool with Children in a Real-World Environment

To evaluate the tool in a real-world environment, a pilot test was conducted with two 6-year-old girls and one 7-year-old boy. The children, who are attending the second and third years of basic general education, respectively, interacted with the tool over several sessions. Following this process, they completed a 13-question survey designed to assess their perceptions based on the following criteria:

- **Interest level:** Andean cultures (C1), images and videos of the Inca and Cañari cultures (C3), and the history of the Inca and Cañari cultures (C8).
- **Sense of pride:** Learning about the Inca and Cañari cultures (C2).
- **Ease of understanding:** The game's activities (C4) and the audio explanations about the characteristics of cultural identity (C9).
- **Learning possibilities:** Using technology (C5), enjoying learning new topics with technological support (C6), and understanding housing in the Inca and Cañari cultures (C7).
- **Perception of specific aspects:** The volume level of the audio indicating cultural characteristics (C10), the robot's movement speed (C11), the robot's size (C12), and the possibility of having the robot at home (C13).

As we can see in Fig. 6, the perceptions of the three children about the educational support tool are summarized across different criteria (C01 to C13). Child 1 and Child 2 generally gave high ratings, indicating positive perceptions about most aspects of the tool, including its educational content, interactivity, and engagement level. Specifically, their ratings are consistently in the 4.55 range, suggesting a strong interest in and understanding of the material. In contrast, Child 3 exhibited a more critical perspective, with lower ratings (between 1 and 3) across several criteria, such as interest in the cultural content (C01C03) and ease of understanding (C04). However, even Child 3 gave slightly higher ratings for some aspects, such as the robot's functionality and learning potential

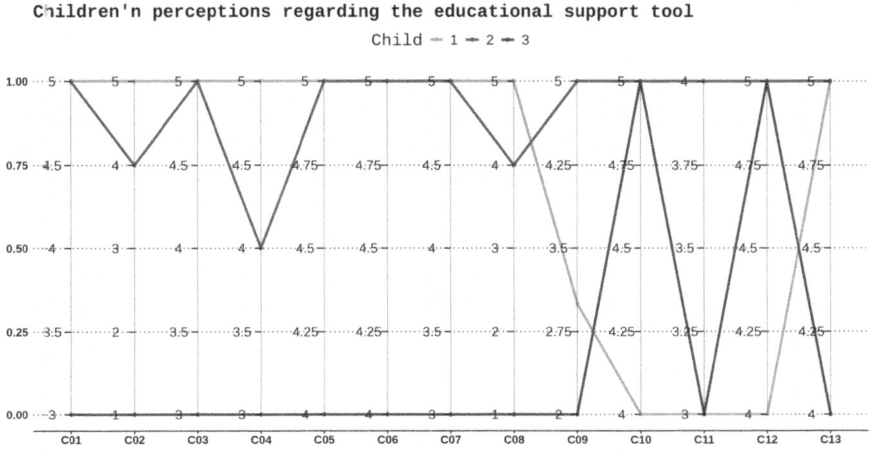

Fig. 6. Children's perception regarding the educational support tool.

(C07C13). The data suggests that while the tool was well-received by most participants, there are areas, particularly in accessibility and engagement, that might need improvement to address varying preferences and learning styles.

5 Conclusions

The development of educational support technologies is fundamental, as it motivates children while effectively recording the various activities conducted in the classroom.

This article has demonstrated that using simple techniques, such as Hu moments in conjunction with capturing overhead images, allows for effective control of the movements performed by a robotic assistant. It has also been shown that, despite being a new tool, there is a moderate consensus among a group of experts with an average of over 21 years of experience regarding the system's potential to support the development of spatial reasoning in children aged 6 to 7 years.

Furthermore, it is important to emphasize that the integration of these resources not only enriches the educational process but also fosters children's interest in their cultural roots, contributing to holistic education. Through playful and visually stimulating activities, children develop essential cognitive skills for their educational growth, underscoring the importance of exploring educational methodologies that combine technology and culture, thereby achieving a more inclusive and effective education.

The following future lines of work are proposed:

- Develop a text-to-speech module that enables spoken commands to be given to the robot to execute specific movements within the model.
- Implement a computer vision module based on deep learning neural networks to replace color markers with two- and three-dimensional objects.

Acknowledgments. This work has been fund by the "Sistemas Inteligentes de Soporte a la Educación (v5)" research project, the Cátedra UNESCO "Tecnologías de apoyo para la Inclusión Educativa" initiative, and the Research Group on Artificial Intelligence and Assistive Technologies (GI-IATa) of the Universidad Politécnica Salesiana, Campus Cuenca.

References

1. Bakala, E., Gerosa, A., Hourcade, J.P., Tejera, G.: Preschool children, robots, and computational thinking: a systematic review. Int. J. Child-Comput. Interact. **29**, 100337 (2021)
2. Berson, I.R., et al.: An exploration of robot programming as a foundation for spatial reasoning and computational thinking in preschoolers' guided play. Early Child. Res. Q. **65**, 57–67 (2023)

3. Brainin, E., Shamir, A., Eden, S.: Robot programming intervention for promoting spatial relations, mental rotation and visual memory of kindergarten children. J. Res. Technol. Educ. **54**(3), 345–358 (2022)
4. Brotóns, E.B.: Programas de desarrollo de la lateralidad, mejora del esquema corporal y organización espaciotemporal. intervención en dificultades de aprendizaje. Procesos y programas de neuropsicología educativa **79** (2015)
5. Förster, J., López, I.: Neurodesarrollo humano: un proceso de cambio continuo de un sistema abierto y sensible al contexto. Revista Médica Clínica Las Condes **33**(4), 338–346 (2022)
6. Gallego Marín, M.A.: La importancia de la estimulación adecuada durante el neurodesarrollo en la primera infancia. Revista senderos pedagógicos **10**(1), 103–120 (2019)
7. He, X., Li, T., Turel, O., Kuang, Y., Zhao, H., He, Q.: The impact of stem education on mathematical development in children aged 5–6 years. Int. J. Educ. Res. **109**, 101795 (2021)
8. Juškevičienė, A., Stupurienė, G., Jevsikova, T.: Computational thinking development through physical computing activities in steam education. Comput. Appl. Eng. Educ. **29**(1), 175–190 (2021)
9. Landis, J.R., Koch, G.G.: The measurement of observer agreement for categorical data. Biometrics, 159–174 (1977)
10. Medina Campos, S.G., Castellón Chévez, G., Sambola, D.M.: Diccionario móvil como estrategia de rescate y conservación lingüísticas de las etnias miskitu y rama de la costa caribe nicaragüense. Wani (81) (2024)
11. Patiño Campoverde, M.M., Arcos Aguilar, M.A., Revelo Quiñonez, N.N., Lema Guanopatin, M.S.: Estimulación sensorial para el desarrollo del pensamiento espacial en niños de 3 a 5 años. Sinergia Académica **7**(1), 187–203 (2024)
12. Robles-Bykbaev, Y.: Social Inequality. IntechOpen, Rijeka (2024). https://doi.org/10.5772/intechopen.100687, https://doi.org/10.5772/intechopen.100687
13. Rodríguez Umaña, L.A., Martínez Baquero, J.E.: Uso de aplicaciones móviles como herramienta de apoyo tecnológico para la enseñanza con metodología steam. Revista Politécnica **18**(36), 75–90 (2022)
14. Sánchez Tendero, E., Cózar Gutiérrez, R., González-Calero Somoza, J.A.: Robótica en la enseñanza de conocimiento e interacción con el entorno. una investigación formativa en educación infantil. RIFOP: Revista interuniversitaria de formación del profesorado: continuación de la antigua Revista de Escuelas Normales **33**(94), 11–28 (2019)
15. Sisman, B., Kucuk, S., Yaman, Y.: The effects of robotics training on children's spatial ability and attitude toward stem. Int. J. Soc. Robot. **13**(2), 379–389 (2021)
16. Wei, Y., Wang, L., Tang, Y., Su, J., Lei, Y., Peng, W.: Influence of programming education modalities on the computational thinking in young children: a comprehensive review and meta-analysis. J. Comput. Assist. Learn. (2024)

Creating a Botnet in a Virtual Environment: A Study Based on the Mirai Code

Luis A. Coronel-Rojas, Fabián R. Cuesta-Quintero, Yesenia Areniz-Arévalo, and Dewar Rico-Bautista(✉)

Universidad Francisco de Paula Santander, Ocaña, Colombia
{lacoronelr,fcuestaq,yareniza,dwricob}@ufpso.edu.co

Abstract. Mirai malware represents a significant threat to Internet of Things (IoT) security, demonstrating its ability to compromise devices through common vulnerabilities such as weak passwords and insecure authentication protocols. This study investigated the functionality and impacts of Mirai through controlled attack simulations, focusing particularly on its ability to orchestrate distributed denial-of-service (DDoS) attacks. The results revealed that Mirai can effectively coordinate networks of compromised devices to launch massive attacks, severely impacting the availability and stability of online services. The operational impact assessment indicated that Mirai-targeted DDoS attacks can saturate critical network resources, resulting in prolonged outages and significant financial losses for affected organizations. Current defense strategies, such as network segmentation and security patching, are crucial but insufficient in the face of Mirai's rapid evolution and adaptability. In addition, the importance of ongoing cybersecurity education and cross-industry collaboration to mitigate the risks associated with IoT botnets is highlighted. In conclusion, this study provides a comprehensive view of the cyber threats represented by Mirai, highlighting the urgency of strengthening cyber defenses and developing innovative solutions to protect critical infrastructure and sensitive data in the IoT ecosystem.

Keywords: vulnerability · mirai code · DDoS attacks and Dos

1 Introduction

In today's digital era, cybersecurity has become a central concern due to the increasing interconnectedness of devices and systems [1]. This technological advancement has brought not only higher levels of efficiency and connectivity but also a proliferation of increasingly sophisticated and persistent cyber threats [2]. Among these threats, botnets have emerged as some of the most worrisome, representing networks of compromised devices under the control of attackers to carry out various malicious activities [3].

In this context, the Mirai malware stands out as a prime example of today's threats. Originally designed to infect Internet of Things (IoT) devices, Mirai is notorious for its ability to launch distributed denial-of-service (DDoS) attacks, severely impacting the availability and functionality of online services and systems [4]. Its evolution and adaptability continue to challenge cybersecurity efforts worldwide [5].

F. R. Narváez et al. (Eds.): SmartTech-IC 2024, CCIS 2392, pp. 232–242, 2026.
https://doi.org/10.1007/978-3-031-98287-3_17

This research project focuses on thoroughly exploring the operation and implications of the Mirai malware, using a controlled virtualized environment to simulate and study its capabilities. Through detailed analysis of Mirai, the study aims to understand its modus operandi and effective defense methods, while also generating critical insights that can strengthen infrastructure protection and user privacy in the contemporary digital environment [6].

The relevance of this study lies in its significant contribution to the field of cybersecurity [7–9]. It addresses critical challenges by providing valuable insights on how to mitigate and prevent threats posed by botnets, particularly the infamous Mirai botnet. Mirai has been responsible for some of the most disruptive and high-profile cyber-attacks in recent years, making its study essential for improving overall internet security [10]. The findings from this research can inform the development of more robust cyber defense strategies, ensuring that networks are better protected against such sophisticated threats.

Moreover, the results obtained from this study can help improve awareness of the vulnerabilities inherent in the massive interconnection of IoT devices [11]. As the IoT ecosystem continues to expand, with billions of devices connected worldwide, the potential attack surface for cybercriminals increases exponentially. Understanding these vulnerabilities is crucial for developing effective countermeasures and enhancing the security of IoT devices [12]. Additionally, the research emphasizes the importance of raising awareness about these vulnerabilities among both consumers and industry stakeholders. By improving awareness, it is possible to foster better security practices and encourage the adoption of more secure technologies, leading to a more resilient digital infrastructure capable of withstanding and recovering from cyber threats [13].

This paper is structured to address each aspect of the project, from the initial setup of the simulation environment to the evaluation of results and final conclusions, with the goal of providing a comprehensive framework for effectively studying and combating botnets in today's digital landscape.

2 Methodology

The methodology of this study focused on thoroughly investigating Mirai malware and its impacts on Internet of Things (IoT) devices through a controlled simulation in a virtualized environment. This approach allowed us to explore the behavior of botnets, their attack capabilities and potential strategies to mitigate these risks [14–16].

2.1 Design of the Simulation Environment

The design of the simulation environment was based on the configuration of virtual machines (VMs) using VirtualBox, selecting operating systems compatible with the Mirai versions investigated [2]. Four different VMs were set up:

Controller Machine (C&C): in charge of sending commands to bot machines and orchestrating attacks.

Bot Machines: Configured to receive instructions from the controlling machine and execute coordinated attacks.

Victim Machine: Simulated to be a vulnerable IoT device, being the target of the attacks.

Each VM was configured with network adapters in bridged mode to simulate a local network, facilitating communication between VMs and allowing access to the Internet to download updates and necessary resources, [17], (see Fig. 1).

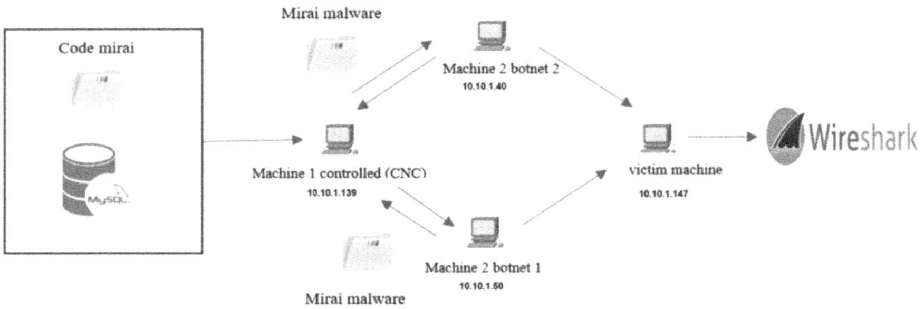

Fig. 1. Design of the Mirai Botnet.

Bot and CnC machines in VirtualBox, (see Fig. 2).

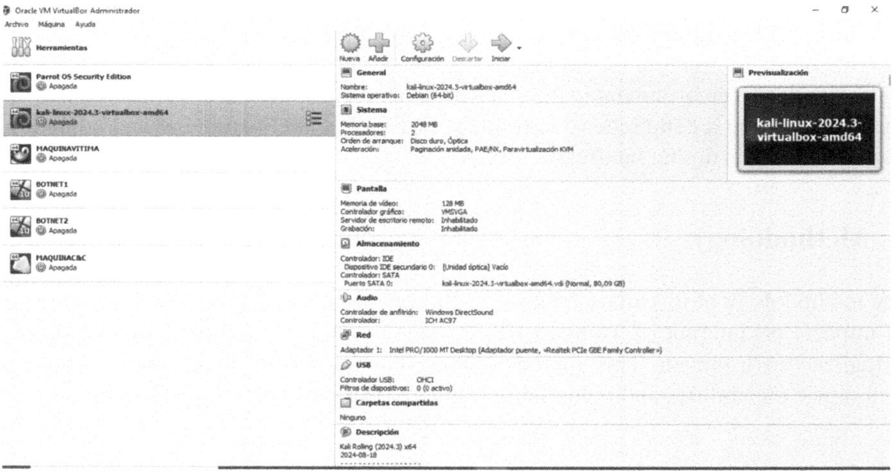

Fig. 2. Bot and CnC machines in VirtualBox.

2.2 Virtual Machine Configuration

To ensure the security and integrity of the simulation environment, rigorous configurations were applied, (see Fig. 3):

Security: non-essential services and ports were disabled, strong passwords were implemented for user accounts, and firewalls were configured to manage incoming and outgoing network traffic effectively [18].

Monitoring: Monitoring software such as Wireshark was installed to capture and analyze network traffic during the simulated attacks, providing crucial data for evaluating the effectiveness of the attacks [19].

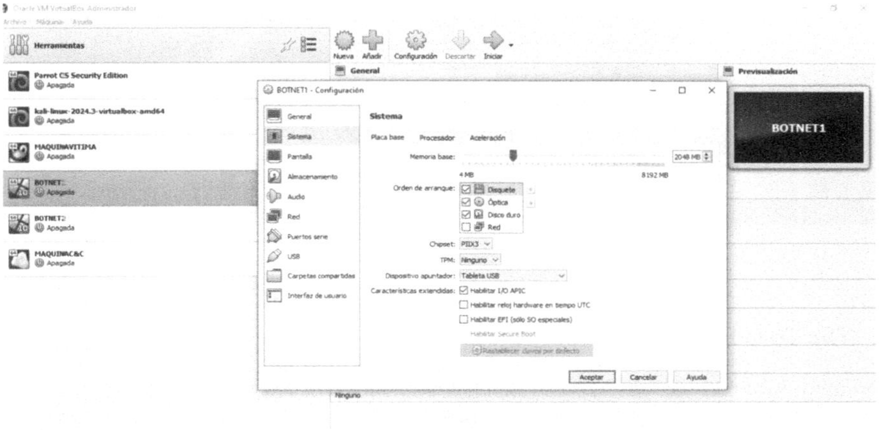

Fig. 3. VirtualBox configuration.

3 Results

The results of this research provide a detailed view of the behavior and impacts of Mirai malware on Internet of Things (IoT) devices, evaluated through controlled botnet simulations and DDoS attacks.

The following are the results obtained in the laboratory tests of the controlled virtual environment for the use of the mirai code. The results obtained were subjected to a detailed analysis to evaluate the effectiveness of the simulated attacks and propose effective defense strategies. It is important to mention that the machines must all be turned on to carry out the necessary tests in the laboratory and obtain the expected results to be analyzed, so the first thing to do is to check that all machine configurations are correct. The following aspects were considered:

3.1 Botnet Implementation and Test Execution

The botnet was implemented using an adapted version of the Mirai malware, designed exclusively for research purposes and not for malicious activities, (see Fig. 4). Effective communication was established between the controlling machine and the bot machines through the C&C protocol, demonstrating the malware's ability to coordinate distributed denial of service (DDoS) attacks [3].

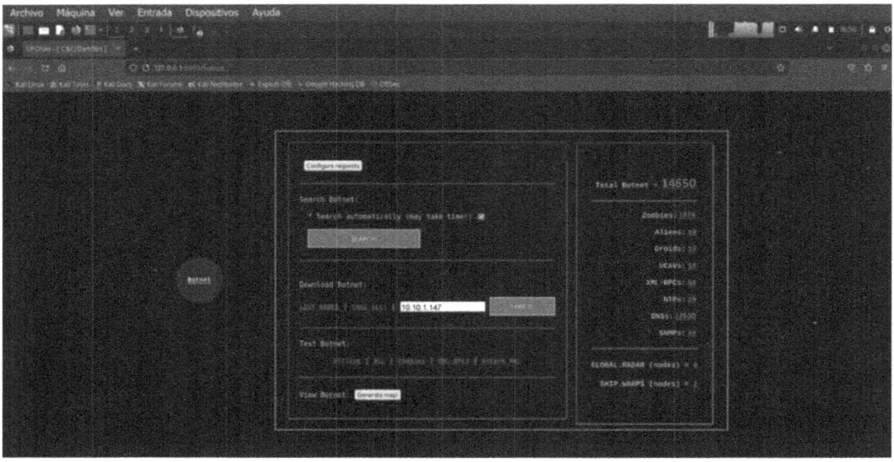

Fig. 4. Botnet and malware startup.

3.2 The Tests Included

Simulated Attacks: various types of DDoS attacks were executed from bot machines to the victim machine, recording and analyzing the impact on service availability and performance of the target system.

Impact Assessment: The resilience of the victim system to the attacks was assessed by observing the utilization of resources such as CPU and bandwidth and analyzing the resilience of the system to abnormal traffic loads [11, 20], (see Fig. 5).

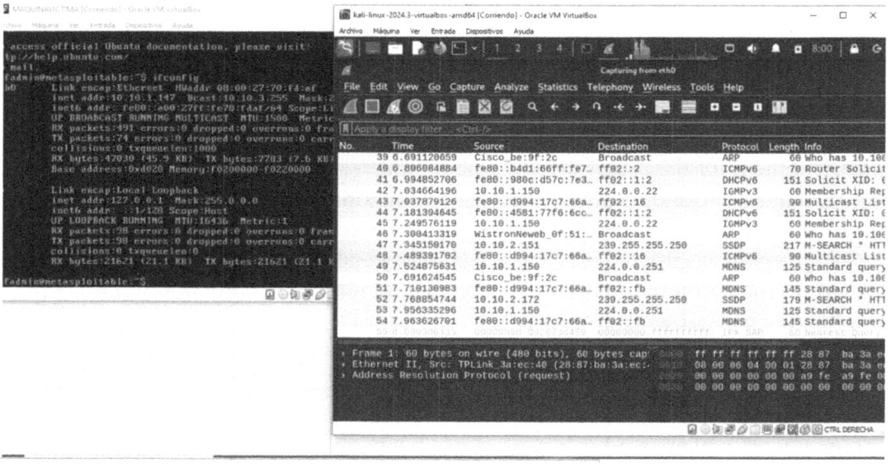

Fig. 5. Running virtual controlled environment.

3.3 Attacker's Console

The following shows the attacker's console in the controlled virtual environment, as illustrated in Fig. 6. This console provides a detailed view of the attack processes, including the commands executed by the attacker, the responses received, and the overall status of the compromised systems.

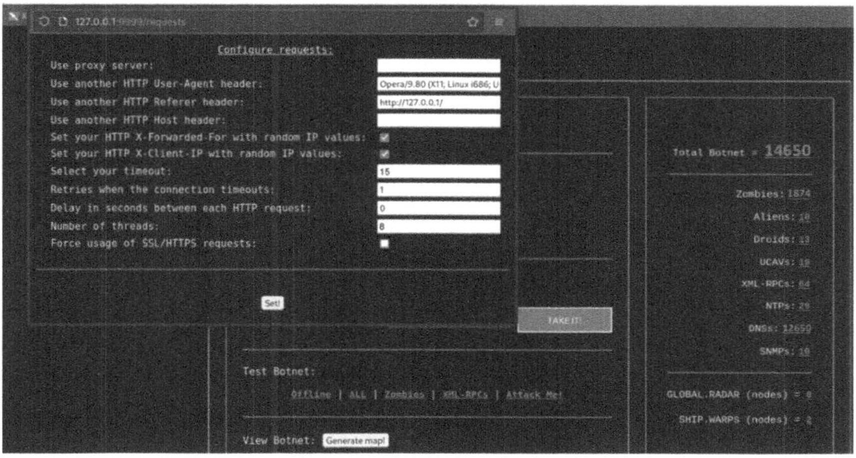

Fig. 6. Attacking console.

In the following Fig. 7, you can see that the list of available attacks that can be performed is displayed.

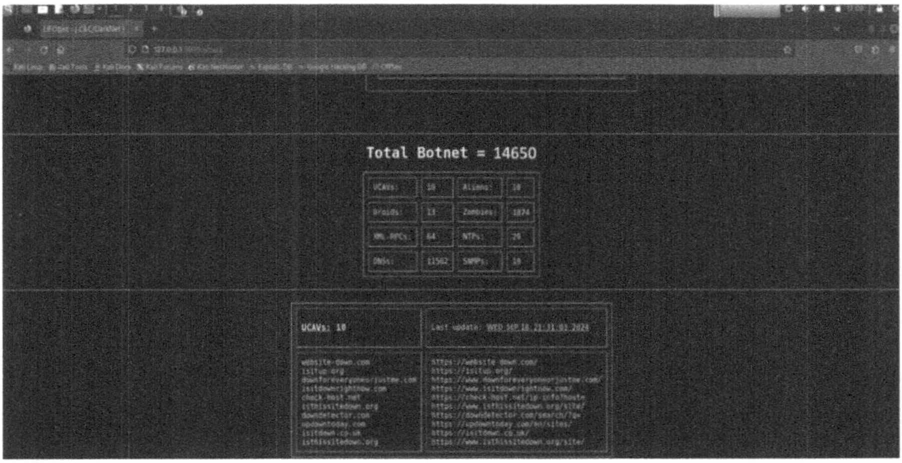

Fig. 7. List of available attacks.

- Propagation and Infectivity of Mirai

Mirai proved to be highly effective at propagating within the simulated network of vulnerable IoT devices. Using automated scanning and exploitation techniques, the malware was able to identify and compromise devices with known vulnerabilities, such as weak default passwords or insecure authentication protocols. This rapid propagation capability underscores the critical importance of securing IoT devices through robust security practices, such as regular firmware updates and implementing strong password policies [1, 21].

- Execution of DDoS Attacks

During the simulated Distributed Denial of Service (DDoS) attacks, Mirai used the compromised devices as bots to generate malicious traffic directed towards the victim machine. This activity resulted in a dramatic increase in system resource usage on the target machine, including high CPU load and network bandwidth. These attacks not only affected the availability of critical services, but also showed how Mirai can effectively coordinate a botnet to maximize the impact on a specific target [11, 20].

The status of the resource in HTTPNULL provides critical information about the current condition and availability of a particular resource in the HTTP environment. This status can indicate whether the resource is accessible, in use, or experiencing any issues that might affect its functionality, (see Fig. 8).

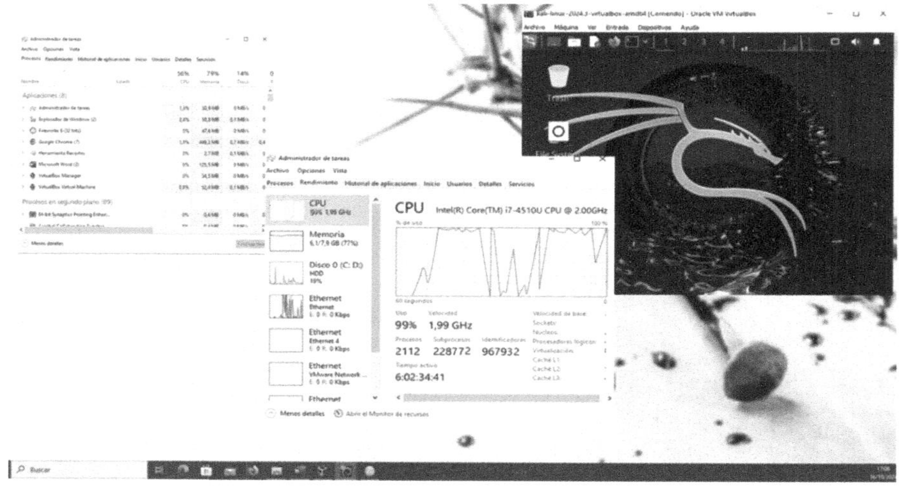

Fig. 8. Status of the resource in HTTPNULL.

3.4 Impact on Infrastructure and System Response

The impact analysis revealed that Mirai attacks can seriously compromise the operational stability and performance of network infrastructure. Service disruptions during DDoS attacks highlight the urgent need for effective mitigation strategies. Furthermore, Mirai's ability to adapt and evade conventional defenses underscores the importance of proactive approaches to cybersecurity, including constant monitoring of network traffic and rapid response to suspicious activity [18], (see Fig. 9).

Fig. 9. Disk space occupied after the test.

3.5 Defense and Mitigation Assessment

Various strategies were explored to defend against and mitigate Mirai attacks, including the implementation of behavior-based traffic filters, frequent security updates for IoT devices, and continued education on secure IoT practices. However, the persistence and constant evolution of Mirai highlight the need for more innovative and collaborative solutions among device manufacturers, service providers, and the cybersecurity community at large [19].

Malware Effectiveness: Mirai's ability to infect vulnerable IoT devices and to expand botnets on a large scale was evaluated.

Infrastructure Impact: Analyzed how the attacks affected service availability, system response and data integrity.

Lessons Learned: Identified common vulnerabilities in IoT devices and recommended measures to improve security and mitigate future attacks, emphasizing the importance of cybersecurity education and secure design of IoT systems [1].

3.6 Ethical Considerations and Limitations

During the development of the research, the ethical principles established by academic institutions and relevant legal regulations were respected. The limitations of the study, such as the restrictions inherent to the virtualized environment and the ethical implications of simulating DDoS attacks, were highlighted, ensuring responsible conduct in cybersecurity research [11, 20], (see Fig. 10).

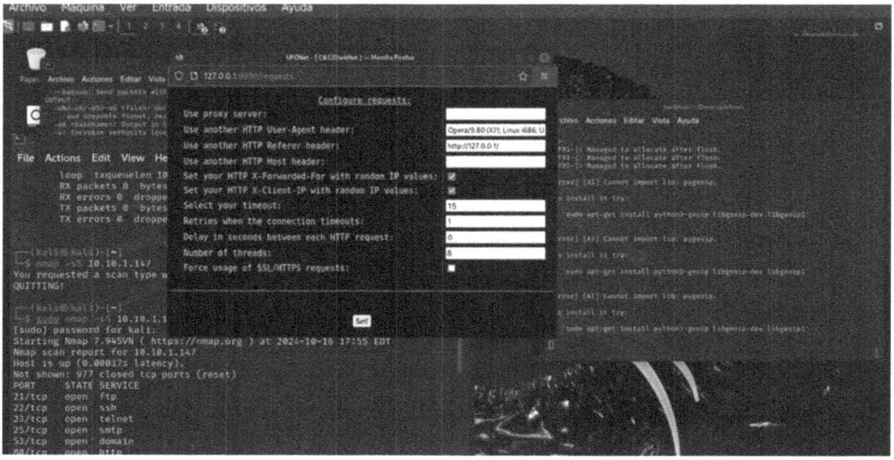

Fig. 10. Console mirai code.

4 Conclusions

The research conducted provides a comprehensive understanding of the challenges and risks associated with Mirai malware in the context of Internet of Things (IoT) devices. From simulating attacks and assessing their impact, the following conclusions can be drawn:

Mirai has proven to be highly effective in infiltrating and compromising vulnerable IoT devices. Its ability to exploit common vulnerabilities, such as weak passwords and insecure authentication protocols, highlights the urgent need for robust security practices to protect these devices.

Simulated Distributed Denial of Service (DDoS) attacks evidence Mirai's ability to coordinate a botnet and direct malicious traffic to specific targets. This results in significant disruption of services, underscoring the importance of preventive measures and rapid incident response.

Impact assessment reveals that Mirai attacks can seriously compromise the operational stability and performance of network infrastructure. Prolonged service disruptions affect the availability and reliability of connected systems, requiring effective mitigation and recovery strategies.

Despite efforts to defend against and mitigate Mirai attacks, malware persistence and adaptability present significant challenges. Current strategies, such as network segmentation and security patching, are critical but must be complemented by continued innovations in cybersecurity and collaboration between different actors in the IoT ecosystem.

This research underscores the need for increased awareness of vulnerabilities in IoT devices and the implementation of proactive security practices. It also highlights the importance of continuing education for both end users and security professionals on emerging threats and best practices to mitigate risks.

References

1. Silva, S.S.C., Silva, R.M.P., Pinto, R.C.G., Salles, R.M.: Botnets: a survey. Comput. Netw. **57**, 378–403 (2013)
2. Stephens, B., Shaghaghi, A., Doss, R., Kanhere, S.S.: Detecting Internet of Things bots: a comparative study. IEEE Access **9**, 160391–160401 (2021)
3. Sinanovic, H., Mrdovic, S.: Analysis of Mirai malicious software. In: 2017 25th International Conference on Software, Telecommunications and Computer Networks (SoftCOM). IEEE, pp 1–5 (2017)
4. Su, Y.-H., Cho, M.C.Y., Huang, H.-C.: False alert buster. In: Proceedings of the 2nd International Conference on Computing and Big Data. ACM, New York, pp 58–62 (2019)
5. Bui, T., Duc, T., Linh Giang, N., Hien, N., Thanh, N., Khanh, N.: A machine learning-based framework for detecting malicious HTTPS traffic. In: Proceedings of the 12th International Symposium on Information and Communication Technology, pp 769–776. ACM, New York (2023)
6. Hallman, R., Bryan, J., Palavicini, G., Divita, J., Romero-Mariona, J.: IoDDoS—The internet of distributed denial of sevice attacks - a case study of the Mirai malware and IoT-based botnets. In: Proceedings of the 2nd International Conference on Internet of Things, Big Data and Security. SCITEPRESS - Science and Technology Publications, pp 47–58 (2017)
7. Palla, T.G., Tayeb, S.: Intelligent Mirai malware detection for IoT nodes. Electronics (Basel) **10**, 1241 (2021)
8. Gopal, T.S., Meerolla, M., Jyostna, G., Reddy Lakshmi Eswari, P., Magesh, E.: Mitigating Mirai malware spreading in IoT environment. In: 2018 International Conference on Advances in Computing, Communications and Informatics (ICACCI), pp 2226–2230. IEEE (2018)
9. Vengatesan, K., Kumar, A., Parthibhan, M., Singhal, A., Rajesh, R.: Analysis of Mirai botnet malware issues and its prediction methods in Internet of Things. In: Pandian, A.P., Senjyu, T., Islam, S.M.S., Wang, H. (eds.) ICCBI - 2018, pp 120–126. Springer, Cham (2020)
10. Bederna, Z., Szadeczky, T.: Cyber espionage through botnets. Secur. J. **33**, 43–62 (2020)
11. Wang, A., Chang, W., Chen, S., Mohaisen, A.: Delving into Internet DDoS attacks by botnets: characterization and analysis. IEEE/ACM Trans. Netw. **26**, 2843–2855 (2018)
12. Griffioen, H., Doerr, C.: Examining Mirai's battle over the Internet of Things. In: Proceedings of the 2020 ACM SIGSAC Conference on Computer and Communications Security. ACM, New York, pp 743–756 (2020)
13. Aslan, Ö., Aktuğ, S.S., Ozkan-Okay, M., Yilmaz, A.A., Akin, E.: A comprehensive review of cyber security vulnerabilities, threats, attacks, and solutions. Electronics (Basel) **12**, 1333 (2023)
14. Haner, J.K., Knake, R.K.: Breaking botnets: a quantitative analysis of individual, technical, isolationist, and multilateral approaches to cybersecurity. J. Cybersecur. (2021). https://doi.org/10.1093/cybsec/tyab003
15. Kabla, A.H.H., Thamrin, A.H., Anbar, M., Manickam, S., Karuppayah, S.: Peer-to-peer botnets: exploring behavioural characteristics and machine/deep learning-based detection. EURASIP J. Inf. Secur. **2024**, 20 (2024)
16. Ogu, E.C., Ojesanmi, O.A., Awodele, O., Kuyoro, S.: A botnets circumspection: the current threat landscape, and what we know so far. Information **10**, 337 (2019)

17. Zhang, X., Upton, O., Beebe, N.L., Choo, K.-K.R.: IoT botnet forensics: a comprehensive digital forensic case study on Mirai botnet servers. Forensic Sci. Int.: Digit. Investig. **32**, 300926 (2020)
18. Alatwi, H.A., Morisset, C.: Realism versus performance for adversarial examples against DL-based NIDS. In: Proceedings of the 38th ACM/SIGAPP Symposium on Applied Computing. ACM, New York, pp 1549–1557 (2023)
19. Apruzzese, G., Andreolini, M., Ferretti, L., Marchetti, M., Colajanni, M.: Modeling realistic adversarial attacks against network intrusion detection systems. Digit. Threats: Res. Pract. **3**, 1–19 (2022)
20. Vlajic, N., Zhou, D.: IoT as a land of opportunity for DDoS hackers. Comput. (Long Beach Calif.) **51**, 26–34 (2018)
21. Alomari, D., Anis, F., Alabdullatif, M., Aljamaan, H.: A survey on botnets attack detection utilizing machine and deep learning models. In: Proceedings of the 27th International Conference on Evaluation and Assessment in Software Engineering, pp 493–498. ACM, New York (2023)

Attention Based Tri-Decoder Framework for Segmentation and Classification of Nuclei in Bladder Histology

Sadia Jabbar Anwar[1], Ibtihaj Ahmad[2(✉)], Umar Saleem[3], Saleem Riaz[3], and Li Ying[1]

[1] School of Computer Science, Northwestern Polytechnical University, Xi'an 710072, Shaanxi, People's Republic of China

[2] National Health and Medical Big Data Research Institute, School of Public Health, Shandong University, Jinan 250012, Shandong, People's Republic of China
ibtihajahmad@sdu.edu.cn

[3] School of Automation, Northwestern Polytechnical University, Xi'an 710072, Shaanxi, People's Republic of China

Abstract. Accurate segmentation and classification of nuclei in histology images of bladder cancer (BC) is crucial for diagnosis and treatment. Hematological analysis gives valuable information about the tumor. However, issues like nuclei overlap and staining inconsistencies make the segmentation and classification challenging. To overcome these challenges, we propose a dual attention-based framework for segmenting and classifying nuclei using a bottom-up tri-decoder approach. Our framework employs three different attention decoder heads to produce semantic, edge, and classification maps. This multi-head attention mechanism enables the model to capture the features and the variations of the images. Additional measures, such as controlled watershed and pixel grouping, are applied to enhance segmentation and classification results. The proposed framework shows better segmentation accuracy and classification reliability with a Dice score of 0.8621 and provides better discrimination between nuclei with an mPQ value of 0.6273. The improved results increase the possibilities of the application of the new AI-based approaches in the diagnosis of bladder cancer and may serve as a basis for further developments in the field of digital pathology.

Keywords: Bladder Cancer · Histology Image · Dual Attention Framework · Tri-decoder · Semantic Segmentation

1 Introduction

Bladder cancer is one of the most common and heterogenic malignancies of the urinary tract responsible for high morbidity and mortality rate with millions of cases every year. The disease varies from mild to highly aggressive diseases such as muscle-invasive cancers hence the need for early diagnosis and right diagnosis

F. R. Narváez et al. (Eds.): SmartTech-IC 2024, CCIS 2392, pp. 243–256, 2026.
https://doi.org/10.1007/978-3-031-98287-3_18

to enhance treatment control and more favorable outcomes [1]. The histopathological examination is considered the gold standard for bladder cancer diagnosis as it provides information about the type and grade of cancer as well as cancer stage, which is crucial for making the treatment plan and predicting the outcomes [18]. However, traditional methods are time consuming and inter observer variability results in variability in diagnosis and management of the patient [23]. This highlights the need for fast and efficient diagnostic procedures [9]. Digital pathology has made a significant change in histopathological examination by allowing Whole Slide Images (WSIs) that present the morphology of tissues at high resolution [21]. However, WSIs present some difficulties because of their size and heterogeneity, therefore, require sophisticated computational tools for analysis. Recent advances in deep learning have resulted in its being a crucial enabler for improving WSI analysis and the field of digital pathology [7].

Applying AI-based methods to digital pathology can improve the diagnostic results and decrease the time needed for detailed examination, which can result in better management of patients and their conditions [14,31]. The current state-of-art deep learning models have been developed to perform diverse image analysis tasks, including nuclei segmentation and classification [15]. Of them, the convolutional-neural-networks (CNNs) have shown promising results in the automation of histological image segmentation and offer reliable tools to pathologists to improve diagnostic processes [16]. The attention mechanisms have been found to be one of the best techniques for enhancing both segmentation and classification in histology image. These mechanisms allow models to attend to the most important areas of an image, which improves feature representation and accuracy [10]. The incorporation of attention mechanisms into the existing deep learning architectures make the model more powerful for by focusing on target area also reduce the training time as well [26]. Compared to other models, attention-based models can capture the differences between similar structures and different staining intensities and perform more accurate segmentation and classification of nuclei [11]. Xie et al. [27] proposed an attention-based CNN that can well combine spatial and channel attention to enhance the segmentation and classification of bladder cancer nuclei. This has been shown to have better performance in dealing with the nuances of staining and tissue architecture that complicate other models. However, these models although efficient are still faced with the challenges of requiring large annotated training sets, and the use of massive computational power.

Since the advent of modern deep-learning, the architecture of U-Net has been highly influential in medical image segmentation as described by the research work of [19]. Subsequent versions have improved the original model in order to address the challenges of histopathological images especially in the context of the detailed and overlapping characteristics of the bladder cancer histology. To make more advance, the research work in [4], introduced a dual attention mechanism within a CNN framework and which has been found to be more effective in the differentiation of nuclei with similar staining patterns. However, the dual attention approach though strong, may not be adequate to solve problems such as the overlapping nuclei misclassification or the problem with extreme variations in staining which are recurrent in histopathology. In histopathological image analysis, multi-decoder architectures have been studied to segment and classify bladder cancer nuclei Multi-decoder network that yields semantic, edge, and classification maps was proposed in [29]. This multi-task technique is helpful in the differentiation of overlapping and differentially stained nuclei in the model. Such models are successful, but the complexity of such models slows the processing and requires more computational power, which is a constraint in clinical environment where time is of essence. To elaborate on this concept, [30], authors apply hybrid decoders which include attention-based mechanisms and traditional decoding techniques. This model improved nuclei segmentation, especially in differentiating closely clustered nuclei from the background tissue. Hierarchical structures and post-processing strategies such as conditional random fields make the models more difficult to use in the real-time diagnostic processes.

Although there has been a great advancement in the use of AI and ML in the segmentation and classification of bladder cancer nuclei, the current methods are still encountering some difficulties. Some of these challenges include the following; variability in staining [17], tissue heterogeneity and complexity [20], computational intensity [3], and model interpretability [8]. In the previous models, new features have been introduced including the attention mechanism. However the attention mechanism needs to be embedded in to multi-decoder architectures. This inclusion can help the multi-decoder architectures to learn the features more efficiently. The reason for selecting multi decoder framework is that We need many decoders, since the simultaneous segmentation and classification can not be achieved using a single decoder. The contributions of this work is as follow.

- Our approach uses a tri-decoder which comprises of three different attention heads to produce semantic, edge, and classification maps.
- This multi-head attention mechanism is developed to meet the requirements of histological image analysis, where heterogeneity in staining, intricate tissue architecture and overlapping nuclei are often encountered.
- Our framework improves the feature extraction capacity and helps to distinguish between the minor differences in the tissue architecture and staining intensity. This is especially important in the case of bladder cancer histology as accurate segmentation and classification of nuclei is vital for the right diagnosis.
- In this work, we also propose a post-processing framework that enhances the reliability of the classification process.

2 Proposed Framework

The proposed framework follows a bottom-up strategy; we build a model that synthesizes primitive features that post-processing techniques transform to enhanced segmentation and classifications [2]. In our previous research, we extend our decoder with more heads to generate the edge map and pixel classification. Despite the fact that these decoders could in principle directly produce instance segmentation, this approach would be less accurate due to such issues as overlapping or only partially stained nuclei, which would increase the false positive rate. To address these issues, we propose a solution which combines intelligently generated edges with semantic segmentation and other derived features, and then undergoes post-processing to produce accurate instance segmentation and classification. Starting with inputting a histological image to our tri-decoder network, it outputs a semantic segmentation, edge maps, and pixel-level classification. We then use a controlled watershed allowing us to obtain instance segmentation, which is then used to fine-tune the final classified nuclei. The detailed working of each block is explained in the following subsections (Fig. 1).

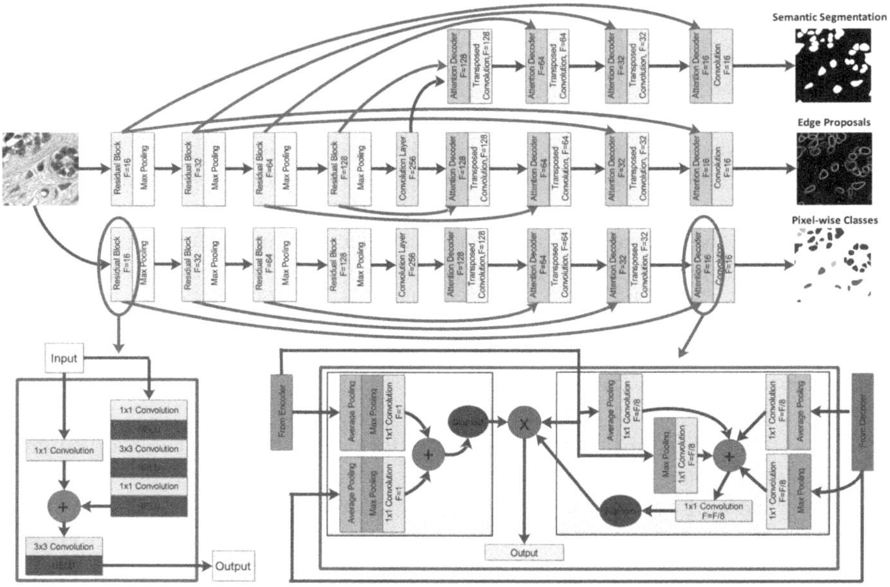

Fig. 1. Overview of the tri-decoder model and the detailed framework of the sub-blocks. The tri decoder model produce three outputs, i.e., semantic segmentation, edge maps, and pixel-level classes.

1. Input layer: The process begins with an input histology image, denoted as $I \in \mathbb{R}^{H \times W \times C}$, where H and W represent the height and width of the image, respectively, and C is the number of channels (e.g., RGB). The goal is to accurately segment and classify the nuclei within this image, which is critical for bladder cancer diagnosis and treatment planning.

2. ResNet Encoder: The input image I is passed through a ResNet encoder, which extracts hierarchical features. The ResNet architecture, composed of convolutional layers, batch normalization, and ReLU activations, is pre-trained on large datasets, enabling it to capture multi-scale features from the image.
Operational Details: The encoder processes the image through a series of residual blocks. As shown Eq. 1, for a given input x, each residual block performs the following operation
$$y = \text{ReLU}\left(x + F\left(x, \{W_i\}\right)\right) \tag{1}$$
where $F(x, \{W_i\})$ represents the convolutional operations within the block, and W_i are the learned weights. The residual connection $x + F(x)$ helps to mitigate the vanishing gradient problem, allowing for deeper networks.
Output: The output of the encoder is a set of feature maps $F_{\text{enc}} \in \mathbb{R}^{H' \times W' \times C'}$, where H', W', and C' denote the reduced height, width, and increased number of channels, respectively.
3. Attention mechanism: The attention block refines the feature maps F_{enc} by enhancing the regions of interest, making it easier for the decoders to accurately segment and classify nuclei.
Operational Details: The Eq. 2 shows, attention mechanism operates by calculating attention weights α for each feature map. These weights are derived using global average pooling (GAP) and global max pooling (GMP):
$$\alpha = \sigma\left(W_1 \cdot \text{GAP}(F_{\text{enc}}) + W_2 \cdot \text{GMP}(F_{\text{enc}})\right) \tag{2}$$
where W_1 and W_2 are learnable weights, and σ is the sigmoid activation function. The refined features are then computed as in Eq. 3:
$$F_{\text{att}} = \alpha \cdot F_{\text{enc}} \tag{3}$$
where $\cdot$ denotes element-wise multiplication.
Output: The output is a set of attention-refined feature maps F_{att}, which are passed to the subsequent decoding stages.
4. Tri-Decoder Heads: The attention-refined feature maps F_{att} are passed through three parallel decoders, each responsible for generating a different type of output. These components are:
   - **Semantic Decoder:** The semantic decoder produces a segmentation map $S \in \mathbb{R}^{H \times W \times 1}$ that delineates the regions containing nuclei. The decoder employs transposed convolutions (also known as deconvolutions) to upsample the feature maps:
   $$S = \sigma(\text{ConvTranspose}(F_{\text{att}})) \tag{4}$$
   - **Edge Decoder:** The edge decoder generates an edge map $E \in \mathbb{R}^{H \times W \times 1}$ that highlights the boundaries of the nuclei.
   Operational Details: Similar to the semantic decoder, the edge decoder upscales the features:
   $$E = \sigma(\text{ConvTranspose}(F_{\text{att}})) \tag{5}$$

- **Classification Decoder:** The classification decoder outputs a pixel-level classification map $C \in \mathbb{R}^{H \times W \times K}$, where K is the number of classes (e.g., cancerous, non-cancerous).
  Operational Details: The classification decoder processes the features through convolutional layers followed by softmax activation:

$$C = \text{softmax}(\text{Conv}(F_{\text{att}})) \tag{6}$$

2.1 Loss Function

Based on the tri-decoder framework, three types of loss functions (l_a, l_b, and l_c) are utilized and each of them has its own corresponding weight (λ_a, λ_b, and λ_c). The overall loss function is formulated as: overall loss function is formulated as:

$$l = \underbrace{\lambda_a l_a}_{\text{Semantic Segmentation}} + \underbrace{\lambda_b l_b}_{\text{edge map}} + \underbrace{\lambda_c l_c}_{\text{pixel-level Class}} \tag{7}$$

Some studies have proposed the use of hybrid loss functions e.g., mutual information and cross-entropy loss functions which have been proven successful. When it comes to semantic segmentation and edge maps, we have applied a special loss function which is known to be more efficient in these cases. This loss function is expressed as: This loss function is expressed as:

$$l_a = \frac{L_{Dice} \times L_{Jaccard}}{L_{Dice} + L_{Jaccard}} \tag{8}$$

This particular formulation has been used based on the fact that it offers better results in improving both the semantic segmentation and edge maps as compared with other typical loss functions. For the classification decoder, we adopt the categorical cross-entropy loss, defined as:For the classification decoder, we adopt the categorical cross-entropy loss, defined as:

$$l_c = -w_d \sum_d t_{c,d} \log(p_{c,d}) \tag{9}$$

In this equation $p_{c,d}$ is the predicted probability for class d of the data point c, $t_{c,d}$ is the corresponding target and w_d is the class-specific weight. These class weights are used to reduce the amounts of disparity that exists in the nuclear categorisations with the weights derived from the ratio of the category to the overall data set. There is no tuning for the weights λ_a , λ_b and λ_c and have been assigned 1,7 and 5 respectively arbitrarily for better results.

2.2 Post-processing for Instance Segmentation and Classification

For nuclei instance segmentation, we use a controlled watershed algorithm as shown in Fig. 2. The first step involves the removal of edge maps that have a probability less than 10 percent, which one has to determine based on testing to give the best results for removing false edges. Afterwards, these filter edge maps are subtracted from the semantic segmentation maps, which assists in fragmenting connected nuclei as well as fixing up the sure foreground regions (foreground markers) of the nuclei. The background markers depicted in the semantic segmentation image are in black. More preferable is if these background markers do not choose with their positions being within proximity to the nuclei edges of the mark. To ensure this, we compute the watershed transform of Euclidean distance transform of sure foreground markers and we can note watershed ridgles. We then integrate the sure foreground, ridgelines and background markers. Finally, we use the marker-controlled watershed algorithm to perform the instance nuclei segmentation.

To reclassify, we employ the segmented instances of nuclei and utilize the tri-decoder network in order to obtain the pixel-level class image and then, crop the related regions derived from the occasion of class reclassification. We then quantify the numbers of pixels in these extracted regions to be associated with each of the classes. It is then assigned to the class which has the highest pixel frequency within the area in subsequent steps. This process is mathematically expressed as a formula represented in Eq. 10:

$$y_c^{\text{ins}} = \max\left(\sum_{(i,j)} x_{c1}(i,j), \sum_{(i,j)} x_{c2}(i,j), \ldots, \sum_{(i,j)} x_{cn}(i,j)\right) \tag{10}$$

Here, y_c^{ins} represents the class c assigned to the instance ins, $x_{cn}(i,j)$ denotes the pixel class at row i, column j, as predicted by the tri-decoder network, and n represents the total number of classes. An illustration of the pixel grouping process is described in Fig. 2. It is to be noted that we classify the cells into five categories: neoplastic (that are tumors), connective, epithelial, dead and inflammatory.

2.3 Evaluation Metrics

For the evaluation of the proposed methods, we use different evaluation metrics for semantic segmentation, instance segmentation and classification. These evaluation metrics are used by other works for the performance comparison. For samantic segmentation, we use Dice score (DS), represented by,

$$\text{Dice} = \frac{2|A \cap B|}{|A| + |B|} \tag{11}$$

where A is the predicted set and B is the ground truth set.

For the instance segmentation, we use binary Panoptic Quality (nPQ)

$$\text{PQ} = \frac{\sum_{(p,g)\in TP} \text{IoU}(p,g)}{|TP| + \frac{1}{2}|FP| + \frac{1}{2}|FN|} \tag{12}$$

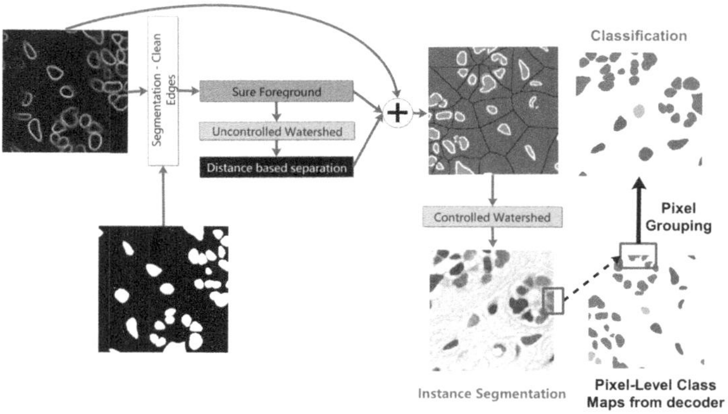

Fig. 2. The proposed post processing method for the instance segmentation and classification.

where TP is the set of true positives (correctly matched predicted and ground truth segments), FP is the set of false positives (unmatched predicted segments), FN is the set of false negatives (unmatched ground truth segments), IoU(p,g) is the Intersection over Union between a matched pair of predicted segment (p) and ground truth segment (g).

For the classification, we use multi-class PQ (mPQ)

$$PQ = \frac{1}{|C|} \sum_{c \in C} \frac{\sum_{(p,g) \in TP_c} \mathrm{IoU}(p,g)}{|TP_c| + \frac{1}{2}|FP_c| + \frac{1}{2}|FN_c|} \tag{13}$$

where C is the set of all classes, TP_c FP_c, and FN_c are the sets of true positives, false positives, and false negatives for class (c), IoU(p,g) is computed as above for each matched pair in class (c).

3 Experiment and Results

We use the PanNuke dataset [5,6], which comprises over 140 patches of H&E-stained bladder tissue. The classes in the dataset include neoplastic, non-neoplastic epithelial, inflammatory, connective tissue, and dead cells. PanNuke is extensively applied in computational pathology research for activities like panoptic segmentation and nuclear morphology studies, supporting developments in cancer diagnostics and automated pathology analysis with its high-quality annotations for segmentation and class labels.

Table 1 presents the detail parameters used during the experiments. These parameters can be used to reproduce the model results. During the training we use data augmentation techniques to increase the size of the dataset. At the start of the training the learning rate is set to 0.005, which is then gradually reduced.

Table 1. The table reports the parameters used during the training of the tri-decoder model.

Loss functions	Semantic Decoder	Hybrid loss
	Edge Decoder	Hybrid loss
	Classification Decoder	Categorical cross entropy
Loss weights		1,7,5
Data Augentation	Flip	vertical and horizontal
Learning rate		0.0005
Learning rate reduction		ReduceLROnPlateau
Optimizer		Adam
Batch size		18

This subsequent section discusses the performance of our proposed attention base tri-decoder method for semantic, instance segmentation tasks as well as cell classification through Fig. 3 and Table 2. The first column in Fig. 3 show image, The second column shows the semantic segmentation. Visual results. The proposed method correctly distinguish the interesting structures within histological images. The black mask shows the regions of interest (which could be cell clusters in a medical imaging scenario) while white is the background. Table I shows the proposed technique achieve high Dice Score (0.8621) compared to other methods. The third column of the visual results contains the instance segmentation. Each cell instance has a unique coloring such that cells can be isolated and counted individually. This is essential in analyzing complicated tissue structures to ensure that overlapping cells are separated. The results show that proposed achieve bPQ score 0.7316 as compared to Mask-RCNN (0.6049) and MicroNet (0.6488). This improvement demonstrates how our model is better at identifying

Table 2. The table reports the semantic segmentation (Dice), instance segmentation (bPQ), and classification (mPQ) performance. Some cells reports N/A, that means that the mentioned end-to-end state-of-the-art models can not generate instances segmentation, while some models do not use semantic segmentation for instance segmentation and classification.

Model	Dice Score	bPQ	mPQ
UNet [25]	0.7901	N/A	0.4825
UNet++ [32]	0.7998	N/A	0.4957
DIST [22]	0.8002	N/A	0.5012
MicroNet [24]	0.8247	0.6488	0.5357
Mask-RCNN [13]	N/A	0.6049	0.5065
HoverNet [12]	0.8494	0.7031	0.5792
PointNuNet [28]	N/A	0.7226	0.6065
Proposed	**0.8621**	**0.7316**	**0.6273**

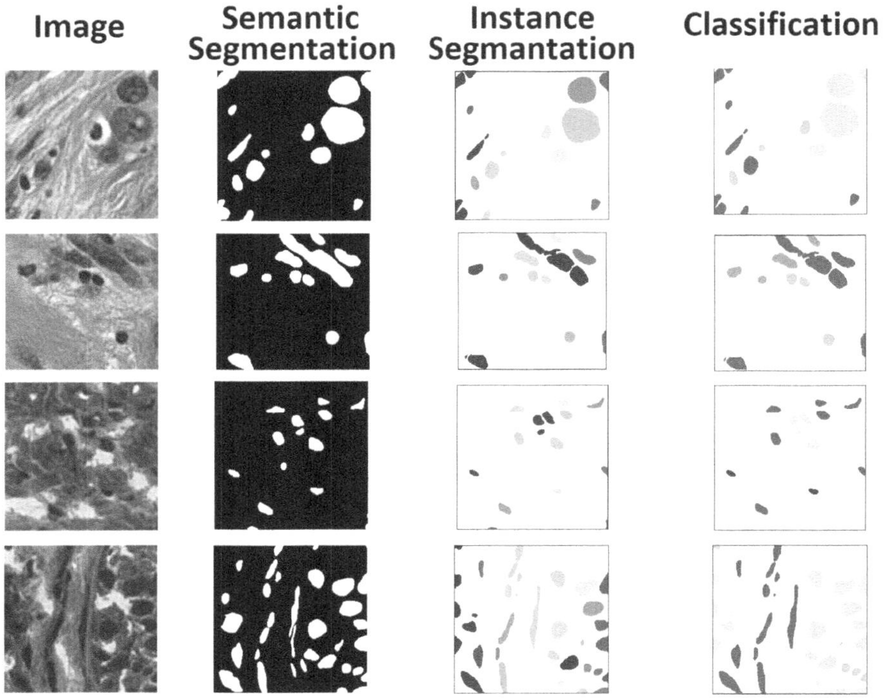

Fig. 3. The figure reports the visual results of semantic segmentation, instance segmentation and classification. The last column in the visual results shows how cells have been classified into five categories: neoplastic (yellow), connective (red), epithelial (green), dead (blue) and inflammatory (cyan). (Color figure online)

and segmenting individual cell instances more accurately, which is critical for count-based analysis and morphological examination downstream purposes.

The fourth column in the visual results shows how cells have been classified into five categories: neoplastic (yellow), connective (red), epithelial (green), dead (blue) and inflammatory (cyan). It is crucial that such cells be accurately classified by the model in order to diagnose a number of pathological conditions. Despite complex tissue morphology, this consistent and unique coloring of that column speaks volumes about its ability to categorize different cell types.

In Table 2, we present quantitative results for comparing our proposed method with several state-of-the-art models. Our proposal has better performance than existing models in terms of semantic segmentation, which had a Dice Score of 0.8621 above HoverNet's 0.8494 as the next best performing model. Furthermore the proposed model can produce instance segmentation, semantic segmentation and classification in contrast to the top state-of-the-art i.e. PointNuNet that can only produce instance segmentation and classification. Regarding instance segmentation, our model achieves a bPQ score of 0.7316 which is much higher compared to other models such as Mask-RCNN (0.6049) or

MicroNet (0.6488) indicating an improved accuracy in detecting and segmenting individual cell instances. Also, with an mPQ score of 0.6273; it further supports the overall precision and robustness observed in our model when dealing with complex tissue structures.

4 Conclusion

This work introduces an improved Attention-based Tri-decoder Framework that is designed for the accurate segmentation and classification of nuclei in histopathological images of bladder cancer. The framework takes a bottom-up approach to address the challenges often associated with histological analysis including the issue of overlapping nuclei, staining differences and tissue heterogeneity. The model incorporates three separate decoder heads which allows for the production of semantic segmentation maps, edge maps and pixel-level classification maps which provides a better understanding of the histology images. The controlled watershed algorithm, which is based on the outputs from the semantic and edge decoders, enhances instance segmentation in a considerable way, thus enabling the precise delineation of nuclei boundaries even under suboptimal conditions. The edge maps improve the model's capacity to solve problems of overlapping and partial staining, which are characteristic of histological images. In addition, by using the pixel grouping strategy together with the classification decoder, the pixel labels are well grouped and achieved, especially where nuclei class is imbalanced as connective tissue and necrotic nuclei. The experiments which were carried out supported our hypothesis that the proposed framework is better than the current solutions as a whole both in segmentation and classification areas. Due to the attention mechanism, and the tri-decoder structure, it is possible to achieve the model with high accuracy, and simultaneously, low computational complexity. The relative solidity of this framework suggests that it may be useful in practical applications of digital pathology where precise and accurate histological assessment is necessary for the optimal management of patient care. Therefore, the Attention-based Tri-decoder Framework provides considerable enhancement in the segmentation and classification of bladder cancer nuclei to enhance diagnostic accuracy and patient care. Since the dataset used in this work have limited number of classes/sub-classes, therefore the model can not be tested for the other sub-classes. The other sub-classes can be included in the future work. This work demonstrates the possibility of increasing the accuracy of histopathological assessment with the help of AI-based solutions and serves as a basis for further development of new methods in the field of digital pathology.

Acknowledgments. This research work was supported by Shandong University, talent funding for "Double First Class Construction" Project No. 10000082492262.

Disclosure of Interests. The authors have no conflict of interest to report regarding the work described in this paper.

References

1. Ahmad, I., Ahmad, M.A., Anwar, S.J.: Transfer learning and dual attention network based nuclei segmentation in head and neck digital cancer histology images. In: 2023 15th International Conference on Electronics, Computers and Artificial Intelligence (ECAI). IEEE (2023). https://doi.org/10.1109/ecai58194.2023.10193937
2. Ahmad, I., Israr, S.M., Islam, Z.U.: A three in one bottom-up framework for simultaneous semantic segmentation, instance segmentation and classification of multi-organ nuclei in digital cancer histology. Image Vis. Comput. **146**, 105047 (2024). https://doi.org/10.1016/j.imavis.2024.105047
3. Azad, R., et al.: Advances in medical image analysis with vision transformers: a comprehensive review. Med. Image Anal. **91**, 103000 (2024). https://doi.org/10.1016/j.media.2023.103000
4. Fu, Z., Li, J., Hua, Z.: DEAU-Net: attention networks based on dual encoder for medical image segmentation. Comput. Biol. Med. **150**, 106197 (2022). https://doi.org/10.1016/j.compbiomed.2022.106197
5. Gamper, J., Koohbanani, N.A., Benes, K., Khuram, A., Rajpoot, N.: Pannuke: an open pan-cancer histology dataset for nuclei instance segmentation and classification. In: European Congress on Digital Pathology, pp. 11–19. Springer (2019)
6. Gamper, J., et al.: Pannuke dataset extension, insights and baselines. arXiv preprint arXiv:2003.10778 (2020)
7. Gao, C., et al.: Transformer based multiple instance learning for WSI breast cancer classification. Biomed. Signal Process. Control **89**, 105755 (2024). https://doi.org/10.1016/j.bspc.2023.105755
8. Gao, Y., Zhou, M., Metaxas, D.N.: UTNet: A Hybrid Transformer Architecture for Medical Image Segmentation, pp. 61–71. Springer International Publishing (2021). https://doi.org/10.1007/978-3-030-87199-4_6
9. Gao, Z., Hong, B., et al.: A semi-supervised multi-task learning framework for cancer classification with weak annotation in whole-slide images. Med. Image Anal. **83**, 102652 (2023). https://doi.org/10.1016/j.media.2022.102652
10. Goceri, E.: Nuclei segmentation using attention aware and adversarial networks. Neurocomputing **579**, 127445 (2024). https://doi.org/10.1016/j.neucom.2024.127445
11. Goswami, N.G., et al.: Current trends of artificial intelligence and applications in digital pathology: a comprehensive review. Int. J. Adv. Appl. Sci. 10(12), 29–41 (2023). https://doi.org/10.21833/ijaas.2023.12.004
12. Graham, S., et al.: Hover-net: simultaneous segmentation and classification of nuclei in multi-tissue histology images. Med. Image Anal. **58**, 101563 (2019). https://doi.org/10.1016/j.media.2019.101563
13. He, K., Gkioxari, G., Dollár, P., Girshick, R.: Mask R-CNN. In: Proceedings of the IEEE international conference on computer vision (2017)
14. Hussain, M.A., Ahmad, I., Shaukat, A., Islam, Z.U.: Leukocytes segmentation and classification in digital microscopic images. In: 2021 4th International Conference on Computing and Information Sciences (ICCIS), pp. 1–6 (2021).https://doi.org/10.1109/ICCIS54243.2021.9676191
15. Islam Sumon, R., et al.: Densely convolutional spatial attention network for nuclei segmentation of histological images for computational pathology. Front. Oncol. **13** (2023). https://doi.org/10.3389/fonc.2023.1009681

16. Jaisakthi, S.M., Desingu, K., Mirunalini, P., Pavya, S., Priyadharshini, N.: A deep learning approach for nucleus segmentation and tumor classification from lung histopathological images. Netw. Model. Anal. Health Inf. Bioinf. **12**(1) (2023). https://doi.org/10.1007/s13721-023-00417-2
17. Li, J., Li, X.: MIU-Net: mix-attention and inception u-net for histopathology image nuclei segmentation. Appl. Sci. **13**(8), 4842 (2023). https://doi.org/10.3390/app13084842
18. Liu, D., et al.: TransFusion: Multi-view Divergent Fusion for Medical Image Segmentation with Transformers, pp. 485–495. Springer Nature Switzerland (2022). https://doi.org/10.1007/978-3-031-16443-9_47
19. Liu, T., Zhang, D., Wang, H., Qi, X.: An Improved U-Net Model for Simultaneous Nuclei Segmentation and Classification, pp. 314–325. Springer Nature Singapore (2024). https://doi.org/10.1007/978-981-97-5597-4_27
20. Mahbod, A., et al.: A dual decoder U-Net-based model for nuclei instance segmentation in hematoxylin and eosin-stained histological images. Front. Med. **9** (2022). https://doi.org/10.3389/fmed.2022.978146
21. Metlek, S., Çetıner, H.: Resunet+: a new convolutional and attention block-based approach for brain tumor segmentation. IEEE Access **11**, 69884–69902 (2023). https://doi.org/10.1109/access.2023.3294179
22. Naylor, P., Lae, M., Reyal, F., Walter, T.: Segmentation of nuclei in histopathology images by deep regression of the distance map. IEEE Trans. Med. Imaging **38**(2), 448–459 (2019). https://doi.org/10.1109/tmi.2018.2865709
23. Rana, M., Bhushan, M.: Machine learning and deep learning approach for medical image analysis: diagnosis to detection. Multimedia Appl. **82**(17), 26731–26769 (2022). https://doi.org/10.1007/s11042-022-14305-w
24. Raza, S.E.A., et al.: Micro-net: a unified model for segmentation of various objects in microscopy images. Med. Image Anal. **52**, 160–173 (2019). https://doi.org/10.1016/j.media.2018.12.003
25. Ronneberger, O., Fischer, P., Brox, T.: U-Net: convolutional networks for biomedical image segmentation. In: Navab, N., Hornegger, J., Wells, W.M., Frangi, A.F. (eds.) MICCAI 2015. LNCS, vol. 9351, pp. 234–241. Springer, Cham (2015). https://doi.org/10.1007/978-3-319-24574-4_28
26. Saleem, U., et al.: Transrul: A transformer-based multihead attention model for enhanced prediction of battery remaining useful life. Energies **17**(16), 3976 (2024). https://doi.org/10.3390/en17163976
27. Xie, Y., et al.: Attention mechanisms in medical image segmentation: a survey (2023), https://arxiv.org/abs/2305.17937
28. Yao, K., Huang, K., Sun, J., Hussain, A., Jude, C.: PointNu-Net: simultaneous multi-tissue histology nuclei segmentation and classification in the clinical wild. IEEE Trans. Emerg. Top. Comput. Intell. (2023)
29. Zhang, J., Zhao, Z., Chen, Y., Liu, H.: Multi-decoder networks for semi-supervised medical image segmentation. In: Proceedings of the 15th International Conference on Digital Image Processing. ICDIP 2023, ACM (2023). https://doi.org/10.1145/3604078.3604098

30. Zhao, T., Fu, C., Tie, M., Sham, C.W., Ma, H.: RGSB-UNet: hybrid deep learning framework for tumour segmentation in digital pathology images. Bioengineering **10**(8), 957 (2023). https://doi.org/10.3390/bioengineering10080957
31. Zheng, Y., et al.: Kernel attention transformer for histopathology whole slide image analysis and assistant cancer diagnosis. IEEE Trans. Med. Imaging **42**(9), 2726–2739 (2023). https://doi.org/10.1109/tmi.2023.3264781
32. Zhou, Z., Siddiquee, M.M.R., Tajbakhsh, N., Liang, J.: UNet++: a nested u-net architecture for medical image segmentation. In: Deep Learning in Medical Image Analysis and Multimodal Learning for Clinical Decision Support, pp. 3–11. Springer International Publishing (2018)

Enhanced Breast Cancer Detection Using Filter-Augmented DenseNet169: Outperforming Traditional CNN Models with Fewer Epochs

Anahí Vaca[1], Paula Pozo[1], Sisa Lluilema[1], Diego Almeida-Galárraga[1], Andrés Tirado-Espín[2], Kevin R. Landázuri[1], Lenin Ramírez-Cando[1], Fernando Villalba-Meneses[1](✉), and Carolina Cadena-Morejón[2]

[1] School of Biological Sciences and Engineering, Yachay University for Experimental Technology and Research (Yachay Tech), Urcuquí 100115, Ecuador
gvillalba@yachaytech.edu.ec

[2] School of Mathematical and Computational Sciences, Yachay University for Experimental Technology and Research (Yachay Tech), Urcuquí 100115, Ecuador

Abstract. Breast cancer detection is crucial for reducing mortality and improving survival rates in women. Convolutional neural networks (CNNs) have demonstrated high accuracy, approximately 95%, in detecting breast cancer in mammograms and magnetic resonance imaging (MRI), which facilitates effective treatments and enhances patient recovery. In this project, we developed a breast cancer detection system using DenseNet169 and a custom CNN architecture. The system employed Gaussian and bilateral filters to enhance image contrast and edges, reducing noise and improving the visualization of tumors and breast tissue. Our model achieved classification accuracy of 63% for distinguishing between benign and malignant images, with training and validation accuracies of 95% and 93%, respectively. This indicates the model's robustness in learning from the dataset with minimal overfitting. Compared to other CNN architectures like AlexNet and ResNet50, our DenseNet-based model required fewer training epochs while maintaining high accuracy, demonstrating the efficiency of the filter-augmented approach. These results suggest significant potential for early breast cancer detection, which could lead to improved patient outcomes and higher survival rates.

Keywords: breast cancer · detection · CNNs · convolutional networks · mammograms

1 Introduction

Breast cancer detection is crucial for reducing mortality rates and increasing survival rates among women affected by this disease. In 2020, approximately 2.3 million women were diagnosed with breast cancer worldwide, underscoring the urgent need for accurate and timely diagnosis [1]. Convolutional neural networks (CNNs) have demonstrated high accuracy, with studies reporting a 95% accuracy rate in detecting breast cancer in

F. R. Narváez et al. (Eds.): SmartTech-IC 2024, CCIS 2392, pp. 257–273, 2026.
https://doi.org/10.1007/978-3-031-98287-3_19

mammograms and magnetic resonance imaging (MRI). High accuracy in early detection enables timely and appropriate treatment, significantly improving patient prognosis and recovery results. Unlike traditional methods, our approach leverages DenseNet and custom CNN architectures, which have shown superior performance in complex image classification tasks. These deep learning models automate and enhance the ability of computers to recognize patterns in medical images, reducing the need for extensive feature extraction and engineering processes typically required by other methods, such as ConvNet [2], ImageNet [3], AlexNet [4], ResNet [5] and DenseNet [6, 7].

This project aims to develop a breast cancer detection system using deep learning techniques. Two types of convolutional neural networks, DenseNet and a custom CNN, were used to analyze medical images. Different preprocessing processes were carried out, including normalization and resizing, to guarantee consistency and comparability of the data. We used two sets of medical image data focused on breast cancer from platforms such as Kaggle, among which were mammograms classified as benign or malignant. The deep learning model was trained thoroughly for 10 epochs and achieved an accuracy of 63% in classifying images as benign or malignant. The training and validation accuracies reached up to 95% and 93%, respectively, without significant evidence of overfitting. The confusion matrix analysis finally showed many correct predictions and few errors [8].

These results underscore the potential of this approach to improve early detection and treatment of breast cancer, allowing medical professionals to provide more effective treatments and improve patient survival rates.

2 State of Art

Breast cancer is a disease where abnormal cells divide uncontrollably, invading and destroying body tissues. It is the most common type of cancer among women globally and the fifth leading cause of cancer-related death worldwide, disproportionately affecting Black and Hispanic women [1, 9, 10]. In 2020, there were approximately 2.3 million new cases, and 685,000 deaths were attributed to breast cancer globally [9]. More recently, in 2022, an estimated 287,850 new cases were reported among American women alone. Breast cancer primarily affects older women, with 83% of diagnoses occurring in those aged 50 or older, and 91% of breast cancer deaths occurring in this age group [1]. The median age for breast cancer diagnosis is 62 years, though this varies slightly by racial and ethnic group: 57 years for Hispanic women, 58 years for Asian-American and Pacific Islander (API) women, 60 years for Black women, 61 years for American Indian and Alaska Native (AIAN) women, and 64 years for white women [1, 10]. These statistics underscore the critical need for targeted prevention and treatment strategies across diverse populations.

Some risk factors that increase the incidence and death rate for breast cancer include advanced age, high body mass index (obesity), tobacco exposure, inadequate physical activity, a diet high in fats, early menarche, advanced age at first childbirth, short periods of breastfeeding, hormone replacement therapy or oral contraceptive use, breast density, and a family history of breast cancer. Countries with high Human Development Index (HDI) values, such as Europe, the United States, Canada, Australia, and Japan, have higher incidence and death rates, showing differences in risk factors, detection strategies, and access to medical treatment. Between 2000 and 2012, the standardized incidence rates for breast cancer significantly increased in South Korea and China, while they decreased in the United States. Conversely, between 2000 and 2015, the standardized death rates increased in China and South Korea, but decreased in the United States, the United Kingdom, and Australia [9, 10].

There are some important differences in the characteristics of breast cancer tumors in different racial and ethnic groups. Black, American Indian and Alaska Native (AIAN), and Hispanic women are less likely to be diagnosed with localized breast cancer compared to Asian American, Pacific Islander (API), and white women. Black women have a higher incidence of distant breast cancer and are more likely to develop high-grade tumors. Additionally, Black women are twice as likely to be diagnosed with triple-negative (HR negative/HER2 negative) breast cancer, a particularly aggressive subtype with fewer treatment options. These tumor differences contribute to the lower survival rates found among black women and highlight the need for more personalized and equitable approaches to breast cancer diagnosis and treatment across racial and ethnic groups [1, 11, 12].

Breast cancer is one of the leading causes of mortality among women worldwide. Consequently, early detection is important to lowering mortality and raising the percentage of women who survive; convolutional neural networks (CNN) are useful in this regard. Because the goal of these networks is to analyze patterns in big databases, they have proven to be highly accurate in finding malignant tumors in MRIs and mammograms. If there is an improvement in the early detection of breast cancer through neural networks, medical professionals could provide appropriate treatments and significantly improve recovery and reduce mortality from breast cancer.

Convolutional neural networks (CNNs) aim to automate and enhance the ability of computers to classify patterns in visual data, being especially effective in object recognition [13–15]. These networks exhibit variations in their architecture to optimize performance through feedback, better adapting to neural data. CNNs are composed of multiple layers, each responsible for extracting different types of features from an image: the initial layers detect simple features like edges and textures, while the final layers identify more complex features and specific patterns. It has been shown that the final layers of CNNs, such as AlexNet, better match higher visual areas in humans and monkeys compared to previous models [13–15].

In medical image analysis, deep neural networks (DNNs) are also employed to improve the accuracy and efficiency of detecting and diagnosing various diseases [16–18]. However, these networks face limitations such as the lack of labeled training data and the need to adapt the networks to the specific characteristics of medical images. These limitations can be mitigated through data preprocessing, using image transformation techniques to increase the variety of the training dataset, and applying dimensionality reduction techniques to simplify image features and enhance training efficiency [16].

The neural network architecture used in medical image analysis primarily includes convolutional neural networks (CNNs) and recurrent neural networks (RNNs). CNNs are effective for pattern detection in images and disease classification, while RNNs are used to analyze image sequences and detect temporal patterns. DNNs are implemented using software frameworks such as Caffe, TensorFlow, MXNet, and Theano, which facilitate the training, visualization, and evaluation of neural networks. The training results of DNNs are evaluated in terms of accuracy, sensitivity, and specificity in disease detection [14–16, 19, 20].

Technological integration in image analysis has significantly advanced the medical field, especially with the use of CNNs and RNNs to detect patterns in images from mammograms, ultrasounds, and MRIs, aiming to classify various diseases and improve their diagnosis. CNNs are particularly effective in identifying features in static images, such as those obtained from mammograms, which are essential for the early detection of breast cancer. In addition to mammography, there are other imaging techniques, such as ultrasound and MRI, which also enhance diagnostic accuracy and efficiency.

Mammography has a sensitivity of 68.75% and a specificity of 69.5% in the diagnosis of breast diseases. On the other hand, contrast-enhanced digital mammography (CEDM) shows greater effectiveness with a sensitivity of 93.75% and a specificity of 91.3%. CEDM is comparable to dynamic contrast-enhanced magnetic resonance imaging (DCE-MRI) in detecting newly diagnosed secondary lesions of breast cancer and fewer false positives. Regarding the evaluation of response to neoadjuvant treatment, in particular, CEDM is more effective than DCE-MRI in terms of sensitivity of 100% and specificity of 84% in predicting complete pathological response. CEDM has a sensitivity and specificity of both 97% for cancer extension compared to DCE-MRI, being 96% and 97%, respectively [21].

Segmentation of breast ultrasound images through clustering techniques includes a variety of processing methods, which are used to differentiate between breast lesions and healthy tissues from the ultrasound. Consequently, it is possible to group pixels with similar characteristics into an area of interest; Therefore, their detection and classification is facilitated. Among the challenges associated with this process we mention noise and variation in image quality in image resolution. Both can be attenuated if combined with appropriate preprocessing techniques before segmentation [22].

The use of magnetic resonance imaging (MRI) in the early detection of breast cancer may be essential in the diagnosis of women who have different degrees of risk of breast cancer, women could present a family history, dense breast tissue or also epithelial atypia. According to the standards of the American College of Radiology (ACR) and the National Comprehensive Cancer Network (NCCN), it is recommended to use MRI especially in women who have different simultaneous risk factors. MRI has greater sensitivity than mammography and digital breast tomosynthesis (DBT) in detecting cancers, especially in women with dense breast tissue, and may reduce the rate of interval cancers. MRI is cost-effective for women at very high risk, such as those with mutations in the BRCA gene, but may not be cost-effective for women at moderate or average risk [23, 24] (Table 1).

Table 1. Comparative Table of Neural Networks for the Detection of Breast Cancer.

Ref	Model	Database (size)	Accuracy
[25]	VGG19	MIAS (322)	97.04%
[26]	Support Vector Machine (SVM)	RSNA (54,713)	92%
[27]	AlexNet	MIAS (322)	88%
[28]	ResNet50	DDSM (55,890)	95%
[29]	denset169	BreakHis (9109)	95%
[30]	LeNet (ReLU)	Kaggle (971)	89,91%
[31]	Hybrid CNN-LSTM	BreakHis(7909)	99%
[32]	CNN-CBR	MIAS (2441)	86.71%
[33]	Image Template Matching	DDSM (439)	85.82%

3 Materials and Methods

In this project, a standard methodology was followed that helped us analyze medical images based on deep learning. The Denset neural network and a convolutional neural network used helped to have breast cancer detection based on two different types of databases, this will help facilitate the detection of this disease, real-time preprocessing, cost reduction and evaluation early. In this way, improve the quality and usefulness of image analysis of patients with breast cancer.

3.1 Data Collection

Data collection was focused on trusted platforms such as Kaggle, where two different medical image databases were obtained. This dataset covers a wide range of mammographic images to ensure robustness in model training. The first database, called MIAS Mammography, is composed of a total of 330 mammograms. These images were divided into two sets: 247 mammograms were allocated for the test set, and the remaining 83 mammograms were assigned to the training set. This approach aims to ensure that the model is effective and to have a more accurate result. In the second database, the data contained 699 medical images where 357 were classified as benign and 342 as malignant. This classification is important to train the model in identifying patterns that distinguish between benign and malignant lesions, contributing to a more accurate classification. The characteristics of these databases are shown in Table 2 [34, 35].

Table 2. Database features

Data base	Amount	Test	Training
MIAS mammography	330	247	83
Mammography	699	340	359

3.2 Medical Image Preprocessing and Deep Learning Architecture Design

In the data preparation process, normalization on a scale of 0 to 255 was performed on the 162 medical images. This adjustment was done by applying a transformation that rescales the pixel intensity values, so that they are all within the standard range. An image size adjustment was performed to ensure that all images had consistent dimensions. The images were adjusted to an ideal size of 256 × 256 pixels, using interpolation techniques such as bilinear and bicubic. Due to this, it was ensured that the neural network model can process the data correctly.

Two types of filters were applied for image segmentation: The Gaussian filter was used to reduce noise and smooth the image, removing unnecessary details that could interfere with the analysis. This filter applies a soft blur using a Gaussian function, applying a convolution, allowing small variations in pixel intensity, such as noise, that are not relevant to the analysis. The smoothing introduced by the Gaussian filter helps reduce distractions in the image without significantly altering the key features. The other type of filter used was the bilateral filter which was used to enhance edges and preserve important details while reducing noise. This filter combines spatial and intensity filtering to keep edges sharp while smoothing the rest of the image. It also helps us dynamically adjust the intensity of smoothing based on brightness differences between pixels, allowing homogeneous regions to be smoothed while edges remain intact [34] (Fig. 1).

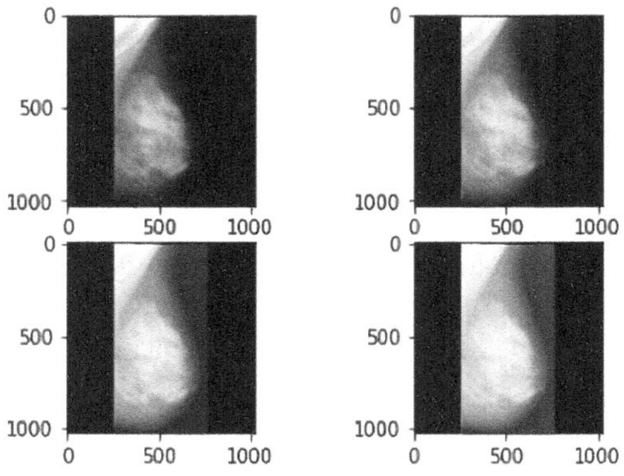

Fig. 1. Visualization of normalized images

Furthermore, this study chose to use 3 distinct architectures such as Denset 169, DenseNet, and a convolutional neural network due to their effectiveness in the field of medical applications, especially in the interpretation of radiographic images and the classification of pathologies. These three architectures were used separately to see if there is a variance in the dataset [35].

The remaining blocks are used in the DenseNet design to help the network learn more complex and essential picture representations. Information can move through the network straight through these leftover blocks, bypassing intermediate stages of processing.

DenseNet architecture emphasizes how crucial it is to have the right values in the output layer for the image size and classifications that are present in the first layer's input. The first layer of the neural network model is examined in depth, revealing the parameters of both the input layer and the output layer. The second layer of the figure presents detailed information about the parameters of the input layer and the functional result obtained in the last layer of the neural network. This approach provides a complete view of data transformation throughout the model. Emphasis is also placed on other core layers of the model, such as "flatten", which is essential for transforming the input data into a 1D matrix before it is processed by the dense layers. The dropout layer adds regularization to the model and prevents overfitting, which helps make the model more efficient when applied to new data and improves generalization. Dense layers are used to build dense connections and learn intricate nonlinear mappings between input and output data. This detailed analysis of the layers provides a comprehensive understanding of how DenseNet processes and learns from data at different stages of the neural network [36]. In addition, the architecture used for a convolutional neural network was based on a series of layers designed to automatically process and learn patterns from structured data, such as our database. This started with convolutional layers, where specialized filters go through the input to detect local features, such as edges or textures. As the network progresses, the layers extract more complex representations until they reach the fully connected layers, which process the necessary features.

3.3 Model Development

In the model development process, several essential libraries were used to ensure code efficiency. Manipulating tabular data and performing data analysis operations were carried out using the Pandas library. Manipulating arrays and performing elementary calculations were made possible by Numpy, providing a solid foundation for effective manipulation of numerical data. For the visualization of images and graphs, the Matplotlib and Seaborn libraries were incorporated, allowing a clear and concise graphical representation of the results obtained during the development process. In addition, the OpenCV (cv2) library was essential for image processing and editing. The OS library, which provides file and directory manipulation capabilities, was an essential component for operating system operations. Regarding the creation and training of the machine learning model, the TensorFlow and Keras libraries were chosen for their ability to handle large amounts of data, supporting deep learning applications, allowing efficient training and evaluation of the model [37].

3.4 Model Training and Validation

The model training process covered all the categories present in the dataset, thus ensuring an optimal result for breast cancer detection. This approach allowed the model to capture and learn specific patterns associated with the various categories, such as "malignant" and "benign", present in the analyzed medical images. Using a convolutional neural network as one of the architectures for this analysis allowed us to observe that by training the model for 10 epochs, it reached an accuracy level of 63%. But by using the DenseNet 169 neural network, the result was an accuracy of 90%, indicating the model's ability to make accurate classifications in a wide variety of cases. At the same time, another DenseNet neural network was used whose accuracy was 94%. This accuracy demonstrates the result of the deep learning used, meaning that the models have acquired a significant understanding of the distinctive pattern present in breast X-rays. Furthermore, the number of training epochs used and the achievement of 63%, 90%, and 93% accuracy are optimal results, but can be adjusted as the requirements and complexity of the problem vary.

4 Results

Breast X-rays image analysis that integrates design with machine learning, Tensor Flow, and deep learning helps make quick diagnoses and allows users to verify information from medical sources. The results were based on the 3 architectures used with the MIAS Mammography database, where the different accuracies that each had according to its architecture were compared.

4.1 Neural Network Model with MIAS Mammography

During the first part of the code, the 330 mammograms from the MIAS mammography database were used. Within this database, there were 247 images for testing and 83 for training. Figure 2a shows the results obtained during the training of the convolutional neural network with the data collected from the MIAS mammograms, and illustrates the accuracy achieved during the training period, highlighting the learning curve over 10 epochs. We can observe that the accuracy results obtained during this training and validation were higher than the 63% achieved with the MIAS mammography database, which justifies the use of the best-ranked database.

However, Fig. 2b shows the loss curves of the model used, analyzing both the training and validation periods. The red curve represents the training loss, which is the loss calculated on the training dataset after each epoch. The blue curve represents the validation loss (val_loss), which is the loss calculated on a separate validation dataset, also after each epoch. Both the training and validation loss continuously decrease as the epochs increase. However, the validation loss is slightly larger than the training loss, suggesting that the model might be overfitting the training data. Despite this, the decrease in the validation loss suggests effective learning without significant overfitting, as evidenced by the loss values remaining stable across all epochs.

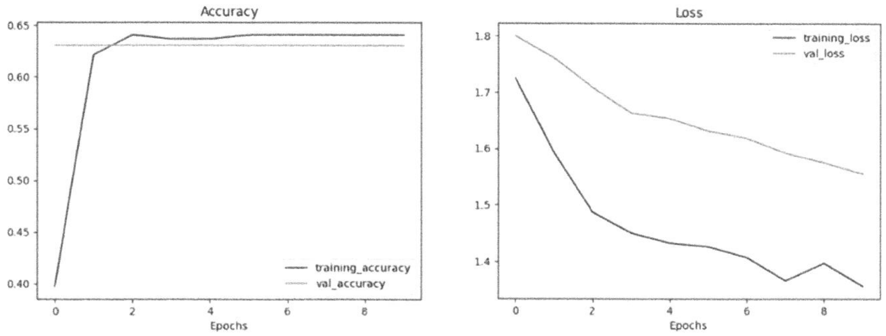

Fig. 2. A) Accuracy in training and validation. B) Loss function in training and validation. (Color figure online)

4.2 Neural Network Model DenseNet 169 with MIAS Mammography

Figure 3 shows the results obtained with the DenseNet 169 architecture, in which its design that directly connects all the layers of a stage using dense connections allowed the flow of information and gradients during training. On the left side, the model accuracy is shown. The blue curve represents the accuracy on the training set, while the orange curve represents the accuracy on the validation set. With these results, we can see that the training accuracy reaches a value close to 90% after 10 epochs, stabilizing around 95% towards the end of training. However, the validation accuracy shows notable variations, staying below the training accuracy and reflecting possible generalization problems. On the right side, the model loss is represented. The blue curve indicates the loss on the training set, which decreases rapidly in the first epochs and stabilizes towards low values, indicating a good learning on the training data. In contrast, the orange curve, corresponding to the validation loss, shows higher values and significant oscillations throughout the training, suggesting some difficulty of the model to generalize to unseen data.

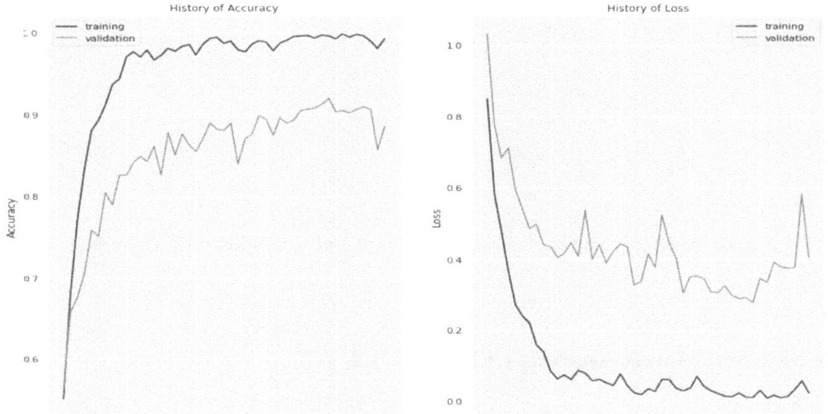

Fig. 3. Accuracy and loss curves with DenseNet 169.

These results show us a typical behavior of deep networks such as DenseNet-169 when faced with limited data sets such as MIAS Mammography.

4.3 Neural Network Model DenseNet

Figure 4 shows the accuracy and loss metrics during training and validation of a neural network model using a combination of two databases: the MIAS Mammography database with 330 images and another database of data with 699 images.

On the left side, the accuracy history is shown, where the training accuracy can be seen to be increasing rapidly and reaching a value close to 95 after about 10 epochs. On the other hand, the validation accuracy is also increasing, at a slower pace, reaching a maximum value of around 93. On the right side, the training loss is observed to be increasing steadily and reaching a low value of around 0.16 at the end of training. The validation loss also decreases and reaches a minimum value of approximately 0.20. Therefore, these results indicate that the model achieved good performance regarding accuracy and loss using the combination of the two databases. It should be noted that the difference between these training and validation curves is relatively small, suggesting that there is no significant overfitting. In addition, the validation accuracy reached a maximum value of around 93%, which shows that the result is optimal for a medical image classification problem.

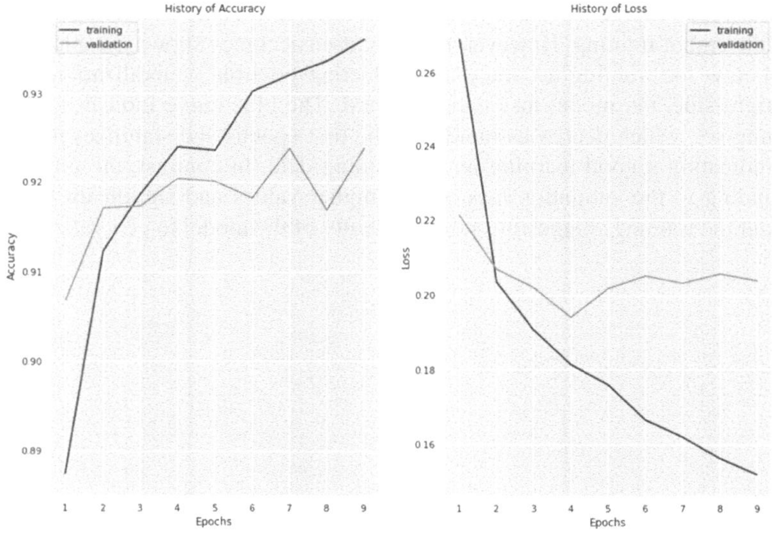

Fig. 4. Accuracy and loss curves in training and validation with DenseNet.

4.4 Confusion Matrix Analysis with DenseNet

Figure 5 shows the analysis of the DenseNet neural network according to the database, the first row and the first column represent the classification. In this case, there are only two classes: "benign" and "malignant." This figure shows a confusion matrix for a binary classification model. The values inside the matrix give us the result that 546 is the number of cases in which the model correctly predicted "benign" when the actual class was "benign" (true negatives). The number of 202 is the number of cases in which the model incorrectly predicted "benign" when the actual class was "malignant" (false negatives). On the contrary, the value 407 means that the neural network correctly predicted "malignant" and 201that the model incorrectly predicted "malignant" when the real class was "benign."

Figure 6 represents how the detection of the medical images was, the rows represent the real classes, while the columns represent the predictions made by the model. The values within the matrix are: 92 cases were correctly classified as "benign", 56 cases were incorrectly classified as "benign" when they were "malignant", 88 cases were correctly classified as "malignant" (true positives), and 36 cases were incorrectly classified as "malignant" when they were actually "benign." This analysis shows us how high values on the main diagonal (92 and 88) and low values outside it (56 and 36), which indicates good performance of the model on the test set.

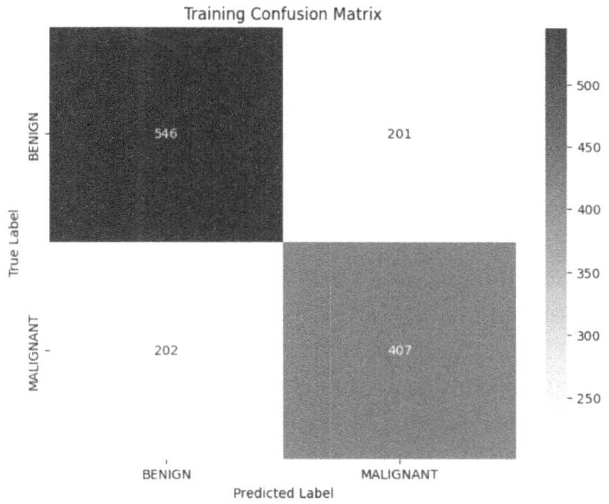

Fig. 5. Training Confusion matrix

The different results obtained in comparison of the convolutional neural network and the DenseNet 169 and DenseNet neural networks are due to the architectures and design of the models. DenseNet, unlike a traditional CNN, uses dense connections between layers, which means that each layer receives information from all previous layers, improving gradient propagation and learning efficiency. This allows DenseNet to learn more complex and deeper representations, leading to significantly better performance in classification tasks, especially when a limited dataset is available. On the other hand, traditional CNN networks, although effective in detecting simple patterns, can face difficulties in capturing features with limited databases, due to which variations in the precision of each model are observed.

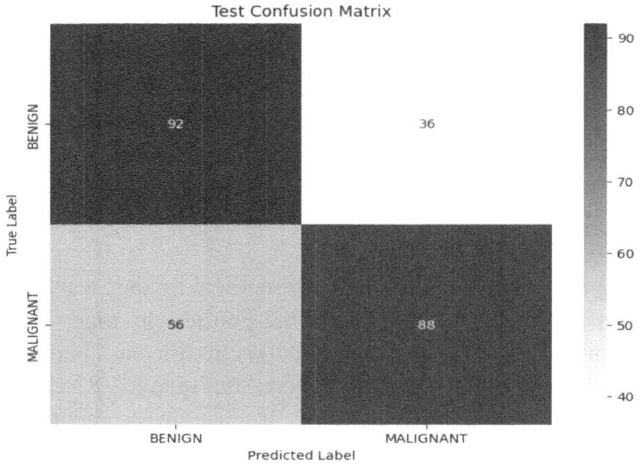

Fig. 6. Test Confusion matrix

5 Discussion

In this study, we applied Gaussian and bilateral filters to the pre-trained DenseNet169 convolutional neural network for breast cancer detection using mammograms. These filters were employed to enhance image contrast and edges, reduce noise, and facilitate the visualization of tumors and breast tissue. This allowed the network to identify patterns more accurately, optimizing cancer detection.

As shown in Table 3, our DenseNet model achieved 93% accuracy with only 9 training epochs, outperforming architectures such as AlexNet, ResNet50, LetNet, CNN-CBR, and Image Template Matching, which presented accuracies of 88%, 95%, 95%, 89.91%, 99%, 86.71%, and 85.82%, respectively. This is because DenseNet169 uses dense and skip connections and requires fewer parameters compared to other deep architecture such as ResNet50, making it more suitable for medical datasets where the number of available images may be limited. While some architectures such as CNN-LSTM achieved higher accuracies (99%), their reliance on a larger number of epochs may increase the risk of overfitting and misclassifications. In contrast, the use of filters in our model proved to be an effective strategy to improve classification accuracy without compromising efficiency [38].

Furthermore, like our application of DenseNet169 for breast cancer detection, other studies have highlighted the potential of deep learning models in medical contexts, such as the quantification of lung lesions in patients with COVID-19 and the detection of neurodegenerative diseases such as Parkinson's [39–41]. These results show us the versatility of these techniques and also increase their importance within clinical diagnosis.

To evaluate the performance of our DenseNet169 model, metrics such as sensitivity, specificity, accuracy, and F1-Score were employed. According to the results presented in Table 4, during training, the model achieved a sensitivity of 0.7299, and in the testing phase, 0.6216. In addition, specificity values of 0.6694 and 0.7096 were obtained, while the F1-Score was 0.8255 and 0.7451 in the training and testing stages, respectively. This demonstrates a good overall performance in classifying medical images.

Table 3. Comparative table of Neural Networks for the Detection of Breast Cancer and the present work

Ref	Model	Accuracy	Epochs	Filter	Data augmentation
[25]	VGG19	97.04%	100	Gaussian	Yes
[26]	Support Vector Machine (SVM)	92%	50	Banks	No
[27]	AlexNet	88%	10	Morphological & gaussian	No
[28]	ResNet50	95%	50	Gaussian & Median Erode	No
[29]	Denset169	95%	44	Banks	No
[30]	LetNet	89,91%	10	Gaussian, median & bilateral	No
[31]	Hybrid CNN-LSTM	99%	200	Gaussian, bilateral, median erode	Yes
[32]	CNN-CBR	86.71%	50	Gaussian & bilateral	No
[33]	Image Template Matching	85.82%	10		No
Our	CNN	63%	9	Gaussian & bilateral	Yes
project	Denset1969	95%	50	Gaussian & bilateral	No
		93%	9	Gaussian & bilateral	No

DenseNet169 stands out as a promising tool for breast cancer diagnosis thanks to its ability to efficiently learn deep features even with limited datasets. Its architecture, based on dense connections, facilitates gradient flow and minimizes the risk of overfitting, making it suitable for medical applications. In this study, with only 9 training epochs, the model achieved an accuracy of 93%, which positions it as a practical alternative to more complex and demanding architectures, such as AlexNet or CNN-LSTM.

Despite the results obtained, the relatively low sensitivity (0.7299 in training and 0.6216 in testing) suggests that the model still requires optimization to reduce the false negative rate and improve the identification of positive cases. This could be achieved by hyperparameter adjustments or data augmentation techniques. Compared to other models, DenseNet169 demonstrated competitive performance and remarkable resistance to overfitting, but still has room for improvement.

In the future, it is recommended to use databases that include images with calcifications, since there is currently little information available on this aspect. With further research in this area, it would be possible to improve early detection and achieve a more accurate classification of cases as benign or malignant. This would allow the full potential of models such as DenseNet169 to be exploited in clinical diagnosis.

Table 4. Comparative table of metrics to evaluate results of the DenseNet169 model.

Model	Accuracy	Sensitivity	Specificity	F1-Score
Training DenseNet	0.95	0.7299	0.6694	0.8255
Test DenseNet	0.93	0.6216	0.7096	0.7451

6 Conclusions

Early and accurate diagnosis of breast cancer is important to improve survival chances, especially when we need to differentiate between healthy, malignant, and suspicious tissues. In this project, we implemented a DenseNet169-based model that achieved 93% accuracy in classifying mammography images, using only 9 training epochs. We incorporated Gaussian and bilateral filters to improve image quality, which helped the model identify complex patterns more effectively. This approach proved to be competitive against other models, even outperforming several existing techniques in terms of simplicity and efficiency.

However, we observed that the sensitivity during testing (0.6216) could be improved to reduce false negatives, as these can have critical consequences in clinical diagnosis. To address this limitation, we recommend exploring additional techniques such as database expansion, hyperparameter tuning, and cross-validation. Furthermore, we believe that including more images with specific features, such as calcifications, could strengthen the model's performance in detecting benign and malignant cases.

This project highlights the ability of deep neural networks, such as DenseNet169, to solve complex medical problems efficiently, even with limited databases. Despite the good results, we must be careful with possible risks of overfitting and continue to optimize the model to ensure its reliability in real-world scenarios. In conclusion, this work represents an important step towards the development of cutting-edge medicine and practices for early diagnosis of breast cancer, providing benefits to healthcare professionals and patients.

References

1. Giaquinto, A.N., et al.: Breast Cancer Statistics, 2022. CA Cancer J. Clin. **72**(6), 524–541 (2022). https://doi.org/10.3322/caac.21754
2. Simonyan, K., Zisserman, A.: Very deep convolutional networks for large-scale image recognition. In: 3rd International Conference on Learning Representations ICLR 2015 - Conference Track Proceedings (2014). https://arxiv.org/abs/1409.1556v6. Accessed 14 June 2024
3. Krizhevsky, A., Sutskever, I., Hinton, G.E.: ImageNet Classification with Deep Convolutional Neural Networks. http://code.google.com/p/cuda-convnet/. Accessed 14 June 2024
4. Nasir, M.U., et al.: Breast cancer prediction empowered with fine-tuning. Comput. Intell. Neurosci. **2022** (2022). https://doi.org/10.1155/2022/5918686
5. Yu, X., Kang, C., Guttery, D.S., Kadry, S., Chen, Y., Zhang, Y.D.: ResNet-SCDA-50 for breast abnormality classification. IEEE/ACM Trans. Comput. Biol. Bioinforma. **18**(1), 94–102 (2021). https://doi.org/10.1109/TCBB.2020.2986544

6. Huang, G., Liu, Z., Van Der Maaten, L., Weinberger, K.Q.: Densely connected convolutional networks. In: Proceedings - 30th IEEE Conference on Computer Vision and Pattern Recognition, CVPR 2017, vol. 2017-January, pp. 2261–2269 (2016). https://doi.org/10.1109/CVPR.2017.243
7. Aguiar-Salazar, E., et al.: Intelligent electromyograph for early detection of myopathy and neuropathy using EMG signals and neural network model. Information and Communication Technologies. TICEC 2022. Communications in Computer and Information Science, vol. 1648, pp. 31–43. Springer, Cham (2022). https://doi.org/10.1007/978-3-031-18272-3_3
8. Michael, E., Ma, H., Li, H., Kulwa, F., Li, J.: Breast cancer segmentation methods: current status and future potentials. Biomed. Res. Int. **2021**(1), 9962109 (2021). https://doi.org/10.1155/2021/9962109
9. Lei, S., et al.: Global patterns of breast cancer incidence and mortality: a population-based cancer registry data analysis from 2000 to 2020. Cancer Commun. **41**(11), 1183–1194 (2021). https://doi.org/10.1002/cac2.12207
10. Kashyap, D., et al.: Global increase in breast cancer incidence: risk factors and preventive measures. Biomed Res. Int. **2022** (2022). https://doi.org/10.1155/2022/9605439
11. Wilkinson, L., Gathani, T.: Understanding breast cancer as a global health concern. Br. J. Radiol. **95**(1130) (2022). https://doi.org/10.1259/BJR.20211033
12. Bodewes, F.T.H., van Asselt, A.A., Dorrius, M.D., Greuter, M.J.W., de Bock, G.H.: Mammographic breast density and the risk of breast cancer: a systematic review and meta-analysis. Breast **66**, 62–68 (2022). https://doi.org/10.1016/J.BREAST.2022.09.007
13. Lindsay, G.W.: Convolutional neural networks as a model of the visual system: past, present, and future. J. Cogn. Neurosci. **33**(10), 2017–2031 (2021). https://doi.org/10.1162/jocn_a_01544
14. Aguiar-Salazar, E., Villalba-Meneses, F., Tirado-Espín, A., Amaguaña-Marmol, D., Almeida-Galárraga, D.: Rapid detection of cardiac pathologies by neural networks using ECG signals (1D) and sECG images (3D). Computation **10**(7), 112 (2022). https://doi.org/10.3390/COMPUTATION10070112
15. Gualsaquí, M.G., et al.: Convolutional neural network for imagine movement classification for neurorehabilitation of upper extremities using low-frequency EEG signals for spinal cord injury. CCIS, vol. 1532, pp. 272–287 (2022). https://doi.org/10.1007/978-3-030-99170-8_20
16. Abdou, M.A.: Literature review: efficient deep neural networks techniques for medical image analysis. Neural Comput. Appl. **34**(8), 5791–5812 (2022). https://doi.org/10.1007/s00521-022-06960-9
17. Matamoros-Alcivar, E., et al.: Implementation of MPC and PID control algorithms to the artificial pancreas for diabetes mellitus type 1. In: Proceedings of the 2021 IEEE International Conference on Machine Learning and Applied Network Technologies. ICMLANT 2021 (2021). https://doi.org/10.1109/ICMLANT53170.2021.9690529
18. Caicho, J., et al.: Diabetic retinopathy: detection and classification using AlexNet, GoogleNet and ResNet50 convolutional neural networks. CCIS, vol. 1532, pp. 259–271 (2022). https://doi.org/10.1007/978-3-030-99170-8_19
19. Tene-Hurtado, D., et al.: Brain tumor segmentation based on 2D U-Net using MRI multi-modalities brain images. Smart Technologies, Systems and Applications. SmartTech-IC 2021. Communications in Computer and Information Science, vol. 1532, pp. 319–331. Springer, Cham (2022). https://doi.org/10.1007/978-3-030-99170-8_25
20. Puchaicela, M., Villalba, F., et al.: Deep learning for glaucoma detection: R-CNN ResNet-50 and image segmentation. Journal of Advances in Information Technology **14**(6), 1186–1197 (2023). https://doi.org/10.12720/jait.14.6.1186-1197
21. Polat, D.S., Evans, W.P., Dogan, B.E.: Contrast-enhanced digital mammography: technique, clinical applications, and pitfalls. American Journal of Roentgenology **215**(5), 1267–1278 (2020). https://doi.org/10.2214/AJR.19.22412

22. Muhammad, M., Zeebaree, D., Brifcani, A.M.A., Saeed, J., Zebari, D.A.: A review on region of interest segmentation based on clustering techniques for breast cancer ultrasound images. J. Appl. Sci. Technol. Trends **1**(3), 78–91 (2020). https://doi.org/10.38094/jastt1328
23. Zhang, Y., et al.: Deep learning-based automatic diagnosis of breast cancer on MRI using mask R-CNN for detection followed by ResNet50 for classification. Acad. Radiol. **30**(Suppl 2), S161–S171 (2023). https://doi.org/10.1016/J.ACRA.2022.12.038
24. Gao, Y., Reig, B., Heacock, L., Bennett, D.L., Heller, S.L., Moy, L.: Magnetic resonance imaging in screening of breast cancer. Radiol. Clin. North Am. **59**(1), 85–98 (2021). https://doi.org/10.1016/J.RCL.2020.09.004
25. Sulaiman, S.N., Hassan, N.A., Isa, I.S., Abdullah, M.F., Soh, Z.H.C., Jusman, Y.: Mass detection in digital mammogram image using Convolutional Neural Network (CNN). In: Proceedings - 2021 11th IEEE International Conference on Control System, Computing and Engineering, ICCSCE 2021, pp. 61–65 (2021). https://doi.org/10.1109/ICCSCE52189.2021.9530945
26. Jafari, Z., Karami, E.: Breast cancer detection in mammography images: a CNN-based approach with feature selection. Information **14**(7), 410 (2023). https://doi.org/10.3390/INFO14070410
27. Krizhevsky, A., Sutskever, I., Hinton, G.E.: ImageNet classification with deep convolutional neural networks. Commun. ACM **60**(6), 84–90 (2017). https://doi.org/10.1145/3065386
28. He, K., Zhang, X., Ren, S., Sun, J.: Deep Residual Learning for Image Recognition, pp. 770–778 (2016). http://image-net.org/challenges/LSVRC/2015/. Accessed 11 June 2024
29. Albalawi, U., Manimurugan, S., Varatharajan, R.: Classification of breast cancer mammogram images using convolution neural network. Concurr. Comput. Pract. Exp. **34**(13), e5803 (2022). https://doi.org/10.1002/CPE.5803
30. Balasubramaniam, S., Velmurugan, Y., Jaganathan, D., Dhanasekaran, S.: A modified LeNet CNN for breast cancer diagnosis in ultrasound images. Diagnostics **13**(17) (2023). https://doi.org/10.3390/DIAGNOSTICS13172746
31. Srikantamurthy, M.M., Rallabandi, V.P.S., Dudekula, D.B., Natarajan, S., Park, J.: Classification of benign and malignant subtypes of breast cancer histopathology imaging using hybrid CNN-LSTM based transfer learning. BMC Med. Imaging **23**(1) (2023). https://doi.org/10.1186/S12880-023-00964-0
32. Bouzar-Benlabiod, L., Harrar, K., Yamoun, L., Khodja, M.Y., Akhloufi, M.A.: A novel breast cancer detection architecture based on a CNN-CBR system for mammogram classification. Comput. Biol. Med. **163** (2023). https://doi.org/10.1016/J.COMPBIOMED.2023.107133
33. Sun, L., Sun, H., Wang, J., Wu, S., Zhao, Y., Xu, Y.: Breast mass detection in mammography based on image template matching and CNN. Sensors (Basel) **21**(8) (2021). https://doi.org/10.3390/S21082855
34. Mader, K.: MIAS Mammography Database. Kaggle Dataset. Available at: https://www.kaggle.com/datasets/kmader/mias-mammography (Accessed: 23 November 2023)
35. Rentsi, A.: Breast cancer classification using DenseNet. Kaggle Notebook. Available at: https://www.kaggle.com/code/angelarentsi/breast-cancer-classification-densenet (Accessed: 23 November 2024)
36. Pawar, S.D., et al.: Multichannel DenseNet architecture for classification of mammographic breast density for breast cancer detection. Front. Public Heal. **10**, 885212 (2022). https://doi.org/10.3389/FPUBH.2022.885212/BIBTEX
37. Saffari, N., et al.: Fully automated breast density segmentation and classification using deep learning. Diagnostics **10**(11), 988 (2020). https://doi.org/10.3390/DIAGNOSTICS10110988
38. Villalba-Meneses, F., et al.: Classification of the pathological range of motion in low back pain using wearable sensors and machine learning. Sensors **24**(3), 831 (2024). https://doi.org/10.3390/S24030831/S1

39. Niles, D.N., et al.: COVID-19 pulmonary lesion classification using CNN software in chest X-ray with quadrant scoring severity parameters. CCIS, vol. 1532, pp. 370–382 (2022). https://doi.org/10.1007/978-3-030-99170-8_27
40. Santos, K., et al.: Detecting Parkinson's disease with convolutional neural networks: voice analysis and deep learning. CCIS, vol. 1885, pp. 324–336 (2023). https://doi.org/10.1007/978-3-031-45438-7_22
41. Villalba-Meneses, F., et al.: BackMov: individualized motion capture-based test to assess low back pain mobility recovery after treatment. Sensors **24**(3), 913 (2024). https://doi.org/10.3390/s24030913

Windowing Based Data Augmentation Techniques to Enhance the Synthesis of Contrast Response in Contrast-Enhanced Spectral Mammography Images

Cristian Restrepo, Kevin Osorno-Castillo, and Gloria M. Díaz(✉)

Facultad de Ingenierías, Instituto Tecnológico Metropolitano, Medellín, Colombia
cristianrestrepo281255@correo.itm.edu.co,
{kevinosorno,gloriadiaz}@itm.edu.co

Abstract. Data augmentation represents a foundational methodological framework within deep learning, aimed at enhancing both the quantity and diversity of training datasets. This approach is particularly critical in the domain of medical imaging, where data availability is frequently limited due to privacy regulations, high acquisition costs, and inherent logistical challenges associated with data collection. This study explores the efficacy of advanced data augmentation techniques on the synthesis of contrast response in contrast-enhanced spectral mammography (CESM) images, employing state-of-the-art image-to-image translation models. The analysis includes conventional data augmentation techniques based on geometric transformations, as well as contrast variation achieved through randomized adjustments of the Window Center (WC) and Window Width (WW) parameters. Among the evaluated techniques, the random adjustment of WC and WW demonstrates superior performance in enhancing the qualitative synthesis of diagnostically relevant regions of interest (ROIs) exhibiting contrast agent responses, particularly in dense breast tissue. Nevertheless, the study highlights that traditional quantitative metrics may inaccurately capture clinical relevance, particularly in scenarios emphasizing the characterization of contrast agent dynamics. The findings underscore the promise of contrast-based augmentation strategies in advancing the generation of diagnostically significant images while simultaneously illuminating the intrinsic constraints of conventional quantitative metrics.

Keywords: Contrast Enhanced Spectral Mammography (CESM) · Window Center and Window Width Adjustments · Data augmentation. · Image-to-image translation

1 Introduction

Breast cancer remains the leading cause of cancer-related mortality among women globally [1], even though it is amenable to treatment when identified

F. R. Narváez et al. (Eds.): SmartTech-IC 2024, CCIS 2392, pp. 274–288, 2026.
https://doi.org/10.1007/978-3-031-98287-3_20

in its initial stages. Among the diverse imaging techniques utilized for detection, full-field digital mammography (FFDM) is still the most extensively employed screening method, attributed to its accessibility and effectiveness. Nevertheless, in women with dense fibroglandular tissue, the sensitivity of this technique is diminished, as the elevated tissue density can obscure lesions, complicating their detection by causing considerable overlap of tissue structures in the acquired images.

Contrast-enhanced spectral mammography (CESM) has recently emerged as a viable alternative to FFDM to enhance the detection of anomalies within dense breast tissues [2]. CESM employs an iodinated contrast agent and captures both low-energy (LE) and high-energy (HE) images, which are subsequently integrated using a weighted logarithmic subtraction algorithm to produce a recombined image (RC). This resulting image accentuates areas exhibiting elevated contrast uptake attributable to the vascularization of tumorous lesions while diminishing the visibility of normal breast tissue [3]. Nevertheless, CESM is associated with a substantial increase in radiation exposure and potential adverse reactions, such as iodine allergies. Furthermore, the need for dual-energy acquisitions (low- and high-energy exposures) introduces additional radiation exposure, raising safety concerns and is currently constrained by limited availability [4].

To overcome these limitations, the implementation of generative models based on deep learning to synthesize contrast-enhanced medical images has been investigated [5,13]. The approach of synthesizing RC images from LE images represents a significant advancement towards generating images that emulate the contrast uptake derived from conventional mammograms, thereby improving both the accessibility and clinical utility of CESM. However, it is widely recognized that deep learning models demand a high computational cost and large volumes of training data for effective generalization. This poses a significant challenge in the context of medical imaging due to the limited availability of data. To address this limitation, data augmentation strategies are commonly implemented, aiming to maximize variability in the training data to improve the generalization capability and robustness of generative models [9].

Data augmentation strategies can be classified into original data transformations and AI-based generated data. In the case of CESM synthesis, AI-based techniques involve the simultaneous and paired creation of LE and RC images, which presents a considerable challenge. Generative models may not accurately capture the complex anatomical and functional relationships between these images, introducing the risk of generating unrealistic or clinically irrelevant patterns. Additionally, artifacts or distortions that compromise data integrity could arise. These deficiencies may negatively affect the training process, compromising both the accuracy and validity of the model in real medical applications. Therefore, it is preferable to use controlled transformations of existing data that reflect real biological variations, such as rotations, scaling, translations, and intensity adjustments, to preserve clinical fidelity and ensure effective model training.

In mammography, variability is related to the scale and contrast values associated with differences in the size and density of breasts among women. Moreover, pixel intensities in medical imaging have physical meanings, which radiologists leverage to highlight anatomical structures by manipulating the window width (WW) and window level (WL) parameters during diagnosis. Thus, this paper proposes to evaluate whether contrast-level data augmentation strategies that simulate actual clinical interpretation conditions,i.e., based on WW and WL variations, contribute to improving the precision and robustness of the synthesis model in comparison with established strategies used in previous works [1].

2 Materials and Methods

The main objective of this study is to evaluate the impact of a data augmentation strategy based on random modifications of WW and WC in the context of image-to-image translation for the synthesis of RC images in CESM, in comparison to established data augmentation techniques commonly used in natural image analysis. To achieve this, three image-to-image translation models were implemented: CycleGAN, Pix2Pix, and Autoencoder, following the implementations detailed in [9]. The selection of these models was based on their ability to synthesize images in scenarios requiring the generation of target domain images from input domain images. This approach is particularly relevant in medical imaging, as these models are highly effective at transforming and preserving the complex features inherent to such data, contributing to a more accurate and clinically meaningful representation in the transformed domain.

Data Augmentation Based on WC and WW Parameter Shifting. In medical imaging, windowing is a technique designed to optimize the visualization and analysis of anatomical structures and specific pathologies. This method adjusts the dynamic range of intensity values in a medical image, enhancing specific regions of interest while suppressing less relevant details. To achieve this, it uses two key parameters: the window width (WW), which defines the range of visible intensity values, and the window center (WC), which sets the midpoint of the range determined by WW [4].

Given its impact on image representation, this technique can be implemented as a data augmentation strategy for training artificial intelligence models. By generating controlled variations in image contrast, it emulates clinical viewing conditions. Figure 1 illustrates the effects of manipulating WC and WW parameters, showcasing how this technique influences the perception of structures and could enhances the sensitivity to contrast of machine learning models.

Baseline Data Augmentation Techniques. In this study, common geometric transformation techniques were applied as baseline data augmentation strategies. Horizontal flipping was used to simulate the natural symmetry between the left and right breasts. Rotations and translations addressed variations due to patient posture, mobility, or differences in acquisition methods that can cause

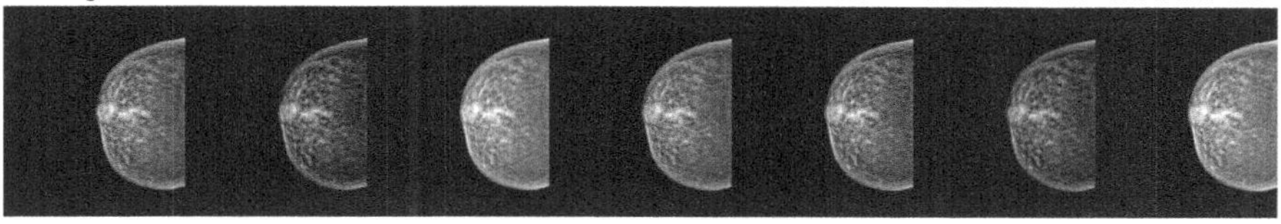

Fig. 1. Variation in LE image rendering is performed by adjusting WC and WW parameters both individually and together. Adjustments of $\pm 5\%$ illustrate their effects on image contrast and visual detail perception.

minor displacements or rotations in anatomical structures. Scaling was also utilized to accommodate dimensional variations in breast lesions and the overall breast, helping the model recognize relevant patterns across different scales.

Additionally, to address potential issues with excessive brightness or darkness in images that can obscure important features, gamma correction was employed in our data augmentation strategies. This technique modifies the tonal intensity of images, creating additional samples that replicate extreme lighting conditions. Such augmentation methods improve the capacity of models to recognize meaningful patterns, regardless of specific details or ideal conditions [11].

2.1 Image Synthesis Models

Deep learning models implemented in this study were selected due to their ability to handle image-to-image translation tasks. These models enable the transformation of images from an input domain (LE) to a target domain (RC), while preserving relevant details and capturing complex features inherent to this type of imagery. The purpose of this transformation is to synthesize the contrast agent response, which is represented in RC images from the features present in LE images.

Pix2Pix. It is a Conditional Generative Adversarial Network (cGAN) designed to address supervised image-to-image translation tasks between domains [8]. This architecture is based on the interaction of two models: a generator and a discriminator. The generator (G) is responsible for learning the transformation of images from the input domain to the target domain. The discriminator evaluates the quality of the images generated by G by comparing them with real images from the target domain.

The Pix2Pix architecture uses a loss function composed of an adversarial loss derived from a conditional Generative Adversarial Network (cGAN) and a reconstruction loss. The adversarial loss, defined by Eq. 1, directs the generation of images that are indistinguishable from actual target domain images, while the reconstruction loss, defined by Eq. 2, assesses the accuracy of the match by minimizing the absolute differences between generated and real images. This combination (Eq. 3) ensures that the generated images maintain visual coherence with the target domain and accurately reproduce the structural and contextual characteristics present in the real images.

$$\mathcal{L}_{cGAN}(G, D) = \mathbb{E}_{x,y}[\log D(x, y)] + \mathbb{E}_{x,\hat{y}}[\log(1 - D(x, \hat{y})))] \tag{1}$$

$$\mathcal{L}_{L1}(G) = \mathbb{E}_{y,\hat{y}}[\|y - \hat{y}\|_1] \tag{2}$$

$$G^* = \arg\min_G \max_D \mathcal{L}_{cGAN}(G, D) + \lambda \mathcal{L}_{L1}(G). \tag{3}$$

In this context, x and y represent the LE and RC images, respectively, while $\hat{y}$ denotes the image generated by the generator G. The hyperparameter λ controls the balance between the different terms in the loss function of the model. This balance is crucial for achieving optimal results in the image translation process, as it influences both the adversarial loss and the reconstruction loss in the overall model training.

CycleGAN. CycleGAN is an architecture designed for unsupervised image translation between unpaired domains, i.e., there is no direct correspondence between images in the input and target domains [10]. Unlike Pix2Pix, CycleGAN uses four models: two generators (G, F) and two discriminators (D_X, D_Y). The generator G converts images from domain X to domain Y, while F performs the inverse transformation, from domain Y to domain X. The discriminators D_X and D_Y evaluate the quality of the generated images, determining whether they belong to the corresponding real domain or are synthetic images created by the generators.

As it is an architecture designed for unsupervised tasks, CycleGAN incorporates a cycle-consistency loss. This loss ensures that if an image from domain X is transformed to domain Y by generator G, and then restored to domain X by the inverse generator F, the result is similar to the original image. Mathematically, this concept is defined by Eq. 4.

$$\mathcal{L}_{\text{cyc}}(G, F) = \mathbb{E}_x[\|F(G(x)) - x\|_1] + \mathbb{E}_y[\|G(F(y)) - y\|_1] \tag{4}$$

In addition to the cycle-consistency loss, CycleGAN optimizes an adversarial loss function for each generator-discriminator pair. For example, for G and D_Y, the adversarial loss function is shown in Eq. 5.

$$\mathcal{L}_{GAN}(G, D_Y, X, Y) = \mathbb{E}_y[\log D_Y(y)] + \mathbb{E}_x[\log(1 - D_Y(G(x)))] \tag{5}$$

Finally, CycleGAN incorporates an identity term in its loss function, aimed at preserving the characteristics of images that already belong to the target domain. This term ensures that if an image from the target domain is processed by the generator designed to transform images into that same domain, the resulting image exhibits no significant alterations compared to its original state. This term is described by Eq. 6.

$$\mathcal{L}_{\text{identity}}(G, F) = \mathbb{E}_y[\|G(y) - y\|_1] + \mathbb{E}_x[\|F(x) - x\|_1] \tag{6}$$

By combining these losses, the total cost function of CycleGAN is expressed by Eq. 7.

$$\begin{aligned}\mathcal{L}(G, F, D_X, D_Y) = \mathcal{L}_{GAN}(G, D_Y, X, Y) + \mathcal{L}_{GAN}(F, D_X, Y, X) \\ + \lambda_{cyc}\mathcal{L}_{cyc}(G, F) + \lambda_{identity}\mathcal{L}_{identity}(G, F)\end{aligned} \tag{7}$$

Autoencoder. An autoencoder is a neural network designed to learn compressed representations of input data and later reconstruct them, making it particularly useful for domain translation tasks between images. An autoencoder consists of two main components: the encoder and the decoder. The encoder reduces the dimensionality of the input image, creating a compact latent representation that captures the most relevant and abstract features of the input domain. The decoder takes this compressed representation and reconstructs the image in the output domain, allowing transformation between domains through the learning of shared essential features. The Eq. 8 defines the loss function of this model, aimed at minimizing the absolute difference between the generated image and the reference image.

$$\mathcal{L}_{L1}(G) = \mathbb{E}_{y,\hat{y}}[\|y - \hat{y}\|_1] \tag{8}$$

where y represents the reference image, and $\hat{y}$ corresponds to the image generated by G after introducing an image from the domain X.

2.2 Data Sets and Image Preprocessing

This study was performed using two public datasets. According to the methodological approach proposed by [9], each synthesis model was initially trained using the CDD-CESM database [12], which is a collection of 2006 high-resolution contrast-enhanced spectral mammography (CESM) JPEG images. Then, the models were fine-tuned for the UCBM-CESM database [14], which consists of 1138 high-resolution CESM images available in DICOM format.

CDD-CESM. The CDD-CESM (Categorized Digital Database for Low-energy and Subtracted Contrast Enhanced Spectral Mammography) dataset was collected at the National Cancer Institute of Cairo University, Egypt, between January 2019 and February 2021. This dataset consists of a total of 1003 image pairs, corresponding to low-energy (LE) and recombined (RC) projections, obtained from 326 female patients aged between 18 and 90 years.

The images in the CDD-CESM dataset have an average resolution of 2355times1315 pixels and are distributed in CC and MLO views. For each patient, up to eight images are included, covering both views for both image types (LE and RC) and both sides of the breast. Additionally, cases with incomplete images are included, either due to mastectomies or technical issues that affected image quality during acquisition. The original format of the images is JPEG, with an 8-bit depth and three color channels.

UCBM-CESM. The UCBM-CESM dataset consists of CESM images acquired at the *Fondazione Policlinico Universitario Campus Bio-Medico* in Rome, between September 2021 and October 2022. The images were obtained using the *GE Healthcare Senographe Pristina* full-field digital mammography system and stored in DICOM format, ensuring the preservation of clinical metadata and image quality. This dataset includes a total of 569 pairs of LE and RC images, corresponding to patients aged between 31 and 90 years.

Regarding spatial resolution, 492 image pairs have a resolution of 2850 × 2396 pixels, while the remaining 77 pairs have a resolution of 2294 × 1916 pixels. The distribution by projection is as follows: 142 image pairs correspond to the craniocaudal (CC) projection of the right breast, 141 pairs belong to the CC projection of the left breast, 146 pairs are from the mediolateral oblique (MLO) projection of the right breast, and 140 pairs are associated with the MLO projection of the left breast.

In addition to the MLO and CC images of both breasts, late-phase acquisitions were performed in 86 patients, capturing images of the same breast and projection. Additional information was extracted from medical reports, including breast density classification according to the BI-RADS system. The distribution of patients across breast density categories is as follows: 65 patients in category A (predominantly fatty tissue), 180 patients in category B (scattered fibroglandular density), 207 patients in category C (heterogeneously dense tissue), and 95 patients in category D (extremely dense tissue).

Image Preprocessing. In order to maintain consistency and uniformity in the data, a series of preprocessing techniques were applied to the images from the two datasets, which differ in storage formats (DICOM for UCBM-CESM and JPEG for CDD-CESM). For the UCBM-CESM dataset, the images were extracted from the DICOM files, and a windowing procedure was applied based on the original window width (WW) and window center (WC) parameters stored in the image metadata. On the other hand, for the CDD-CESM dataset, the images in JPEG format with three color channels were converted to grayscale.

Since CESM images typically have a rectangular aspect ratio, zero-padding was applied to transform them into square images. This step was necessary because models like CycleGAN and Pix2Pix require input images with uniform dimensions to ensure that the proportions of structures in the images are correctly maintained during the learning and generation processes.

Considering the high spatial resolution of CESM images and the high computational cost associated with training deep learning models on images of these dimensions, the images were resized to 512 × 512 pixels. This adjustment significantly reduced computational requirements while maintaining a suitable resolution to preserve the relevant characteristics of the images needed for effective model training.

Following this, the image values were scaled from 0 to 1 using Min-Max normalization. This process utilized the minimum and maximum values specific to the data type storing the images in each dataset. For the UCBM-CESM dataset, a range of 0 to 4095 was employed for normalization, whereas the CDD-CESM dataset utilized a range of 0 to 255 as reference points for this scaling.

2.3 Performance Evaluation

The performance of data augmentation methods in generating the contrast-agent response in RC images was assessed using widely accepted similarity metrics from the current state of the art. These metrics include Visual Information Fidelity, Structural Similarity Index Measure, Mean Squared Error, and Peak Signal-to-Noise Ratio.

To ensure that the analysis focused on breast tissue, a breast mask was generated using a thresholding method. This procedure allowed for the segmentation and delimitation of the region of interest while excluding the background. Additionally, to calculate Visual Information Fidelity, a breast region crop was applied using a bounding box. These quantitative evaluation methods focused on breast tissue help eliminate much of the residual background, thereby minimizing the inherent biases associated with the background in such images during metric evaluation.

Visual Information Fidelity (VIF). This metric quantifies the loss of visual information by measuring the mutual information shared between a reference image and the generated image. It then normalizes the visual information extracted from the distorted image relative to the reference image, enabling an assessment of the relative image quality in terms of perceptual fidelity [6].

$$VIF = \frac{I(X;Y) + I(X;Z)}{I(X;Y)} \tag{9}$$

where $I(X;Y)$ is the mutual information between the reference image X and the generated image Y, and Z represents the distortion.

Structural Similarity Index Measure (SSIM). The SSIM quantifies the structural similarity between two images by evaluating three key components: luminance, contrast, and structure. This metric is designed to align with human visual perception, providing a value between 0 and 1, where 1 represents an exact match between the compared images [7].

$$SSIM(x,y) = \frac{(2\mu_x\mu_y + C_1)(2\sigma_{xy} + C_2)}{(\mu_x^2 + \mu_y^2 + C_1)(\sigma_x^2 + \sigma_y^2 + C_2)} \tag{10}$$

where μ_x and μ_y are the means of the images, σ_x^2 and σ_y^2 are the variances, and σ_{xy} is the covariance between x and y.

Mean Square Error (MSE). The MSE is a measure that calculates the mean squared error between the pixel values of a reference image and the generated image. A low MSE value indicates precise correspondence between the images.

$$MSE = \frac{1}{N}\sum_{i=1}^{N}(y_i - \hat{y}_i)^2 \tag{11}$$

where y is the reference image, $\hat{y}$ is the generated image, and N is the total number of pixels.

Peak Signal-to-Noise Ratio. The Peak Signal-to-Noise Ratio (PSNR) is a metric that quantifies the relationship between the maximum possible value of an image and the noise level present in the generated image. The value of this metric is expressed in decibels (dB), and higher values indicate better quality of the generated image.

$$PSNR = 10 \cdot \log_{10}\left(\frac{R^2}{MSE(y, \hat{y})}\right) \tag{12}$$

where R is the maximum possible value of the signal (for example, 255 for 8-bit images).

3 Experimental Results

3.1 Experimental Setup

Setup of Synthesis Models. The training process of the deep learning models was conducted in two stages: pretraining and fine-tuning, in accordance with the methodology described in [9].

During the pretraining phase, the models were initialized and trained using the CDD-CESM dataset, which provides a broad representation of the global features present in the RC images. This procedure allowed the models to learn patterns related to the global structure of the images. During this phase, we did not carry out any data augmentation operations since the image format of the CDD-CESM dataset prohibits the execution of the windowing process.

In the fine-tuning stage, the pre-trained models were adjusted using the UCBM-CESM dataset. During this phase, both baseline data augmentation operations and those based on random adjustments of the WW and WC parameters were implemented. The DICOM format of this dataset enabled dynamic modifications of the windowing parameters, introducing additional variability in the images.

Both in the pretraining and fine-tuning stages, the models were trained on an NVIDIA GeForce RTX 2070 GPU. The dataset was partitioned by patient, using a stratified random selection based on breast density. This approach ensured that the distribution of breast density categories was representative in each set, thereby ensuring a balanced and consistent evaluation of the models' performance in different clinical scenarios. The images of patients were distributed as follows: 80% for training, 5% for validation, and 15% for testing.

The models were trained for 200 epochs in both stages: pretraining and fine-tuning. Key hyperparameters, such as the gains associated with the loss functions and the learning rates, were configured following the methodology described in [9]. With respect to batch size, it was adjusted according to the specific characteristics of each model: a batch size of 4 for the Autoencoder, 16 for Pix2Pix, and 1 for CycleGAN.

Configuration of Data Augmentation Strategies. Four combinations of data augmentation techniques were implemented, including both conventional geometric transformations and image contrast manipulations. The first combination included horizontal flipping, rotation, zoom, and translation. These geometric transformations were selected due to their widespread use in the state of the art. In the second combination, gamma correction and zoom adjustment were implemented to simulate variable lighting conditions and variations in breast size dimensions.

Similarly, the third combination incorporated random adjustments of WW and WC parameters during windowing with zoom. This approach introduces dynamic variations in perceived contrast in the LE images, along with scale modifications, thereby improving the representation of data diversity.

Finally, the fourth combination integrated the geometric transformations from the first combination with contrast manipulation through windowing. This set included variations in image orientation and scale, as well as dynamic contrast adjustments, offering a comprehensive strategy to maximize variability and robustness in the dataset. The configuration of the action ranges of these techniques is shown in Table 1.

Table 1. Range of application of the data augmentation techniques used in this study.

Operation	Range of action
Translation (T)	$[-10\%, +10\%]$ in both directions
Zoom (Z)	$[0.9, 1.1]$ (90% a 110%)
Mirror (F)	horizontal (flip)
Rotation (R)	$[-15, +15]$
Gamma correction (G)	$[0, 2.0]$
Adjustment of WC and WW (V)	$[-2\%, +2\%]$

3.2 Quantitative Results

Table 2 presents a comparison of the quantitative metrics obtained by applying different combinations of data augmentation techniques to the three image translation models: Pix2Pix, CycleGAN, and Autoencoder. These metrics were calculated on the test set of the UCBM-CESM dataset, evaluating the effectiveness of each model in image synthesis. Each augmentation combination reflects a specific approach, incorporating geometric transformations such as rotation, translation, and zoom, along with contrast variations through random adjustments of WC and WW parameters during windowing, as well as gamma correction. These results allow for an analysis of the impact of data augmentation strategies on model performance.

In the case of the geometric transformations (F, R, T, and Z), better performance is observed across all evaluated models in the MSE and PSNR metrics. This result suggests that these transformations, by introducing variations in orientation, position, and scale, help the models capture fundamental image patterns, thereby reducing reconstruction errors and improving the signal-to-noise ratio.

The SSIM metric shows that the complete geometric transformations (F, R, T, and Z) maximize the preservation of key structures in the Pix2Pix and Autoencoder models, while contrast adjustments (G and Z, V and Z) excel in the performance of the CycleGAN model, which is more sensitive to intensity variations. This uniform SSIM behavior could be attributed to the repetitive and structured nature of the RC images used, which makes it easier for the models to learn defined patterns, generating images with robust global structures. However, the limited ability of SSIM to discriminate subtle variations associated with the contrast-agent response highlights the need for complementary, more sensitive metrics.

The VIF analysis highlights that combinations of operations based solely on contrast adjustments (G and Z or V and Z) tend to improve visual fidelity more than complete geometric transformations, especially in the Pix2Pix and CycleGAN models. This may be because contrast adjustments emphasize key visual differences in specific regions, such as the ROIs, which are critical in the synthesis of RC images.

3.3 Qualitative Results

Figures 2 and 3 illustrate the visual comparison of RC images generated by the models under various combinations of data augmentation strategies, analyzing their impact on preserving key structures. Figure 2 depicts a case with breast density C (heterogeneously dense), while Fig. 3 represents a patient with breast density A (predominantly fatty tissue). In both cases, a region with contrast uptake is identified in the RC image. Particularly in Fig. 2, the lesion is obscured by fibroglandular tissue in the LE image but becomes clearly visible in the RC image due to contrast uptake.

Although the Autoencoder model achieved the highest PSNR and SSIM metrics, it is evident in both cases that it fails to synthesize the contrast uptake in the RC images, limiting its ability to reproduce key features associated with intensity variations induced by contrast.

Table 2. Quantitative comparison of data augmentation techniques applied to image-to-image translation models (Pix2Pix, CycleGAN, Autoencoder) for CR image synthesis. Each row reflects a combination of techniques: geometric transformations (F: horizontal reflection, R: rotation, T: translation, Z: zoom) and contrast variations (V: fenestration, G: gamma adjustment). Bold values indicate the best performance per metric for each model.

Model	Operations	MSE	PSNR	SSIM	VIF
Pix2Pix	F, R, T, Z	**0.0019 ± 0.00003**	**27.754 ± 0.12**	**0.9080 ± 0.006**	0.521 ± 0.005
	F, R, V, Z	0.0020 ± 0.00004	27.591 ± 0.13	0.9076 ± 0.005	0.519 ± 0.005
	G, Z	0.0020 ± 0.00005	27.417 ± 0.13	0.9023 ± 0.005	**0.524 ± 0.005**
	V, Z	0.0022 ± 0.00006	27.089 ± 0.14	0.8973 ± 0.005	0.521 ± 0.005
CycleGAN	F, R, T, Z	**0.0023 ± 0.00007**	**26.417 ± 0.12**	0.8860 ± 0.005	0.177 ± 0.004
	F, R, V, Z	0.0024 ± 0.00006	25.912 ± 0.13	0.8840 ± 0.005	0.187 ± 0.004
	G, Z	0.0025 ± 0.00006	25.951 ± 0.12	0.8900 ± 0.005	0.182 ± 0.004
	V, Z	0.0025 ± 0.00007	26.132 ± 0.11	**0.8900 ± 0.005**	**0.202 ± 0.004**
Autoencoder	F, R, T, Z	**0.0021 ± 0.00005**	**28.165 ± 0.13**	**0.9257 ± 0.006**	0.249 ± 0.005
	F, R, V, Z	0.0021 ± 0.00004	27.945 ± 0.12	0.9244 ± 0.006	0.242 ± 0.005
	G, Z	0.0027 ± 0.00005	26.968 ± 0.13	0.9159 ± 0.006	**0.223 ± 0.005**
	V, Z	0.0021 ± 0.00006	27.999 ± 0.12	0.9255 ± 0.006	0.245 ± 0.005

This behavior extends to cases where full geometric transformations (F, R, T, Z) are applied. While these transformations achieved the best results in quantitative metrics, they show variability in terms of clarity and preservation of details in the ROIs. Specifically, Fig. 2 shows that all models using this combination of transformations fail to detect the hidden lesion. In the case of Fig. 3, only the CycleGAN model detects the lesion, suggesting that this outcome is more related to the model's inherent characteristics than to the specific combination of data augmentation. This is evidenced by CycleGAN's consistent performance across all data augmentation strategy combinations, where it successfully identifies the lesion.

Contrast adjustment through random variations in WW and WC improves the representation of the ROIs in the Pix2Pix and CycleGAN models. In Fig. 2, Pix2Pix detects the hidden lesion in combinations including contrast adjustment (G and Z, V and Z, F, R, V and Z), although it generates contrast responses classifiable as false positives. For CycleGAN, only the (V and Z) combination synthesizes the ROI more accurately, producing fewer false positives compared to Pix2Pix. In Fig. 3, combinations incorporating contrast adjustment more faithfully reproduce the lesion characteristics in both models. These observations support the hypothesis that contrast variations contribute to highlighting visual differences between breast tissue and regions with contrast agent uptake, better preserving key ROI characteristics compared to geometric transformations.

These results highlight a significant limitation of commonly used quantitative similarity metrics in the state of the art. This issue can be attributed to an inherent bias of these metrics towards analyzing the entire image, contrasting with clinical relevance, which lies in the ability to accurately generate the contrast response in RC images. In this context, class imbalance becomes a critical challenge, as a large portion of the image corresponds to healthy breast tissue, while the ROIs represent a minimal proportion. This causes the specific analysis

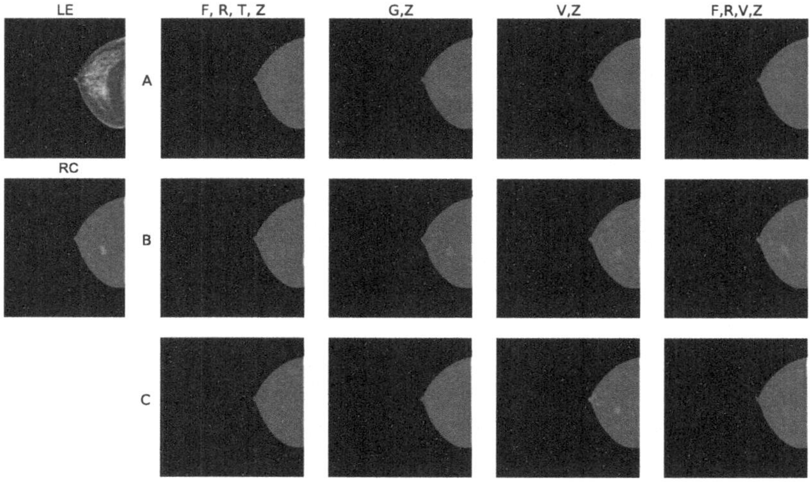

Fig. 2. Visual comparison of images generated by translation models under different data augmentation strategies is divided into three sections: **A** shows results from the Autoencoder, **B** displays Pix2Pix outputs, and **C** presents CycleGAN results.

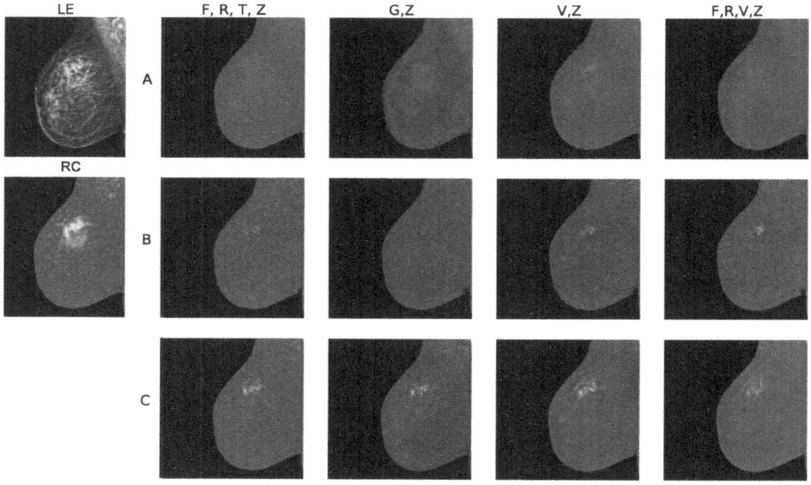

Fig. 3. Visual comparison of the images generated by the image translation models under the proposed combinations of data augmentation strategies is presented in three sections: **A** shows the images generated by the Autoencoder model, **B** the images generated by the Pix2Pix model, and **C** the results corresponding to the CycleGAN model.

of the ROIs to be diluted in the global evaluation performed by these metrics, reducing their capacity to adequately assess clinically relevant key features.

4 Conclusions and Future Work

This study analyzed the impact of various data augmentation strategies on the synthesis of contrast agent response in CESM images using deep learning models. The results revealed that data augmentation strategies based on contrast variation, particularly the random manipulation of WC and WW parameters within the windowing technique, were the most effective in qualitatively improving the synthesis of regions exhibiting contrast agent response. However, the current quantitative metrics (MSE, PSNR, SSIM, and VIF) were insufficient for accurately evaluating the clinical performance of the models in regions with contrast agent uptake, limiting the full interpretation of the findings. To consolidate and expand the obtained results, the development of quantitative metrics specific to the analysis of clinically relevant regions is proposed. Additionally, clinical validation with expert radiologists is necessary to assess the practical utility of the synthetic images and their ability to improve diagnostic accuracy in real-world contexts.

References

1. Gomaa, M.M., Kamal, R.M., Vancamberg, L.: AI-Based cancer detection model for contrast-enhanced mammography. Bioengineering **10**(8), 974 (2023). https://doi.org/10.3390/bioengineering10080974
2. Pötsch, N., Vatteroni, G., Clauser, P., et al.: Contrast-enhanced mammography versus contrast-enhanced breast MRI: A systematic review and meta-analysis. Radiology **305**(1), 94–103 (2022). https://doi.org/10.1148/radiol.212530
3. Zheng, T., Lin, F., Li, X., et al.: Deep learning-enabled fully automated pipeline system for segmentation and classification of single-mass breast lesions using contrast-enhanced mammography: A prospective multicentre study. EClinicalMedicine **58**, 101913 (2023). https://doi.org/10.1016/j.eclinm.2023.101913
4. Zhang, S., Shao, H., Li, W., et al.: Intra-and peritumoral radiomics for predicting malignant BiRADS category 4 breast lesions on contrast-enhanced spectral mammography: A multicenter study. Eur. Radiol. **33**, 5411–5422 (2023). https://doi.org/10.1007/s00330-023-09513-3
5. Cozzi, A., Magni, V., Zanardo, M., et al.: Contrast-enhanced mammography: A systematic review and meta-analysis of diagnostic performance. Radiology **302**(3), 568–581 (2022). https://doi.org/10.1148/radiol.211412
6. Sheikh, H.R., Bovik, A.C.: Image Information and Visual Quality. IEEE Trans. Image Process. **15**(5), 1193–1201 (2006). https://doi.org/10.1109/TIP.2005.862074
7. Wang, Z., Bovik, A.C.: Image quality assessment: From error visibility to structural similarity. IEEE Trans. Image Process. **13**(2), 600–612 (2004). https://doi.org/10.1109/TIP.2004.824104
8. Isola, P., Zhu, J., Zhou, T., Alexei A., Efros.: Image-to-Image translation with conditional adversarial networks. In: IEEE Conference on Computer Vision and Pattern Recognition (CVPR), 2017

9. Rofena, A., et al.: “A deep learning approach for virtual contrast enhancement in Contrast Enhanced Spectral Mammography,” Computerized Medical Imaging and Graphics, vol. 116, 102398, 2024.https://doi.org/10.1016/j.compmedimag.2024.102398
10. Zhu, J., Park, T., Isola, P., Efros, A.A.: "Unpaired image-to-image translation using cycle-consistent adversarial networks." In: Proceedings of the IEEE international conference on computer vision, 2017
11. Garcea, F., Serra, A., Lamberti, F., Morra, L.: Data augmentation for medical imaging: A systematic literature review. Dipartimento di Automatica e Informatica, Politecnico di Torino, C.so Duca degli Abruzzi, 24, Torino, 10129, Italy (2023)
12. Khaled, R., et al.: Categorized contrast enhanced mammography dataset for diagnostic and artificial intelligence research. Scientific Data **9**(1), 122 (2022). https://doi.org/10.1038/s41597-022-01238-0
13. Cañaveral, S., Mera-Banguero, C., Fonnegra, R. D.: Síntesis de imagen médica postcontraste en estudios de DCE-MRI de mama usando aprendizaje profundo. TecnoLógicas, 27(60), e3052 (2024). https://doi.org/10.22430/22565337.3052
14. “CESM@UCBM – CoSBi”. CoSBi – Computer Systems and Bioinformatics. Accedido el 28 de noviembre de 2024. [En línea]. Disponible: http://www.cosbi-lab.it/cesmucbm/

Smart Systems

Detection of DDoS Attacks in Computer Networks Using Deep Learning

Jimmy Calle, Rodolfo Bojorque(✉), Andrea Plaza, and Pilar Morquecho

Universidad Politécnica Salesiana, Cuenca 010102, Ecuador
jcalleg@est.ups.edu.ec, {rbojorque,aplaza,mmorquechoy}@ups.edu.ec

Abstract. Nowadays the security of communication networks has gained increasing significance with the advancement and expansion of large-scale networks like the Internet. Consequently, developing new and efficient systems for detecting malicious traffic, particularly that generated by Distributed Denial of Service attacks among the most severe threats has become a key research focus. This study presents the design and implementation of a system for classifying malicious traffic using Deep Learning architectures, specifically focusing on the CICIDS2017 public dataset. Despite working with sophisticated architectures, the Multilayer Perceptron Artificial Neural Network and its simplicity demonstrated the best classification performance over this dataset. Experimental results indicate that the classifier system achieves satisfactory outcomes, as evidenced by the F1 Score metric, following data analysis and preprocessing steps like class balancing before applying the Deep Learning model. F1 Score was chosen as the primary metric for evaluating model efficiency due to its connection with other crucial metrics, such as Precision and Recall, and the necessity of avoiding false positives and negatives due to the network traffic.

Keywords: Deep Learning · DDoS Traffic Classifier · Class Balancing

1 Introduction

The growth in the development and innovation of communication networks provides new and improved ways of communication. However, this rapid growth has been affected by an increasing number and variety of attacks on computer networks [3]. One of the main attacks on communication networks is known as Distributed Denial of Service (DDoS).

DDoS attacks create unauthorized traffic through multiple synchronized requests from different points in the network, thus compromising one of the main premises of computer network security: information availability. This type of attack prevents legitimate traffic from reaching a network resource by saturating the bandwidth or exhausting the machine's system resources, causing

F. R. Narváez et al. (Eds.): SmartTech-IC 2024, CCIS 2392, pp. 291–305, 2026.
https://doi.org/10.1007/978-3-031-98287-3_21

a denial of service [15]. Systems designed to address these network availability issues are capable of detecting the anomalous traffic flow of DDoS attacks, blocking it, and thus preventing the collapse of services.

The detection of these types of attacks has been implemented with a large number of systems that employ classification and anomaly detection procedures, with machine learning methods being among the most popular [1]. Currently, Deep Learning, a subset of machine learning, offers new perspectives for network traffic analysis and attack detection due to its ability to recognize highly complex information, as malicious traffic can contain a variety of characteristics [9,25]. The effectiveness of classification depends on the models and the dataset used for their structuring and training [12].

For our approach, we used the dataset CICIDS2017 [24] since is a popular open dataset with different applications of malicious traffic. The dataset consists of 8 files of traffic data collected over 5 days, containing 14 classes of cyberattacks, including DDoS. This dataset is one of the most popular as studies show it possesses characteristics very close to real-life scenarios [6]. Like many datasets, CICIDS2017 requires preprocessing procedures before being used in the construction of the classifier system, as it may contain data errors or unbalanced information that could affect classification and bias the results toward a predominant class [20]. Our approach shows that applying a preprocessing phase allows us to use simple models to predict DDoS attacks. The DDoS Attacks over CICIDS2017 datasets have a wide literature [1,13,25].

This document is divided as follows: Sect. 2 establishes a theoretical framework detailing key concepts such as Deep Learning models, the structure of the CICIDS2017 dataset, data augmentation, and the metrics used to analyze and evaluate the models. Section 3 presents the methodology of this research. Section 4 presents the results obtained, Sect. 4 discusses these results, and finally, Sect. 5 provides the conclusions.

2 Theorical Framework

In recent decades, the advancement and improvement of algorithms for analyzing large amounts of data have not been limited to statistical analysis for predicting behaviors. Thanks to the application of artificial intelligence, underlying fields such as machine learning have been developed, which aim to create new methods for automatic information analysis.

2.1 Deep Learning

With the availability of larger and more varied information, such as open databases consisting of millions of data points, there is a need to apply algorithms that can abstract more features and solve more complex problems, leading to the development of deep learning.

Deep Learning consists of algorithms that abstract complex features from large amounts of data, which would otherwise be difficult to perform manually but are manageable for a computational system [10]. Unlike machine learning, deep Learning performs learning directly from data in a very high-dimensional space, whereas machine learning requires preprocessing to extract key features to perform tasks effectively [22]. The more data available, the better and more accurate the models become, especially for classification tasks [5].

Deep Learning is generally associated with deep neural networks composed of multiple hidden layers that enable the learning of complex features from data, thus allowing them to solve nonlinear problems. However, there is no consensus or established standard for determining the number of layers required to consider a network as deep [23]. Each layer identifies a specific feature from the input data, and this information is passed to the next layer. Together with the application of activation functions, this provides non-linearity in feature recognition, resulting in high-level recognition and consequently high-precision results.

Deep Learning requires a large amount of information to train a model and thus necessitates substantial computational processing power, which can be provided by processing units such as Graphics Processing Units (GPUs) to handle information quickly [29]. GPUs were originally developed for high-quality graphics applications, such as in video games, due to their parallel information processing capability provided by their numerous cores, in contrast to Central Processing Units (CPUs), which process information sequentially. Since image processing on a GPU involves managing information in matrix form, it is applicable in the field of Deep Learning, which also requires handling large amounts of data organized in a matrix format [14].

Depending on the use case or problem to be addressed through Deep Learning, various models or neural network architectures [28] may be utilized, among which we can cite the following:

Multilayer Perceptron (MLP). MLP networks consist of an input layer, a set of hidden layers, and an output layer, all fully connected without lateral connections. Learning is performed through Backpropagation algorithms, which are among the most important methods used in an MLP.

According to [30] Neurons in one layer connect to neurons in the next layer, forming a Feedforward network. The most commonly used activation functions are the sigmoid and hyperbolic tangent functions. Currently, in Deep Learning, functions such as ReLU and Leaky ReLU are used, providing non-linearity to feature extraction and classification solutions [7]. These features endow the MLP with the properties of a universal approximator.

The number of hidden layers that these networks should have depends on the researcher's experience, and no rule determines the appropriate number; in practice, it is often determined through trial and error. This number frequently depends on the problem being addressed. The number of neurons in the input layer corresponds to the independent variables to be represented, while the categorical variable determines the output layer [11].

Convolutional Neural Network (CNN). This is a type of artificial neural network with multiple layers that performs exceptionally well in image recognition and classification. Other applications include computer vision and speech recognition. These networks apply the mathematical principle known as convolution, which involves taking groups of adjacent pixels from an image and operating them through a dot product with another small matrix called a kernel. Multiple kernels can be used as filters to extract specific features from an image, constituting an initial mapping of the input image. Subsequently, subsampling techniques are applied to reduce and extract the main features from the mapping, with pooling layers commonly used today. This process can be repeated with additional convolution operations to enable the model to recognize more complex shapes in images [2].

Recurrent Neural Network (RNN). An RNN is a network composed of neurons with feedback connections, which can be between themselves or with other neurons. This way, at a given moment, neurons can receive information from the network input, neurons from previous layers, and from previous time steps of contiguous connections. This property gives the network a form of memory, making it ideal for sequential analysis such as text, language, sound, and video analysis, where context from past information is required [21]. The issue with these networks relates to the number of training steps performed, as the importance of previous steps diminishes for the current output, a phenomenon known as vanishing gradient [17].

Long Short Term Memory (LSTM). LSTM networks are a type of RNN that can retain information from previous states not only for a short time but also for much longer periods [30]. An LSTM cell consists of state blocks through which the signal flows while being regulated by input, forget, and output gates [28]. LSTM networks are an evolution of RNNs as they address the vanishing gradient problem. They have had a significant impact on applications such as handwriting recognition and speech recognition.

2.2 CICIDS2017

The public dataset CICIDS2017, provided by the Canadian Cybersecurity Institute at the University of New Brunswick, Canada [24], offers a list of recent attacks and information on attacks with real-world characteristics. This dataset can be utilized for the development of systems to defend networks against intrusion activities.

The CICIDS2017 dataset comprises 3.1 million data flow records collected over a span of 5 days, divided into a total of 8 data files [31]. These were generated by fictitious attack networks and victim networks structured with a wide variety of devices, operating systems, and attack tools, applying common network profiles to achieve scenarios very close to real-life situations. The captured traffic within the dataset corresponds to the following labels:

- BENIGN
- DoS Hulk
- PortScan
- DDoS
- DoS GoldenEye
- FTP-Patator
- SSH-Patator
- DoS slowloris
- DoS Slowhttptest
- Bot
- Web Attack – Brute Force
- Web Attack – XSS
- Infiltration
- Web Attack – SQL Injection
- Heartbleed

The download link for the dataset files, presented in various download formats, is available on the University of New Brunswick website https://www.unb.ca/cic/datasets/ids-2017.html according to the work [24], distributed in files according to [19].

Among the main characteristics of this dataset are 2,830,540 traffic instances, each with 79 attributes (after error removal), distributed across 15 classes [19]. As shown in Fig. 1, some classes have a higher number of instances, which results in an imbalanced dataset. This imbalance will require data preprocessing techniques such as balancing to prevent training issues in the classifier system, such as bias towards any majority class.

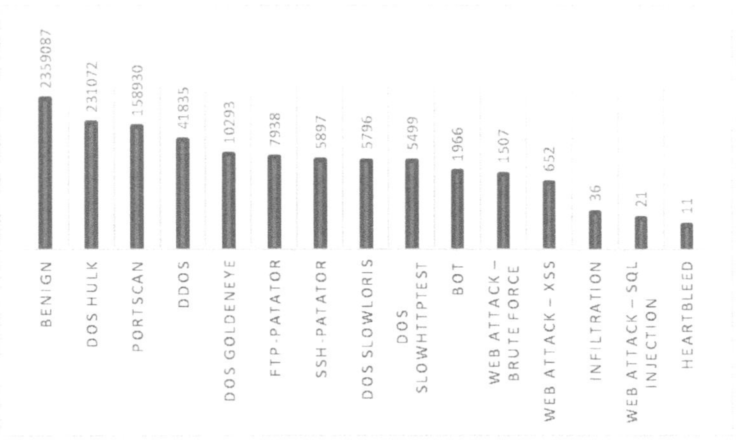

Fig. 1. Traffic Distribution of CICIDS2017

Among the data balancing techniques is data re-labeling [19], which involves equalizing the number of data points for each class in order to avoid bias towards any predominant class.

2.3 Data Augmentation

Data augmentation is a technique primarily applied to image processing when dealing with a limited dataset [4]. It involves increasing the number of samples in the original dataset while maintaining their labels by applying subtle transformations or deformations to each instance in the dataset (images), which are then added to the original dataset. This results in a larger dataset that can be used to train a model. Among the data augmentation techniques for images, those described in [27] can be indicated. In the current traffic data analysis case, the principle of information augmentation is applied by adding a small percentage of random information to the traffic data, which is then incorporated into the total dataset.

2.4 Evaluation Tools

Confusion Matrix. The confusion matrix is composed of the predictions made by the classifier compared to the actual corresponding data, allowing for the analysis of the performance of a supervised learning algorithm. The values that make up the matrix are: True Negatives (TN), True Positives (TP), False Positives (FP), and False Negatives (FN) [26]. Table 1 illustrates the construction of a confusion matrix for binary classification with the aforementioned terms.

Table 1. Constitution of a binary confusion matrix

	Prediction		
		Negative class	*Positive class*
Reality	Negative class	True Negative (TN)	False Positive (FP)
Reality	Positive class	False Negative (FN)	True Positive (TP)

Evaluation Metrics. Evaluation metrics allow for the assessment of a classifier's performance. The choice of an algorithm or model will depend on the values provided by these metrics, based on the needs or application of the classification [8,16]. Below are the equations for the evaluation metrics that will be used in this study.

$$precision = \frac{TP}{TP + FP} \tag{1}$$

$$recall = \frac{TP}{TP + FN} \tag{2}$$

$$F1score = 2 * \frac{precision * recall}{precision + recall} \tag{3}$$

$$accuracy = \frac{TP + TN}{TP + TN + FP + FN} \tag{4}$$

T-SNE Analysis. The t-distributed Stochastic Neighbor Embedding (T-SNE) analysis is an algorithm for representing high-dimensional data in 2 or 3 dimensions to facilitate visualization and analysis [18]. The algorithm maps the data and measures the similarities between high-dimensional points using a Gaussian distribution within a specified area for each point. When two points have a similar distribution, they are considered similar. Subsequently, the algorithm attempts to reproduce this similarity in a lower-dimensional space, aiming to preserve the original distribution [18].

3 Methodology

3.1 Cleaning of CICIDS2017

Since the CICIDS2017 dataset is divided into 8 files, the relevance of working with a single data source was assessed, and the data was consolidated into a single file, resulting in a matrix of 2,427,193 rows with 79 attributes plus a final column of labels. Column names and labels with typographical errors were corrected to avoid discrepancies. Additionally, 334 rows containing NULL values were removed, and 1,132 rows with infinite values were also removed, resulting in a final dataset of 2,425,727 rows.

3.2 Data Selection

The data to be analyzed in subsequent stages is cleaned due to the imbalance present in the CICIDS2017 dataset. Figure 2 shows the distribution of the original dataset and the predominance of benign data, represented by red points; this is a graph generated using T-SNE processing.

For this reason, data balancing is performed to prevent classification bias towards the predominant class. Minor classes contributing little information are merged to create a new class called "Other." Additionally, the data for the newly created classes is adjusted to ensure equal amounts of information, using data augmentation techniques applied to classes with less information. Figure 3 illustrates the distribution of information after re-labeling and adjustment, resulting in a balanced dataset with 500,000 samples and three generated classes: "Benign," "DDoS," and "Other." This figure shows a more even distribution of the information.

3.3 Dataset Preparation

The dataset undergoes a final procedure to facilitate model training, reduce computational load during the process, and enhance efficiency. In this phase, attribute scaling is performed using "Robust Scaling," which is based on percentiles to mitigate the influence of outliers. Additionally, the labels for each class are encoded, converting the class names into numerical values; this encoding replaces class names with integers starting from 0. Finally, the dataset is split, with 80% of the data allocated for training and 20% for testing from the total CICIDS2017 dataset.

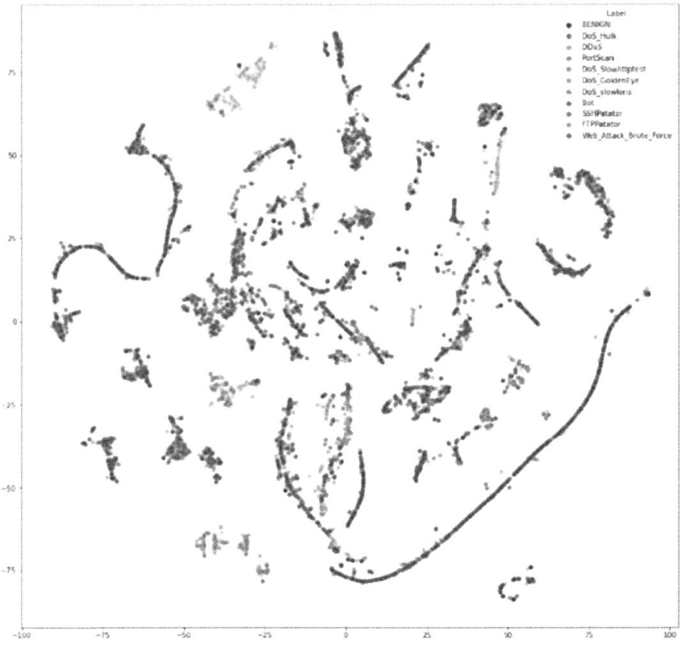

Fig. 2. T-SNE graphic of traffic CICIDS2017's distribution

3.4 Neural Network Architecture

The task of detecting benign and anomalous traffic is fundamentally a classification problem. For this, we rely on Deep Learning, which enables the abstraction and processing of large amounts of information contained in the CICIDS2017 dataset. Deep Learning typically involves networks with a large number of hidden layers; however, the number of layers depends on the complexity of the training data and the non-linearity of the classification. This study requires a simple neural network known as a Feedforward Neural Network with a Backpropagation algorithm, consisting of 3 layers, which constitutes a type of Multilayer Perceptron (MLP). This network will be used to classify each of the classes presented, whether the complete set of 15 classes or the adjusted dataset with 3 classes. This type of classification, represented by labels, constitutes a supervised learning scenario.

The input layer consists of 78 neurons, corresponding to the 78 attributes of the dataset. The hidden layers will vary according to the test models, ranging from 1 to 3 layers with 64, 128, or 256 neurons each. The output layer will consist of 3 or 15 neurons, depending on whether we wish to classify the 14 attacks plus the benign class or only the "DDoS" attack along with benign and other attacks. The activation functions used in the hidden layers are ReLU, while the SoftMax function is used for the output layer. When constructing a model with 3 hidden layers, the activation functions are alternated as ReLU-

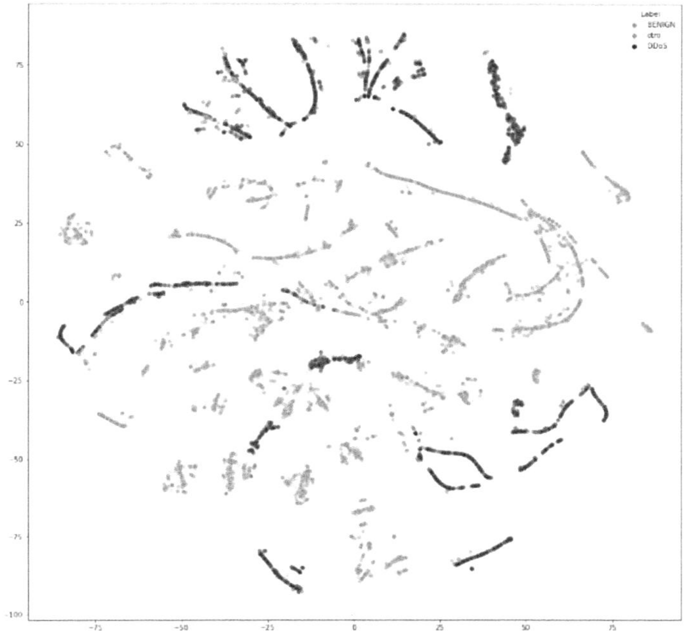

Fig. 3. Distribution of the dataset with 500000 data in each class

Sigmoid-ReLU to introduce non-linearity into the model and provide complex solutions. A Dropout parameter of 0.2 is used to reduce overfitting and improve the network's accuracy. For classification problems, the Adam optimizer and Sparse Categorical Crossentropy loss function are typically used. By default, the models are configured with 100 Epochs (which means 100 passes over all the data). However, to avoid overfitting, EarlyStopping is enabled to automatically determine the number of Epochs and halt training if no improvement is observed after 10 iterations.

3.5 Evaluation Models

The models are constructed using Python, which supports numerous scientific libraries for deep learning applications, such as TensorFlow and its Keras library for neural network configuration, and Sklearn for dataset management, including scaling, encoding, and splitting. Eight test models are created to build the classifier, with variations in the dataset and neural network model to analyze the effectiveness of the classification by verifying the evaluation metric values. The description of the models is presented in Table 2.

3.6 Evaluation Criteria

A DDoS traffic classifier requires a minimum number of False Negatives, meaning the system must avoid predicting traffic as non-DDoS (benign or other types) when it is indeed DDoS. Failure to do so may lead to the collapse of a system by allowing DDoS attack traffic mistakenly identified as benign.

Table 2. Description of the 8 classification test models

Model	Dataset	Neural Network (layers)
1	All tags	Flatten 78, Dense 67 - relu, Dense 15 âĂŞ softmax
2	Relabeling classes and reducing the Benign class	Flatten 78, Dense 67 - relu, Dense 3–softmax
3	Relabeling classes and reducing the Benign class	Flatten 78, Dense 128 - relu, Dense 64 – Sigmoid, Dense 32 - relu, Dense 3 – softmax
4	Relabeling classes and reducing the Benign class	Flatten 78, Dense 128 - relu, Dense 3 – softmax
5	Relabeling classes and reducing the Benign class	Flatten 78, Dense 128 - relu, Dense 128 – relu, Dense 3 softmax
6	Relabeling classes and reducing the Benign class	Flatten 78, Dense 256 - relu, Dense 3 – softmax
7	Relabeling classes and balancing classes 500000 samples	Flatten 78, Dense 128 - relu, Dense 3 – softmax
8	Dataset pruning according to DDoS, three classes at 128000	Flatten 78, Dense 128 - relu, Dense 3 – softmax

The number of False Positives detected should have a more permissive tolerance, meaning the detection of DDoS traffic when it is benign can be allowed. This tolerance is feasible within the limits of the system being protected, as excessive False Positives in DDoS traffic may incur processing costs. Therefore, both False Negatives and False Positives should remain low to maintain system effectiveness. Metrics that evaluate these rates are Precision and Recall, as shown in Eq. (1) and (2). By keeping "FP" and "FN" values low, the Precision and Recall rates will be high, respectively.

A metric that efficiently combines both values for quick system assessment is the F1-Score, which compares combined performance through a harmonic mean of these two metrics, as shown in Eq. (3). Therefore, this study will serve as a key indicator of the system's performance.

4 Results and Discussion

After analyzing 8 models with various modifications to the CICIDS2017 dataset, the following observations were made.

Table 3 shows that Model 1 has an Accuracy of 91.033%, which appears acceptable at first glance. However, it is important to consider that we are working with an imbalanced dataset where the majority of the data is labeled as "Benign," which causes the classifier to be biased towards the predominant class. This is evidenced by a low Precision value of 78.017%. Therefore, although the Accuracy metric is one of the most commonly used, it is not the best indicator of classifier quality. This is further demonstrated by a very low F1 Score of 48.5%.

Table 3. Traffic classifier evaluation metrics

Model	Accuracy	Precision	Recall	F1 Score
1	0,9103	0,7802	0,4546	0,4850
2	0,9659	0,9800	0,9456	0,9615
3	0,9448	0,9684	0,9082	0,9342
4	0,9663	0,9805	0,9459	0,9618
5	0,9542	0,9734	0,9319	0,9505
6	0,9638	0,9784	0,9436	0,9596
7	0,9319	0,9415	0,9318	0,9332
8	0,9266	0,9370	0,9266	0,9280

Table 4. DDoS traffic evaluation

Model	Precision	Recall	F1 Score
1	0,8684	0,3597	0,5087
2	0,9995	0,9046	0,9497
3	0,9960	0,8241	0,9019
4	0,9997	0,9048	0,9499
5	0,9975	0,9013	0,9470
6	0,9988	0,9044	0,9493
7	0,9996	0,9050	0,9500
8	1,0000	0,9029	0,9489

Upon analyzing the confusion matrix data for the DDoS class in Table 5, it can be observed that there is a relatively small number of False Negatives (235). However, there is also a relatively small number of True Positives, indicating that the classifier is not recognizing all DDoS traffic values. This issue arises due to the substantial amount of information present in other classes, reflected in a high number of True Negatives (484,759). Therefore, the performance of this model is not very satisfactory.

The best results are provided by Model 4, which consists of three classes: "Benign," "DDoS," and "Other," with the "Benign" class reduced to 500,000 data points. This model achieves a Recall of 94.59%, a Precision of 98.05%, and an F1-Score of 96.18%, as shown in Table 3. For the "DDoS" class, which is the class of interest, Model 4 attains a Recall of 90.48% and a Precision of 99.97%, as observed in Table 4. These results demonstrate that the design of the DDoS attack traffic classifier is within acceptable values, thanks to the preprocessing of the dataset performed before the training phase.

Table 5, which consolidates the confusion matrix values for all models, illustrates the classifier's behavior in detecting DDoS traffic, applying the evaluation criteria described in Sect. 4.6. These results are consistent with the good performance of Models 2 and 4, as they achieve the lowest False Negative values.

Table 5. DDoS Class confusion matrix values for each model

Model	FN	FP	TN	TP
1	235	20	484759	132
2	2443	12	152423	23167
3	4056	85	152350	21104
4	2438	8	152427	23172
5	2528	57	152378	23082
6	2448	27	152408	23162
7	9474	36	200225	90265
8	4506	85	152350	21104

It should also be noted that the best neural network model is represented by the MLP model with a single hidden layer of 128 neurons. Tests conducted with models featuring 2 and 3 hidden layers (Models 3 and 5) did not yield satisfactory results. Therefore, the model with an input layer of 78 neurons, a hidden layer of 128 neurons, and an output layer of 3 neurons fully connected (Model 4) demonstrates the best classification performance for the preprocessed dataset. However, for application in a real system, one might consider a model with a 64-neuron hidden layer (Model 2), as its metric values are very similar to those of the 128-neuron model and may offer less computational cost for real-world application.

It is also evident that the Precision, Recall, and F1 Score metrics differ significantly in models using the original unbalanced dataset (Model 1). This demonstrates that executing models with a dataset containing a large number of unbalanced classes does not provide useful information and results in low

Precision. Similarly, reducing the dataset dimension to 128,000 samples (Model 8) also decreases the amount of useful information, as evidenced by low Precision and Accuracy values, as shown in Table 3.

Increasing the number of hidden layers or neurons does not improve the evaluation metrics of the system, as this elevated number of layers tends to overfit the model and does not generalize well to unknown data. Therefore, the optimal neural network representation consists of a hidden layer with between 67 and 128 neurons.

5 Conclusions

Machine Learning methods, especially Deep Learning techniques, have the capability to extract and learn a large number of features from a dataset. As the complexity of the analysis increases, deeper neural networks are required to handle more complex multidimensional spaces.

The importance of preprocessing information before presenting it to a Deep Learning model is evident. This phase constitutes the most labor-intensive part of achieving acceptable results during classification.

This work demonstrates that having more information does not always equate to better model training, especially with unbalanced or "skewed" datasets as referred to in specialized literature. In this case, it was necessary to significantly and randomly trim data representing benign traffic, as the models efficiently learned to recognize benign traffic but achieved high false-negative rates in the presence of different types of attacks. The objective of our work is to detect distributed denial-of-service attacks.

Different scaling techniques or combinations of scaling techniques could be applied to each column or attribute of the dataset as a proposed improvement. Given that the input data contain heterogeneous values across different ranges relative to other variables, this mismatch can lead algorithms to focus more on large values and ignore smaller ones, causing them to get stuck in local minima, slowing down learning, and increasing computational costs. Therefore, scaling input variables is a preparatory data technique before presenting them to a model. Normalization or scaling of a dataset is a common practice among estimators. Outliers often negatively influence the mean and variance; in such cases, the median and interquartile range provided by RobustScaler yield better results.

References

1. Abdulrahman, A.A., Ibrahem, M.K.: Evaluation of ddos attacks detection in a cicids2017 dataset based on classification algorithms. Iraqi J. Inf. Commun. Technol. (IJICT) **1**(3) (2018)
2. Albawi, S., Mohammed, T., Al-Zawi, S.: Understanding of a convolutional neural network. In: 2017 International Conference on Engineering and Technology (ICET), pp. 1–6, 21 August 2017

3. Aslan, Ö., Aktuğ, S.S., Ozkan-Okay, M., Yilmaz, A.A., Akin, E.: A comprehensive review of cyber security vulnerabilities, threats, attacks, and solutions. Electronics **12**(6), 1333 (2023)
4. Bonandrini, V., Bercher, J.F., Zangar, N.: Machine learning methods for anomaly detection in iot networks, with illustrations. In: Boumerdassi, S., Renault, É., Mühlethaler, P. (eds.) Machine Learning for Networking, pp. 287–295. Springer International Publishing, Cham (2020)
5. Emmert-Streib, F., Yang, Z., Feng, H., Tripathi, S., Dehmer, M.: An introductory review of deep learning for prediction models with big data. Front. Artif. Intell. **3**, 4 (2020)
6. Gharib, A., Sharafaldin, I., Lashkari, A.H., Ghorbani, A.A.: An evaluation framework for intrusion detection dataset. In: 2016 International Conference on Information Science and Security (ICISS), pp. 1–6. IEEE (2016)
7. Ghayoumi, M.: Generative Adversarial Networks in Practice. CRC Press, Boca Raton (2023)
8. Hossin, M., Sulaiman, M.N.: A review on evaluation metrics for data classification evaluations. Int. J. Data Min. Knowl. Manag. Process **5**(2), 1 (2015)
9. Hussein, T.: Deep learning-based ddos detection in network traffic data. Int. J. Electr. Comput. Eng. Syst. **15**(5), 407–414 (2024). https://doi.org/10.32985/ijeces.15.5.3, https://ijeces.ferit.hr/index.php/ijeces/article/view/3150
10. IBM: What is deep learning? (June 2024). https://www.ibm.com/topics/deep-learning
11. Isa, I., Saad, Z., Omar, S., Osman, M., Ahmad, K., Sakim, H.M.: Suitable mlp network activation functions for breast cancer and thyroid disease detection. In: 2010 Second International Conference on Computational Intelligence, Modelling and Simulation, pp. 39–44. IEEE (2010)
12. Javaid, A., Niyaz, Q., Sun, W., Alam, M.: A deep learning approach for network intrusion detection system. In: Proceedings of the 9th EAI International Conference on Bio-inspired Information and Communications Technologies (formerly BIONETICS), pp. 21–26 (2016)
13. Kareem, M.I., Jasim, M.N.: Ddos attack detection using lightweight partial decision tree algorithm. In: 2022 International Conference on Computer Science and Software Engineering (CSASE), pp. 362–367. IEEE (2022)
14. Kimm, H., Paik, I., Kimm, H.: Performance comparision of tpu, gpu, cpu on google colaboratory over distributed deep learning. In: 2021 IEEE 14th International Symposium on Embedded Multicore/Many-core Systems-on-Chip (MCSoC), pp. 312–319. IEEE (2021)
15. Kumar, D., Pateriya, R., Gupta, R.K., Dehalwar, V., Sharma, A.: Ddos detection using deep learning. Procedia Comput. Sci. **218**, 2420–2429 (2023). https://doi.org/10.1016/j.procs.2023.01.217, https://www.sciencedirect.com/science/article/pii/S187705092300217X, international Conference on Machine Learning and Data Engineering
16. Kumar, G.: Evaluation metrics for intrusion detection systems-a study. Evaluation **2**(11), 11–7 (2014)
17. Kvita, B.J.: Image captioning with recurrent neural networks (2016)
18. Van der Maaten, L., Hinton, G.: Visualizing data using t-sne. J. Mach. Learn. Res. **9**(11) (2008)
19. Panigrahi, R., Borah, S.: A detailed analysis of cicids2017 dataset for designing intrusion detection systems. Int. J. Eng. Technol. **7**(3.24), 479–482 (2018)

20. Sahu, S.K., Sarangi, S., Jena, S.K.: A detail analysis on intrusion detection datasets. In: 2014 IEEE International Advance Computing Conference (IACC), pp. 1348–1353. IEEE (2014)
21. Salem, F.M.: Recurrent Neural Networks. Springer (2022)
22. Saputra, N.A., Riza, L.S., Setiawan, A., Hamidah, I.: A systematic review for classification and selection of deep learning methods. Decis. Anal. J. **12**, 100489 (2024)
23. Schmidhuber, J.: Deep learning in neural networks: an overview. Neural Netw. **61**, 85–117 (2015)
24. Sharafaldin, I., Lashkari, A.H., Ghorbani, A.A., et al.: Toward generating a new intrusion detection dataset and intrusion traffic characterization. ICISSp **1**, 108–116 (2018)
25. Shieh, C.S., Nguyen, T.T., Horng, M.F.: Detection of unknown ddos attack using convolutional neural networks featuring geometrical metric. Mathematics **11**(9), 2145 (2023)
26. Shijie, J., Ping, W., Peiyi, J., Siping, H.: Research on data augmentation for image classification based on convolution neural networks. In: 2017 Chinese Automation Congress (CAC), pp. 4165–4170. IEEE (2017)
27. Shorten, C., Khoshgoftaar, T.M.: A survey on image data augmentation for deep learning. J. Big Data **6**(1), 1–48 (2019)
28. Shrestha, A., Mahmood, A.: Review of deep learning algorithms and architectures. IEEE Access **7**, 53040–53065 (2019)
29. Smys, S., Chen, J., Shakya, S.: Survey on neural network architectures with deep learning. J. Soft Comput. Paradigm (JSCP) **2**(03), 186–194 (2020)
30. Wang, Z., Sun, T., Hu, K., Zhang, Y., Yu, X., Li, Y.: A deep learning semantic segmentation method for landslide scene based on transformer architecture. Sustainability **14**(23) (2022). https://doi.org/10.3390/su142316311, https://www.mdpi.com/2071-1050/14/23/16311
31. Zegeye, W.K., Dean, R.A., Moazzami, F.: Multi-layer hidden Markov model based intrusion detection system. Mach. Learn. Knowl. Extr. **1**(1), 265–286 (2019)

Exploring New Horizons on the Interpretation of PCA Using LLM for Data Analysis

Victor Saquicela(✉), Kenneth Palacio-Baus, Mercy Orellana Bravo, and Mauricio Espinoza-Mejía

Department of Computer Science, Department of Electrical, Electronic Engineering and Telecommunications, Departamento de Economía, Empresa y Desarrollo Sostenible, University of Cuenca, Cuenca, Ecuador
{victor.saquicela,kenneth.palacio,mercy.orellana, mauricio.espinoza}@ucuenca.edu.ec

Abstract. This paper proposes an innovative approach to address the challenge of semantic interpretation of principal components generated by the widely used Principal Component Analysis (PCA) on complex datasets. We propose a novel method that incorporates large language models (LLM) into the interpretation process. This approach aims to bridge the gap between the statistical complexity of PCA and the practical applicability of latent variables. Our initial results demonstrate the effectiveness and promising precision that this approach can achieve in translating complex mathematical relationships into contextually rich semantic interpretation. This work represents a significant step towards improving interpretability in data science, and a valuable resource to facilitate informed decision making and understanding in diverse research and data analysis contexts.

Keywords: PCA · LLM · Interpretation

1 Introduction

In the fascinating field of Data Science, Principal Component Analysis (PCA) has emerged as an essential tool for distilling complex patterns in vast data sets. On top of the mathematical robustness found in PCA [10], there exists a significant challenge on attempting to attribute semantic meaning to the resulting components. Although it is possible to derive interpretation and understanding directly from numerical relationships, it is clear that this task may be complicated when it is necessary to assign meaningful contexts to the latent variables revealed by PCA.

In the context of the use of PCA, giving useful meaning to the principal components is often limited to mathematical explanations and statistical variations.

Supported by VIUC.

F. R. Narváez et al. (Eds.): SmartTech-IC 2024, CCIS 2392, pp. 306–321, 2026.
https://doi.org/10.1007/978-3-031-98287-3_22

Although this approach is valuable for data analysts, there still exists an open gap when it comes to translate the results for researchers and decision makers from a non-mathematical viewpoint. The root of the problem lies on the lack of a formal process to add semantic meaning to such resulting components. This places researchers at the intersection of converting numerical relationships into practical and relevant interpretations.

Although we present preliminary –yet promising– results, we discovered that the best path to conduct research towards addressing the challenge of PCA interpretation lies on the innovative inclusion of large language models (LLM). This way, we propose a versatile approach that combines the mathematical robustness of PCA with the semantic richness of language models. This method not only preserves the important statistical properties inherent of PCA, but also pushes the interpretation up to a more accessible and meaningful level for researchers in a wider specialization spectrum. Ultimately, this integration maintains the mathematical integrity of the analysis providing at the same time a deeper and more applicable understanding of the intricate components generated by PCA. Though our approach shows promising results, we recognize that further empirical studies must be conducted in order to evaluate the effectiveness of the proposed approach on various datasets and different contexts, and quantify how the incorporation of LLM improves semantic interpretation compared to traditional methods.

The remaining of this article is organized as follows: in Sect. 2, the background and related work is covered. In Sect. 3, a case-scenario is described. The proposed procedure is presented in Sect. 4, which outlines its main components and workflows. Finally, in Sect. 5, we present conclusions and future work.

2 Background and Related Works

In this section we review some key concepts useful for the presentation and understanding of our proposal, as well as the most relevant related works.

2.1 Background

PCA is a multivariate analysis technique that seeks to transform a set of statistically correlated variables into a new set of uncorrelated variables called principal components [7]. These components capture the largest variance present in the data, allowing a more compact representation of information and facilitating the identification of patterns and trends.

The implementation of PCA involves computing the eigenvectors and eigenvalues of the covariance matrix of the original data. Eigenvectors represent the main directions of statistical variation, whereas eigenvalues indicate the magnitude of the variance in those directions.

The main applications of PCA are: dimensionality reduction to manage the curse of dimensionality; pattern analysis and outlier detection; data compression while maintaining essential information.

The powerful feature of dimensionality reduction derived from the use of PCA on complex data sets is subject to certain conditions that must be met to obtain meaningful results. First, it is essential that variables in the data set are linearly correlated since PCA is based on the covariance between variables. In addition, it is assumed that there exists a smooth continuous relationship between the variables, since PCA seeks to capture joint variation in the data. Another important condition is that variables must have significant variance. PCA works best when the variables show substantial variability, since its main objective is to identify the directions in which the data exhibit the highest variability. If some variables have low or constant variance, they may not contribute significantly to the analysis and could be discarded. Finally, it is crucial to work with outliers-free data sets, since outliers may disturb the identification of the main directions of variation. This happens because outliers may have a disproportionate impact on the estimation of principal components, which would ultimately affect the quality of dimensionality reduction.

The other element of our proposal involves the use of LLM, which are tools developed in the field of natural language processing (NLP) that assign probability values to sequences of words. These models are handful on understanding and generating text, being fundamental building blocks in tasks such as machine translation, text summarization and text generation. Language Models are categorized as *N-grams*: Simple models that consider the probability of word occurrence based on the last n words; *Transformer-Based Models*: More advanced architectures, such as GPT (Generative Pre-trained Transformer), that learn contextual representations of words. Among the relevant applications of LLM it is worth mentioning: speech recognition, machine translation, autonomous text generation, among others.

We have envisioned a promising research niche resulting from the integration of PCA and LLM towards the goal of improving the interpretation of the components obtained in PCA by matching them with human-understandable meaning. To this end, language models are used to provide semantic context to latent variables, facilitating the understanding of relationships and patterns discovered by PCA in complex datasets. This approach may have significant implications for components meaning interpretability and practical usefulness in dimensionality reduction techniques.

Natural interpretation of principal components refers to assigning a specific (human-understandable) meaning to each component resulting from principal component analysis (PCA). This can be challenging, though it is fundamental to understand what the new variables represent and how they relate to the original ones. This issue is relevant to the interpretability and explainability of models in several ways:

- **Assigning Meanings to Components**: Each principal component is a linear combination of the original variables. To interpret each component, the coefficients. To interpret each component, the coefficients (or loadings) of the original variables on each component are examined. Variables with high coefficients (positive or negative) have the greatest influence on that component.

Analysis of these coefficients may reveal significant patterns or characteristics of the data.
- **Explainability in Predictive Models**: In predictive models, principal components can be used as explanatory variables. The interpretation of these components can help to understand how and why a model makes certain predictions. This is essential for model explainability, as it allows users to understand the inner workings of the model.
- **Dimensionality Reduction and Interpretability**: PCA is commonly used to reduce the dimensionality of the data while maintaining most of the variability. By reducing the number of variables, the model is simplified, which can improve interpretability. However, for the model to be interpretable, it is crucial to understand what each principal component represents.
- **Data Visualization and Understanding**: Principal component interpretation facilitates the visualization of complex data in a lower dimensional space. This helps to identify patterns, clusters or trends that may not be evident in the original variable space.

2.2 Related Works

The authors [2] discuss the need for interpretability in the field of machine learning and propose a taxonomy of evaluation using three approaches: application-based, human-based, and function-based. The goal of the paper is to establish a rigorous definition and evaluation of interpretability in machine learning. The authors also address interpretability in the context of machine learning models, by exploring strategies to make the models more interpretable and understandable. Though the article is not specifically focused on the interpretation of principal components generated by PCA, it provides an overview of the challenges and approaches to interpretation in data science, which is relevant to this proposal, see also [9].

Article [4] addresses the lack of explanation in decision support systems using a black boxes approach and exploring ways to balance accuracy and interpretability. A classification of the problems related to the explanation and types of black boxes is also presented, guiding researchers to relevant proposals according to their needs. The proposed classification aims to address open questions in black box model based research. The semantic interpretation of principal components generated by PCA has been a persistent challenge in data science. Up to date, related literature has approached this problem from a mathematical, geometric and statistical perspective [3,5,6,8], leaving a significant gap in terms of contextual meaning assignment.

A recent work interpreting machine learning results using LLM is presented in [1], which highlights the challenge of analyzing complex biomedical and healthcare data for researchers without computer science training by means of *Aliro*, an open-source software package with a user-friendly web interface. Leveraging LLM, Aliro allows users to interact with their data, retrieve and execute code seamlessly, accelerating new insights discovery. The software includes a pre-trained machine learning recommendation system for automated algorithm and hyperparameter selection, along with visualization of evaluated models and data.

The work described in [11] demonstrates the powerful synergy between PCA loadings (feature weights corresponding to the principal components), transformer predictions, and state-of-the-art large language models (LLMs). Specifically, the authors find that while each component provides substantial predictive insight, their combination provides a paradigm shift in how we approach accident prediction. They conclude that the semiotic richness of LLMs not only refines predictions, but also provides discernible, actionable insights that are fundamental to field implementation and real-time use.

The innovative approach we propose in this article brings up an interesting combination that takes advantage of the power of Principal Component Analysis (PCA) and the interpretability of Language Models (LLM), aiming to assign human–readable meaning to the resulting components. To date, and to the best of the knowledge of the authors, we found that literature lacks research considering merging these two paradigms, which highlights the uniqueness and novelty of this proposal. Our approach involves the use of pre-trained language models to generate semantic descriptions of the original variables, thus, true human-readable meaning can be assigned to each PCA principal component. This approach seeks to overcome the limitations of the conventional linear interpretation inherent of PCA, which can be achieved by capitalizing on the ability of LLMs to contextualize and coherently describe domain-specific terms.

Although language model interpretation has experienced important progress in recent years, its application to PCA constitutes uncharted territory. The scarcity of previous work on the topic underscores the innovation behind this proposal, suggesting a path towards a richer and more accessible interpretation of PCA results. The effectiveness of this approach will depend on the quality of the language model and the consistency of the generated descriptions, highlighting the importance of the validation and refinement stages, which could be performed through collaboration with domain experts. This approach represents not only a bold step up in the interpretation of PCA results, but also an exciting opportunity to open new perspectives in understanding complex data in diverse contexts.

3 Scenario

We consider a sample scenario used to illustrate the application of our approach. Note that this scenario can be easily changed and modified to test our proposal out for any desired context. Consider a data scientist, who is working on an ambitious data analysis project. The scientist faces a complex and multidimensional dataset containing crucial information for the research. In order to reveal underlying patterns and understand the hidden structure of the data, the scientist decides to apply Principal Component Analysis (PCA). Nonetheless, the project is not limited to use of the conventional PCA approach alone, since additional semantic complexities, can be captured recognizing the richness of natural language and the ability of Language Models (LLM). Thus, the scientis incorporates LLM into the analysis. The final goal is thus to go beyond dimensionality reduction and to assign a meaningful explanation to the principal components generated by PCA through the power of language models.

As progress in the research is made, the challenge of interpreting these components effectively arises. The scientist may now use advanced strategies, such as examining coefficients, analyzing correlations, and collaborating closely with domain experts on interpreting results. In addition, innovative techniques that leverage LLMs can be also used to explore the semantics of variables and reveal hidden connections.

This research path not only seeks to simplify the model, but also to deepen the understanding of the data through semantic interpretation regardless of the field from which data is analyzed. The final result is a unique and powerful approach that combines the mathematical structure of PCA with the richness of natural language, providing a more complete and meaningful view of data. This scenario highlights the intersection between advanced statistical techniques and the power of semantic interpretation, taking data analysis to new levels of depth and understanding.

4 Procedure for Interpreting Components Using LLM

In this section we present the procedure of assigning meaning to the components extracted from the dataset as shown in Fig. 1. Each component of the proposal is described below:

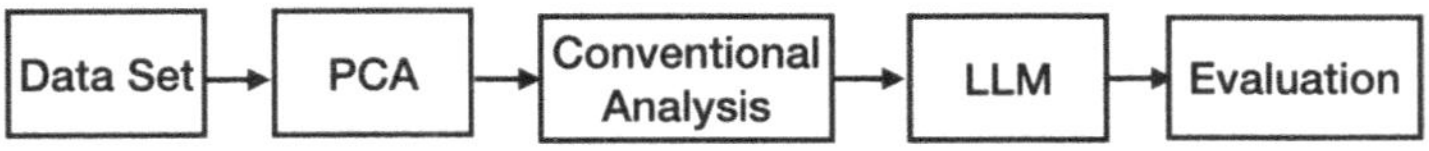

Fig. 1. Procedure for Interpreting Components using LLM

4.1 Data Set

The data set proposed in this research may originate from different forms, including surveys, data tables, databases, among others. This dataset comprises n variables with m observations. We consider each variable representing a business question, and the diversity found in the answers reflecting multiple user observations allows addressing the inherent complexity of the data. In this paper, the data set is assumed to have an $m \times n$ matrix form.

Based on the described problem and data set, we proceed to exemplify and present a more rigorous formalization. In the example used, we focus on a dataset that has a natural language description and is formally defined as:

$$D \triangleq \{\text{Problem description}\} \tag{1}$$

where (D) is the description of the problem in natural language.

To clarify the approach proposed in this paper, a concrete example will be used: in this case D has the following description: We use a data set called USArrests[1], this data set contains statistics, in arrests per $100,000$ residents for assault, murder, and rape in each of the 50 US states in 1973. Also given is the percent of the population living in urban areas. Table 1 shows the description of each variable representing the problem discussed.

The Set of Variables (V) representing the dataset, is defined as

$$V = \{1, 2, 3, \ldots, n\} \tag{2}$$

Table 1. Variables of USArrests dataset

Variable	Data type	Description
Murder	numeric	Murder arrests (per 100,000)
Assault	numeric	Assault arrests (per 100,000)
UrbanPop	numeric	Percent urban population
Rape	numeric	Rape arrests (per 100,000)

Values taken by each of the variables (V) are defined as the Instance Set (I).

$$I = \{1, 2, 3, \ldots, m\} \tag{3}$$

Together the variables and instances define a matrix Data Matrix (M)

$$M = \{(i, j, \text{value}) \mid i \in I, j \in V\} \tag{4}$$

where location (i, j) indicates the value of a variable. Where value is the assessment to the j-th variable, and in the i-th instance (observation).

Each of the variables has a natural language name and is defined as the set of variable names (NV)

$$NV = \{\text{Variable name 1}, \text{Variable name 2}, \ldots\} \tag{5}$$

Thus, the *i-th variable* has a natural language name and is defined as the set of variable names (NV). For the example used, NV = {Murder, Assault, UrbanPop,Rape}

The association of variables with names (VN) is defined as.

$$VN = \{(j, \text{Variable name}) \mid j \in V\} \tag{6}$$

where j represents the location of the variable in M and its respective name in natural language.

Each variable has a Natural Language definition (DV) formally defined as

$$DV = \{\text{Definition of variable 1}, \text{Definition of variable 2}, \ldots\} \tag{7}$$

[1] https://www.kaggle.com/datasets/halimedogan/usarrests.

For the example used, we have:
DV = {"Murder arrest (per 100000)","Assault arrests (per 100000)",
"Percent urban population","Rape arrests (per 100000)" }

In summary, the data set includes the problem description (D), the set of variables (V), the set of instances (I), the data matrix (M), the variable names (NV), the association of variables with names (VN), and the natural language variable definitions (DV). This representation provides a complete structure for understanding and addressing the problem, from an initial description to the detailed variable definitions. It should be emphasized that this modeling generalizes to any data set in a matrix form.

4.2 PCA

The PCA application process is performed to reduce the dimensionality of the data set and to identify the principal components that capture the greatest variability in the data set. The sequence of steps to achieve this comprises the following:

1. Data Normalization: to ensure that all variables have the same scale and contribute equally to the analysis. If variables are not standardized, meaning they do not have zero mean and a standard deviation of 1 before performing the PCA study, the Assault variable will dominate most of the principal components, because the unit of measure indicates large numbers compared to the other variables.
2. Covariance Matrix Calculation: to understand the relationships between variables and their contribution to the total variability.
3. Calculation of eigenvectors and eigenvalues: these represent the direction and magnitude of variability in the data, respectively.
4. Principal Component Ordering: the principal components are ordered according to the amount of variability they explain.
5. Selection of Relevant Components: based on the cumulative proportion of variance explained and specific research criteria.

It should be noted that the Kaiser-Meyer-Olkin (KMO) test, which is a fundamental tool in factor analysis, including Principal Component Analysis (PCA), is used to determine whether it is possible to apply PCA to the data set. This test provides a measure of the adequacy of the sample for factor analysis, assessing whether the correlations between variables are strong enough to justify the use of dimensionality reduction techniques. The KMO result is expressed as a coefficient ranging from 0 to 1. A value close to 1 suggests that the variables are sufficiently correlated to proceed with PCA. In interpretation, values greater than 0.6 or 0.7 are considered to indicate an appropriate adequacy of the data for factor analysis. In the example used, the value of KMO is 0.65.

Additionally, Bartlett's test of sphericity is an essential tool to determine whether the correlation matrix between variables is different from the identity matrix, which would be indicative of the presence of significant correlations. It is particularly relevant when considering the application of techniques such as PCA. If Bartlett's test yields a significantly low p-value (generally less than 0.05), the null hypothesis that the matrix is an identity matrix is rejected, suggesting that there is sufficient correlation between variables to justify the use of PCA. This test provides crucial statistical validation before embarking on dimensionality reduction using PCA. In the example used, the value of Barlett is 0.00000000000000006868423.

We use the formalization previously established in the data set description for the component extraction process, assuming the steps described in this section.

The principal component extraction process is defined as

$$CP \triangleq \mathrm{PCA}(M), \tag{8}$$

where CP is the set of principal components resulting from applying PCA to the data matrix M.

For each principal component $c \in CP$, the weights of the original variables in that component are analyzed to understand which variables have a significant contribution. Formally,

$$w_{c,j} = \text{Variable weight } j \text{ in the component } c \tag{9}$$

Table 2 shows the results of the PCA algorithm execution. It shows the values of the weights of each component with respect to each of the variables.

Table 2. Components

	PC1	PC2	PC3	PC4
Murder	−0.5358995	0.4181809	−0.3412327	−0.64922780
Assault	−0.5831836	0.1879856	−0.2681484	0.74340748
UrbanPop	-0.2781909	−0.8728062	−0.3780158	0.13387773
Rape	−0.5434321	−0.1673186	0.8177779	0.08902432

4.3 Conventional Analysis

Conventionally, the analysis resulting from the application of PCA proceeds by:

- Identifying the variables with the highest weights in each component which helps to determine the characteristics that contribute most to that dimension. Thus, each component C is composed of a subset of variables V that contribute most to the component;
- A manual procedure is made where domain knowledge and variable definitions are used to interpret what aspect of the problem or phenomenon each principal component represents. In addition, plotting the principal components may be included to provide a visual representation of how the original variables contribute to each component. Also, the variance explained by each component can be considered to assess its relative importance in explaining the total variability in the data;

- If possible, validate the interpretations obtained with domain experts to ensure consistency and relevance;
- Consider the magnitude of the loading coefficients, as these indicate the importance of each original variable in the construction of each principal component. Variables with high loading coefficients are those that contribute most to the variability of the component;
- Examine the direction of the loading coefficients, these can be positive or negative. Positive coefficients indicate that the original variables are positively correlated with the component, while negative coefficients indicate that they are negatively correlated;
- Finally, use biplot graphs to visualize the relationship between the principal components and the original variables. These plots can be useful to identify groups of variables that are correlated with each other.

The above method is often performed by researchers with the objective of assigning meaning to the components identified by PCA, however, matching them to substantial meaning can be considered as a totally subjective assignment.

Analyzing in detail the vector of weights that form each component can be helpful on interpreting what type of information each component collects. For example, the first and second components are the result of the following linear combination of the original variables:

$PC1 = -0.5358995 \cdot \text{Murder} - 0.5831836 \cdot \text{Assault} - 0.2781909 \cdot \text{UrbanPop} - 0.5434321 \cdot \text{Rape}$

$PC2 = 0.4181809 \cdot \text{Murder} + 0.1879856 \cdot \text{Assault} - 0.8728062 \cdot \text{UrbanPop} - 0.1673186 \cdot \text{Rape}$

In the first component, weights assigned to Assault, Murder and Rape variables are approximately equal to each other and considerably higher than that assigned to UrbanPoP. This indicates that the first component captures mainly information related to **violent crime**. In contrast, the second component is characterized by a significantly higher weight for the UrbanPoP variable, suggesting that it primarily reflects the **level of urbanization** of the state. While in this example the interpretation of the components is relatively clear, this is not always the case in all instances.

4.4 Assigning Meaning to Components Using Language Models

The core of our proposal lies on the integration of Language Models (LLM) in the analysis. This is carried out at this point to add a semantic layer to the interpretation process of the principal components generated by PCA. This involves a semantic mapping to the Principal Components for which, Language Models are applied to understand the relationship between the components and the keywords present in the original variables.

The combination of PCA and Language Models not only allows dimensionality reduction, but also enriches the interpretation with semantic meaning, providing a more complete and understandable view of the data set.

The variables and sets used in the process of assigning meaning to the principal components are represented as follows:

1. D - Description of the problem.
2. CP - Set of principal components obtained after PCA.
3. c_i - A specific principal component, where each $c_i \in (CP)$.
4. V_{c_i} - Set of variables selected in the component c_i.
5. NV_{c_i} - Set of names of the variables selected in c_i.
6. DV_{c_i} - Set of definitions of the variables selected in c_i.
7. S_{c_i} - Meaning assigned to the component c_i by the LLM process.

Given problem description D , and CP as the set of principal components obtained after applying PCA, the process of assigning meaning to the principal components is formalized as follows:

1. For each major component $c_i \in CP$:
   (a) Obtain the set of selected variables V_{c_i} in c_i from the defined threshold.
   (b) Get the set of names of the selected variables NV_{c_i} in c_i.
   (c) Get the set of definitions of the selected variables DV_{c_i} in c_i.
   (d) Send as input to an LLM process the description of the problem D, V_{c_i}, NV_{c_i}, and DV_{c_i}.
   (e) Get the meaning assigned S_{c_i} to the component c_i by the LLM process.
2. The final result is the set of meanings assigned to all principal components S_{c_i}.

A prompt is then constructed to send to the language model (LLM) to obtain a possible meaning for the principal component c_1. Based on the description of the problem and the principal component c_1 together with the description of the meaning of each variable, it is asked to provide a possible meaning for c_1.

For the creation of the prompt, different alternatives can be proposed according to the description of the problem, the definition of the variables and possible enrichments of the context in general. In addition, the contribution of each of the variables to the components should be considered, that is, the construction of the prompt should reflect the importance of each variable to the component.

The creation of prompts will be developed strategically, employing various engineering strategies to optimize the interaction with the model. This approach will allow controlled experiments to be conducted, with the clear goal of refining the prompt formulation. Versatile experimentation will help us discern the most effective tactics, gradually refining the prompts to obtain more accurate and desired responses from the model. Constant iteration and adaptation based on the results obtained will be essential in this process, helping to maximize the effectiveness of the selected prompt.

In the example presented in this paper, the prompt generated from D, NV and DV is integrated with the components resulting from the PCA analysis. Each component c is associated with the original variables with the highest loading, called Vc. These variables, are in turn related to NV and DV.

The prompt generated is as follows:
In the context of the interpretation of the components generated by PCA, a method is proposed where PCA is related to LLM. The problem is formulated as follows: D **describes the dataset,** NV **are the names of the variables,** DV **are the descriptions of each variable,** C **are the component results of PCA,** Vc **are the original variables with the highest representativeness of the component, there is a relation between** Vc **and the original ones. In the example used** D**, we use a data set called USArrests, this data set contains statistics, in arrests per 100,000 residents for assault, murder, and rape in each of the 50 US states in 1973. Also given is the percent of the population living in urban areas.**

"NV = {Murder, Assault, UrbanPop, Rape},
"DV= {"Murder arrest (per 100000)", "Assault arrests (per 100000)", "Percent urban population", "Rape arrests (per 100000)"},
the two components possess the following loadings: $PC1 = -0.5358995 \cdot \text{Murder} - 0.5831836 \cdot \text{Assault} - 0.2781909 \cdot \text{UrbanPop} - 0.5434321 \cdot \text{Rape}$,
$PC2 = +0.4181809 \cdot \text{Murder} + 0.1879856 \cdot \text{Assault} - 0.8728062 \cdot \text{UrbanPop} - 0.1673186 \cdot \text{Rape}$.
Based on this description, the prompt generates a meaning for both components.

The result of the PROMPT run in CHATGPT indicates the following: To interpret the principal components (PC1 and PC2) generated by Principal Component Analysis (PCA) in the context of the USArrests dataset, we analyze the weights associated with each component and see how the original variables contribute to each one of them.

Analysis of PC1:

- Negative loadings (weights): All variables have negative loadings, indicating that this principal component decreases with the increase of any of the variables (Murder, Assault, UrbanPop, Rape).
- Most representative variables: The variables "Assault" (–0.5831836), "Rape" (–0.5434321) and "Murder" (–0.5358995) have the highest loadings in absolute value, suggesting that this component is most influenced by these three variables.

PC1 can be interpreted as a general measure of the **violent crime rate** in U.S. states in 1973. As the value of PC1 decreases, the arrest rate for murder, assault and rape tends to increase. The "UrbanPop" variable also contributes, although to a lesser extent, indicating that there is a slight relationship between urbanization and violent crime.

Analysis of PC2 :

- Negative loadings ((weights)): Again, all variables have negative loadings, but "UrbanPop" has a much higher loading in absolute value (-0.8728062) compared to the other variables.
- Most representative variable: The variable "UrbanPop" is the most representative of this component, suggesting that PC2 is more influenced by the percentage of urban population.

PC2 can be interpreted as a **measure of urbanization** in the U.S. states in 1973. As the value of PC2 decreases, the percentage of urban population tends to increase. Although the variables "Murder," "Assault," and "Rape" also contribute, their influence is minor, suggesting that PC2 primarily captures variability related to urbanization rather than criminality.

As can be seen, the results from traditional analysis, where each component and its loadings are analyzed manually, coincide semantically with the results obtained through an automatic process using LLM. This corroborates our proposal to automate the process of assigning meaning to each component resulting from the PCA analysis.

4.5 Evaluation

At the heart of this paper lies our proposal of a rigorous evaluation process designed to support and validate our innovative approach. Starting from the meticulous selection of PCA studies to blind peer review, each phase of this process stands as an essential pillar to highlight the uniqueness and relevance of our language modeling approach. This procedure is not limited to a mere comparison of results, but stands as a concrete demonstration of the distinctive contribution our model makes to principal component interpretation in the data analysis landscape. This introduction aims to outline the structure and essence of our evaluation journey, highlighting not only the action and innovation, but also the direct relevance of each step in the context of our paper. The evaluation process to be followed is detailed below.

PCA Study Selection and Human Evaluation: This is a crucial step, where we carefully select relevant PCA studies that serve as a basis for comparing the interpretations generated by our LLM-based approach. In addition, human interpretations associated with these components are acquired, thus establishing a critical standard for the evaluation of our innovative method. In this case, the explanation of the process has been guided by an example.

Comparison to LLM Results: The essence of our paper lies on a comprehensive comparison between the interpretations provided by the language model and human interpretations derived from previous PCA studies. This analysis not only highlights similarities and differences, but also highlights the added value that the LLM can bring to the component interpretation process. As illustrated in the example presented, the results of the manual process of component interpretation and the automatic process for assigning meaning exhibits semantic similarity.

Expert Evaluator Set: Within the dynamics of a paper, a selected group of domain experts will be convened, who play a fundamental role in validating the innovation presented. Their impartiality and expertise are essential to provide an objective assessment of the interpretations generated by our approach and the traditional ones.

5 Conclusions and Future Work

In this paper, a rigorous compilation of expert assessments and observations has been made. Moreover, our detailed analysis reveals not only areas of agreement and disagreement, but also underlines the innovation and potential impact of the LLM-based approach.

The integration of linguistic models into the principal component interpretation process represents a significant advance in overcoming the challenge of assigning semantic meanings to the latent variables uncovered by PCA. The ability to translate complex mathematical relationships into contextually relevant semantic interpretations not only facilitates understanding, but also enhances informed decision making. This approach provides researchers and analysts with a manageable, yet powerful tool to explore and understand the latent dimensions in their datasets in a more accessible way.

From this starting point, several research paths will be explored in the upcoming future to further improve the presented approach:

First, we aim to incorporate cross-validation and bench-marking techniques along with other interpretation methodologies to further strengthen confidence of the results. In addition, ongoing expert feedback will be collected and the model will be adapted to different settings to improve the robustness of the approach and it generalization.

Second, future research will be conducted on data sets where neither the problem nor the definition of the variables are clear. The data for each variable will be analyzed to reach conclusions regarding possible meanings.

Third, we seek to generate specific metrics designed to quantify the quality of interpretations. These metrics, are specially adapted to the context of the study, and will serve as objective tools to evaluate and compare the effectiveness of LLM compared against traditional methods.

Finally, a blind evaluation will be carried out by experts who, without prior knowledge of the source of the interpretations, will make critical judgments on their consistency and relevance. This blind evaluation will reinforce the validity and objectivity of the approach.

The results of this study support the central thesis of the article: that LLM integration significantly improves component interpretation compared to traditional methods. This proposition highlights the challenges and opportunities encountered when exploiting LLMs in making sense of PCA. Acknowledging that further experimentation is required to validate our claims in a general manner, our findings suggest a favorable path of research based on the proposal presented in this article. Note that our methodology can be tested in multiple scenarios and data sets for which PCA interpretation results have been already generated using conventional methods supported by human experts.

This research contributes to the field of data science and highlights the need for further research to improve the interpretation of components with linguistic models. The recommendations presented point to areas of improvement and future avenues of research with the aim to build on and extend this innovative approach. It is expected that this work will serve as a foundation for future research exploring the potential of LLMs on improving complex data understanding and analysis.

Acknowledgements. This paper is the result of a research carried out within the framework of the project "ANÁLISIS DEL IMPACTO DE LAS PRÁCTICAS SOCIOTÉCNICAS Y DEL ACCESO A LAS TIC EN LOS PROCESOS Y PRÁCTICAS EDUCATIVAS EN LA UNIVERSIDAD DE CUENCA EN EL CONTEXTO DE LA PANDEMIA POR COVID-19", financed by the VIUC.

References

1. Choi, H., Moran, J., Matsumoto, N., Hernandez, M., Moore, J.: Aliro: an automated machine learning tool leveraging large language models. Bioinformatics **39**(10) (2013). https://doi.org/10.1093/bioinformatics/btad606
2. Doshi-Velez, F., Kim, B.: Towards a rigorous science of interpretable machine learning (2017)
3. Gniazdowski, Z.: New interpretation of principal components analysis. Zeszyty Naukowe Warszawskiej Wyższej Szkoły Informatyki **11**, 43–65 (2017). https://doi.org/10.26348/znwwsi.16.43
4. Guidotti, R., Monreale, A., Ruggieri, S., Turini, F., Giannotti, F., Pedreschi, D.: A survey of methods for explaining black box models. ACM Comput. Surv. **8** (2018). https://doi.org/10.1145/3236009
5. Jeong, D., Jeong, C., Ziemkiewicz, W., Ribarsky, R.A.C.: Understanding principal component analysis using a visual analytics tool, vol. 1 (2010)
6. Jolliffe, I.: Rotation and interpretation of principal components. Principal Component Analysis, pp. 269–298 (2002)
7. Jolliffe, I., Cadima, J.: Principal component analysis: a review and recent developments. Philos. Trans. R. Soc. A: Math. Phys. Eng. Sci. **374**(20150202) (2016). https://doi.org/10.1098/rsta.2015.0202
8. Krafty, R., Zhang, J., Siegle, G., D'Andrea, W.: Interpretable principal component analysis for multilevel multivariate functional data. 2020 Fall Central Sectional Meeting (2020)

9. Molnar, C., Casalicchio, G., Bischl, B.: Interpretable machine learning – a brief history, state-of-the-art and challenges. In: ECML PKDD 2020 Workshops, pp. 417–431 (2017)
10. Ringnér, M.: What is principal component analysis? Nat. Biotechnol. **26**(3), 303–304 (2008). https://doi.org/10.1038/nbt0308-303
11. Zarzà, I., Curtò, J., Roig, G., Calafate, C.: Llm multimodal traffic accident forecasting. Sensors **23** (2023). https://www.mdpi.com/1424-8220/23/22/9225

ChatBanker: A Chatbot for Efficient Management of Bank Documents

Jorge Cordero(✉), Edgar Martínez, Jandri Villavicencio, and Luis Barba-Guaman

Universidad Técnica Particular de Loja, San Cayetano Alto, Loja, Ecuador
{jmcordero,edmartinez8,jgvillavicencio4,lrbarba}@utpl.edu.ec

Abstract. Efficient document management is important to optimize operational processes and ensure fast access to the information contained therein. Chatbots are increasingly being used in different sectors, as their implementation opens up promising opportunities to improve access to information. This research presents ChatBanker, a chatbot developed to efficiently manage documents in the banking sector. The main objective is to improve the accessibility and retrieval of document information by using natural language processing (NLP) technologies, the OpenAI API and optical character recognition. The methodology includes segmentation and embedding of PDF content using embeddings, enabling accurate responses to user queries. The results demonstrate ChatBanker's ability to process multiple documents simultaneously, providing accurate responses based on semantic similarity. ChatBanker achieves a 92% response accuracy and reduces information search time by 70%, demonstrating its effectiveness. The chatbot highlights its potential to significantly improve operational efficiency and user satisfaction in document management tasks. These results underscore ChatBanker's practical value as an artificial intelligence-driven solution for document-intensive environments.

Keywords: Chatbot · Banking Documents · Natural Language Processing · Optical Character Recognition · Artificial Intelligence

1 Introduction

Today, banks, companies, the education sector, the medical sector, and governments have adopted chatbots as strategies for business development and competitiveness. In banking, efficient document management is a critical task that directly impacts the operability and quality of customer service. With the progressive digitization of banking processes, the amount of documents in digital format, especially PDF, has increased exponentially. The manual search and management of these documents represent a significant challenge, resulting in slow response times, errors in the search for information and a decrease in worker productivity. In this context, the implementation of emerging technologies that optimize document management becomes essential to maintain competitiveness and efficiency in the banking sector.

The use of chatbots based on Natural Language Processing (NLP) and Optical Character Recognition (OCR) has shown promising results in various fields, improving user

F. R. Narváez et al. (Eds.): SmartTech-IC 2024, CCIS 2392, pp. 322–334, 2026.
https://doi.org/10.1007/978-3-031-98287-3_23

interaction and operational efficiency. However, its specific application in banking document management is still limited and requires exploration. ChatBanker emerges as an innovative solution to address this problem, offering a chatbot capable of handling PDF documents efficiently and accurately, improving the accessibility and retrieval of relevant information for banking process specialists.

Existing literature on chatbots highlights their benefits in terms of efficiency and user satisfaction. For example, several studies demonstrate how chatbots can automate routine tasks and provide fast and accurate responses to user queries [1, 2]. In addition, other research emphasizes the potential of NLP to understand and process natural language, enabling chatbots to interact more effectively with users [3]. However, these studies do not specifically address the application of these technologies in banking document management, leaving a gap that ChatBanker seeks to fill.

The objective of this study is to design and evaluate ChatBanker, a chatbot that uses NLP technologies, embeddings, consine similarity and the OpenAI API to improve the management of banking documents in PDF format. This chatbot not only has the ability to process multiple documents simultaneously but can also provide accurate answers based on semantic similarity, thus optimizing the time and resources of banking specialists. Unlike existing approaches, ChatBanker uniquely integrates advanced artificial intelligence techniques to address the specific challenges of banking automation, such as handling diverse document formats and improving query efficiency. This practical application underscores its potential to transform document-intensive processes within financial institutions.

The importance of this work lies in its potential to transform the way banks manage their documents, providing a tool that improves operational efficiency and user satisfaction. By implementing ChatBanker, it is expected to significantly reduce information search times, minimize errors and free up human resources for higher value-added tasks. Ultimately, this study contributes to the advancement of technology in banking and offers a practical solution to a persistent problem in document management.

This paper is structured as follows: after the introduction, Sect. 2 presents a review of related work; Sect. 3 details the methodology used; Sect. 4 describes the proposed work; Sect. 5 presents the results and discussion; and finally, the conclusions of the study and future directions for research are presented.

2 Related Work

The use and popularity of chatbots have steadily increased in recent years [4, 5]. Chatbots are implemented in several areas, mainly for customer service [6–8]. The implementation of chatbots in document management is recent and is being welcomed with the emergence of large language models. The following is a review of the most relevant works in this area, although they are few, their main contributions and limitations are highlighted.

In [9] they conducted a systematic review on the techniques and algorithms used in the implementation of chatbots, focusing on the state-of-the-art services that improve the performance of these systems. They identified that deep learning and reinforcement learning are widely used techniques to understand user requests and generate appropriate responses. On the other hand, in [10] they analyzed the advantages and challenges of chatbots in public administration and document management-based services. They highlight that these systems can automate tasks, provide customer services and improve governance, but they also face significant challenges such as difficulty in handling complex tasks and unstructured documents.

The development of AI-based chatbots has shown significant benefits, but also presents several challenges. In [11] they discuss the positive impact of a voice-based chatbot on customer satisfaction and competitive advantage in banks by being an innovative service, while highlighting issues such as security, regulatory compliance, integration, and infrastructure limitations. Likewise, in [12] they explore the factors influencing consumer acceptance of chatbots in the banking industry, highlighting the importance of perceived compatibility and usability in the adoption of this technology. These insights are important for understanding the potential and limitations of implementing ChatBanker in a similar context, with the goal of improving document accessibility and operational efficiency.

The use of large-scale language models (LLMs) such as GPT for financial applications has been explored with promising results. For example, in [13] they demonstrate the ability of ChatGPT to significantly assist in financial research by generating research insights when complemented with domain expertise. In addition, studies on multimodal models show how incorporating design information into documents can significantly increase performance in bank document classification [14]. Also, recent research has shown that LLMs can be adapted to specific domains by connecting to a corpus of trusted documents and using embeddings, improving the contextualization and accuracy of the generated answers [15]. These studies emphasize the transformative potential of LLMs in financial services, reinforcing the relevance of using advanced AI models in ChatBanker for efficient document management and information retrieval in the banking sector.

In the specific context of banking document management, chatbots can improve efficiency in document retrieval and categorization. However, their effectiveness depends largely on the accuracy of the training and the quality of the data used for their development [16]. Although they achieved significant improvements in response accuracy, they faced challenges related to integrating the chatbot into existing systems and adapting to changes in document structure.

Our work differs from these studies by focusing specifically on the development of a chatbot for bank document management, using a combination of information retrieval and generation techniques. In addition, it focuses on addressing the challenges of integration and adaptation, by using an agile methodology and collaborating with experts from the banking sector to ensure the relevance and effectiveness of the developed chatbot. This practical approach combines training with user-supplied documents and the generation of answers through semantic similarity, offering an innovative and efficient solution for document management in banking environments.

3 Methodology

The present study was conducted using an experimental design based on the Scrum methodology, which is known for its agile approach and ability to manage software projects efficiently [17]. The implementation of Scrum allowed for continuous iteration and rapid adaptation to changes, ensuring that the chatbot development was aligned with user needs.

3.1 Requirements Analysis

A thorough analysis of the requirements and expectations of the banking process specialists was conducted to identify the key areas where a chatbot could improve document management in the banking sector. This analysis included literature review, interviews with industry experts and surveys to identify opportunities for improvement and to understand the main challenges and requirements in document management. The information gathered allowed defining the essential functionalities of the chatbot and identifying priority areas for improvement.

3.2 Functional and Non-functional Requirements

Based on the needs analysis, the functional and non-functional requirements of the chatbot were defined. Functional requirements specify the capabilities that the system must have to meet user needs, such as the ability to process and retrieve information from bank documents. Non-functional requirements, on the other hand, include aspects such as security, scalability and system performance.

3.3 Epics, User Stories, Case Studies and Sprints

Within the methodology selected for the chatbot development such as Scrum, the correct definition of epics, user stories and sprints are fundamental. The chatbot development was structured around epics, which are large bodies of work that can be divided into smaller user stories. Each user story describes specific functionality from the end user's perspective. Detailed use cases were developed to describe the interactions between users and the chatbot. These use cases helped to clearly define how the chatbot should behave in different scenarios, from searching for specific documents to retrieving information based on complex queries. Development was carried out in sprints, short work cycles that allow continuous delivery of increments of functional software. Each sprint was carefully planned, defining specific objectives and deliverables to ensure the steady progress of the project.

3.4 Stakeholders and Users

Within the operational framework of the ChatBanker solution for banks, several actors play crucial roles in ensuring its functionality and usability. These include end users, administrators, and external systems such as the OpenAI API. Each of these players uniquely contributes to the system ecosystem, from managing documents to administering the chatbot and providing advanced natural language processing capabilities to generate contextualized and accurate responses.

Chatbot users are critical within the banking environment, especially in this case process specialists. These professionals were previously tasked with manually querying large physical repositories for specific information. With ChatBanker, they now have the ability to upload PDF documents, perform advanced queries and get accurate answers efficiently. This solution not only streamlines access to critical data, but also improves productivity by significantly reducing the time spent searching for information.

3.5 Technology Integration

The implementation of the chatbot involved the integration of several advanced technologies. NLP was used to understand and respond to user queries, the OpenAI API to continuously improve the accuracy of responses, and OCR to extract information from scanned documents. Segmentation and embedding of PDF content was performed using embeddings, allowing for accurate answers based on semantic similarity. To enhance reproducibility, we have included code snippets illustrating the embedding generation process and OCR integration. These examples highlight the use of the OpenAI API and the specific configurations employed in the system.

3.6 Statistical Analysis of Performance

The chatbot's performance is evaluated through various interactions carried out by a total of 125 users, who together make 500 queries based on 20 PDF documents from different areas, such as economics, programming, banking procedures and literature, the variety of topics is intended to ensure that the chatbot responds effectively to a wide variety of contexts. Each user asks four questions to evaluate the accuracy and reaction time of the system.

The chatbot has a 92% accuracy in responses, standing out for its effectiveness in most of the queries made. Response times vary between 4 and 6 s after applying some optimizations, which is a great improvement compared to the initial 11–12 s.

4 Proposed Work

The development of ChatBanker was carried out using the agile Scrum methodology. This methodology allows for continuous adaptation and evolution of the project, ensuring that end-user requirements are met and that a high quality functional chatbot is delivered.

4.1 Arquitecture of ChatBanker

The ChatBanker architectural model was designed to ensure efficient interaction between system components, facilitating document processing and the generation of precise responses.

Figure 1 presents the architecture defined for the ChatBanker implementation. The chatbot is built using the Django framework due to its robust structure, development security features and seamless integration capabilities with various technologies and algorithms. The database used is MySQLite3, chosen for its compatibility with the framework, speed and ease of use. This integration is facilitated through the Python programming language, which guarantees a robust and structured architecture.

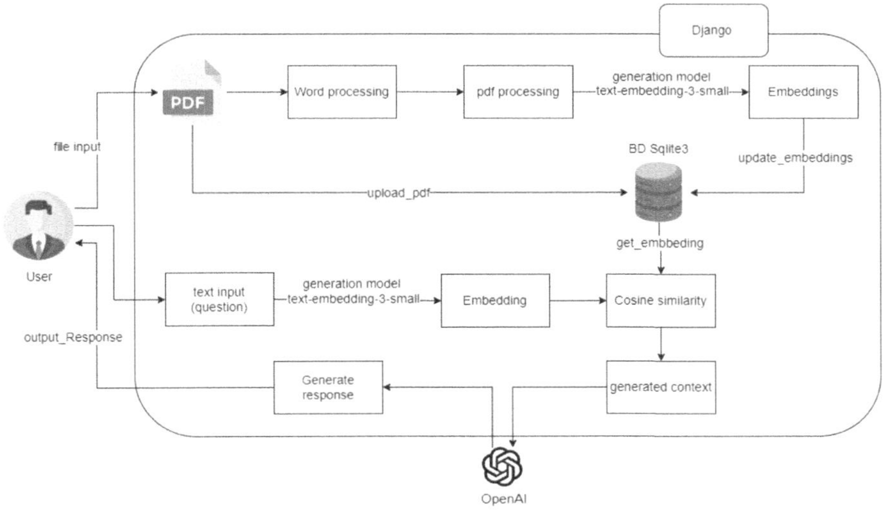

Fig. 1. Architecture of ChatBanker for document management.

In this architecture the user initiates the operation of Chatbanker, providing the knowledge base and executing the queries to the chatbot. In addition, both administrator and user roles are highlighted. The administrator's primary responsibility is to upload PDF documents into the system. Upon uploading, the system analyzes the document to determine if it is a textual document or a scanned image. For scanned documents, ChatBanker employs Optical Character Recognition (OCR) to detect and extract text. Once the text is extracted, word processing techniques are applied to generate key ideas from the document. These ideas are then segmented into conceptual fractions. Using the OpenAI API and the "text-embedding-3-small" model, the system generates vector structures (embeddings) that represent these ideas. These embeddings, along with the textual content and reference to the original PDF, are stored in the SQLite3 database.

The system uses the OpenAI API and the "text-embedding-3-large" embeddings model to process PDF documents and extract key ideas using natural language processing techniques. These ideas are segmented into related text fractions, which are converted into 3072-dimensional vector structures (embed-dings). These embeddings, together with the original textual content and its reference to the PDF, are stored in a SQLite3 database, serving as organized knowledge sources for further use.

When a user inputs a query, the system generates an embedding for the question in the same manner as the document embeddings. The cosine similarity algorithm is then utilized to find the closest semantic match between the user's query embedding and the stored document embeddings. The closest match is identified by comparing the vector matrices of the knowledge base embeddings and the user's query embedding. Upon identifying the closest semantic similarity, the system leverages the OpenAI API once more, utilizing the GPT-3.5-turbo model to generate a user-friendly response. This response is then presented to the user through an intuitive graphical interface, ensuring an accessible and efficient interaction.

4.2 ChatBanker Graphical Interface

Figure 2 shows the graphical interface of the chatbot which is designed to provide an intuitive user experience that facilitates interaction and document management.

Fig. 2. ChatBanker main view.

The main view shows a welcome greeting, which allows establishing a friendly dialogue from the start. It also provides a brief description of the purpose of the chatbot.

The user can interact via the main functionality buttons. The "*Cargar PDF*" option allows users to upload PDF documents, and the "*PDF cargados*" option allows access to a list of files that have been previously uploaded. The user can interact directly with the chatbot by entering their instruction or prompt in the text box that is labeled "Escribe tu consulta ..." and clicking "*Enviar*" or pressing Enter. In addition, this interface is being optimized for voice command queries by selecting the "*Hablar*" button.

4.3 Functional and Non-functional Requirements of ChatBanker

This section summarizes the most relevant functional and non-functional requirements for the development of ChatBanker, providing a clear and concise overview of the essential capabilities that the system must have to meet end-user expectations and ensure its robustness and efficiency.

Table 1 shows the functional requirements cover the basic capabilities of the system, such as PDF document loading and processing, text extraction and tokenization, embedding generation and storage, and retrieval and display of relevant information.

Table 1. Summary of main functional requirements.

Functional Requirements	Description
PDF Document Upload	Enable uploading of PDF documents through an intuitive interface
Information Extraction	Extract information contained in PDF documents
Embeddings Generation	Convert text into numeric vectors (embeddings)
Embeddings Comparison	Compare question embeddings with stored embeddings to find similarities
Information Retrieval	Provide relevant information based on the comparison of embeddings
Generating Responses	Generate consistent answers to user queries

Table 2 shows the non-functional requirements focus on ensuring the efficiency, scalability, security and accessibility of the system, including specific parameters such as processing time, latency, availability and compatibility with different browsers.

Table 2. Summary of main non-functional requirements.

Non-functional requirements	Description
Fast Processing	Process PDF documents in a maximum time of 20 s
Scalability	Handle an increase in the number of documents and queries
Accessibility	Comply with accessibility regulations
Security	Implement user authentication and activity logging

4.4 Deployment

The development of ChatBanker was carried out using the agile Scrum methodology, ensuring incremental and continuous delivery of functionality [18]. Several epics were defined, including PDF file management, text processing and analysis, embedding generation and storage, user interface, query and response system, and administration. Each epic was broken down into user stories. In total, nine user stories were defined, below are described some that have high priority, for example: "HU01: As a user, I want to upload PDF files to get the information I am looking for" and "HU05: As a developer, I want to convert the main ideas of the PDFs into embeddings to store and search them efficiently", and "HU07: As a user, I want to ask questions about the content of the uploaded PDFs and get accurate answers". Use cases were detailed, such as loading PDF documents, extracting main ideas, and generating answers to user queries. This approach allowed for structured development, focused on user needs.

Planning in Scrum is essential because it establishes the basis for the work to be done in each Sprint, aligning the team's activities with the needs and priorities of the stakeholders and users. Stakeholders, represented mainly by the Product Owner, include all project stakeholders, such as customers, product managers and other stakeholders. The users, who are the people who will interact directly with the final product, have their expectations and requirements captured in user stories. This planning process includes defining acceptance criteria for each user story, ensuring that users' needs and expectations are adequately met.

4.5 ChatBanker Stakeholders and Users

In the development of ChatBanker, several key actors are identified, each playing roles essential to the functionality and usability of the chatbot. Among the authors are the end user, the administrator and the OpenAI API. The end user is the banking process specialists who need to access and query information stored in physical documents. Its main functionalities include loading PDF documents into the system and performing complex queries on banking information. The administrator is in charge of managing ChatBanker within the bank and his functions include setting access permissions, managing document versions and supervising the general operation of the chatbot. Another player is the OpenAI API used to provide advanced natural language processing capabilities, generating accurate and relevant responses from queries.

ChatBanker is designed to be used by various users within the banking environment. Particularly by technical users who are the banking process specialists who previously queried information in physical repositories. Their expectations include reducing search time, quickly accessing accurate documents and performing complex queries efficiently.

This structuring ensures that each actor and user has defined roles and expectations, facilitating efficient and productive use of the chatbot.

5 Results and Discussion

The results of this study demonstrate that ChatBanker is an effective tool for bank document management. The improvements in accuracy, efficiency and user satisfaction highlight the potential of ChatBanker as an effective and practical solution for financial institutions. Error analysis revealed challenges in handling documents with complex formatting or low-quality scans, where OCR accuracy impacts performance. Addressing these challenges will require optimization of OCR capabilities and preprocessing techniques.

5.1 Interaction with ChatBanker

Figure 3 shows an example of a question asked to the chatbot and the response provided by the chatbot, including reference to the source document of the response. This example illustrates ChatBanker's ability to process queries and extract accurate and relevant information from multiple documents.

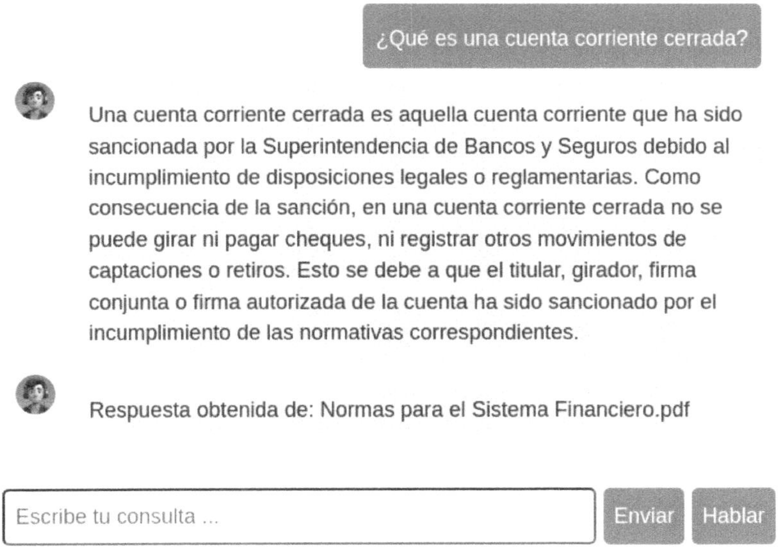

Fig. 3. Example of interaction with ChatBanker.

5.2 Response Accuracy

Using the GPT-3.5-turbo model and the embedding generation API, ChatBanker achieved 92% accuracy in understanding and answering specific queries based on PDF documents. This accuracy was validated through a set of tests that included frequently asked questions and complex queries.

5.3 Information Search Efficiency

ChatBanker significantly reduced the time required to locate and process specific information within PDF documents. Compared to manual search, the chatbot proved to be 70% faster on average, representing a marked improvement in operational efficiency. Despite these gains, the system's dependence on document quality and OCR accuracy remains a limitation, underscoring the need for continuous improvement in these areas.

5.4 User Satisfaction

The fundamental goal of usability testing is to help developers produce more usable products. Usability testing remains a central way of determining whether users accomplish their goals. Usability testing helps determine user satisfaction with the system, including complexity, ease of use, dialogue flow functioning, consistency, reliability, and integration [19]. A usability score of 90% was obtained by applying the SUS questionnaire to evaluate the implemented case study. ChatBanker is rated as "Good". The result reflects that the customer experience is influenced by their ability to use the technology, given that many of the people who interacted and evaluated the usability of the system were specialists in banking processes. Overall, the chatbot proved to be acceptable; therefore, it is useful, easy to use and can be implemented in the banking environment.

5.5 Statistical Analysis

The accuracy of the answers generated by ChatBanker was evaluated in terms of semantic similarity to user queries. Table 3 presents the results of evaluating the accuracy and response time. The average accuracy was 92%, with a standard deviation of 2.5%, indicating high consistency in the chatbot responses. In addition, the average response time was 2.5 s per query, demonstrating the efficiency of the chatbot. To further validate the system's performance, precision and recall metrics were calculated, offering a deeper understanding of its ability to retrieve relevant information accurately. These metrics highlight the robustness of ChatBanker in handling diverse query types.

Table 3. Evaluation of the chatbot's accuracy and response time.

Metrics	Mean value	Standard deviation
Response accuracy	92%	2,5%
Response time	2.5 s	0,2 s

Student's t-tests were performed to compare the efficiency of ChatBanker with traditional document management methods. The results showed a statistically significant improvement ($p < 0.05$) in the speed and accuracy of information access when using ChatBanker. In addition, linear regression analysis showed a strong positive correlation between the use of ChatBanker and reduced document search time. This analysis confirms the practical significance of the chatbot's implementation in enhancing document retrieval processes within banking environments.

5.6 Significance of the Findings

The findings of this research are significant and provide a meaningful contribution to the field of process automation in the banking industry through the use of advanced artificial intelligence technologies. ChatBanker is important for several aspects. For example, it is efficient in document management, overcoming the limitations of manual methods for obtaining information. The accuracy of the responses generated and the fast average response time highlight the chatbot's ability to improve operational efficiency. These results align with previous studies that have shown the potential of chatbots and natural language processing technologies to automate administrative tasks and reduce information access time [20]. The implementation of ChatBanker facilitates real-time information access and optimizes the bank's internal processes, which can lead to increased productivity and reduced operational costs.

This study is not without limitations. The evaluation of ChatBanker was conducted in a controlled environment, which may not fully reflect actual usage conditions in different banking scenarios. In addition, the set of documents and query types used in the testing was limited, which may restrict the generalizability of the results. Future work should address these limitations by evaluating the chatbot in diverse operating environments and expanding the variety of documents and queries to validate and improve the current findings.

6 Conclusions and Future Work

The implementation of ChatBanker for the efficient management of banking documents has proven to be a significant innovation in the optimization of processes within the financial sector. The results obtained confirm that ChatBanker is effective in improving accuracy, speed and satisfaction in document management.

ChatBanker has demonstrated a 70% improvement in the efficiency of searching and processing information within PDF documents, compared to traditional manual methods. This improvement reduces the time required to complete queries, contributing to more effective and reliable document management.

The chatbot has proven its ability to effectively handle a wide variety of document types and queries. This helps to ensure that the information provided to users is accurate, thus increasing confidence in the chatbot.

The chatbot's adaptability to different types of documents and queries underscores its versatility and potential to be integrated into various banking and financial environments. In addition, the integration of additional features such as sentiment analysis and personalization can offer further improvements to the user experience and accuracy of responses.

SUS questionnaire usability tests allow us to measure system satisfaction. According to the results, the ChatBanker implementation is widely accepted, which encourages financial institutions to integrate it for accurate and fast document queries. The high user satisfaction rate of 90% highlights ChatBanker's effectiveness in providing an intuitive and efficient user experience. The user-friendly interface and the ability to handle natural language queries are key aspects that contribute to a positive experience.

The results of this study provide a solid foundation for further research in the field of chatbots in document management. Future research could consider a wider diversity of documents and usage scenarios to validate and improve on the current findings.

References

1. Adamopoulou, E., Moussiades, L.: Chatbots: history, technology, and applications. Mach. Learn. Appl. **2**, 100006 (2020). https://doi.org/10.1016/j.mlwa.2020.100006
2. Okonkwo, C.W., Ade-Ibijola, A.: Chatbots applications in education: a systematic review. Comput. Educ.: Artif. Intell. **2**, 100033 (2021). https://doi.org/10.1016/j.caeai.2021.100033
3. Abdulla, H., Eltahir, A.M., Alwahaishi, S., Saghair, K., Platos, J., Snasel, V.: Chatbots development using natural language processing: a review. In: 2022 26th International Conference on Circuits, Systems, Communications and Computers (CSCC), pp. 122–128 (2022). https://doi.org/10.1109/CSCC55931.2022.00030

4. Sanjaya, W., Calvin, M.R., Meiliana, F.M.: Systematic literature review on implementation of chatbots for commerce use. Procedia Comput. Sci. **227**, 432–438 (2023). https://doi.org/10.1016/j.procs.2023.10.543
5. Casheekar, A., Lahiri, A., Rath, K., Prabhakar, K.S., Srinivasan, K.: A contemporary review on chatbots, AI-powered virtual conversational agents, ChatGPT: applications, open challenges and future research directions. Comput. Sci. Rev. **52**, 100632 (2024). https://doi.org/10.1016/j.cosrev.2024.100632
6. Misischia, C.V., Poecze, F., Strauss, C.: Chatbots in customer service: their relevance and impact on service quality. Procedia Comput. Sci. **201**, 421–428 (2022). https://doi.org/10.1016/j.procs.2022.03.055
7. Cordero, J., Barba-Guaman, L., Guamán, F.: Use of chatbots for customer service in MSMEs. Appl. Comput. Inform. ahead-of-print (2022).https://doi.org/10.1108/ACI-06-2022-0148
8. Cordero, J., Toledo, A., Guamán, F., Barba-Guamán, L.: Use of chatbots for user service in higher education institutions. In: 2020 15th Iberian Conference on Information Systems and Technologies (CISTI), pp. 1–6 (2020). https://doi.org/10.23919/CISTI49556.2020.9141108
9. Mohamad Suhaili, S., Salim, N., Jambli, M.N.: Service chatbots: a systematic review. Expert Syst. Appl. **184**, 115461 (2021). https://doi.org/10.1016/j.eswa.2021.115461
10. Nirala, K.K., Singh, N.K., Purani, V.S.: A survey on providing customer and public administration based services using AI: chatbot. Multimed. Tools Appl. **81**, 22215–22246 (2022). https://doi.org/10.1007/s11042-021-11458-y
11. Anaya, L., Braizat, A., Al-Ani, R.: Implementing AI-based chatbot: benefits and challenges. Procedia Comput. Sci. **239**, 1173–1179 (2024). https://doi.org/10.1016/j.procs.2024.06.284
12. Alt, M.-A., Vizeli, I., Săplăcan, Z.: Banking with a chatbot – a study on technology acceptance. Studia Universitatis Babes-Bolyai Oeconomica **66**, 13–35 (2021). https://doi.org/10.2478/subboec-2021-0002
13. Dowling, M., Lucey, B.: ChatGPT for (finance) research: the Bananarama Conjecture. Financ. Res. Lett. **53**, 103662 (2023). https://doi.org/10.1016/j.frl.2023.103662
14. Gerling, C., Lessmann, S.: Multimodal Document Analytics for Banking Process Automation (2023). https://arxiv.org/abs/2307.11845
15. Yager, K.G.: Domain-specific chatbots for science using embeddings. Digit. Discov. **2**, 1850–1861 (2023). https://doi.org/10.1039/d3dd00112a
16. Chong, T., Yu, T., Keeling, D.I., de Ruyter, K.: AI-chatbots on the services frontline addressing the challenges and opportunities of agency. J. Retail. Consum. Serv. **63**, 102735 (2021). https://doi.org/10.1016/j.jretconser.2021.102735
17. Srivastava, A., Bhardwaj, S., Saraswat, S.: SCRUM model for agile methodology. In: 2017 International Conference on Computing, Communication and Automation (ICCCA), pp. 864–869 (2017)
18. Anwer, F., Aftab, S., Shah, S.S.M., Waheed, U.: Comparative analysis of two popular agile process models: extreme programming and scrum. Int. J. Comput. Sci. Telecommun. **8**, 1–7 (2017)
19. Lewis, J.R., Sauro, J.: Usability and user experience: design and evaluation. In: Handbook of Human Factors and Ergonomics, pp. 972–1015 (2021)
20. Majumder, S., Mondal, A.: Are chatbots really useful for human resource management? Int. J. Speech Technol. **24**, 969–977 (2021). https://doi.org/10.1007/s10772-021-09834-y

Application of Machine Learning Algorithms to Detect Fake News in the Peruvian Context

Diego Yoshiro Dongo Esquivel(✉), E. Gladys Cutipa Arapa, and Rony Villafuerte Serna

Professional School of Computer and Systems Engineering, Universidad Nacional de San Antonio Abad del Cusco, Av. de La Cultura 773, Cusco, Cusco, Peru
{160543,efraina.cutipa,rony.villafuerte}@unsaac.edu.pe
https://www.unsaac.edu.pe

Abstract. The expansion of the internet and social media has transformed the way society accesses information, also facilitating the spread of fake news. In the Peruvian context, where linguistic and cultural patterns present unique characteristics, addressing this issue becomes a significant challenge. This work develops a model for fake news detection based on machine learning algorithms, specifically *Naive Bayes* and *Support Vector Machine*, using a locally generated dataset with posts obtained from the Twitter API. Through a methodological approach that includes data cleaning, feature selection, and parameter optimization, the *Naive Bayes* model achieved an accuracy of 95.40%, outperforming *Support Vector Machine* with an accuracy of 90.45%. The research demonstrates that the quality and representativeness of the dataset are critical to the performance of the models. Additionally, this contribution not only offers an innovative approach adapted to the local context but also opens possibilities for future applications in sentiment analysis and natural language processing in Peru.

Keywords: Fake news · Machine learning · *Naive Bayes* · *Support Vector Machine*

1 Introduction

The spread of fake news is one of the most pressing challenges of contemporary society, with significant impacts on political, economic, and social spheres. This problem has been exacerbated by the exponential growth of social media platforms, which enable the rapid dissemination of information without proper verification. In the Peruvian context, this issue is further intensified due to linguistic diversity, informal communication styles, and high social polarization, particularly during critical events such as electoral processes or public health emergencies.

Globally, various studies have addressed the detection of fake news using machine learning techniques, achieving high levels of accuracy by applying

F. R. Narváez et al. (Eds.): SmartTech-IC 2024, CCIS 2392, pp. 335–346, 2026.
https://doi.org/10.1007/978-3-031-98287-3_24

advanced models. However, much of this research has focused on Anglo-Saxon contexts or international datasets, which fail to capture the peculiarities of local language and information sources. In contrast, this study focuses on the construction and analysis of a dataset specifically tailored to the Peruvian context, overcoming challenges related to the lack of labeled datasets and language heterogeneity.

The goal of this research is to develop a machine learning-based predictive model for fake news detection, utilizing *Naive Bayes* (NB) and *Support Vector Machine* (SVM) algorithms. These methods were selected for their effectiveness and applicability in text classification tasks. The implementation of these models aims not only to improve the quality of information in the Peruvian digital ecosystem but also to contribute to the advancement of knowledge in data analysis within regional contexts.

Additionally, this research examines the limitations of classical models in comparison to more advanced approaches and discusses how dataset characteristics and optimization processes directly influence the obtained results. Finally, this study has the potential to serve as a reference for the development of similar tools in other regional contexts across Latin America, where linguistic and sociocultural conditions present unique challenges.

2 Related Work

Manually classifying fake news requires expertise and specialized skills to identify anomalies in the text. Research conducted by the University of Engineering and Technology in Peshawar, Pakistan, has shown that graph theory and machine learning techniques can be effective in identifying key sources involved in the spread of fake news. By using a linear *Support Vector Machine* on various datasets, accuracies ranged from 31% to 98%, depending on the dataset used. Additionally, advanced feature extraction techniques, such as those implemented with the *LIWC2015* software, resulted in a significant increase in accuracy, reaching up to 99% with *Random Forest* and 98% with SVM. [1]

The study conducted by the Research and Graduate Division of the Polytechnic University of Tulancingo and the Mechatronics Department of the Polytechnic University of Pachuca, Hidalgo, Mexico [2], investigates the automatic detection of fake news using traditional textual representations and deep learning techniques. The study employed a dataset comprising two collections of news from the *FakeDeS 2020* and *FakeDeS 2021* competitions in Mexico. Models, including SVM, LR, and RF, were trained with 70% of the data and evaluated on the remaining 30%. The analysis revealed that model performance depends significantly on textual representation features and algorithm configuration. Results showed an accuracy of 77.97% for the SVM classifier on the 2021 corpus, lower than that for the 2020 corpus, suggesting difficulties in adapting to thematic and linguistic variations. Despite thorough analysis, the evaluated models did not surpass the performance of the reference model.

On the other hand, Florida State University, USA, developed a *Deep Diffusive Network* model that leverages the network structure of articles, creators, and news topics to improve accuracy in fake news detection. The model, tested on the *PolitiFact* dataset, demonstrated outstanding performance by integrating information from multiple sources through a model called the *Gate Diffusive Unit* (GDU), which enables effective fusion of diverse inputs to identify false content [3].

Additionally, a study conducted by the School of Computer Science at Fudan University, Shanghai, China, introduced the LLM-GAN model, an innovative architecture that combines *Generative Adversarial Networks* and *Large Language Models* (LLMs) for explainable fake news detection [4]. Experiments conducted on real-world datasets such as *Weibo21* and *GossipCop* achieved strong metrics, with a macro F1 score of 80.40% on *Weibo21* and 82.30% on *GossipCop*. This model delivered clear and easily understandable explanations for its predictions.

Finally, in a study conducted by Zayed University, United Arab Emirates, the *WEKA* software was used with classifiers such as *Naive Bayes*, *BayesNet*, and *Logistic* to analyze data extracted from social networks and websites like Facebook and Reddit. The results showed high accuracy in detecting fake news sources, reaching up to 98.7% with *Naive Bayes* [5].

3 Methodological Approach

The methodology employed in this study is based on the creation and use of a specific dataset of digital posts from Peruvian news outlets to train a predictive model for detecting fake news. The process began with data collection from November 2021 to January 2023, using the Twitter API to gather both true and fake news. This data was cleaned and processed to eliminate inconsistencies and ensure the quality of the information.

The predictive model was trained using the NB and SVM algorithms, widely known for their high accuracy in text classification. The methodology follows the structure of *Knowledge Discovery in Databases* (KDD), which includes domain understanding, data collection and mining to discover patterns, and the interpretation and documentation of results [6].

In the case of SVM, the selection of parameters, such as the value of the C parameter and the kernel, was performed empirically. Various configurations were tested to identify the ones that optimized the model's accuracy.

Both the dataset and the developed model not only allow for accurate detection of fake news, but also have the potential to be used in future research on sentiment analysis and natural language processing in the Peruvian context.

4 Dataset Preparation

4.1 Data Extraction

The dataset was generated using the Twitter API to collect posts from selected accounts of Peruvian news outlets. The necessary credentials were generated to access the API, enabling the extraction of up to two million tweets per month.

This process is detailed in [7], which provides a comprehensive guide on using the Twitter API for data collection in natural language processing projects.

The creation of this dataset was essential, as, up until the time of this research, there was no specific Spanish-language dataset containing news from Peruvian media. This posed a significant barrier to the automated analysis of fake news in the local context, as datasets available in other languages or regions did not reflect the linguistic, cultural, and thematic peculiarities of Peru. Therefore, the need to create a local and representative dataset arose in order to effectively address the challenge of detecting fake news in the Peruvian context.

The process began with the selection of Twitter accounts from reliable news outlets in Peru, based on a study by the *Reuters Institute* that evaluated the credibility of different media sources [8]. Figure 1 shows the trust percentage of these news outlets, and Table 1 lists the news outlets selected for the project due to their high credibility.

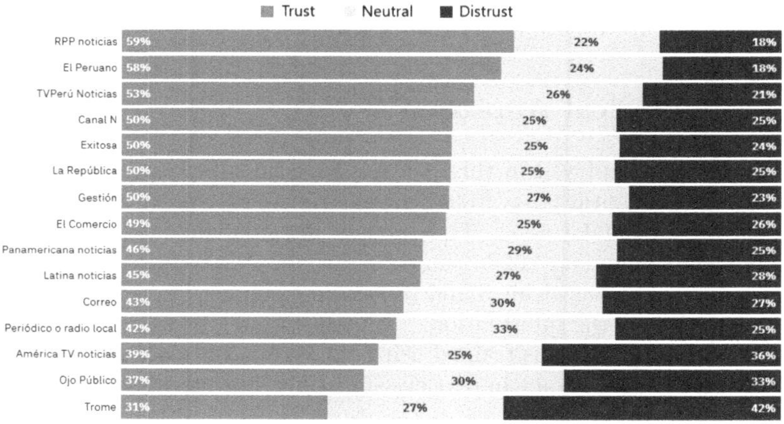

Fig. 1. Confidence percentage of selected media by the *Reuters Institute*. Source: [8]. Trust score of Peruvian news outlets

Simultaneously, Twitter accounts with low credibility were identified, characterized by posts that are often personal comments or unsupported information. Table 2 provides details on these accounts.

Data extraction was performed using a Python script, leveraging the TweePy library to connect to the Twitter API. The latest thousand tweets from each account were retrieved, filtering out those with fewer than 40 words to ensure the dataset's quality. Table 3 presents a sample of the retrieved tweets.

4.2 Data Preprocessing

After extraction, a noise-cleaning process was performed, during which non-useful elements such as emojis, hashtags, and URLs were removed using regular

Table 1. Peruvian news outlets labeled as reliable in the project

	News outlet	Twitter user	Credibility
1	RPP	@RPPNoticias	59%
2	Diario El Peruano	@DiarioElPeruano	58%
3	TV Perú Noticias	@noticias_tvperu	53%
4	Canal N	@canalN_	50%
5	Exitosa Noticias	@exitosape	50%
6	La República	@larepublica_pe	50%
7	Diario Gestión	@Gestionpe	50%
8	El Comercio	@elcomercio_peru	49%
9	Panamericana noticias	@PTV_Noticias	46%
10	Latina Noticias	@Latina_Noticias	45%

Table 2. Peruvian news outlets labeled as deceptive in the project

	News outlet	Twitter user	Seniority
1	MalditaTernua	@malditaternura	2020
2	PolloFarsantePe	@PolloFarsantePe	2021
3	JusticieroPE	@justicierope	2021
4	el_analista2020	@el_analista2020	2020
5	Lord	@blackdragon1802	2010
6	Sinmermelada	@Sinmermelada3	2021
7	Derecha Unida	@derecha_Unida_	2022
8	el comentarista	@elcomentaristam	2021
9	Rafael Rey Rey	@reyreysincorona	2011
10	El Joker	@eljokerpe	2021

expressions. This step was crucial to ensure that the data was in optimal condition for training the predictive model. Additionally, stop words, or words that do not prcvide significant value to the predictive analysis, were removed, following best practices recommended in natural language processing [9].

5 Development of Predictive Models

5.1 Naive Bayes

The *Naive Bayes* (NB) model is a simple yet effective probabilistic classifier that calculates the probabilities of each news item based on the words present [10]. The model was implemented in Python using Google Colab, a platform well-suited for machine learning projects.

Word Histogram. To optimize the performance of the NB classifier, word histograms were created for each class of news (true and fake). These histograms,

Table 3. Sample of tweets retrieved using the Twitter API

Label	Text	Creation Date
true	Una banda de delincuentes asaltó a una mujer que acababa de recoger a su hijo del colegio en San Juan de Lurigancho. Al momento de la captura se les encontró un arma de fuego.	2022-08-18 02:26:37
fake	Este sujeto funge de periodista y se encarga de hacer el registro de todos los compañeros para que después sean atacados. Ojo con él. Hoy en el ataque de la Resistencia a la feria de niños llegó con el bloque fascista.	2022-05-15 04:30:50

generated after a noise-cleaning process that removed irrelevant words such as news outlet names and monosyllables, allow for the calculation of the probability of each word appearing in the news. Figures 2a and 2b display the top 10 most frequently used terms in both news sets. As observed, the most frequent tokens are not necessarily the most distinctive.

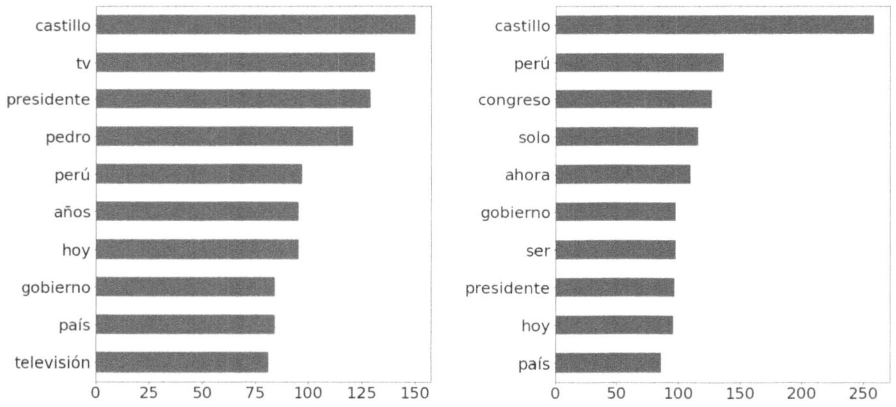

(a) Regarding the cluster of real news (b) Regarding the cluster of fake news

Fig. 2. Top 10 most used words for each class

On the other hand, highly characteristic words for each class were identified using a differentiation ratio, which improved prediction accuracy. This analysis revealed that certain terms, although less frequent, are much more indicative of a particular class, as shown in Fig. 3.

Table 4 provides a practical example of how the NB algorithm works, showing how the individual probabilities of each word in a new text are calculated and how the total probability is determined to classify the news as true or fake.

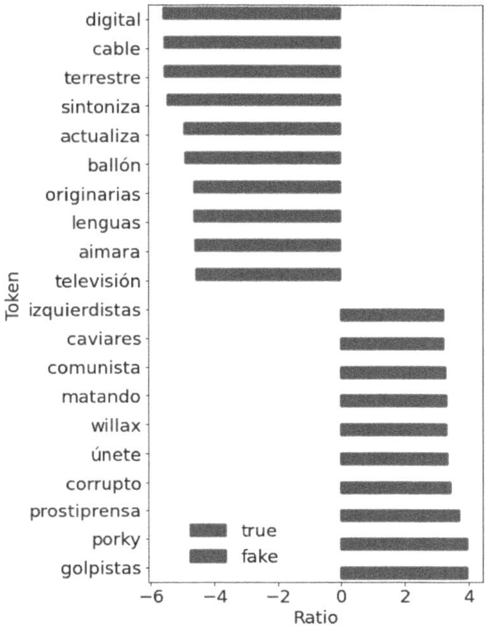

Fig. 3. Top 10 most differentiating words for each class

Table 4. Example of how the NB algorithm works

Text					Prop. V	Prob. V
Las	personas	sufrieron	un	accidente	0.4455	3.9723×10^{-12}
	14.19×10^{-4}	0.424×10^{-4}		1.482×10^{-4}		
Text					Prop. F	Prob. F
Las	personas	sufrieron	un	accidente	0.5545	0.8127×10^{-12}
	7.674×10^{-4}	0.357×10^{-4}		0.535×10^{-4}		

5.2 Support Vector Machine

Data Exploration. *Support Vector Machine* (SVM) is a good alternative for predicting the truthfulness of texts, expanding the approach used in NB. To implement the model, a detailed analysis of the content of the data collections was carried out, studying aspects such as text length, the proportion of stop words, the most frequent terms, and the frequency of grammatical elements. Certain differences were discovered, such as the more varied use of words in true news compared to the repetitive use of words in fake news. Additionally, a slight positive correlation was observed between the words used in both classes, identifying unique words in each. This analysis formed the basis for building the SVM model.

Feature Extraction. It is a critical stage in the construction of the dataset for SVM and plays a key role in the accuracy of the final prediction. Without precise feature extraction, it is challenging to achieve accurate and reliable results in the model. As mentioned by [11], the main difficulty in detecting fake news lies in identifying the features that distinguish them from true news.

Features related to sentiment, emotional, and hate analysis were included, using the *PySentimiento* library. True news tends to be neutral or show less aggression compared to fake news, which displays higher levels of hate, aggression, and anger, as shown in Figs. 4 and 5. The use of non-dictionary words was also analyzed, assuming that fake news is less formal and contains more grammatical errors. Despite the richness of the features, it was observed that the generated clusters were not fully differentiating, which presents a challenge for the model.

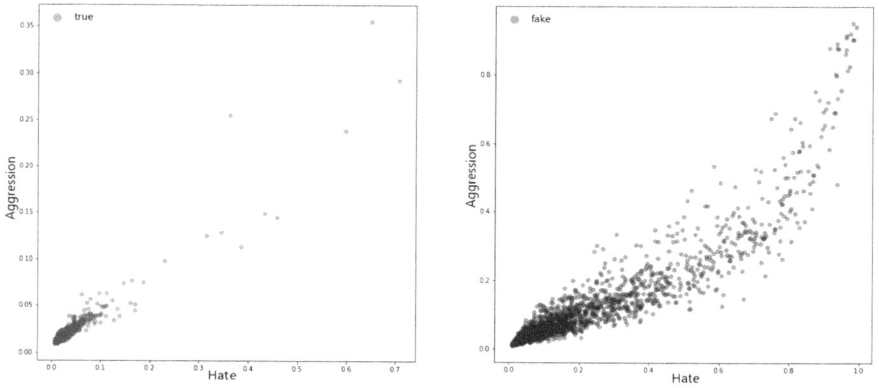

(a) Cluster of true news

(b) Cluster of fake news

Fig. 4. Clusters of news regarding the Hate-Aggression pair

6 Experimental Evaluation

6.1 Naive Bayes

A dataset of 4326 news articles was used, divided into 80% for training and 20% for validation. This approach allowed for optimizing the model's accuracy, achieving a 95.4% accuracy rate.

To evaluate the model's performance, a confusion matrix was constructed using the validation set, comparing the model's predictions with the actual labels. The confusion matrix, presented in Table 5, shows that the model correctly predicted 94.99% of true news and 95.73% of fake news, as detailed below:

- True news correctly classified as true: 322 (94.99%).

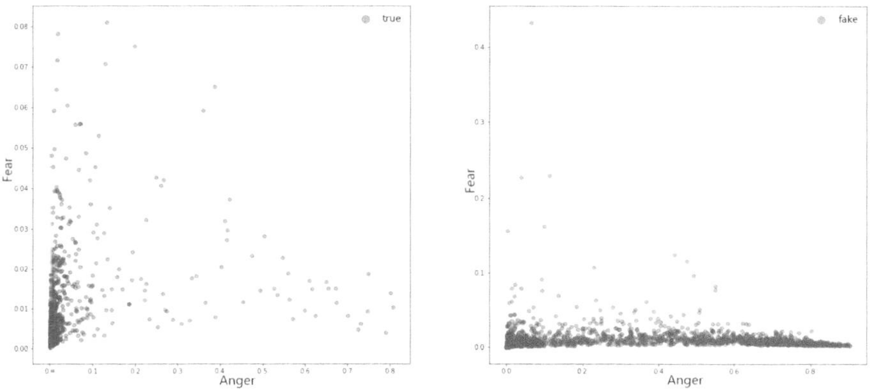

(a) Cluster of true news

(b) Cluster of fake news

Fig. 5. Clusters of news regarding the Anger-Fear pair

Table 5. Confusion matrix for the *Naive Bayes* algorithm

		Prediction	
		True	Fake
Original label	True	322	17
	Fake	18	404

- Fake news correctly classified as fake: 404 (95.73%).
- True news incorrectly classified as fake: 17 (5.01%).
- Fake news incorrectly classified as true: 18 (4.27%).

These results indicate that, although the model demonstrates a high level of accuracy, factors such as syntax and word repetition can influence the precision of its predictions.

6.2 Support Vector Machine

Unlike *Naive Bayes*, the SVM algorithm allows for more detailed adjustments through the configuration of multiple parameters, which can significantly influence the model's performance. To optimize its performance, empirical tests were conducted using various parameter configurations, including the selection of different kernels and the variation of the C parameter, which controls the penalty for classification errors. The selection of these parameters was not based on an explicit theoretical model but rather on experimentation with different values to find the configuration that provided the best results in terms of accuracy.

It was observed that the use of a polynomial kernel with C in the range of 10 to 100 produced the best results, achieving an accuracy of up to 90.7%, as shown in Table 6. However, this empirical selection also revealed that the

SVM model requires a greater number of differentiating features to improve its predictive capacity. The variability in the results suggests that, to further enhance the model's accuracy, the selection and extraction of features should be further optimized, which will be the focus of future research.

Table 6. Comparison of SVM Parameter Configurations

C	Lineal	Gaussiano	Polinomial
1	0.8819	0.8643	0.8944
10	0.8869	0.8894	0.9070
100	0.8894	0.8869	0.8995

The resulting confusion matrix, shown in Table 7, indicates a higher proportion of errors compared to the *Naive Bayes* algorithm:

Table 7. Confusion matrix of SVM using optimal configuration

		Prediction	
		True	Fake
Original label	True	369	50
	Fake	25	352

- True news correctly classified as true: 369 (88.07%).
- Fake news correctly classified as fake: 352 (93.37%).
- True news incorrectly classified as fake: 50 (11.93%).
- Fake news incorrectly classified as true: 25 (6.63%).

The tests conducted using SVM demonstrated that, while achieving considerable accuracy, its predictive capability is inferior to that of NB. This is partly attributed to the complexity of the problem and the need for more precise distinguishing features.

7 Discussion of Results

The study successfully generated an adequate dataset, achieving an accuracy of 95.40% with the *Naive Bayes* classifier and 90.45% with the *Support Vector Machine* (SVM). However, it was observed that the accuracy of the SVM model heavily depends on the quality of the extracted features, underscoring the need to enhance data sources and consider the inclusion of more distinctive features.

7.1 Comparison with Previous Work

Compared to previous studies, the results obtained are consistent, although with slight variations due to differences in the contexts of the datasets used. For example, the use of tools like *LIWC2015* and *WEKA* in other works showed similar accuracies; however, our approach relied on open-source libraries and custom scripts, achieving good results. The main difference lies in the data sources: while other studies focused on broader and more specific datasets like *Politifact*, our dataset was based on news from multiple Peruvian media outlets, which presented a greater challenge for classification due to the wide variety of writing styles and topics covered.

7.2 Complications During the Research

The generation of the dataset faced several complications. First, data collection was impacted by global events, which altered the perception and classification of topics initially considered false or science fiction. Additionally, the suspension of Twitter accounts spreading fake news reduced access to data sources, affecting the project's coverage. Lastly, technical issues related to data encoding arose, and challenges were encountered in detecting patterns in modified words meant to evade censorship, which were addressed through the development of regular expressions and spelling analysis techniques.

7.3 Limitations of the Implemented Algorithms

Naive Bayes showed limitations by not considering the context of words, leading to incorrect classifications in some cases. The algorithm evaluates words individually, without taking into account their context, which can result in the misclassification of meaningless word sets. Additionally, the frequent repetition of certain words in the analyzed texts can negatively impact the model's accuracy, changing the label of the news to an incorrect class if the repeated words do not correspond to the correct label.

On the other hand, the implementation of *Support Vector Machine* required detailed analysis and selection of optimal features to improve its accuracy. The use of standard libraries did not provide the necessary flexibility, and the identification of differentiating features between true and fake news proved to be a challenge. Some data mining software did not meet expectations. Solving the sentiment analysis issues, including the influence of punctuation marks, improved the model's accuracy, but the optimal determination of parameters for the SVM remains an extensive and complex process.

8 Conclusions

1. One of the biggest challenges was finding reliable sources of information to gather the news and generate the dataset.

2. Libraries such as SAS and *PySentimiento* were used for feature extraction, and noise cleaning was performed to improve data quality, which increased the accuracy of the final results.
3. The results obtained through benchmarking tests showed a high level of accuracy in the developed model, specifically achieving 95.4% accuracy with the *Naive Bayes* classifier and 90.45% with the *Support Vector Machine* optimizer.
4. The limitations of each algorithm were identified: *Naive Bayes* struggled to capture the context of words, leading to classification errors, while *Support Vector Machine* requires a larger number of differentiating features to improve the accuracy of its predictions.

Acknowledgments. To my family and advisors, for enriching this project.

References

1. Ahmad, I., Yousaf, M., Yousaf, S.: Fake News Detection Using Machine Learning Ensemble Methods. Hindawi, Peshawar, Pakistan (2020)
2. Espejel, R., Calderón, S., Ortega, M., Camacho, B., Márquez, V.: Detección automática de noticias falsas usando representaciones textuales tradicionales y soluciones basadas en aprendizaje profundo. Hidalgo, México: Pädi Boletín Científico de Ciencias Básicas e Ingenierías del ICBI, 2022, vol. 10, no. 3
3. Zhang, J., Dong, B., Yu, P.S.: FAKEDETECTOR: Effective Fake News Detection with Deep Diffusive Neural Network. The University Press of Florida, Florida, USA (2019)
4. Wang, Y., et al.: Llm-gan: construct generative adversarial network through large language models for explainable fake news detection, *arXiv*, 2024. https://arxiv.org/abs/2409.01787
5. Aldwairi, M., Alwahedi, A.: Detecting Fake News in Social Media Networks. Elsevier, Abu Dhabi, Emiratos Árabes Unidos (2018)
6. Witten, I.H., Frank, E., Hall, M.A.: Data Mining: Practical Machine Learning Tools and Techniques, 4th edn. Morgan Kaufmann, San Francisco, CA (2017)
7. Russell, M.A., Mining the Social Web: Data Mining Facebook, Twitter, LinkedIn, Instagram, GitHub, and More, 3rd ed. O'Reilly Media, Sebastopol, 2019
8. Chacón, L.M.C.: La cobertura electoral partidista y la creciente hostilidad hacia la prensa contribuyeron a la disminución de la confianza en los medios de perú en un año en el que se convirtió en el país con la mayor tasa de mortalidad por covid-19 del mundo, 2022. https://reutersinstitute.politics.ox.ac.uk/es/digital-news-report/2022/peru. Accessed 31 June 2023
9. Jurafsky, D., Martin, J.H.: Speech and Language Processing, 3rd ed. Prentice Hall, Hoboken (2023)
10. Alpaydin, E.: Introduction to Machine Learning. MIT press, Cambridge (2014)
11. Xue, J., Wang, Y., Tian, Y., Li, Y., Shi, L., Wei, L.: Detecting fake news by exploring the consistency of multimodal data. Inf. Process. Manag. **58**(5) (2021). https://doi.org/10.1016/j.ipm.2021.102610

Use of an Annotation Method for Spanish-Language Tweets Concerning corruption in Peru

Contreras Ruiz Daniel[1], Idrogo Diaz Johann[2], Cánepa Pérez Carlos[1,2], and Guzmán Monteza Yudi[1,2](✉)

[1] Universidad Nacional Mayor de San Marcos, Lima, Perú
yudi.guzman@unmsm.edu.pe

[2] Ciudad Universitaria, Av. Germán Amezaga s/n, Lima, Perú

Abstract. Corruption is a phenomenon in most countries worldwide, creating obstacles to social, political, and economic development. This research aims to utilize social media platforms like Twitter to gather data on crimes in Peru against public administration and, through an annotation guide and a data-driven annotation process, develop a reliable corpus for classifying crimes into 12 categories. Additionally, this study seeks to increase the availability of Spanish-language datasets, facilitating the identification and classification of corruption-related topics in Peru. The dataset construction process involved extracting text from Twitter using tools such as Snscrape, Tweepy, and manual extraction, resulting in 3,692 records. The annotation method employed included designing an annotation process and creating an annotation guide. Three iterations achieved a final Cohen's Kappa coefficient of 0.922, indicating an almost perfect agreement. The most frequent crime types identified were Influence Peddling, Collusion, Illicit Enrichment, and Bribery.

Keywords: Annotation process · Annotation guides · Cohen's Kappa coefficient · Twitter (X) · Corruption

1 Introduction

Corruption is omnipresent in most countries worldwide, creating significant obstacles to social, political, and economic development. According to the Citizen Perception of Governance, Democracy, and Trust in Institutions report for July to December 2023, corruption and crime are highlighted as the country's main issues, with 55% and 38%, respectively. Regarding the level of trust in national institutions, political parties showed around 93% distrust, the Congress of the Republic 91%, the Anti-Corruption Prosecutor's Office 74%, and radio and television 79% [1].

Our societies are currently undergoing various changes due to digital advancements, and social networks have become valuable data sources for research and analysis. [16] presents a ranking of social media platforms, placing Facebook in the top position with 16.33% of all users, followed by YouTube with 13.34%, WhatsApp and Instagram at

F. R. Narváez et al. (Eds.): SmartTech-IC 2024, CCIS 2392, pp. 347–361, 2026.
https://doi.org/10.1007/978-3-031-98287-3_25

10.71%, and TikTok slightly lower at 8.37%. It is worth noting that popular platforms tend to focus on entertainment and messaging, leaving microblogging sites like Twitter (X) and Reddit lower in the rankings.

In the case of Peru, Fig. 1 illustrates some of the most popular social media platforms [17].

Fig. 1. Web traffic from social networks in Peru, Data Reports, 2024

In [18], the use of X (formerly Twitter) is highlighted for immediate access to news related to health services. Similarly, [19] analyzed approximately 596,000 tweets to examine attitudes and sentiments towards the HPV vaccine. In [20], natural language processing (NLP) techniques were employed to analyze comments on social media, exploring interpretations of financial education.

The web hosts diverse data on various topics, necessitating its structuring to systematize and derive meaningful insights. This article focuses on tweet analysis, aiming to implement an annotation method for Spanish texts and construct a dataset under the supervised learning approach for studies on the classification and identification of corruption-related crimes. Furthermore, the dataset is designed to expand over time, incorporating crimes not covered in this study but present in other countries within the region. The resulting corpus consists of over 3,500 tweets, evaluated for reliability using Cohen's Kappa coefficient.

2 Context and Related Work

The Corruption Perception Index (CPI) is calculated using data from 13 external sources, including the World Bank and the World Economic Forum [2]. In 2023, Peru scored 33 on the CPI, ranking 121st globally [3], underscoring the country's high corruption levels.

In [4], the reactions of the Colombian population to the 2021 national strike were analyzed, with all opinions extracted from X (formerly Twitter). Similarly, [22] explored X and other Brazilian portals to construct a corpus analyzing how public opinion influences perceptions of corruption, identifying certain crime types. In [6], user opinions and reactions on social media were used to analyze the popularity of two fast-food brands and conduct sentiment analysis. Additionally, [8] developed a dataset for identifying argumentative texts in general elections, sourcing data from Twitter.

Data extraction methods were explored in [5], including web crawlers, HTTP programming, HTML parsing, and tree-based techniques. Meanwhile, [21] collected X data using a streaming API for a social network analysis project in Colombia. The data collection approach in this work combines hybrid methods, integrating web scraping techniques (using a Python-developed script), X's official API, and manual extraction.

Annotation-focused studies include [7], which created annotation guidelines for tagging cooking recipes, and [8], which proposed and evaluated an annotation method based on an adapted argumentation model and data-driven annotation processes from Twitter. In [15], a sentiment analysis-oriented dataset on biodiversity was developed with labeled data. Similarly, [11] used semi-supervised bootstrapping to create a corpus of potentially suicidal messages, and [14] introduced RUN-AS, an annotation scheme for categorizing global reliability as "Reliable" or "Unreliable."

3 Dataset Construction

This section details the process followed to construct the dataset. Across three extraction rounds, approximately 3,480 tweets were initially gathered. However, some tweets referenced multiple crimes within their content. To address this issue, tweets were segmented systematically, ensuring their original context was preserved during the division process. As a result, the dataset comprises a total of 3,692 records.

3.1 Text Extraction

The text extraction process was carried out using three different methods, detailed as follows:

- **Snscrape**: An open-source tool.
- **Tweepy**: Twitter's official API.
- **Manual Search**: Directly conducted to supplement automated methods.

Table 1 provides a summary of the data obtained through each method.

Table 1. The number of tweets obtained by extraction methods.

Method	Tweets obtained
Snscrape	2880
Tweepy	181
Manual Search	500
Total	**3561**

The text collection was carried out using two tools: Snscrape and Tweepy. Snscrape is a handy scraper for collecting information from social networks such as Facebook, Instagram, Mastodon, Reddit, Telegram, Twitter, VKontakte, and Weibo. The tool is available on GitHub, and its link is as follows: https://github.com/JustAnotherArchivist/snscrape. This tool was chosen because it offers a free and efficient way to quickly gather a large volume of tweets by utilizing Twitter's search functionality. Using Snscrape, approximately 2800 records were obtained.

Due to Elon Musk's recent acquisition of Twitter and the subsequent changes in the company's policies, several platforms and tools used to gather content from Twitter faced restrictions and became practically obsolete. To address this issue, Twitter's own API was used to access more data. However, another challenge arose, as the available data could only be extracted within seven days. Despite this, around 180 additional records were obtained.

Following the established workflow, as shown in Fig. 2, it was necessary to collect more tweets to supplement the data already gathered. Using the Twitter API was not viable due to the cost of the basic plan, which is $100 per month and only allows for the extraction of tweets published within the last seven days. With this limitation, only 181 tweets were obtained during approximately three weeks. Since no open-source tools were available, and the Twitter API, given its cost, did not yield worthwhile results, it was decided to manually select an additional 500 tweets, which were subsequently added to the final corpus.

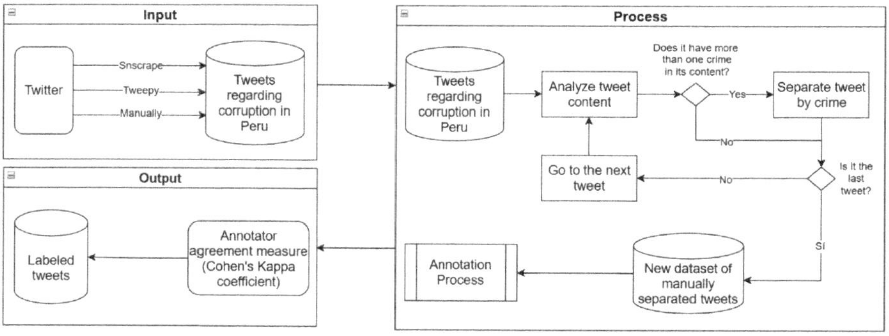

Fig. 2. Workflow for Tweet Labeling

Table 2. Crimes Against Public Administration According to the Government of Peru Portal

Number	Class
1	Abuse of authority
2	Unlawful collection
3	Bribery
4	Collusion
5	Extortion
6	Illicit enrichment
7	Embezzlement of funds
8	Incompatible negotiation or improper use of office
9	Illegal appointment or acceptance of a position
10	Illegal sponsorship
11	Misappropriation
12	Influence peddling

It is essential to mention that the results obtained using the methods listed in Table 1 underwent some modifications, which caused the number of records to either increase or decrease. These changes include eliminating identical or very similar records and splitting a tweet that contains more than one of the crimes considered in Table 2. Below, in Table 3, we provide an example of how a tweet was split.

Table 3. Division of a Crime

Original tweet	Trabajadores de la Biblioteca Nacional denuncian abuso de autoridad y despilfarro en el gasto público ► https://t.co/1uZEB4ecwX https://t.co/ck4pmT3GRc
Manually divided tweets	Trabajadores de la Biblioteca Nacional denuncian abuso de autoridad ► https://t.co/1uZEB4ecwX https://t.co/ck4pmT3GRc Trabajadores de la Biblioteca Nacional denuncian despilfarro en el gasto público ► https://t.co/1uZEB4ecwX https://t.co/ck4pmT3GRc

Finally, in Table 4, we see the result of the tweets obtained by each data extraction method.

Table 4. A final number of tweets was obtained through extraction methods.

Method	Obtained tweets	Tweets after modifications
Snscrape	2880	3000
Tweepy	181	145
Manual Search	500	547
Total	**3561**	**3692**

4 Annotation Method

The annotation method used for constructing the dataset, adapted from the work done by [8], consists of three main components. However, for this work, only two components were used: the annotation process, carried out by a supervisor and two annotators, and the creation of the annotation guide. The annotation process begins with developing the first version of the annotation guide based on research related to each offense listed in Table 2.

4.1 Annotation Process

The annotation process followed the theoretical framework outlined by [9] and the application presented in [8]. The annotation process consists of two main aspects: the first is the double-blind method, which ensures that annotators are not influenced by annotations made by others (annotators); the second is the Kappa coefficient, which guarantees a reliability test for the level of agreement between annotators, with a k value > 0.60 accepted as substantial agreement [9].

Communication between annotators was only conducted to discuss and modify the annotation guide if necessary, and no interaction occurred beyond that.

The annotation process involves two types of participants: a supervisor and an annotator. For this study, since two participants (authors of the article) were involved, the supervisor performed both roles, supervisor and annotator. The developed annotation process is shown in Fig. 3.

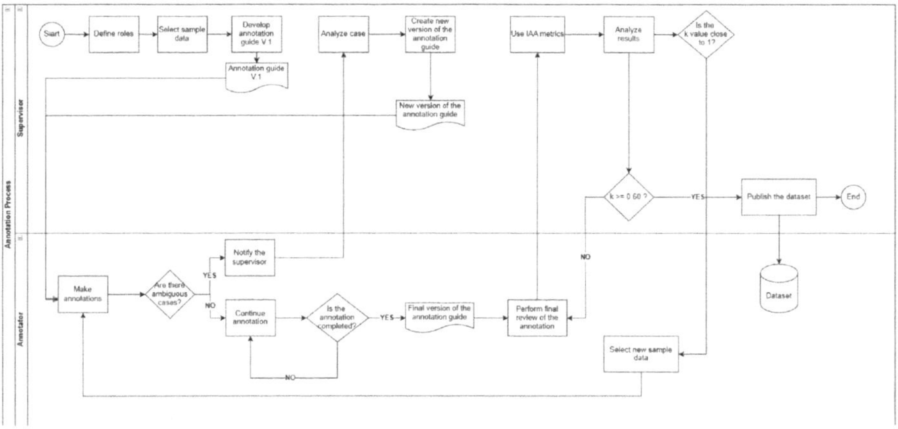

Fig. 3. Annotation Process

The process is detailed as follows:

1. The roles of annotator and supervisor are defined. After selecting a sample of 500 tweets from an approximate total of 3800, the first version of the annotation guide is created based on these tweets and additional research. The supervisor then instructs the annotators on the general aspects of the guide, communication protocol, and the annotation method to be used. If any annotator has doubts, they notify the supervisor, who analyzes the case and updates the guide if necessary.
2. The annotators proceed to annotate the dataset according to the most recent version of the Annotation Guide provided by the supervisor. The annotator notifies the supervisor if any ambiguous or unclear cases are identified. The case is analyzed, and the Annotation Guide is updated accordingly. Afterward, the annotators continue the process using the new version of the guide. This step is repeated if further exceptional cases not covered in the guide are identified.
3. Once the entire corpus has been annotated, a final review is conducted based on the latest version of the Annotation Guide. The guide is saved, and the validation process using the Inter-Annotator Agreement (IAA) method is carried out.
4. The IAA method is applied, specifically Cohen's Kappa coefficient (k). Two scenarios are considered at this point:

   – If the k value is greater than or equal to 0.60, it is considered that the annotators have substantial agreement, and the corpus is ready for publication.
   – If the k value is close to 1, a new sample of approximately 500 tweets, external to the corpus being classified, is taken for re-evaluation, and the process returns to step 2.

4.2 Development of the Annotation Guide

As described in [8], the Annotation Guide was created due to the iterative annotation process. This guide provides the directives for classifying a tweet into categories corresponding to the crimes previously outlined in Table 2.

Version 2.0 of the guide, shown in Table 5, differs from its first version in only two aspects. The first change is explicitly adding the crime's name to search for within the tweet's content. The second change incorporates former public officials, not just current officeholders, as part of the classification criteria.

Table 5. Version 2.0 of the Annotation Guide

Class	Annotation Guide
Abuse of authority	1. The tweet includes the phrase "abuse of authority" in its wording. 2. When the tweet shows that a public official or former official harmed someone arbitrarily by misusing their powers. 3. When the verb "to commit" is used actively, it means that the public officials themselves are committing the abusive act. 4. When the verb "to order" expresses a causal relationship between i) the public official who ordered, ii) the authority they overstepped, and iii) the harmful, abusive act.
Class	**Annotation Guide**
Unlawful collection	1. El tuit incluye la frase "cobro indebido" en su redacción 2. El contenido del tuit involucra a un funcionario o ex-funcionario público que exige o hace pagar o entregar contribuciones no debidas o en cantidad que excede a la tarifa legal. 3. El contenido del tuit sugiere pagos ilícitos a cambio de servicios gubernamentales o favores.

(continued)

Table 5. (*continued*)

	4. Cuando el tuit menciona transacciones monetarias sospechosas vinculadas a cargos públicos.

Class	**Annotation Guide**
Bribery	1. The tweet includes the phrase "bribery" or "coima" in its wording. 2. When the tweet involves a public servant or former public servant requesting, offering, or accepting compensation for neglecting their administrative duties in favor of a third party. 3. When the tweet shows the undue influence of financial factors in government decisions. 4. When the tweet's content suggests exchanging personal benefits for governmental actions.

Class	**Annotation Guide**
Collusion	1. The tweet includes the phrase "collusion" in its wording. 2. When the tweet mentions secret agreements between public and private entities for mutual benefit. 3. When the tweet's content shows manipulation of government processes to favor specific interests. 4. The tweet shows a public servant making a deal with a third party to defraud the state in public contracts for goods, works, or services entrusted to them.

Class	**Annotation Guide**
Extortion	1. the tweet includes the phrase "extortion" in its wording. 2. The tweet shows that a public official or former official, abusing their position, forces or induces someone to give or promise, either for themselves or for another, an asset or financial benefit in an improper manner. 3. When the tweet's content contains expressions that suggest threats or pressures from a public official to obtain personal benefits.

Class	**Annotation Guide**
Illicit enrichment	1. The tweet includes the phrase "illicit enrichment" in its wording. 2. The tweet's content suggests a significant and unjustified increase in the wealth of public officials. 3. The tweet's content presents expressions that denote possessions or luxurious lifestyles incompatible with the known income of public officials.

(*continued*)

Table 5. (*continued*)

Class	Annotation Guide
	4. The tweet refers to investigations on the origin of a public official's fortune.
Class	**Annotation Guide**
Embezzlement of funds	1. The tweet includes the phrase " embezzlement of funds" in its wording. 2. The tweet's content mentions public officials' improper use of public resources for personal purposes. 3. The tweet expresses the diversion of government funds for unauthorized activities. 4. The tweet mentions irregularities or complaints regarding the financial management of public institutions.
Class	**Annotation Guide**
Incompatible negotiation or improper use of office	1. The tweet includes the phrase "incompatible negotiation" or "improper use of office" in its wording. 2. The tweet mentions actions by public officials or former public officials that directly benefit companies or individuals with whom they have a relationship. 3. When the tweet includes expressions about violating ethical rules in making governmental decisions. 4. When the tweet contains messages suggesting conflicts of interest between public duties and personal or business relationships.
Class	**Annotation Guide**
Illegal appointment or acceptance of a position	1. The tweet includes the phrase "illegal appointment to position" or "illegal acceptance of position" in its wording. 2. The tweet mentions appointments to public office without meeting legal requirements. 3. When the tweet contains expressions about nepotism or undue favors in the assignment of positions. 4. When the tweet suggests cases of individuals holding positions for which they are not qualified.
Class	**Annotation Guide**
Illegal sponsorship	1. The tweet includes the phrase "illegal sponsorship" in its wording. 2. The tweet mentions actions by officials or former officials that benefit companies or individuals in which they have personal interests. 3. When the tweet refers to misusing position to favor certain sponsors.

(*continued*)

Table 5. (*continued*)

Class	Annotation Guide
	4. When the tweet suggests secret agreements between officials, former officials, and sponsors to gain benefits.
Class	**Annotation Guide**
Misappropriation	1. The tweet includes the phrase " Misappropriation" in its wording. 2. The tweet mentions the improper appropriation of public assets by officials. 3. When the tweet refers to the personal use of government resources. 4. When the tweet contains phrases about cases of officials or former officials directly benefiting from public property.
Class	**Annotation Guide**
Influence peddling	1. The tweet includes the phrase "influence peddling" in its wording. 2. The tweet mentions the improper use of connections to obtain favors or benefits. 3. When the tweet contains expressions suggesting governmental decisions' manipulation through undue influences. 4. When the tweet implies the exchange of influences to secure contracts or opportunities.
Class	**Annotation Guide**
Not Related	1. The tweet's content is unrelated to any of the previously mentioned crimes. 2. The tweet's content is unrelated to Peru's political context.

5 Analysis and Interpretation of the Results of the Applied Metrics

5.1 Result of the First Annotation

For the first iteration, 3,145 tweets were used for annotation, and the results were measured using Cohen's Kappa coefficient. After calculating this coefficient to measure the agreement between the two annotators, a concordance index of approximately 0.937 was obtained. This high result was the explicit presence of the exact word or phrase in the tweet content, indicating the class to which it belongs. In this sense, the annotators likely agreed on most of the tweets due to the clarity of the content.

Given that this result was very high, a second test was conducted with 547 new tweets (Fig. 4).

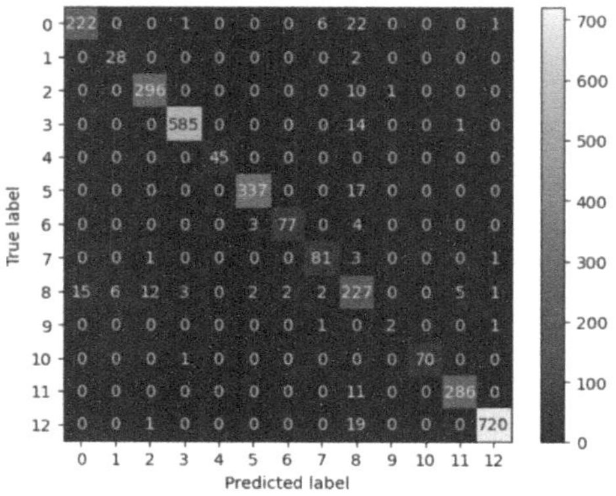

Fig. 4. Confusion Matrix Between Annotators 1 and 2

5.2 Result of the Second Annotation

This iteration repeated the same process as the first but with 547 tweets. The objective of this iteration was to validate the result of the first annotation since it was very high. After obtaining the coefficient result for this iteration, the value was 0.836. Due to this outcome, it was decided to merge the dataset from the first iteration with the second one and proceed to perform the annotation process again (Fig. 5).

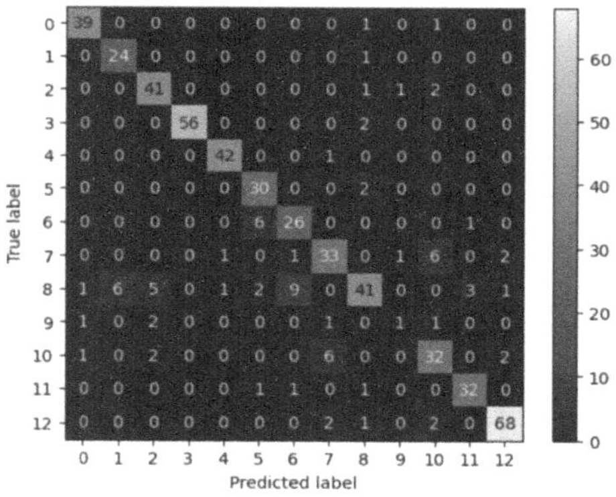

Fig. 5. Confusion Matrix Between Annotators 1 and 2

5.3 Result of the Third Annotation

By merging both datasets, a total of 3,692 tweets was obtained. The annotation process was repeated for this new dataset, resulting in a Cohen coefficient of 0.922. Although the results were higher than usual, this was due to the content of the tweets and their ease of being labeled. For this reason, the second iteration was carried out to observe whether the results from the first iteration were repeated. The objective of this final iteration was to combine both results to create a larger dataset and achieve a coefficient lower than the first one due to the result of the second iteration (Fig. 6).

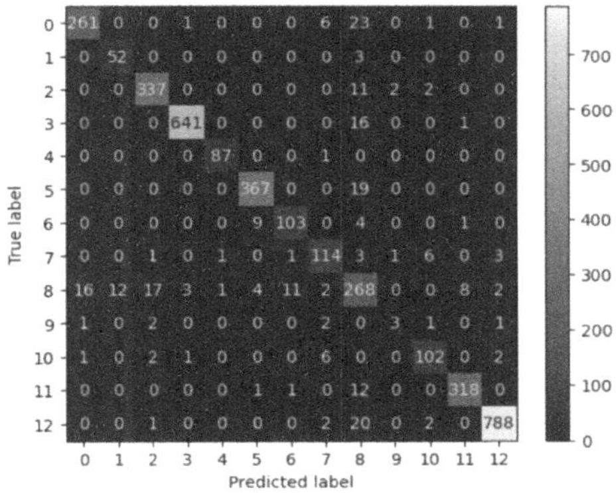

Fig. 6. Confusion Matrix Between Annotators 1 and 2

Finally, comparing the annotation method used in this study with those in [8] and [9], although this study worked with more classes, only two versions of the annotation guide were created. In contrast, [9] utilized nine versions of the guide. Additionally, the results obtained in this study exhibited a higher degree of reliability, primarily due to the ease of labeling caused by the content of the tweets.

6 Conclusions and Future Work

- The literature review did not reveal any datasets specifically focused on identifying corruption crimes against public administration in Spanish-speaking contexts. This highlights the value of the dataset developed in this study, which includes types of corruption crimes in Peru.
- The text extraction process encountered several challenges due to changes in the policies of platform X, which made free access to its content difficult.
- Despite difficulties accessing the content, a Spanish-language dataset related to corruption crimes in Peru was successfully built. The most frequent crimes in the dataset were Influence Peddling (788), Collusion (641), Illicit Enrichment (367), and Bribery (337).
- The constructed dataset adds value to the topic of corruption by providing a unique resource that facilitates understanding and analysis of the frequency and context of these crimes on social media.
- The annotation method is crucial for building a reliable corruption dataset based on supervised learning.
- In the first iteration of the annotation method, a very high percentage of agreement was obtained, with a concordance index of 0.937. In the second iteration, the agreement index was 0.836. In the final iteration of the process, the index was 0.922. This

demonstrates that the first result was influenced by the ease of labeling tweets due to their content.
- Having a Spanish-language corruption dataset opens up new opportunities for future data science studies focusing on corruption as a central theme.
- This dataset presents new opportunities for research in data science, particularly for predictive analysis and modeling patterns of corruption in Spanish-speaking contexts.
- The dataset allows for future expansion, including crimes and additional variables from other countries in the region, to serve as a reference tool for identifying and analyzing corruption at a regional level.

References

1. Instituto Nacional de Estadística e Informática: Perú: Percepción Ciudadana sobre Gobernabilidad, Democracia y Confianza en las Instituciones (Informe técnico N°1 - Febrero 2024). INEI, Lima (2023). Disponible en: https://www.inei.gob.pe/media/MenuRecursivo/boletines/informe-tecnico-de-gobernabilidad-jul-dic-2023-febrero-2024-28-febrero.pdf. Accessed 01 Mar 2024
2. Transparencia Internacional: El índice de percepción de la corrupción 2022 revela escasos avances contra la corrupción en un contexto mundial cada vez más violento. Transparencia Internacional (2023). Disponible en: https://www.transparency.org/es/press/2022-corruption-perceptions-index-reveals-scant-progress-against-corruption-as-world-becomes-more-violent. Accessed 31 Jan 2023
3. Transparencia Internacional: Índice de percepción de corrupción. Disponible en, 2023. https://www.transparency.org/en/cpi/2023
4. Aramburo, R.F.P., Moreira, M.Â.L., Fávero, L.P.L., Costa, I.P.A., dos Santos, M.: Data science in social politics with particular emphasis on sentiment analysis. Procedia Comput. Sci. **214**, 420–427 (2022). https://doi.org/10.1016/j.procs.2022.11.194
5. Parvez, M., Tasneem, K., Rajendra, S., Bodke, K.: Analysis of different web data extraction techniques. In: 2018 International Conference on Smart City and Emerging Technology (ICSCET), pp. 1–7. IEEE, Mumbai (2018). https://doi.org/10.1109/ICSCET.2018.8537333
6. El Rahman, S.A., AlOtaibi, F.A., AlShehri, W.A.: Sentiment analysis of twitter data. In: 2019 International Conference on Computer and Information Sciences (ICCIS), pp. 1–4. IEEE, Sakaka (2019). https://doi.org/10.1109/ICCISci.2019.8716464
7. Yamakata, Y., Tajima, K., Mori, S.: A case study on start-up of dataset construction: in case of recipe named entity corpus. In: 2018 IEEE International Conference on Big Data (Big Data), pp. 3564–3567. IEEE, Seattle (2018). https://doi.org/10.1109/BigData.2018.8622382
8. Guzman, Y.: Assessment of an annotation method for the detection of Spanish argumentative, non-argumentative, and their components. Telemat. Inform. Rep. **11**, 100068 (2023). https://doi.org/10.1016/j.teler.2023.100068
9. Urpay-Camasi, J., Garcia-Calderon, J., Shiguihara, P.: A method to construct guidelines for Spanish comments annotation for sentiment analysis. In: 2021 IEEE Sciences and Humanities International Research Conference (SHIRCON), pp. 1–4. IEEE, Lima (2021). https://doi.org/10.1109/SHIRCON53068.2021.9652313
10. Moraton, L., Lavid, J.: Stance and engagement in English and Spanish journalistic texts: towards a reliable annotation scheme for linguistic and computational purposes. Studia Linguistica Universitatis Iagellonicae Cracoviensis **135**(1), 29–45 (2018)
11. Acuña Caicedo, R.W., Gómez Soriano, J.M., Melgar Sasieta, H.A.: Bootstrapping semi-supervised annotation method for potential suicidal messages. Internet Interv. **28**, 100519 (2022). https://doi.org/10.1016/j.invent.2022.100519

12. Chamid, A.A., Widowati, Kusumaningrum, R.: Labeling consistency test of multi-label data for aspect and sentiment classification using the Cohen kappa method. Ingénierie des Systèmes d'Information **29**(1), 161–167 (2024). https://doi.org/10.18280/isi.290118
13. Balouchzahi, F., Sidorov, G., Gelbukh, A.: PolyHope: two-level hope speech detection from tweets. Expert Syst. Appl. **225**, 120078 (2023). https://doi.org/10.1016/j.eswa.2023.120078
14. Bonet-Jover, A., Sepúlveda-Torres, R., Saquete, E., et al.: RUN-AS: a novel approach to annotate news reliability for disinformation detection. Lang. Resour. Eval. **58**, 609–639 (2024). https://doi.org/10.1007/s10579-023-09678-9
15. Uliniansyah, M.T., Budi, I., Nurfadhilah, E., Afra, D.I.N., Santosa, A., Latief, A.D., et al.: Twitter dataset on public sentiments towards biodiversity policy in Indonesia. Data Brief **52**, 109890 (2024). https://doi.org/10.1016/j.dib.2023.109890
16. Fernández, R.: Ranking mundial de redes sociales por número de usuarios activos mensuales en 2024. Statista (2024). Disponible en: https://es.statista.com/estadisticas/600712/ranking-mundial-de-redes-sociales-por-numero-de-usuarios/#statisticContainer. Accessed 18 June 2024
17. Kemp, S.: DIGITAL 2024: PERU. Data Reportal (2024). Disponible en: https://datareportal.com/reports/digital-2024-peru. Accessed 23 Feb 2024
18. Usman, M., et al.: Analyzing patients satisfaction level for medical services using Twitter data. PeerJ Comput. Sci. **10**, e1697 (2024). https://doi.org/10.7717/peerj-cs.1697
19. Boucher, J.C., et al.: HPV vaccine narratives on Twitter during the COVID-19 pandemic: a social network, thematic, and sentiment analysis. BMC Public Health **23**, 694 (2023). https://doi.org/10.1186/s12889-023-15615-w
20. Muñoz-Céspedes, E., Ibar-Alonso, R., de Lorenzo Ros, S.: Financial literacy and sustainable consumer behavior. Sustainability **13**(16), 9145 (2021). https://doi.org/10.3390/su1316914
21. Rodríguez Rojas, S.A.: #Paro21denoviembre: un análisis de redes sociales sobre las interacciones y protagonistas de la actividad política en Twitter. Análisis Político **33**(98), 44–65 (2020). https://doi.org/10.15446/anpol.v33n98.89409
22. Souza, C.S.: How is corruption portrayed in the Brazilian media? An analysis of corruption in news portals and twitter. Corvinus J. Sociol. Soc. Policy **14**(1), 175–199 (2023). https://doi.org/10.14267/CJSSP.2023.1.8

Detecting Fake News and Fact-Checking in Tweets Using Spanish Language Models: A Case Study with Ecuador Chequea and Ecuador Verifica

Mariuxi Toapanta-Bernabé[1,2(✉)], Miguel Ángel García-Cumbreras[2], and L. Alfonso Ureña-López[2]

[1] Universidad de Guayaquil, Guayaquil, Ecuador
mariuxi.toapantab@ug.edu.ec
[2] CEATIC. Department of Computer Science, Universidad de Jaén. Campus Las Lagunillas, 23071 Jaén, Spain
{magc,laurena}@ujaen.es

Abstract. Currently, verifying news content before its dissemination poses a significant challenge due to its rapid spread and ease of replication. These factors contribute to the proliferation of fake news. Collaborative initiatives like Duke Reporters' Lab and the International Fact-Checking Network have been established to enhance the accuracy of fact-checking to combat various forms of disinformation. The accredited fact-checking platforms in Ecuador are "Ecuador Chequea" and "Ecuador Verifica".

This paper details the outcomes from five transformer-based models, namely BETO, MarIA, RoBERTuito, BERTuit, and BERTin, for classifying fake news in Spanish. The rating system of "Ecuador Chequea" and "Ecuador Verifica" validated the news gathered from these platforms' accounts on the social network X, including tweets generated between January 2020 and March 2024. The findings validate that in terms of accuracy, recall, precision, and F1 score, the MarIA language model outperforms other Spanish-based models such as BERTin, RoBERTuito, BETO, and BERTuit.

Keywords: Fact-checking grading system · Fake news · Fact-checker · Spanish Language Models · Text Classification

1 Introduction

Over the last decade, the phenomenon of "fake news" has underscored the increasing global need for data verification, also known as Fact-Checking [1]. For the Collins Dictionary, it is "false information, often sensational, disseminated under the guise of news" while the Oxford Dictionary defines it as "news that conveys or incorporates false, fabricated, or deliberately misleading information, or that is characterized or accused of doing so".

F. R. Narváez et al. (Eds.): SmartTech-IC 2024, CCIS 2392, pp. 362–376, 2026.
https://doi.org/10.1007/978-3-031-98287-3_26

1.1 Fact-Checking Organizations

To support Fact-Checking initiatives, the Poynter Institute established the International Fact-Checking Network (IFCN) in 2015, which adheres to the Code of Principles. It is a journalistic research institute of the Sanford School of Public Policy at Duke University, whose main projects focus on fact-checking [8]. It brings together a growing community of data verifiers worldwide and advocates for factual information in the global fight against misinformation [2].

On the other hand, the Duke Reporters' Lab was founded in 2011 [3]. Comprised of five guiding principles that signatories of the IFCN commit to uphold: 1) a commitment to independence and impartiality; 2) transparency of sources; 3) transparency in funding; 4) transparency with methodology; and 5) a commitment to open and honest correction [7]. Both organizations offer a verification map, that facilitates the identification of fact-checkers globally, thus providing a valuable resource for consultation [9].

1.2 Fact-Checking in Ecuador

In October 2016, "Ecuador Chequea" was founded, becoming the first Ecuadorian media dedicated exclusively to verifying public discourse and deceptive content circulating on the Internet. This portal is part of a global data verification network that includes, among others, "Chequeado from Argentina", a pioneering project in Latin America that has provided training to the "Ecuador Chequea" team. Additionally, it is a member of "Latam Chequea" and has obtained certification from the IFCN [4].

"Ecuador Verifica" is an initiative coordinated by "Ecuador Chequea" that emerged to combat misinformation in the 2021 presidential elections. The National Democratic Institute (NDI), an international cooperation organization committed to the fight against misinformation [6], supports this coalition that brings together media outlets, civil society organizations (CSOs), and universities to verify political discourse and promote transparency in public institutions. It is a global geographical representation where sites accredited for verification by the IFCN or Duke Reporters' Lab are registered [5].

1.3 Fact-Checking Rating System

The methodology applied by "Ecuador Chequea" for the verification process is internationally certified and endorsed by the IFCN. As of July 19, 2021, "Ecuador Verifica" adopted the same methodology established by "Ecuador Chequea", which is available on their official websites. The methodology used by "Ecuador Chequea"[1] and "Ecuador Verifica"[2] detail their rating system to verify news as "cierto", "falso", "alterado", "engañoso", "impreciso", "sátira", "inverificable" (in English "true", 'false', 'altered', 'misleading', 'inaccurate', 'satire', 'unverifiable', 'unverifiable', 'false', 'misleading', 'inaccurate', 'satire', 'unverifiable'). Figure 1 shows the rating system of both initiatives.

[1] https://ecuadorchequea.com/metodologia/.
[2] https://ecuadorverifica.org/metodologia/.

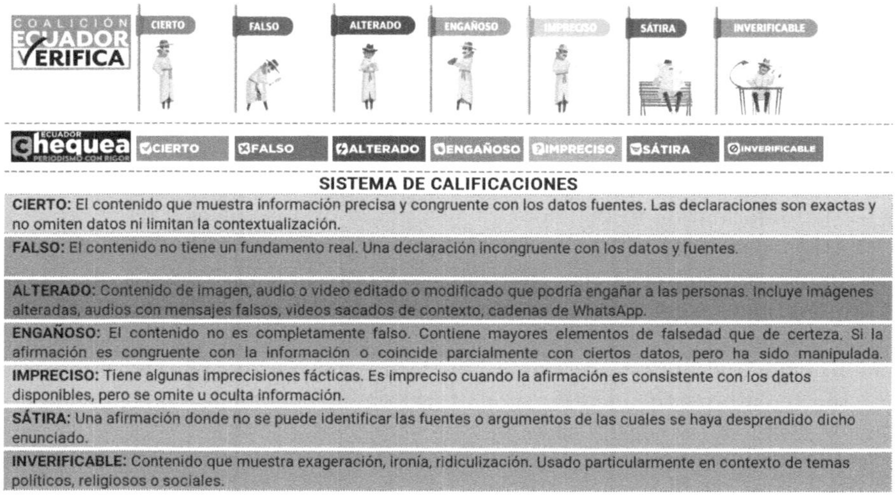

Fig. 1. "Ecuador Chequea" and "Ecuador Verifica" Rating System. Source: "Ecuador Chequea" and "Ecuador Verifica" webpages.

1.4 Research Objectives and Research Questions

The following are the research objectives and research questions of this work:

- **RO1**. To conduct a rigorous and equitable evaluation of various Spanish language models using a dataset of verified news from "Ecuador Chequea" and "Ecuador Verifica", to compare their quality and effectiveness in accurately detecting fake news. RQ1. How can these Spanish language models be evaluated to determine their performance in detecting fake news within the Ecuadorian context?
- **RO2**. To analyze the performance of these models through key metrics such as accuracy, recall, precision, and F1-score, identifying the most effective models in handling Spanish language social media data. RQ2. When analyzed through these metrics, what are the strengths and limitations of the Spanish language models, and how do they detect fake news in tweets?
- **RO3**. To ensure that the dataset and code are accessible for further research, enabling reproducibility and future studies in this area. RQ3. How can the provision of an accessible dataset and code facilitate additional investigations and ensure the reproducibility of results in the detection of fake news in Spanish-language contexts?

The article is organized into six main sections. Section 2 begins with a comprehensive review of significant research on Spanish language models. Next, Sect. 3 describes the dataset used for training, the preprocessing techniques applied to tweets, and details the experimental setup. Section 4 presents the evaluation results of the language models, followed by Sect. 5 offers an in-depth analysis of the models' performance and behavior. Finally, Sect. 6 concludes with the main findings and suggestions for future research directions

2 Related Work in Natural Language Processing

2.1 Language Models in Natural Language Processing

Recent advances in NLP have led to a paradigm shift, rendering many older techniques obsolete. Deep Learning is now being used to tackle challenges like fake news detection [10], and transformer architectures have revolutionized various NLP tasks, outperforming previous recurrent neural network models [11]. While many pre-trained models are available in English—driven largely by large companies due to high development and training costs [12–14]—there remains a shortage of high-quality Spanish language models. Despite Spanish being the second most spoken language, available models are less effective because of the limited quality and volume of Spanish corpora, as well as high costs that restrict development to large corporations. Furthermore, model performance degrades when applied to different domains, such as Twitter, where informal language and slang are common, and pre-trained models for Spanish user-generated text are either unavailable or difficult to locate in popular repositories like Hugging Face's model hub [15].

2.2 Spanish Pre-trained Model

The use of pre-trained models for Spanish text has seen significant advancements in the last years.

BETO. It is a version of BERT trained on an extensive Spanish text corpus, marking the first pre-trained model for the Spanish language [16]. Created in late 2019 by researchers from the University of Chile, the model was trained on a collection of corpora including Wikipedia and the OPUS Spanish corpus [17], and was later evaluated on the GLUES dataset, comparing favorably to the multilingual BERT. With approximately 110 million parameters, the model is similar to a BERT Base.

TWil-BERT. This language model, named TWil-BERT, is a specialization of BERT for the Spanish language and the Twitter domain. This specialization involves training a BERT model from scratch to obtain coherent and contextualized embeddings of tweets in Spanish [18].

MarIA. It is a family of Spanish language models providing public resources for the industry and the scientific community. MarIA currently includes Spanish language models RoBERTa-base, RoBERTa-large, GPT2, and GPT2-large, which can be considered the largest and best models for Spanish. The models have been pre-trained using a massive corpus of 570GB of clean texts, comprising 135 billion words extracted from the Spanish Web Archive built by the National Library of Spain between 2009 and 2019 [12].

RoBERTuito. This language model is a specialization of BERT for both the Spanish language and the Twitter domain, named TWil-BERT. This specialization consists of training a BERT model from scratch to obtain coherent and contextualized embeddings of tweets in Spanish [15].

RigoBERTa. It is a state-of-the-art language model for Spanish developed by the Institute of Knowledge Engineering (IIC) capable of adapting to different language domains (legal, health, etc.) to enhance NLP applications in specific fields. RigoBERTa is trained on a well-curated corpus formed from different subcorpora with key characteristics. It follows the DeBERTa architecture, which has several advantages over other similar-sized architectures like BERT or RoBERTa [13].

BERTuit. The largest transformer proposed to date for the Spanish language, BERTuit, has been pre-trained on a large dataset of 230 million Spanish tweets using the RoBERTa optimization. The proposed resource enables the identification of fake news propagators on Twitter and detecting such users. It can be used in applications focused on this social network that aim to combat the spread of misinformation [19].

BERTin. It is a model produced during the Flax/Jax Community Week. The BERTIN model is a RoBERTa-large with 24 layers, 16 heads, 1024 hidden units, and 355M parameters. It was trained from scratch on the Spanish portion of the mC4 dataset [20].

2.3 Pre-trained Generalist Models Vs. Domain-Specific Models

Pre-trained generalist models (e.g., BERT, GPT-3) have broad capabilities [19,21–25] but can fall short in scenarios requiring fine-grained, domain-specific linguistic nuances. In contrast, domain-specific models like MarIA and BERTuit are fine-tuned on targeted data, which provides them with several distinct advantages:

- **Domain-Specific Context and Vocabulary**. These models are trained on texts that capture the precise terminology and language usage within a particular domain. For instance, MarIA leverages diverse Spanish texts—including Wikipedia and news—while BERTuit specializes in the informal language of Spanish tweets, leading to more accurate handling of specialized vocabulary.
- **Enhanced Semantic Understanding**. By focusing on domain-relevant content, these models excel at disambiguating polysemous words and interpreting technical jargon. This improved semantic understanding minimizes misinterpretations, especially in complex texts such as legal or medical documents.
- **Adaptation to Language Styles and Structures**. Domain-specific models can adapt to their target domains' distinct syntactic and stylistic features. BERTuit, for example, is adept at processing the fragmented and informal style common on social media, whereas MarIA is better suited to the formal language of scholarly articles.

- **Noise Reduction in Learning**. Training exclusively on domain-relevant data helps these models avoid extraneous patterns, resulting in more efficient learning and higher precision compared to generalist models exposed to a wide range of irrelevant information.
- **Effective Knowledge Transfer within the Domain**. Once trained on a particular domain, these models can transfer foundational knowledge to related subdomains (e.g., from general medical language to specialized fields like cardiology), further enhancing their performance.

2.4 Size and Specificity of the Training Corpus in Domain-Specific Models

The size and specificity of the training corpus are crucial factors that impact the effectiveness of Spanish NLP models like MarIA and BERTuit in detecting fake news. Larger training corpora allow models to capture a wider range of linguistic patterns, improving their ability to generalize and accurately detect fake news, especially on dynamic platforms like Twitter. Domain-specific corpora enhance precision by training models on the particular vocabulary, context, and patterns of a specific domain (e.g., politics or health), making them more effective in identifying misinformation in those areas.

Research supports that models trained on large, domain-specific data perform better in fake news detection [26]. This approach maximizes accuracy and allows models to handle diverse misinformation more effectively [27].

2.5 Advantages and Disadvantages of Preprocessing and Fine-Tuning in NLP for Social Media Analysis

Preprocessing and fine-tuning techniques offer clear advantages in adapting NLP models to the unique and often complex language used on social media, making them particularly effective for tasks such as fake news detection in Spanish. Models like MarIA and BERTuit benefit from these techniques by achieving greater accuracy and domain-specific understanding. However, these methods risk amplifying biases, losing important contextual information, and requiring significant expertise and computational resources to implement effectively. Striking the right balance between thorough preprocessing and maintaining linguistic nuances is essential for ensuring that these models remain accurate and unbiased, providing reliable results in dynamic environments like Twitter.

Advantages

- Better Handling of Informal Language: Fine-tuning models like BERTuit allows them to capture the nuances of social media language, improving accuracy in text analysis [26].
- Adaptation to Specific Domains: Models like MarIA perform better when fine-tuned with domain-specific data, making them more effective in detecting fake news in targeted contexts [26].

- Efficiency: Preprocessing reduces noise and saves computational resources, enhancing the training process for large datasets [27].

Disadvantages

- Loss of Important Information: Overly aggressive preprocessing can remove crucial context, such as emojis, affecting sentiment analysis [27].
- Risk of Bias: Fine-tuning can amplify biases present in the training data, leading to skewed results [27].
- Complexity: Fine-tuning requires high-quality data and expertise, making implementing it more challenging.

3 Materials and Methods

3.1 Dataset

The dataset comprises posts on social network X that were verified by "Ecuador Chequea" @ecuadorchequea and "Ecuador Verifica" @ecuadorverifica between January 1, 2020, and March 25, 2024. The Apify platform, which extracts data from websites, is used to collect data from tweets on the social network X. Tasks are created with the required filters for execution. After completing the task, the information from the tweets is downloaded in CSV format.

3.2 Cleaning and Preprocessing

The data standardization process known as Text Normalization removed irrelevant elements, such as links, mentions, hashtags, emojis, and punctuation marks, and preprocessed the text using a series of regular expressions. The tweet-preprocessor library is used for data cleaning instead of writing the tweet-cleaning logic. The clean method performs tweet cleaning by removing URLs, mentions, reserved words (RT, FAV), hashtags, emojis, smileys, and numbers by default unless you specify only some of the options. Continuing the cleaning process, the text is converted to lowercase, punctuation marks and extra spaces are removed.

Next, the preprocessing process is carried out.

1. Tokenization. We use TweetTokenizer, which is a specialized tokenizer designed to handle tweets and other social media texts.
2. Stopwords. We use the NLTK library to remove empty words using the Spanish corpus.
3. Lemmatization. We use the STANZA library[3]. This text normalization technique aims to reduce words to their root (lemma).

3.3 Experiments Design

The Spanish news corpus contains 1340 news items in Spanish, consisting of 580 "falso" ("false"), 314 "cierto" ("true"), 221 "engañoso" ("misleading"), 149 "impreciso" ("inaccurate"), 26 "sí pero" [4] ("yes, but"), 26 "inverificable" ("unverifiable"),

[3] https://stanfordnlp.github.io/stanza/.

[4] This category was in a previous version.

"sátira" ("satire") and "insostenible" ("untenable"). Figure 2 shows through a chart the corresponding distribution for each news item in a chart.

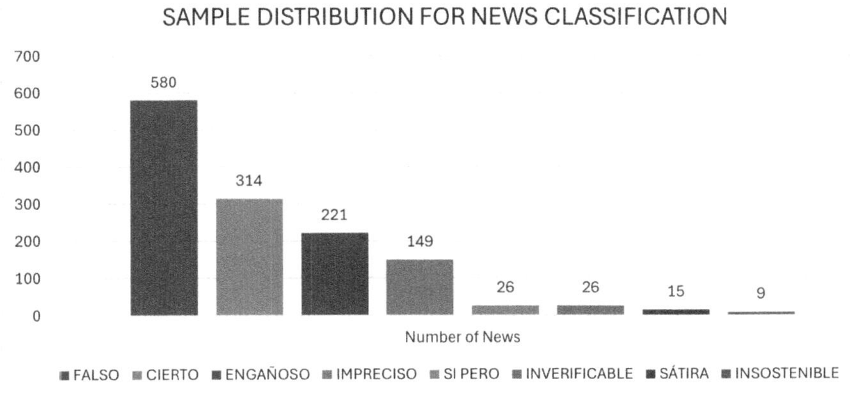

Fig. 2. Sample distribution for "Ecuador Chequea" and "Ecuador Verifica" news classification.

The dataset split was set to an 80% train and 20% test ratio. Based on the outcomes of the initial analysis, among the techniques for balancing the dataset, over-sampling of the minority classes was chosen, which led to the use of SMOTE (Synthetic Minority Over-sampling Technique). Table 1 shows the values after balancing the dataset.

Fine-tuning a pre-trained model and adjusting TrainingArguments are crucial steps in a machine learning project, especially when working with language models like BERT, GPT, or RoBERTa. TrainingArguments is a class provided by the Hugging Face's transformers library, offering a comprehensive set of parameters for configuring the training process of machine learning models, particularly those related to NLP. The most frequent values are explained below:

- output_dir. Specifies the directory where the model checkpoints and training outputs will be saved. This is essential for model persistence and later evaluation or use.
- per_device_train_batch_size. Determines the batch size for training on each device (GPU/CPU). Smaller batch sizes require less memory but can lead to longer training times and potentially more noise during the training process.
- per_device_eval_batch_size. Sets the batch size for evaluation on each device. This is similar to per_device_train_batch_size but used during the model evaluation phase.
- num_train_epochs. Defines the total number of training epochs. An epoch represents one complete pass through the entire training dataset. Adjusting the number of epochs can affect the model's performance and training time.

Table 1. Training arguments for transformers-based models.

Classification News	Number of News
FALSO	580
CIERTO	580
ENGAÑOSO	580
IMPRECISO	580
SI PERO	580
INVERIFICABLE	580
SáTIRA	580
INSOSTENIBLE	580
Total	**4640**

- warmup_steps. The number of steps to increase the learning rate from 0 to the initial learning rate set via learning_rate. This can help improve model performance and stability in the initial phase of training.
- weight_decay. A regularization parameter to prevent overfitting by applying penalties on large weights during optimization. Adjusting this can help improve the generalization of the model.
- learning_rate. The initial learning rate for the optimizer. The choice of learning rate can significantly impact model performance and convergence speed.
- evaluation strategy. Determines when the model evaluation should occur. Options include“no” (no evaluation), “steps” (after a set number of training steps), and “epoch” (after each training epoch).
- save_strategy. Similar to evaluation_strategy, but for saving model checkpoints. This can be set to “no”, “steps”, or “epoch”.
- logging_dir. Directory where the training logs will be stored. Useful for monitoring the training process through tools like TensorBoard.
- logging_steps. is a parameter within TrainingArguments that specifies the frequency at which training, and evaluation metrics are logged. This parameter is particularly useful for monitoring the model's performance and the training process in real-time or through logging frameworks like TensorBoard.
- load_best_model_at_end. Whether to load the model checkpoint with the highest evaluation metric or the final model at the end of training. Useful for automatically selecting the best model.
- metric_for_best_model. Specifies the metric to use when load_best_model_at_end is True. The model with the best value of this metric will be loaded at the end.

Table 2 shows the parameterized values in Training arguments for Fine-tuning a pre-trained model.

4 Results

This section shows the results obtained in this research work.

4.1 Model Fine-Tuned

According to the results, the MarIA model outperformed the other models, achieving an Accuracy of 0.9601, indicating its high efficiency in correctly classifying fake news, as shown in Table 4. Additionally, the metrics obtained during the training of the remaining models are detailed in Table 3 providing a comprehensive comparison of their performance.

5 Discussion

Research involving Spanish language models for text classification, specifically in the detection of fake news, has achieved notable results using datasets drawn from verified tweets by "Ecuador Chequea" and "Ecuador Verifica". The experiments were designed to assess how effectively these models can classify news based solely on text data from the social network X, without incorporating multimedia elements, following the fact-checking criteria established by these Ecuadorian verifiers.

The study focused on rigorously evaluating the models' ability to classify news as "cierto", "falso", "alterado", "engañoso", "impreciso", "sátira" and "inverificable", adhering strictly to the verification methodologies employed by "Ecuador Chequea" and "Ecuador Verifica". This process is crucial for understanding the nuances of misinformation in the Spanish language, especially within the Ecuadorian context, where fake news can impact public discourse.

5.1 Performance Metrics

The performance metrics —accuracy, precision, recall, and F1-score— offer a comprehensive view of how effectively the Spanish language models can handle text-based analysis on the social network X. These metrics not only provide valuable insights into the strengths and potential improvements of the models when applied to real-world fact-checking and verification tasks but also highlight their potential as powerful tools in the fight against disinformation. The ability of these models to distinguish between factual and fabricated content with such high accuracy and precision is crucial for automating the detection of fake news, thereby enhancing the reliability of information disseminated across digital platforms.

Accuracy. The model achieved an accuracy rate of 0.9601, demonstrating a high degree of reliability in correctly identifying the veracity of news across the entire test dataset. This metric reflects the model's overall effectiveness in accurately classifying both genuine (true) and misleading (fake) news, making it a strong candidate for real-world applications.

Table 2. Training arguments for transformers-based models.

Model	Training arguments
MarIA[a]	`output_dir='./results', per_device_train_batch_size=16, warmup_steps=500, weight_decay=0.01, learning_rate=1e-5, evaluation_strategy="epoch", save_strategy='epoch', logging_dir='./logs', logging_steps=100, load_best_model_at_end=True, metric_for_best_model="accuracy"`
BETO[b]	`output_dir='./results', per_device_train_batch_size=16, per_device_eval_batch_size=64, num_train_epochs=4, warmup_steps=500, weight_decay=0.01, learning_rate=1e-5, evaluation_strategy="epoch", save_strategy='epoch', logging_dir='./logs', logging_steps=100, lload_best_model_at_end=True, metric_for_best_model="accuracy"`
RoBERTuito[c]	`output_dir='./results', per_device_train_batch_size=8, per_device_eval_batch_size=8, num_train_epochs=3, warmup_steps=500, weight_decay=0.01, learning_rate=2e-5, evaluation_strategy="epoch", save_strategy='epoch', logging_dir='./logs', logging_steps=100, load_best_model_at_end=True, metric_for_best_model="accuracy"`
BERTuit[d]	`output_dir='./results', per_device_train_batch_size=8, per_device_eval_batch_size=8, num_train_epochs=3, warmup_steps=500, weight_decay=0.01, learning_rate=2e-5, evaluation_strategy="epoch", save_strategy='epoch', logging_dir='./logs', logging_steps=100, load_best_model_at_end=True, metric_for_best_model="accuracy"`
BERTin[e]	`output_dir='./results', per_device_train_batch_size=8, per_device_eval_batch_size=8, num_train_epochs=3, warmup_steps=500, weight_decay=0.01, learning_rate=1e-5, evaluation_strategy="epoch", save_strategy='epoch', logging_dir='./logs', logging_steps=100, load_best_model_at_end=True, metric_for_best_model="accuracy"`

[a] bert-base-spanish-wwm-uncased https://huggingface.co/dccuchile/bert-base-spanish-wwm-uncased

[b] PlanTL-GOB-ES/roberta-base-bne https://huggingface.co/PlanTL-GOB-ES/roberta-base-bne

[c] pysentimiento/robertuito-base-cased https://huggingface.co/pysentimiento/robertuito-base-cased

[d] bertin-project/bertin-roberta-base-spanish https://huggingface.co/bertin-project/bertin-roberta-base-spanish

[e] bertin-project/bertin-roberta-base-spanish https://huggingface.co/bertin-project/bertin-roberta-base-spanishc

Table 3. Train Output Models

Modelo	Epoch	Training Loss	Validation Loss	Accuracy	Precision	Recall	F1 Score
BETO	1	1.9099	1.460454	0.575431	0.519867	0.575431	0.517765
	2	0.9221	0.627142	0.789871	0.792705	0.789871	0.780918
	3	0.5125	0.306508	0.911638	0.914206	0.911638	0.910657
	4	0.2155	0.225540	0.935345	0.934864	0.935345	0.934516
MarIA	1	0.0398	0.185121	0.954741	0.954894	0.954741	0.953861
	2	0.0156	0.350760	0.929957	0.943936	0.929957	0.926845
	3	0.0280	0.214479	0.960129	0.959850	0.960129	0.959735
RoBERTuito	1	0.8486	0.591580	0.782328	0.827286	0.782328	0.772328
	2	0.2734	0.257701	0.906250	0.908591	0.906250	0.901669
	3	0.1322	0.211828	0.935345	0.935905	0.935345	0.933532
BERTuit	1	0.3602	0.348519	0.881466	0.887611	0.881466	0.872059
	2	0.1818	0.259604	0.923491	0.924281	0.923491	0.920490
	3	0.1032	0.254212	0.934267	0.933133	0.934267	0.932568
BERTin	1	1.1841	0.801565	0.693966	0.750559	0.693966	0.664146
	2	0.2706	0.205788	0.937500	0.938318	0.937500	0.936755
	3	0.0640	0.150867	0.954741	0.954394	0.954741	0.954364

Table 4. Train Ouput Models

Model	Accuracy	Precision	Recall	F1 Score
BETO	0.9353	0.9349	0.9353	0.9345
MarIA	0.9601	0.9599	0.9601	0.9597
RoBERTuito	0.9353	0.9359	0.9353	0.9335
BERTuit	0.9343	0.9331	0.9343	0.9326
BERTin	0.9547	0.9544	0.9547	0.9544

Precision. With a precision score of 0.9599, the model effectively returns relevant results, indicating that when it classifies news as fake, it is accurate 95.99% of the time. This high precision is essential for minimizing false positives, ensuring that legitimate news is not incorrectly flagged as fake, which is critical for maintaining credibility in content moderation.

Recall. The model's recall score of 0.9601 indicates its strong ability to identify nearly all instances of fake news within the dataset. In practical terms, this means the model successfully captures 96.01% of fake news cases, showcasing its efficiency in detecting a broad spectrum of misleading content with minimal oversight.

F1-score. The model achieved an F1-score of 0.9597, which represents the harmonic mean of precision and recall. This balanced metric confirms the robustness and overall effectiveness of the model, indicating that it maintains both high precision and recall. An F1-score close to 1 underscores the model's reliability in distinguishing between truthful and false content.

5.2 Implications of MarIA in Combating Misinformation

MarIA, with an accuracy of 96.01%, emerges as a powerful tool for automating fact-checking processes, enabling scalable strategies to combat misinformation across diverse sectors [10,12]. In education, MarIA can enhance academic integrity by assessing the reliability of information and fostering critical thinking among students and educators [1]. In public health, its ability to identify false claims on sensitive topics such as vaccines and therapies reinforces trust in healthcare organizations [10,27]. Additionally, with an F1-score of 95.97%, MarIA shows promise in improving content moderation on social media platforms by enabling real-time analysis for safer digital ecosystems [11,15]. Despite its strong performance metrics—precision at 95.99% and recall at 96.01%—the model's deployment must address ethical challenges, including ensuring unbiased training data and continuous updates to adapt to evolving misinformation tactics [11,27].

6 Conclusions and Further Work

This study demonstrates the remarkable performance of the MarIA model in detecting fake news in Spanish, outperforming other state-of-the-art models such as BETO, RoBERTuito, and BERTuit. Achieving an accuracy of 96.01%, precision of 95.99%, recall of 96.01%, and an F1-score of 95.97%, MarIA stands out as a highly reliable tool for classifying misinformation based solely on textual content. These results confirm the effectiveness of domain-specific models in addressing misinformation within the Ecuadorian context.

By adhering to the rigorous methodologies of Ecuador Chequea and Ecuador Verifica, aligned with IFCN standards, MarIA ensures both accuracy and consistency in its classifications, covering categories such as "cierto", "falso", "alterado", "engañoso", "impreciso", "sátira", "inverificable" (in English "true", 'false', 'altered', 'misleading', 'inaccurate', 'satire', 'unverifiable', 'unverifiable', 'false', 'misleading', 'inaccurate', 'satire', 'unverifiable').

MarIA's robust performance highlights its ability to automate fact-checking in sectors such as education, public health, and social media regulation. This emphasizes the vital role of advanced NLP tools in enhancing the reliability of digital information and combating misinformation. Future research should focus on refining these models and addressing the emerging challenges within these domains. For further work, the following is suggested:

- **Dataset Expansion:** Broaden the dataset by collecting more verified tweets from @ecuadorchequea and @ecuadorverifica to improve analysis robustness.

- **Additional Tweet Elements:** Incorporate metadata and user interaction patterns to gain a more comprehensive understanding of tweet context.
- **Labeling Guide:** Develop a detailed labeling guide to standardize the annotation process, ensuring consistency and reliability in future analyses.
- **Labeling Feature Integration:** Embed a labeling function within the Support System for Fact-Checkers that aligns with the rating criteria of Ecuador Chequea and Ecuador Verifica.
- **Model Deployment:** Utilize the trained language models within the Support System to provide advanced fact-checking tools and enhance tweet verification accuracy.

Acknowledgements. This research is part of the proposal submitted under the Call for Research Project Proposals of the Internal Competitive Fund (FCI) 2023. The project was approved by the Research Council of the Faculty of Industrial Engineering on February 22, 2023; the Advisory Council for Research, Postgraduate Studies, and Internationalization on August 23, 2023, through resolution No. CCIPI-SE-009-01-2023; and the Higher University Council of the University of Guayaquil on September 14, 2023, via resolution No. R-CSU-UG-SE34-313-14-09-2023. Also, CONSENSO (PID2021-122263OBC21), MODERATES (TED2021-130145B-I00), and SocialTOX (PDC2022-133146-C21) funded by Plan Nacional I+D+i from the Spanish Government.

References

1. Ireton, C., Posetti, J.: Periodismo, "Noticias Falsas" & Desinformación: Manual de Educación y Capacitación en Periodismo. Organización de las Naciones Unidas para la Educación, la Ciencia y la Cultura (UNESCO), República Dominicana (2020)
2. Verified signatories of the IFCN. https://www.ifcncodeofprinciples.poynter.org/signatories. Accessed 4 Feb 2024
3. Duke Reporters' Lab About. https://reporterslab.org/about-the-lab/. Accessed 4 Feb 2024
4. Ecuador Chequea History. https://ecuadorchequea.com/historia/. Accessed 4 Feb 2024
5. Ecuador Verifica About. https://ecuadorverifica.org/quienes-somos/. Accessed 4 Feb 2024
6. International Fact-Checking Network (IFCN). https://www.poynter.org/ifcn/. Accessed 4 Feb 2024
7. The commitments of Code of Principles IFCN. https://www.ifcncodeofprinciples.poynter.org/. Accessed 4 Feb 2024
8. Duke Reporters' Lab Global Fact-Checking sites. https://reporterslab.org/fact-checking/. Accessed 4 Feb 2024
9. Universidad de Las Américas UDLA Channel Chequea. https://www.udla.edu.ec/2021/03/udla-channel-chequea-esta-en-el-mapa-de-verificadores-de-duke-reporters-lab/. Accessed 22 Mar 2021
10. Martínez-Gallego, K., álvarez-Ortiz, A., Arias-Londoño, J.: Fake news detection in spanish using deep learning techniques. ArXiv abs/2110.06461, 1–10 (2021)

11. Vaswani, A., et al.: attention is all you need. In: 31st Annual Conference on Neural Information Processing Systems (NIPS 2017), pp. 5999–6009. Curran Associates Inc., New York (2018)
12. Gutiérrez-Fandiño, A., et al.: MarIA: spanish language models. Procesamiento del Lenguaje Natural **68**(68), 39–60 (2022)
13. Vaca Serrano, A., et al.: Rigoberta: A state-of-the-art language model for spanish. ArXiv **abs/2205.10233**, 1–15 (2022)
14. Agerri, R., Agirre, E.: Lessons learned from the evaluation of Spanish Language Models. Procesamiento del Lenguaje Nat. **70**(70), 157–170 (2023)
15. Pérez, J., Furman, D., Alonso Alemany, L., Luque, F.: RoBERTuito: a pre-trained language model for social media text in Spanish. In: 13th Conference on Language Resources and Evaluation (LREC 2022), pp. 7235—7243. European Language Resources Association, Paris (2022)
16. Cañete, J., Chaperon, G., Fuentes, R., Ho, J.-H., Kang, H., Pérez, J.: Spanish pre-trained BERT model and evaluation data. In: PML4DC Workshop at ICLR 2020, pp. 1—10. Curran Associates Inc., New York (2020)
17. Tiedemann, J., Thottingal, S.: OPUS-MT – Building open translation services for the World. In: 22nd Annual Conference of the European Association for Machine Translation, pp. 479–480. Curran Associates Inc., New York (2020)
18. González, J., Hurtado, L., Pla, F.: TWilBert: pre-trained deep bidirectional transformers for Spanish twitter. Neurocomputing **426**, 58–69 (2021)
19. Huertas-Tato, J., Martin, A., Camacho, D.: BERTuit: understanding spanish language in twitter through a native transformer. Expert. Syst. **40**(9), e13404 (2023)
20. De la Rosa, J., et al.: Bertin: Efficient pre-training of a Spanish language model using perplexity sampling. Procesamiento del Lenguaje Nat. **68**(68), 13—23 (2022)
21. Sarker, I.H.: AI-based modeling: techniques, applications and research issues towards automation, intelligent and smart systems. SN Comput. Sci. **3**(2), 1–20 (2022). https://doi.org/10.1007/s42979-022-01043-x
22. Martinez-Rico, J.R., Araujo, L., Martinez-Romo, J.: Building a framework for fake news detection in the health domain. PLoS ONE **19**(7), e0305362 (2024)
23. Sellami, R., Sadat, F., Beluith, L.: Intelligent natural language processing: trends and applications. Springer International Publishing, Cham (2018)
24. Sarker, I.H.: Deep learning: a comprehensive overview on techniques, taxonomy, applications and research directions. SN Comput. Sci. **2**(6), 1–20 (2021). https://doi.org/10.1007/s42979-021-00815-1
25. Ding, J., Li, B., Xu, C., Qiao, Y., Zhang, L.: Diagnosing crop diseases based on domain-adaptive pre-training BERT of electronic medical records. Appl. Intell. **53**(12), 15979–15992 (2023)
26. Peña, A., et al.: Leveraging large language models for topic classification in the domain of public affairs. In: Coustaty, M., Fornés, A. (eds.) International Conference on Document Analysis and Recognition, ICDAR, vol. 1, pp. 20–33, Springer Nature Switzerland, Cham (2023). https://doi.org/10.1007/978-3-031-41498-5_2
27. Garrido-Muñoz, I., Martínez-Santiago, F., Montejo-Ráez, A.: MarIA and BETO are sexist: Evaluating gender bias in large language models for Spanish. Lang. Resour. Eval. **58**(4), 1387–1417 (2024)

Detection of Automatically Generated Texts: A Classification-Based Approach and Text Features

César Espin-Riofrio[1](✉), Joel Alejandro Barba-Salazar[1], Edison Cruz-Navarrete[1], Mariuxi Del Carmen Toapanta Bernabé[1], Oswaldo Vergara-Bello[1], Pamela Carriel-Castillo[1], Irving Garzón-Soledispa[1], and Arturo Montejo-Ráez[2]

[1] University of Guayaquil, Guayaquil 090510, Ecuador
{cesar.espinr,joel.barbas,edison.cruzn,mariuxi.toapantab, oswaldo.vergarab,pamela.carrielc,irvin.garzons}@ug.edu.ec
[2] University of Jaén, 23071 Jaén, Spain
amontejo@ujaen.es

Abstract. The development of language models capable of generating text with a high degree of similarity to human-written content presents significant challenges regarding the authenticity and reliability of information, both online and in academic and professional contexts. These models have raised concerns due to the difficulty in distinguishing between human and machine-generated content, which impacts the evaluation and consumption of information. This study proposes a method based on machine learning and Natural Language Processing (NLP) techniques to differentiate texts written by humans from those generated by machines. The approach focuses on analyzing textual features such as phrasal patterns, the use of discourse markers, and punctuation signs. The multilingual dataset from the IberLEF 2024 task was used, which includes texts in Spanish, English, Catalan, Basque, Galician, and Portuguese, covering various domains such as news and essays, generated by models like GPT and LLaMA. Classification algorithms such as Random Forest, Multilayer Perceptron, and XGBoost were employed, along with an ensemble model combining these methods. The ensemble model outperformed the others, followed by Random Forest. The results are promising and highlight the effectiveness of the proposed method, as well as the relevance of textual features in model learning.

Keywords: Generated text · Phrasal features · Natural Language Processing

1 Introduction

The proliferation of text generators has led to a significant increase in the amount of automatically generated text, posing serious challenges regarding the reliability and authenticity of information, both online and in professional and academic environments. UNESCO has emphasized the importance of detecting such texts due to the severe problems they may pose in terms of information integrity, highlighting that automatic text

F. R. Narváez et al. (Eds.): SmartTech-IC 2024, CCIS 2392, pp. 377–389, 2026.
https://doi.org/10.1007/978-3-031-98287-3_27

detectors are essential to preserving this integrity [1]. The detection of automatically generated texts has become an indispensable need to address the challenge of distinguishing between human-written content and that created by machines.

The identification of automatically generated texts has become a crucial necessity for tackling the challenge of differentiating between texts produced by humans and those crafted by machines. By analyzing linguistic and stylistic patterns, the goal is to detect automatically generated texts to combat misinformation, plagiarism, and other forms of information manipulation. Natural Language Processing (NLP) provides the ability to understand, interpret, and generate human language more efficiently [2].

The detection of automatically generated texts is an evolving field, driven by the rapid advancement of generative AI models. While there are effective tools available, such as GLTR (Giant Language Model Test Room), DetectGPT, and GPTZero, challenges remain, primarily due to the models' increasing ability to mimic human writing styles with greater precision. The development of new techniques based on linguistic features, combined with machine learning models and explainability approaches, appears to be the path toward continuous improvement in the detection of AI-generated texts.

GLTR [3] employs advanced metrics to analyze and identify texts, highlighting words based on their perplexity. In this way, GLTR assists users in detecting patterns that may indicate whether a text was generated by a language model.

Tools like StyloAI and Grover employ stylistometric techniques, which involve analyzing the stylistic features of a text (such as sentence length, use of connectors, and other linguistic aspects). These models can detect differences between human writing styles and outputs generated by AI models. The advantages of these tools lie in their ability to identify stylistic patterns that are specific to generative models.

The research in [4] uses stylistometric techniques to develop StyloAI, a model specifically designed to identify texts automatically created by AI. This model analyzes and classifies texts using 31 stylistometric features, thereby enhancing the ability to distinguish between AI-generated and human-written content. Similarly, [5] uses a stylometric classifier called Grover-Mega, which aims to differentiate between real and fake texts generated by language models. Grover-Mega can detect false information produced by language models in two key scenarios: news expansion and article modification.

Several studies address the detection of automatically generated texts using a variety of techniques and methods. For example, [6] uses BERT [7] to identify AI-generated text, while [8] employs a combination of models such as BERT, ELMo [9], XLNet [10], PanGu-α [11], and GROVER. These models are integrated with feature-based strategies, linguistic analysis, and statistical techniques to detect deviations from natural language, such as n-gram frequencies, and examine both linguistic and statistical traits of the generated texts. Meanwhile, [12] employs BERT models and a feed-forward neural network for the detection of automatically generated texts, experimenting with different layers of BERT embeddings and presenting prediction systems for texts in both English and Spanish. Similarly, [13] describes a detection system called "stacking ensemble," which combines multiple Transformer models [14], such as ALBERT [15], ELECTRA [16], RoBERTa [17], and XLNet, through a Logistic Regression classifier, achieving an accuracy of 0.9555, outperforming individual models. [18] uses a range of techniques and methods for detecting generated texts, highlighting the use of RoBERTa adapted to technical texts from various domains, which allows for the detection of generated text at the paragraph level by evaluating sentences within it.

Additionally, [19] proposes a classification model based on XGBoost [20] to automatically detect essays generated by ChatGPT. Two feature extraction schemes were experimented with: TF-IDF [21] and a manually designed feature set, achieving 96% accuracy in detecting texts generated by ChatGPT. On the other hand, [22] introduced the DetectGPT method, which compares its efficacy with several methods based on token probabilities, token ranges, and predictive entropy. The test results showed that DetectGPT outperformed other methods, achieving an average accuracy of 80% in detecting machine-generated texts. In [23], the use of deep language model techniques, such as GPT-2, is explored for both text generation and detection, focusing on the creation of unfiltered tweets. To assess its detection capability, textual features are combined with tweet metadata, account information, and embedded media.

Several approaches focus on the extraction of linguistic features for detection. These methods can be integrated into supervised classification models, where the model learns to identify differences between human-written and generated texts based on these features.

This research proposes an approach based on the extraction of phraseological features, such as word and phrase frequency, sentence and paragraph length, lexical diversity (vocabulary variety), etc., as well as language usage features like connectors and punctuation marks. These features are used to train various models, offering a promising alternative for the detection of automatically generated texts through machine learning classification methods.

2 Method

We conducted a comprehensive analysis of existing methods that utilize techniques related to the extraction of phraseological features for identifying automatically generated texts, drawing from a variety of key publications in the field. Based on this analysis, we propose a novel methodology that leverages the extraction of several linguistic features, including phraseological patterns (PHR), the frequency of connector usage (CON), and the frequency of punctuation marks (PUN).

To implement this approach, we first compiled a language-specific list of the most used textual connectors in the dataset. Additionally, we identified the most frequently occurring punctuation marks across all the texts in the dataset. This step ensures that the features we extract are both language-dependent and reflective of general punctuation usage.

During the training phase, we performed a series of ablation experiments to assess the impact of each feature on model performance. Specifically, we conducted multiple trials in which we isolated and tested each feature individually. Additionally, we performed tests in which we excluded one feature at a time, leaving the remaining features to be combined. The objective of these tests was twofold: first, to determine which specific feature had the most significant impact on improving model performance, and second, to assess whether the combination of all features—either in full or as subsets—yielded the best results.

These extracted features were then used to train a variety of classification models. Once trained, the models were applied to make predictions on the test texts, allowing us to evaluate their performance in identifying whether a text was generated by an AI model or written by a human. By comparing the performance of different models, we were able to identify which model produced the most accurate predictions.

Figure 1 provides a visual representation of the proposed method, outlining the sequential phases of feature extraction, model training, prediction, and evaluation. This methodology demonstrates how the integration of phraseological and linguistic features, combined with advanced machine learning techniques, can contribute to more accurate and reliable detection of automatically generated texts.

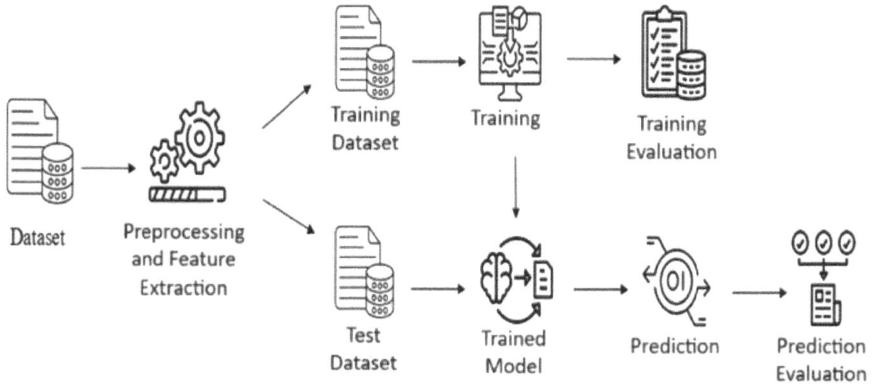

Fig. 1. Diagram of the proposed method

2.1 Dataset

The dataset used in this study is the one provided by [24] for the IberAuTexTification challenge of IberLEF 2024 [25], which focuses on identifying automatically generated texts in different languages (Spanish, Catalan, Basque, Galician, Portuguese, and English) from various models (GPT [26], LLaMA [27], Coral [28], Command [29], Falcon [30], MPT [31]). The dataset includes texts from different domains, such as news articles, reviews, emails, essays, and sources like Wikipedia, WikiHow, and tweets. Table 1 details the distribution of texts by language for training and testing.

Table 1. Dataset distribution by language

Language	Train	Test
Catalan	16474	8014
English	25773	10325
Spanish	22353	9110
Basque	13583	5520
Galician	11450	1392
Portuguese	20030	9004
Total	109663	43365

The target variable labels each text as "generated" or "human". Figure 2 shows a sample from the initial training dataset.

	id	text	label
0	15442	Es un tribunal de suprema instanza que forma p...	generated
1	26409	Això de tindrer la platgeta tant prou era un p...	human
2	12777	Doug mcadam es un científico estadista estadou...	generated
3	63467	El president de la generalitat, carles puigdem...	generated
4	41050	Traídas de francia, tan estrafalarias que una ...	generated
...	...	...	...
109658	76637	Bere burua egokitzen saiatu zuen, aurreko mome...	generated
109659	107183	Benquerida compañeira e amiga, para nós é moi ...	human
109660	144741	The irish president has signed the "long-await...	generated
109661	1202	Pedro de alvarado y contreras "tonatiuh" (bada...	human
109662	21996	Sure! wikipedia articles should be well-writte...	generated

109663 rows × 3 columns

Fig. 2. Sample of the initial training dataset

2.2 Preprocessing

The preprocessing included cleaning and removing emojis, mentions, hashtags, and URLs. A key step was encoding the target labels ("generated" as 0 and "human" as 1).

fastText [32] was used to automatically identify the language of the texts with a minimal error rate, which was manually corrected. The "one-hot encoder" technique was used to individually encode the languages, which were then incorporated as features for training. Figure 3 illustrates the preprocessed data.

	id	text	label	lang	ca	en	es	eu	gl	pt
0	15442	Es un tribunal de suprema instanza que forma p...	0	ca	1	0	0	0	0	0
1	26409	Aixó de tindrer la platgeta tant prou era un p...	1	ca	1	0	0	0	0	0
2	12777	Doug mcadam es un científico estadista estadou...	0	es	0	0	1	0	0	0
3	63467	El president de la generalitat, carles puigdem...	0	ca	1	0	0	0	0	0
4	41050	Traídas de francia, tan estrafalarias que una ...	0	es	0	0	1	0	0	0
...	...	...	...	...	...	...	...	...	...	...
109586	76637	Bere burua egokitzen saiatu zuen, aurreko mome...	0	eu	0	0	0	1	0	0
109587	107183	Benquerida compañeira e amiga, para nós é moi ...	1	gl	0	0	0	0	1	0
109588	144741	The irish president has signed the "long-await...	0	en	0	1	0	0	0	0
109589	1202	Pedro de alvarado y contreras "tonatiuh" (bada...	1	es	0	0	1	0	0	0
109590	21996	Sure! wikipedia articles should be well-writte...	0	en	0	1	0	0	0	0

109591 rows × 10 columns

Fig. 3. Preprocessed data

3 Text Features

Feature extraction focused on four aspects:

Phrasal Analysis. Average word length, average sentence length, sentence length standard deviation, average word count per paragraph, words per paragraph, sentence count per paragraph, lexical diversity of words.

Lexical Diversity. Measures the variety of unique words in the text relative to the total number of words. This metric helps capture the richness of the vocabulary used in the document.

Average Word Length. Calculates the average length of words in the text, providing an insight into the complexity of the language used. This can indicate the presence of more technical or complex vocabulary.

Average Sentence Length. Determines the average number of words per sentence in the text. This feature is indicative of sentence structure and can be useful in identifying the overall complexity of writing.

Sentence Length Standard Deviation. Represents the standard deviation of sentence lengths in the text. This measure reflects the variability in sentence structure, with a higher value indicating more variation in sentence lengths.

Average Words per Paragraph Length. Calculates the average number of words per paragraph in the text. This feature can highlight the typical length of paragraphs, which may vary between human-written and machine-generated text.

Variance in Words per Paragraph Length. Measures the variability in the number of words per paragraph in the text. Higher variance may suggest a less structured or more inconsistent style, which can be a distinguishing factor between human and automatically generated writing.

Document Length. Indicates the total number of words or characters in the entire document. This feature provides a basic overview of the length of the text, which can be relevant for identifying patterns typical of longer or shorter documents.

Punctuation Analysis. Frequency of punctuation usage.

Connector Analysis. Frequency of connector usage by language.

The frequency of punctuation marks and connectors was determined based on a list obtained from authoritative sources, such as the Real Academia Española (RAE) [33] for the Spanish language, as well as other language-specific analyses for the other mentioned languages.

The feature analysis provided a detailed representation of the texts, aiding the identification of patterns for the learning of the models used. Figures 4 and 5 show a sample of the extracted features from the texts.

	id	text	label	lang	ca	en	es	eu	gl	pt	...	,	;	:	¡	!
0	73360	Desde el nacimiento de sus hijos, los padres h...	0	es	0	0	1	0	0	0	...	12.145749	0.000000	0.000000	0.0	0.000000
1	78[illegible]81	olha gata! só passei por aqui pra te desejar ...	1	pt	0	0	0	0	0	1	...	8.333333	0.000000	0.000000	0.0	8.333333
2	16620	Meu bebê amou, podemos levar a cadeirinha pra ...	1	pt	0	0	0	0	0	1	...	12.121212	0.000000	0.000000	0.0	24.242424
3	52768	Nigel farage said he did not declare the £450,...	1	en	0	1	0	0	0	0	...	7.103825	0.000000	0.546448	0.0	0.000000
4	36737	Esta obra de marcrista é unha revelación cruda...	0	gl	0	0	0	0	1	0	...	5.612722	0.000000	0.000000	0.0	0.000000
...	...	...	...	...	...	...	...	...	...	...	...	...	...	...	...	...
87723	3822	I have been a loyal customer for quite a while...	0	en	0	1	0	0	0	0	...	8.353222	0.000000	0.000000	0.0	0.000000
87724	74048	Era dia claro, não sei onde estávamos; via ao ...	1	pt	0	0	0	0	0	1	...	17.704518	4.884005	0.000000	0.0	0.000000
87725	63468	Y, sara, tú encárgate de que todo el personal ...	1	es	0	0	1	0	0	0	...	6.071119	0.000000	0.000000	0.0	0.000000
87726	117639	Ainda não instalei mas ela é realmente linda !...	1	pt	0	0	0	0	0	1	...	0.000000	0.000000	0.000000	0.0	20.000000
87727	1187	¿qué haces, luci? ¿qué haces? le preguntaba co...	0	es	0	0	1	0	0	0	...	18.430034	0.000000	0.000000	0.0	0.000000

87728 rows × 590 columns

Fig. 4. Sample of punctuation usage in each text

	id	text	label	MeanWordLen	LexicalDiversity	MeanSentenceLen	StdevSentenceLen	MeanParagraphLen	DocumentLen	WordsPerParagraph	SentencesPerParagraph
0	15442	Es un tribunal de suprema instanza que forma p...	0	5.012658	46.416382	26.333333	12.247449	237	1462	237	9
1	26409	Això de tindrer la platgeta tant prou era un p...	1	4.692308	100.000000	13.000000	0.000000	13	75	13	1
2	12777	Doug mcadam es un científico estadista estadou...	0	5.411429	52.261307	25.000000	11.722993	175	1138	175	7
3	63467	El president de la generalitat, carles puigdem...	0	5.090909	49.025974	24.000000	4.954337	264	1637	264	11
4	41050	Traídas de francia, tan estrafalarias que una ...	0	4.579545	58.333333	29.333333	7.408704	88	496	88	3
...	...	...	...	...	...	...	...	...	...	...	...
109658	76637	Bere burua egokitzen salatu zuen, aurreko mome...	0	5.840000	56.147541	11.764706	3.352425	200	1395	200	17
109659	107183	Benquerida compañeira e amiga, para nós é moi ...	1	4.460000	81.481481	16.666667	7.760298	50	274	50	3
109660	144741	The irish president has signed the "long-await...	0	4.754342	40.000000	23.705882	8.803507	403	2359	403	17
109661	1202	Pedro de alvarado y contreras "tonatiuh" (bada...	1	4.685990	42.126789	103.500000	60.168513	414	2423	414	4
109662	21996	Sure! wikipedia articles should be well-writte...	0	4.679348	42.533937	19.631579	11.183684	373	2152	368	19

Fig. 5. Sample of Linguistic Features in Each Tex

4 Experimentation

Several tests were conducted during the experimentation phase, combining the extracted features, as well as ablation tests, to determine which features had the greatest influence on model learning and to verify which model achieved the best results.

4.1 Training

Three classification models were selected for training, based on their success in previous experiments [34]: Random Forest (RF) [35], Extreme Gradient Boosting (XGB) [20], and Multi-Layer Perceptron (MLP) [36]. An ensemble model (denoted as ENS) was created by combining these models using a "soft" voting classifier technique. The preprocessed dataset was split into 80–20 partitions for training and testing, respectively.

The training phase was evaluated using 10-fold cross-validation, which provided the metrics for all models, including the ensemble.

4.2 Prediction

Prediction was carried out using all models with the test dataset, from which the features were also extracted. These predictions were thoroughly evaluated by comparing them with the target labels, which allowed us to assess the effectiveness of the method in detecting automatically generated texts. This analysis helped validate the performance of each model and its ability to accurately distinguish between generated and human-written texts.

5 Results

The metrics used, along with their results, for evaluating the training process are detailed in Table 2. This table provides a clear view of the different indicators used to measure model performance and training effectiveness.

Table 2. Training results

Model	Accuracy	Precision	Recall	F1-Weighted
RF	0.882526	0.882141	0.881604	0.882485
MLP	0.851624	0.851407	0.850702	0.851539
XGB	0.865120	0.864283	0.865053	0.865192
ENS	0.887234	0.886716	0.886707	0.887232

Based on the tests, it was found that the "ensemble" model performed best across all metrics, followed by Random Forest. MLP had the lowest performance among all models. Figure 6 provides a graphical representation of the model performances, highlighting the ensemble model in red as the best.

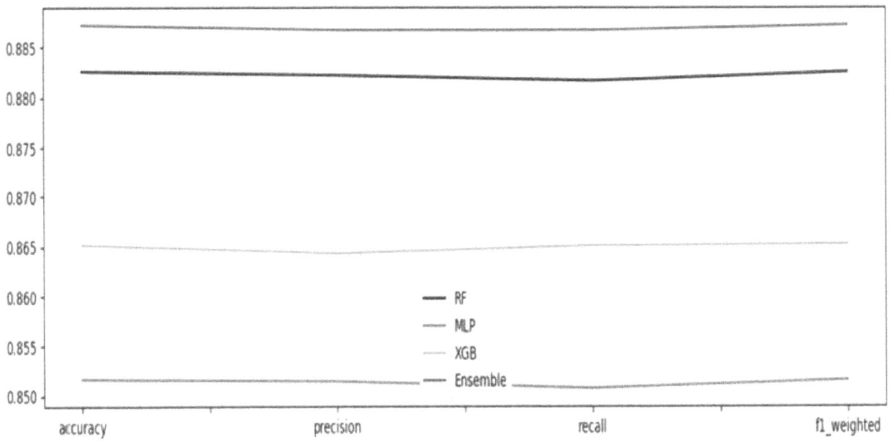

Fig. 6. Graphical representation of model performance

Table 3 shows the results of the ablation tests for feature combination. On one hand, the results are presented using only a specific set of features (ONLY), and on the other hand, excluding that feature (WITHOUT) to use the combination of the remaining ones. It can be observed that combining all the features (ALL) yields the best results.

Table 3. Ablation test results for feature combinations

	ONLY				WITHOUT			
		precision	recall	f1-w		precision	recall	f1-w
PHR	RF	0.809781	0.809921	0.809695	RF	0.861744	0.861761	0.861611
	MLP	0.802902	0.802307	0.801516	MLP	0.808922	0.807186	0.805999
	XGB	0.797181	0.797201	0.796738	XGB	0.837352	0.837414	0.837374
	ENS	0.814060	0.814070	0.813710	ENS	0.856403	0.855925	0.855541
PUN	RF	0.734500	0.734874	0.734487	RF	0.876029	0.876032	0.875911
	MLP	0.717074	0.714312	0.710494	MLP	0.842046	0.842110	0.842067
	XGB	0.726320	0.725163	0.722780	XGB	0.850543	0.850362	0.850422
	ENS	0.743730	0.742944	0.741235	ENS	0.876871	0.876898	0.876881
CON	RF	0.740018	0.740300	0.739551	RF	0.885484	0.885469	0.885476
	MLP	0.735476	0.734920	0.735102	MLP	0.867318	0.866548	0.866135
	XGB	0.711609	0.712078	0.71114	XGB	0.864521	0.864451	0.864479
	ENS	0.750195	0.750376	0.750258	ENS	0.883555	0.883600	0.883556
ALL	RF	0.886205	0.886244	0.886184				
	MLP	0.860437	0.860484	0.860359				
	XGB	0.865662	0.865408	0.865478				
	ENS	**0.889947**	**0.889983**	**0.889954**				

6 Discussion

By combining all the extracted features, the models' performance in prediction was significantly improved, with the ensemble model standing out. Using the features together, the ensemble model achieved an F1 score of 0.889954, followed by the Random Forest model with an F1 of 0.886184. When considering only the phraseological and punctuation features—excluding connectors—Random Forest maintained solid performance, achieving an F1 score of 0.885476.

During the training phase, it was consistently observed that both the ensemble model and Random Forest outperformed the other evaluated models. Among all the tests conducted, the Multi-Layer Perceptron (MLP) model exhibited the lowest performance, though still within an acceptable range.

Ablation tests allowed for the determination of the weight of each feature in the models' learning and prediction processes, as well as the models' performance in each specific test.

Limitations that may affect the model's performance are mainly due to the presence of texts in different languages. In this context, we use language-specific features such as textual connectors for each language.

The use of advanced techniques such as voting classification and cross-validation was crucial in the construction of the ensemble model and the thorough evaluation of performance during training. These techniques not only optimized the models but also ensured the stability and robustness of the results, reflecting a comprehensive approach to the detection of automatically generated texts.

7 Conclusions

A machine learning-based method using classification models was developed to identify whether a text has been written by a human or generated automatically. The ensemble model, combining the strengths of Random Forest, XGBoost, and Multi-Layer Perceptron, demonstrated superior performance, achieving the highest accuracy in classifying automatically generated texts. Among the individual models, Random Forest outperformed the others in terms of key performance metrics, such as accuracy, precision, and F1 score, establishing itself as a particularly powerful tool for this task.

The approach incorporated a comprehensive set of linguistic features, including phraseological elements, frequency of punctuation marks, and the use of textual connectors. These features allowed the identification of distinctive patterns that differentiated human-authored texts from machine-generated ones. The analysis revealed that the combination of these features was pivotal in enhancing the model's performance, as each feature provided complementary insights into the characteristics of the texts. Specifically, the integration of phraseological patterns, punctuation usage, and connector frequency contributed to the robustness of the classification models and was fundamental to their optimization during training.

The results highlight that traditional classification models, when combined with well-chosen linguistic features, are highly effective in distinguishing between human and AI-generated texts. The ensemble model was able to leverage the full potential of these features, leading to a significant improvement in the model's accuracy. Furthermore, the results from feature ablation tests confirmed that the use of all the extracted features—rather than relying on individual features—was essential for obtaining the best classification outcomes.

To overcome the limitations arising from texts in different languages, future experiments could explore using language-independent text features, such as the use of n-grams for TF-IDF and bag of words.

This study provides compelling evidence that a combination of linguistic features, alongside advanced machine learning techniques, is a promising direction for improving the detection of automatically generated texts. The findings suggest that future research could focus on refining these models further, exploring additional features, and testing the method across diverse datasets and languages. As AI-generated texts continue to evolve in complexity, these approaches will play an increasingly critical role in ensuring the accurate identification of machine-generated content.

References

1. Holmes, W., Hui, Z., Miao, F., Ronghuai, H., et al AI and education: guidance for policymakers
2. Manjarrés-Betancur, R.A., Echeverri-Torres, M.M.: Asistente virtual académico utilizando tecnologías cognitivas de procesamiento de lengua-je natural. Revista Politécnica **16**, 85–95 (2020). https://doi.org/10.33571/rpolitec.v16n31a7

3. Gehrmann, S., Strobelt, H., Rush, A.M.: GLTR: statistical detection and visualization of generated text (2019)
4. Opara, C.: StyloAI: Distinguishing AI-generated content with sty-lometric analysis (2024)
5. Schuster, T., Schuster, R., Shah, D.J., Barzilay, R.: The limitations of stylometry for detecting machine-generated fake news (2020). https://doi.org/10.1162/COLI
6. Wang, H., Li, J., Li, Z.: AI-Generated text detection and classification based on bert deep learning algorithm
7. Devlin, J., Chang, M-.W., Lee, K., et al.: BERT: Pre-training of deep bidirec-tional transformers for language understanding
8. Valiaiev, D.: Detection of machine-generated text: literature survey (2023)
9. Peters, M.E., Neumann, M., Iyyer, M., et al.: Deep contextualized word representations (2018)
10. Yang, Z., Dai, Z., Yang, Y., et al.: XLNet: generalized autoregressive pretraining for language understanding (2019)
11. Zeng, W., Ren, X., Su, T., et al.: PanGu-α: Large-scale auto-regressive pretrained chinese language models with auto-parallel computation (2021)
12. Espin-Riofrio, C., Ortiz-Zambrano, J., Montejo-Ráez, A.: SINAI at autexTification in IberLEF 2023: combining all layer embeddings for automatically generated texts (2023)
13. Nguyen, D., Naing, K.M.N., Joshi, A.: Stacking the Odds: transformer-based ensemble for AI-generated text detection (2023)
14. Vaswani, A., Brain, G., Shazeer, N., et al.: Attention is all you need
15. Lan, Z., Chen, M., Goodman, S., et al.: ALBERT: a lite bert for self-supervised learning of language representations (2019)
16. Clark, K., Luong, M-.T., Le, Q.V.: Manning CD (2020) ELECTRA: pre-training text encoders as discriminators rather than generators
17. Liu, Y., Ott, M., Goyal, N., et al.: RoBERTa: a robustly optimized bert pretraining approach (2019)
18. Rodriguez, J.D., Hay, T., Gros, D., et al.: Cross-domain detection of GPT-2-Generated technical text
19. Canhasi, E., Shijaku, R.: ChatGPT generated text detection. https://doi.org/10.13140/RG.2.2.21317.52960
20. Chen, T., Guestrin, C.: XGBoost: A scalable tree boosting system. In: Proceedings of the ACM SIGKDD International Conference on Knowledge Discovery and Data Mining. Association for Computing Ma-chinery, pp 785–794 (2016)
21. Jones, K.S.: A statistical interpretation of term specificity and its application in retrieval. J. Docum. **60**, 11–21 (2004)
22. Mitchell, E., Lee, Y., Khazatsky, A., et al.: DetectGPT: zero-shot ma-chine-generated text detection using probability curvature (2023)
23. Tourille, J., Sow, B., Popescu, A.: Automatic detection of bot-generated tweets. In: Proceedings of the 1st International Workshop on Mul-timedia AI against Disinformation (MAD '22), June 27, 2022, Newark, NJ, USA 1:44–51 (2022). https://doi.org/10.1145/3512732.3533584ï
24. González, J.Á., Sarvazyan, A.M., Franco-Salvador, M., et al.: IberAuTe-xTification (test dataset) (1.0.0). Zenodo (2024). https://doi.org/10.5281/zenodo.11034382. Accessed 17 Jul 2024
25. Chiruzzo, L., Jiménez-Zafra, S., Rangel, F.: IberLEF. In Proceedings of the Iberian Languages Evaluation Forum (IberLEF 2024), co-located with the 40th Conference of the Spanish Society for Natural Language Pro-cessing (SEPLN 2024), CEUR-WS.org (2024)
26. Openai, A.R., Openai, K.N., Openai, T.S., Openai, I.S.: Improving language un-derstanding by generative pre-training
27. Touvron, H., Lavril, T., Izacard, G., et al.: LLaMA: open and efficient foundation language models (2023)

28. Mckay C (2023) Cohere Unveils Coral, An Enterprise-Focused Genera-tive AI Assistant. https://www.maginative.com/article/cohere-unveils-coral-an-enterprise-focused-generative-ai-assistant/ Accessed 13 Aug 2024
29. Wang, P., Zeng, F., Qian, Y.: A Survey on deep learning-based spatio-temporal action detection (2023)
30. Wei, H., Chen, Z.: Improving generalization of image captioning with unsupervised prompt learning (2023)
31. Meyer, L.A., Romero, S., Bertoli, G., et al.: How effective is multifactor authentication at deterring cyberattacks? (2023)
32. Joulin, A., Grave, E., Bojanowski, P., et al.: Fasttext.Zip: Compressing Text Classification Models
33. RAE (2010) signos ortográficos | Diccionario panhispánico de dudas | RAE - ASALE. Real Academia Española
34. Espin-Riofrio, C., Murillo-Cepeda, V., García-Zambrano, D., et al.: News categorisation based on pre-trained transformer models. In: Pro-ceedings of the LACCEI international Multi-conference for Engineering, Education and Technology. Latin American and Caribbean Consortium of Engineering Institutions (2023)
35. Breiman, L.: Random Forests (2001)
36. Olmedo, M.T.C., Paegelow, M., Mas, J.F., Escobar, F.: Geomatic ap-proaches for modeling land change scenarios. An introduction. In: Lec-ture Notes in Geoinformation and Cartography. Springer Science and Business Media Deutschland GmbH, pp 1–8 (2018)

Polyglot Persistence in Heterogeneous NoSQL Database Systems with Python

Diana Martinez-Mosquera(✉), Rosa Navarrete, Lorena Recalde, and Andres Andrade-Cabrera

Escuela Politécnica Nacional, Quito, Ecuador
diana.martinez@epn.edu.ec

Abstract. Modern applications often require functionalities that single types of database systems cannot adequately fulfil, prompting the use of multiple types of databases for effective data management. Polyglot persistence enables the integration of various data storage technologies within a single application, leveraging the strengths of each system. This approach, however, introduces complexities in design and implementation, increasing programming complexity and necessitating knowledge of multiple languages. This article presents a practical method for achieving application-coordinated polyglot persistence across key-value, column-oriented, and document-oriented NoSQL databases, specifically focusing on Redis, Cassandra, and MongoDB, using Python. Our proposed three-layer architecture enhances data management and analytics by utilizing Jupyter Notebooks for interactive applications and employing Python libraries for orchestration, integrating specialized NoSQL databases. We encountered specific challenges, such as memory overload in Cassandra during complex query operations, which highlights the limitations in scalability under certain conditions. Additionally, our findings indicate significant variations in query execution times, with MongoDB demonstrating the fastest responses and Cassandra showing delays when handling complex queries. Using the SSB from TPC-H with a dataset of 6,000,000 entries, we evaluated loading times and query execution performance. This study aims to serve as a comprehensive guide for researchers and industry professionals seeking to implement a unified interface across heterogeneous NoSQL engines, providing insights into both the potentials and hurdles of polyglot persistence.

Keywords: databases · heterogeneous · NoSQL · polyglot persistence · python · SSB dataset evaluation · NoSQL database performance · polyglot database systems

1 Introduction

Modern applications often require functionalities beyond what single types of database systems cannot provide, necessitating the use of multiple types of

F. R. Narváez et al. (Eds.): SmartTech-IC 2024, CCIS 2392, pp. 390–404, 2026.
https://doi.org/10.1007/978-3-031-98287-3_28

databases for effective data management. Polyglot persistence allows the integration of various data storage technologies within a single application, leveraging each system's strengths to handle different types of data and operations [1,2]. However, this approach introduces significant complexities in design and implementation, increasing programming challenges and necessitating knowledge of multiple programming languages [1–4].

The use of application-coordinated polyglot persistence, microservices, polyglot database services, and multi-model databases are various architectural approaches each presenting unique challenges and benefits. For example, microservices simplify development by allowing individual services to use their own databases, supported by modern technologies like IaaS and PaaS, which aid in scaling and management [5]. Conversely, polyglot database services provide a unified API to manage data across different systems, simplifying interactions but potentially limiting flexibility [5].

Multi-model databases attempt to integrate multiple data models into a single system, efficient in some operations but limited in others, such as record updates [6–8]. Furthermore, the landscape of database technologies comprises Relational, NoSQL, and NewSQL databases, each catering to specific requirements ranging from complex transactions in financial systems to horizontal scalability in social networks [9,10]. NoSQL is generally considered the more mature technology compared to NewSQL [11]. NoSQL technologies, such as MongoDB [12], Redis [13], and Cassandra [14], offer solutions for managing large volumes of diverse data types and are widely adopted by leading tech companies [15–17].

This study focuses on polyglot persistence using these NoSQL solutions, aiming to streamline data management across different systems through a unified interface or standardized query language, utilizing Python for its widespread adoption in data analytics [18,19] . By leveraging the Star Schema Benchmark (SSB), based on the Transaction Processing Performance Council H (TPC-H) Benchmark, this research evaluates the performance of loading and querying data across heterogeneous NoSQL databases, proposing an efficient approach for their management and integration [20,21].

The remainder of this paper is organized as follows. First, the Related Work examines various research proposals. Second, the Materials and Methods section details the process of using Python to load and query heterogeneous NoSQL databases. Third, the Results section showcases the achievable queries and their execution times. Finally, the last section presents the conclusions and outlines future work.

2 Related Work

Research on polyglot persistence has explored various database combinations to address the diverse needs of modern applications. Studies like those by Landuyit et al. (2023) using the UniBench framework have demonstrated that the efficacy of polyglot and multi-model databases varies based on data types, queries, and underlying data models, with specific databases like ArangoDB and OrientDB excelling in document, graph, and key-value storage but lacking support for column-oriented databases and Python [22].

Further analysis by Kulkarni et al. (2020) have compared these approaches in handling unstructured datasets, revealing scenarios where each model provides distinct advantages [7]. Additionally, the application of polyglot persistence in sectors like healthcare has proven effective in reducing latency and improving performance as demonstrated by studies such as those by Prasad (2013) and Kaur (2015), who highlight the benefits of tailored database solutions for healthcare data management [23,24].

Integrations of relational and NoSQL databases have also shown performance improvements in big data applications, supporting efficient data migration and system integration [25]. However, the implementation of polyglot persistence faces challenges such as the need for multiple programming languages and maintaining system consistency [3]. This study builds on these findings by offering a unified approach using Python to manage NoSQL databases, aiming to simplify the polyglot persistence model while enhancing database interaction and processing capabilities in diverse application domains.

While Prasad and Sha (2013) underscore the benefits of polyglot persistence in healthcare Information Systems (HIS), emphasizing tailored database solutions to enhance performance and reduce latency [23], our study expands on these concepts by integrating a broader range of NoSQL technologies. Unlike the referenced study, which may focus on specific implementations or configurations, our approach employs a novel integration of diverse database technologies, leveraging modern programming frameworks to address and solve unique data storage challenges inherent in healthcare systems. Our methodology distinguishes itself by focusing on the synergy between multiple NoSQL databases through Python, which facilitates a more dynamic and adaptable system architecture, better suited to the evolving demands of modern healthcare data analytics.

Recent studies in 2023 and 2024 have further explored the capabilities of NoSQL databases in handling extensive data sets. Khan et al. (2023) provide an in-depth comparison of HBase and Cassandra, using the YCSB benchmark to evaluate performance in cloud environments. Their findings highlight the robust scalability of Cassandra, which aligns with our observations of improved performance in polyglot configurations [26]. Similarly, Mohan et al. (2024) assess MongoDB, Redis, Kudu, and ArangoDB across various OLAP workloads. Their benchmarking approach, utilizing Koalabench, underscores the need for diverse data processing strategies, reinforcing our polyglot persistence model's flexibility and efficiency [27]. These contemporary analyses not only validate our approach but also underscore the ongoing evolution of database technologies in supporting complex analytical tasks.

Ye et al. (2024) contrast polyglot persistence strategies with multi-model databases, focusing on their application in multithreaded operations and complex query handling. Their benchmark, MDBench, is particularly insightful for our work, as it emphasizes the superior adaptability and resource efficiency of polyglot systems in diverse scenarios [28]. Incorporating these findings, our study suggests that polyglot persistence, especially when integrated with Python and Jupyter, offers significant advantages over traditional multi-model databases in terms of development flexibility and operational efficiency.

3 Materials and Methods

Research [29] suggests that an effective and viable approach to implementing polyglot persistence involves using a unified query language. In this context, Python libraries stand out as a universal solution due to their seamless integration with various NoSQL databases such as Redis, Cassandra, and MongoDB. Python not only facilitates interaction with multiple technologies but also simplifies data management in complex architectures, providing invaluable flexibility in polyglot environments.

As mentioned in Sect. 1: Introduction, this approach emphasizes Application-Coordinated Polyglot Persistence, where Python acts as a central interface to directly manage connections and operations across multiple NoSQL databases. This methodology enables flexibility and control in environments where different databases excel at specific tasks, such as MongoDB for document-based storage, Redis for in-memory key-value operations, and Cassandra for handling high-throughput distributed data.

By using Python as the orchestration layer, this approach eliminates the need for complex middleware, ensuring that the application can natively interact with each database using libraries that are tailored to their respective APIs. Moreover, Python's versatility allows developers to customize and scale their solutions without being locked into a single database paradigm, offering significant advantages in heterogeneous data environments. The hardware architecture supporting this implementation comprises (Table 1):

Table 1. Hardware Architecture Supporting the Implementation

Component	Specification
Operating System	Ubuntu 20.04.5 LTS x86_64
CPU	Intel Xeon E5-2690 v3 (10 cores) @ 2.593 GHz
Memory	5496 MiB/32111 MiB
Python Version	Python 3.11.7

This proposed polyglot persistence approach integrates an architecture, where three layers are highlighted:

1. Application: Includes Jupyter Notebooks that provide an interactive and collaborative environment for data exploration, visualization, and analysis. By incorporating notebooks into the persistence system, users can execute ad-hoc queries, perform analytics, and derive insights directly within the same platform.

2. Python Orchestration: Python libraries are used here to manage connections and operations between the application and the databases.
3. NoSQL Database: Includes MongoDB (for document-based storage), Redis (for in-memory key-value operations), and Cassandra (for high-throughput distributed data).

Figure 1 illustrates the detailed layers and their connections between a Jupyter Notebook, Python, and various NoSQL databases, highlighting the ports and libraries used for querying.

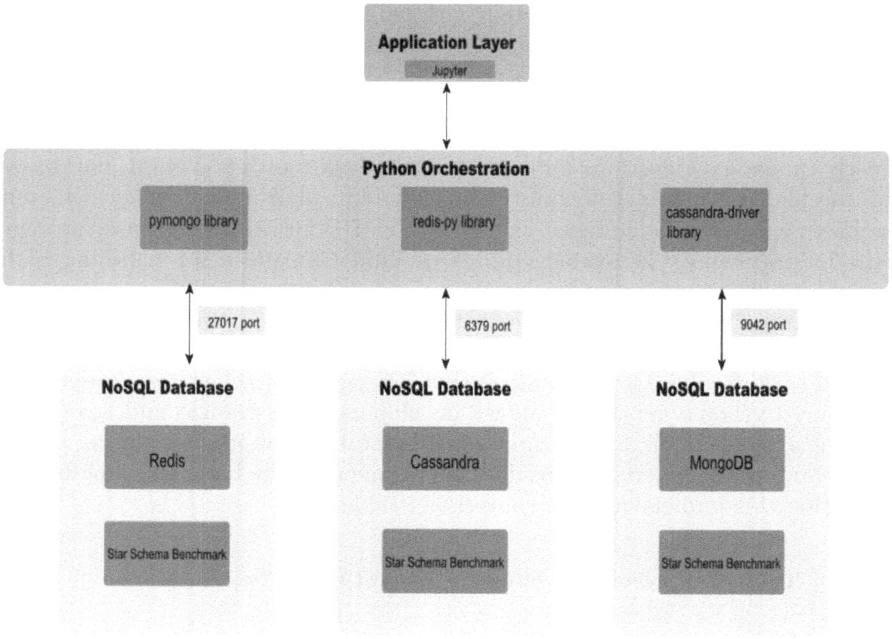

Fig. 1. Connection from Jupyter Notebook to NoSQL databases for queries

This setup allows users to perform ad-hoc queries, execute analytics, and generate insights directly within the Jupyter Notebook environment, leveraging the flexibility and capabilities of multiple NoSQL databases. The seamless integration illustrated in the Fig. 1 highlights the power of using a unified platform for polyglot persistence.

The SSB from TPC-H [20], a trusted tool for Big Data assessments widely used for research and industry, was employed to test the persistence layer with a dataset of 6,000,000 entries. This large-scale benchmark ensures that the system's scalability and performance under significant load are rigorously evaluated, reinforcing the reliability of the polyglot persistence strategy.

Our selection of databases and operations for evaluation was strategically informed by the goals of optimizing data warehousing performance, as emphasized by the SSB [20]. The SSB focuses on operations that minimize disk access and simplify queries through schema denormalization. Accordingly, we chose MongoDB for its efficiency in document storage, Redis for its rapid data retrieval capabilities, and Cassandra for its robustness in distributed data management. These databases were specifically selected for their proven performance in handling large datasets and their alignment with the SSB principles, which are crucial for assessing the efficiency and scalability of polyglot persistence systems. By adopting these principles, we aim to minimize disk access and simplify the processing of queries in our system, enhancing overall performance and manageability.

3.1 Preprocessing the SSB Dataset

The SSB script from TPC-H generates five tables: customer, dates, lineorder, part, and supplier in TBL format, which can be interpreted as CSV after adding the appropriate headers, as shown in Fig. 2.

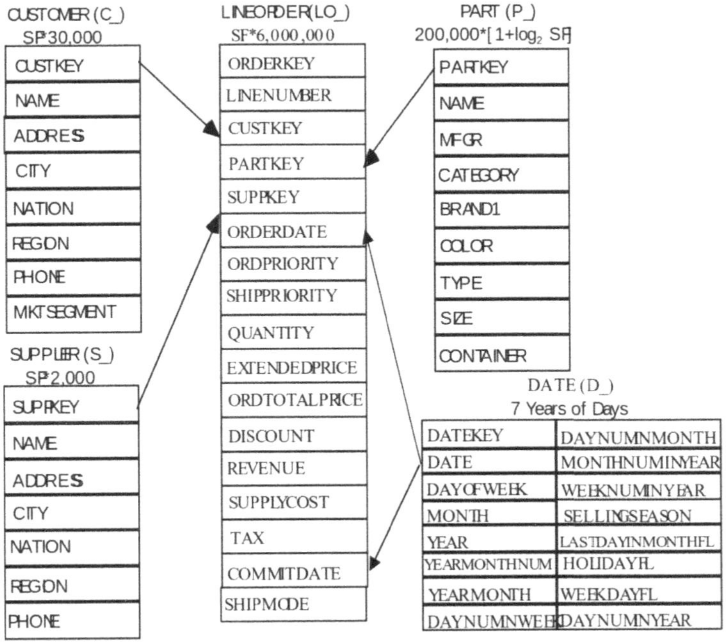

Fig. 2. SSB Schema [20]

To load the tables into various types of NoSQL databases, it was necessary to parse the TBL files into a JSON file. Figure 3 provides a visual representation of the workflow of the Python script used to read data from the TBL files, construct nested JSON objects, and write them to a single JSON file. The steps include:

- Loading CSV Data: The script loads the data from TBL files and creates dictionaries for quick lookups.
- Constructing JSON Objects: Each record from the lineorder.tbl file is enriched with related data from the other tables (customer, part, supplier, and dates).
- Writing to JSON: The enriched data are written into a file (all_lineorders.json) as a JSON array. The final file size was approximately 9.4ĠB due to the redundancy in the data.

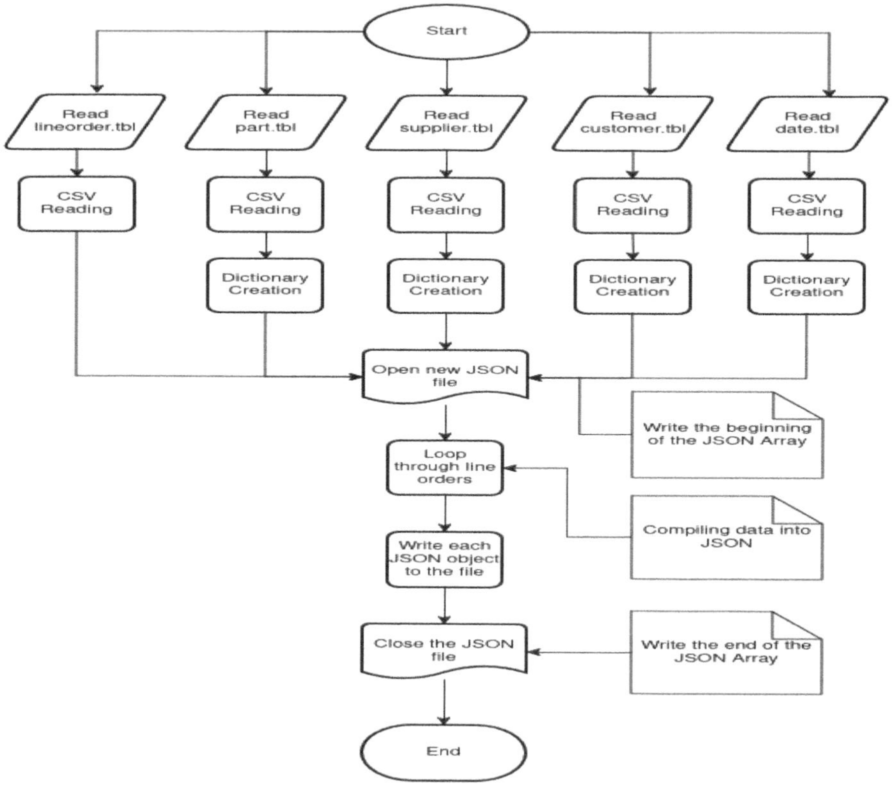

Fig. 3. Flowchart of the Python script workflow

3.2 Loading SSB Data into NoSQL Databases

Once the JSON files were obtained, they were loaded into the NoSQL databases Redis, Cassandra, and MongoDB. For Redis, the JSON file is opened and read line by line, skipping the initial formatting characters. Each line is then parsed into a JSON object suitable for storage in Redis. The data is stored with unique keys in Redis, where each key corresponds to a specific record, incremented with a counter.

To optimize the process, unnecessary characters like trailing commas are removed before storing the data. Throughout the loading process, a progress bar tracks the number of lines processed, and at the end, the total time taken and the number of JSON objects loaded are displayed to provide an overview of the operation's performance. The full implementation of the JSON loading process to Redis with Python can be found in the respective GitHub repository [30].

For Cassandra, the file is read line by line, skipping unnecessary formatting, and each line is converted into a Python dictionary representing the data. The nested fields in the JSON format are converted to match Cassandra's User Defined Types (UDTs) to ensure compatibility with the database schema. For each record, a custom INSERT query is constructed, mapping each field from the JSON data to its corresponding column in Cassandra. The query is then executed to insert the data into the database.

Throughout the process, unnecessary characters, such as commas, are removed to maintain proper formatting. This approach ensures that the data is correctly formatted and inserted into the appropriate fields within the Cassandra table. For the detailed code and steps on how to load JSON files into Cassandra using Python, refer to the repository on GitHub [31].

For MongoFB, a connection is established with a specific database and collection first. Then, the JSON file is opened and read line by line, converting each line into an object suitable for storage. The data is temporarily accumulated in batches, and once a certain batch size is reached, it is inserted into the database.

This optimizes performance by reducing the number of individual insertion operations. Finally, any remaining data is loaded to ensure everything is stored properly. For the complete algorithm and implementation details on how to load JSONs into MongoDB using Python in a Jupyter notebook, please refer to the corresponding code hosted on GitHub [32].

3.3 Querying NoSQL Data from Jupyter

We conducted a series of operations from Jupyter to assess the performance of the polyglot persistence system across various NoSQL databases. These operations included common database interactions such as search, insert, update, delete, and complex aggregations to analyze data.

Operations executed on MongoDB involved basic Create, Read, Update, Delete (CRUD) functionalities and complex queries like aggregation to calculate revenues from specific orders. These operations demonstrate MongoDB's capabilities in handling both simple document retrievals and more complex, conditional data manipulations. The Python code used for querying MongoDB in Jupyter is available in the repository [32].

For Redis, we performed actions on JSON objects, including retrieval, creation, modification, and deletion. Additional operations included indexing JSON documents and performing aggregations based on specific conditions. These tasks highlight Redis's strength in managing JSON data structures quickly and efficiently. The implementation details can be found in the repository [30].

For Cassandra, the queries focused on basic data retrieval, data insertion, and updates, alongside more complex queries such as data filtering and counting rows based on specific conditions. These operations underscore Cassandra's use in scenarios requiring robust data handling capabilities. The complete querying script is available in the repository [31].

These operations, executed from a Jupyter Notebook environment using Python, underline the versatility and challenges of managing data across different NoSQL databases and provide a practical perspective on polyglot persistence implementations. Our methodology provides a dynamic integration strategy that leverages Jupyter Notebooks and Python libraries to enhance data accessibility and real-time analytics capabilities.

4 Results

As mentioned earlier, a dataset comprising 6,000,000 entries from the SSB benchmark was utilized. Table 2 presents the data loading times for these entries across various NoSQL databases and is depicted graphically in Fig. 4.

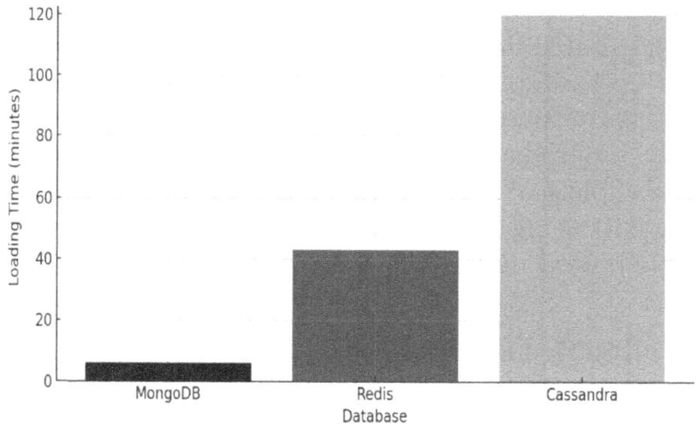

Fig. 4. Data Loading Process Durations across MongoDB, Redis, and Cassandra.

Based on the data loading times summarized in Table 2, significant performance differences between the NoSQL databases are evident. MongoDB exhibited the fastest loading time, requiring approximately 6 min to process the dataset. In contrast, Redis took around 43 min, while Cassandra demonstrated the longest loading time of approximately 2 h. Despite these varying loading times, the results confirm the feasibility of a polyglot persistence approach, enabling the use of Python to load data into these different types of NoSQL databases.

Tables 3, 4, and 5 present the executed queries along with their corresponding execution times for Redis, Cassandra, and MongoDB, respectively.

Table 2. Data Loading Process Durations

Database	Loading Time
MongoDB	˜6 min
Redis	˜43 min
Cassandra	˜2 h

For every type of database, queries were generally executed within seconds; however, queries involving complex aggregations displayed more distinct behaviours, as shown in Fig. 5.

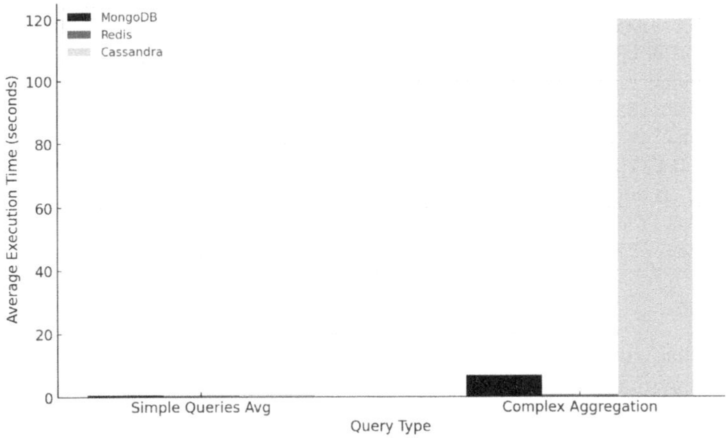

Fig. 5. Comparison of Average Execution Times for Simple and Complex Queries across MongoDB, Redis, and Cassandra.

For MongoDB, although the query was straightforward, it required approximately six seconds to produce results. In the case of Redis, it was necessary first to create an index and then execute the aggregate function, which took about 0.5 s. This efficiency stems from Redis needing to load all JSONs into memory initially, leading to 100% of memory usage during the operation.

Conversely, Cassandra presented several limitations: while it supports the SUM function for aggregation, it cannot perform multiplication between two columns, nor can it access columns within nested JSON structures. Additionally,

Table 3. Redis Commands in Python for Jupyter

Query	Execution Time (s)
client.json_get(‘lineitem:1743’, path=‘.L_ORDERKEY’)	< 1 (s)
client.json_get(‘lineitem:1743’)	< 1 (s)
client.json_set(‘newkey’, ‘.’, ‘{‘‘field’’: ‘‘value’’}’)	< 1 (s)
client.json_set(‘lineitem:1743’, path=‘.L_ORDERKEY’, value=‘‘new_value’’)	< 1 (s)
client.delete(‘lineitem:1743’)	< 1 (s)
client.json_mget(‘lineitem:1743’, paths=[‘.L_SHIPMODE’, ‘.L_SHIPINSTRUCT’])	< 1 (s)
client.exists(‘lineitem:1743’)	< 1 (s)
client.ft().create_index(‘lineorder-idx’, ‘ON JSON PREFIX 1 ‘‘lineorder:’’ SCHEMA $.LO_ORDERKEY AS LO_ORDERKEY NUMERIC $.LO_EXTENDEDPRICE AS LO_EXTENDEDPRICE NUMERIC $.LO_DISCOUNT AS LO_DISCOUNT NUMERIC $.LO_ORDERDATE.D_YEAR AS D_YEAR TEXT $.LO_QUANTITY AS LO_QUANTITY NUMERIC’)	< 1 (s)
client.ft().aggregate(‘lineorder-idx’, ‘*’, load=[‘@LO_ORDERKEY’, ‘@LO_EXTENDEDPRICE’, ‘@LO_DISCOUNT’, ‘@D_YEAR’, ‘@LO_QUANTITY’], filters=[‘@D_YEAR == ‘‘1993’’’, ‘@LO_DISCOUNT >= 1 && @LO_DISCOUNT <= 3’, ‘@LO_QUANTITY < 25’], apply=[‘@LO_EXTENDEDPRICE * @LO_DISCOUNT AS revenue’], group_by={‘properties’: [‘@D_YEAR’], ‘reducers’: [(‘SUM’, 1, ‘revenue’, ‘total_revenue’)]})	0.51 (s)

despite only utilizing directly accessible table columns, the aggregation process in Cassandra was unsuccessful. It exceeded the system's available memory capacity and consequently failed to execute.

4.1 Performance Analysis of Complex Queries

The evaluation highlighted significant challenges associated with complex queries, particularly within Cassandra. During stress tests involving heavy aggregation queries, Cassandra experienced notable failures, primarily due to memory overloads when handling large datasets. Detailed analysis indicates that Cassandra's memory heap could not efficiently manage the sudden spike in data retrieval demands, leading to prolonged response times and eventual system crashes.

Table 4. Cassandra Commands in Python for Jupyter

Query	Execution Time (s)
session.execute(‘‘SELECT field FROM table WHERE key = ‘value’ ALLOW FILTERING’’)	< 1 (s)
session.execute(‘‘SELECT * FROM table WHERE key = ‘value’ ALLOW FILTERING’’)	< 1 (s)
session.execute(‘‘INSERT INTO table (key, field, value) VALUES (‘key’, ‘field’, ‘value’)’’	< 1 (s)
session.execute(‘‘UPDATE table SET field = ‘value’ WHERE key = ‘value’’’)	< 1 (s)
session.execute(‘‘DELETE FROM table WHERE key = ‘value’’’)	< 1 (s)
session.execute(‘‘SELECT field1, field2 FROM table WHERE key = ‘value’ ALLOW FILTERING’’)	< 1 (s)
session.execute(‘‘SELECT COUNT(*) FROM table WHERE key = ‘value’ ALLOW FILTERING’’).one()[0] > 0	< 1 (s)
session.execute(‘‘SELECT SUM(lo_extendedprice * lo_discount) as revenue FROM json.lineorders WHERE lo_discount >= 1 AND lo_discount <= 3 AND lo_quantity < 25 AND lo_orderdate.d_year = 1993 ALLOW FILTERING;’’)	MEMORY OVERLOADED

Table 5. MongoDB in Python for Jupyter

Query	Execution Time (s)
collection.find({ ‘key’: ‘value’ }, { ‘field’: 1 })	< 1 (s)
collection.find({ ‘key’: ‘value’ })	< 1 (s)
collection.insert_one({ ‘key’: key, ‘field’: field, ‘value’: value })	< 1 (s)
collection.update_one({ ‘key’: ‘value’ }, { ‘$set’: { ‘field’: ‘value’ } })	< 1 (s)
collection.delete_one({ ‘key’: ‘value’ })	< 1 (s)
collection.find({ ‘key’: ‘value’ }, { ‘field1’: 1, ‘field2’: 1 })	< 1 (s)
collection.find({ ‘key’: ‘value’ }).limit(1).count() > 0	< 1 (s)
collection.aggregate([{ $match: { ‘‘LO_ORDERDATE.D_YEAR’’: ‘‘1993’’, ‘‘LO_DISCOUNT’’: {$gte: 1, $lte: 3}, ‘‘LO_QUANTITY’’: {$gte: 25} }}, {$group: {_id: null, revenue: {$sum: {$multiply: [‘‘$LO_EXTENDEDPRICE’’, ‘‘$LO_DISCOUNT’’]}}}}]);	6.75 (s)

5 Conclusions and Future Work

The adoption of various NoSQL databases can enhance an organization's ability to address specific use cases. This article presented a practical approach to achieving Application-coordinated polyglot persistence across key-value, column-oriented, and document-oriented, NoSQL databases, highlighting Redis, Cassandra, and MongoDB as prominent NoSQL solutions, using Python as a unified query language within the Jupyter environment.

This proposed polyglot persistence approach combines a three-layer architecture that enhances data management and analytics across heterogeneous NoSQL databases. By leveraging Jupyter Notebooks for an interactive application layer, employing Python libraries for seamless orchestration, and utilizing specialized NoSQL databases for distinct data storage needs.

Utilizing the SSB from TPC-H with a dataset of 6,000,000 entries, we evaluated both the loading times and query execution times. MongoDB exhibited the best performance in terms of loading times. For simple queries, such as searching, inserting, updating, and deleting, all databases achieved execution times of less than one second. However, for aggregation queries, Redis demonstrated the shortest execution time, while Cassandra faced memory overload issues that hindered the execution of complex aggregations.

Our study aims to serve as a guide for researchers and industry professionals in utilizing a unified interface across various NoSQL database engines. The insights gathered on query performance and resource utilization highlight opportunities for optimization, especially concerning complex queries involving aggregations and advanced operations.

Future work will tackle the identified gaps in our research. We aim to enhance data synchronization and transactional integrity across diverse databases to address specific technical challenges and ensure consistent data handling. A refined experimental design will be implemented, incorporating rigorous statistical analyses to robustly compare database performance under varied conditions. This effort will extend to addressing Cassandra's memory overload issues and will broaden our study's scientific quality by offering deeper empirical insights and a thorough discussion of our findings. Moreover, we plan to expand our approach to include graph-oriented databases like Neo4J, broadening the applicability and flexibility of our polyglot persistence solutions.

References

1. Singhal, H., Saxena, A., Mittal, N., Dabas, C., Kaur, P.: PolyGlot persistence for microservices-based applications. Int. J. Inf. Technol. Syst. Approach **14**, 17–32 (2021). https://doi.org/10.4018/IJITSA.2021010102
2. Lajam, O., Mohammed, S.: Revisiting polyglot persistence: from principles to practice. Int. J. Adv. Comput. Sci. Appl. **12**, 872–882 (2022). https://doi.org/10.14569/ijacsa.2022.0130599
3. Deka, G.C.: NoSQL polyglot persistence. Adv. Comput. **109**, 357–390 (2018). https://doi.org/10.1016/BS.ADCOM.2017.08.003

4. Zdepski, C., Bini, T., Matos, S.: An Approach for Modeling Polyglot Persistence, pp. 120–126 (2018). https://doi.org/10.5220/0006684901200126
5. Gessert, F., Wingerath, W., Ritter, N., Gessert, F., Wingerath, W., Ritter, N.: Polyglot persistence in data management. In: Fast and Scalable Cloud Data Management, pp. 149–174 (2020)
6. Oliveira, F., Cura, L.: Performance evaluation of NoSQL multi-model data stores in polyglot persistence applications. In: International Database Engineering & Applications Symposium (2016). https://doi.org/10.1145/2938503.2938518
7. Kulkarni, N.: Review of Nosql databases and performance comparison between multimodel and polyglot persistence approach. Int. J. Sci. Technol. Res. **9**, 1522–1527 (2020)
8. Messaoudi, C., Fissoune, R., Badir, H.: A performance evaluation of NoSQL databases to manage proteomics data. Int. J. Data Min. Bioinform. **21**, 70–89 (2018). https://doi.org/10.1504/IJDMB.2018.10016724
9. Meier, A. and Kaufmann, M. (2019). SQL & NoSQL databases, pp. 123-142
10. Őzsu, M. T., Valduriez, P., Őzsu, M.T., Valduriez, P.: NoSQL, NewSQL, and polystores. In: Principles of Distributed Database Systems, pp. 519–558 (2020)
11. Chung, J., Chang, M., Phang, S.: Recent advances and benchmarking of NewSQL for OLTP and OLAP in the big data age. In: 2023 IEEE 13th Symposium on Computer Applications & Industrial Electronics (ISCAIE), pp. 168–174 (2023). https://doi.org/10.1109/ISCAIE57739.2023.10164996
12. MongoDB. MongoDB Atlas - Cloud Database Service. https://www.mongodb.com/es/. Accessed 14 July 2024
13. Redis. Redis - Open-source, in-memory data structure store. Available at: https://redis.io/es/. Accessed: July 14, 2024
14. Apache Cassandra. Apache Cassandra - Highly scalable distributed database. https://cassandra.apache.org/_/index.html. Accessed 14 July 2024
15. Martinez-Mosquera, D., Navarrete, R., Luján-Mora, S., Recalde, L., Andrade-Cabrera, A.: Integrating OLAP with NoSQL databases in big data environments: systematic mapping. Big Data Cogn. Comput. **8**, 64 (2024). https://doi.org/10.3390/bdcc8060064
16. Arshad, M., Brohi, M.N., Soomro, T.R., Ghazal, T.M., Alzoubi, H.M., Alshurideh, M.: Nosql: future of bigdata analytics characteristics and comparison with rdbms. In: The Effect of Information Technology on Business and Marketing Intelligence Systems, pp. 1927–1951 (2023)
17. Martinez-Mosquera, D., Navarrete, R., Lujan-Mora, S.: Modeling and management big data in databases–a systematic literature review. Sustainability **12**, 634 (2020). https://doi.org/10.3390/su12020634
18. Statista. Worldwide Developer Survey - Most Used Programming Languages 2024. https://www.statista.com/statistics/793628/worldwide-developer-survey-most-used-languages/. Accessed 14 July 2024
19. Santana, L., Mello, R.: A middleware for polyglot persistence of RDF data into NoSQL databases. In: 2019 IEEE 20th International Conference on Information Reuse and Integration for Data Science (IRI), pp. 237–244 (2019). https://doi.org/10.1109/IRI.2019.00046
20. O'Neil, P., O'Neil, B., Chen, X.: 1. Star Schema Based on TPC-H'. Accessed 14 July 2024
21. TPC Benchmark^{TM}H (TPC-H). TPC-H Benchmark - Decision Support Benchmark. https://www.tpc.org/tpch/. Accessed 14 July 2024

22. Landuyt, D., Benaouda, J., Reniers, V., Rafique, A., Joosen, W.: A comparative performance evaluation of multi-model NoSQL databases and polyglot persistence. In: Proceedings of the 38th ACM/SIGAPP Symposium on Applied Computing (2023). https://doi.org/10.1145/3555776.3577645
23. Prasad, S., Sha, M.: NextGen data persistence pattern in healthcare: polyglot persistence. In: 2013 Fourth International Conference On Computing, Communications And Networking Technologies (ICCCNT), pp. 1–8 (2013)
24. Kaur, K., Rani, R.: A smart polyglot solution for big data in healthcare. IT Prof. **17**, 48–55 (2015). https://doi.org/10.1109/MITP.2015.111
25. Pokorný, J.: Integration of relational and NoSQL databases. Vietnam. J. Comput. Sci. **6**, 389–405 (2018). https://doi.org/10.1007/978-3-319-75420-8_4
26. Khan, N., Ahmad, N., Sharma, N., Niazy, M.: A study of performance evaluation and comparison of NoSQL database choosing for big data: HBase and cassandra using YCSB. IOSR J. Comput. Eng. **6**, 1–12 (2023)
27. Mohan, R., Kanmani, R., Ganesan, K., Ramasubramanian, N.: Evaluating NoSQL databases for OLAP workloads: a benchmarking study of MongoDB, Redis, Kudu and ArangoDB (2024)
28. Ye, F., Sheng, X., Nedjah, N., Sun, J., Zhang, P.: A benchmark for performance evaluation of a multi-model database vs. polyglot persistence. J. Datab. Manag. (JDM) **34**, 1–20 (2023)
29. Khine, P.P., Wang, Z.: A review of polyglot persistence in the big data world. Information **10**(4), 141 (2019). https://doi.org/10.3390/info10040141
30. Andrade-Cabrera, A.: Redis Scripts on GitHub. https://github.com/andr3slelouch/PolyglotPersistenceNoSQLScripts/blob/main/RedisDBScripts.md. Accessed 23 Nov 2024
31. Andrade-Cabrera, A.: Cassandra Scripts on GitHub. https://github.com/andr3slelouch/PolyglotPersistenceNoSQLScripts/blob/main/CassandraDBScripts.md. Accessed 23 Nov 2024
32. Andrade-Cabrera, A.: MongoDB Scripts on GitHub. https://github.com/andr3slelouch/PolyglotPersistenceNoSQLScripts/blob/main/MongoDBScripts.md. Accessed 23 Nov 2024

An Intelligent Mobile Navigation System for Visually Impaired People Using Computer Vision and Deep Learning for Multi-label Classification in Park Environments

Remigio Hurtado(✉) and Christian Delgado

Universidad Politécnica Salesiana, Cuenca, Ecuador
rhurtadoo@ups.edu.ec
http://www.ups.edu.ec

Abstract. Individuals with visual impairments encounter considerable difficulties when navigating outdoor environments, where limited accessible information can lead to accidents or discomfort. To address this issue, an intelligent system is proposed, utilizing deep learning and computer vision to assist users with visual impairments in safely navigating park environments. The system adopts a structured machine learning approach, comprising phases of data preprocessing, model training, and evaluation. The dataset used in this study, though small and self-collected, includes images of common park elements such as benches, trees, and vehicles. This limited dataset presents an opportunity to explore transfer learning and fine-tuning techniques to improve model performance. Several convolutional neural network (CNN) models are evaluated using classification metrics like Hamming Loss, which is especially important for multi-label classification tasks. Results show promising accuracy and effective performance in real-world applications. Future work will aim to expand the dataset, include additional object categories, and enhance system adaptability by integrating advanced sensory inputs and incorporating user feedback.

Keywords: Deep Learning · Multi-Label Classification · Assistive Technology · Computer Vision · Visually Impaired Navigation · Transfer Learning

1 Introduction

The **problem** of visual impairment affects a significant portion of the global population, leading to challenges in navigating and interacting with environments such as parks [1]. Visually impaired individuals often struggle with recognizing signs, avoiding obstacles, and finding their way through public spaces. These difficulties not only impact their ability to enjoy recreational areas but also affect their overall quality of life [2]. Addressing these challenges requires innovative

F. R. Narváez et al. (Eds.): SmartTech-IC 2024, CCIS 2392, pp. 405–419, 2026.
https://doi.org/10.1007/978-3-031-98287-3_29

solutions that leverage modern technologies to enhance accessibility and independence. The **purpose** of this research is to support visually impaired individuals by developing an intelligent system deployed in a mobile application that leverages machine learning (ML) and computer vision technologies. This system aims to enhance accessibility and independence by providing assistance and navigation support. Specifically, it focuses on recognizing signage, detecting obstacles, and guiding users through park environments. The approach integrates advanced computer vision techniques and deep learning models to interpret visual data and deliver actionable feedback to users. Our method adheres to the CRISP-DM (Cross-Industry Standard Process for Data Mining) framework, which structures the development process into phases including data understanding, data preparation, modeling, evaluation, and deployment [3,4]. This structured approach ensures systematic development and deployment of the predictive models. The core of our system relies on convolutional neural networks (CNNs) and other deep learning techniques, optimized for high performance in recognizing and classifying visual information [5,6].

Machine learning, a subset of artificial intelligence, involves training algorithms to recognize patterns and make decisions based on data. In classification problems, models are trained to categorize input data into predefined classes. There are three primary types of classification problems: binary, multiclass, and multi-label classification. Binary classification involves distinguishing between two classes, where each data point belongs to one of the two categories. Multiclass classification involves multiple classes, but each data point belongs to a single class. Multi-label classification, which is particularly relevant to our application, allows data points to be assigned multiple labels simultaneously. For example, an image of a park might contain a bench, a dog, and a car, each of which needs to be identified and classified. This capability is crucial for creating a comprehensive assistive tool that can accurately describe a variety of objects and features present in the environment [7,8]. In the context of supporting visually impaired individuals, machine learning plays a critical role in enhancing safety and accessibility within park environments. The identification and classification of key elements such as vehicles, trees, people, and benches are essential to providing a comprehensive and reliable navigation aid. Vehicles pose significant safety concerns, and detecting their presence and movement is crucial for avoiding traffic-related hazards. Trees, serving as natural landmarks, assist in spatial orientation and provide sensory enrichment, while the detection of other park visitors facilitates social interaction and helps prevent collisions. Benches offer resting points, essential for planning routes and ensuring a comfortable park experience. By focusing on these four categories—vehicles, trees, people, and benches—this initial work aims to address the most immediate needs of visually impaired users, ensuring that the developed application provides targeted and effective assistance in navigating park environments.

The development process includes several key steps:

- **Model Development:** Techniques such as deep learning and transfer learning are employed to enhance model performance, especially given the challenges of limited training data [9].

- **Optimization and Evaluation:** The models are fine-tuned and evaluated to ensure they provide reliable predictions. Hyperparameter optimization is performed to achieve the best possible performance.
- **Deployment:** The trained models are integrated into a mobile application that provides feedback to users, helping them navigate and interact with their environment more effectively.

The results obtained from our experiments demonstrate the effectiveness of the application in improving park navigation for visually impaired users. The main contributions of this research are:

- **Intelligent Navigation Support:** Development of a mobile application that provides assistance and navigation support in park environments.
- **Intelligent Image Classification System:** Development of a system that captures images and classifies them using machine learning, with integration for voice command activation and text-to-speech feedback for enhanced accessibility.
- **Systematic Methodology:** Application of the CRISP-DM approach for structured development, including comprehensive phases for data collection, preparation, model training, and evaluation.
- **Advanced Multi-Label Classification Algorithm:** Design and implementation of a multi-label classification algorithm using CNNs and Transfer Learning, with a focus on adapting pre-trained models for improved accuracy and handling of self-collected datasets.
- **Performance Optimization:** Demonstration of significant performance improvements through Transfer Learning with MobileNet, including enhanced accuracy and reduced Hamming Loss, illustrating the benefits of transfer learning and fine-tuning for small or specialized datasets.

The remainder of this paper is organized as follows: Sect. 2 reviews related work in the field. Section 3 describes the developed intelligent system using machine learning, detailing the framework, methodology, and general algorithm. Section 4 presents a comprehensive analysis of the results, including dataset description, optimization parameters, and evaluation of the models. Finally, Sect. 5 concludes the paper with a summary of findings and future directions.

2 Related Work

This section presents related work closely aligned with the approach of integrating machine learning with mobile applications designed to assist visually impaired individuals. Various studies have explored methodologies, frameworks, and case studies that are pertinent to this research.

In [10], the development of deep learning models is described, focusing on the introduction of convolutional neural networks (CNNs) as a pivotal point in the evolution of artificial intelligence, particularly for unmanned vehicles. Computer vision technology, which is integral to our work, has been extensively applied across various fields, including facial recognition, autonomous driving, medical image recognition, and voice recognition. The study [11] proposes determining optimal placement considerations to improve detection accuracy in people recognition using background subtraction, cascade detectors, and optical flow techniques. This work highlights the importance of environmental characterization in enhancing detection performance, which is relevant to our context of identifying objects and people in park environments.

In [12], a mobile application is developed utilizing deep learning-based computer vision techniques to determine the fermentation level of cocoa beans. The application achieves an accuracy of 86%, demonstrating the potential of mobile applications powered by ML for decision-making in specialized tasks, akin to our goal of assisting visually impaired users. The study [9] conducts research on artificial intelligence and deep learning to identify plant species. The study concludes that increasing training time, enhancing image quality, or expanding the training dataset can significantly improve recognition accuracy, which parallels our use of transfer learning to enhance model performance despite limited training data. In [13] the detection and post-processing of inscriptions and coats of arms on building facades using neural networks and computer vision is addressed. The YOLOv5 model is found to be suitable for real-time detection tasks, achieving satisfactory accuracy.This study underscores the importance of selecting appropriate ML models for specific tasks, a principle applied here by choosing CNNs for the intended application.

The study [14] presents a mobile application that employs deep learning for text recognition, aimed at supporting individuals with visual impairments. The work demonstrates the feasibility of deploying ML models on mobile devices to assist in everyday tasks, which directly aligns with our research objective. Similarly, in [15], a CNN-based system is developed for object detection to aid visually impaired users in indoor navigation. The study highlights the use of mobile platforms for real-time object detection.

Another relevant work is [16], which explores the application of CNNs for the recognition of Braille characters in images, supporting visually impaired individuals in reading and writing tasks. This study emphasizes the adaptability of CNNs for tasks requiring high precision, which is relevant to our application in recognizing park features. In [17], the development of a mobile application for obstacle detection using CNNs is described, focusing on providing auditory feedback to visually impaired users. The study demonstrates the effectiveness of combining deep learning with auditory interfaces, a strategy also employed to deliver feedback to users. Finally, the research [18] presents a mobile application for real-time text recognition and translation, aimed at assisting visually impaired individuals in reading.

Our approach introduces an innovative integration of machine learning with mobile applications, specifically designed to enhance park accessibility for visually impaired users. Unlike previous work that primarily focuses on either indoor navigation or specialized tasks, our system addresses outdoor environments by recognizing a wide range of objects—vehicles, trees, people, and benches—that are crucial for safe and enjoyable park experiences. Additionally, our use of transfer learning and multi-label classification distinguishes our work by improving accuracy and efficiency in detecting multiple relevant objects simultaneously. This combination of techniques ensures a robust and practical solution that directly addresses the unique challenges faced by visually impaired individuals in park settings.

3 Intelligent System

In this section, the developed intelligent system for capturing images and classifying them using machine learning is presented, as shown in the high-level view of the system elements and their interactions in Fig. 1. The system can be triggered either by a voice command or by pressing one of the volume buttons on the device. Once the image is captured, the application consumes a machine learning service to classify the image with multiple labels, identifying all elements present in the image. The prediction is then transformed into a user-friendly format, initially as text and subsequently converted into speech for audio feedback to the user. The machine learning method follows the CRISP-DM approach [4] to ensure systematic and comprehensive development. The method is designed to provide robust and accurate image classification, facilitating user interaction through intuitive voice commands and responsive feedback systems, based on advanced machine learning techniques such as transfer learning and fine-tuning. The machine learning method is detailed through its different phases in Fig. 2.

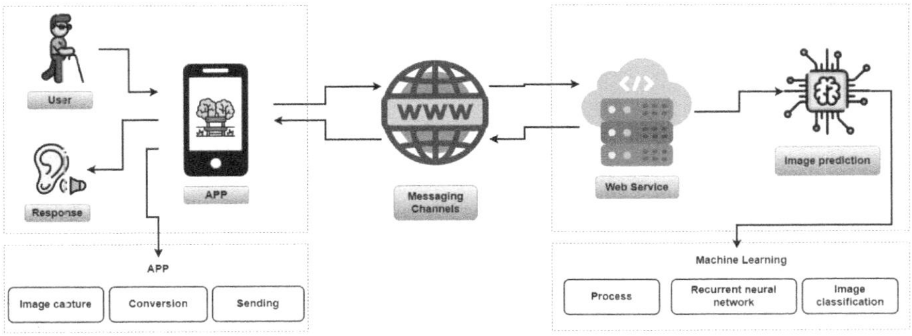

Fig. 1. Intelligent system for capturing images and classifying them using machine learning.

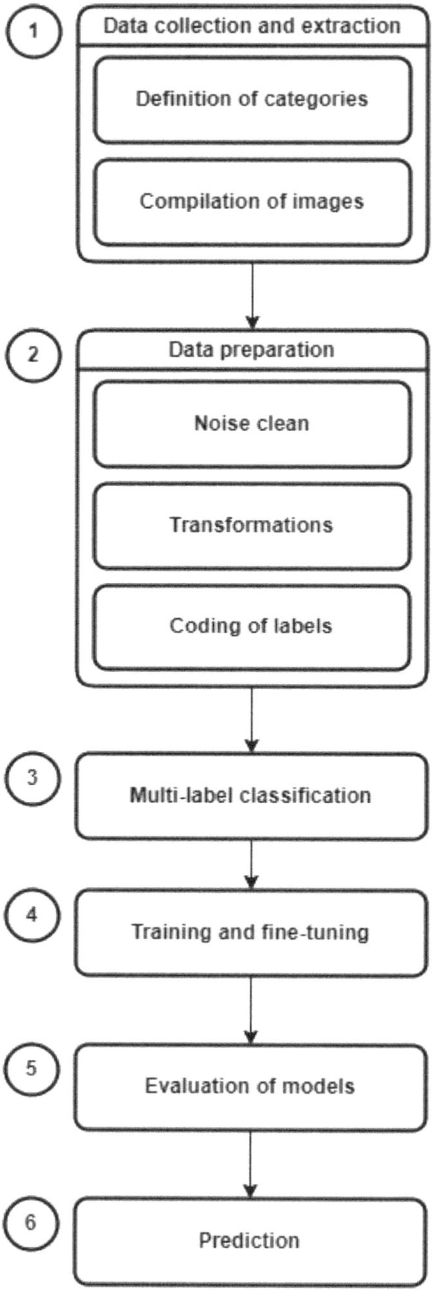

Fig. 2. Proposed method following CRISP-DM process for image capture and classification.

The general algorithm formalizes the method applied to our specific problem (Table 1).

Table 1. General algorithm following the CRISP-DM methodology for multi-label classification

General Algorithm
Input: Image Dataset
Phase 1: Data Collection and Extraction
1. Define categories for image classification.
2. Compile images from various sources.
Phase 2: Data Preparation
3. Apply noise reduction techniques to enhance image quality.
4. Resize images to ensure uniform dimensions.
5. Generate and encode labels using folder names with a multi-label binarizer.
Phase 3: Multi-label Classification
6. Build CNN model with convolutional and pooling layers.
7. Flatten output from the convolutional layers for dense layer processing.
8. Add dense layers, including a 64-neuron layer, for classification.
9. Utilize sigmoid activation in the output layer for multi-label classification.
10. Incorporate transfer learning by importing a pre-trained model.
11. Add custom layers to adapt the pre-trained model for the specific task.
Phase 4: Model Training and Fine-Tuning
12. Train the model on the dataset, adjusting weights to minimize loss.
13. Fine-tune the model's hyperparameters and layers to optimize performance.
Phase 5: Model Evaluation
14. Evaluate model performance using accuracy, precision, recall, and F1 score.
15. Identify the most accurate model for deployment.
Phase 6: Prediction
16. Test the model with new images to identify detected objects.
Output: Image Labels

To understand the proposed algorithm for multi-label image classification, it's helpful to follow its six main phases, each crucial for the effectiveness of the final model.

The **first phase** focuses on data collection and initial organization. The dataset used in this study is proprietary and was self-collected specifically for the purpose of this research. Images were captured in real-world park environments, focusing on the four key classes required for recognition in the proposed system: vehicles, trees, people, and benches. These images were taken using a standard camera device, with a careful selection of diverse locations and scenes to ensure the dataset represented a variety of environmental conditions typically encountered in park settings. Given the scope of the project and available resources, the dataset is relatively small, consisting of several hundred images per class. This limitation posed a challenge in training machine learning models, as deep learning algorithms generally require large, labeled datasets to perform well. To mitigate the impact of this limited dataset, the approach of transfer learning was adopted. By leveraging pre-trained models on large, general-purpose datasets (such as ImageNet), the model was able to learn general features that could be transferred to the specific task of classifying park-related objects. Transfer learning allows the model to benefit from the knowledge learned in other domains, making it more effective even with a small, domain-specific dataset. This dataset was carefully labeled according to the categories of interest: vehicles, trees, people, and benches. Each image was manually annotated, ensuring that the classification labels accurately reflected the objects present in the image. The images were then processed and prepared for training, following a structured data preparation pipeline that included noise reduction, resizing, and label encoding.

In the **second phase**, the goal is to prepare the data for effective processing. Noise reduction techniques are applied to enhance the image quality by removing unwanted elements while preserving essential details. Following this, images are resized to ensure uniform dimensions, facilitating subsequent processing. Finally, labels are generated and encoded based on the folder names in the dataset, using a multi-label binarizer to appropriately classify and store images for training and testing. The **third phase** is crucial for building the classification model. It starts with designing a Convolutional Neural Network (CNN) architecture that includes convolutional layers to extract important features from the images, such as edges and textures. Pooling layers then reduce the dimensionality of the feature maps, maintaining essential information while improving the model's efficiency. The output from the convolutional layers is flattened into a 1D vector for processing in dense layers, which include a layer with 64 neurons to capture complex patterns necessary for classification. The final output layer uses a sigmoid activation function for multi-label classification. Additionally, transfer learning techniques are applied by importing a pre-trained model and adding custom layers to tailor it to the specific dataset and classification task, thereby enhancing classification accuracy.

Once the model is designed, the **training phase** begins with the dataset. During this phase, the model's weights are adjusted to minimize loss and improve performance. Following this, hyperparameters and additional layers are fine-tuned to optimize the model's accuracy and generalization, ensuring it can effectively handle new data. The **evaluation phase** is essential for measuring the model's effectiveness. Metrics such as accuracy, precision, recall, and F1 score are used to assess performance, allowing for the identification of the most accurate model for deployment and ensuring reliable predictions. Finally, in the **prediction phase**, the model is tested with new images to identify which objects from the defined categories are detected. This step verifies the model's ability to handle unseen data and evaluates its performance in real-world conditions. Each of these phases is interdependent and contributes to the overall success of the algorithm, ensuring that the multi-label classification model is effective and accurate in labeling images.

4 Experiments, Results and Discussion

This section provides a comprehensive analysis of the results obtained, including a description of the dataset, quality measures, optimization parameters of the predictive models, and model evaluation. The discussion covers the optimization of hyperparameters and the evaluation through quality measures, with particular emphasis on the superior performance of the CNN model that incorporates transfer learning and fine-tuning to adapt to the self-collected dataset. The functionality and effectiveness of the implemented system are highlighted, concluding with a demonstration of the model's ability to perform multi-label classification on images.

The experimental design follows the methodology and architectures outlined in [5,19,20]. The dataset used in this study is described in Table 2, highlighting its characteristics.

Table 2. Description of the dataset

Dataset	Number of Images	Dimensions	Labels
self-collected dataset	152	(128×128)	tree car bench person

The optimization parameters of the predictive models are presented in Table 3, which shows the values of the hyperparameters. These parameters are adjusted using techniques such as Grid Search and Random Search to find the optimal settings for each method. The quality metrics employed in this analysis include Precision, Recall, Accuracy and F1-Score, which are commonly used in machine learning, particularly for classification tasks. In addition, the Hamming Loss quality metric has been used to provide a way to evaluate the performance of a multi-label classification model. The study also employs the K-Folds cross-validation technique with K set to 20, which ensures a robust evaluation of the methods and mitigates the risk of overfitting. The optimal parameter values for the models are highlighted in Table 3.

$$\text{Precision} = \frac{TP}{TP + FP} \tag{1}$$

$$\text{Recall} = \frac{TP}{TP + FN} \tag{2}$$

$$\text{F1-Score} = \frac{2 \cdot (\text{Precision} \cdot \text{Recall})}{\text{Precision} + \text{Recall}} \tag{3}$$

$$\text{Accuracy} = \frac{TP + TN}{TP + TN + FP + FN} \tag{4}$$

$$\text{Hamming Loss} = \frac{1}{N \times L} \sum_{i=1}^{N} \sum_{j=1}^{L} I(y_{ij} \neq \hat{y}_{ij}) \tag{5}$$

where TP, TN, FP, and FN are the numbers of True Positives, True Negatives, False Positives, and False Negatives, respectively. **Hamming Loss** is a measure of the fraction of incorrect labels to the total number of labels. It calculates the proportion of misclassified labels in multi-label classification problems. Specifically, it is defined as:

- N: The number of samples.
- L: The number of labels per sample.
- y_{ij}: The true label for sample i and label j.
- $\hat{y}_{ij}$: The predicted label for sample i and label j.
- $I(\cdot)$: An indicator function that equals 1 if the condition inside is true and 0 otherwise.

The Hamming Loss provides a way to evaluate the performance of a multi-label classification model by considering the fraction of labels that are incorrectly predicted across all labels and samples. The lower the Hamming Loss, the better the model's performance in accurately predicting labels.

The analysis reveals a significant enhancement in model performance when applying Transfer Learning with MobileNet, compared to a standard CNN approach. As shown in Table 4, the CNN with MobileNet achieved an impressive accuracy of 0.812, a notable increase from the 0.419 accuracy obtained with the traditional CNN model. This improvement is particularly valuable in the context of using self-collected datasets, which are typically smaller and less varied than standard datasets. Transfer Learning proves crucial for optimizing model performance with limited data. MobileNet, with its pre-trained weights and efficient architecture, adapts effectively to the specifics of our self-collected dataset. This adaptation is evident in the reduced Hamming Loss from 0.3145 to 0.125, demonstrating the model's superior ability to handle multi-label classification tasks with higher accuracy. Fine-tuning further enhances this advantage by allowing the model to adjust its pre-trained features to the unique characteristics of the new dataset. This process ensures that the model can accommodate the specific nuances of the self-collected data, leading to more accurate and reliable predictions. Thus, the synergy of Transfer Learning and fine-tuning represents a robust strategy for overcoming the limitations of small or specialized datasets.

Table 3. Optimization parameters for CNN models

Model	Parameters
CNN (No Pre-training)	epochs: 10, 20, 30, **50**, 80, 100 batch size: 32, **64**, 128 optimizers: SGD, **Adam**, RMSProp functions: Sigmoid, Hyperbolic Tangent, **ReLU** **Activation:** Conv1: ReLU; Conv2: ReLU; Conv3: ReLU; Dense1: ReLU **Dropout:** Conv1: 0, 0.1, 0.2, **0.3**, 0.4; Dense1: 0, 0.1, **0.2**, 0.3 **Output Layer:** Dense Layer: **64** neurons; Activation: Sigmoid
CNN with Transfer Learning (MobileNet)	epochs: 10, 20, 30, **50**, 80, 100 batch size: 32, **64**, 128 optimizers: SGD, **Adam**, RMSProp functions: Sigmoid, Hyperbolic Tangent, **ReLU** **Activation:** MobileNet: **ReLU** **Dropout:** GlobalMaxPool: 0, 0.1, **0.2**, 0.3 **Output Layer:** Dense Layer: **64** neurons; Activation: Sigmoid

Table 4. Results with CNN models

Model	Accuracy	Precision	Recall	F1-Score	Hamming Loss
CNN	0.419	0.6825	0.6935	0.6880	0.3145
CNN (MobileNet)	0.812	0.875	0.875	0.875	0.125

The implementation of MobileNet through Transfer Learning in a Python-based web service, accessed via a mobile application, has resulted in a powerful and efficient solution for image description. This setup provides notable benefits in efficiency, accessibility, and scalability. However, it also necessitates meticulous management of security, network latency, and continuous model updates. The robust web service and accessible mobile application collaborate effectively to enhance user experience and make a meaningful impact on individuals with visual impairments.

The most relevant outcome of this implementation is illustrated in Fig. 3. The figure demonstrates how the application, powered by the model, successfully identifies and classifies three elements: a person, a bench, and a tree. This functionality not only establishes a solid foundation for image description and support for visually impaired users but also opens avenues for future improvements. The system is designed to integrate additional images, develop new personalized services, and continually enhance accessibility and user experience. Future developments will emphasize incorporating new models, expanding fea-

Fig. 3. Demonstration of the application's performance using the MobileNet-based Transfer Learning model. The figure shows the successful identification and classification of three objects in a test image: a person, a bench, and a tree. This result highlights the model's accuracy and effectiveness in image recognition.

tures, and fostering collaboration with communities and experts. This comprehensive approach will ensure the system's ongoing relevance and maximize its positive societal impact.

Despite the advancements made in the development of this navigation system for visually impaired individuals, there are some technical limitations that need to be addressed to improve its performance and scalability in varied environments. Currently, the system is optimized to work in park environments, which present a specific set of visual characteristics. However, the variability in environmental conditions, such as terrain diversity (grass fields, paved paths, gravel areas, etc.), weather conditions (rain, fog, direct sunlight), and the presence of different types of obstacles, could affect the model's accuracy. Additional effort is needed to adapt the system to other urban and rural settings with diverse visual and dynamic characteristics, such as traffic zones or areas with high population density. Moreover, the system's scalability at a global level or across different parks and cities requires expanding the dataset and integrating models that can generalize better in varied contexts, ensuring that model adaptation and performance are not compromised in environments with configurations or characteristics different from current park settings.

5 Conclusions

This work involves the development and implementation of an intelligent system based on deep learning and computer vision to assist visually impaired individuals in navigating park environments. Utilizing advanced multi-label classification techniques and transfer learning, the system demonstrates accurate identification of key environmental elements, such as vehicles, trees, people, and benches, providing contextual assistance to users. Following the CRISP-DM methodology, convolutional neural network models were systematically optimized and evaluated to maximize performance under limited data conditions. The results show significant improvements in accuracy and a reduction in Hamming Loss, underscoring the effectiveness of the techniques employed. Future developments will expand the system to cover additional object categories and enhance user-system interaction by integrating new sensory modalities and feedback mechanisms. Moreover, the scope of the system will be extended to assist individuals with various other conditions beyond visual impairment, including adults with low vision, individuals with mobility issues, and those with other disabilities that affect their ability to navigate and interact with outdoor environments. This expansion aims to improve the system's accessibility and functionality, enhancing independence and quality of life for a more diverse group of users. The integration of features such as voice-controlled navigation, haptic feedback for mobility challenges, and multi-modal interfaces tailored to different sensory impairments will ensure the system's flexibility and effectiveness across a wide range of real-world contexts.

Data Availibility Statement. Data used for training and validation of the models presented in this study are available upon request. Interested researchers can contact the corresponding author for details on accessing the dataset.

References

1. World Health Organization. Blindness and Visual Impairment. World Health Organization (2023). https://www.who.int/news-room/fact-sheets/detail/blindness-and-visual-impairment
2. Consejo Nacional para la Igualdad de Discapacidades. Estadísticas de Discapacidad. Consejo Nacional para la Igualdad de Discapacidades (2023). https://www.consejodiscapacidades.gob.ec/estadisticas-de-discapacidad
3. IBM Corporation. CRISP-DM Overview. IBM Corporation (2021). https://www.ibm.com/docs/es/spss-modeler/saas?topic=dm-crisp-help-overview
4. Wirth, R., Hipp, J.: CRISP-DM: towards a standard process model for data mining. In: Proceedings of the 4th International Conference on the Practical Applications of Knowledge Discovery and Data Mining, vol. 1 (2000)
5. Hurtado, R., Guzmán, S., Muñoz, A.: An architecture and a new deep learning method for head and neck cancer prognosis by analyzing serial positron emission tomography images. In: Conference on Cloud Computing, Big Data and Emerging Topics. Springer, Cham (2023). DOI: https://doi.org/10.1007/978-3-031-40942-4_10
6. Jara-Gavilanes, A., Hurtado-Ortiz, R., Guzmán-Ortiz, S.: Lung cancer detection using positron emission tomography images through convolutional and recurrent neural networks. In: 2023 XLIX Latin American Computer Conference (CLEI). IEEE (2023)
7. Dembczynski, K., et al.: On label dependence and loss minimization in multi-label classification. Mach. Learn. **88**(2), 209–233 (2012)
8. Herrera, F., Charte, F., Rivera, A.J., del Jesus, M.J.: Multilabel Classification. Springer, Cham (2016). https://doi.org/10.1007/978-3-319-41111-8
9. Guo, J.: Research on artificial intelligence: deep learning to identify plant species. In: Proceedings of the International Conference on Machine Learning and Knowledge Engineering (2022). https://doi.org/10.1109/MLKE55170.2022.00017.
10. Qiu, H., et al.: Development of deep learning models and CNN introduction. J. Artif. Intell. Res. **45**, 123–135 (2021)
11. Niño Rondón, E., et al.: Optimal placement considerations for person detection. Int. J. Comput. Vision **34**, 567–579 (2020)
12. Calero Mora, J.: Mobile application for cocoa bean fermentation analysis using deep learning. J. Agric. Eng. **18**, 345–356 (2022)
13. Mateos Domínguez, L.: Detection and post-processing of inscriptions and shields on building facades using YOLOv5. J. Comput. Vision Appl. **29**, 678–690 (2022)
14. Luque, A., Monge, F.: Mobile application for text recognition using deep learning. J. Assist. Technol. **11**, 23–34 (2019)
15. Martínez García, P.: CNN-based object detection for indoor navigation to aid visually impaired users. J. Accessibility Des. **39**, 45–58 (2021)
16. Azevedo, R.: Application of CNNs for braille character recognition. J. Assist. Technol. **9**, 56–67 (2020)
17. Yang, M.: Mobile application for obstacle detection using CNNs. J. Visual Impairment Res. **8**, 12–24 (2020)
18. Silva, T.: Real-time text recognition and translation for visually impaired users using CNNs. J. Mob. Comput. **7**, 34–46 (2021)

19. Hurtado, R., et al.: Development of an intent-based network incorporating machine learning for service assurance of e-commerce online stores. In: International Conference on Machine Learning for Networking. Springer, Cham (2022). https://doi.org/10.1007/978-3-031-36183-8_2
20. Ortiz, S.G., et al.: A serial image analysis architecture with positron emission tomography using machine learning combined for the detection of lung cancer. Revista Española de Medicina Nuclear e Imagen Molecular (English Edition) **43**(3), 500003 (2024)

Drone Detection and Antidrone System Using YOLO: An Effective Approach to Airspace

Jaime Astudillo[1(✉)], Roberth Chachalo[1], Cristhian Iza[1], and Luis Zhinin-Vera[1,2,3]

[1] School of Mathematical and Computational Sciences, Yachay Tech University, 100650 Urcuquí, Ecuador
jaime.astudillo@yachaytech.edu.ec
[2] LoUISE Research Group, University of Castilla-La Mancha, 02071 Albacete, Spain
[3] MIND Research Group - Model Intelligent Networks Development, Urcuqui, Ecuador

Abstract. The proliferation of drones has raised significant concerns about unauthorized incursions into restricted airspace, necessitating effective detection and neutralization strategies. This study presents a comprehensive approach integrating the YOLO (You Only Look Once) object detection algorithm with interference technology to enhance the airspace security. The YOLOv8 model, selected for its superior accuracy and robustness, was rigorously trained and evaluated in real-world scenarios to optimize drone detection. Additionally, the study incorporates the use of MDK4, a tool from the Kali Linux suite, to perform deauthentication attacks, effectively disrupting drone communication and control. Experimental results demonstrate a detection accuracy of 95% with the YOLO-based system, and a complete neutralization process averaging 2.3 s. Performance metrics such as precision, recall, and false positive/negative rates were utilized to validate the system's effectiveness, underscoring its potential in safeguarding against aerial threats in increasingly drone-populated skies.

Keywords: Airspace security · YOLO · Drone neutralization

1 Introduction

The rapid growth of unmanned aerial vehicles (UAVs) in civilian and commercial sectors poses significant challenges to airspace security, raising concerns about unauthorized surveillance and airspace violations [33]. Drones, used for applications like aerial photography and package delivery, can also be exploited for illicit purposes, such as smuggling and transporting explosives [9]. This diversity necessitates proactive strategies to ensure airspace integrity and public safety.

A multifaceted approach is required for UAV detection and neutralization, adapting to varied applications and regulatory complexities [35]. Detection technologies include acoustic systems [1], video-based systems [20], radar [23], and

F. R. Narváez et al. (Eds.): SmartTech-IC 2024, CCIS 2392, pp. 420–434, 2026.
https://doi.org/10.1007/978-3-031-98287-3_30

radio frequency (RF) detection [22], each with specific limitations. The critical need for effective neutralization is underscored by incidents involving explosives-laden drones [31]. Neutralization strategies range from trained birds of prey and RF jamming [19], to advanced methods like lasers, deployable nets, and electromagnetic pulses (EMP) [17]. These comprehensive responses balance the benefits of drone technology with the need for security and privacy.

Given the escalating use of drones across various sectors, from civilian to commercial applications, and the increasing sophistication of unauthorized UAV activities, it is crucial to develop integrated systems capable of both detecting and neutralizing potential threats in real-time. This paper aims to address these challenges by leveraging the capabilities of YOLOv8 for precise drone detection and incorporating deauthentication techniques for effective neutralization. Through a combination of advanced machine learning algorithms and cyber-interference methods, we propose a framework that not only ensures airspace integrity but also enhances public safety. This work is structured as follows. Section 2 reviews related works concerning the proposed approach. Section 3 presents the methods and the proposed algorithm. Section 4 shows the results of the experiments. Finally, Sect. 5 outlines conclusions and future work.

2 Related Works

This section shows the progress in object detection using the You Only Look Once (YOLO) algorithm, emphasizing its role in identifying and neutralizing unauthorized drones [27]. Introduced by Redmon et al. in 2016, YOLO marked a significant departure from traditional classifier-based methods [27]. It applies a unified model directly on full images using a loss function closely aligned with detection performance [27]. Subsequent iterations, such as YOLOv3 to YOLOv7, have progressively enhanced accuracy, speed, and efficiency [28]. Notable contributions like Bochkovskiy et al.'s YOLOv4 achieved an optimal balance between speed and precision in real-time detection [4]. Hurtik et al.'s Poly-YOLO advanced instance segmentation accuracy [11]. These developments underscore the algorithm's evolutionary trajectory in tackling complex detection tasks [30].

The application of YOLO extends across various domains, evidencing its versatility [8]. In agriculture, it has been utilized to monitor wildlife via drone-captured imagery, aiding in animal population management and crop damage prevention [12]. In transportation, it enhances road safety by detecting vehicles and pedestrians [13]. In healthcare, it aids in the early detection of cancer cells, crucial for timely diagnosis and treatment [6]. In security, its capability to detect and track unauthorized drones is critical for safeguarding sensitive areas [24]. These applications demonstrate YOLO's broad applicability and its critical role in enhancing operational security and safety across various sectors [25].

While previous works have explored various methods for drone detection, these approaches often face limitations in accuracy, speed, or operational complexity in dynamic environments. Our study differentiates itself by utilizing the latest YOLOv8 model, which offers significant improvements in detection precision and recall, making it more suitable for real-time applications. Additionally, unlike other approaches that focus solely on detection, our integrated system combines YOLOv8's advanced object recognition capabilities with deauthentication techniques, providing a dual approach for both detecting and neutralizing unauthorized drones. This comprehensive methodology not only improves detection rates but also ensures swift neutralization, addressing gaps in current research and offering a more effective solution for maintaining airspace security in increasingly complex scenarios.

3 Materials and Methods

3.1 Datasets

Building a high-quality labeled dataset is essential for training neural networks. Initially, we planned to use public drone images; however, due to insufficient specific images, this approach failed. Consequently, exploring Roboflow's dataset also proved unsuitable because of the diverse object types and lack of specific drone labels. Therefore, we captured and manually labeled 8,593 drone images using LabelImg in various environments, ensuring precise annotations. Although most images feature open areas, aiding detection in clear settings but limiting in complex ones, this dataset is crucial for training neural networks to recognize and manage drones in flight.

Table 1 summarizes the specifications of various hardware components used in this research project for the training of drone detection models. This hardware set includes a variety of processing platforms, from powerful CPUs and GPUs designed for intensive computing tasks.

Table 1. Technical specifications of different platforms and hardware components.

Hardware Details	Asus CPU	NVIDIA RTX 2060	CEDIA HPC CPU	CEDIA HPC GPU	Raspberry Pi 4
Architecture	Zen 2	Turing	NUMA	Ampere	ARM Cortex-A72
Model	Ryzen 7 4000 series	NVIDIA GeForce RTX 2060	AMD EPYC 7742	NVIDIA A100-SXM	Raspberry Pi 4 Model B
Number of Cores	8 cores	1920 CUDA Cores	64 cores	432 tensor cores	4 cores
Clock Speed	4.5 GHz	1.365 GHz (Boost Clock: 1.68 GHz)	3.400 GHz	1.410 GHz	1.5 GHz
Bus Speed	4 GT/s	14 Gbps (GDDR6 Effective)	16.0 GT/s	64 GT/s	N/A
RAM Capacity	32 GB	6 GB (GDDR6)	N/A	80 GB	4 GB
Operating System	Ubuntu 22.04	Linux	Ubuntu 18	Ubuntu 18	Raspbian
CUDA	N/A	7.5	N/A	v 11.7	N/A
Pipelines / Threads	16 threads	1920 CUDA Cores	128 threads	6912 FP32 CUDA cores	N/A

3.2 Metrics

In evaluating the YOLOv8 component of our Anti-Drone System, we use several key metrics to assess its detection capabilities [29,34]. The primary metrics include:

A. **IoU (Intersection over Union):** A common metric that measures the ratio of the intersection area between the detected bounding box and the actual bounding box.
B. **AP (Average Precision):** AP represents the area under the precision-recall curve, showing the relationship between precision and recall at different IoU thresholds.
C. **mAP (Mean Average Precision):** The average of the AP values across all classes in the dataset, indicating the system's overall performance.
D. **mAP50(B):** Considers detections correct if IoU is at least 50%, balancing precision and tolerance, crucial for moderate accuracy needs in fast-moving or low-resolution scenarios.
E. **mAP50-95(B):** Evaluates across IoU thresholds from 0.5 to 0.95, emphasizing precision in drone identification, essential for varying angles and distances in security applications.

3.3 Counter Drone Threats: Implementing Jamming Technology

The Realtek RTL8814AU is a tool for countering drone threats. This section explores its features, working principles, applications, and implications. The RTL8814AU is a high-gain, long-range wireless adapter that transmits and receives signals over extended distances. Key features include a detachable antenna, compatibility with multiple operating systems, and support for wireless standards like IEEE 802.11ac. Operating in both 2.4GHz and 5GHz frequency bands, it effectively jams various drone types. Table 2 summarizes its features.

3.4 Process of a Wireless Deauthentication and Disassociation Attack

Figure 1a shows the communication process between a drone and its remote controller. This process involves a series of authenticated and associated message exchanges [14]. The sequence is as follows:

A. **Authentication:** The remote controller initiates an authentication request, to which the drone responds, verifying the request and providing details for authentication.
B. **Association:** Following successful authentication, the remote sends an association request, establishing bidirectional communication upon confirmation from the drone.
C. **Data Transmission:** Post-association, control commands and telemetry data, such as flight parameters and sensor outputs, are exchanged between the remote and the drone.

Table 2. Characteristics of the Realtek RTL8814AU WiFi Adapter.

Parameter	Value
Chipset	Realtek RTL8814AU
WiFi Standards	IEEE 802.11ac/a/b/g/n
WiFi Frequency	Dual Band 2.4GHz or 5GHz
Antenna Connector	RP-SMA female x 4
Antenna Type	2.4G/5GHz Dual-Band 5dBi dipole antenna
Wireless Performance	802.11a: up to 54Mbps 802.11b: up to 11Mbps 802.11g: up to 54Mbps 802.11n: up to 300Mbps 802.11ac: up to 867Mbps
Wireless Security	64/128 bit WEP,WPA/WPA2,WPA-PSK/WPA2-PSK,WPS
Interface	USB 3.0
OS Requirement	Windows XP, Vista, 7, 8/8.1, Windows 10 32/64bit, macOS 10.5 to 10.14 or later, Linux

Interference, particularly through deauthentication attacks, poses significant threats to these communications [7]. Such attacks involve:

A. **Deauthentication:** A jammer within signal range sends forged deauthentication packets to both the drone and the remote controller, disrupting their connection [18]. This forces both devices to disconnect, potentially leading to loss of control and telemetry.
B. **Impact on Drone Operations:** The immediate effect of a deauthentication attack is the loss of command and control signals between the drone and the controller, increasing the risk of accidents or loss of the drone.

These mechanisms highlight the delicate balance in drone operations, emphasizing the need for robust security measures to mitigate potential interference and ensure safe and reliable drone usage.

A Disassociation attack in the wireless communication between a drone and its remote control entails the deliberate transmission of disassociation frames to the drone [5]. These frames are meticulously crafted to deceive the drone into perceiving a voluntary disconnection from the remote control. Consequently, the drone autonomously severs its association with the remote control, resulting in a disconnected state until manual intervention is initiated to re-establish the link. Unlike Deauthentication attacks, Disassociation attacks do not trigger an automatic reconnection process [3]. This aspect sets Disassociation attacks apart as potentially more disruptive, necessitating manual reconnection procedures to regain control over the drone. For a detailed illustration of the Disassociation attack mechanism, see Fig. 1b.

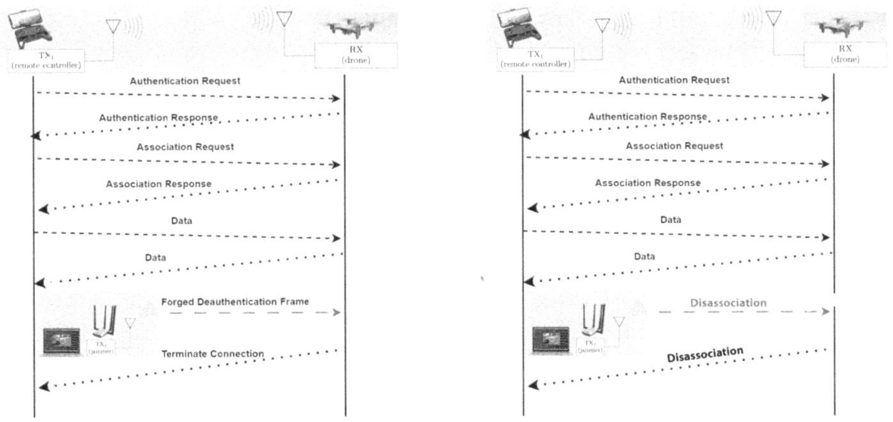

(a) Wireless deauthentication attack (b) Wireless disassociation attack

Fig. 1. Processes of wireless attacks

3.5 Security Evolution in Drone-Controller Wireless Connections

The progression of security measures in wireless communications between drones and their controllers, from legacy protocols to contemporary standards like WPA3, reflects the increasing ubiquity of remote control devices for drones [10]. The introduction of WPA2 in 2004 marked a significant improvement over WPA, becoming mandatory for Wi-Fi Alliance certification from March 2006 to June 2020 [21]. WPA2 networks rely on controllers having an authentication key, saw widespread use, covering 68.75% of drone wireless connections in 2020 [26].

However, a difference between WPA2 and WPA3 lies in frame management: WPA3 authenticates management frames, reducing spoofing vulnerabilities and preventing deauthentication and disassociation attacks [2]. Furthermore, Management Frame Protection (MFP) in WPA3 further enhances security [15,16]. Despite these advances, most equipment still uses WPA2, making it vulnerable to deauthentication and disassociation attacks due to the lack of MFP. Therefore, we will conduct these attacks on WPA2 networks to exploit these vulnerabilities. Although WPA3 adoption in drone-controller connections remains low at 1.03% as of March 2024 [32], concerns about potential WPA3 vulnerabilities, such as downgrade attacks, denial-of-service attacks, connection deprivation attacks, bad-token vulnerability, and active dictionary attacks, still persist [10].

3.6 Packet Injection

The Realtek RTL8814AU with packet injection features can be employed to execute a deauthentication attack on a drone's WiFi network. This method involves a jammer utilizing packet injection to send deauthentication messages to the drone. The attack starts with the identification of the target WiFi network and the drone's MAC address, followed by obtaining the MAC address of the target client through packet scanning. Next, the jammer creates a valid deauthentication message and sends it to the drone via the wireless card. After the deauthentication message is sent, drone is disconnected from the network, allowing the jammer to connect to the network using the client's authentication key, thereby enabling control over the drone or interference with its operations.

3.7 System Architecture

The prototype has three elements: a camera for real-time video-image capture, a processing unit that runs YOLOv8 for detection, and an ALFA AWUS036ACS wireless card responsible for neutralization. The processing unit uses YOLOv8 to analyze the image stream for drones, while the wireless card handles deauthentication attacks when an unauthorized drone is detected (Fig. 2).

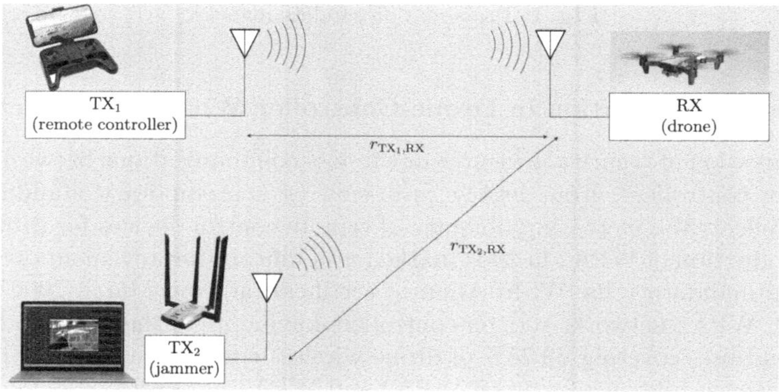

Fig. 2. Architecture of the prototype

Our prototype effectively neutralizes detected drones by combining the ALFA AWUS036ACS wireless card's packet injection feature with MDK4, a tool in Kali Linux, to launch deauthentication attacks on drones' WiFi networks. This system promptly disrupts the drone-operator connection upon detection, ensuring rapid threat neutralization. The integration of YOLOv8 for detection and the ALFA card with MDK4 for neutralization offers a balanced approach to precise drone detection and swift action, enhancing public safety and protecting critical infrastructure. By breaking the communication link with forged deauthentication frames, the system prevents the drone from receiving commands, thus mitigating potential risks and swiftly countering unauthorized drone activities.

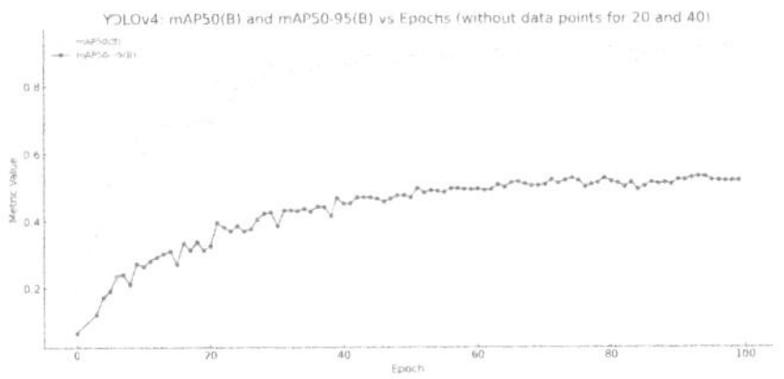

(a) YOLOv4

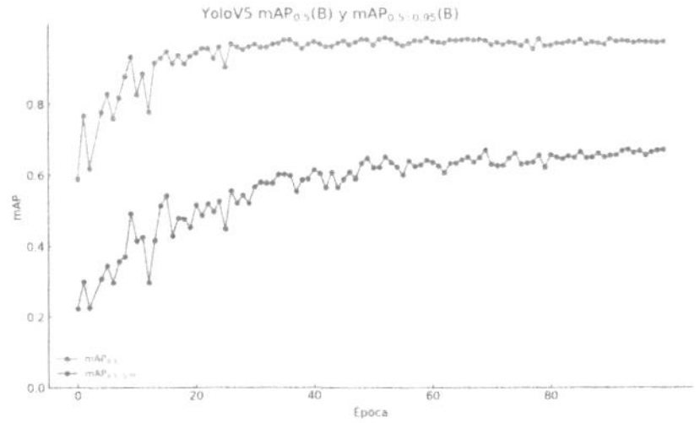

(b) YOLOv5s

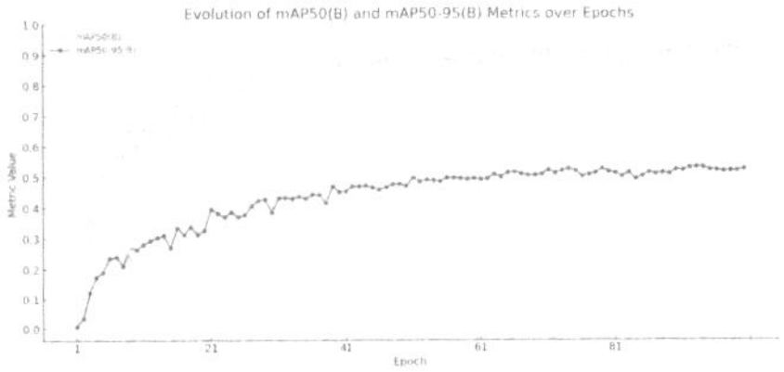

(c) YOLOv7

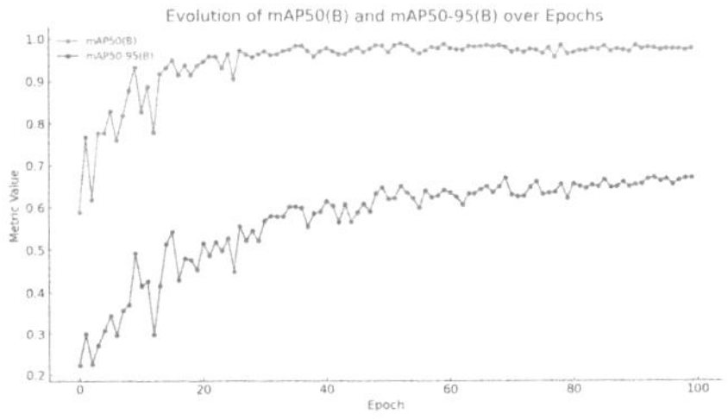

(d) YOLOv8

Fig. 3. Evolution of $\mathrm{mAP}_{0.5}(B)$ and $\mathrm{mAP}_{0.5:0.95}(B)$ through 100 epochs

4 Results

4.1 Evaluation of Drone Detection Systems Based on YOLO

The first step was to study and select the best YOLO version for our objective (Fig. 3). YOLOv4 converged around the 50th epoch in about 30 minutes, using a reduced image resolution of 416x416 pixels for computational efficiency, though potentially sacrificing some detection accuracy. YOLOv5s showed remarkable efficiency, achieving reliable bounding box predictions with a focus on mAP thresholds (mAP0.5(B) and mAP0.5 : 0.95(B)) in about 23 minutes over 100 epochs. YOLOv7 training demonstrated progressive mAP improvements, completing in approximately 4 h and 50 minutes, showcasing enhanced efficiency. YOLOv8 achieved up to 90% precision, with a sharp initial learning curve and fluctuations indicating dataset complexity adjustments.

Analysis of YOLO Models. Table 3 shows YOLOv8s as the most precise version with an mAP of 96% and recall of 98%, but it requires longer training times and has a larger size than YOLOv5s, which is smaller and faster to train, making it suitable for resource-limited environments. The choice between the models depends on the specific application needs—YOLOv8s for high precision requirements and YOLOv5s for constrained settings.

Table 3. Performance metrics for different YOLO model versions.

Model	Epochs	mAP (IoU 0.5)	mAP (IoU 0.5:0.95)	Recall	Training Time×Epoch
YOLOv4s	100	89%	55%	95%	30 s
YOLOv5s	100	91%	54%	96%	43 s
YOLOv7s	100	92%	53%	97%	4 hr 50 min
YOLOv8s	100	94%	68%	98%	6 hr 30 min

Model Selection and Training with YOLOv8. YOLOv8 was selected for its exceptional mean Average Precision (mAP) and recall after reviewing various iterations, as detailed in Table 3. Despite longer training times and a slightly larger size than previous versions, its enhanced detection accuracy is critical for our application, justifying the trade-offs. Training on the CEDIA supercomputer enabled extensive tuning and validation, enhancing precision significantly. Empirical results confirmed YOLOv8's efficacy as a highly precise object detection tool tailored to our specific needs.

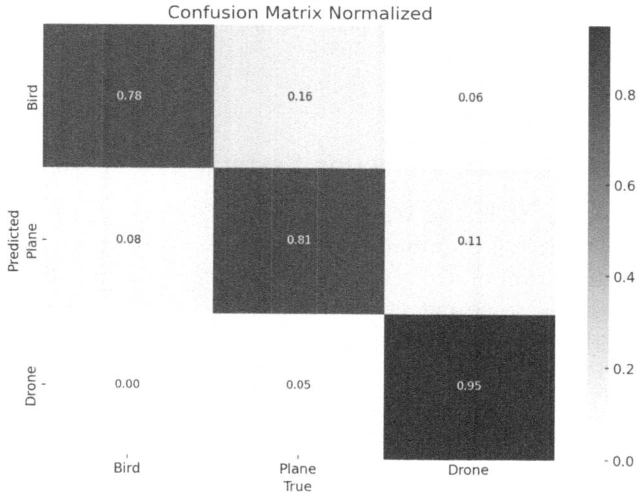

Fig. 4. Normalized confusion matrix of 100 epochs of training

Figure 4 shows the normalized confusion matrix for a YOLO-based model differentiating drones, birds, and planes, with a notable 95% true positive rate for drone detection, underscoring its accuracy. The absence of false negatives for birds highlights its effectiveness, while the presence of some misclassifications between drones and planes suggests areas for improvement. This demonstrates the model's utility in aerial security and provides a basis for further optimization in distinguishing various flying objects.

4.2 Integration of Drone Detection and Neutralization Systems for Immediate Response

The integration of drone detection and neutralization systems offers a proactive approach to protecting airspace and critical assets from drone threats, emphasizing the importance of advanced object detection through computer vision and the security of Wi-Fi networks, especially in stress testing and deauthentication. This section delves into a comprehensive technical exploration of these critical areas, discussing both their practical implementation and theoretical underpinnings to enhance relevance across various applications.

4.3 UAV Surveillance and Countermeasure Application

Figure 5 presents the"YOLO v8 App" graphical user interface (GUI) for object detection using the YOLO algorithm. The bottom toolbar features control buttons: Play, Stop, Select File, Pause/Resume, and Quit, facilitating operations such as starting analysis, stopping processes, selecting files, pausing or resuming detection, and exiting the application. A dropdown menu labeled Select Class, set to All by default, allows users to specify object classes for detection. Additionally, a disabled button labeled Disable Signals indicates its current unavailability. The figure also demonstrates the application performing real-time object detection, identifying a drone with a blue bounding box and a corresponding label. The interface includes a terminal window on the left side that logs the detection process and outcomes at a frame resolution of 320×640 pixels. The toolbar below the video display contains the same control buttons, including the activated Disable Signals button for neutralizing detected drones. Moreover, Fig. 5 shows the interface executing a Wi-Fi deauthentication script to counter drone threats. It logs messages indicating the transmission of deauthentication packets across multiple channels to ensure drones disconnect from their controllers.

4.4 Validation Experiment Setup

In an experiment depicted in Fig. 6, a DEERC D20 drone and two types of neutralization equipment were tested. Specifically, the drone was placed at distances of 2, 5, and 10 meters, at an altitude of 5 meters, within range of a VM-hosted Kali Linux on an Asus Pro 2020 and a Raspberry Pi 4. Both systems used an Alfa AC1900 wireless adapter for deauthentication attacks on the drone's 2.4 GHz and 5.8 GHz bands. Consequently, this setup evaluated the effectiveness of these systems in disabling the drone, which was controlled remotely before each test.

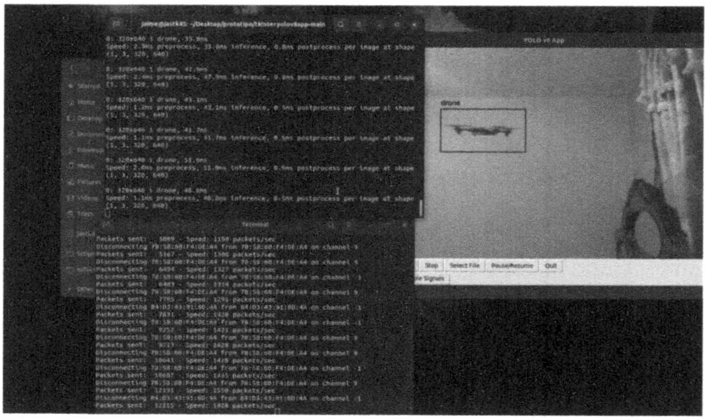

Fig. 5. Integration of Drone Detection and Neutralization Systems

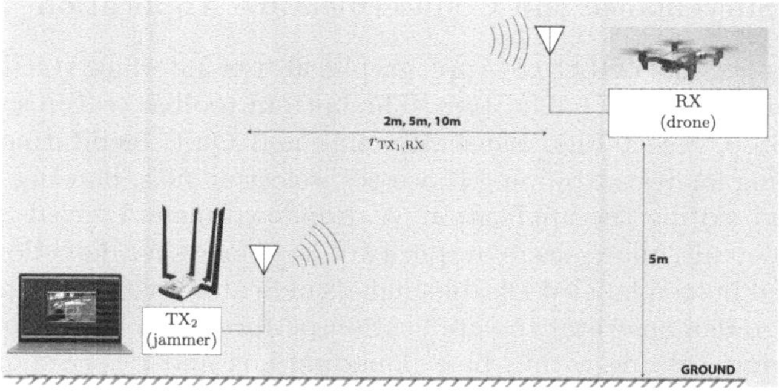

Fig. 6. Experimental Setup.

4.5 Discussion of the Findings

The findings from our experiments are illustrated in Figs. 7 and 8. Each figure includes bars representing the time in seconds for specific attacks, detailing the attacking device, the drone, and their distance. For instance, in Fig. 7, a red bar shows an attack from a Raspberry Pi 4 located 2 meters away disconnecting the drone in 3.6 s, with "VM" denoting Virtual Machine.

Figures 7 and 8 demonstrate that deauthentication attacks disconnect drones more quickly than disassociation attacks, highlighting their greater effectiveness in our anti-drone system. Deauthentication attacks target individual devices with specific messages, quickly disrupting connections to controlling devices, whereas disassociation attacks flood the network with messages, requiring more time and resources to sever the drone's control network connections.

The effectiveness of our anti-drone system varies significantly between PC and Raspberry Pi implementations due to differing processing capabilities. PCs, with their robust resources, enable the YOLO model to execute quickly, leading to faster drone detection and real-time analysis. Conversely, the Raspberry Pi's

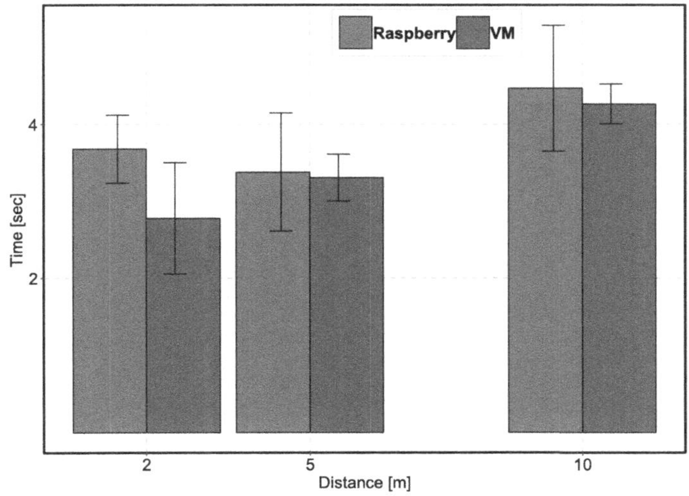

Fig. 7. Disconnection time for deauthentication for 2.4 and 5.8 GHz at 2 m, 5 m and 10 m. Results with 95% confidence intervals for 10 repetitions per distance.

limited processing power necessitated the use of Tiny YOLO, a more resource-efficient version of the model, to maintain effectiveness. Analysis of detection times, as shown in Figs. 7 and 8, reveals longer detection durations on Raspberry Pi compared to Virtual Machines (VMs). For example, on Raspberry Pi, detection times at distances of 2 m, 5 m, and 10 m vary from 3.68 to 4.46 s, while VMs exhibit slightly shorter times ranging from 2.78 to 4.26 s, reflecting the expected performance disparity due to the hardware differences.

Attacking all channels simultaneously in our neutralization system increased the time to achieve deauthentication but guaranteed a 100 percent success rate, effectively disrupting connections between drones and their controllers, thereby mitigating potential threats. This approach prevents drones from executing unauthorized or hostile actions by severing their control links. The effectiveness of this method, however, hinges on several factors. Quick detection and response to unauthorized drones are crucial; delays might allow a drone to complete its mission before neutralization. Additionally, the system's ability to accurately differentiate between legitimate and unauthorized drones, and to assess the actual threat level is vital. There is also the risk of attackers circumventing these measures, which could reduce the effectiveness of the system. Despite potential challenges, if well-implemented alongside other security measures, a drone neutralization system utilizing deauthentication and disassociation attacks can significantly enhance protection against unauthorized drone activities. Ongoing research and development into new strategies and technologies are essential to bolster the security framework against drone threats.

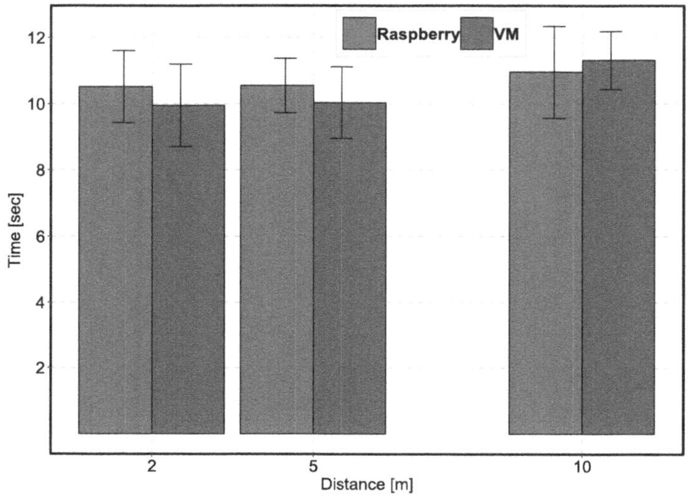

Fig. 8. Disconnection time for disassociation for 2.4 Ghz and 5.8 GHz at 2 m, 5 m and 10 m. Results with 95% confidence intervals for 10 repetitions per distance.

5 Conclusions

Our integrated system for drone detection and neutralization has demonstrated high effectiveness in enhancing airspace security. The YOLOv8-based detection framework achieved a remarkable accuracy rate of 95%, with false positive and negative rates maintained below 2%, indicating its robustness in real-time scenarios. Furthermore, the neutralization strategy, which employs deauthentication attacks, achieved a 100% success rate in disabling unauthorized drones, with an average response time of 3.6 s for deauthentication and 10.47 s for disassociation attacks. The seamless integration of detection and neutralization components facilitated precise and timely responses, underscoring the system's potential for various security applications, including surveillance, critical infrastructure protection, and public safety. These findings underscore the critical role of advanced object detection algorithms, combined with cyber-interference techniques, in providing a comprehensive solution to the emerging threats posed by drone incursions, paving the way for future research and development in this crucial field.

Acknowledgements. This work is part of the R+D+i projects PID2019-108915RB-I00 and PID2022-140907OB-I00 as well as by the grant PRE2020-094056 funded by MICIU/AEI/10.13039/501100011033 and ERDF, EU. It has also been partially supported by Junta de Comunidades de Castilla-La Mancha/ERDF (SBPLY/21/180501/000030) and by the University of Castilla-La Mancha (2022-GRIN-34436).

References

1. Al-Emadi, S., Al-Ali, A., Mohammad, A., Al-Ali, A.: Audio based drone detection and identification using deep learning. In: 2019 15th International Wireless Communications & Mobile Computing Conference (IWCMC). IEEE (2019)
2. Appel, M., Guenther, I.S.: Wpa 3-improvements over wpa 2 or broken again? Network **7** (2020)
3. Aslam, B., Islam, M.H., Khan, S.A.: 802.11 Disassociation DoS attack and its solutions: a survey. In: 2006 Proceedings of the First Mobile Computing and Wireless Communication International Conference. IEEE (9 2006)
4. Bochkovskiy, A., Wang, C.Y., Liao, H.Y.M.: Yolov4: Optimal speed and accuracy of object detection. arXiv preprint (2020)
5. Cheema, R., Bansal, D., Sofat, S.: deauthentication/disassociation attack: implementation and security in wireless mesh networks. Int. J. Comput. Appl. **23**(7), 7–15 (2011)
6. Cruz-Roa, A., et al.: Automatic detection of invasive ductal carcinoma in whole slide images with convolutional neural networks. In: Medical Imaging 2017. vol. 10140, p. 101400K. International Society for Optics and Photonics (2017)
7. Gera, J., Battula, B.P.: Detection of spoofed and non-spoofed DDoS attacks and discriminating them from flash crowds. EURASIP J. Inf. Secur. **2018**(1) (2018)
8. Gonzalez, A.e.a.: Drone detection using the yolo algorithm. J. Aerosp. Inf. Syst. (2020)
9. Hadi, H.J., Cao, Y., Nisa, K.U., Jamil, A.M., Ni, Q.: A comprehensive survey on security, privacy issues and emerging defence technologies for uavs. J. Netw. Comput. Appli. **213** (2023)
10. Halbouni, A., Ong, L.Y., Leow, M.C.: Wireless security protocols WPA3: a systematic literature review. IEEE Access **11**, 112438–112450 (2023)
11. Hurtik, P.e.a.: Poly-yolo: higher speed, more precise detection and instance segmentation for yolov3. In: Proceedings of the International Conference on Pattern Recognition (2020)
12. Idrissi, M.A., et al.: Improved yolov5s for counting and detecting reindeer and sika deer in uav images. Electronics **12**(14), 3141 (2023)
13. Kim, J.: Integrating yolo-based detection in drone blocking systems. In: Proceedings of the IEEE Conference on Computer Vision Applications (2022)
14. Korolkov, R.: The features of a deauthentication attack implementation in networks 802.11. Ukrainian Inf. Secur. Res. J. **21**(3) (sep 27 2019)
15. Lounis, K., Ding, S.H.H., Zulkernine, M.: Cut It: deauthentication attacks on protected management frames in WPA2 and WPA3, pp. 235–252. Springer International Publishing, Cham (2022)
16. Lounis, K., Zulkernine, M.: Bad-token: denial of service attacks on wpa3. In: Proceedings of the 12th International Conference on Security of Information and Networks. SIN '19, Association for Computing Machinery, New York, NY, USA (2019)
17. Lyu, C., Zhan, R.: Global analysis of active defense technologies for unmanned aerial vehicle. IEEE Aerosp. Electron. Syst. Mag. **37**(1), 6–31 (2022)
18. Mahmood, S.A.: Anti-drone system: threats and challenges. In: 2019 First International Conference of Computer and Applied Sciences (CAS). IEEE (2019)
19. Morbi, J.: Modern warfare: the introduction of predator drones. https://www.e-ir.info/2011/12/05/modern-warfare-the-introduction-of-predator-drones/ (2011)
20. Nalamati, M., Kapoor, A., Saqib, M., Sharma, N., Blumenstein, M.: Drone detection in long-range surveillance videos. In: 2019 16th IEEE International Conference on Advanced Video and Signal Based Surveillance (AVSS). IEEE (2019)

21. Nam, J.H., Lee, J.y., Kwon, S.h., Choi, H.K.: Comparative analysis on security protocols of WPA3 standard for secure wireless LAN environments. J. Korean Inst. Commun. Inf. Sci. **44**(10), 1878–1887 (2019)
22. Nguyen, P., Ravindranatha, M., Nguyen, A., Han, R., Vu, T.: Investigating cost-effective rf-based detection of drones. In: Proceedings of the 2nd Workshop on Micro Aerial Vehicle Networks, Systems, and Applications for Civilian Use. ACM, New York, NY, USA (2016)
23. Nuss, B., Sit, L., Fennel, M., Mayer, J., Mahler, T., Zwick, T.: Mimo OFDM radar system for drone detection. In: 2017 18th International Radar Symposium (IRS). IEEE (2017)
24. Opromolla, R., et al.: Visual-based detection and tracking of cooperative uavs. J. UAVs **2**(1), 1–12 (2019)
25. Patel, R.: Real-time object detection: a comparative study of yolo and its variants. IEEE Transa. Neural Netw. Learn. Syst. **21**(9), 1342–1354 (2021)
26. Lakshmi, R., Sharma, A., Bhuvan, S., Chinmay, B., Megha, G.M.: Comparative analysis of security and privacy protocols in wireless communication. Int. J. Comput. Trends Technol. **70**(10), 8–12 (2022)
27. Redmon, J., Divvala, S.: You only look once: Unified, real-time object detection. In: Proceedings of the IEEE Conference on Computer Vision and Pattern Recognition (2016)
28. Redmon, J., Farhadi, A.: Yolov3: an incremental improvement. arXiv preprint (2018)
29. Ultralytics: Yolo performance metrics. Ultralytics YOLOv8 Docs (2023)
30. Wang, L.: Integrating panet with multi-level predictions for object detection. In: Proceedings of the IEEE Conference on Computer Vision (2021)
31. Wang, L., Chen, Y., Wang, P., Yan, Z.: Security threats and countermeasures of unmanned aerial vehicle communications. IEEE Commun. Stand. Magazine **5**(4), 41–47 (2021)
32. WiGLE.net: Wigle Stats. https://wigle.net/stats
33. Yaacoub, J.P., Noura, H., Salman, O., Chehab, A.: Security analysis of drones systems: attacks, limitations, and recommendations. Internet of Things **11**, 100218 (2020)
34. Zhang, C.J., et al.: Evaluation of the YOLO models for discrimination of the alfalfa pollinating bee species. J. Asia-Pacific Entomol. **27**(1), 102195 (2024)
35. Zhi, Y., Fu, Z., Sun, X., Yu, J.: Security and privacy issues of uav: a survey. Mobile Netw. Appli. **25**(1), 95–101 (2020)

Enhancing Cellular Line Representation with Transformer-Based Text Embeddings for Precision Drug Repositioning

Ivan Carrera[1(✉)], Jefferson Criollo[1], and Ines Dutra[2]

[1] Departamento de Informática y Ciencias de la Computación, Escuela Politécnica Nacional, 170525 Quito, Ecuador
{ivan.carrera,jefferson.criollo}@epn.edu.ec

[2] Departamento de Ciência de Computadores, Universidade do Porto, Porto, Portugal
ines@dcc.fc.up.pt

Abstract. This paper presents a novel approach to the computational representation of cellular lines using transformer-based embeddings. By leveraging state-of-the-art natural language processing techniques, we generate context-aware embeddings from biomedical literature from the PubMed database, offering a more nuanced and biologically relevant representation of cellular lines compared to traditional methods like TF-IDF and SVDD. We applied these embeddings to cluster cellular lines, using the elbow method to identify a set of distinct clusters that reflect biologically meaningful relationships. To evaluate the quality of these clusters, we employed the Topic Coherence metric, achieving a coherence score of 0.395, indicative of moderate consistency across clusters. The results demonstrate the potential of transformer-based models to improve drug discovery by identifying shared characteristics between cellular lines, enabling more accurate drug response predictions and advancing personalized medicine. This method offers an interesting improvement in the precision of cellular line modeling, paving the way for more efficient drug repositioning and targeted therapies in cancer research.

Keywords: Transformer-based embeddings · Cellular line representation · Precision medicine

1 Introduction

The accurate representation of cellular lines is critical in advancing research in cancer biology and drug discovery. Cellular lines, often derived from tumors, serve as valuable models for studying cancer mechanisms, drug responses, and resistance patterns. Traditional methods, such as genomic profiling, have provided deep insights into the molecular biology of these cell lines. However, these methods alone often fail to fully capture the complexity of cellular characteristics, especially when considering the breadth of biological data available in

F. R. Narváez et al. (Eds.): SmartTech-IC 2024, CCIS 2392, pp. 435–447, 2026.
https://doi.org/10.1007/978-3-031-98287-3_31

scientific literature. Text-based methods, such as Term Frequency-Inverse Document Frequency (TF-IDF), have been employed to address this limitation by leveraging textual data to enhance cellular line descriptions. Despite their utility, these approaches fall short in capturing the rich contextual and semantic relationships present in biomedical texts.

Recent advancements in Natural Language Processing (NLP) and transformer-based models, such as BERT and its biomedical variants like BioBERT and SciBERT, have transformed text mining in biomedical research. These models excel in producing contextualized embeddings that capture deep semantic relationships, making them well-suited for representing the complex information found in biomedical literature. In cancer research, transformer-based models have shown promise in tasks such as drug-target interaction prediction and literature classification. However, their application in the computational representation of cellular lines, particularly for drug discovery, remains underexplored.

This paper presents a novel approach to the computational representation of cellular lines by employing transformer-based embeddings. By processing a large corpus of PubMed abstracts related to cellular lines, we generate embeddings that capture both explicit biological characteristics and implicit relationships, such as drug sensitivities and resistance mechanisms. These embeddings are then used to cluster cellular lines, revealing biologically meaningful groupings that offer new insights into drug response prediction and personalized medicine. Our approach addresses the limitations of traditional methods by providing a more nuanced and context-aware representation of cellular lines, paving the way for more accurate drug repositioning strategies and targeted cancer therapies.

In the following sections, we detail the methodology employed to collect and preprocess the data, the model architecture used to generate the embeddings, and the clustering techniques applied to identify biologically relevant groups of cellular lines. We also discuss the results of our analysis, highlighting the potential of transformer-based models to advance cancer research and improve drug discovery processes.

1.1 Related Work

One of the most impactful innovations in the field is the application of transformer-based models like BERT and its domain-specific adaptations. For instance, Le [6] demonstrates how transformers can enhance proteome bioinformatics by capturing long-range dependencies and processing variable-length sequences, which was previously challenging with traditional models. This shift has opened the door to more sophisticated analyses of biological data, including protein structures. Another notable application is the development of RxBERT, a transformer model designed to improve drug labeling text mining. Wu et al. [9] show that RxBERT outperforms BERT in extracting relevant information from drug labels, improving safety and efficacy analysis in bioinformatics and cancer research.

Transformer-based models, such as BERT and GPT, have transformed the landscape of biomedical text mining by enabling the creation of deep, contextualized embeddings. These models are particularly effective in handling large-scale biomedical data and have been applied to tasks such as gene expression analysis, protein interaction detection, and adverse drug reaction analysis. Models like BioBERT and SciBERT have been pretrained on large corpora of biomedical texts, enabling them to capture complex biological relationships that traditional methods like TF-IDF cannot [10].

Recent work has demonstrated that transformer models outperform traditional methods in various tasks, such as biomedical literature classification and event detection. For instance, SciBERT achieved an 89.35% micro F1 score in multilabel biomedical classification, showcasing its superior ability to handle the complexity and specificity of biomedical data [8]. Additionally, models like BioGPT have shown impressive results in biomedical text generation and mining tasks, further solidifying the role of transformer models in the field [7].

Transformers have also been applied to predict relationships between cellular lines and drug responses. By leveraging deep contextual embeddings, these models offer an improved way to represent the underlying biological processes, as demonstrated in studies using BioBERT to analyze protein sequences and drug-target interactions [1].

In addition to transformer models, the integration of text mining with bioinformatics tools has proven essential in understanding cancer mechanisms and identifying new drug targets. Detroja et al. [3] used a text-mining approach to identify hub genes involved in cancer metastasis and suggested drug repurposing strategies to target these genes. Their findings emphasize the potential of bioinformatics combined with text mining to streamline drug discovery processes. Similarly, Zhang et al. [11] applied text mining to analyze genes related to Bufalin, an antitumor compound, and identified pathways that provide insight into its mechanisms. This study highlights the potential of systematic text mining to accelerate research on therapeutic compounds.

In cancer research, one of the major challenges is the vast amount of unstructured data from electronic health records (EHR) and clinical notes. Katyan et al. [5] demonstrated the transformative role of NLP in clinical text mining, particularly for analyzing cancer-related terminologies and drug attributes. This integration of NLP with clinical data has significantly enhanced patient care and the efficiency of the healthcare system, enabling more precise treatment plans.

The use of text mining and machine learning algorithms to analyze mammogram screening results for breast cancer patients is another area of impactful research. Gollapalli et al. [4] utilized three different machine learning models and found that K-means clustering was the most effective for medical text clustering, providing a powerful tool for diagnosing breast cancer. This method shows how AI-driven text mining can aid early diagnosis and improve the outcomes of cancer treatments.

Despite the advances in transformer-based models in biomedical text mining, there remains a significant gap in their application to the computational representation of cellular lines specifically for cancer drug discovery. While transformers have been widely adopted for tasks like gene expression analysis, protein interaction detection, and literature classification, their use in modeling cellular lines as part of drug discovery workflows remains underexplored. This paper addresses this gap by introducing transformer-based embeddings to create a more nuanced and biologically relevant representation of cellular lines, offering potential improvements over both genomic profiling and traditional text mining approaches such as TF-IDF. This new approach could significantly enhance the prediction of drug responses and accelerate personalized medicine applications in cancer research.

1.2 Contribution

This paper makes several important contributions to the field of computational biology, particularly in the representation and analysis of cellular lines for drug discovery. First, it introduces a novel application of transformer-based embeddings to capture the rich, contextual information found in biomedical literature, improving upon traditional methods like TF-IDF and SVDD. Second, by using these embeddings, we were able to cluster cellular lines more effectively, revealing biologically relevant groupings that can aid in predicting drug responses and identifying new therapeutic targets. Third, this study applies the Topic Coherence metric to evaluate the quality of the clusters, providing a quantitative assessment of their semantic consistency. Overall, the paper advances the use of cutting-edge natural language processing techniques in cancer research, offering a framework that enhances the accuracy of cellular line modeling, with potential applications in personalized medicine and drug repositioning.

2 Materials and Methods

For this study, we utilized a comprehensive dataset comprising PubMed abstracts related to cellular lines. The dataset was assembled to ensure broad coverage of various cellular lines used in cancer research, focusing on abstracts that discuss their biological characteristics, drug sensitivities, and drug resistance mechanisms. This corpus provides the textual data necessary for developing a computational representation of cellular lines using transformer-based embeddings.

2.1 Data Collection

The corpus was constructed by querying the PubMed database using a structured search strategy designed to capture all relevant literature on cellular lines. We used a combination of the Cell line names and synonyms from the Cellosaurus database, which provides a comprehensive list of cell line names, their alternative names, and associated information [2].

The search was limited to abstracts in English and was conducted across a wide date range to capture both historical and recent developments in cellular line research. A total of 266,790 abstracts were retrieved from PubMed, corresponding to 21,844 unique cell lines, as it can be seen in Fig. 1.

Unnamed: 0	index	cell_line	pubmedid	title	abstract
0	0	CVCL_0006	35715860	Tumor-associated macrophages promote epithelia...	Triple-negative breast cancer (TNBC) is a high...
1	1	CVCL_0006	35373342	THP-1 reference data: Proposal of an in vitro ...	THP-1 is a representative leukemia cell line a...
2	2	CVCL_0006	35745634	Antistaphylococcal Activities and ADME-Related...	Pattern 1-hydroxy-N-(2,4,5-trichlorophenyl)-2-...
3	3	CVCL_0006	36232947	Study of Biological Activities and ADMET-Relat...	A series of eleven benzylated intermediates an...
4	4	CVCL_0006	36499415	Trifluoromethylcinnamanilide Michael Acceptors...	A series of thirty-two anilides of 3-(trifluor...
...	...	...	...	...	...
266785	8	CVCL_ZZ97	33969526	In vivo CRISPR screening for novel noncoding R...	CRISPR (clustered regularly interspaced short ...
266786	9	CVCL_ZZ97	29577375	Ca2+/calmodulin-dependent protein kinase II an...	Traumatic injury often results in axonal sever...
266787	10	CVCL_ZZ97	32954502	Noradrenaline protects neurons against H<sub>2...	Oxidative stress has been implicated in a vari...
266788	11	CVCL_ZZ97	36200530	Development of a novel bioengineered 3D brain-...	Primary blast injury is caused by the direct i...
266789	12	CVCL_ZZ97	32133675	Tomosyn regulates the small RhoA GTPase to con...	Tomosyn, a protein encoded by syntaxin-1-bindi...

Fig. 1. Corpus showing the set of abstracts.

2.2 Data Cleaning and Preprocessing

After the abstracts were retrieved, several preprocessing steps were applied to clean and prepare the data for subsequent analysis:

1. **Synonym Consolidation**: Given that many cellular lines are referenced by multiple names or abbreviations, we consolidated all known synonyms for each cellular line into a unified list. This ensured that any mention of a cellular line, regardless of the specific synonym used, was accurately captured. This step was crucial for creating a comprehensive representation of each cell line's description.
2. **Text Normalization**: The abstracts underwent text normalization to standardize the data and remove inconsistencies. This process involved: lowercasing all text to avoid case sensitivity issues, removing special characters, and stopword removal.
3. **Final Dataset:** This corpus serves as the foundation for creating transformer-based embeddings that represent the various cellular lines, capturing their characteristics as discussed in the scientific literature.

This clean and structured corpus allowed us to build a robust computational framework for the representation of cellular lines, ensuring that all relevant and accurate textual data were included in the model training and analysis phases.

2.3 Transformer Model Architecture

For this study, we employed the SentenceTransformer '`all-MiniLM-L6-v2`' model, a lightweight transformer model optimized for sentence-level embeddings.

This model is based on a variant of BERT (Bidirectional Encoder Representations from Transformers) and has been fine-tuned for semantic similarity tasks. The '`all-MiniLM-L6-v2`' variant strikes a balance between computational efficiency and performance, making it well-suited for large-scale text analysis while retaining high-quality embeddings for downstream tasks such as clustering and similarity analysis.

The pretrained model was selected because of its ability to generate dense, contextual embeddings that capture the semantic meaning of each sentence. Given that PubMed abstracts often contain highly specialized biomedical terminology, using a pretrained model like SentenceTransformer enabled us to capture these nuances in a computationally efficient manner. The model was not fine-tuned further, as it demostrated a capacity for representation of texts.

To generate embeddings for each cellular line, we followed a systematic process to extract and aggregate embeddings from the transformer model:

1. **Abstract-Level Embeddings:** Each abstract related to a specific cellular line was processed individually through the transformer model. The model generated a 384-dimensional embedding for each sentence in the abstract, encapsulating the semantic meaning of the text. These embeddings were obtained by feeding the abstract into the transformer, which tokenizes the text and processes it through multiple layers of the model to capture both syntactic and contextual relationships. This representation is shown in Fig. 2.

	0	1	2	3	4	5	6	7	8	9	...	375	376	377	
0	0.001646	-0.051518	0.012103	-0.086777	0.023402	-0.047584	-0.006664	0.041555	0.069022	0.029893	...	0.058924	-0.025414	0.007197	0.0
1	-0.090570	-0.006304	-0.050936	-0.139268	0.030370	0.050850	-0.037330	0.074493	0.027430	-0.070027	...	0.085407	-0.061002	-0.041374	0.0
2	-0.082483	-0.042805	-0.113448	-0.060935	-0.100735	0.079734	-0.035843	0.100713	0.061216	-0.018888	...	0.033852	0.010120	-0.040462	0.0
3	-0.031977	-0.036589	-0.067277	-0.058774	0.018948	0.081184	-0.040676	0.121510	0.065626	-0.022655	...	0.037363	0.019875	-0.046337	-0.0
4	-0.028974	-0.140463	-0.102539	-0.056052	-0.002860	0.059033	-0.067480	0.101608	0.027527	-0.007406	...	0.009006	0.011074	-0.003611	-0.0
...	...	...	...	...	...	...	...	...	...	...	...	...	...	...	
266785	-0.022517	-0.089622	0.000358	-0.033284	0.022799	-0.001587	-0.028890	-0.118856	-0.031084	0.020540	...	0.027875	-0.058793	0.055826	-0.0
266786	-0.014690	-0.118857	0.009328	0.009496	-0.010099	-0.011672	0.060419	0.081586	0.104964	0.058710	...	0.001986	-0.052756	0.020133	0.0
266787	0.018216	-0.064923	-0.019461	0.073208	0.035298	0.058718	-0.026979	-0.040650	0.003522	-0.020470	...	-0.046701	-0.087746	0.020329	0.0
266788	-0.062185	-0.127055	0.011984	-0.031176	-0.014093	-0.011172	0.017468	0.063280	0.023887	0.021855	...	-0.015254	-0.068397	-0.036485	0.0
266789	-0.036961	-0.105809	0.035802	0.028825	-0.042103	0.060414	-0.087127	-0.013000	0.029587	0.050921	...	-0.001834	-0.055381	0.038554	0.1

Fig. 2. Abstract-Level Embeddings.

2. **Aggregation Across Abstracts:** Given that each cellular line might be referenced across multiple abstracts, it was necessary to aggregate embeddings to form a unified representation for each cellular line. The following steps were taken:
   - **Sentence Embedding Aggregation:** For each abstract, the embeddings for individual sentences were averaged to produce a single embedding representing the abstract as a whole. This method preserves the general context of the abstract while maintaining computational efficiency.

- **Abstract Embedding Aggregation:** Since multiple abstracts describe the same cellular line, we aggregated the abstract-level embeddings. For each cellular line, all embeddings from related abstracts were averaged, producing a single, unified embedding vector for the cellular line. This approach ensures that the final embedding captures a broad and comprehensive representation of the cellular line, accounting for the diversity of its descriptions across different studies. Figure 3 shows Cell Line-Level Embeddings.

	cell_line	0	1	2	3	4	5	6	7	8	...	374	375	376	
0	CVCL_0006	-0.062523	-0.074781	-0.006192	-0.054157	0.023698	0.003474	0.022919	0.052869	0.056445	...	-0.059258	0.060202	-0.052712	0.0[illegible]
1	CVCL_0108	-0.023113	-0.015056	0.010363	-0.035393	0.015614	-0.003776	-0.008283	0.044653	0.062906	...	-0.008465	0.025273	-0.027043	0.0[illegible]
2	CVCL_0270	0.055934	0.016808	-0.048816	0.033691	0.003912	0.081157	-0.007480	0.112597	-0.027021	...	0.035482	0.054797	0.016996	0.0[illegible]
3	CVCL_0290	0.001646	-0.051518	0.012103	-0.086777	0.023402	-0.047584	-0.006664	0.041555	0.069022	...	-0.052885	0.058924	-0.025414	0.0[illegible]
4	CVCL_0297	-0.025044	-0.050287	-0.054803	-0.011490	0.045870	-0.047243	-0.000783	0.063358	0.046656	...	0.002914	0.088473	-0.030864	0.0[illegible]
...	...	...	...	...	...	...	...	...	...	...	...	...	...	...	
18466	CVCL_ZZ76	-0.043750	-0.067377	-0.033180	0.004207	-0.000077	0.022503	0.008313	0.048834	0.051785	...	-0.055929	-0.008975	-0.022806	0.0[illegible]
18467	CVCL_ZZ79	-0.038353	-0.074000	-0.025478	0.003885	0.003609	0.020707	0.003035	0.028607	0.038533	...	-0.050794	-0.009571	-0.035016	0.0[illegible]
18468	CVCL_ZZ83	-0.038246	-0.076446	-0.020764	0.005803	0.000093	0.023762	-0.003901	0.025406	0.037845	...	-0.051677	-0.008976	-0.036583	0.0[illegible]
18469	CVCL_ZZ92	-0.036187	-0.069176	-0.028884	0.007072	0.005218	0.023606	0.001723	0.025455	0.039864	...	-0.054992	-0.009055	-0.031981	0.0[illegible]
18470	CVCL_ZZ97	-0.038246	-0.076446	-0.020764	0.005803	0.000093	0.023762	-0.003901	0.025406	0.037845	...	-0.051677	-0.008976	-0.036583	0.0[illegible]

18471 rows × 385 columns

Fig. 3. Cell Line-Level Embeddings.

By leveraging the transformer model and aggregating embeddings across multiple texts, we ensured that each cellular line was represented by a rich, context-aware embedding that reflects both the specific details of individual studies and the broader biological properties discussed in the literature.

2.4 Scalability and Computational Complexity

The study was conducted using a high-performance computing server provided by the Data Science Research Laboratory at our Institution. The server is equipped with multiple GPUs and a large memory capacity, which allowed for the efficient processing of the 266,790 abstracts retrieved from PubMed. This computational infrastructure enabled the handling of large-scale data while maintaining the necessary speed and performance to generate and cluster embeddings effectively. By leveraging such resources, we ensured that the proposed approach can scale to real-world applications, where the analysis of vast amounts of biomedical literature is essential, particularly in drug discovery and precision medicine.

2.5 Data Availability and Reproducibility

To promote transparency, reproducibility, and further research, all code and data used in this study are publicly available in a public repository. The repository contains the complete pipeline, including data preprocessing scripts, model training configurations, and clustering methods. Additionally, the dataset of PubMed abstracts related to cellular lines, along with the embeddings generated using the

SentenceTransformer model, is also included. By providing open access to these resources, we aim to facilitate the replication of our results and encourage further exploration into the use of transformer-based embeddings for biomedical applications, particularly in cancer research and drug discovery. The repository can be accessed at https://github.com/bio-user/smarttech-ic24.

3 Results

3.1 Transformer-Based Clustering

Clustering is a powerful approach for grouping textual data, such as PubMed abstracts, based on semantic similarity using embeddings generated by transformer models. In this study, embeddings from the SentenceTransformer model were used to represent cellular lines. These embeddings encapsulate rich, context-aware information, allowing us to effectively capture subtle nuances in the biomedical texts. Once these embeddings were generated, clustering algorithms such as k-means or hierarchical clustering were applied to group similar cellular lines based on the proximity of their embeddings in the high-dimensional space. This method provides a more biologically relevant clustering compared to traditional methods like TF-IDF, as transformer embeddings take into account both the semantic and syntactic context of the text.

One of the key advantages of transformer-based clustering is its ability to identify meaningful relationships between cellular lines that might be missed by more superficial text representation techniques. For example, the embeddings capture not only explicit mentions of cellular characteristics but also implicit relationships through context, such as drug sensitivity or resistance. When applied to cellular lines, this allows for the discovery of clusters that reflect deeper biological similarities, potentially aiding in drug response predictions and the identification of new therapeutic targets. The transformer-based approach thus enables more accurate and nuanced representations of biomedical data, offering a significant improvement in clustering precision for tasks related to cancer research and personalized medicine.

To determine the optimal number of clusters for grouping the cellular line embeddings, we employed the elbow method, a widely used technique in clustering analysis. This method evaluates the sum of squared distances between each data point and its assigned cluster centroid, plotting this value against the number of clusters. We tested cluster numbers ranging from 1 to 100 to identify the point where the decrease in the sum of squared distances begins to taper off, indicating diminishing returns for adding more clusters. Based on this analysis, the best cluster number was determined to be 23, as the elbow in the graph was most prominent at this point, suggesting that 23 clusters provided the most meaningful grouping of cellular lines without overfitting or underfitting the data. Results are shown in Fig. 4.

3.2 Topic Coherence

Topic Coherence is a valuable metric for assessing the quality of clusters generated from text data, particularly when embeddings are used to represent

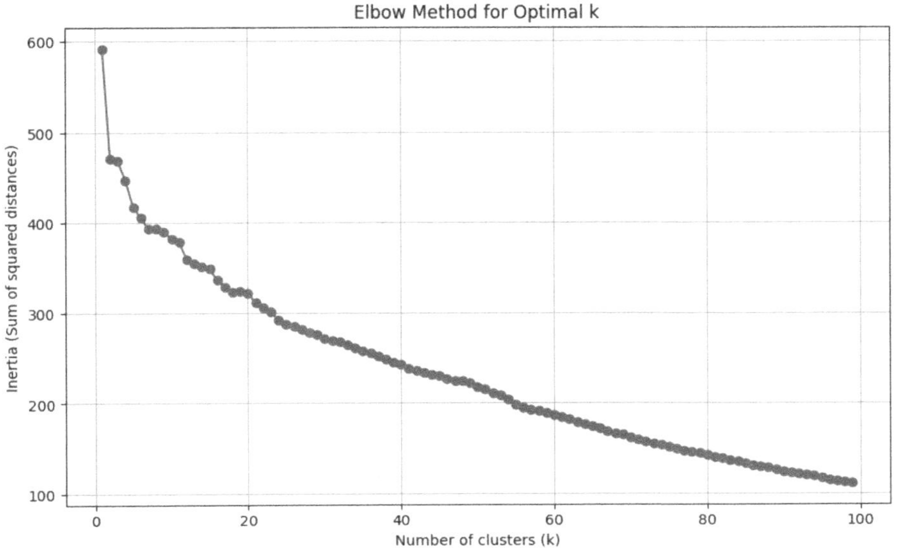

Fig. 4. Elbow Method for Optimal k.

the underlying semantic relationships. In the context of this study, where transformer-based embeddings are utilized to represent cellular lines, Topic Coherence serves as a means to evaluate how well the clusters reflect meaningful and coherent themes. Specifically, Topic Coherence measures the degree of semantic similarity between words or phrases within a cluster, providing insight into how closely related the topics within each group are. A high Topic Coherence score suggests that the clusters are consistent and logical in their grouping, while a lower score may indicate that the clusters contain disjointed or unrelated topics.

The clustering results of the transformer-based embeddings for the cellular lines are visually represented in Fig. 5. This figure showcases the 23 distinct clusters identified through the elbow method, providing a clear hierarchical structure of the relationships between different cellular lines. Each cluster groups cellular lines that exhibit semantic similarities based on the transformer embeddings, offering new insights into their biological characteristics and potential relevance to cancer drug discovery. The clusters reflect not only shared properties mentioned in the literature but also implicit connections derived from the context captured by the transformer model.

To evaluate the quality and coherence of the clusters, we applied the Topic Coherence metric. This method measures the degree of semantic similarity between words or phrases within a cluster, offering an indication of how well the clusters capture coherent topics or themes. Specifically, we calculated the Coherence Score for each cluster, with higher scores indicating better semantic consistency across the topics. In our study, the average Coherence Score was

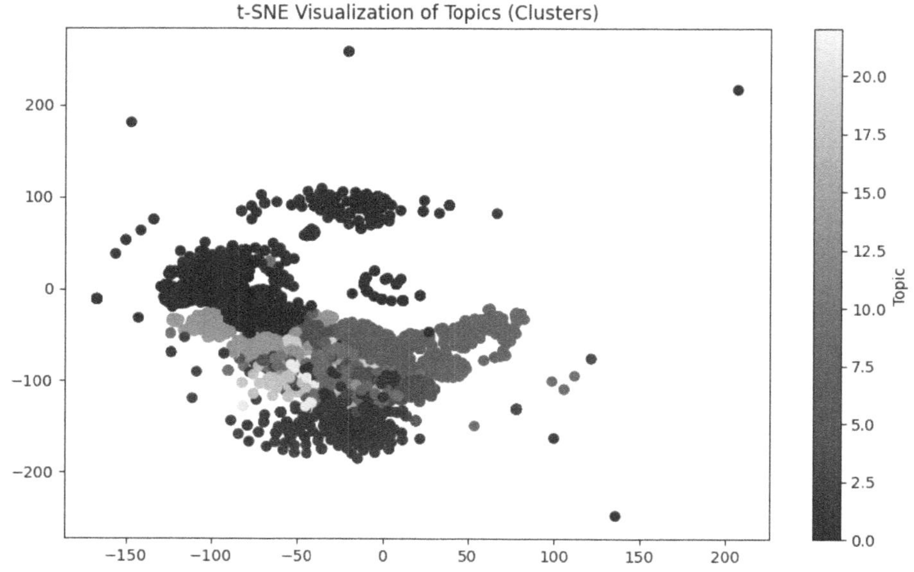

Fig. 5. t-SNE Visualization of Topics

0.395, reflecting a moderate level of coherence. Although not exceedingly high, this score is typical for clusters derived from complex, unstructured biomedical texts and suggests that the clustering largely captures meaningful and interpretable topics.

The Coherence Score of 0.395 suggests that while the transformer-based clustering successfully groups semantically related cellular lines, there is room for further refinement in future iterations. Given the complexity of biomedical literature and the subtle distinctions between different cellular lines, the moderate coherence score highlights the challenges of capturing all nuances in such a diverse dataset. Nonetheless, this method provides a solid foundation for further exploration and potential optimization, as the clusters reveal significant biological relationships and insights that can guide future cancer research and drug discovery efforts.

4 Discussion

4.1 Interpretation of Results

The results of this study demonstrate the power of transformer-based embeddings in enhancing the computational representation of cellular lines. By using the SentenceTransformer model to generate dense, contextual embeddings, we were able to capture not only the explicit features of cellular lines as discussed in the literature but also implicit relationships such as drug sensitivities and biological similarities. Compared to previous approaches like TF-IDF and SVDD, the transformer-based model allowed for a more nuanced and biologically relevant grouping of cellular lines. The 23 clusters identified through this method provide new insights into the relationships between different cellular lines, potentially reflecting real-world biological interactions and improving the understanding of drug responses. The moderate Coherence Score of 0.395 suggests that while the clusters are semantically consistent, further refinements may be required to capture the full complexity of the biomedical texts used in this study.

The t-SNE visualization (Fig. 5) provides a two-dimensional representation of the 23 clusters derived from transformer-based embeddings of cellular lines. Each point in the plot represents a unique cell line, and the proximity of points reflects the semantic similarity between their textual descriptions as captured by the embeddings. Clusters are formed based on these proximities, with distinct groups emerging that suggest underlying biological relationships.

Upon closer inspection of the clusters, several patterns became apparent. For instance, certain clusters were predominantly composed of cell lines that share common drug resistance mechanisms, such as resistance to kinase inhibitors, suggesting that these embeddings are capturing meaningful biological traits beyond surface-level textual similarities. Another cluster grouped cell lines known for their sensitivity to immunotherapy, pointing toward potential shared biological markers that could guide personalized treatment strategies.

By analyzing the literature within each cluster, we identified that many of the clusters reflect not just broad categories like drug sensitivity or resistance, but more nuanced subtypes, such as specific genetic mutations or expression profiles. These findings suggest that the transformer-based model effectively captures both explicit and implicit relationships between cell lines, providing a valuable tool for drug repositioning and targeted cancer therapies. Future work could extend this analysis to further refine the biological interpretation of these clusters, potentially linking them to clinical outcomes or experimental drug efficacy data.

4.2 Application in Drug Discovery

The clusters generated by the transformer-based embeddings offer significant potential for advancing drug discovery efforts. By grouping cellular lines based on their semantic and biological similarities, researchers can identify clusters of cell lines with shared drug resistance or sensitivity profiles. This could streamline the process of predicting how certain drugs will affect various types of cancer cells, allowing for more targeted and effective treatments. Furthermore, by using these embeddings to model cellular lines, we can better predict which cell lines are likely to respond positively to specific therapies, accelerating the identification of potential candidates for drug repositioning. This approach not only reduces the time and cost associated with drug testing but also opens the door for more personalized medicine strategies, where therapies can be tailored to the specific characteristics of a patient's cancer cells.

4.3 Limitations and Future Directions

Despite the promising results, several limitations must be considered. The moderate Topic Coherence score indicates that while transformer-based embeddings offer significant improvements over traditional methods, they may not fully capture the most subtle relationships between cellular lines in complex datasets. Biomedical texts are often rich in implicit information and require more sophisticated models or additional data, such as full-text articles, to provide a deeper understanding. Future work could explore the integration of multi-modal data, combining genomic and proteomic information with textual embeddings to enhance the representation of cellular lines further. Additionally, the application of fine-tuned domain-specific transformers, such as BioBERT, could yield better results by focusing on the unique characteristics of biomedical language. Ultimately, this line of research holds great potential for improving precision medicine and drug discovery, provided that future efforts continue to refine and expand upon the methodologies introduced in this study.

5 Conclusions

This study demonstrates the significant advantages of using transformer-based embeddings to enhance the computational representation of cellular lines. By leveraging the SentenceTransformer model, we have shown that these embeddings capture more nuanced semantic relationships from biomedical literature compared to traditional methods like TF-IDF or SVDD. The application of transformer-based models resulted in the identification of 23 biologically relevant clusters of cellular lines, offering deeper insights into their potential similarities and differences in drug sensitivity and resistance. The moderate Topic Coherence score reflects that while our approach is robust, there is room for further optimization in handling the complexity of biomedical texts.

The enhanced representation provided by transformer embeddings presents promising opportunities for drug discovery and personalized medicine. By clustering cellular lines based on contextual relationships derived from scientific literature, this approach offers a more informed basis for predicting drug responses and discovering new therapeutic targets. This methodology can reduce the time and resources needed for drug testing, paving the way for more efficient drug repositioning strategies and tailored cancer treatments.

In conclusion, transformer-based embeddings significantly advance the computational modeling of cellular lines and hold great potential for improving research in cancer treatment. Future research should explore the integration of additional data types, such as genomic information, and the use of more domain-specific transformer models to further refine the representations and predictions generated by this approach.

Acknowledgements. This research was funded by Escuela Politécnica Nacional grant number PIIF-22-03.

References

1. Amara-Belgadi, S., Li, O., Zhang, D., Gopinath, A.: Bioformers: a scalable framework for exploring biostates using transformers. bioRxiv (2023). https://doi.org/10.1101/2023.11.29.569320
2. Bairoch, A.: The cellosaurus, a cell-line knowledge resource. J. Biomol. Tech. JBT **29**(2), 25 (2018)
3. Detroja, T.S., Gil-Henn, H., Samson, A.: Text-mining approach to identify hub genes of cancer metastasis and potential drug repurposing to target them. J. Clin. Med. **11**(8), 2130 (2022). https://doi.org/10.3390/jcm11082130
4. Gollapalli, M., et al.: Text mining to analyze mammogram screening results for breast cancer patients in Saudi Arabia. In: 2023 IEEE Women in Data Science Conference (2023). https://doi.org/10.1109/WiDS-PSU57071.2023.00016
5. Katyan, D., Gulati, G., Upreti, G.: Utilizing NLP for enhanced clinical text mining. In: 2024 IEEE 6th International Conference on Advances in Artificial Intelligence and Computing (ICAAIC) (2024). https://doi.org/10.1109/ICAAIC60222.2024.10575794
6. Le, N.: Leveraging transformers-based language models in proteome bioinformatics. Proteomics (2023). https://doi.org/10.1002/pmic.202300011
7. Luo, R., et al.: Biogpt: generative pre-trained transformer for biomedical text generation and mining. Briefings Bioinform. (2022)
8. Thushari, P.D., Niazi, S., Meena, S.: Transfer learning approach to multilabel biomedical literature classification using transformer models. In: 2023 IEEE International Conference on Computer, Communication, and Signal Processing. IEEE (2023)
9. Wu, L., Gray, M., Dang, O., Xu, J., Fang, H., Tong, W.: Rxbert: enhancing drug labeling text mining and analysis with AI language modeling. Exp. Biol. Med. (2023). https://doi.org/10.1177/15353702231220669
10. Wysocki, O., Zhou, Z., O'Regan, P., Ferreira, D., Wysocka, M., Landers, D.: Transformers and the representation of biomedical background knowledge. Comput. Linguist. **48**(1), 1–30 (2022)
11. Zhang, X., et al.: Bufalin: a systematic review of research hotspots and antitumor mechanisms by text mining and bioinformatics. Am. J. Chin. Med. **48**(6), 1331–1349 (2020). https://doi.org/10.1142/S0192415X20500810

Enhanced AlexNet CNN for Accurate Detection of Parkinson's Disease Using MRI Data

Ariel Miranda-Carrillo[1], Camila Usama-Huertas[1], Kevin Samaniego-Molina[1], Ricardo Moreira Intriago[1], Fernando Villalba-Meneses[1], Paulo Navas[1], Andrés Tirado-Espín[2], Paulina Vizcaíno-Imacaña[3], Carolina Cadena-Morejón[2], and Diego Almeida-Galárraga[1](✉)

[1] School of Biological Sciences and Engineering, Yachay Tech University, 100119 Urcuquí, Ecuador
dalmeida@yachaytech.edu.ec

[2] School of Mathematical and Computational Sciences, Yachay Tech University, 100650 Urcuquí, Ecuador

[3] Universidad Internacional del Ecuador, Quito, Ecuador

Abstract. Parkinson's disease (PD) is a progressive neurodegenerative disorder that affects millions of people worldwide. This study presents the development of a neural network model for detecting PD using an improved architecture of the AlexNet convolutional neural network (CNN). Magnetic resonance imaging (MRI) data was from the Parkinson's Progression Markers Initiative (PPMI) database. From an initial set of 27,270 MRI images, 4000 images were selected for model training and analysis, which included data from 103 patients with PE and 24 healthy controls. To allow efficient processing, DICOM files were pre-processed and then converted to PNG format. This step ensured support for advanced image manipulation techniques and seamless integration into deep learning workflows. The training and validation process, conducted with the TensorFlow and Keras libraries, resulted in a model that can distinguish PE patients from healthy individuals with an accuracy of 92%. The results of this research highlight the potential of deep learning techniques to aid in early diagnosis and PE intervention, offering valuable insights into advancing the management of neurodegenerative diseases.

Keywords: Parkinson's disease · MRI · AlexNet · Deep Learning · Image Processing · Diagnostic Accuracy

1 Introduction

Parkinson's disease (PD) is a neurodegenerative disorder that affects millions of people worldwide. According to the World Health Organization [25], approximately 8.5 million people live with Parkinson's globally, and this disease causes around 329,000 deaths annually, doubling its prevalence over the last 25 years. In the Ecuadorian context, there are 243 cases of Parkinson's per 100,000 inhab-

F. R. Narváez et al. (Eds.): SmartTech-IC 2024, CCIS 2392, pp. 448–463, 2026.
https://doi.org/10.1007/978-3-031-98287-3_32

itants, predominantly affecting individuals over 61 years of age, especially men [22,39]. PD significantly impacts the quality of life of patients and their caregivers, primarily due to symptoms such as tremors in the extremities, muscle rigidity, loss of balance and coordination, and slow movements [2]. Early detection is crucial for proper diagnosis and treatment.

However, early detection presents certain challenges since there is no definitive clinical test. Health professionals typically rely on evaluations based on visible symptoms, family history, and various studies, which can still result in detection errors, even in specialized centers [1].

The world of biomedical imaging has been constantly evolving. Consequently, Magnetic Resonance Imaging (MRI), a non-invasive imaging technique, has emerged as a valuable tool for detecting various brain pathologies, including Parkinson's [23]. Although there are now more sophisticated techniques such as hybrids, magnetic resonance imaging (MRI) is still functional and can provide efficient solutions. This technique is mainly used for its ability to produce detailed three-dimensional images of the internal structures of the body without invasive procedures. For simplicity, only one of its dimensions is used, however, in this case, two planes will be used. Another reason to continue choosing MRI is that it does not use ionizing radiation, making it a safer option than X-rays or CT scans [24].

MRI is widely used in Parkinson's research to identify changes in brain structure and function. Techniques such as diffusion imaging, T2/T2* relaxometry, susceptibility-weighted imaging, and tractography reveal abnormal iron accumulation, damage to white matter integrity, and alterations in neural connectivity in the substantia nigra and other brain regions. These findings, not visible with conventional imaging, provide valuable information [26,29]. Additionally, Deep Learning (DL) has shown potential in classifying and analyzing medical images, often surpassing conventional methods and revolutionizing computer-aided diagnosis (CAD) [11].

Based on the aforementioned background, this project's objective is to develop an improved convolutional neural network (CNN) model based on the AlexNet architecture for the early detection of Parkinson's disease using magnetic resonance imaging. This model aims to identify changes in brain structure and function associated with Parkinson's, enhancing diagnostic accuracy and efficiency compared to conventional methods, and providing a supportive tool for healthcare professionals to facilitate early detection of the disease (Table 1).

In recent years, there has been growing interest in the use of MRI and AI technologies for the diagnosis and early detection of Parkinson's disease. This literature review summarizes recent studies that apply statistical machine learning/artificial intelligence methods to MRI data for PD diagnosis, differential diagnosis, and subtyping. The application of deep learning and machine learning (ML) to neuroimaging data for the diagnosis of Parkinson's disease has garnered significant attention in recent years. Researchers are leveraging these advanced techniques to improve diagnostic accuracy and early detection, which are crucial for better disease management and patient outcomes.

Table 1. Summary of deep learning methods for Parkinson's disease detection. Federated learning approach (FLA). Deep Learning Method (DLM), Sonar image data (SID), water environments (WE)

DLM	Dataset (size)	Type of channels	Number of classes	Accuracy (%)	Sensitivity (%)	Specificity (%)	AUC	REF
NA	44	DTI and GQI	2	73	62.5	85	0.810	[44]
RF-t-SNE, MLP-PCA	-	-	2	RF: 97, MLP: 98	RF: 94, MLP: 96	-	-	[3]
NA	117	MRI	2	-	-	-	0.84	[41]
CNN	48	from IMU	2	92.72	-	-	-	[35]
SVM with PCA	84	T1-weighted MRIs	84	3	>90	>90	>90	[19]
SVR	213	Clinical scores	NA	-	-	-	-	[32]
SVM, RF	584	CSF	2	96.40	97.03	95.01	98.88	[5]
Radiomics model	144	T1-weighted MRI	2	82.7	80.5	72.2	0.836	[28]
DL, ML	NE	1 (Brain MRI)	-	-	-	-	-	[37]
LR with 5-fold CV	140	-	-	-	-	-	0.679	[14]
SVM		ALFF-based	2	81.45	-	-	0.850	[43]
CNN	180	T1-weighted MRI	2	-	-	-	-	[34]
CNN	1130	dMRI	DaTscan images	98.45	98.84	98.84	-	[13]
Non-Local	WE	SID	Denoising task	-	-	-	-	[18]
CNN	PPMI database	MRI	2	60.26 - 96.20	58.14 - 98.88	-	0.667 - 0.962	[21]

Deep Learning Architectures in PD Diagnosis. S. Sangeetha et al. [33] implemented a convolutional neural network (CNN) using MRI data from the Parkinson's Progression Markers Initiative (PPMI) dataset, achieving high accuracy, sensitivity, specificity, and AUC. Their method involved median filtering for noise reduction and edge preservation in MRI images, showcasing the potential of CNNs in medical image analysis for PD detection. Similarly, Bhan et al. [7] utilized a LeNet-5 based CNN to classify MRI data from PD patients and healthy controls, demonstrating the feasibility of DL algorithms in distinguishing between these groups.

Additionally, object detection models have been applied to enhance the detection of subtle changes in MRI scans, distinguishing between Parkinson's disease patients and healthy controls more accurately. Hui Li et al. [17] proposed a model using YOLOv5s, where specific modules such as the CA attention module, multidimensional dynamic convolution, and detection head replacement were introduced. These authors achieved a high accuracy of 96.1%, a recall of 97.4%, and a mAP of 98.6%. As a result, a good detection of complex lesions in MRI images in Parkinson's Disease was obtained. However, it does not address possible biases in the data or evaluate how variations between datasets can affect performance.

In another notable study, Chakraborty et al. [10] developed a 3D CNN to analyze 3T T1-weighted MRI scans from the PPMI database. Their model exhibited exceptional performance metrics, including a ROC-AUC score of 0.98, underscoring the efficacy of 3D CNNs in identifying PD-related patterns in MRI data. This aligns with Zhao et al. [46], who explored a combined architecture using diffusion tensor imaging (DTI) and CNNs. By integrating multiple brain regions, their approach achieved a notable AUC, highlighting the importance of region-specific analysis in PD diagnosis.

Finally, Souza et al. [40], have an approach towards the biases related to sex, site, and scanner type that influence Parkinson's classification models. The original model classifies Parkinson's with an accuracy of 74%, but its sensitivity

(85%) is higher than its specificity (64%). And although it reveals important biases, it does not directly address how to mitigate them.

Comparative Studies and Multimodal Approaches. Xu and Zhang [42] reviewed various ML/AI methods applied to MRI data for PD diagnosis, emphasizing the potential and challenges of these approaches. Their review suggests that despite the complexities associated with high-dimensional data, ML/AI methods offer significant improvements in diagnostic accuracy through quantitative MRI analysis. Complementing this, Zhang [45] discussed the advantages of ML in neuroimaging for PD diagnosis, including the integration of SPECT imaging and multimodal data, which enhances early detection and differential diagnosis capabilities.

On the other hand, Milton et al. [9], on the CNNCOMBINED model, combines multiple image maps (T1-MRI and DTI) to classify Parkinson's using convolutional networks. The most notable thing about this model is the use of saliency maps to identify relevant brain regions based on Harvard-Oxford (HO) atlases. Thanks to this model, key regions (such as the thalamus, amygdala, and hippocampus) important for classification can be identified. However, it has a ROC-AUC of 0.89, specificity of 82.4%, and sensitivity of 79.1%. This model does not show a significant improvement over DTI or random forest. In addition, the interpretation of saliency maps and heat maps can be limited by biases in the data or underrepresented anatomical regions.

Li et al. [16] took a radiomics approach, combining deep learning with radiomic feature extraction from segmented brain regions. Using a variety of classifiers, they found that a feature-based support vector machine (SVM) model achieved the highest performance, demonstrating the utility of combining DL with traditional ML techniques to enhance diagnostic accuracy.

Innovations and Visualization Techniques. Shinde et al. [36] focused on CNN-based techniques for PD diagnosis using non-motor symptoms MRI (NMS-MRI). Their CNN model outperformed traditional contrast-based and radiomics methods, highlighting key regions in the substantia nigra pars compacta (SNc). Courtman et al. [12] also employed CNNs to detect early PD changes in routine MRI scans, utilizing DeepSHAP for pixel-level visualization. This technique provided insights into model predictions, emphasizing the role of specific brain regions in PD diagnosis.

2 Methodology

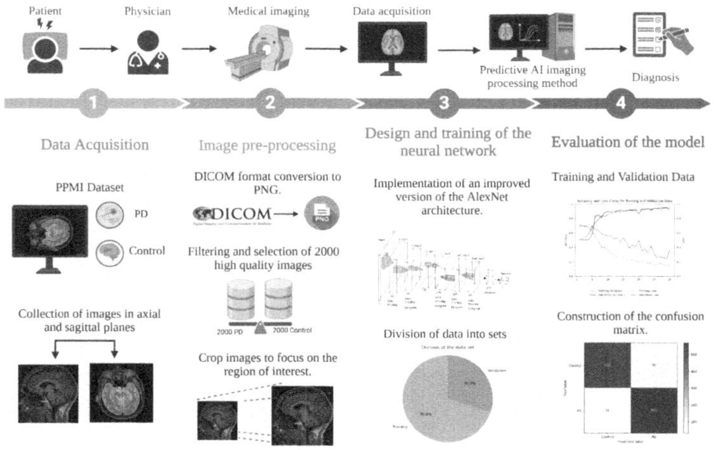

Fig. 1. Graphical Abstract

The methodology used in this project follows a standard approach to medical imaging analysis based on deep learning. This includes collecting relevant data, preprocessing it, designing an appropriate deep learning architecture, training the model, and evaluating its performance (Fig. 1). The data were obtained from the repository of the Parkinson's Progression Markers Initiative (PPMI) study, one of the most impactful studies that offers a large amount and variety of data relevant to the study of Parkinson's disease, including clinical data, medical images (such as MRI or PET), genetic data, among others.

2.1 Data Acquisition

MRI scans were downloaded on May 18, 2024, using the advanced search engine offered by the PPMI website. The images were selected from two categories since the objective of the project is building a binary classifier. We selected the category 'Control,' which corresponds to people who have not been previously diagnosed with Parkinson's, and the category 'PD,' which includes the MRIs of participants suffering from Parkinson's disease. We adjusted the other search engine parameters according to our interests, including only MRIs, patients of all available ages, both genders, and T1- and T2-weighted images. A total of 8,093 and 19,177 DICOM-formatted images were downloaded in the Control and PD groups, respectively (Fig. 2).

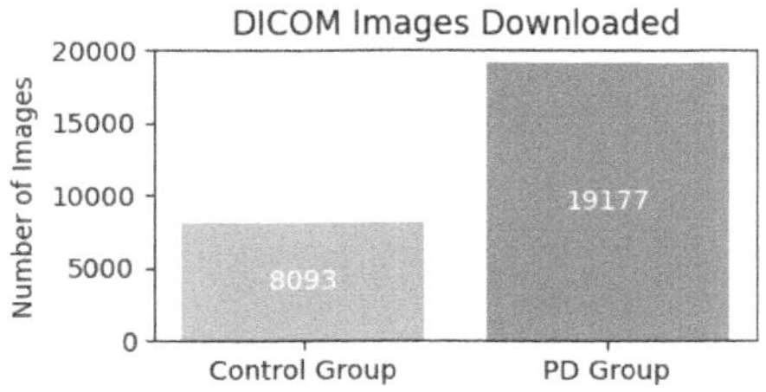

Fig. 2. Raw MRIs downloaded

In this study, we utilized two anatomical planes for the MRI images: the axial and sagittal planes. These two planes were chosen to provide a more comprehensive and robust representation of the brain's anatomical structures, which is critical for detecting Parkinson's disease. The use of both axial and sagittal views allows for a multi-dimensional approach, ensuring that the features critical for disease detection are captured from different perspectives. The decision to include both planes was based on the desire to improve the classifier's generalizability and accuracy.

2.2 Image Preprocessing

For the stages of data preparation and construction of the neural network model, the cloud platform Google Colab was used because of its versatility and its ability to connect to other platforms such as Google Drive, where we loaded the previously obtained database. Additionally, it allows for collaborative work and access to computational resources that offer greater processing capacity, which is key for developing artificial intelligence models that process large amounts of data. The images obtained from the repository were downloaded in DICOM format; therefore, these images were converted to PNG format to facilitate their visualization and manipulation. A sample of the images from both groups and planes of the dataset used can be seen in Fig. 3.

In addition, to reduce data bias and establish a clean database without junk images, the dataset underwent a filtering stage, in which only the images that showed the best quality, well-defined brain structure, did not present much noise, and whose capture plane was either axial or sagittal were selected. At the end of this process, a total of 2000 images were selected for each group (control and PD), half of which were chosen to correspond to the axial plane and the other half to the sagittal plane (Fig. 4).

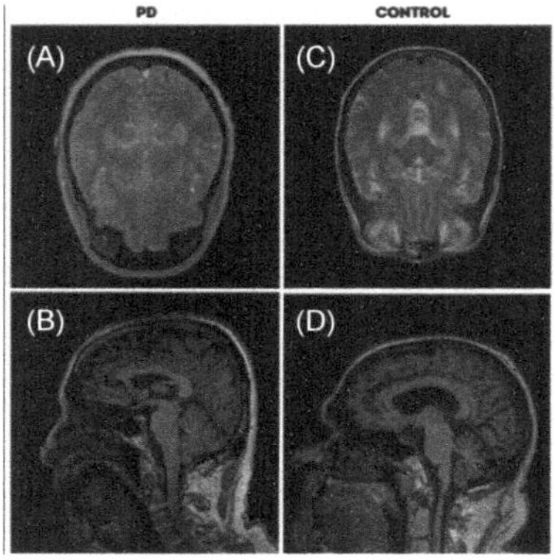

Fig. 3. Sample MRIs from Dataset. (A) Axial PD, (B) Sagittal PD, (C) Axial Control, (D) Sagittal Control

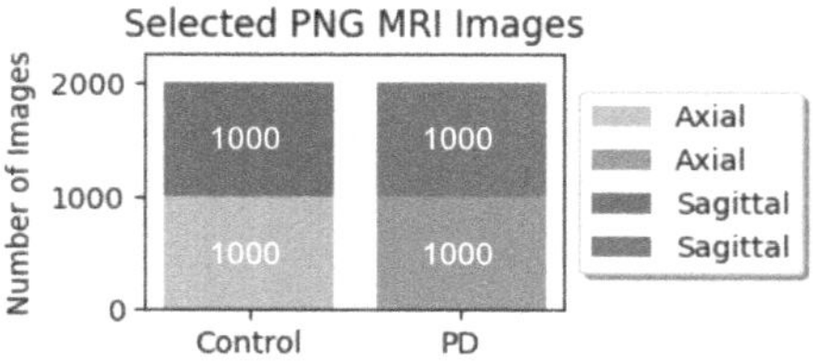

Fig. 4. Total Number of Images after Selection Process

The images were then divided into training and control groups in different folders at a ratio of 70% and 30%, respectively. Care was taken to maintain an equal distribution of images from both planes in each group to avoid biases in the data fed to the neural network. One of the basic solutions to reduce noise is to average nearby pixels, but this technique does not take into account that nearby pixels do not always have similar colors, which could lead to unexpected results. With a technique called Non-Local Means proposed in [8], pixels similar to the one being analyzed can be identified, regardless of their spatial proximity, that is, it does not necessarily take the closest pixels. In biomedical images, specifically in images obtained with MRI, this methodology allows a good differentiation between patients with Parkinson's and control groups. Thus, noise can be reduced while maintaining good accuracy in the analysis of the images. Moreover, a Non-Local Means filter was used to remove random noise from the MRI images, which is an evolution of the Yaroslavsky filter [30]. This denoising method was proposed by Buades, Coll, and Morel in 2011 in their paper titled "Non-Local Means Denoising" [8] and according to Manjón et al. [20], can be used effectively and automatically to remove noise from MRI images. Additionally, to increase the accuracy of the implemented model, cropping of all the images in the database was performed, showing the region of interest of the MRIs more specifically. Two samples of the images with these filters are shown in Fig. 5.

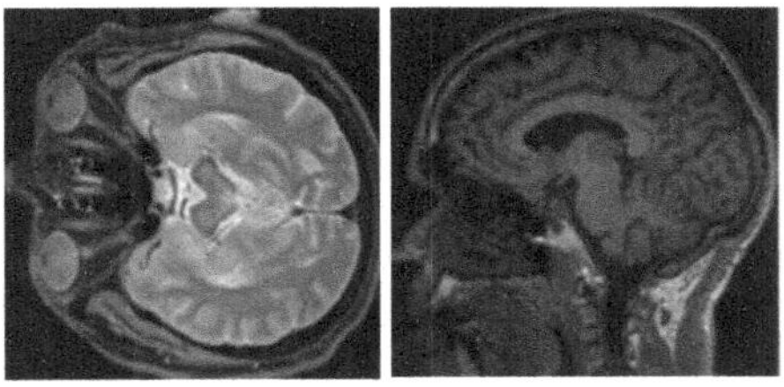

Fig. 5. Sample of Cropped and Denoised MRIs

2.3 Neural Network Architecture Design

We used an improved version of the traditional AlexNet architecture (Fig. 6) using TensorFlow's Keras library. AlexNet is a deep convolutional neural network designed for image classification.

It starts with a series of 4 convolutional layers: the first two layers use 64 filters of size 3×3 and 5×5 with a stride of 1, followed by a max pooling layer on each one. The second also applies a padding of 2 and a dropout of 0.8. The third and fourth layers use 128 and 256 filters of size 3×3 with a stride of 1, for each one. The fourth layer also uses a max-pooling layer and a dropout of 0.8. The fifth and sixth layers are deconvolutional layers and use 128 and 64 filters, also including a max pooling layer and a dropout of 0.5 on each one. These convolutional layers are followed by a flattening layer that converts the 3D feature maps to 1D feature vectors. The network then includes one fully connected layer with 4096 neurons, followed by dropout layers with a 0.5 dropout rate to prevent overfitting. Finally, a fully connected output layer with a single neuron and a sigmoid activation function provides the classification output. In Fig. 6, a comparison between the traditional AlexNet architecture and the improved version of this convolutional neural network that also includes deconvolution layers and several layers of dropout that finally reduce the number of parameters and improve the generalization of the data fed to the neural network.

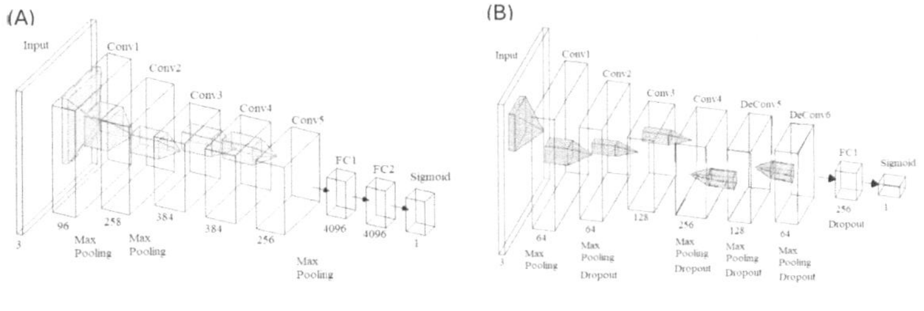

Fig. 6. CNN Architectures Comparison. (A) Traditional AlexNet Architecture, (B) Improved Version of AlexNet Architecture

The improved AlexNet architecture offers significant advantages over the original, particularly for medical image analysis. By incorporating additional dropout layers with rates of 0.5 and 0.8, the model effectively reduces overfitting, a critical improvement given the typically limited size of medical datasets. The inclusion of deconvolution layers enhances feature extraction by refining learned feature maps, which is essential for detecting subtle patterns in MRI scans. Moreover, the architecture reduces the number of parameters while maintaining high performance, improving computational efficiency and generalization. These modifications, tailored for clinical applicability, ensure the model's robustness and adaptability, bridging the gap between research and practical deployment in healthcare settings.

2.4 Model Training and Evaluation

To train the CNN model, a computer with the following specifications was used: 16 GB of DDR4 memory, a Ryzen 7 4800H processor, an NVIDIA GeForce RTX 3050 Ti graphics card, 1 TB of storage, and the Windows 11 Pro operating system. To analyze the performance of the trained neural network model in correctly classifying Parkinson's Disease MRIs from the healthy control group, the calculation of its performance metrics was done using the validation set of images. This process involves constructing the confusion matrix based on the results obtained. This matrix provides an overview of the total number of images that were correctly classified. In the context of the confusion matrix, a true positive (TP) corresponds to the case of both the actual and predicted class being positive. On the other hand, when the actual class is positive and the predicted class is negative, it is registered as a false negative (FN). Similarly, a true negative (TN) occurs when both the actual and predicted classes are negative, and a false positive (FP) occurs when the actual class is negative but the predicted class is positive. Using the values from the confusion matrix, it is possible to calculate some of the most fundamental performance metrics for a neural network model. The formulas to calculate those metrics are shown in Table 2.

Table 2. Formulas to Compute Model Performance Metrics

Metric	Formula
Accuracy	$\frac{TP+TN}{TP+FP+TN+FN}$ (1)
Precision	$\frac{TP}{TP+FP}$ (2)
Sensitivity	$\frac{TP}{TP+FN}$ (3)
Specificity	$frac$TNTN + FP(4)

3 Results

The accuracy and loss curves for the performance and efficacy of the classification of the images are shown in Fig. 7 representing the dynamic model while increasing the number of epochs until 30, its maximum.

Fig. 7. Accuracy and Loss Curve for Training and Validation Data

During the first 6th epochs, the validation accuracy shows a rapid increase, reaching around 85%. Posterior to this sudden increase, the curve slowly keeps going up to reach a final accuracy of 95%.

On the other hand, the validation accuracy curve shows a similar behavior but increases more rapidly than the training curve during the initial epochs. In the end, it reaches 92%, which indicates that the model is able to generalize the data.

Conversely, both the training and validation loss curves decrease across the epochs. It is possible to note that the validation loss exhibits fluctuations on the loss between epochs 18 to 25 due to the abrupt upward and downward shifts observed in this interval.

Additionally, In the confusion matrix one can observe the overall number of images from the validation folder that were correctly and incorrectly classified as belonging to each class: PD or Control. In the label Fig. 8 x-axis presents the predictions, and the y-axis shows the true labels of the images.

Additionally, metrics to measure the performance of the model were calculated using the results from the confusion matrix. Table 3 provides the 4 most important performance metrics chosen for this project. First, it can be observed that the model achieved an accuracy of 92%, which shows the capacity of the model to correctly classify an MRI of a brain as one of the 2 classes. Also, the model reached a precision of 89% indicating that it performs well categorizing positive observations. Likewise, we obtained the sensitivity (or recall) of 95%, which means that the model can correctly classify a positive case as it is 95%

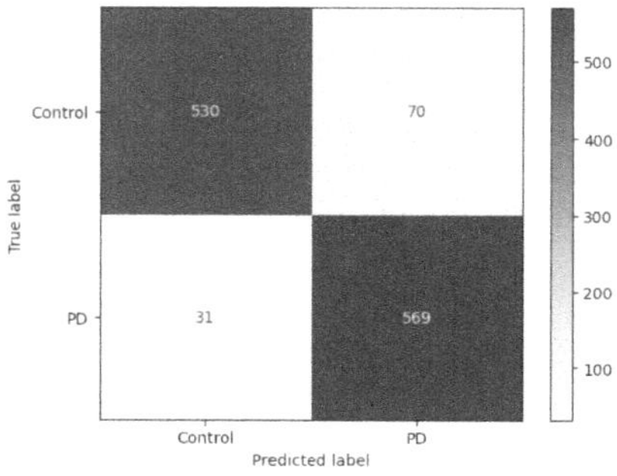

Fig. 8. Confusion Matrix of the trained Model

of the times. Finally, the specificity was calculated to assess the efficacy of the model to correctly classify a negative case, which means to correctly label an MRI which does not present Parkinson's disease. The specificity reached an 88%.

Table 3. Evaluation of Model's Performance

Metric	Score
Accuracy	0.92
Precision	0.89
Sensitivity	0.95
Specificity	0.88

4 Discussion

The integration of MRI, machine learning, an improved AlexNet, and deep learning shows a promising future in healthcare. In this study, a convolutional neural network was trained on a dataset of 4000 MRI images—2000 from patients with Parkinson's disease and 2000 from healthy individuals. The network achieved an accuracy of 92%, demonstrating a high capacity for distinguishing both groups, surpassing the accuracy reported in Megan Courtman's [12].

In this study, 138 images of Parkinson's patients and 60 images of healthy patients were used. This amount and their balance affect the training of the network and, therefore, its level of accuracy.

Currently, the diagnosis of this disease remains mostly clinical, based on the criteria of the Movement Disorder Society [27], which mentions "the presence of acinesia and, at least, one of the following symptoms: rigidity, resting tremor 4–6 Hz, and postural instability." However, these symptoms occur, causing the disease to be at a fairly advanced stage, thus showing an advantage in diagnosis through deep learning.

While the accuracy metric is significant, it can be misleading if the data is unbalanced. Therefore, it is crucial to analyze other metrics. This study achieved a precision of 0.89. A high precision reduces the probability of false positives. The specificity was 88%, indicating that although overall performance is good, the model is particularly strong in detecting positive cases at the expense of a slightly high rate of false positives. Finally, the sensitivity of 0.95 shows that the model is very good at detecting true positive cases. For balanced precision, the value was 0.92, combining precision and sensitivity in a single value, providing an overview of the model. However, this also implies that about 11% of cases predicted as positive are false positives, which could lead to unnecessary concern for some patients. Research in artificial intelligence, machine learning, and deep learning is currently focused on the interpretability of black box models [34]. For this reason, the development of a 3D class activation map that pays attention to the region of black matter (SNc) is significant. Focusing the model on a specific area may be necessary to recognize disease markers and predict more accurately.

Noise removal and normalization in MRI images aid in improving input data quality and making it easier for the CNN model to extract important features. This method emphasizes the importance of preprocessing for creating machine learning models in the medical field, where precision and dependability are crucial. Additionally, incorporating data augmentation methods in training offers a wider variety of instances for the model, helping to avoid overfitting and enhancing the model's capacity to generalize to unfamiliar data. Table 4 compares several relevant studies in Parkinson's disease detection using different datasets and machine learning methods. Each study demonstrates variations in accuracy and sensitivity, underscoring the impact of methodology and dataset on the diagnostic precision of Parkinson's disease.

Table 4. Comparison between related studies

Study	Dataset	Method	Accuracy	Sensitivity	Specificity	Processing Time
This Study	PPMI	AlexNet-based CNN	92	95	-	3 h
[38]	PPMI	AlexNet CNN	88.9	89.3	88.4	-
[6]	NTU Dataset	DenseNet-LSTM	90.0	90.0	93.8	-
[36]	NMS-MRI	CNN	80.0	86.0	70.0	-
[4]	PD Dataset from Leeds Teaching Hospitals NHS Trust	CNN	95.02	-	98.31	-
[15]	PPMI	CNN	89.23	90.27	89.03	1 h
[31]	PPMI	ANN	94.0	100	88.0	-

5 Conclusions

This study successfully implemented an improved version of the AlexNet convolutional neural network to detect Parkinson's disease from MRI scans. By employing advanced image processing techniques like NL Means denoising and enhancing the AlexNet architecture with deconvolution layers and dropout, the model achieved robust performance metrics: an accuracy of 92%, precision of 89%, sensitivity of 95%, and specificity of 88%. The CNN model was trained on a balanced dataset comprising 2000 images each from Parkinson's disease patients and healthy controls. This balanced dataset and the refined network architecture contributed to reducing overfitting and enhancing generalization, demonstrating significant potential for early and effective diagnosis of Parkinson's disease.

The findings from this project show promise for enhancing Parkinson's disease detection by leveraging non-invasive techniques like MRI, offering a faster and more affordable alternative to other methods. Additionally, using the usage of MRI of two planes provides the model with a more comprehensive perspective, enabling it to better learn the complex patterns associated with the disease. Early and accurate detection can facilitate timely intervention, potentially slowing disease progression and enhancing patient quality of life. The deployment of the trained model in clinical settings could improve diagnostic accuracy, especially in regions lacking specialized neurological expertise. Future research directions include integrating multimodal data from the PPMI database, such as combining MRI images with clinical, genetic, and demographic data, to develop a more comprehensive diagnostic model.

Moreover, the study proposes future efforts to create a practical impact, such as developing a support platform for Parkinson's patients in Ecuador. This initiative aims to fill the gap in dedicated outreach and support systems for Parkinson's disease in the country. The envisioned platform, titled "Red Ecuatoriana de Apoyo para pacientes con Parkinson," will not only provide information but also allow individuals to upload MRI images for assessment, aiding in early detection and management. In conclusion, while the results are promising, ongoing research and refinement of the approach are essential. By expanding to include multimodal data and advancing technological platforms for patient support, this study aims to make significant strides in Parkinson's disease diagnosis and care.

References

1. Magnetic resonance imaging for the diagnosis of Parkinson's disease. J. Neural Transm. **124**(8), 915–964 (2017). https://doi.org/10.1007/s00702-017-1717-8. https://www.ncbi.nlm.nih.gov/pubmed/28378231
2. Parkinson's disease: causes, symptoms, and treatments (2022). https://www.nia.nih.gov/health/parkinsons-disease/parkinsons-disease-causes-symptoms-and-treatments#:~:text=Many%20people%20with%20Parkinson

3. Alalayah, K.M., Senan, E.M., Atlam, H.F., Ahmed, I.A., Shatnawi, H.: Automatic and early detection of Parkinson's disease by analyzing acoustic signals using classification algorithms based on recursive feature elimination method. Diagnostics **13**(11), 1924 (2023). https://doi.org/10.3390/diagnostics13111924
4. Alissa, M., et al.: Parkinson's disease diagnosis using convolutional neural networks and figure-copying tasks. Neural Comput. Appl. **34**(2), 1433–1453 (2021). https://doi.org/10.1007/s00521-021-06469-7
5. Almgren, H., et al.: Machine learning-based prediction of longitudinal cognitive decline in early Parkinson's disease using multimodal features. Sci. Rep. **13**(1), 13193 (2023). https://doi.org/10.1038/s41598-023-37644-6
6. Basnin, N., Nahar, N., Anika, F.A., Hossain, M.S., Andersson, K.: Deep learning approach to classify Parkinson's disease from MRI samples. In: Mahmud, M., Kaiser, M.S., Vassanelli, S., Dai, Q., Zhong, N. (eds.) BI 2021. LNCS (LNAI), vol. 12960, pp. 536–547. Springer, Cham (2021). https://doi.org/10.1007/978-3-030-86993-9_48
7. Bhan, A., Kapoor, S., Gulati, M., Goyal, A.: Early diagnosis of Parkinson's disease in brain MRI using deep learning algorithm. In: 2021 Third International Conference on Intelligent Communication Technologies and Virtual Mobile Networks (ICICV) (2021). https://doi.org/10.1109/icicv50876.2021.9388571
8. Buades, A., Coll, B., Morel, J.M.: Non-local means denoising. Image Process. On Line **1**, 208–212 (2011)
9. Camacho, M., et al.: Exploiting macro- and micro-structural brain changes for improved Parkinson's disease classification from MRI data. NPJ Parkinson's Dis. **10**(1) (2024). https://doi.org/10.1038/s41531-024-00647-9. https://www.nature.com/articles/s41531-024-00647-9
10. Chakraborty, S., Aich, S., Kim, H.C.: Detection of Parkinson's disease from 3T T1 weighted MRI scans using 3D convolutional neural network. Diagnostics **10**(6), 402 (2020). https://doi.org/10.3390/diagnostics10060402
11. Chan, H.-P., Samala, R.K., Hadjiiski, L.M., Zhou, C.: Deep learning in medical image analysis. In: Lee, G., Fujita, H. (eds.) Deep Learning in Medical Image Analysis. AEMB, vol. 1213, pp. 3–21. Springer, Cham (2020). https://doi.org/10.1007/978-3-030-33128-3_1
12. Courtman, M., et al.: 095 artificial intelligence based detection of Parkinson's disease in magnetic resonance imaging brain scans. J. Neurol. Neurosurg. Psychiatry **93**(9), e2 (2022). https://doi.org/10.1136/jnnp-2022-abn2.139. https://jnnp.bmj.com/content/93/9/e2.45
13. Erdaş, î, Sümer, E.: A fully automated approach involving neuroimaging and deep learning for Parkinson's disease detection and severity prediction. PeerJ Comput. Sci. **9**, e1485 (2023). https://doi.org/10.7717/peerj-cs.1485
14. Garcia Santa Cruz, B., Husch, A., Hertel, F.: Machine learning models for diagnosis and prognosis of Parkinson's disease using brain imaging: general overview, main challenges, and future directions. Front. Aging Neurosci. **15**, 1216163 (2023). https://doi.org/10.3389/fnagi.2023.1216163
15. Kaur, S., Aggarwal, H., Rani, R.: Diagnosis of Parkinson's disease using deep CNN with transfer learning and data augmentation. Multimedia Tools Appl. **80**(7), 10113–10139 (2020). https://doi.org/10.1007/s11042-020-10114-1
16. Li, C., et al.: Automatic diagnosis of Parkinson's disease using artificial intelligence base on routine T1-weighted MRI. Front. Med. **10**, 130–350 (2023). https://doi.org/10.3389/fmed.2023.1303501. https://pubmed.ncbi.nlm.nih.gov/38249966/
17. Li, H., Yang, Z., Qi, W., Yu, X., Wu, J., Li, H.: Parkinson's image detection and classification based on deep learning. BMC Med. Imaging **24**(1), 187 (2024)

18. Li, S., Zhao, J., Zhang, H., Bi, Z., Qu, S.: A non-local low-rank algorithm for sub-bottom profile sonar image denoising. Remote Sens. **12**(14), 2336 (2020). https://doi.org/10.3390/rs12142336
19. Lin, C.H., Wang, F.C., Kuo, T.Y., Huang, P.W., Chen, S.F., Fu, L.C.: Early detection of Parkinson's disease by neural network models. IEEE Access **10**, 19033–19044 (2022). https://doi.org/10.1109/ACCESS.2022.3150774
20. Manjón, J.V., Carbonell-Caballero, J., Lull, J.J., García-Martí, G., Martí-Bonmatí, L., Robles, M.: MRI denoising using non-local means. Med. Image Anal. **12**(4), 514–523 (2008)
21. Marino, S., et al.: Magnetic resonance imaging markers for early diagnosis of Parkinson's disease. Neural Regeneration Res. **7**(8), 611–619 (2012). https://doi.org/10.3969/j.issn.1673-5374.2012.08.009
22. Montalvo Herdoíza, J.P., Montalvo Perero, P.S., Alvear Toala, L.E., Intriago Mercado, E.R., Moreira-Vera, D.V.: Prevalencia de la enfermedad de parkinson: Estudio puerta-puerta en la provincia de manabí-ecuador. Revista Ecuatoriana de Neurología (2017). https://revecuatneurol.com/magazine_issue_article/prevalencia-de-la-enfermedad-de-parkinson-estudio-puerta-puerta-en-la-provincia-de-manabi-ecuador-prevalence-parkinsons-disease-door-door-study-manabi-ecuador/
23. Mozhdehfarahbakhsh, A., Chitsazian, S., Chakrabarti, P., Chakrabarti, T., Kateb, B., Nami, M.: An MRI-based deep learning model to predict Parkinson's disease stages. MedRXIV (2021). https://doi.org/10.1101/2021.02.19.21252081
24. NIH. https://www.nibib.nih.gov/science-education/science-topics/magnetic-resonance-imaging-mri
25. World Health Organization: Parkinson disease (2023). https://www.who.int/news-room/fact-sheets/detail/parkinson-disease
26. University of Oxford: MRI brain scans detect people with early Parkinson's | University of Oxford (2014). https://www.ox.ac.uk/news/2014-06-12-mri-brain-scans-detect-people-early-parkinsons
27. Postuma, R.B., et al.: MDS clinical diagnostic criteria for Parkinson's disease. Mov. Disord. **30**(12), 1591–1601 (2015)
28. Prashanth, R., Roy, S.D., Mandal, P.K., Ghosh, S.: High-accuracy detection of early Parkinson's disease through multimodal features and machine learning. Int. J. Med. Inform. **90**, 13–21 (2016). https://doi.org/10.1016/j.ijmedinf.2016.03.001
29. Pyatigorskaya, N., Gallea, C., Garcia-Lorenzo, D., Vidailhet, M., Lehericy, S.: A review of the use of magnetic resonance imaging in Parkinson's disease. Ther. Adv. Neurol. Disord. **7**(4), 206–220 (2014). https://doi.org/10.1177/1756285613511507. https://www.ncbi.nlm.nih.gov/pmc/articles/PMC4082302/
30. Rosenfeld, A.: Digital Picture Processing. Academic Press (1976)
31. Rumman, M., Tasneem, A.N., Farzana, S., Pavel, M.I., Alam, M.A.: Early detection of Parkinson's disease using image processing and artificial neural network. In: 2018 Joint 7th International Conference on Informatics, Electronics & Vision (ICIEV) and 2018 2nd International Conference on Imaging, Vision & Pattern Recognition (icIVPR) (2018). https://doi.org/10.1109/iciev.2018.8641081
32. Salvatore, C., et al.: Machine learning on brain MRI data for differential diagnosis of Parkinson's disease and progressive supranuclear palsy. J. Neurosci. Methods **222**, 230–237 (2014). https://doi.org/10.1016/j.jneumeth.2013.11.016. https://www.sciencedirect.com/science/article/pii/S0165027013003993
33. Sangeetha, S., Baskar, K., Kalaivaani, P., Kumaravel, T.: Deep learning-based early Parkinson's disease detection from brain MRI image (2023). https://doi.org/10.1109/iciccs56967.2023.10142754

34. Shi, D., et al.: Machine learning for detecting Parkinson's disease by resting-state functional magnetic resonance imaging: a multicenter radiomics analysis. Front. Aging Neurosci. **14**, 806828 (2022). https://doi.org/10.3389/fnagi.2022.806828
35. Shin, N., et al.: Cortical thickness from MRI to predict conversion from mild cognitive impairment to dementia in Parkinson disease: a machine learning–based model. Radiology **300**(2), 390–399 (2021). https://doi.org/10.1148/radiol.2021203383
36. Shinde, S., et al.: Predictive markers for Parkinson's disease using deep neural nets on neuromelanin sensitive MRI. NeuroImage: Clin. **22**, 101748 (2019). https://doi.org/10.1016/j.nicl.2019.101748. https://www.ncbi.nlm.nih.gov/pmc/articles/PMC6417260/
37. Shu, Z., et al.: Predicting the progression of Parkinson's disease using conventional MRI and machine learning: an application of radiomic biomarkers in whole-brain white matter. Magn. Reson. Med. **85**(3), 1611–1624 (2020). https://doi.org/10.1002/mrm.28522
38. Sivaranjini, S., Sujatha, C.M.: Deep learning based diagnosis of Parkinson's disease using convolutional neural network. Multimedia Tools Appl. (2019). https://doi.org/10.1007/s11042-019-7469-8
39. Solano Cayo, A.A., Carlosama Males, A.E.: Propiocepción en el entrenamiento de la marcha en pacientes con parkinson (2023). http://dspace.unach.edu.ec/handle/51000/10588
40. Souza, R., et al.: Identifying biases in a multicenter MRI database for Parkinson's disease classification: is the disease classifier a secret site classifier? IEEE J. Biomed. Health Inform. **28**(4), 2047–2054 (2024). https://doi.org/10.1109/jbhi.2024.3352513. https://ieeexplore.ieee.org/abstract/document/10388228
41. Tessitore, A., Cirillo, M., De Micco, R.: Functional connectivity signatures of Parkinson's disease. J. Parkinsons Dis. **9**(4), 637–652 (2019). https://doi.org/10.3233/JPD-191592
42. Xu, J., Zhang, M.: Use of magnetic resonance imaging and artificial intelligence in studies of diagnosis of Parkinson's disease. ACS Chem. Neurosci. **10**(6), 2658–2667 (2019). https://doi.org/10.1021/acschemneuro.9b00207. https://pubmed.ncbi.nlm.nih.gov/31083923/
43. Ya, Y., et al.: Machine learning models for diagnosis of Parkinson's disease using multiple structural magnetic resonance imaging features. Front. Aging Neurosci. **14**, 808520 (2022). https://doi.org/10.3389/fnagi.2022.808520
44. Yuzkan, S., et al.: Utility of diffusion tensor imaging and generalized q-sampling imaging for predicting short-term clinical effect of deep brain stimulation in Parkinson's disease. Acta Neurochirurgica **166**(1) (2024). https://doi.org/10.1007/s00701-024-06096-w
45. Zhang, J.: Mining imaging and clinical data with machine learning approaches for the diagnosis and early detection of Parkinson's disease. NPJ Parkinson's Dis. **8**(1) (2022). https://doi.org/10.1038/s41531-021-00266-8
46. Zhao, H., et al.: Deep learning based diagnosis of Parkinson's disease using diffusion magnetic resonance imaging. Brain Imaging Behav. **16**(4), 1749–1760 (2022)

Author Index

F. R. Narváez et al. (Eds.): SmartTech-IC 2024, CCIS 2392, pp. 465–468, 2026.
https://doi.org/10.1007/978-3-031-98287-3

The manufacturer's authorised representative in the EU is Springer Nature Customer Service Centre GmbH, Europaplatz 3, 69115 Heidelberg, Germany. If you have any concerns regarding our products, please contact ProductSafety@springernature.com

Printed and bound by CPI Group (UK) Ltd, Croydon, CR0 4YY
01/10/2026
02225952-0016